COMMONLY USED SYMBOLS

SYMBOL	TERM	PAGE WHERE SYMBOL FIRST INTRODUCED
Y	GDP	29
C	Consumption	29
I	Investment	29
G	Government spending	29
X	Net exports	29
F	Government transfers	42
Q	Interest on the government debt	42
T	Taxes	42
V	Net factor payments from abroad	42
S_p	Private saving	42
S_g	Government saving	42
S_r	Rest of world saving	42
U	Unemployment	77
U^*	Natural rate of unemployment	77
Y^*	Potential GDP	77
N	Employment	89
K	Captial stock	89
A	Technology	89
W	Wage	91
P	Price level	91
N^*	Full employment	93
n	Labor force growth rate	100
s	Net saving rate	101
H	Human capital	148
Y_d	Disposable income	170
b	Marginal propensity to consume	170
t	Tax rate	171
m	Marginal propensity to import	182
R	Interest rate	194
M	Money demand/supply	194
π	Rate of inflation	223
π^e	Expected inflation	223
R^*	Equilibrium real interest rate	245
Y_p	Permanent disposable income	279
E	Exchange rate	329
P_W	Rest of the world price level	330
p^*	Target inflation rate	438
r	Federal funds rate	439
$\hat{Y}$	% deviation of Y from Y^*	439
Z	Exogenous price shock	447

MACROECONOMICS

SIXTH EDITION

MACROECONOMICS
economic growth, fluctuations, and policy

SIXTH EDITION

robert e. hall and david h. papell

W • W • NORTON & COMPANY
NEW YORK • LONDON

W. W. Norton & Company has been independent since its founding in 1923, when William Warder Norton and Mary D. Herter Norton first published lectures delivered at the People's Institute, the adult education division of New York City's Cooper Union. The Nortons soon expanded their program beyond the Institute, publishing books by celebrated academics from America and abroad. By mid-century, the two major pillars of Norton's publishing program—trade books and college texts—were firmly established. In the 1950s, the Norton family transferred control of the company to its employees, and today—with a staff of four hundred and a comparable number of trade, college, and professional titles published each year—W. W. Norton & Company stands as the largest and oldest publishing house owned wholly by its employees.

Composition by GGS Book Services, Atlantic Highlands.
Manufacturing by Quebecor, Taunton.
Book design by Sandy Watanabe.
Editor: Karl Bakeman
Project Editor: Christopher Miragliotta
Director of Manufacturing, College: Roy Tedoff

Library of Congress Cataloging-in-Publication Data

Hall, Robert Ernest, 1943–
    Macroeconomics / Robert E. Hall, David H. Papell.—6th ed.
        p. cm.
    Fifth ed. by Robert Ernest Hall and John B. Taylor.
    Includes bibliographical references and index.
    ISBN 0-393-97515-0
    1. Macroeconomics. I. Papell, David H. II. Title.

HB172.5.H35   2005
339—dc22

                                    2004063573

W. W. Norton & Company, Inc., 500 Fifth Avenue, New York, N.Y. 10110
    www.wwnorton.com

W. W. Norton & Company Ltd., Castle House, 75/76 Wells Street, London W1T 3QT

1 2 3 4 5 6 7 8 9 0

To Bonnie, Darci, and Marisa

CONTENTS

PREFACE

What policies enable an impoverished tropical country to promote economic growth and raise its standard of living, and what policies lead to further poverty? If a country experiences high inflation, why is it costly to bring inflation down? Why have many countries, including the United States, experienced improved economic performance since the mid-1980s? The answers to these questions, and many more, comprise the subject of macroeconomics. As economic theory, facts and policies change, so must economics textbooks. In this sixth edition, we have incorporated key new developments in macroeconomics while keeping to the basic goal since our first edition: to capture the spirit and content of modern macroeconomics in a form that is manageable at the intermediate level.

The sixth edition represents the most extensive revision of the text since its inception, starting with a new author: David Papell of the University of Houston. Most intermediate textbooks focus on economic fluctuations, with occasional chapters on growth, international, and policy. In contrast, we provide balanced coverage in three areas: economic growth, economic fluctuations, and economic policy, while retaining the text's traditional strengths in unemployment and the microfoundations of macroeconomics. We integrate international aspects of macroeconomics throughout the text. Economic fluctuations are discussed in the context of an open economy, and we include chapters on the international aspects of growth, policy, and microfoundations. We continue to keep the length of the book short so that the material can be covered in one semester.

Economic Growth

Students and faculty have expressed enthusiasm for the book's strong emphasis on long-term economic growth. This desire for greater emphasis on economic growth reflects changes in the field of macroeconomics and changes in the real world, as the problem of slow growth around the world has proved to be more and more persistent. In this sixth edition we expand the coverage of economic growth from two to three chapters by moving beyond the Solow and endogenous growth models to encompass exciting new areas of research.

For most of recorded history, there was no economic growth, and very low growth rates continue to characterize parts of the world today. We therefore start with Malthus, and show how today's advanced countries progressed through Malthusian stagnation to the industrial revolution, the demographic transition, and the modern growth regime. We analyze how technology affects growth in both the Solow and endogenous growth models, but we also discuss the neoclassical growth revival—recent work that argues that an augmented Solow model, rather than the endogenous growth model, provides a better explanation of the facts of economic growth.

The experience of economic growth around the world ranges from miracles to tragedies. In an entirely new chapter, we first document the process of convergence for industrialized countries and divergence for the world as a whole. We discuss research that attempts to explain why some countries grow faster and others grow slower, and see how this research has been translated into economic policymaking. Finally, we look at the relation between geography and growth. Temperate countries grow faster than tropical countries, and we discuss very recent work that attempts to understand whether the explanation is based on geography or on institutions.

Economic Fluctuations

Economic fluctuations—recessions and booms—continue to be a key theme of the book. Recessions cause serious hardship and economic loss. We continue to view them, however, as temporary departures of the economy from its full-employment long-run growth path. We take the view that many types of shocks are responsible for departures of the economy from its long-run path. These include changes in monetary and fiscal policies, as well as sudden increases in world oil prices, a factor that was of great importance in the 1974–1975 and 1981–1982 recessions.

In our view full employment is not restored immediately after a shock because the economy adjusts slowly, with the sluggishness primarily due to price and wage rigidity. We study rigidities within an overall framework in which expectations and other features of people's behavior are basically rational, and we provide a microeconomic account of the way in which price and wage rigidities delay the return to full employment.

As in the earlier editions, we develop a complete model of economic fluctuations. The model, developed in a three-chapter sequence, focuses on three major ideas: the fundamental determinants of output in the long run, the determination of output and employment in the short run through the aggregate demand curve and the predetermined price, and the process of price adjustment that takes the economy back to the long-run growth path after a shock causes a recession or boom.

Economic Policy

During the past two decades, the United States has experienced greatly improved macroeconomic performance—lower inflation and smaller output fluctuations—compared with the 1970s. Changes in the conduct of monetary policy, which can be explained using the coefficients of a monetary policy rule by which the Federal Reserve Board raises the real interest rate when inflation increases above its target level or when output rises above its long-run potential level, are the most probable cause of the improved performance. This policy rule, most often called the Taylor rule, is the centerpiece for a three-chapter sequence on macroeconomic policy.

We begin by discussing the Taylor rule and show that it provides a good depiction of how the Federal Reserve Board has set interest rates since the mid-1980s. We emphasize the importance of the Taylor principle: when inflation rises, the Fed needs to raise the nominal interest rate more than point-for-point, so that the real interest rate rises. We then develop a model of macroeconomic policy that combines the IS curve and the price adjustment process, introduced earlier when we analyzed economic fluctuations, with the Taylor rule. While using only simple algebra, this model closely resembles macroeconomic models used by researchers today. We show, using the Taylor rule, how changes in monetary policy can explain the improvement in macroeconomic performance in the United States since the mid-1980s.

We next analyze normative aspects of macroeconomic policy. Using a framework where policymakers attempt to minimize a combination of deviations of inflation from its target level and GDP from its potential level, we show how the Taylor rule falls within the class of optimal policies. The analysis is conducted using the model of macroeconomic policy so that students can progress easily from positive to normative considerations. Finally, we analyze macroeconomic policymaking in the world economy. We discuss the macroeconomic policy trilemma—the impossibility of a country simultaneously having fixed exchange rates, free movement of capital, and an independent monetary policy—and show how the Taylor rule is incompatible with fixing exchange rates. We show how other countries that have adopted monetary policies that obey the Taylor principle—Australia, Canada, and the United Kingdom—have experienced improvements in macroeconomic performance similar to that experienced by the United States. We also analyze the deterioration in macroeconomic performance in Japan in the 1990s and early 2000s and the problems of deflation.

Distinctive Features at a Glance

A number of important features have made this book work well in the classroom:

- Consistent development of a *complete macroeconomic model*, with short-run fluctuations, price adjustment, and long-run growth. The production function, which is the centerpiece for studying economic growth, is used to determine potential output when considering economic fluctuations. The IS curve, introduced for the study of economic fluctuations, continues to be used later for the analysis of macroeconomic policy.

- Thorough examination of how macroeconomics is used in *practical policy applications*, with an analysis of both positive and normative aspects of macroeconomic policymaking.

- Consistent *numerical values* of the coefficients of the complete model to give a sense of the magnitudes involved and provide a bridge between the text and the end-of-chapter problems.

- A *MacroSolve Web site* that displays the same complete model and permits many kinds of experiments with the model.

- Extensive analysis of *long-run growth*, with discussion of the determinants of long-run growth before describing fluctuations around the growth path.

- Treating the *price level as a predetermined variable* when explaining short-run departures of the economy from its growth path.

- Extensive coverage of the *international* aspects of macroeconomics, including economic growth and macroeconomic policy in the world economy.

- Considering the United States as an *open economy* throughout the book, rather than adding trade and exchange rates late in the book.

- Attention to the *microeconomic foundations* of all subjects discussed, with careful exposition of the empirical regularities of the U.S. economy at the start of each chapter on microfoundations.

Summary of Pedagogical Features

With the new edition, *Macroeconomics* has been completely redesigned to give it a more open and contemporary feel. In addition to the new look, *Macroeconomics* includes many pedagogical features that enhance the student's understanding of the material:

- *New integrated MacroSolve exercise icons.* Each chapter in the book features icons indicating topics that are addressed in the exercises on the Macro-Solve Web site. Updated with the most recent data, MacroSolve allows students to experiment with the models developed in the text and includes multiple choice questions to guide them through each exercise.

- *Summary boxes.* Key ideas are drawn together at appropriate places within each chapter. The boxes serve a reinforcing function by allowing readers to check their understanding of one aspect of the analysis before tackling new material. And they also serve a review function; they help readers locate the building blocks of the analysis without reading entire chapters.

- *Topic boxes.* Special concepts that are related to the discussion in the text are introduced. These include computing growth rates, quarterly gross domestic product statistics, budget projects, indexing taxes, and the relationship between graphs and algebra. The boxes also present discussion of historical examples, current policy issues, and other illustrations of points in the text.

- *Research in Practice boxes.* In order to highlight how research is used in practice, a series of policy essays have been placed at appropriate spots throughout the text. We portray how successful, or unsuccessful, each application has been.

- *End-of-chapter problems.* At the end of each chapter there are numerical and analytical questions for review. The numerical problems require the use of a hand calculator and usually take some time. We have found these useful for special projects. The analytical questions can be done with graphs or simple algebra.

- *Parallel graphical and algebraic presentation.* In most cases arguments are presented in both graphical and algebraic form. We have found that some students learn better with graphs and some learn better with algebra, especially if the algebra is presented in a way that does not intimidate. Graphical arguments are not necessarily easier for all students, and the algebra is provided to help those with a preference for algebra. Of course, graphical presentation usually helps with the intuition, and we expect even the less graphically inclined students to learn basic diagrams. A special effort has been made to demonstrate that graphs and algebra are just two ways to describe the same economic concepts.

- *Real-world examples.* Seeing how economic theory works in practice is the best way to learn. Too often, however, these lessons of experience are placed at some distance from the analysis, with the result that students often sense that a barrier exists between macroeconomic models and the real world from which they are drawn. We have chosen to make the performance of the economy an integral aspect of the exposition, with new concepts constantly illuminated by examples.

Student Resources

- An excellent *Study Guide* prepared by Sarah Culver of the University of Alabama at Birmingham and David Papell of the University of Houston is available for student purchase.

- *MacroSolve Web site* (www.wwnorton.com/web/macrosolve). The Macro-Solve program, now available in a new online version, includes interactive versions of the economic growth, economic fluctuations, and economic policy models developed in the text and has received rave reviews from students and teachers.

Instructor Resources

- The *Instructor's Manual* has been revised by David Gillette of Truman State University and includes a *Test-Item File* of roughly 800 questions, which is available in electronic format with the publisher's test-making program, *Norton TestMaker*.

- Powerpoint slides are available at www.wwnorton.com/nrl.

A Guided Tour

The book starts with a short course in macroeconomic analysis in the first three parts. In Part I we introduce the basic macroeconomic facts to be explained. The introductory chapter (Chapter 1) discusses the variables that macroeconomics endeavors to explain—real GDP, inflation, unemployment, nominal and real interest rates, and the money supply—and provides a core of practical macroeconomics that introduces themes used throughout the text. Chapter 2 discusses macroeconomic measurement, including the new "chain-weighted" GDP, which is now the main measure of real output in the national income and product accounts. The problem of unemployment has also received renewed attention in macroeconomics in the 2000s, as high unemployment in the several years following the recession of 2001 has concerned both the public and the policymakers. Unemployment and labor market dynamics are analyzed in Chapter 3, where the process of job creation and job destruction is explored.

In Part II we analyze long-run growth. We begin Chapter 4 with the production function, the determination of potential GDP, and the determination of the natural rate of unemployment. We continue to use the production function to develop the Malthusian model, where no growth occurs, and the Solow growth model. Technology and economic growth is considered in Chapter 5, both exogenously and endogenously determined. We discuss sources of growth using the Solow growth accounting formula, evidence for endogenous and neo-classical growth models, and reasons for the growth in productivity in the 1990s and early 2000s. Economic growth around the world is the subject of Chapter 6. The question of why are some countries so rich and others so poor is one of the most interesting topics in macroeconomics, and we discuss convergence: how GDP per capita narrows among countries over time; and divergence: how GDP per capita widens. We consider cross-country growth, and study the aug-mented Solow model. We end with an analysis of geography, institutions, and growth—a topic of extensive current research among economists.

Then in Part III we delve into the reasons for the departures of the econ-omy from its long-run growth path. We start in Chapter 7 with the consump-tion function, net export function, and the multiplier. In Chapter 8, we use the IS-LM apparatus to derive the aggregate demand curve and explain the deter-mination of output in the short run when the price level is predetermined. The path to full employment is governed by the price-adjustment process, intro-duced in Chapter 9. Our analysis shuttles back and forth from price adjust-ment to output determination. Once the price level has adjusted, output is found at the point of the new price level on the aggregate demand curve. We do not drop the predetermined-price assumption when we trace the econ-omy's move to its long-run path. IS-LM remains our theory of output determi-nation in each period of the dynamic analysis.

The expositional simplification we achieve in this way is enormous. We do not feel that the empirical evidence justifies the complexity of simultaneous determination of prices and output in each period. There is certainly no con-tradiction to the predetermined-price assumption if the period is a quarter of a year, and the assumption is valid as a close approximation if the period is a full year.

The adaptation of price adjustment to inflation ranks high among the ideas that have evolved in macroeconomics over the past two decades. We avoid characterizing this adaptation solely as a matter of changing expectations. Even with rational expectations, price adjustment depends partly on recent inflation experience, since contracts and other rigidities prevent quick adjustments. We discuss how the adaptation of expectations to inflation depends on how prices and wages are set.

After the short course in macroeconomic analysis, we go on to develop the micro foundations of aggregate demand in Part IV. At the start of each chapter we present the key facts or puzzles that need to be explained. At the end of each chapter we look at the implications for the complete macro model. The con-sumption chapter (Chapter 10) develops a forward-looking theory of consump-tion based on the life-cycle and permanent-income formulations, emphasizing the role of rational expectations. By establishing an intertemporal budget con-straint, we avoid present discounted values and forbidding summations. Chapter 11, on investment, focuses on Dale Jorgensen's model. The foreign trade chapter (Chapter 12) focuses on flexible exchange rates, with a rational expectations model of the exchange rate as its centerpiece. Chapter 13, on government, presents material on the deficit and government debt alongside a standard treatment of automatic stabilizers and related subjects. When the intertemporal budget constraint for the government is presented, the idea is already familiar to the student from consumption and investment. Chapter 14, on the monetary system, takes up money demand and describes the role of the Federal Reserve in determining the money supply and the short-run interest rate. Chapter 15 considers market-clearing or equilibrium views of price rigidity, including Robert Lucas's imperfect information model of aggregate supply, and also considers alternative views that emphasize wage contracts or sticky prices.

Part V pulls the analysis together into a comprehensive treatment of macroeconomic policy evaluation. Chapter 16 introduces the Taylor rule and the Taylor principle. The Taylor rule is first combined with the IS curve, introduced in Chapter 8, to derive the macroeconomic policy curve. The price adjustment line, introduced in Chapter 9, is then added to comprise the macroeconomic policy model. The model is used to analyze events such as a boom, disinflation, and an oil price shock, and to study macroeconomic performance for the United States. Chapter 17 takes up normative policy issues such as time inconsistency, targets and instruments, and the rational expectations critique of policy evaluation. The inflation/unemployment trade-off appears as a policy frontier between output stability and price stability, and the normative aspects of the Taylor rule are studied. Chapter 18 considers macroeconomic policy in the world economy, including a review of the history of the international monetary system and an analysis of how countries conduct exchange rate policies today. Monetary policy rules in the world economy are studied, including the demise of fixed exchange rates and the role of the exchange rate in the Taylor rule. The improved macroeconomic performance of three countries—Australia, Canada, and the United Kingdom—that have adopted monetary policies similar to the Taylor rule, are studied and contrasted with the deterioration of Japan's macroeconomic performance in the 1990s and early 2000s.

Acknowledgments

We thank the students, teaching assistants, and instructors in numerous sections of intermediate macro at Stanford and Houston for their many helpful comments and corrections throughout the development of this book. We are also deeply grateful to the many teachers and students at other universities who wrote to us with comments on earlier editions. The book is immeasurably better than it would have been without their feedback. In particular, we would like to single out the following: Francis Ahking, University of Connecticut; Ugur Aker, Hiram College; Robert Barry, College of William and Mary; Dan Ben-David, Tel-Aviv University; Ernst Berndt, Massachusetts Institute of Technology; Olivier Blanchard, Massachusetts Institute of Technology; Dwight M. Blood, Brigham Young University; Ronald Bodkin, University of Ottawa; Robert K. Brown, Texas Tech University; Menzie Chinn, University of Wisconsin–Madison; Norman G.

Clifford, University of Kansas; Gregory Crawford, Stanford University; Sarah Culver, University of Alabama–Birmingham; Betty Daniel, SUNY–Albany; Paul Emberton, Texas State University; Wilfred J. Ethier, University of Pennsylvania; George Evans,University of Oregon; Craig Furfine,Federal Reserve Bank of Chicago; Rajendra Gangadean, Stanford University; David Gillette, Truman State University; Frederick Goddard, University of Florida; Peter Gomori, St. Francis College (New York); Rae-Joan B. Goodman, U.S. Naval Academy; Harvey Gram, City University of New York; Howard Gruenspecht, Carnegie-Mellon University; Joseph Guerin, St. Joseph's University; John Haltiwanger, University of Maryland; James Hamilton, University of California, San Diego; Hsiang-ling Han, Babson College; Daniel Himarios, University of Texas at Arlington; Brad Humphreys, University of Maryland; Takatoshi Ito, University of Tokyo; Charles I. Jones, University of California–Berkeley; Demetrius Kantarelis, Assumption College; Chulsoo Kim, Sookmyung Women's University; Stephen R. King, Chemical Bank; Michael Knetter,University of Wisconsin–Madison; John Laitner, Unversity of Michigan; Julia Lane, American University; Bennett McCallum, Carnegie-Mellon University; Basil Moore, Wesleyan University; Roger Morefield, University of St. Thomas; Richard F. Muth, Emory University; David Nelson, Western Washington University; Neil B. Niman, University of New Hampshire; Ian Novos, University of Southern California; Ernest H. Oksanen, McMaster University; Edmund S. Phelps, Columbia University; Mikko Puhakka, Cornell University; Garey Ramey, University of California, San Diego; Duane J. Rosa, West Texas State University; Michael Sattinger, SUNY-Albany; Edward Trubac, University of Notre Dame; J. Kirker Stephens, University of Oklahoma; Michael Truscott, University of Tampa; Nora Underwood, University of California–Davis; Larkin Warner, Oklahoma State University; Shinichi Watanabe, University of Kansas; Akila Weerapana, Wellesley College; John Williams,Federal Reserve Bank of San Francisco; and Hou-Mu Wu, Tulane University; Steven Yamarik, Tufts University.

Finally, we would like to thank Karl Bakeman, Ed Parsons, Drake McFeely, Donald Lamm, Jack Repcheck, and Joan Benham of W. W. Norton for outstanding editorial help and advice.

D.H.P.
Houston, Texas
June 2004

INTRODUCTION

PART ONE

ECONOMIC GROWTH, FLUCTUATIONS, AND POLICY

The economy grows, evolves, and fluctuates. In some years, jobs and production grow rapidly. In others, the economy grows slowly or even shrinks. Over the past 30 years, the average growth of the United States economy, measured as the total production of goods and services, has been about 3.2 percent per year. However, growth of the U.S. economy, along with most other economies, fluctuates widely around the long-term average from year to year. In some years, such as in the United States in 2000 and 2001, growth turns down, workers lose jobs, and unemployment and poverty rise. In other years, the economy advances more rapidly than the average of 3.2 percent per year. For instance, in the United States from 1997 through 1999, production rose by more than 4.0 percent each year: Jobs grew rapidly and unemployment fell.

Following the longest peacetime expansion in United States history, which started in 1991, economic growth turned down in 2000. While stronger growth returned in 2002, the recovery was slow and unemployment continued to rise until growth accelerated in 2003. The cycle of recession and recovery in 2001–2003 occurred many times before. In the last few decades, there have been economic contractions in 1970, 1974–1975, 1980, 1982, and 1990–1991. Following each of these contractions were years of unusually high growth as the economy recovered. Growth was above average for the seven consecutive years from 1983 through 1989 and the five consecutive years from 1996 through 2000, two of the longest periods of above-average growth in U.S. history. But history shows that booms and slumps are temporary. Even the long boom of the 1980s and 1990s was interrupted by the recession of 1990–1991 and came to an end with the recession of 2001.

The short-run fluctuations, or cycles of expansions, recessions, and recoveries, occur against the backdrop of persistent, long-run rates of economic growth. Yet, these long-run growth rates are subject to change. During the 1950s and 1960s, the U.S. economy enjoyed high growth rates. In the 1970s, growth rates fell, only to rise again in the 1980s and 1990s. Overall, there has been considerable improvement in macroeconomic performance from the 1970s to the mid-1980s and beyond. In addition to higher growth rates, the frequency and severity of recessions have diminished. The improvements in macroeconomic performance are clearly related to improvements in the conduct of macroeconomic policy. The lessons that we learned regarding macroeconomic policy transcend the state of the economy at any particular point in time and provide reason for optimism regarding macroeconomic performance in the first decades of the 2000s.

1.1 | MACROECONOMICS AND ITS USES

Macroeconomics tries to explain how and why the economy grows and fluctuates over time. The general upward path of the economy is the result of slow-moving forces—increasing population, more factories and machines, and better technology. The long-run upward path is not smooth. It occurs as a series of **business cycles**—recurrent cycles of expansions, recessions, and recoveries. Macroeconomics tries to explain growth and fluctuations using the standard principles of economic analysis.

The other branch of economics is **microeconomics**—the study of the behavior of individual consumers, firms, and markets. Microeconomics differs from macroeconomics in two ways. First, microeconomics is more concerned with how individual markets differ than with how the economy as a whole grows and fluctuates over time. Second, macroeconomics explains the determination of variables, including national income, the price level, and interest rates, that microeconomics considers given. Although it has different objectives, macroeconomics employs the basic ideas of microeconomics. When

macroeconomists try to explain growth and fluctuations, they look at the behavior of consumers and firms, the organization of labor markets and industry,
the workings of financial markets, and even the machinations of government.
They rely on microeconomics to do so. Good microeconomics is a necessary
but not sufficient condition for good macroeconomics.

Although long-run economic growth and short-term fluctuations have
dominated discussions of economic performance in recent years, other important variables change as the macroeconomy grows and fluctuates. For example,
inflation and interest rates in the United States rose toward the end of the
1983–1988 high growth period and declined as production and employment
fell in 1990 and 1991. Interest rates rose in 1994–1999, then fell again in 2000
and 2001. Although the high inflation of the 1970s is a faded memory, it is important to remember that it caused great harm to the economy, and ending it
brought on the pain of two recessions in the early 1980s. Exchange rates and
the foreign trade deficit, as well as inflation and interest rates, are all part of the
natural focus of macroeconomics.

What is macroeconomics good for? One answer is that macroeconomics
is essential for good economic policy. Used appropriately by policy makers, it
has the potential greatly to improve economic welfare in the United States
and other countries, including the less-developed economies of Africa, Asia,
and Latin America and the newly emerging market economies of Eastern Europe and the former Soviet Union. Consider the following applications of
macroeconomics.

Macroeconomics can help policy makers decide what to do to help avert
recessions and ensure that recessions are as short and mild as possible when
they occur. Fluctuations are not unique to the last 25 years. They have been
recorded for hundreds of years in the United States and other countries, and
they will undoubtedly continue into the future. Hence, the possibility of another recession in the economy remains a continual concern to policy makers.
When the next recession strikes, it will have substantial effects on our welfare,
just as the last one did. Unemployment and poverty rise in all recessions. Even
those who do not lose their jobs may be forced into part-time jobs. The lower
income throughout the nation reduces the funds available to make new investments that fuel long-term growth.

Macroeconomics can also help policy makers sort through various government spending and tax proposals to increase long-term economic growth. Production *per hour* by U.S. workers grew by only 1.5 percent per year between
1973 and 1996, way down from the 2.7 percent per year from 1959 to 1973.
After 1973, the labor force expanded rapidly, as the postwar baby boom generation entered the workforce and more women chose to work outside the
home. Therefore, the slowdown of *total* production was moderate, although
total production would have increased substantially if the rate of production
per hour had not fallen.

Macroeconomics can help policy makers keep inflation low and stable
without making the economy unstable in the short run. Many analysts feel that
low and stable inflation is essential for strong long-term economic growth.

Suggestions about how government institutions can be designed to best ensure low and stable inflation are some of the more important recent contributions of macroeconomics.

Finally, macroeconomics tells us how broad policy changes affect the types of goods produced in the economy. Even when overall economic growth is relatively smooth, there are major fluctuations in the kinds of goods being produced. For example, during the 1990s, production of defense and nondefense goods for the federal government shrank, while the production of goods for investment soared. During this same period of steady overall growth consumption continued to rise. These developments in the government and investment sectors of the economy represented sharp reversals of developments from the 1980s. As we will see, they led to large changes in the trade deficit. The trade deficit rose in the 1990s. Explaining the trade deficit is one of the responsibilities of macroeconomics.

1.2 | RECENT MACROECONOMIC PERFORMANCE

MACROSOLVE
EXERCISE

Figure 1.1 documents the fluctuations of the U.S. economy over the last 35 years. The red line in the figure traces **real gross domestic product (GDP),** a concept we examine in more detail in the next chapter. Real GDP measures the actual physical production of cars, trucks, TV sets, rock concerts, Hollywood films, medical care, and every other good or service that people in the United States produce for trade with one another or the rest of the world. We get real GDP by summing up the dollar value of production, then adjusting for any price changes that have occurred from year to year. Frequently, real GDP is simply called *real output,* as it represents the total output of goods in the economy.

The vertical axis in Figure 1.1 shows the values of real GDP in 1996 dollars; the horizontal axis indicates the year. GDP rose fairly consistently during this period at an average growth rate of 3.2 percent. Figure 1.1, as well as many other figures in the book, uses a logarithmic scale to denote real GDP. The advantage of using a logarithmic scale is that a constant growth rate is plotted as a straight line. Growth in the labor force and the capital stock, the two key inputs to production, accounted for part of the total growth. The rest came from technological improvements. The gray line in the chart indicates the steady upward trend that underlies the behavior of real GDP; it measures the amount of output that would have been produced had the economy been in neither boom nor recession.

During the period shown in Figure 1.1, the U.S. economy experienced six **recessions**—periods when real GDP declines. The recessions are highlighted with boxes in the figure. Recessions follow **expansions** (periods when real

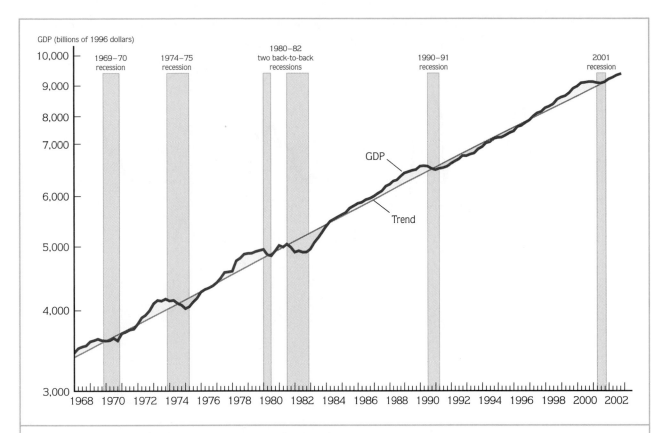

Figure 1.1 **REAL GDP IN THE UNITED STATES, 1968–2002**

The red line shows what has happened to real GDP. The gray line shows what real GDP would have looked like if it had grown smoothly at about 3.2 percent per year during the period instead of fluctuating as it did.

SOURCE: *Economic Report of the President*, 2003, Table B-2.

GDP is above its trend) and in turn are followed by **recoveries** (periods of positive growth with the economy still below its trend). Recessions start just after the *peak* of the previous expansion. The end of each recession is called a *trough*.

Figure 1.2 gives a more-detailed look at the deviations of real GDP from its trend. The ups and downs are exactly the same as in Figure 1.1, but the *percentage* deviations of real GDP from trend are shown.

Fluctuations do not occur at regular intervals. They certainly cannot be anticipated with great accuracy, and this is what makes macroeconomic forecasting both difficult and interesting. For example, the recovery that began in 1992 was very long, whereas the recovery that began in 1980 was short.

Figure 1.3 gives a longer perspective on the growth and fluctuations in economic activity, showing the ups and downs in the economy over the last 92

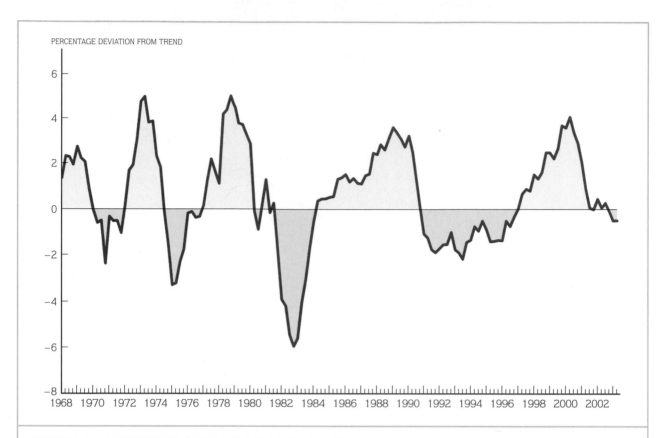

PERCENTAGE DEVIATION FROM TREND

FIGURE 1.2   FLUCTUATIONS OF REAL GDP AROUND ITS SMOOTH TREND

The chart shows the *percentage* deviations of real GDP from its trend. Real GDP was about 3 percent below its trend in 1975 and almost 6 percent below its trend in 1982.

years. The most noticeable single fluctuation during this period was the downturn during the Great Depression of the early 1930s. Note, however, that the recession in the early 1920s and the subsequent boom in the late 1920s were also comparatively large in magnitude. Although economic fluctuations in the United States have not ceased, they appear to have diminished in magnitude compared with this earlier period.

Employment

Fluctuations in employment follow closely the fluctuations in real GDP. Figure 1.4 shows the ratio of employed workers to the working-age population for the same period covered by Figure 1.1. Employment fell rapidly as the economy went through each of the six recessions during this period. Firms laid off workers as the economy's production fell and hired fewer new workers. As the

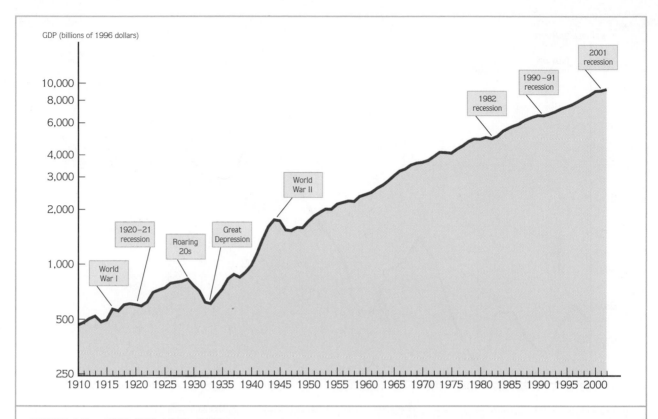

FIGURE 1.3   REAL GDP, 1910–2002

The largest decline in real GDP occurred from 1929 to 1933, the years of the Great Depression. Another important contraction occurred in the early 1920s. Both were more serious than any recession since 1950.

SOURCE: Angus Maddison, *Monitoring the World Economy: 1820–1992* (Paris: Organization for Economic Cooperation and Development, 1995).

economy began to recover after each downturn, employment again grew as firms called workers back to work and hired many new workers. This close association between production and employment as the economy fluctuates is a key fact of macroeconomics. It is why recurrent recessions are serious social problems, because they involve large-scale job loss.

Mirroring the fluctuations in employment are the fluctuations in the **unemployment rate,** the percentage of those in the labor force who are not working but looking for work. When employment falls, the unemployment rate rises as workers are laid off. Figure 1.5 shows the unemployment rate. In 1982, the unemployment rate rose to nearly 10 percent. In 1989, it fell to about 5 percent. Unemployment rose again, reaching over 7 percent for 1992, and then gradually declined to 4 percent by 2000 before rising again in 2001 and 2002.

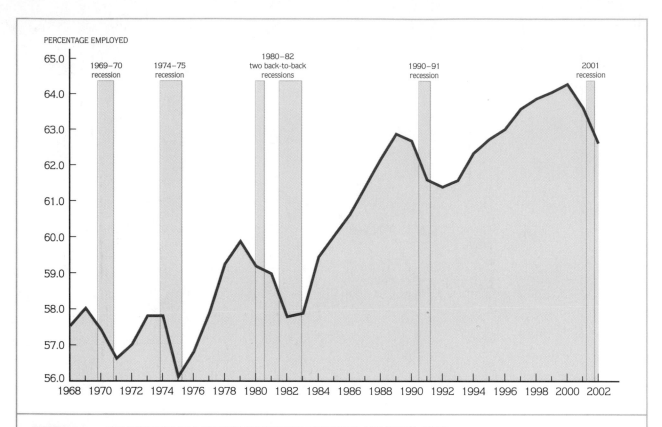

FIGURE 1.4   **EMPLOYMENT AS A PERCENTAGE OF THE WORKING-AGE POPULATION**

Recessions are periods of declining employment, measured as a fraction of the working-age population. Because of the fluctuations in employment, recessions influence a large fraction of the public. The percentage of the working-age population who are working reached an all-time high in 2000.

SOURCE: *Economic Report of the President,* 2003, Table B-35.

Inflation

Another important fact of economic fluctuations is their correlation with the rate of **inflation**—the percentage change in the average price of all goods and services in the economy. In general, prices tend to rise faster when the economy is operating near its peak. Conversely, prices tend to rise less rapidly when the economy is near a trough. These rises and falls lag behind the fluctuations in real GDP.

Figure 1.6 shows the rate of inflation. One of the most striking aspects of inflation is that it was much higher and much more volatile in the 1970s than in the 1980s and 1990s. This is clearly demonstrated in the chart. Almost all the significant increases in the rate of inflation preceded recession periods. Declines in inflation usually follow recessions. Do increases in inflation cause recessions? Are recessions a necessary part of the disinflation process? These are two central concerns of this book.

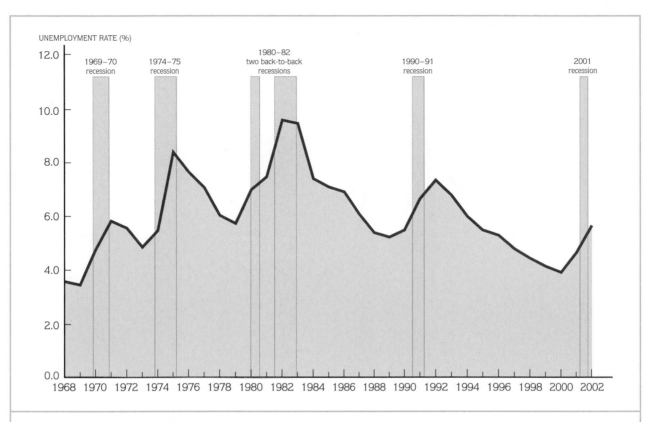

FIGURE 1.5   THE UNEMPLOYMENT RATE

The unemployment rate rises during recessions and falls during recoveries.

SOURCE: *Economic Report of the President*, 2003, Table B-42.

Interest Rates

Interest rates also tend to fluctuate over the business cycle. The interest rate is the amount charged for a loan by a bank or other lender per dollar per year, expressed as a percent. For instance, if you borrow $100 and repay $110 a year from now, the interest rate is 10 percent. Figure 1.7 shows one representative interest rate, the federal funds rate, during the same period we previously considered. The federal funds rate measures how much banks pay to borrow funds from each other overnight. As we will see, the federal funds rate is a key measure of the effect of the Federal Reserve Board, the central bank of the United States. Interest rates rose with inflation in the 1970s and fell as inflation declined in the 1980s and 1990s. Interest rates usually rise with inflation to compensate lenders for the falling purchasing power of the dollar.

However, the fluctuations in interest rates during recessions are most dramatic. Interest rates are *procyclical;* they move together with output, rising

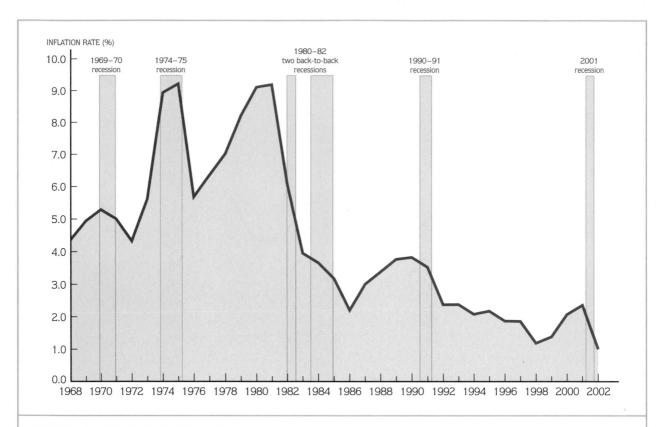

FIGURE 1.6   THE RATE OF INFLATION

Inflation was high and volatile in the 1970s. In the 1980s, it declined and remained relatively steady. Bursts of inflation have preceded or accompanied recessions. Typically, inflation subsides during and just after recessions.

SOURCE: *Economic Report of the President,* 2003, GDP deflator in Table B-3.

during booms and falling during recessions. They are also one of the most volatile macroeconomic variables, and the most difficult to predict. Nevertheless, as Figure 1.7 makes clear, these interest-rate fluctuations are intimately related to the fluctuations in production and employment. A thorough understanding of interest-rate behavior is crucial to any explanation of economic fluctuations.

The **real interest rate** is the interest rate minus the expected rate of inflation. The real interest rate is a key variable in macroeconomics because, as we will see, it strongly influences real GDP. Figure 1.8 shows the real interest rate. Because inflation has been positive for the United States, the real interest rate is lower than the interest rate. While the real interest rate is generally positive, for a few years in the 1970s, inflation was higher than the interest rate and the real interest rate was negative.

A variable closely related to the interest rate is the money supply. The **money supply** consists of currency and the deposits people have at banks and

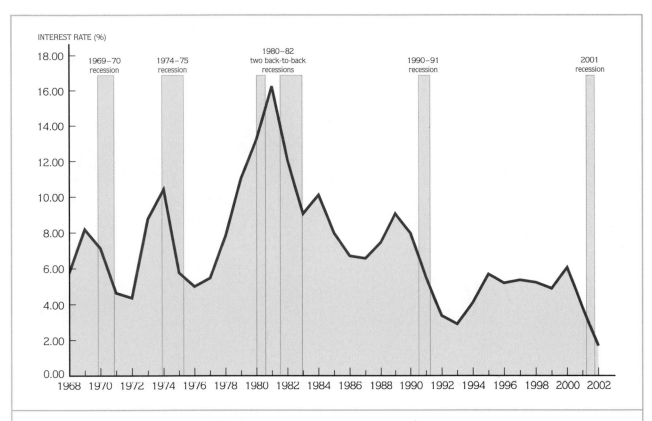

FIGURE 1.7   THE FEDERAL FUNDS INTEREST RATE

Like other interest rates, the federal funds rate reaches a peak just before a recession and then usually falls sharply.

SOURCE: *Economic Report of the President*, 2003, B-73.

certain other financial institutions. It is controlled by the Federal Reserve Board. The behavior of the money supply is shown in Figure 1.9. The chart shows the money supply divided by the price level, or *real money*. There seems to be a relationship between money and the timing of recessions and booms. The relationship suggests that changes in the money supply may be a cause of the fluctuations in the economy.

The ideas, theories, and models we study in this book endeavor to explain why GDP and employment fluctuate so much. They also try to provide reasons for the cyclical movements of inflation, interest rates, and the money supply as well as a number of other macroeconomic variables.

Growth and Fluctuations

1. In most years, the economy grows. The long-run growth path of the economy depends on population growth, capital accumulation, and technological progress.

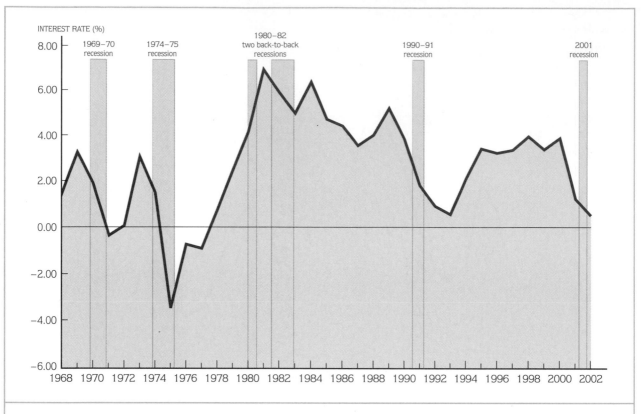

INTEREST RATE (%)

FIGURE 1.8   THE REAL INTEREST RATE

The real interest rate is the federal funds interest rate minus the rate of inflation.

SOURCE: *Economic Report of the President,* 2003, B-3 and B-73.

2. The economy undergoes recessions, recoveries, and other fluctuations at irregular intervals. Recessions are periods of contracting economic activity; recoveries are periods of above-average economic growth following a recession.

3. The physical volume of output—measured by real GDP—contracts in a recession and expands in a recovery.

4. Employment moves closely with output. Recessions are periods of job loss, that is, rising unemployment.

5. The period between World War I and World War II saw two very large contractions. Recessions have continued since World War II. In the early 1980s, the overall contraction was the worst since the Great Depression. The recessions of 1990–1991 and 2001 were less severe.

6. Inflation generally increases before a recession and subsides in the wake of a recession.

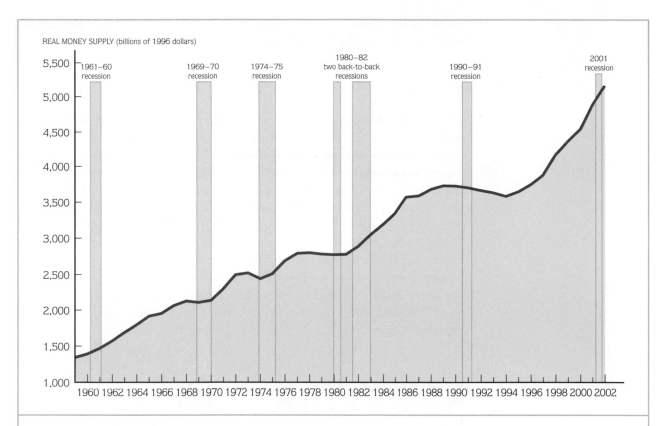

REAL MONEY SUPPLY (billions of 1996 dollars)

FIGURE 1.9   THE MONEY SUPPLY

The money supply divided by the price level—real money—seems to decline before recessions. The general trend in real money is positive because the growth in the economy creates a need for more money to assist in buying and selling goods.

SOURCE: *Economic Report of the President*, 2003, Tables B-3 and B-69.

7. Interest rates usually reach a peak just before a recession starts and then fall considerably during the recession.

1.3 EXPLAINING ECONOMIC GROWTH AND FLUCTUATIONS: A PREVIEW

The aim of this book is to develop a theory to explain both the short- and long-term movements of the economy. Recall that *long-run growth* refers to the general upward trend path of real GDP, shown in Figure 1.1, while *economic fluctuations* refer to the shorter-run movements of real GDP around that path.

In developing an explanation of how the economy grows and fluctuates, the macroeconomist constructs a *model*, a description of the economy expressed in graphs or equations. It shows how the decisions of households and firms interact with each other in markets to determine output and other variables.

The Model of Long-Run Growth

Macroeconomists use a long-run growth model to study the general upward path of the economy over time. The growth model focuses on the amount of labor and capital that go into the production of goods and services. Labor and capital work together to produce output. Most of the output is consumed by households; the rest is invested by businesses in new factories and equipment or is used by government. In focusing on the upward path of the economy, the growth model does not dwell on how the economy adjusts to temporary shocks, such as brief wars or financial turmoil. This is an oversimplification, because such shocks are frequent and the economy is always in the process of adjusting to one shock or another. After developing the long-run growth model, we consider the adjustment process through which the economy responds to shocks. We describe a complete model that considers temporary fluctuations, adjustment over time, and the process of growth in the long run.

GROWTH RATES

Macroeconomics gives a lot of attention to growth rates. Often, the recent change in a variable is the most important aspect that macroeconomics needs to discuss. For example, real GDP grows rapidly during an expansion and has a negative growth rate during a recession. One growth rate, that of the price level, even has a special name, the *rate of inflation*.

The growth rate of a variable between two periods, in percent, is defined as *the change in the variable divided by the value of the variable in the first period multiplied by 100*. Hence, the growth rate of real GDP from 1999 to 2000 is

$100 \times$ (real GDP in 2000 − real GDP in 1999)/(real GDP in 1999)
  = 100 (9224.0 − 8856.5)/(8856.5)
  = 100 (367.5)/(8856.5)
  = 4.1 percent.

Growth rates are usually converted to "annual rates" because everyone is used to annual rates. For a change from one year to the next, the growth rate is already at an annual rate. For the growth rate from one quarter to the next, the annual rate is approximated by multiplying the quarterly growth rate by 4.

One of the sources of growth is rising employment. The population grows over time, and at least in the past four decades, a growing fraction of the population chooses to work outside the home. With more labor available, the economy produces more output. A second source is increases in the stock of plant, equipment, and other capital: Workers produce more when they have more tools to work with. A third source of growth is improved technology. During recent years, the output of the economy has grown at least 1 percent per year from improved methods of production. Between 1996 and 2000, technological improvement ran at a much higher pace of about 2.5 percent per year.

In addition to describing the sources of growth in total output, the growth model explains the division of output among alternative uses. Consumption is the main use of output. Investment in new capital—plant and equipment—is a second. The government uses output, especially for defense. Finally, the rest of the world supplies us with output, in the form of goods imported from other countries, and the United States provides output to other countries in the form of exported goods. The interest rate plays the central role in dividing output among these uses. When the need for the government to use output is particularly strong—for example, when military spending is high—the interest rate is high. Then, the high interest rate induces businesses to limit or defer their investment. Exports fall and imports rise when the interest rate is high. And households may defer some types of consumption, such as buying new cars, when the interest rate is high.

The growth model provides a baseline for judging macroeconomic performance even in the short run. The level of **potential GDP** is the amount of GDP the economy produces according to the growth model. Although fluctuations not considered by the growth model cause actual GDP to depart from potential, the potential level is a baseline that actual GDP returns toward, once a temporary fluctuation subsides.

The Model of Fluctuations

Look back at Figure 1.1. Actual GDP is the red line and potential GDP is the gray line. During recessions, actual GDP drops below potential, and during booms actual GDP rises above potential. These fluctuations are transitory—the smooth potential GDP line describes how GDP behaves in the longer run. The model of fluctuations explains why there are temporary movements. In particular, it considers why the economy contracts sharply during recessions, when employment falls and unemployment rises as well.

What kinds of forces cause recessions and booms? Some originate from private sources in this country. In some years, there is a spontaneous decline in the amount that families spend on cars, appliances, and houses, or businesses spend on new plant and equipment. Another source of shocks is public policy. The Federal Reserve has a powerful influence because it controls the money supply and interest rates. Congress sets income taxes and these affect consumption; business taxes are an important determinant of investment spending.

Some shocks reach the United States from world markets—the oil market has been the most important source of this type in the past few decades.

Certain important characteristics of the economy affect the way these shocks influence output and employment. In an ideal economy where prices and wages could adjust immediately to new conditions, many of these shocks would probably have little effect on total output (they would still affect the distribution of output, however). The fluctuations model pays particular attention to the role of slow price and wage adjustment in amplifying and extending the effects of shocks. Once the price and wage adjustment occurs, the economy moves back to potential. The factors considered in the fluctuations model do not affect the long-run trends of the economy.

The Model of Macroeconomic Policy

Look back once more at Figure 1.1. Between 1970 and 1983, there were four recessions, and two of these (in 1974–1975 and 1982–1983) caused large increases in unemployment. Between 1984 and 2000, in contrast, there was only one recession, in 1990–1991, and that recession was relatively short and mild. Now look at Figure 1.6. The rate of inflation was much higher during the 1970s than after the early 1980s.

What caused the improvement in macroeconomic performance between the 1970s and the mid-1980s and beyond? While this question remains controversial, it is clear that changes in the conduct of **monetary policy**—movements of the interest rate and money supply determined by the Federal Reserve Board—have been the most important determinant of the improvement in macroeconomic performance. Since the mid-1980s, the Fed has conducted policy in a way that can be described by a **monetary policy rule,** in which the real interest rate is increased when inflation rises and when GDP exceeds potential GDP. During the 1970s, the Fed did not follow such a rule.

Economists use the macroeconomic policy model to study policy making by the Fed for two purposes. *Positive macroeconomics* studies "what is," how the Fed actually conducts monetary policy. *Normative macroeconomics* studies "what should be," whether or not a proposed monetary policy rule is optimal. The monetary policy rule, where the real interest rate is increased when inflation rises and when GDP exceeds potential GDP, scores well on both counts: It accurately describes actual Fed behavior and falls within a class of optimal monetary policy rules.

Growth and Fluctuations

1. Economists use the long-run growth model to study the general upward path of the economy over time.

2. In the growth model, the level of output is determined by labor, capital, and technical know-how; the economy grows as these determinants become more plentiful.

3. The path of output from the growth model is called potential GDP.

4. The economy experiences booms and recessions, when actual GDP is above or below potential; these departures from potential are temporary.

5. An important reason for the time it takes for the economy to return to potential GDP is slow price and wage adjustment.

6. The Fed conducts monetary policy according to a rule where the real interest rate is increased when inflation rises and when GDP exceeds potential GDP.

1.4 | A CORE OF PRACTICAL MACROECONOMICS

Macroeconomics has always been an area of great controversy and debate. Sometimes, it appears as though macroeconomists are divided into armed camps, fighting pitched battles among competing schools of thought. Yet there is a set of key principles—a core—of macroeconomics about which there is wide agreement. This core is practical in the sense that it has beneficial effects on macroeconomic policy, especially monetary policy, and has resulted in improvements over the last 20 years. In fact, new econometric models in operation at the Fed largely reflect this core. The five key principles are as follows:[1]

The Long-Run Growth Rate

Over the long term, growth in the productivity of labor depends on the growth of capital per hour of work and the growth of technology. If one adds to this growth in the productivity of labor an estimate of growth in the labor force itself, one gets an estimate of the long-run growth rate of real GDP, or what is typically referred to as *potential GDP growth*. This principle, the essence of neoclassical growth theory, provides a way to estimate and discuss the sources of long-term economic growth.

The principle has immense practical importance. Economists regularly use this approach to get estimates of potential GDP growth. Most now estimate this growth to be about 2–2.5 percent a year for the United States. The approach is also central to increasing economic growth for the world's poorest countries. Small differences in growth rates lead, over time, to large differences in standards of living. While, in principle, developing countries should grow faster than the United States, many poor countries, especially in Africa, have grown much slower. Promoting economic growth among the world's poorest countries has become an important focus of U.S. macroeconomic policy making.

---

[1] See John B. Taylor, "A Core of Practical Macroeconomics," *American Economic Review*, May, 1997, 233–235.

Inflation and Unemployment in the Long Term

There is no long-term trade-off between the rate of inflation and the rate of unemployment. A shift by the central bank to a higher rate of money growth simply results in more inflation in the long run, with the unemployment rate remaining unchanged. This is no longer controversial. In the 1960s, inflation was low and unemployment was between 5 and 6 percent; in the 1970s, inflation was high and unemployment was no lower; and in the 1990s and early 2000s, inflation was low again and unemployment had not increased. This principle has had a major practical impact on policy. It implies that central banks should pick a long-run target range for inflation and stick with it. Many central banks around the world are doing just that, either explicitly or implicitly.

Inflation and Unemployment in the Short Term

There is a short-run trade-off between the rate of inflation and the rate of unemployment. The existence of a short-run trade-off has practical implications for policy. Monetary policy should keep the growth of aggregate demand stable to prevent fluctuations in real output and inflation. In fact, the improvements in monetary policy during the past 20 years have led to much more stable macroeconomic conditions. The United States experienced, back to back, the two longest peacetime expansions (1982–1990 and 1991–2000) in U.S. history, separated by one of the mildest recessions (1990–1991). Greater stability of monetary policy is largely responsible for this record-breaking macroeconomic stability. Recessions are typically preceded by a run-up of inflation; by keeping inflation from rising in the first place, the chance of such recessions is diminished.

Rational Expectations

People's expectations are highly responsive to policy; therefore, expectations matter for assessing the impact of monetary and fiscal policy. The most feasible empirical way to model this principle is the rational expectations approach. The hypothesis of **rational expectations** holds that firms and consumers make the most of the information available to them. By introducing rational expectations into fully estimated econometric models and then simulating the models for different policies, the response of expectations to changes in policy can be reasonably approximated.

This principle also has an impact on practice. Macroeconomic models with rational expectations now in use at the Fed can estimate the effects on interest rates of expected future budget deficits. These models can help guide monetary decisions about interest rates when a plan for budget deficit reduction (like those in 1990 and 1993 in the United States) is being considered. Another example of the practical relevance of this principle is the great emphasis placed on credibility by central banks today. According to the rational expectations approach, there are advantages to credibility in both monetary policy and fiscal policy. For example, a disinflation has lower short-run costs if policy is credible. Similarly, a plan to reduce the budget deficit has a smaller short-run contractionary effect if it is credible.

Monetary Policy Rules

Monetary policy makers should follow clear procedures and not administer onetime jolts. This fifth principle follows from the first four principles. A monetary policy rule describes how the central bank changes an instrument of monetary policy, usually the overnight interest rate, in response to developments in the economy. One policy rule that accurately describes the actions of the Fed since the mid-1980s is known as the **Taylor rule.** It describes the Fed as raising the overnight interest rate when inflation exceeds an inflation target and when GDP exceeds potential GDP. The size of the interest rate responses matters greatly. Moving the overnight interest rate more than one for one with the inflation rate, so that the real interest rate rises when inflation increases, is an essential property of a good policy rule. The importance of raising the real interest rate when inflation rises to the conduct of monetary policy is sometimes known as the **Taylor principle.**

Recently, practical interest in policy rules has increased. In a speech given at the January 2004 American Economic Association meetings, Federal Reserve Board chair Alan Greenspan emphasized that a key objective of monetary policy is to ensure that the response to incipient changes in inflation is forceful enough and that, in the face of incipient inflation, nominal interest rates must move up more than one for one.[2] Federal Reserve Board governors Laurence Meyer and Janet Yellen have described in detail how policy rules can be helpful in the formulation of monetary policy, and the Fed staff now uses a stochastic simulation of alternative policy rules on a regular basis. Monetary policy rules are also used for private sector forecasting. Many business economists have noted the similarity between the actions of the Fed and other central banks to the outcomes implied by certain policy rules.

1.5 | THE MACROECONOMIC MODEL USED IN THIS BOOK

Although many alternative theories are discussed, a main model appears throughout this book. The model *combines* the model of long-run economic growth, the model of short-run economic fluctuations, and the model of macroeconomic policy previewed in this chapter. The model assumes that classical principles describe the growth trend of the economy in the longer run. Supplies of labor and capital, and the process of innovation and technical progress, are important parts of the longer-run growth model. Recessions are

---

[2] See Alan Greenspan, "Risk and Uncertainty in Monetary Policy," *American Economic Review,* May 2004, 33–40.

HOW DID TODAY'S MACROECONOMISTS COME TO STUDY ECONOMICS?

Macroeconomists began studying economics for many different reasons. Some got interested because the hardships of the Great Depression of the 1930s touched them personally. For others it was pure chance. But, whatever the reason, they all liked it and stuck with it.*

Robert E. Lucas, Jr.

I have always liked to think about social problems. It may have something to do with my family. We always argued about politics and social issues. I studied history. . . . But I came around to the view that economic forces are central forces in history, and started trying some economics. It was a big shock to me to find books in English that were incomprehensible to me . . . [Like] Keynes's *General Theory*. I still can't read Keynes. [Laughter] I realized I couldn't pick it up as an amateur. So I got into economics in a professional way and got my Ph.D. at Chicago.

Thomas J. Sargent

[Long pause and hesitation] I liked it when we studied it in college. But also I was truly curious, ever since I was a kid, about what caused depressions. The Great Depression had a big effect on me: a lot of people in my family got wiped out. My grandfather ran a quarry in the construction business, and he got wiped out. My other grandfather was in the radio business, and he got wiped out. It was the common story.

Paul Romer

I was a math and physics major at the University of Chicago. I took my first economics course in my senior year because I was planning to go to law school. I did well in the class and the professor encouraged me to go on to graduate school to study economics. Economics offered some of the same intellectual appeal as physics—it uses simple mathematical models to understand how the world works—and in contrast to physics, it was an area of academic study where I could actually get a job.

Kenneth Rogoff

[Who retired as an international chess grandmaster at the age of 25] Being a chess player is much more like being an artist. It's a bohemian life, and I could have gone that way. But I am happy I chose to pursue economics. Why did I give up chess? The reason was threefold: I wanted to do something more important with my life; I didn't want to travel so much; and I didn't think it was great for my social life. Then, of course, I became an academic economist, which seemed to share the same three faults.

* See Arjo Klamer, *Conversations with Economists* (Totowa, N.J.: Rowman and Allanheld, 1984) for Lucas and Sargent; Brian Snowden and Howard Vane, *Conversations with Leading Economists* (Cheltenham, UK: Edward Elgar, 1999) for Romer; and *IMF Survey*, November 26, 2001, for Rogoff.

temporary departures from the growth path. Because of price and wage stickiness, the economy does not return immediately to potential GDP after a shock.

We call this the *complete model*, because it combines the elements of modern macroeconomics that we feel are essential to explaining growth, fluctuations, and policy. The complete model is developed in Chapters 4 through 9, with the important microeconomic foundations and more advanced policy analysis provided later in the book. In developing the complete model, we begin with the determinants of long-term potential growth (Chapters 4 through 6) and then discuss departures from the potential growth path (Chapters 7 through 9). The book continues with microeconomic foundations (Chapters 10–15) and macroeconomic policy (Chapters 16–18).

REVIEW AND PRACTICE

Major Points

1. The economy fluctuates around its long-run growth path. These fluctuations, however, are not symmetric. Output and employment expand and contract at irregular intervals.

2. Other measures of the state of the economy, such as interest rates and inflation, also exhibit fluctuations.

3. The long-run growth model is used to study the general upward path of the economy over time. The level of potential GDP is the amount of GDP that the economy will produce according to the model of long-run growth.

4. The model of fluctuations explains departures of the economy from its long-run growth path.

5. There is no long-term trade-off between the rate of inflation and the rate of unemployment.

6. There is a short-run trade-off between the rate of inflation and the rate of unemployment, and the existence of this trade-off has practical implications for policy.

7. Monetary policy in the United States since the mid-1980s is well-described by a rule where the Fed increases the real interest rate when inflation rises and when GDP exceeds potential GDP.

Key Terms and Concepts

macroeconomics	interest rates
business cycles	real interest rate
microeconomics	money supply
real gross domestic product (GDP)	potential GDP
recessions	monetary policy
expansions	monetary policy rule
recoveries	rational expectations
unemployment rate	Taylor rule
inflation	Taylor principle

Questions for Discussion and Review

1. What is the difference between potential GDP and real GDP?

2. What are the determinants of potential GDP?

3. How have economic fluctuations changed during the last 90 years?

4. What is a monetary policy rule?

5. What is the difference between positive and normative macroeconomics?

6. What is the hypothesis of rational expectations?

7. What policy rule accurately describes the actions of the Fed since the mid-1980s?

Problems

NUMERICAL

1. Real output in the United Kingdom from 1960 through 2002 follows. All data are in billions of 2000 pounds.

1960	355.9	1975	529.4	1990	750.7
1961	364.6	1976	543.6	1991	740.4
1962	368.9	1977	556.9	1992	741.9
1963	387.8	1978	575.2	1993	759.1
1964	409.4	1979	590.7	1994	792.7
1965	418.9	1980	578.6	1995	815.2
1966	427.1	1981	570.2	1996	837.2
1967	437.7	1982	581.1	1997	864.7
1968	456.2	1983	601.7	1998	891.7
1969	465.8	1984	617.2	1999	916.6
1970	476.4	1985	639.2	2000	951.3
1971	486.1	1986	664.5	2001	971.6
1972	503.6	1987	694.7	2002	987.9
1973	539.6	1988	729.2		
1974	532.2	1989	745.0		

(a) Plot U.K. real output over the 42-year period. Put real output on the vertical axis of the graph and the year on the horizontal axis.

(b) Estimate potential output by drawing a smooth trend line through the points on the graph. Identify any shifts in the trend of potential. By what percent did real output grow during this period?

(c) Identify the fluctuations of real output around potential output. How many complete (peak-to-peak) economic fluctuations occurred during this period? How does the frequency of economic fluctuations during this period compare with that of the United States during the same period?

2. We have the following data on interest rates and the price level (in the United States) for the years 1977–2002:

YEAR	PRICE LEVEL	INTEREST RATES (PERCENT)
1977	60.6	5.6
1978	65.2	7.6
1979	72.6	10.0
1980	82.4	11.4
1981	90.9	13.8
1982	96.5	11.1
1983	99.6	8.8
1984	103.9	9.8
1985	107.6	7.7
1986	109.6	6.1
1987	113.6	6.1
1988	118.3	7.0
1989	124.0	8.0
1990	130.7	7.5
1991	136.2	5.5
1992	140.3	3.6
1993	144.5	3.1
1994	148.2	4.7
1995	152.4	5.6
1996	156.9	5.1
1997	160.5	5.2
1998	163.0	4.9
1999	166.6	4.8
2000	172.2	5.9
2001	177.1	3.4
2002	179.9	1.7

(a) Calculate the rate of inflation for the years 1978–2002.

(b) Calculate the expected rate of inflation for the years 1979–2002 assuming (i) people expect the rate of inflation to be the average rate of inflation in the two previous years and (ii) people have perfect foresight and expected inflation just equals actual inflation.

(c) For each of the assumptions in part b, calculate the real interest rate for the years 1977–2002.

(d) In light of this example, explain why economists have such a difficult time measuring the real interest rate.

(e) How do you think people forecast inflation? What information do they use? Do you think they systematically underestimate changes in the price level?

ANALYTICAL

1. Starting from a peak, describe a typical macroeconomic fluctuation.

2. Describe the determinants of potential GDP growth.

3. There is no long-term trade-off between the rate of inflation and the rate of unemployment. What are the implications of this principle on the conduct of monetary policy?

4. There is a short-run trade-off between the rate of inflation and the rate of unemployment. What are the implications of this principle on the conduct of monetary policy?

5. Describe the five core principles economists agree on.

MEASURING ECONOMIC PERFORMANCE

In Chapter 1, we examined the behavior of several key macroeconomic variables—production, employment, and inflation. In this chapter we show how these and other important variables are defined and measured.

2.1 | GROSS DOMESTIC PRODUCT

We begin with gross domestic product. GDP refers to production during a particular time period, which we will usually take to be a year or a quarter of a year. It is the *flow* of new products during the year or quarter, measured in dollars. When we adjust GDP for the effects of inflation, we get real GDP, the measure of physical output discussed in Chapter 1.

There are three different ways to think about and measure GDP. First, we can measure *spending* on goods and services by different groups—households, businesses, government, and foreigners. Second, we can measure *production* in different industries—agriculture, mining, manufacturing, and so on. Last, we can measure the total wage and profit *income* earned by different groups producing GDP. Each of these measures has its special purpose, but they all add up to the same thing. We consider each in turn in the next three sections.

How do we know that the total amount of spending is equal to the total value of production, which in turn is equal to the total amount of income? Think about an individual firm. Suppose the value of its production is $1 million. Suppose that spending by consumers on the firm's product is $900,000. For accounting purposes, we treat the remaining $100,000 as spending. It is the firm's investment in inventories of its own goods, included as part of total investment. Both at the level of the firm and the level of the whole economy, the equality of production and spending is the result of considering inventory investment as part of spending; that is, spending = $900,000 + $100,000 = $1,000,000 = production.

The equality of the value of production and income also derives from accounting principles. Our firm takes in $900,000 in one year. In addition, we add in the $100,000 value of its inventory accumulation as sales, for a total value of production of $1 million. The firm pays out $450,000 in wages. That amount is counted in the incomes of the workers. The firm pays $50,000 in interest, which is counted in the incomes of whoever lent money to the firm. It pays $400,000 for its raw materials, which is counted in the incomes of the sellers of materials or their employees. The residual, $1,000,000 − $450,000 − $50,000 − $400,000 = $100,000, is the profit earned by the owner of the firm and counts as part of the owner's income. All the receipts of the firm from its sales are paid out to somebody as income. The value of production and the total amount of income generated are the same.

As a result of the two accounting rules—including inventories in spending and computing profit as the residual between sales and expenses—it is always true that production, spending, and income are exactly the same. This kind of relation is called an *identity;* it is the inevitable outcome of the accounting system, not a statement about how the economy works.

The alternative measures of GDP are gathered together in the national income and product accounts (NIPA). Economists and statisticians at the Bureau of Economic Analysis (BEA), an agency of the United States government in Washington, DC, are responsible for collecting the GDP data and publishing the NIPA. Many of the ideas behind the GDP were developed by the late Simon Kuznets of Harvard University. He won the Nobel Prize in economics in 1971 for this work.

2.2 | MEASURING GDP THROUGH SPENDING

Total spending on goods and services produced by Americans during any period can be broken down as follows:

> Gross domestic product = Consumption
> + Investment
> + Government purchases
> + Net exports (or exports minus imports).

Using symbols, this key identity can be written on one line:

$$Y = C + I + G + X,$$

where Y = Gross domestic product
C = Consumption
I = Investment
G = Government spending
X = Net exports (exports minus imports).

Consumption

Consumption is defined as spending by *households*. It includes purchases of (1) *durable goods*, such as washing machines, stereos, and cars; (2) *nondurable goods*, such as food, clothing, and gasoline; and (3) *services*, such as haircuts, medical care, and education. However, the measurement of consumption does not consist simply of blindly summing all purchases made by households during a given time period. To be included in the consumption portion of GDP, the goods purchased must be new purchases. Items purchased used, such as a resold computer or a car auctioned used, are excluded in the calculation of consumption. Additionally, spending on new houses is the only type of household spending that is not included in consumption. Instead it is included in fixed investment. Consumption was the primary force behind economic growth in 2002, rising at an annual rate of about 3 percent. Spending on consumer durables, particularly automobiles, was especially strong.

Investment

Investment is the sum of spending by firms on goods such as plant, equipment, and inventories and spending by households on housing. We separate total investment into fixed investment and inventory investment. **Fixed investment** is the purchase of new factories, machines, and houses. **Inventory investment** is the change in inventories at business firms from one year to another. We first discuss fixed investment.

FIXED INVESTMENT   Fixed investment is broken down into nonresidential fixed investment and residential fixed investment. **Nonresidential fixed investment** is spending on structures and equipment for use in business. Steel mills, office buildings, and power plants are examples of structures. Trucks, lathes, and computers are examples of equipment. **Residential fixed investment** is spending on construction of new houses and apartment buildings. The term *fixed* connotes that these types of investment goods will be around for a long time and distinguishes them from inventory investment, which is much more temporary, as we will see. The term *fixed* is conventionally dropped when the meaning is implicit from the context, and we follow this convention.

Investment is a *flow* of new capital during the year that is added to the *stock* of capital. The **capital stock** is the total physical amount of productive capital in the economy; it includes all the buildings, equipment, and houses. The capital stock increases from one year to the next as a result of investment. However, because the capital stock is constantly wearing out, part of the investment reported in each year's GDP is actually devoted to replacing worn-out capital, not increasing the capital stock. What is reported in GDP is *gross* investment. This accounts for the term *gross* in GDP. Statisticians have a number of ways of estimating the loss of the existing capital stock from one year to the next. This loss is called **depreciation. Net investment** is defined as follows:

$$\text{Net investment} = \text{Gross investment} - \text{Depreciation.}$$

We have the following relation:

Capital stock at the end of this year = Capital stock at the end of last year
− Depreciation during this year
+ Gross investment during this year.

By rearranging this equation and putting in the definition of net investment, we have:

Net investment = Capital stock at the end of this year
− Capital stock at the end of last year.

These equations hold whether we are looking at total investment or separately at nonresidential and residential investment.

INVENTORY INVESTMENT   Now consider inventory investment, which is simply the change in the stock of inventories held at businesses.

Inventory investment this year = Stock of inventories at the end of this year
− Stock of inventories at the end of last year.

For example, when a publisher produces and stores 10,000 copies of a newly printed book in its warehouse, the books are counted in GDP as inventory investment. Even though no one has yet purchased the books, they must be counted in GDP because they have been produced. If subsequently you purchase a book directly from the publisher, consumption is up by one book and inventory investment is down by one book; GDP does not change, nor should it, since there is no new production. When the publisher sells a book to a bookstore, the publisher's inventory investment is down by one book and the bookstore's inventory investment is up by one book. Total inventory investment does not change and neither does GDP.

Inventory investment is positive when inventories are increasing and negative when inventories are decreasing. In 2000, a year of strong growth, inventory investment was $64 billion. In 2001, a recession year, it was −$60 billion. If inventory investment were not added to spending when computing GDP, we would underestimate production when inventory investment was positive, as in 2000, because spending would be less than production; similarly, we would overestimate production when inventory investment was negative, as in 2001, because spending would be more than production.

As the data for 2000 and 2001 show, inventory investment adds to the fluctuations of GDP. Final sales is a measure that excludes inventory investment. *Final sales* is defined as GDP minus inventory investment. Final sales fluctuates less than GDP.

Government Purchases

Government purchases are the sum of federal government and state and local government purchases of goods and services. In 2000, state and local government purchases were 65 percent of total government purchases. These purchases include items such as schools, road construction, and military hardware. However, it should be noted that government purchases are only part of the total government *outlays* included in the government budget. When measuring government purchases, economists exclude transfer payments of income from the government to individuals; this includes items such as welfare payments and interest payments on public debt. These items are excluded since they do not reflect production.

The distinction between consumption, investment, and government purchases is based primarily on the type of purchaser rather than on the type of product purchased. If a Chevrolet is purchased by a household, it goes into consumption—as a consumer durable. If it is purchased for use by a business, it goes into investment—as business fixed investment in equipment. If it is purchased by government, it goes into government purchases. The only exception to this rule is residential investment, which includes all housing purchases whether by households, businesses, or government.

Imports and Exports

The United States has an open economy. An *open economy* is one with substantial interaction with other countries. The United States has experienced a growing volume of transactions with the rest of the world, and GDP has to take these into account. **Exports** are goods and services produced in the United States and purchased by foreign consumers, businesses, or governments. **Imports** are goods and services produced abroad and purchased by United States consumers, businesses, or governments. Since exports are produced in the United States, they are counted as part of GDP even though they are not part of domestic consumption, investment, or government purchases. Since imports are produced abroad, they are not counted as part of GDP even though they are part of domestic consumption, investment, or government purchases.

For these reasons, imports are subtracted from spending and exports are added to spending when computing GDP. In other words, only *net exports*, that is, *exports less imports*, are added to the total volume of spending when computing GDP. The total of net exports is sometimes referred to as the *trade balance*. When net exports are positive there is a *trade surplus*. When net exports are negative there is a *trade deficit*. The United States had a very large trade deficit in the early 2000s. There is another complication in computing imports and exports. Only part of United States exports represent goods and services *produced* by Americans. The other part has been imported to the United States and then sold abroad, perhaps as part of manufactured products. For example, General Motors might put a radio imported from Japan into a Chevrolet that is exported to Mexico. We want to subtract the radio from the exported car if we are measuring goods produced by Americans.

The Recent Composition of Spending

Table 2.1 breaks down U.S. GDP for 2002. Consumption is the biggest component—about two-thirds—of GDP. Services is the biggest component of consumption—about 59 percent. Services (restaurants, utilities, housing, transportation, medical care, and the like) have been growing as a share of consumption. In the early 1950s, services accounted for less than a third of consumption. Medical services have grown most rapidly.

Fixed investment is about 15 percent of GDP. Nonresidential fixed investment is much larger than residential fixed investment. Government purchases are larger than investment, at about 19 percent of GDP. Imports are about 14 percent of GDP. Exports are 10 percent of GDP. Foreign trade is now a much bigger factor in the United States than it was 20 or 30 years ago. In the early 1950s, exports and imports each were about 5 percent of GDP.

TABLE 2.1

GROSS DOMESTIC PRODUCT IN 2002— THE SPENDING SIDE (BILLIONS OF DOLLARS)

Gross domestic product	10445.6
Consumption	7301.9
Durables	871.7
Nondurables	2115.0
Services	4315.2
Investment	1593.0
Fixed Investment	1589.3
Nonresidential	1117.5
Residental	471.8
Inventory investment	3.6
Government purchases	1973.3
Net Exports	−422.5
Exports	1015.8
Imports	1438.2
Final sales	10266.5

Note: Final sales is GDP less inventory investment. Details in the table may not add to totals because of rounding.
SOURCE: U.S. Department of Commerce, *Survey of Current Business*, March 2003, p. d-2.

BRINGING ASTRONOMICAL NUMBERS DOWN TO EARTH

Table 2.1 shows that GDP was $10,445.6 billion, or about $10.4 trillion, in 2002. With all the zeros this looks like $10,445,600,000,000. An astrophysicist would write it 10.4456×10^{12} dollars. How can we make intuitive sense of such large numbers?

The best way to bring numbers like these down to size is simply to divide by the population; that is, to calculate GDP per person, or GDP per capita. The population in the United States in 2002 was 289 million. GDP per capita in the United States is therefore $36,144 (10,445,600,000,000/289,000,000 = 36,143.94). U.S. consumption in 2002 was $7,301.9 billion.

This amounts to about $25,266 per capita for food, clothing, transportation, and other consumer items. On average, every man, woman, and child in the United States consumed $25,266 of goods and services in 2002.

Government purchases of goods and services were $1,973.3 billion in 2002. This amounted to $6,828 per capita for national defense, schools, highways, police, and so on. Net exports were −$422.5 billion in 2002, or about −$1,462 per capita. In other words, on average, every person in the United States bought $1,462 more goods that were made abroad than they made goods that were sold abroad.

These shares fluctuate from year to year, but the two-thirds consumption share is fairly typical of recent years in the United States. Inventory investment and net exports fluctuate dramatically and can be negative as well as positive; no year is typical. Since exports were smaller than imports in 2002, net exports were negative. Final sales were less than GDP in 2002, since inventory investment was positive.

Which Spending Items Should Be Included?

In deciding which spending items to include in computing GDP, we must be careful to avoid double counting. For example, the purchase of a 10-year-old house should not be counted; that house was counted 10 years ago when it was constructed. Similarly, the purchase of the assets of Mobil Oil by Exxon should not be counted; the Mobil building in Pittsburgh and Mobil's offshore oil rigs were included in business fixed investment when they were built.

To avoid double counting, we also do not include the purchase of **intermediate goods.** These are goods that are converted into other goods in the production process (for example, steel is an intermediate good used in the production of cars). We include only **final goods,** such as the cars themselves. The value of the steel is included in GDP as part of a car when someone buys the car. The purchases of steel by automobile manufacturers are not counted.

In computing GDP, we value different types of goods, such as apples and oranges, using the price of each good that is paid by the purchaser. The price includes sales and excise taxes. If apples cost twice as much as oranges, then each apple contributes twice as much to GDP as each orange.

Real GDP

GDP is a dollar measure of production or final goods and services during one year. Comparing one year with another, we run into the problem that the dollar is not a stable measure of purchasing power. For example, in the 1970s, GDP rose a great deal, not because the economy was actually growing rapidly but because the dollar was inflating. As this example suggests, the measure of GDP (what we have used to measure production up to this point) fails to be an adequate representation of production for comparison across time. Therefore, to correct this discrepancy and make GDP comparisons across years, we need a measure of output that adjusts for inflation. We want *GDP in constant dollars*, or as we generally call it, **real GDP.** In contrast, the GDP we looked at so far is sometimes called **nominal GDP.** From 1970 to 2000, nominal GDP grew by 850 percent, from $1,039.7 billion to $9,872.9 billion. During the same period, real GDP grew by about 158 percent. The conversion from nominal to real makes a big difference.

The concept of real GDP is straightforward. We want to measure consumption, investment, government purchases, and exports in physical rather

CHAIN-WEIGHTED GDP

The calculation of GDP starts with data on many components of consumption, investment, and other categories. The data show the dollar flows of purchases and the prices. For each component, the real flow of purchases is the dollar flow divided by the price. How should we calculate total real consumption, total real investment, and total real GDP? In the past, the answer was to choose a base year. Real quantities in the base year are taken to be the dollar quantities in that year. The prices are set to 1 in the base year. For later years, the national income and product accounts compute real quantities by dividing the dollar amounts by the prices. Then, the real totals are the sums of the real components.

The traditional procedure has the defect that, as the years go by, it gives too much weight to components whose prices have fallen. The category that has caused the most trouble is computers. The easiest way to see the problem and the solution is in an example. Suppose that investment consists of computers and dump trucks and the basic data over a four-year period are as follows:

YEAR	DOLLAR PURCHASES		PRICES	
	COMPUTERS	DUMP TRUCKS	COMPUTERS	DUMP TRUCKS
1	100	106	1.00	1.00
2	105	98	0.80	1.05
3	103	104	0.60	1.10
4	99	100	0.40	1.15

The traditional calculations are

	REAL QUANTITIES			
YEAR	COMPUTERS	DUMP TRUCKS	TOTAL REAL INVESTMENT	INVESTMENT DEFLATOR
1	100.0	106.0	206.0	1.000
2	131.3	93.3	224.6	0.904
3	171.7	94.5	266.2	0.778
4	247.5	87.0	334.5	0.595

The weighting problem is evident: Although, in year 4, dollar spending on computers is slightly below spending on dump trucks, the real quantity of computers is almost three times as large.

The solution to this problem has been known for many decades. For two adjacent years, we can calculate the rate of growth of each real component. Then, we can calculate the rate of growth of the aggregate as the weighted sum of the individual real growth rates, using the current dollar spending flows to derive weights. Finally, we can cumulate the growth rates to get the real aggregate. Below are the calculations for the investment example:

The result of keeping the weights in line with the relative dollar spending is to reduce the growth in total real investment and raise the growth in the deflator. The use of a fixed earlier year invariably gives too optimistic a picture about real growth. For the period 1988–1994, the bias in the traditional approach is about 0.4 percent—the traditional measure of real GDP growth was 15.3 percent and the new chain-weighted measure was 14.8 percent.

YEAR	WEIGHT FOR COMPUTERS	GROWTH RATE OF TOTAL REAL INVESTMENT	CUMULATED TOTAL REAL INVESTMENT	INVESTMENT DEFLATOR
1	0.485		206.0	1.000
2	0.517	0.017	209.6	0.969
3	0.498	0.046	219.4	0.943
4	0.497	0.061	233.2	0.853

than dollar units. Further, we want to subtract imports in the same physical units, so that real GDP is a measure of production.

To compute consumption in real terms, the national income statisticians gather data on the prices of consumption goods in great detail. They take the data on the corresponding detailed flows of goods to consumers and restate them in 1996 dollars. For example, suppose the retail price of a typical shirt rose from $10.00 in 1996 to $12.00 in 2000. The flow of shirts to consumers was $3 billion in 1996 and $5 billion in 2000. Consumption of shirts in real terms was $3 billion in 1996 dollars in 1996 and $4.17 billion in 1996 dollars in 2000. The $4.17 billion is computed as

$$(5 \text{ billion 2000 dollars}) \times [(10/12) \text{ 1996 dollars per 2000 dollar}]$$
$$= 4.17 \text{ billion 1996 dollars.}$$

The same type of adjustment for price change is applied to each detailed category of consumption, investment, government purchases, exports, and imports. Then real GDP is real consumption plus real investment plus real government purchases plus real exports less real imports.

2.3 | MEASURING GDP THROUGH PRODUCTION: VALUE ADDED

GDP can also be computed by adding up production of goods and services in different industries. As we observed on the spending side, we must avoid counting the same items more than once. Many industries specialize in the production of intermediate goods used in the production of other goods. If we want each industry's production to include the contribution of those industries to total GDP, then we want to take the production of intermediate goods into account.

The concept of **value added** was developed to prevent double counting and attribute to each industry a part of GDP. The value added by a firm is the difference between the revenue the firm earns by selling its products and the amount it pays for the products of other firms it uses as intermediate goods. It is a measure of the value that is added to each product by firms at each stage of production.

For General Motors, for example, value added is the revenue from selling cars less the amount it pays for steel, glass, and the other inputs it buys. For a car dealer, value added is the revenue from selling cars less the wholesale cost of the cars. Wages, rents, interest, and profits are what make up value added at each firm.

GDP is the sum of the value added by all the firms located in the United States. If a firm sells a final product, the sale appears in that firm's value added but does not appear anywhere else. On the other hand, if a firm sells its output as an input for another firm, that sale appears negatively in the other firm's value added. Products sold by one firm to another are called *intermediate goods.* When the two firms are added together in the process of computing GDP, sales of intermediate goods wash out. When a firm imports a good, the transaction appears negatively in that firm's value added but does not appear positively in the value added of any U.S. firm.

A breakdown of real GDP in terms of the value added by various industries is given in Table 2.2 for 1987 and 2001. These figures tell some interesting stories about the modern U.S. economy. Services and finance, insurance, and real estate are the two largest sectors, and the wholesale and retail trade sector, whose function is to take produced goods and make them available to the public, is a close third. The manufacturing sector is also large.

Near the bottom of the list is a small item called *statistical discrepancy.* Although the value-added computation of GDP should give the same answer as total spending, in practice measurement errors cause a slight discrepancy between the two.

TABLE 2.2

VALUE ADDED, BY INDUSTRY, IN 1987 AND 2001 (BILLIONS OF 1996 DOLLARS)

	1987	PERCENT	2001	PERCENT
GDP	6113		9215	
Agriculture	110	1.80	164	1.78
Mining	99	1.61	107	1.16
Construction	278	4.55	372	4.04
Manufacturing	1046	17.12	1490	16.17
Transportation and utilities	460	7.53	781	8.47
Wholesale and retail trade	866	14.16	1700	18.45
Finance, insurance, and real estate	1169	19.13	1844	20.01
Services	1181	19.32	1843	20.00
Government	938	15.34	1108	12.02
Statistical discrepancy	4	0.07	−108	−1.18

SOURCE: *Economic Report of the President,* 2003, Table B-13.

2.4 | MEASURING GDP THROUGH INCOME

The Americans who produce GDP receive income for their work. This income provides a third way to compute GDP. To see the relation between GDP and income, think again about the value added of a car dealer. Value added is the difference between the revenue from selling cars and the wholesale cost of cars. That difference must be somebody's income. Part of the difference is the wages the car dealer pays to salespeople and mechanics. Another part is the rent that the car dealer pays to a landlord for the use of the showroom and garage. Another part is the interest that the car dealer pays to a bank for loans to finance inventory. The rest of the difference is profit, which goes into the income of the owner of the car dealership. All of a firm's value added is either rent, interest, or profit. Since we know that the sum of all firms' value added is GDP, the sum of all incomes must also equal GDP.

Why national income is different from GDP

Because of taxes and certain other complications, there are several concepts of income. The most comprehensive is **national income.** It is a broad measure of the incomes of Americans, including income taxes and several other items that are deducted before people receive actual payments. There are three important reasons why national income is different from GDP. First, some Americans earn at least part of their income abroad, and some have invested capital abroad and earn income on that capital. This income from work or capital is called *factor income from the rest of the world*. It must be added to GDP to get a measure of income. On the other hand, some of U.S. GDP is earned by foreigners who work in the United States or who have invested capital in the United States. This, called *factor income to the rest of the world*, must be subtracted from GDP to get a measure of income. GDP plus factor income from the rest of the world minus factor income to the rest of the world is called the *gross national product* (GNP). It is a measure of goods and services purchased by Americans rather than in America.

GNP

A second reason that GDP is different from national income is that depreciation must be subtracted to get national income. A third is that national income is measured in terms of the prices firms receive for the products they sell, whereas GDP is measured in terms of the prices paid by purchasers. Prices received differ from prices paid by the amount of sales and excise taxes.

There are two other minor conceptual differences. Business transfer payments (such as business gifts) are deducted from national income. Subsidies paid by the government to the businesses it runs are added to national income.

Finally, there is the statistical discrepancy. Conceptually, the income calculation should be numerically the same as the spending calculation of GDP. But, because of measurement errors, there is a small discrepancy. (This discrepancy is identical to the discrepancy in the calculation of value added, which attributes incomes to the various industries.)

The relation between GDP and national income is shown in Table 2.3.

TABLE 2.3

RELATION BETWEEN GDP AND NATIONAL INCOME IN 2001 (BILLIONS OF DOLLARS)

Gross domestic product	10208.1
plus: Net factor payments	−5.3
equals: Gross national product	10202.8
less: Depreciation	1351.4
equals: Net national product	8851.4
less: Sales and excise taxes	794
less: Business transfers	44.6
less: Statistical discrepancy	−149.8
plus: Net subsidies to government business	54.8
equals: National income	8217.5

SOURCE: U.S. Department of Commerce, *Survey of Current Business*, May 2002, p. D-5.

Government and businesses also raise and lower the incomes of some people. The NIPA contain two concepts of income that take account of these diversions and augmentations. **Personal income** is total income received by the public before income taxes, and **disposable personal income** is total income after income taxes.

For wage income, the social security tax is one of the important differences between wages paid by businesses and wages received by workers. The aggregate amount of social security tax, called *contributions for social insurance*, is one of the items subtracted from national income to get personal income.

All the profits of corporations are included in national income, but only the cash payments of dividends by corporations are included in personal income. The difference between profits and dividends consists of *retained earnings* and the income taxes paid by corporations. These two items are excluded from personal income.

People have two important sources of income other than the production of goods and services. First, the government pays social security and other benefits. Second, people receive interest from the government debt and other nonbusiness sources. Both are included in personal income. Note that social security contributions by employers are taken out of personal income, but the benefits financed by the contributions are added back into personal income.

The relationship among the three concepts of income is shown in Table 2.4. Disposable personal income was $7,417.3 billion, or $26,023 per capita. Consumption per capita was $24,786, so all but $1,237 of income per capita was consumed.

TABLE 2.4

NATIONAL INCOME, PERSONAL INCOME, AND PERSONAL DISPOSABLE INCOME IN 2001 (BILLIONS OF DOLLARS)

National income	8217.5
less: Contributions for social insurance	731.2
less: Corporate retained earnings	1321.4
plus: Nonbusiness interest	1409.9
plus: Transfer payments from government and business	1148.8
equals: Personal income	8723.5
less: Income taxes	1306.2
equals: Personal disposable income	7417.3

Note: Wage accruals less disbursements, a trivial accounting item, is omitted from the list of adjustments to national income.
SOURCE: U.S. Department of Commerce, *Survey of Current Business*, May 2002, pp. D-5 and D-7.

How much of national income is earned by workers and how much is profit? Table 2.5 shows the breakdown for 2001. About 73 percent of national income was earned by labor; this includes payments to workers in wages and salaries as well as fringe benefits. The profit share includes not only corporate profits but also rental income, proprietors' income, and net interest income. Since labor plus profits exhausts income, the profit share was 27 percent in 2001. These relative shares are fairly stable from year to year. In 1970, the labor share of national income was 74 percent.

TABLE 2.5

LABOR AND PROFIT SHARES OF NATIONAL INCOME IN 2001 (BILLIONS OF DOLLARS)

Compensation of employees	6010	Labor share 73 percent
Proprietors' income	743.5	
Rental income of persons	142.6	
Corporate profits	767.1	Profit share 27 percent
Net interest	554.3	
National income	8217.5	

SOURCE: U.S. Department of Commerce, *Survey of Current Business*, May 2002, p. D-6.

The National Income and Product Accounts

1. Gross domestic product (GDP) is the production of goods and services in the United States. The spending, value added, and factor income measures of GDP are all equal.

2. Consumption, investment, government purchases, and net exports are the four basic components of spending. Consumption is the largest component and investment is the most volatile component.

3. The investment component of GDP includes the replacement of depreciating capital. It is thus gross investment. Net investment is gross investment less depreciation.

4. Real GDP is a measure of production adjusted for the effects of inflation. It measures the physical volume of production. Nominal GDP measures the dollar volume of production.

5. Final sales is GDP less inventory investment. It fluctuates less than GDP.

6. To avoid double counting, we measure the contribution of each industry by its value added and do not include any goods produced in an earlier year.

7. Disposable personal income is the amount of national income available for households to spend. It excludes retained earnings of corporations. It includes what is left of wage and salary income, fringe benefits, rents, dividends, interest, and small business income after all taxes are paid to governments.

2.5 | SAVING AND INVESTMENT

Saving is defined as income minus consumption. An important principle is that *saving must equal investment*. To see this, consider first a closed economy with no government and therefore no taxes. Then,

$$\text{Spending on GDP} = \text{Consumption} + \text{Investment}.$$

Also, from the definition of saving,

$$\text{Income} = \text{Saving} + \text{Consumption}.$$

Since spending on GDP equals income, we know that

$$\text{Consumption} + \text{Investment} = \text{Saving} + \text{Consumption}$$

or

$$\boxed{\text{Investment} = \text{Saving.}}$$

The equality of saving and investment follows from none other than the definitions of GDP and income. As long as the statisticians adhere to these definitions, there is no possibility that investment can ever differ from saving. We don't have to say, "If our theories hold, saving and investment are equal." No matter how investors and consumers behave, saving and investment are equal.

Saving and Investment in an Open Economy

Some more symbols save space in the explanation of saving and investment in an open economy. Let

F = Government transfers to the private sector
Q = Interest on the government debt
T = Taxes
V = Factor income and transfer payments from abroad (net)
S_p = Private saving (saving of the private sector)
S_g = Government saving
S_r = Rest of world saving;

and recall that we previously defined

Y = GDP
C = Consumption
I = Investment
G = Government spending
X = Net exports.

PRIVATE SAVING   From the definition of saving, we know that private saving is disposable income $(Y + V + F + Q - T)$ minus consumption (C):

$$S_p = (Y + V + F + Q - T) - C. \tag{2.1}$$

GOVERNMENT SAVING   Government saving equals income (tax receipts, net of transfer payments and interest payments) minus purchases of goods and services:

$$S_g = (T - F - Q) - G. \tag{2.2}$$

$+S_g \qquad -S_g$

Government saving is also called the government **budget surplus** or **budget deficit**. The budget is in surplus when G is less than $(T - F - Q)$ and in deficit when G is greater than $(T - F - Q)$.

REST OF THE WORLD SAVING The rest of the world saving in the United States is defined as payments received from the United States less payments made to the United States. We need to keep track of three types of payments. Payments received from the United States include (1) payments for our imports, (2) factor payments to foreigners, and (3) transfer payments to foreigners. Payments made to the United States include (1) payments for our exports, (2) factor payments to Americans, and (3) transfer payments to Americans.

Rest of the world saving is the sum of the net payments for each type: (1) imports less exports, or *net* exports with the sign reversed, (2) factor payments to foreigners less factor payments from foreigners, or *net* factor income from abroad with the sign reversed, and (3) transfer payments to foreigners less transfer payments to Americans, or *net* transfer payments from abroad with the sign reversed. In terms of our notation, (1) is equal to $-X$, and (2) plus (3) is equal to $-V$. Therefore,

$$S_r = -X - V. \tag{2.3}$$

The sum $V + X$ is sometimes called *net foreign investment of the United States*. Recall that X is the *trade surplus* (if positive) or *deficit* (if negative). As we describe in the next section, $V + X$ is the *surplus* (or *deficit*) on the *current account*. Hence, foreign saving is positive in the United States when the United States is running a current account deficit. The rest of the world saving is used to either buy financial assets in the United States or reduce foreign financial liabilities. Either is called a *capital inflow*. Put another way, the United States finances any excess of imports over exports by borrowing from abroad. Then, rest of the world lending is equal to U.S. borrowing.

For the three sectors as a whole, saving must equal investment. The sum of the three sectors' saving is

$$I = S_p + S_g + S_r = Y - C - G - X$$

$$S_p + S_g + S_r = (Y + V + F + Q - T)$$
$$- C + (T - F - Q - G) - V - X. \tag{2.4}$$

Everything cancels out on the right-hand side except $Y - C - G - X$, which from the income identity is equal to investment, I. Thus, private saving plus government saving plus saving from the rest of the world equals investment. This identity is of great importance in interpreting movements in investment and saving. Because of large shifts in the saving of these three sectors in recent years, the identity deserves particular emphasis, as is illustrated in Table 2.6.

Table 2.6 shows investment in the United States in 2002 and where the saving came from. *National saving* is the sum of private plus government saving and in 2002 equaled $1,573.7 billion. Investment in factories and equipment in the United States was $2,069.3 billion, larger than national saving because of the willingness of foreigners to save in the United States.

Figure 2.1 shows the trends in investment and saving since 1980. Except in the recession year 1991, investment has been greater than national saving,

TABLE 2.6

GROSS SAVING AND INVESTMENT, 2002
(BILLIONS OF DOLLARS)

National saving $(S_p + S_g)$	1573.7
plus: Foreign saving (S_r)	495.6
equals: Investment (I)	2069.3

SOURCE: *Economic Report of the President*, 2003, Table B-32.

so that foreign saving has been positive. Foreign saving is related to the trade deficit. As the gap between investment and national saving rose in the 1990s and the early-2000s, the trade deficit also rose. Figure 2.1 shows how dramatic that pattern was. Figure 2.2 shows how the trade deficit (X) has the same pattern.

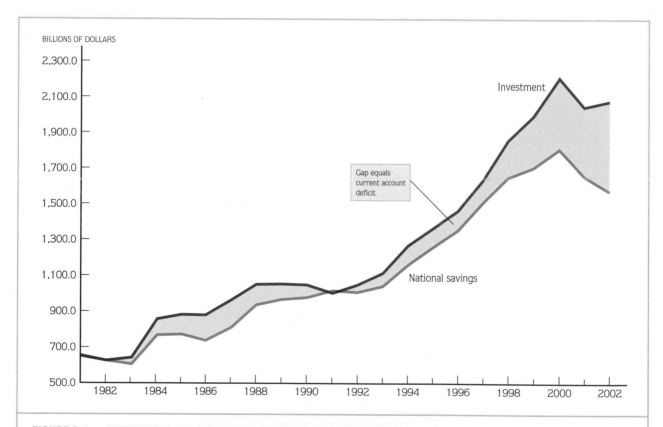

FIGURE 2.1   INVESTMENT AND NATIONAL SAVING IN THE UNITED STATES

The gap between investment and national saving (private plus government saving) rose and then fell during the 1980s. It rose again in the 1990s and early-2000s. The gap equals the current account deficit.

SOURCE: *Economic Report of the President*, 2003, Table B-32.

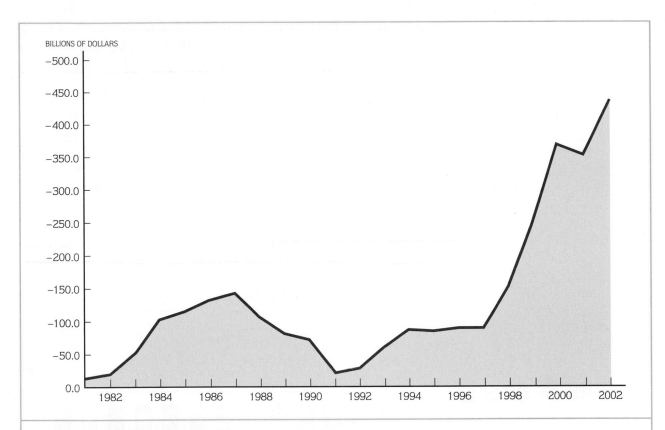

FIGURE 2.2   U.S. TRADE DEFICIT

The trade deficit is closely related to the gap between investment and national saving shown in Figure 2.1. As the gap widened, so did the trade deficit. (The gap equals $X + V$, where X is the trade deficit and V is other net payments to foreigners.)

SOURCE: *Economic Report of the President*, 2003, Table B-1.

2.6 | TRANSACTIONS WITH THE REST OF THE WORLD: THE BALANCE OF PAYMENT ACCOUNTS AND THE EXCHANGE RATE

The balance of payments accounts record transactions between Americans and the rest of the world. International transactions are divided into *current account transactions* and *financial account transactions*. The **current account** keeps track of net exports of goods and services, net interest payments, and net international transfers such as government grants and remittances (when a worker in a foreign country sends money home). The **financial account** keeps track of borrowing and lending. When an American lends to a foreigner, by making a loan, buying a bond, or some similar transaction, the lending appears with a negative sign in the financial account. When an American borrows by taking out a loan in another country or selling stocks and bonds, the borrowing appears with a positive sign. The term *balance of payments* refers to both the current account and the financial account.

An important principle of the balance of payments accounts is that the current account and the financial account should sum to zero. When the United States imports more than it exports, it is borrowing from the rest of the world to finance its current account deficit. There should be a positive balance in the financial account equal in magnitude to the current account deficit. This principle is what underlies Equation 2.3. When Americans buy more goods and services than they sell, they become more indebted to the rest of the world. To finance this debt, they must borrow from abroad. Figure 2.3 shows the net effect of U.S. borrowing and lending abroad since 1982. The U.S. current account deficit means that we are increasing our net indebtedness to

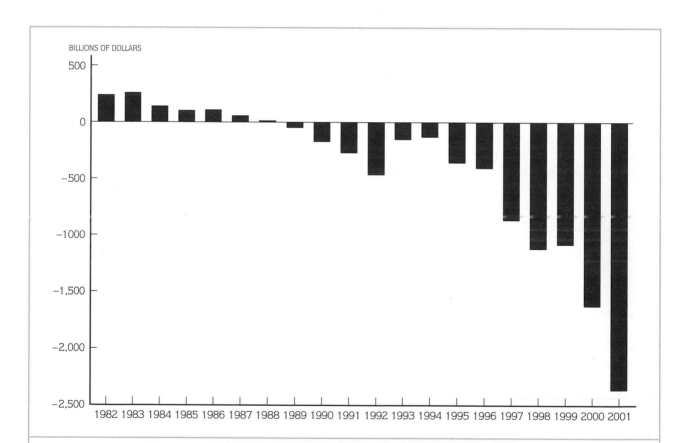

FIGURE 2.3   NET CREDITOR/DEBTOR POSITION OF THE UNITED STATES

Data series on U.S. assets at market values shows that the United States has moved from being a creditor nation to being a debtor nation in the last 15 years.

SOURCE: *Economic Report of the President,* 2003, Table B-10.

foreigners. Our net asset position—assets less liabilities—went from positive to negative.

The Exchange Rate

Transactions with other countries require that U.S. dollars be exchanged for foreign currency—euros, Japanese yen, Canadian dollars, and so on. The **exchange rate** is the price at which these exchanges of dollars for foreign currencies take place. The dollar exchange rate measures the *price of dollars* in terms of foreign currencies. For example, the exchange rate between the U.S. dollar and the Japanese yen in the last quarter of 2002 was 122 yen per dollar. That is, one could go to a bank and get 122 yen with 1 dollar. The *price* of 1 dollar was 122 yen. When Americans purchase foreign goods, such as a cup of coffee in Tokyo, they must pay for these goods with foreign currency, such as yen. Hence, the exchange rate is important for international transactions. A cup of coffee that costs 244 yen in Tokyo would cost an American 2 dollars if the exchange rate is 122 yen per dollar. If the exchange rate rises to 244 yen per dollar, that same cup of coffee would cost 1 dollar.

The exchange rate determines how expensive foreign goods are compared with American goods. When the exchange rate rises, foreign goods become cheaper compared with home goods. As we will see in Chapter 8, this causes Americans to buy more goods abroad and foreigners to buy fewer goods in the United States.

Starting in 2002, 12 European countries, including France, Germany, and Italy, combined their national currencies into a single European currency, the **euro.** This is one of the most important developments in the world economy in the past 50 years. Where tourists, importers and exporters, and currency traders once had to contend with French francs, German marks, and Italian lira, there is now one currency.

Figure 2.4 shows the mark/dollar exchange rate, which is now determined by the euro/dollar exchange rate, along with the yen/dollar exchange rate. Note that both exchange rates fluctuate by large amounts. Some of these fluctuations are associated with the fluctuations in real GDP in the United States. For example, the dollar fell during the boom in economic activity in the late 1970s and rose during the slump in economic activity in the early 1980s. But there are many other movements in the exchange rate. During the period from 1973 to 2002, the dollar generally fell relative to the yen. As we will see, this was a result of the higher rate of inflation in the United States than Japan during these years.

2.7 | MEASURING INFLATION

The national income and product accounts discussed at the beginning of this chapter are important measures of economic performance. But two other measures—inflation and employment—are released to the public at more

MACROSOLVE
EXERCISE

FIGURE 2.4   MARK/DOLLAR AND YEN/DOLLAR EXCHANGE RATES

The exchange rate has had large fluctuations during the last 30 years. Some of these fluctuations are associated with the movements in U.S. output. The dollar fell during the boom of the late 1970s and rose during the slump of the early 1980s. Other fluctuations seem unrelated to the state of the U.S. economy.

SOURCE: International Monetary Fund, IFS CD-ROM.

frequent intervals and form the basis of most policy initiatives. Data on inflation and employment are released every month.

Almost everybody watches the rate of inflation. It is a major indicator of how the economy is doing, and changes in inflation are related to fluctuations in real GDP. The *rate of inflation* is defined as the percentage rate of change in the general price level from one period to the next. The general price level is a measure of the purchasing power of the dollar, or the amount of goods and services the dollar can buy. For example, one measure of the price level was 180 in 2002, which means that the same basket of goods that cost $100 in 1983 cost $180 in 2002. In this example, 1983 is the base year. There are two approaches to measuring the general price level: constructing **price indexes** directly from data on the prices of thousands of goods and services, and calculating **deflators** by dividing a component of nominal GDP by the same component of real GDP.

measuring gen. price level

Price Indexes

A price index is a ratio showing the price of a basket of goods and services in various years in relation to the price of the basket in a base year. The index is 100 in the base year and correspondingly higher in later years if the prices of the things in the basket have risen. The most conspicuous price index is the **consumer price index (CPI).** This index measures the cost of living for a typical urban family. The Bureau of Labor Statistics (BLS) of the Department of Labor computes it in the following way: Once every 10 years or so, the BLS makes a survey of the buying habits of American families. The survey covers not only the products they buy in stores but other expenditures like the purchases of houses. Then, the BLS makes a long list of goods and services whose prices they can determine once a month. From the survey of buying habits, they estimate the quantities of each item bought by the average family. The list includes tomato soup, for example. However, the amount of tomato soup in the CPI basket is greater than the fraction of income that the typical family spends on tomato soup. The price of tomato soup is considered representative of the prices of similar products that are not included in the index.

Every month, the BLS sends surveyors into stores to write down the actual prices of goods and services. When discounts are available, they take them into account. The BLS is particularly careful about new car prices, because cars play a large role in the price index and few people actually pay the sticker price for a new car.

Each month, the BLS computes the new level of the price index by using the detailed prices to compute the cost of the CPI basket. The basket is chosen so that its price was 100 in 1983, which means that the index had the value 100 in 1983. In 2002, the index was 179.9, so prices rose by 80 percent over 19 years. Some prices rose more than others. The 2002 level of the medical care price index was 285.6, while the level for energy was only 121.9. Both started at 100 in 1983.

Figure 2.5 shows the rate of inflation, the percent change in the U.S. price level as measured by the CPI, since 1968. Inflation was moderate in the early 1960s but, as shown in Figure 2.5, gained momentum in the late 1960s and early 1970s and reached two peaks in 1974 and 1980. Inflation moderated in the early 1980s and has been low since then.

The CPI is the most widely used measure of the purchasing power of the dollar. When people make an agreement that is set in dollars and want to protect themselves against inflation, they can write in a provision that payments rise in proportion to the increase in the CPI. This practice, called *cost-of-living adjustment* (COLA), is used for social security payments and in some collective-bargaining agreements that spell out the terms of employment for unionized workers.

The government puts out another major price index in addition to the CPI. It is called the **producer price index (PPI).** Instead of measuring the prices actually paid by consumers, the PPI measures the prices charged by producers at various stages in the production process. There is no clear basis for

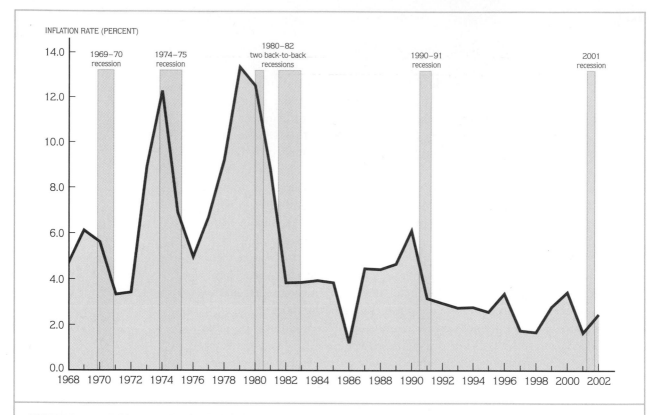

FIGURE 2.5　CONSUMER PRICE INFLATION

The consumer price index measures the price of a bundle of goods and services representative of the purchases of a typical family. The chart shows the percent change in this index (December to December) for each year.

SOURCE: *Economic Report of the President,* 2003, Table B-63.

the choice of weights for the PPI, comparable to the market basket that gives the weights for the CPI. As a result, there is much less interest in the monthly value of the PPI. However, the BLS reports all the detailed prices going into the PPI, and these prices and the price indexes computed from them are the best source of information about prices of crude materials and intermediate goods. Some economists think that the PPI for crude materials is one of the most sensitive early warning indicators of future inflation.

Deflators

The construction of data on nominal and real GDP results in another type of price index. The purpose of measuring real GDP is to get rid of the price effects in nominal GDP. Therefore, the ratio of nominal GDP to real GDP is a measure of prices. It is called the *GDP implicit price deflator*. For example, in 2000, nominal GDP was $9,872.9 billion. Real GDP was $9,224 billion 1996 dollars. The GDP deflator for 2000 was $100 \times 9,872.9/9,224 = 107$. That is, with a base of 100 in 1996, the price level according to the GDP deflator was 107.

Each component for GDP has a deflator. For example, the ratio of nominal consumption to real consumption is the *consumption deflator*. It is widely used as an alternative to the CPI as a measure of the cost of living.

Inflation, Price Indexes, and Deflators

1. Inflation is the rate of increase in the price level. The price level is an average of all prices in the economy.

2. There are two types of measures of the price level: price indexes and deflators. The consumer price index (CPI) and the producer price index (PPI) are the two major price indexes. The weights on the individual prices in the CPI are based on a survey of consumer buying habits. The GDP deflator is the ratio of nominal GDP to real GDP. It is a measure of the prices of all goods and services produced in America.

3. The CPI is used for cost-of-living adjustments in many union contracts and in many government programs.

2.8 | MEASURING EMPLOYMENT AND WAGES

Employment falls along with production during recessions and rises again during recoveries. Over the long haul, employment grows along with potential GDP as firms hire more workers to produce the growing output. Information on employment in the United States comes from two surveys, one of *households* and the other of *establishments*—the offices, factories, stores, mines, and other places where people work.

The household survey, called the *Current Population Survey*, is conducted each month by the Bureau of the Census, and the data are tabulated and reported by the BLS. About 100,000 adults are interviewed each month to find out whether they are employed during the calendar week that includes the 12th of the month. Everyone who worked an hour or more during that week is counted as employed for that month. The results are blown up by multiplying by about 1,000 so that they are good estimates of the total number of workers employed that month in the whole economy (each person in the survey stands for a little over 1,000 people in the population). Some other people who did not work, notably those on vacation, are also counted as employed.

Total civilian employment by this measure was 134.3 million in 2002, up almost 16 million from its level in 1992. Between 2000 and 2002, employment fell by almost a million, whereas in normal years, it rises by several million. The expansion that started in 1992 involved substantial growth in employment, as expansions generally do. On the other hand, employment falls during recessions, as it did in 1982 and 1991.

The establishment survey interviews employers to find out the number of people on the payroll at each workplace. The survey excludes farm employees. Because it is based on payrolls, it also omits people who are self-employed. Total nonagricultural payroll employment was 134.3 million people in December 2002.

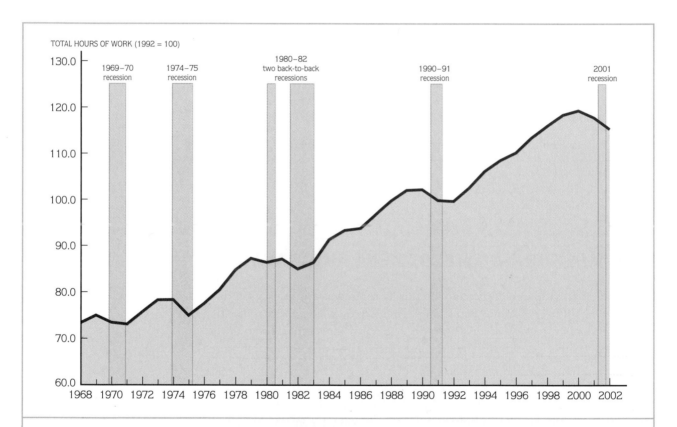

FIGURE 2.6   GROWTH AND FLUCTUATIONS OF HOURS WORKED

The total amount of work performed in the United States, measured by the hours of all workers, fluctuates along with the business cycle. In each of the six recessions shown here—1969–70, 1974–75, 1980, 1981–82, 1990–91, and 2001—total hours declined. In general, total hours have been growing. Growth was particularly strong from 1975 to 1979, from 1982 to 1988, and from 1992 to 2000.

SOURCE: *Economic Report of the President*, 2003, Table B-49.

Hours per Week and Total Hours

The number of hours worked each week varies among workers and over time. Some people normally work only a few hours a week and others work 60 to 70 hours. The average worker now puts in about 34 hours per week, while the average factory worker puts in about 41 hours. Also, the number of hours per week falls during recessions and rises during expansions. When demand is booming, many workers are asked, or choose, to work overtime. Average weekly hours fell from 34.5 hours per week in July 1990 to 34.0 in April 1991 and rose back to 34.5 by 1993 in the recovery. The data also verify the fact that the average workweek has declined over the long term. Average weekly hours fell from about 39 hours per week in 1959 to about 34 hours per week now, and average weekly hours in manufacturing have remained steady at about 40 hours per week since 1959.

For all these reasons, employment by itself is not a complete measure of labor input to the economy. Total hours of work—the number of people working multiplied by the hours of work of the average worker—is a better measure. The BLS index of total hours for the business sector is shown in Figure 2.6 for the period from 1968 to 2002. The upward trend in hours is clear in the figure, but so are the fluctuations. When the level of real output of the economy declines, total hours of work decline. The workforce feels the effects of a recession in the form of fewer hours of work per week; they feel it as well in the possibility of being laid off. In either case, their pay declines even if the wage rate does not change.

REVIEW AND PRACTICE

Major Points

1. There are three ways to measure and think about GDP: the spending side, the production side, and the income side. The components of spending are consumption, investment, government spending, and net exports. The components of production are the values added by each industry. The components of income are wages, profits, and interest.

2. Real GDP is the physical volume of production, after the effects of rising prices have been removed. Real GDP growth has averaged about 3.2 percent per year during the last 35 years, but there have been many fluctuations. Potential GDP is real GDP after the economic fluctuations have been removed. Nominal GDP is just GDP without adjustment for inflation or economic fluctuations.

3. Value added by a firm is the difference between the revenue of the firm and its purchase of goods and services from other firms. It is the firm's contribution to GDP. GDP for the whole economy is the sum of values added across all producers.

4. Depreciation is the loss of capital from wear and tear. Net investment is gross investment less depreciation.

5. Conceptually, income and production are equal. All value added is somebody's income. The national accounts use various measures of income. National income is GDP less depreciation and less sales and excise taxes and adjusted for net factor payments. Personal income is national income less social security taxes and corporate retained earnings plus transfer payments and interest paid by the government to consumers. Disposable personal income is personal income less income taxes.

6. The international accounts, called the *balance of payments accounts*, consist of a current account and a financial account. The two sum to zero. The current account is in surplus when the United States exports more than it imports. At the same time, the financial account is in deficit—capital is flowing out because the United States must be lending to the rest of the world if the United States imports less than it exports.

7. The exchange rate is crucial for international transactions. It is the price of dollars in terms of foreign currency. When the exchange rate rises, more foreign currency can be bought with each dollar. This makes foreign goods cheaper in terms of dollars.

8. An important implication of the equality of income and product is the equality of saving and investment. Investment always equals private saving plus the government surplus plus the capital inflow from abroad.

9. The consumer price index is the number of dollars required to purchase a market basket of goods and services typical of the consumption patterns of Americans.

10. Price indexes called *deflators* can be calculated by dividing a component of nominal GDP by the same component of real GDP. The consumption deflator is widely used by economists as an alternative to the CPI. The overall GDP deflator is a measure of the price of domestic production; it does not include the price of imports.

11. The best measure of total labor input to the economy is the total number of hours worked by all workers each year. That measure tends to fluctuate in the same direction as real GDP.

12. A good measure of hourly wages is total labor earnings divided by total hours worked. The real wage is the ratio of the hourly wage to the price level.

Key Terms and Concepts

consumption	nominal GDP
investment	value added
fixed investment	national income
inventory investment	personal income
nonresidential fixed investment	disposable personal income
residential fixed investment	budget surplus
capital stock	budget deficit
depreciation	current account
net investment	financial account
government purchases	exchange rate
imports	euro
exports	price indexes
intermediate goods	deflators
final goods	consumer price index (CPI)
real GDP	producer price index (PPI)

Questions for Discussion and Review

1. Explain why spending on GDP is equal to income earned from producing GDP.

2. Identify which of the following are flows and which are stocks: consumption; government bonds outstanding at the end of last year; government purchases; inventories; inventory investment; depreciation; factories and equipment in the United States on December 31, 2004; the budget deficit.

3. Explain how real GDP is calculated.

4. Which components of spending fluctuate the most over the cycle?

5. What is the difference between high prices and inflation?

Problems

NUMERICAL

1. The following are data for the U.S. economy for 2000 in billions of dollars:

Net rental income of persons[1]	141.6
Depreciation	1,241.3
Compensation of employees	5,715.2
Personal consumption expenditures	6,728.4
Sales and excise taxes	762.7

[1]Adjusted for capital consumption.

Business transfer payments	43.9
Statistical discrepancy	−130.4
Gross private domestic investment	1,767.5
Exports of goods and services	1,102.9
Net subsidies of government business	37.6
Government purchases of goods and services	1,741.0
Imports of goods and services	1,466.9
Net interest	532.7
Proprietors' income	715.0
Corporate profits	876.4
Net factor income from rest of world	−12.1

    a. Compute GDP using the spending approach.

    b. Compute net domestic product.

    c. Compute national income two ways.

2. Fill in the blanks.

    a. If investment is $1,100 billion, private saving is $1,050 billion, and capital inflow from abroad is $100 billion, then the government budget deficit is ____ billion.

    b. If the stock of inventories in the economy is $1,000 billion at the end of 2008 and $1,050 billion at the end of 2009, then inventory investment for 2008 is ____ billion.

    c. If production by Americans and American capital abroad is $80 billion and GNP is $7,000 billion, then GDP is ____.

3. Consider a closed economy with the following expenditure totals for a year:

Consumption	1,300
Investment	500
Government purchases	500
Government tax receipts	400
Depreciation	200

Suppose that the financial assets in the economy consist of money and bonds. Assume that money equals 500 at the start of the year and that government bonds equal 700 at the start of the year.

    a. Assuming that 90 percent of government deficits are financed by bonds, calculate the new levels of bond and money holdings for the private sector and for the government.

    b. Show how the total change in government liabilities—money (M) + bonds (B)—can be computed in two ways.

4. The consumer price index for the 1978–82 period and the GDP deflator follow. This was a period of unusually high, but declining, inflation. (The CPI is equal to 100 in the base years, 1982–84; the GDP deflator is equal to 100 in the base year 1987.)

	CPI	GDP DEFLATOR
1978	65.2	60.3
1979	72.6	65.5
1980	82.4	71.7
1981	90.9	78.9
1982	96.5	83.8

a. Calculate the rate of inflation according to both measures from 1979 through 1982. What might explain the differences between the two?

b. Suppose that the hourly wage rate for a group of workers that sign an employment contract for the three-year period starting in 1979 is indexed to the CPI according to the formula

$$\Delta W/W = 0.03 + 0.5 \, \Delta CPI/CPI.$$

Calculate the actual increase in wages during each year of the contract period. If the wage is $12.00 in 1979, what was it in 1980, 1981, and 1982? What happens to the real wage measured in terms of the CPI?

c. Repeat your calculations with 0.03 reduced to 0 and 0.5 increased to 1. What indexing formula would the workers' employer have preferred? Is there any reason for the employer to have been happy with the other formula before the actual inflation experience was known?

5. The CPI is calculated for a fixed market basket. It measures the change in the cost of the market basket from the base year until the current year. An index with the market basket fixed in the first year, like the CPI, is called a *Laspeyres index*. An alternative index, the Paasche index, is based on a market basket in the end year. It measures the change in the cost of a market basket fixed in the end year. Suppose that the base year is 2003. Suppose that the market basket contains only two items, peanut butter and gasoline, and the quantities consumed in 2006 and 2007 are

	PEANUT BUTTER	GASOLINE
2006	100 jars	50 gallons
2007	150 jars	45 gallons

Suppose that the price of peanut butter increases from $1.00 per jar in 2006 to $1.20 per jar in 2007 and the price of gasoline increases from $0.50 per gallon to $2.00 per gallon.

a. Calculate the rate of inflation for the Laspeyres (CPI) index and the Paasche index.

b. Will inflation calculated using the Laspeyres index always exceed inflation calculated with the Paasche index? (Hint: Use standard indifference curve analysis.)

c. Workers often receive an adjustment in their wages equal to only a fraction of inflation as calculated using the CPI. In view of the preceding analysis, explain why workers would likely be better off than they were before if they were fully compensated for inflation. Would this also be the case if inflation was calculated using the Paasche index?

ANALYTICAL

1. Identify which of the following purchases is counted as part of GDP: You purchase a used lawn mower at a garage sale. General Motors purchases tires from Goodyear to equip new Chevrolets. General Motors purchases tires from Goodyear to replace worn tires on executives' company cars. A neighbor hires you to baby-sit for an evening. You purchase a share of AT&T. A neighbor breaks your window with a golf ball, and you purchase a new window. You pay your tuition for the semester.

2. As part of its drive to replace welfare with workfare, the government decides to redesignate $100 billion in welfare benefits as government wages. The recipients become government employees.

   a. For each of the methods used in calculating GDP, describe the effect of this policy change.

   b. Suppose now that the workfare recipients are removed from the government payroll and moved into the payroll of the newly incorporated Workfare, Inc. As part of its support for the workfare program, the government stands ready to subsidize Workfare, Inc., if its sales do not cover its costs. Since Workfare, Inc., has no products to sell, the subsidy ends up being the full $100 billion. How does this arrangement affect your answers to part a?

3. Suppose that automobile purchases were to be treated like housing purchases in the national income accounts. How would that affect saving? Investment?

4. Determine whether the following statements are true or false and explain why.

   a. The trade deficit is equal to the government budget deficit plus investment less private domestic saving.

b. If GDP were measured at the prices firms receive for the products they sell, then sales and excise taxes would not be subtracted from GDP in computing national income.

c. The importance of different goods in GDP is determined by their relative price; for example, the production of one ounce of gold counts much more in GDP than the production of one ounce of steel.

5. In 2001, spending by Americans on personal consumption, private investment, and government operations totaled 104 percent of GDP. How is that possible?

6. Explain how the trade deficit in the 1980s helped finance the large government budget deficit as well as the large increase in private gross investment in the United States. Should Americans care whether foreigners or other Americans hold the U.S. public debt?

7. Suppose initially that exports are zero and imports are $100 billion. Then assume that the government places a ban on imports. Assume that the spending habits of consumers, firms, and government remain the same (i.e., they spend the same amount but substitute domestic goods for imports).

a. What happens to GDP?

b. What happens to each category of savings (assume taxes remain unchanged)?

c. Does total savings still equal investment?

8. Suppose that, in a given year, U.S. foreign trade consists of some consumer importing a single Toyota Camry for $20,000 (2.3 million yen). Here are some possible financial transactions to accompany the purchase: (i) The consumer pays with $20,000, which Toyota puts in its American bank account. (ii) The consumer pays with 2.3 million yen that happens to be in a Japanese bank account. (iii) The consumer pays with $20,000; Toyota invests the proceeds in U.S. Treasury bills. (iv) The consumer purchases 2.3 million yen on the foreign exchange market from some anonymous American foreign exchange trader and then pays for the car.

a. Is the United States running a current account surplus or deficit?

b. For each of the financial transactions just described, explain the effect the transaction has on the U.S. financial account. What is the sum of the current account and financial account balances?

9. Net domestic product is considered to be a better measure of welfare than GDP, since it adjusts for the fact that part of GDP must be devoted to replacing physical capital worn out during the course of the year. If we took this principle of adjusting for depreciation more seriously, what other expenditures would you want to deduct from GDP to get a clearer measure of net national product?

10. With the exception of housing expenditure, consumption and investment spending are delineated by the decision-making unit responsible for each type of expenditure. An alternative accounting scheme might be based on the durability of goods. Suppose investment was equal to total expenditures on goods that last one year or more. All other expenditures count as consumption. How would this revised scheme affect consumption, investment, depreciation, and the capital stock relative to the current accounting system? Which system do you think is more informative and why? Which system would be more costly to manage?

UNEMPLOYMENT, JOB CREATION, AND JOB DESTRUCTION

U nemployment is a key variable in macroeconomics. The most significant aspect of a recession is that people are thrown out of work and become unemployed. In a bad recession, 1 worker out of 10 is unemployed. Even in normal times, 5 or 6 percent of the labor force is unemployed in the United States; and unemployment has been even higher in most European countries for the past 20 years. In booms, a low unemployment rate—4 or even 3 percent—is a sign of plentiful jobs for workers and recruitment problems for some employers. One of the most important questions in macroeconomics is why the economy does not provide work for the entire labor force. Even in the best of times, some people are unemployed.

In this chapter, we develop a unified view of unemployment that deals with the amount of unemployment in normal times (the natural rate of unemployment) and the bursts of higher unemployment that occur during recessions. Our discussion of unemployment is an important element of both the long-run growth model and the short-run fluctuations model. In the growth model, the natural rate of unemployment is a limit on the amount of labor available as an input to production. In the fluctuations model, unemployment can change rapidly over time. The factors that cause production to fall in a recession also cause unemployment to rise, sometimes dramatically.

3.1 | MEASURING UNEMPLOYMENT

MACROSOLVE
EXERCISE

The unemployed are people looking for work and available for work but who have not found jobs. A principal purpose of the Current Population Survey (discussed in Chapter 2 as one of the main sources of information about workers) is to determine how many people are unemployed each month. The survey counts you as unemployed if you did not work at all during the survey week and are looking for work. In each survey, several million people are found to be unemployed. The **labor force** is defined as the number of people 16 years of age or over who are either working or unemployed. The **unemployment rate** is the percentage of the labor force that is unemployed.

Millions of people are not working but are not counted as unemployed. They are considered *out of the labor force* because they are retired, in school, at home looking after their own children, sick, or not looking for work for some other reason. The *labor force participation rate* is the percentage of the working-age population in the labor force.

The survey data can also be used to tell us the reasons for unemployment—a job loss, a quit, or simply someone who just entered the labor force. Of the 5.9 million people unemployed in January 2001, 46 percent had lost their jobs, 14 percent had quit, and 40 percent had newly entered or reentered the labor force. In a year with more unemployment, 1992, 56 percent of the unemployed had lost their jobs.

Another important fact about the labor market is that, at any given time, not everybody who is in the labor force and available for work is actually employed. Unemployment is a feature of the economy even when supply and demand appear to be in balance. In February 1996, a good period for the economy, 5.5 percent of the labor force was unemployed during the typical week. Unemployment rises in recessions and falls in booms, but there is a certain level of unemployment called the **natural rate of unemployment.** The natural rate is the amount of unemployment when the labor market is in equilibrium. One simple measure of the natural rate is the average rate of unemployment over several decades. The natural rate appears to lie between 5 and 6 percent in the United States.

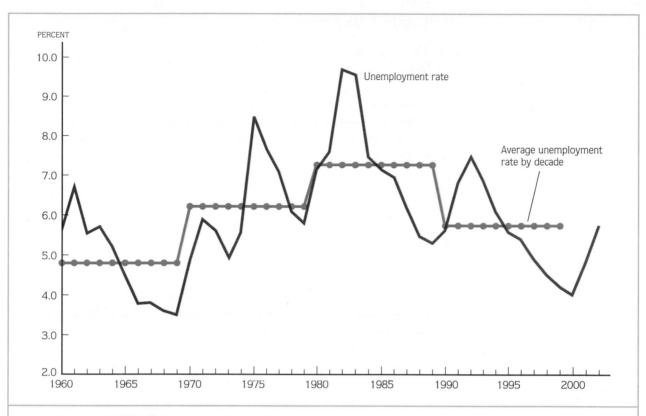

PERCENT

FIGURE 3.1   UNEMPLOYMENT IN THE UNITED STATES

The unemployment rate in the United States has fluctuated between 3 and 10 percent since 1960. Average unemployment was relatively low in the 1960s, rose in the 1970s and early 1980s, and fell during the mid-1980s through the early 2000s. Unemployment rises during recessions and falls during expansions.

SOURCE: *Economic Report of the President*, 2003, Table B-42.

Figure 3.1 shows the history of unemployment in the United States from 1960 to 2003. The years with the highest rates of unemployment, 1975 and 1982, were the years of the two largest recessions in the United States since the Great Depression. Unemployment also rose following the 1990–91 and 2001 recessions. Figure 3.1 also depicts decade-by-decade averages for the 1960s, 1970s, 1980s, and 1990s. The average unemployment rates rose in the 1970s and 1980s but fell in the 1990s. The natural rate of unemployment is not constant—it can change over time. Most economists conclude that the natural rate of unemployment for the United States was about 5 percent in the 1950s and 1960s, rose to over 6 percent in the 1970s and 1980s, and fell to between 5 and 6 percent in the 1990s and 2000s.

Measuring Unemployment

1. The unemployed are looking for work, available for work, but have not yet found jobs.

2. Unemployment is measured in a national survey of households.

3. When the labor market is in balance, there is still some unemployment. The natural rate of unemployment is between 5 and 6 percent in the United States.

3.2 | FLOWS INTO AND OUT OF UNEMPLOYMENT

Flows into and out of unemployment are huge—every month, almost 3 percent of the labor force becomes newly unemployed, well over 3 million people. And in most months, about the same number of people leave unemployment. With 3 percent of the labor force becoming unemployed each month and a normal unemployment rate of less than 6 percent, most of the unemployed do not stay that way very long. Normal spells of unemployment last for a few weeks, although a small fraction of spells last for many months.

If you are 16 years of age or over, you are either employed, unemployed, or out of the labor force. There are many types of flows among these three categories. If you are employed and either lose or quit your job, you become unemployed if you look for another job and out of the labor force if you do not look for work, say because you retire, go back to school, or stay at home to take care of your children. If you are unemployed, you become employed if you find a job and out of the labor force if you stop looking for a job, say because you return to school, retire, or become a *discouraged worker*—someone out of work who stops looking for work. If you are out of the labor force, you become employed if you find a job and unemployed if you start looking for but do not find a job, say because you graduate from college, no longer wish to stay at home and take care of your children, or no longer wish to be retired and are looking for but have not yet found work.

To understand the determination of the unemployment rate that results from these high flows into and out of unemployment, it helps to go through a simple mathematical exercise. We let

$l =$ the **job-losing rate,** the ratio of the number of people who become unemployed in a month to the labor force in that month.

$f =$ the **job-finding rate,** the fraction of the unemployed who leave unemployment in a month.

$u =$ the unemployment rate, the fraction of the labor force that is unemployed.

The flow into unemployment is the job-losing rate l and the flow out of unemployment is the product of the unemployment rate u and the job-finding rate f; the flow is uf. The flow of increasing unemployment is the difference between the inflow l and the outflow, uf; the flow is $l - uf$. So, to understand why unemployment rises in a recession, we need to know why the inflow rate to unemployment, l, is high and why the outflow rate from unemployment, uf, is low.

Before we look at recessions, though, we want to consider normal conditions. Suppose unemployment does not change from one month to the next, as we would expect to be true in normal conditions. Then, the inflow must equal the outflow:

$$l = uf \qquad\qquad (3.1)$$

This can be solved for the unemployment rate:

$$u = \frac{l}{f} \qquad\qquad (3.2)$$

The unemployment rate is just the ratio of the job-losing rate, l, to the job-finding rate, f. An economy with a large job-losing rate or a small job-finding rate has a high unemployment rate. We can break down our discussion of the determinants of the natural rate of unemployment into two parts: determinants of the rate at which people lose jobs and determinants of the rate at which they find jobs. To be more precise, these are the rate at which people become unemployed (since some people become unemployed without losing jobs) and the rate at which they leave unemployment (since some people leave the labor force while they are unemployed and do not find jobs).

Even in normal times, there are substantial flows into and out of unemployment. One good way to measure normal conditions is to take averages over fairly long periods. For the period 1990 through 2002, average conditions were as follows:

Job-losing rate, l	2.2 percent per month
Job-finding rate, f	39 percent per month
Unemployment rate, u	5.6 percent of labor force

By this measure, the natural rate of unemployment was 5.6 percent. An average over a longer period including the low-unemployment years of the 1950s and 1960s and the high unemployment years of the 1970s and 1980s would be around 5.5 percent.

Flows into Unemployment

How do workers become unemployed? We break down the sources of new unemployment into the following three categories:

1. Job destruction

2. Job loss without destruction

3. Personal transitions

Job destruction is the result of an employer's decision to terminate a position, dismissing the worker without refilling the job.[1] Job destruction often takes the form of plant closings or elimination of second shifts. Recessions generally have a burst of job destruction around the time that output is declining most rapidly. Even in normal times, rates of job destruction are high—in the average month from 1972 through 1988, almost 2 percent of all jobs in manufacturing were destroyed. In the early-2000s, job destruction from outsourcing of high technology jobs to foreign countries, especially India, became a high-profile issue, although the impact on unemployment was not large.

Job destruction occurs when individual plants or firms are no longer viable and have to be shut down or scaled back. In normal times, there is somewhat more job creation than destruction, so employment grows along with the labor force. Part of the source of chronic job destruction and creation is continual shifts across industries. In any year, there are contractions in some industries and expansions in others, as the economy adjusts to changes in world markets and consumer preferences. For example, in 1994, a year of strong overall growth in employment, more jobs were destroyed than were created in mining, nondurables manufacturing, and the federal government. Even more job destruction occurs within industries, as dynamic new firms displace the losers.

Job loss without destruction occurs when a worker loses a job but the employer does not reduce total employment. Either the discharged worker is replaced directly or another worker is hired and duties are reorganized. There are massive flows of this type of job loss. Over 5 percent of workers lose their jobs each month.[2] Although this figure includes job destruction and situations where workers quit jobs voluntarily, it is likely that over half of the flow is job loss without destruction. Many of these losses involve explicitly temporary work, including summer employment for students. The construction industry is a large contributor to this category—contractors hire and lay off workers with particular skills with great frequency.

Personal transitions cause people to quit their jobs. For example, a graduating student may quit a part-time after-school job and look for full-time work. Although flows of job quitters are large, quits are not an important flow into unemployment—only 13 percent of the newly unemployed have quit jobs. Much more important is the transition from nonwork activities. Almost half the newly unemployed were previously out of the labor force. The decision to look for work after being in school, sick, or involved in home activities is a major source of the flow into unemployment. In economies or markets where

---

[1] See Steven J. Davis, John C. Haltiwanger, and Scott Schuh, *Job Creation and Destruction* (Cambridge, MA: MIT Press, 1996).

[2] Patricia M. Anderson and Bruce D. Meyer, "The Extent and Consequences of Job Turnover," *Brookings Papers on Economic Activity, Microeconomics* (1994), pp. 177–236.

people frequently change their roles in the economy, flows into unemployment are higher.

Flows out of Unemployment

About two-thirds of the flow out of unemployment is the result of successful job search; one-third of those who stop being unemployed decide to leave the labor force.[3] Therefore, the major determinant of the flow out of unemployment is the job-finding rate. That rate is the result of interaction of the availability of jobs, on the one hand, and the strategies that job seekers use to find jobs, on the other hand.

Jobs are constantly available because of the natural flows out of jobs that we just discussed. First, in normal times, there is a flow of job creation at the same rate of about 2 percent per month that jobs are destroyed. In the same industries where some firms are shutting plants and terminating workers, other firms are opening up new plants and hiring workers. Job creation is actually more stable over the business cycle than job destruction.[4] Even in the most severe part of a contraction, when the job destruction rate skyrockets, job creation continues at levels not far below normal.

Just as there are job losses that occur without job destruction, there are flows of new hires that occur without job creation. Workers whose jobs ended normally, as in temporary work, or who quit to return to school or take other jobs, need to be replaced.

Hence, at all times, jobs are available to absorb the unemployed. Though evidence is scant, it appears that the number of jobs available at any one time is far lower than the number of people looking for work. Nonetheless, in normal times, most of the unemployed find jobs in a month or two. The reason we know this is that job vacancies last only a week or two, on the average. The flow of new vacancies is huge. The typical job seeker keeps in touch with employers who might offer suitable jobs and waits until one opens up. The employer considers applicants quickly and makes a hire. Job seekers remain unemployed until they win suitable jobs.

The strategies followed by job seekers are the other important determinant of the speed at which they find work and thus of the flow out of unemployment. Economists have looked carefully at optimal strategies that workers should follow. The result has been a body of thinking called **search theory**.[5] One of the basic assumptions in search theory is that wages and working conditions vary across jobs. An optimal job-seeking strategy would not be to take the first job that comes along—it probably is one at the nearest fast-food restaurant. Instead, the job seeker should balance the benefit of starting an

[3] Olivier J. Blanchard and Peter Diamond, "The Cyclical Behavior of the Gross Flows of U.S. Workers," *Brookings Papers on Economic Activity*, Vol. 2 (1990), pp. 85–143.

[4] See Davis, Haltiwanger, and Schuh, *Job Creation and Destruction*.

[5] See Christopher A. Pissarides, *Equilibrium Unemployment Theory* (Cambridge and Oxford, England: Basil Blackwell, 1990).

available job right away against the benefit of taking a better job that comes along later, net of the cost of waiting. An improvement in wages can justify a long wait. For example, if you have an offer at $350 per week for a job immediately available, but think that a job paying $400 per week (14 percent higher) will probably take six weeks to find, and you expect to hold either job until a year from now, it will be better to hold out for the better job. You will make $350 × 52 = $18,200 in the lower-paying job against $400 × 46 = $18,400 in the better job with six more weeks of unemployment.

Search theory portrays the activities of job seekers as economically rational, just like other household decisions. We can establish links between the economic environment of job seekers and their job-finding rates by using search theory. Then, we can use Equation 3.2 to draw conclusions about how that environment affects the unemployment rate.

First, the job-finding rate depends on the availability of jobs. If there are large numbers of job seekers and a small flow of new jobs, the probability is small that one job seeker will both find out about a particular new job *and* be offered that job. Second, the job-finding rate depends on the amount of variation there is in the wages and working conditions for jobs. What matters is the chances of getting a really good job. If there is a small but significant chance that a job will come along that is much better than the typical one, the rational searcher will wait quite a while for that job to materialize. Job-finding rates in such markets—for example, the market for corporate executives—are low. On the other hand, if all jobs are basically the same, the job seeker will want to take the first one offered. Job-finding rates are high in such markets—for example, in the market for temporary office work. Third, the job-finding rate depends on the cost of waiting until a better job offer is made. If the cost is low, people have a smaller incentive to find jobs and so lower job-finding rates. Similarly, a program that subsidized people for looking for work would lengthen their period of search and lower their job-finding rates. Finally, the job-finding rate is lower for jobs that are expected to last a long time. It pays to look for months for a career job but not for a temporary job.

Unemployment Flows

1. About 3 percent of the labor force becomes newly unemployed in the average month.

2. When the unemployment rate is neither rising nor falling, it is given by a formula: the ratio of the job-losing rate to the job-finding rate.

3. A major source of unemployment, especially in recessions, is job destruction. A job is destroyed if the worker holding it is laid off and nobody is hired to replace the worker.

4. The unemployed either find jobs or leave the labor force. About 39 percent of the unemployed depart unemployment in the average month.

3.3 | THE NATURAL RATE OF UNEMPLOYMENT

In normal times—when real GDP is equal to potential GDP—unemployment is not zero. Recall that the unemployment rate equals the natural rate in normal times. When workers enter the labor force for the first time or after a spell out of the labor force, they need some time to find a job. During this period they are counted as unemployed. Similarly, when workers quit their jobs, there frequently is a span of time before they find new jobs. Movements from one job to another are particularly common for young workers, as they find out what type of job they are best suited for. This is one reason why young workers have higher unemployment rates than older workers. In addition, some low-skilled workers are frequently unemployed. Additional training for such workers would reduce the unemployment rate.

Recall that the formula in Equation 3.2 applies when the unemployment rate is steady, neither rising or falling. Therefore, the formula describes the natural rate because in normal times the unemployment rate is holding steady. In words, it is

$$\text{Natural rate of unemployment} = \frac{\text{Job-losing rate}}{\text{Job-finding rate}} = \frac{l}{f}. \qquad (3.3)$$

The natural rate is high in a labor market that has high rates of inflow and low rates of outflow. Economies with high rates of job destruction and creation have high rates of inflow to unemployment and therefore high natural rates. High rates of personal turnover contribute to the numerator and thus also raise the natural rate.

The natural rate also is high in an economy or market with a low job-finding rate, the denominator in the equation for the natural rate. Economists have identified four special factors that may lower job-finding rates and thus raise the natural rate.

EFFICIENCY WAGES[6]   According to the "efficiency wage" view, the employment relationship works best when workers feel that their current jobs are valuable. In this view, a valuable job is one that pays well above what the worker could earn from looking for another job, including the cost of search. If the job is valuable, the threat to fire a worker is effective as a way to get the worker to perform. One way for an employer to make its jobs valuable is to pay higher wages than other employers. But not every firm can pay more than other firms. As firms bid up wages to make their jobs valuable, they reduce the number of jobs available (because labor demand slopes downward) and increase the number of people looking for those jobs (because labor supply slopes upward). Job-finding rates are lower in that setting. Jobs are valuable because fired workers face long periods of search to find new jobs. In a labor market where the efficiency wage

---

[6] See George A. Akerlof and Janet L. Yellen, *Efficiency Wage Models of the Labor Market* (New York: Cambridge University Press, 1986); and Andrew Weiss, *Efficiency Wages: Models of Unemployment, Layoffs, and Wage Dispersion* (Princeton, NJ: Princeton University Press, 1990).

LOW UNEMPLOYMENT	HIGH UNEMPLOYMENT
Worker's perspective: Wage at current job: $400 per week. Wage at next job: $400 per week. Time required to find next job: 1 week. Loss if fired from this job: $400.	*Worker's perspective:* Wage at current job: $400 per week. Wage at next job: $400 per week. Time required to find next job: 15 weeks. Loss if fired from this job: $6,000.
Conclusion: I don't have to work too hard at this job because I lose only $400 if I am fired and have to move to another job.	*Conclusion:* I better work hard at this job because I lose $6,000 if I am fired and have to move to another job.
Employer's perspective: I should raise the worker's pay because under present conditions, the worker has no reason to work hard.	*Employer's perspective:* I don't need to change the worker's pay, because under present conditions, the worker has a good reason to work hard.
Conclusion: The market cannot stay like this because all employers will raise wages.	***Conclusion:*** The market can stay like this because employers will keep wages at this level.

FIGURE 3.2   COMPARISON OF LOW- AND HIGH-UNEMPLOYMENT LABOR MARKETS IN THE EFFICIENCY WAGE MODEL

The left side considers a labor market where employers want to make it expensive for workers to leave their jobs. But it is easy for the workers to find new jobs, because jobs are plentiful and it will take only a week to find one. Employers will then raise wages. The left side does not depict an equilibrium. On the right side, it is difficult to find new jobs and a worker sacrifices $6,000 by losing the current job. Employers feel no need to change wages. The labor market is in equilibrium with high unemployment.

theory applies, firms have numerous applicants on the spot for every job opening and job seekers find job offers few and far between. Figure 3.2 illustrates the difference between a low-unemployment labor market and a high-unemployment one where the assumptions of efficiency-wage theory apply. Only the right column, with high unemployment, can be an equilibrium in the market.

UNION WAGE PREMIUMS   Labor unions may also raise the natural rate. How? One purpose of labor unions is to improve wages and working conditions. In markets where unions are successful, the same type of asymmetry predicted by the efficiency wage theory would hold. Firms find hundreds of applicants for good union jobs and job seekers find opportunities for union jobs to be rare. As we note in our discussion of the search model, it is worth searching longer if there is a small chance of getting a really good job. So an economy with successful unions probably has a higher natural rate of unemployment, according to this line of thought.

MINIMUM WAGES   The government intervenes in labor markets for low-wage workers in much the same way that unions do for more-skilled workers. If there is rigorous enforcement of minimum wages at levels well above what would otherwise occur, the jobs affected by the minimum wage are harder to find. To the extent that the legal minimum wage is low relative to wages in general and to the extent that employers simply ignore the law, the minimum wage may not raise the natural rate by very much.

UNEMPLOYMENT INSURANCE   Some workers receive payments from the unemployment insurance system during periods of job search—in January 2001, 5.9 million workers were unemployed and 3.1 million of them drew benefits. Because the benefits are paid to replace lost earnings during unemployment, they are a subsidy for job search. Recall the earlier example, where you would be willing to wait six weeks for a better job. Suppose instead that you received $200 per week in unemployment benefits. Then it would pay to search for as long as 12 weeks for the $400 per week job instead of settling for the $350 per week job right away. You would make $18,200 from the lower-wage job over the year, but $200 × 12 + $400 × 40 = $18,400 from the unemployment benefits and the higher-wage job. Therefore, unemployment insurance makes the unemployed choosier in accepting lower-wage jobs and encourages search strategies with lower job-finding rates. Of course, the motive for the unemployment insurance system is to help workers deal with the sudden loss of income that goes with unemployment. Lengthening of the job search and the consequent increase in the natural rate are side effects.

Why Does the Natural Rate Change over Time?

The forces that determine the natural rate are not immutable. As they change, we would expect the natural rate to change. The natural rate should be high if an unusual restructuring of the economy is in progress, with high rates of job destruction in shrinking industries and job creation in expanding ones. Large changes in defense spending might be one source of this type of restructuring. The natural rate should be high if the labor force has an unusual proportion of younger workers with higher rates of personal transition. Declining unionization may lower the natural rate. Higher minimum wages and higher unemployment benefits would raise the natural rate.

Over the past 15 years, most of these trends would suggest a lowering of the natural rate. The majority of the baby boom generation are now over 40, a time of low turnover. Unionization of the workforce has declined dramatically. The minimum wage has not grown as fast as wages in general. A declining fraction of the unemployed receive benefits, and benefits have not risen in relation to wages. Despite much disagreement about change in the natural rate among economists, some evidence supports the hypothesis of a decline. Unemployment was above 6 percent in the expansion of the late 1970s, even when other conditions, such as worsening inflation, suggested that the economy was in a boom. By contrast, unemployment in the expansion years of the late 1990s fell below 5 percent, without worsening inflation.

The Natural Rate of Unemployment

1. The natural rate of unemployment is the amount of unemployment in normal times and is around 5 or 6 percent.

2. Forces tending to raise the natural rate are efficiency wage setting, union wage premiums, minimum wages, and unemployment insurance.

3. The determinants of the natural rate vary over time. The natural rate rose in the 1970s and fell in the 1990s.

European Unemployment

Unemployment in the United States is characterized by short-run fluctuations and long-run trends. Unemployment rises during recessions and falls during expansions and booms. The natural rate of unemployment, the rate of unemployment in normal times, is subject to long-run trends. The natural rate of unemployment rose during the 1970s and 1980s, but fell during the 1990s to nearly its level in the 1960s.

European unemployment has behaved very differently. Unemployment rates for the three largest continental European countries—France, Germany, and Italy—are shown in Figure 3.3. Like the United States, unemployment rose during the recessions of the mid-1970s, early 1980s, and early 1990s. Unlike the United States, however, unemployment during the subsequent expansions did not fall back to its previous levels. The natural rate of unemployment in Europe rose during the 1970s, 1980s, and 1990s, and is now much higher than during the 1960s.[7]

Why did the natural rate of unemployment decrease in the 1990s in the United States but not in Europe? In this section, we discussed reasons why the natural rate of unemployment is not equal to zero. Several of these reasons—the fraction of the labor force that belong to unions, the minimum wage relative to wages in general, the level of unemployment insurance benefits relative to wages, and the duration of unemployment insurance benefits—decreased in the United States over time but not as much, if at all, in Europe. These factors have lowered the natural rate of unemployment in the United States but not in Europe.

Figure 3.3 also shows that, during the early 2000s, unemployment in the three European countries declined from their mid-1990s peaks. The elimination

[7] See David H. Papell, Christian J. Murray, and Hala Ghiblawi, "The Structure of Unemployment," *Review of Economics and Statistics*, Vol. 82, May 2000, pp. 309–315.

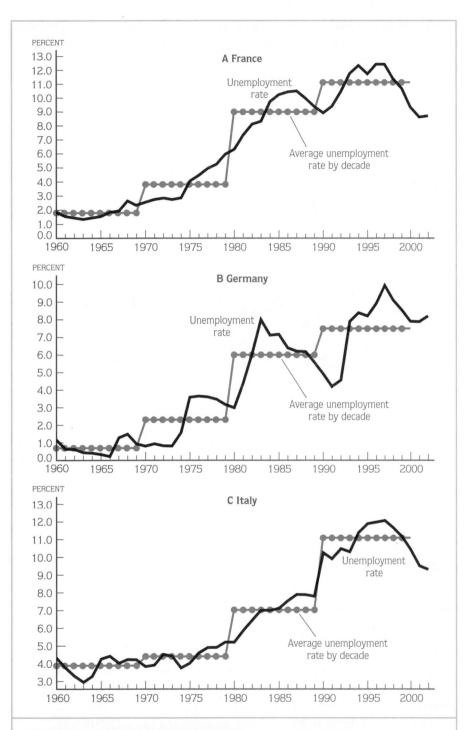

FIGURE 3.3   EUROPEAN UNEMPLOYMENT

European unemployment rose from the 1960s to the 1970s. In contrast with the United States, unemployment in Europe continued to rise in the 1980s and 1990s.

SOURCE: *OECD Main Economic Indicators.*

of capital and exchange controls in Europe, culminating with the establish-ment of a single currency, the euro, should increase competitiveness and help decrease long-term unemployment. Unless Europe's labor market institutions become more like those in the United States, however, it seems unlikely that the natural rate of unemployment in Europe will fall to the level in the United States.

3.4 | UNEMPLOYMENT IN RECESSIONS AND BOOMS

Figure 3.1 shows how the unemployment rate fluctuated since 1960. Unem-ployment moves with the business cycle. In booms, when real GDP is high rel-ative to potential GDP, unemployment is low. In recessions, unemployment rises sharply and then declines more gradually as the recovery gets under way.

We can analyze fluctuations in unemployment in the framework devel-oped in the first section. Recall that the number of people becoming unem-ployed each month in relation to the labor force is the inflow rate l. The number leaving unemployment, in relation to the labor force, is uf, the product of the unemployment rate u and the rate at which people depart from unem-ployment f. The rate at which unemployment rises, in relation to the labor force, is $l - uf$. If we know the starting unemployment rate and the inflow and outflow rates, we can compute the increase in unemployment. Then we can update the unemployment rate and repeat the process. To put it differently, we can think of today's unemployment rate as the result of the history of inflows and outflows. Because most spells of unemployment last only a month or two, today's unemployment rate actually depends on the history of inflows and out-flows only during the last six months or so.

Changes in the Unemployment Flows

By far the most important source of changes in inflows to unemployment is job destruction. Figure 3.4 shows the job destruction rate in manufacturing.[8] Occasionally, job destruction skyrockets. The peaks in 1975, 1980, 1982, and 1991 coincided with recessions. The peaks in 1985 and 1986 occurred during expansions; the one in 1986 may have been triggered by the collapse of oil prices in that year. Rates of inflow to unemployment jump up during these episodes of job destruction. As is shown in Figure 3.1, the unemployment rate jumps up as well, because inflows to unemployment exceed outflows.

---

[8] Calculation of the job-destruction rate requires processing data on individual plants. The data are available in suitable form only for manufacturing and only for the period 1972–1994..

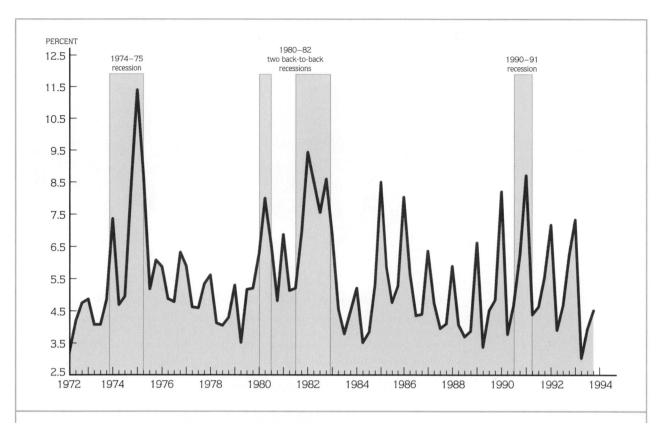

PERCENT

1974–75
recession

1980–82
two back-to-back
recessions

1990–91
recession

FIGURE 3.4   JOB DESTRUCTION RATE IN MANUFACTURING

Each month, between 1.5 and 3.5 percent of jobs in manufacturing are destroyed by plant shutdowns, elimination of shifts, or other sources of reduced employment. The job-destruction rate reaches sharp peaks in recession years such as 1980, 1982, and 1991. But even in years of good conditions in the labor market, many jobs are destroyed. Job destruction is a major source of unemployment, especially in recessions.

SOURCE: Davis, Haltiwanger, and Schuh, *Job Creation and Destruction,* 1996, and C. J. Krizan, Census Bureau.

Inflow rates to unemployment remain high after a burst of job destruction.[9] There are secondary effects from the displacement of workers. For example, a worker who is terminated in a plant closing may take temporary work after a period of search. When the temporary job is over, the worker will once again become unemployed. The secondary effects of the job destruction from a serious recession, such as that of 1982, appear to last for several years.

Outflows from unemployment also decline after a burst of job destruction. When job-finding rates are high, the fraction of unemployed workers who remain unemployed for extended periods is low. When outflows from unemployment occur more slowly, the fraction of long-term unemployed rises. Figure 3.5 compares unemployment duration in a good year, 1999, and a weak

[9] See Robert E. Hall, "Lost Jobs," *Brookings Papers on Economic Activity*, Vol. 1 (1995), pp. 221–273.

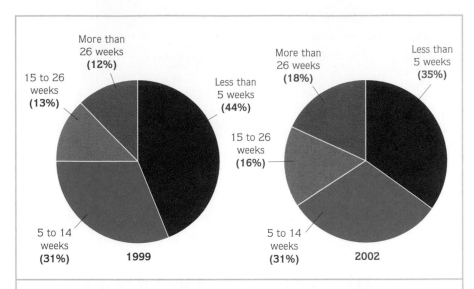

FIGURE 3.5   UNEMPLOYMENT DURATION IN A SLUMP AND IN A BOOM

The pie charts show the percentage of workers unemployed for different lengths of time in a bad year just at the end of a recession (2002) and in a good year just before the start of a recession (1999). Long-term unemployment is relatively high in a bad year. Job-finding rates are higher in good years.

SOURCE: *Economic Report of the President*, 2003, Table B-44.

year in the aftermath of a recession, 2002. In 2002, 18 percent of the unemployed had been looking for work for more than 26 weeks, compared to only 12 percent in a good year, 1999. People find jobs more rapidly in strong markets than in weak markets. The main difference is that job seekers compete with more rivals for each job opening when unemployment is high.

The overall story of fluctuations in unemployment starts with a burst of job destruction, resulting from an oil price shock, financial crisis, or other adverse development. Unemployment jumps upward. It remains at levels above the natural rate for several years after the shock. During this period, there are continuing unusually high flows into unemployment from the secondary effects of the shock, as workers have second and third spells of unemployment after their displacement in the original job destruction. Another factor holding unemployment above the natural rate is that job-finding rates are lower for several years after the shock.

Okun's Law

A useful shorthand formula closely approximates the cyclical relationship between unemployment and real GDP. Commonly called **Okun's law,** after its discoverer, Arthur Okun, the law says that, for each percentage point by which

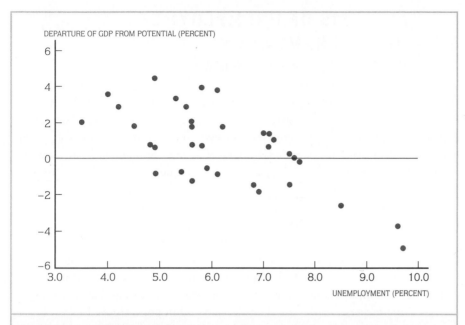

FIGURE 3.6 OKUN'S LAW

The movements in unemployment are closely related to the movements in the percentage departures of real GDP from potential GDP. The slope of the relationship is roughly 3 percentage points of real GDP for each percent of unemployment.

the unemployment rate is above the natural rate, real GDP is 3 percent below potential GDP. The percentage departure of GDP from potential is called the **GDP gap.**

The equation that describes Okun's law is

$$(Y - Y^*)/Y^* = -3(U - U^*),$$ (3.4)

where Y is GDP, Y^* is potential GDP, U is the unemployment rate, and U^* is the natural rate of unemployment. For example, if the unemployment rate U is 7.5 percent and the natural rate of unemployment U^* is 5.5 percent, real GDP is 6 percent below its potential, so that the GDP gap is minus 6 percent. The historical accuracy of Okun's Law is illustrated in Figure 3.6.

Fluctuations in Unemployment

1. Unemployment in the United States fluctuates from 3 percent of the labor force in the sharpest booms to 10 percent in the worst recessions.

2. The unemployment rate is closely related to the deviations of real GDP from potential GDP. This relation is called *Okun's law.*

3.5 | ANALYSIS OF UNEMPLOYMENT IN THE FRAMEWORK OF SUPPLY AND DEMAND

Why do so many people lose their jobs in recessions? Why does unemployment linger for several years after a recession? Why doesn't the labor market adjust quickly to provide employment for everyone willing to work at the market wage? Why isn't the standard model of supply and demand an accurate model of the labor market? These are central questions of macroeconomic analysis.

The discussion earlier in this chapter showed what happens during the extended period when unemployment is high, during and after a recession, without completely answering these central questions. Instead of closing plants and destroying jobs, for example, employers could lower wages in order to keep marginal plants in business. And employers could hire aggressively during periods of high unemployment, when job seekers are numerous and jobs are easy to fill, and pay workers a little less than they would in good times. In search theory, job seekers should set their sights a little lower when jobs are hard to find.

Standard principles of economics seem to suggest that the incentives to correct excess unemployment are strong. Figure 3.7 shows the standard labor supply and demand diagram, with employment N on the horizontal axis and the real wage W/P on the vertical axis. (We will review the derivation of this diagram in Chapter 4.) However, unlike in Chapter 4, we now consider the possibility that there is unemployment; that is, the actual level of employment in a recession (N_R) is less than the equilibrium level of employment (N^*).

One reason why employment might be at the low level N_R rather than at the equilibrium level N^* is that the real wage W/P is above its equilibrium level. Then, the quantity of labor demand by firms on their labor demand curves is N_R. The real wage could be above equilibrium because of government restrictions on wages or slow adjustment of wages. High unemployment in Germany, France, and Spain in the mid-1990s may have been the result of excess real wages, for example.

Regardless of the level of the real wage in Figure 3.7, when employment is below the equilibrium level, there are incentives facing employers, workers, or both to raise the amount of work. The difference between the marginal product of labor (the labor demand schedule) and the real wage is the incentive facing the

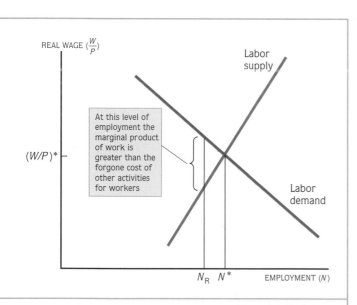

FIGURE 3.7   INCENTIVES WHEN EMPLOYMENT IS BELOW EQUILIBRIUM

If employment is at the recession level, employers and workers have incentives to increase the amount of work. The incentives are measured in dollars per hour on the vertical (real-wage) axis.

RESEARCH IN PRACTICE
A Silver Lining to the Storm Clouds of Recession?

Recessions are times of hardship for unemployed workers and lower average incomes for people in general. But economists have been looking at the benefit side as well.* The benefits arise because recessions are times when the economy has a chance to regroup and reorganize. There are two branches to this line of thought. One says that booms tend to keep outdated plants in operation and recessions are times to prune them out and expand modern plants. The other says that recessions are times when firms have less incentive to produce output and therefore a lower opportunity cost for reorganizing. In both cases, there is no claim that recessions are desirable, only that the economy is good at figuring out useful alternative activities during recessions.

In the "cleansing" view, firms wait until a recession to shut down old-fashioned plants. The market can respond to lower demand both by reducing the rate of opening of new plants and by shutting down old ones. In the cleansing model, the second effect is the more important. This property of the cleansing model is in line with the evidence that a disproportionate fraction of employment reductions in recessions take the form of increased job destruction rather than reduced job creation.

The second view has been called the "pit stop" model of recessions. In auto racing, cars are required to slow down when the yellow light is on because of an accident. Drivers often choose yellow-light periods to make pit stops to refuel and change tires. Relative to the situation when the green light is on and they can drive as fast as possible, the opportunity cost of a pit stop is lower when the yellow light is on. A recession is like a yellow-light period. It is less profitable to produce and sell output, so firms and workers have lower opportunity costs for other activities. Restructuring is an activity that is cheaper in a recession. During restructuring, firms lay off workers who are not well matched to their current jobs. These workers enter the labor market and search for new jobs that are better matches. Recessions and the periods of high unemployment that follow them are times when the economy is building better organizations, getting ready for the next burst of demand for output.†

Whatever the merit of these views, the flows through the labor market are much greater during recessions and their aftermaths than in booms. In 1982, a year of severe recession, 3.5 percent of the labor force became newly unemployed each month. In 1994, a year of favorable and improving conditions, only 2.1 percent of the labor force became newly unemployed each month. The labor market was called on to handle about 70 percent *more* matching of job seekers to jobs in the recession year than in the good year. Even if there proves to be little support for the optimistic view that finding new jobs for so many extra workers is good for the economy, our thinking about recessions should always keep in mind how much bigger the flows are in the labor market during recessions. If the market could not handle the higher flows, recessions would be even harder on job losers than they are in today's U.S. economy.

*Ricardo J. Caballero and Mohamad L. Hammour, "The Cleansing Effect of Recessions," *American Economic Review* 84 (December 1994): 1350–1368.

†Robert E. Hall, "Labor Demand, Labor Supply, and Employment Volatility," *NBER Macroeconomics Annual*, 1991, pp. 17–47.

employer. One added worker increases the firm's revenue by the marginal product, but the worker has to be paid only the real wage. The difference is a profit opportunity for the firm; it provides an economic incentive to expand output.

The difference between the real wage and the worker's value of time (the labor supply schedule) is the incentive facing the worker. Another hour of work earns the worker the real wage, but the cost (forgone time in other activities) is a smaller amount. The difference is an economic opportunity for the worker; it provides an economic incentive to increase hours worked.

Both firms and workers have incentives to raise employment when employment is at a recession level, below equilibrium. How long it takes for these incentives to bring about an expansion of employment back to equilibrium is a question macroeconomists debate frequently and intensely. For now, we simply make the practical observation that employment frequently drops below its equilibrium level, especially in recessions. It takes several years for employment to return to equilibrium. We conclude that incentives operate slowly over years, not days, weeks, or months. Until incentives do their job, the level of employment can remain below equilibrium. In Chapters 7 through 9, we develop a short-run model to describe the transitory departures of the economy from its long-run growth path.

The Labor Market Out of Equilibrium

1. When level of employment is lower than the full-employment level, firms and workers face incentives to expand employment.

2. These incentives take time to operate. High unemployment can persist for several years.

REVIEW AND PRACTICE

Major Points

1. Unemployment is measured in a survey of households. A person is counted as unemployed if he or she is available for work and looking for work but has not yet found a job.

2. There are substantial flows into and out of unemployment. The unemployment rate is the ratio of the job-losing rate to the job-finding rate.

3. The natural rate of unemployment is the amount that prevails in normal times, around 5 or 6 percent.

4. The flow into unemployment comes from job destruction, other job losses, and personal transitions that cause people to quit jobs and look for new ones.

5. The flow out of unemployment depends on the job-finding rate, which averages 39 percent per month.

6. The efficiency wage model offers one reason for low job-finding rates. If jobs are easy to find, employers raise wages to motivate their workers.

7. Union wage premiums and the minimum wage are other reasons why jobs may be hard to find.

8. Unemployment insurance causes job seekers to be choosier and thus lowers job-finding rates.

9. Unemployment moves over the business cycle. In recessions, it rises as high as 10 percent, and in booms, it falls as low as 3 percent.

10. Okun's law describes the relation between unemployment and real GDP. For each percentage point by which unemployment is above the natural rate, real GDP is 3 percent below potential.

11. When unemployment is high during a recession, there are incentives to put more workers to work—the marginal product of labor exceeds the real wage.

12. It takes several years for the level of employment to respond to incentives and to return to normal after a recession.

Key Terms and Concepts

labor force   job-finding rate
unemployment rate   search theory
natural rate of unemployment   Okun's law
job-losing rate   GDP gap

Questions for Discussion and Review

1. What is the difference between being unemployed and not working? Give some examples of people not at work who are not unemployed.

2. What situations cause workers to become unemployed?

3. Explain why, when the unemployment rate is steady, it is equal to the ratio of the job-losing rate to the job-finding rate.

4. What factors determine the job-finding rate?

5. List four factors that tend to raise the natural rate of unemployment.

6. How has the natural rate of unemployment differed between Europe and the United States since the 1960s? What accounts for the differences?

7. Explain why unemployment falls when output rises. In the process, mention what happens to employment.

8. Explain the role of labor supply and labor demand in determining the incentives to return to equilibrium.

Problems

NUMERICAL

1. In a particular month, the labor force is 130 million, there are 9.1 million unemployed workers, the job-losing rate is 3 percent per month, and the job-finding rate is 40 percent per month. How many people will be unemployed next month? At what unemployment rate would the number of unemployed remain the same from one month to the next?

2. A firm finds the following relationship between the amount that workers lose if they are fired and workers' productivity:

DOLLARS LOST BY WORKER AS A RESULT OF BEING FIRED	IMPROVEMENT IN PRODUCTIVITY BECAUSE WORKERS WORK HARDER TO AVOID LOSING THEIR JOBS (EXTRA DOLLARS OF PROFIT TO FIRM)
1000	1000
2000	3500
3000	5000
4000	5500

Workers are paid $500 per week at other firms and all jobs last 50 weeks.

(a) If there is no unemployment, so workers can find jobs instantly at other firms, how much will this firm pay its workers?

(b) How many weeks of job search are needed so that this firm will pay its workers no more than they could get at other jobs?

(c) What is the natural rate of unemployment in this labor market if all firms are in the same situation?

3. Suppose that Okun's law relating unemployment and GDP is given by

$$(Y - Y^*)/Y^* = -3(U - U^*),$$

where U is the unemployment rate, U^* is the natural rate of unemployment, Y is GDP, and Y^* is potential GDP. Unemployment is measured as a fraction. Suppose that the natural rate is 6 percent; that is, $U^* = 0.06$.

(a) Calculate the GDP gap for each of the years in 1990–95 using the following unemployment data: U = 5.6, 6.8, 7.5, 6.9, 6.1 and 5.6 percent, respectively.

(b) GDP for these same years is as follows: $5,744, $5,917, $6,244, $6,550, $6,931, and $7,246 billion. Using these data and your answers to part a, calculate potential GDP for each of these years. What is the average growth rate of potential GDP?

ANALYTICAL

1. Discuss briefly how each of the following changes would affect the natural rate of unemployment.

   (a) The economy enters a period of little structural change and all industries are growing at about the same rate.

   (b) Schools operate for the full year, so no students are looking for summer work.

   (c) The Internet lists all the jobs available in the whole country, so it is easier for job seekers to locate potential jobs.

   (d) People who quit their jobs are drafted into low-wage community-service jobs.

   (e) In addition to unemployment insurance, the unemployed receive a bonus for finding new jobs; the bonus is greater if the job is found in the first few weeks of search and declines with the duration of search.

2. Okun's law suggests that, over the course of the business cycle, a change in the unemployment rate of 1 percentage point will be accompanied by a 3 percent change in output. Using the formula

$$Y = (Y/H)(H/N)(1 - U)L,$$

where Y/H is output per hour worked, H/N is hours per worker, N is the number of employed workers, U is the unemployment rate, and L is the labor force, explain in what direction and why some of the factors other than Y and U might change. (Note that, if W 5 XYZ, then for small changes the percentage change in W is given by the sum of the percentage changes in X, Y, and Z. Note also that 1 2 U 5 N/L and a change in the unemployment rate of 1 percentage point corresponds to approximately a 1 percent change in N/L.)

ECONOMIC GROWTH

PART Two

LONG-RUN ECONOMIC GROWTH

CHAPTER 4

Long-run economic growth is the study of the general upward path of output over time. Small differences in the economic growth rate make enormous differences in economic well-being. At the beginning of the 19th century, real GDP per capita in the United States was 2.5 times as large as in India. Over the next two centuries, real GDP per capita grew at 1.6 percent per year in the United States but only 0.54 percent per year in India. By the beginning of the 21st century, real GDP per capita in the United States was 16 times as large as India. As Robert Lucas of the University of Chicago, who won the Nobel Prize in 1995, wrote, "The consequences for human welfare involved in questions like these are simply staggering: Once one starts to think about them, it is hard to think about anything else."[1]

It does not take centuries for differences in economic growth rates to matter. A convenient rule of thumb, called the *rule of 70*, is that a country growing at g percent per year doubles its GDP per capita approximately every $70/g$ years. A country growing at 4 percent per year will see its GDP per capita double in 17.5 years, while a country growing at 2 percent per year will see its GDP per capita double in 35 years. Seemingly small changes in growth rates translate over time to very large differences in GDP per capita.

The **long-run growth model** is designed to explain differences in growth rates across countries and over time. Issues involving economic growth are so important that we spend three chapters studying them. In this chapter, we begin by introducing the determinants of economic growth. We then consider why there was no economic growth until the 19th century and study the relation between saving and growth. Chapter 5 focuses on technology: the engine of sustained growth. Chapter 6 considers growth in the world economy.

The long-run growth model does not try to explain the departures of the economy from its growth trend. It describes the economy in a state where supply and demand for both goods and workers are in balance. Wages and prices move as needed to equate supply and demand. Incentives have their full effect in inducing an efficient level of production. Unlike the economic fluctuations model, which is examined in Chapters 7 through 9, the long-run growth model abstracts from short-run fluctuations and does not try to explain important events like the 2001 recession and the increase in unemployment that occurred at that time. We use it to project economic conditions in the more distant future and understand variations in growth rates.

4.1 | THE DETERMINANTS OF ECONOMIC GROWTH

MACROSOLVE
EXERCISE

There are three important determinants of the long-run growth path of output:

1. *Labor*—the people available for work

2. *Capital*—equipment, structures, and other productive facilities

3. *Technology*—the knowledge about how to use labor and capital to produce goods and services.

Labor

Growth in the number of people available for work is an important source of the growth of GDP. Since the 1970s, growth in the number of workers has been strong as the post–World War II baby boom generation came of working

---

[1] Robert E. Lucas, "On the Mechanics of Economic Development," *Journal of Monetary Economics*, Vol. 22 (July 1988), p. 3–42.

age and women entered the labor market in large numbers. In the future, growth in the number of workers is expected to be weaker.

Not everybody in the population is in the labor force. It is against the law for children to work; many adults are in school, working at home, or in retirement; and quite a few others are unable to work because they are disabled or sick. Some people are committed to working full-time no matter what the incentives; others choose the level of their work effort depending on the incentives provided by the labor market. About 67 percent of the working-age population was in the labor force in 2001. This percentage—the **labor force participation rate**—has been steadily increasing during the last 20 years, primarily because of increasing participation rates for women.

If we subtract the number of unemployed workers from the number of workers in the labor force, we get the number of workers employed. Production depends not only on the number of workers employed but also on the amount of hours they work each year. Hence, when looking at the effects of employment on production and growth, we count only the hours that workers actually work. The total number of hours worked in the economy in a given year is what we mean by *labor input*. We frequently refer to labor input simply as employment and label it N.

Capital

In any given year, the volume of physical capital—aircraft factories, computers, trucks, tractors, barns, clothing stores, and so forth—is determined by investment in previous years. An increase in the amount of capital in the economy enables the economy to produce more output. For example, a farmer with a tractor can produce tons more wheat than a farmer without a tractor. Boeing could not produce any 767s without manufacturing plants. The capital stock increases from one year to the next as long as gross investment is greater than the depreciation of the capital stock. As long as net investment is positive, the capital stock grows. However, any investment project undertaken this year to increase the capital stock will not add to the stock until the project is complete, a process that takes time. We use the symbol K for the existing capital stock.

Technology

The third determinant of production—technology—tells us how much output can be produced from the amount of labor and capital used in production. Technology includes anything that influences the productivity of workers or capital. It includes technology in the usual sense of the word, such as a communications technology that enables a firm to fax a supplier an order form rather than send it by regular mail. It also includes how efficiently businesses are organized and managed.

We use the symbol A to represent technology. Technology is perhaps the most abstract of the three determinants of growth, and it is more difficult to measure than labor and capital. Fortunately, many vivid examples can reduce the level of abstraction, such as the following automobile example.

HENRY FORD'S ASSEMBLY LINE   One of the great—and most visible—technological advances of the 20th century was Henry Ford's idea of mass production through the assembly line. Mass production greatly increased the productivity of workers and capital employed in the automobile industry, and eventually other industries as well. It represents an example of an increase in technology—an increase in A.

Ford's innovation occurred in 1913 at his Highland Park factory in Detroit, where he arranged an assembly line in which cars moved past workers who remained in place, rather than having the workers move around the factory. Observers at the time calculated that this one technological advance reduced the time it took a group of workers to assemble the major components into a complete car from $12\frac{1}{2}$ to $1\frac{1}{2}$ hours! With this increase in productivity it is not surprising that Ford could double wages to $5 a day and still cut prices.

Technological change increases the productivity of both labor and capital. Labor and capital are factors of production. Technological change may increase the productivity of both factors in a neutral way such that their marginal productivities increase in the same proportion. It is then useful to define technological change as something that increases *total factor productivity*.

The Production Function

A simple way to represent how the three determinants of production combine to produce output is through the **production function,** which shows how much output can be produced from given amounts of labor, capital, and technology. The production function can be represented using symbols as follows:

$$Y = F(N, K, A). \qquad \text{The Production Function} \qquad (4.1)$$

This is simply shorthand notation for saying that output Y depends on employment N, capital K, and technology A. (Reading out loud we say "Y is a function F of N, K, and A.") The notation F followed by variables listed in parentheses means a general function of those variables. With such a notation we are not specific about what the function actually looks like, whether it is linear, the square root of N, or whatever.

The production function relates output to employment, capital, and technology, whatever their levels. It tells us how much real GDP would be produced, for example, if there were a very severe depression and only half the normal number of people were at work.

Figure 4.1 shows how production depends on labor for a given capital stock and a given level of technology. The production function curves toward the horizontal axis. The **marginal product of labor** is the additional output produced by one additional unit of work. The marginal product of labor is the

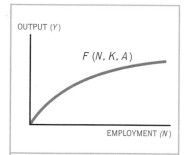

FIGURE 4.1   THE PRODUCTION FUNCTION IN TERMS OF LABOR INPUT

With a given capital stock and technology, the volume of output produced from various levels of employment N shows the diminishing marginal product of labor.

slope of the production function in Figure 4.1. Note how the production function gets less steep as more labor is employed. This means that the marginal product of labor declines as the amount of employment increases.

4.2 | FULL EMPLOYMENT AND POTENTIAL GDP

The growth model assumes that the economy is at full employment, with the quantity of labor demanded equal to the quantity of labor supplied. We define *potential GDP* as the amount of production that occurs when labor is fully employed. To determine potential GDP, therefore, we must calculate the level of N corresponding to full employment. For now, we consider the level of technology A and the level of capital K as given. To find N, we consider the demand for, and supply of, labor.

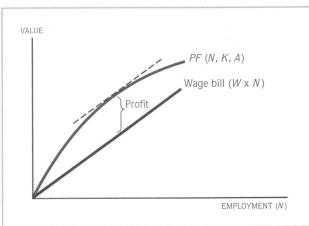

FIGURE 4.2   PROFIT MAXIMIZATION

Profit is the difference between the value of output, P times $F(N, K, A)$, and the wage bill, W times N. It reaches a maximum when the slope of P times $F(N, K, A)$ equals the slope of W times N; that is, the value of the marginal product of labor equals the wage.

The Demand for Labor

A first principle of microeconomics is that a profit-maximizing firm in a competitive market chooses the level of employment where *the marginal product of labor equals the real wage*. The **real wage** is the dollar wage W divided by the price level P, that is, W/P. If firms have employment below this level, the marginal product of labor exceeds the real wage and an opportunity for improved profit exists. A firm could hire a worker for the wage W, produce more output in the amount given by the marginal product of labor, sell that output at price P, and make a profit on the deal. Firms pursue this opportunity for profit until their additional hiring pushes the marginal product of labor down to the real wage. The point of maximum profit is shown in Figure 4.2.

The demand function for labor is a negative function of the real wage because the marginal product of labor declines with increased labor input, as shown in Figure 4.3.

The Supply of Labor

The supply of labor is determined by the decisions of individual workers about how much of their time to spend working. The real wage measures the incentive to work. At higher real wages, those already at work want to work more. In addition, a higher real wage may draw people into the workforce who would

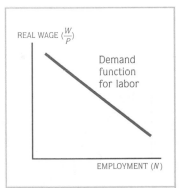

FIGURE 4.3   THE DEMAND FUNCTION FOR LABOR

The demand function for labor is a downward-sloping relation between the real wage, W/P, and the level of employment, N. For each real wage, it gives the level of employment that firms choose by equating the marginal product of labor to the real wage.

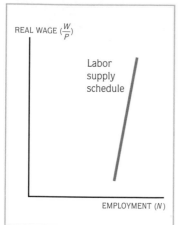

FIGURE 4.4   LONG-RUN LABOR SUPPLY SCHEDULE

The labor supply schedule gives the amount of labor offered in the labor market for various levels of the real wage. When real wages rise permanently, the incentive to work is greater, but people have more income, and this tends to offset the incentive. The evidence suggests that the long-run labor supply schedule is almost vertical.

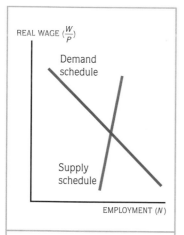

FIGURE 4.5   LABOR MARKET EQUILIBRIUM

In the model with perfectly flexible wages and prices, the real wage is determined by the intersection of the supply and demand curves for labor.

not work at all with a lower real wage. A higher real wage has an incentive effect toward more work. For most people, however, wages are the dominant source of income. When wages rise permanently, they are better off. People who are better off choose to spend more time at home and away from the job. On this account, permanently higher real wages bring lower labor supply. Microeconomic theory labels these two contrasting influences the *substitution effect* and the *income effect*.

SUBSTITUTION EFFECT   As something becomes more expensive, people substitute away from it. In the case of labor supply, as time at home becomes more expensive (as its opportunity cost, the real wage, rises), people substitute away from time at home and toward time in the labor market. To put it another way, the real wage provides an incentive for work, and people substitute toward work when the real wage rises.

INCOME EFFECT   As income rises, people tend to consume more of most things. In this case, they consume more of their own time at home and offer less of their time in the labor market. Permanently higher real wages make people better off, and they work less on that account.

The long-run labor supply schedule, illustrated in Figure 4.4, shows the net effect of these two offsetting influences. Research by a number of economists has agreed rather closely that the net effect of the two influences of real wage on labor supply is roughly zero.[2] However, it is important to keep in mind that the agreement is that the *net effect* is approximately zero, not that each of its components is zero. The substitution effect, prompting people to work more when the real wage rises, has been shown to be strong in some studies. In these studies, the income effect happens to be equally strong in the opposite direction.

Full Employment

Another principle of microeconomics is that employment is at the intersection of the labor supply and labor demand schedules. The equilibrium is shown in Figure 4.5. On the vertical axis is the real wage, which is the ratio W/P of the dollar wage to the price level. In equilibrium at the real wage W/P, the quantity of labor N chosen by firms equals the quantity supplied by the public. In Figure 4.5, the labor market is in a standard microeconomic equilibrium. Every worker is able to find a job. If the real wage were too high to provide jobs for everyone interested, the real wage would fall. The fall would stimulate labor demand by firms and discourage work effort by workers. The real wage would

---

[2] The most recent econometric studies have used experimental data or panel data of the type we describe in Chapter 10 in our analysis of consumption. A useful survey of available results is found in John Pencavel, "Labor Supply of Men: A Survey," in Orley Ashenfelter, ed., *Handbook of Labor Economics* (Amsterdam: North-Holland, 1987).

fall immediately to the point where the supply and demand curves intersect and everybody had work.

We define **full employment,** N^*, as the volume of employment at the intersection of supply and demand in Figure 4.5. It is the total amount of work that would be done if each worker could find a job after a brief search and earn as much as similar workers are already earning. Note that full employment is not the absolute maximum amount of work that the population is capable of doing. It is the amount people want to work given the real wage that employers are willing to pay. If productivity rises, so that the labor demand schedule shifts upward, the equilibrium level of employment rises. Moreover, as the population grows, the labor supply schedule shifts to the right and equilibrium employment rises.

Potential GDP

Potential GDP, denoted by Y^*, is the amount of output produced when the labor market is at full employment:

$$Y^* = F(N^*, K, A). \tag{4.2}$$

The level of output, Y^*, is the amount of output that would be produced if everybody who wanted to work could find a job. For this reason, Y^* is also frequently called the **full-employment level of output.** Recall that in Figures 1.1 and 1.2, we compared actual GDP with estimates of potential GDP. We found that potential GDP grows steadily, whereas actual GDP fluctuates around a growth trend.

In Chapter 3, we defined the *natural rate of unemployment* as the amount of unemployment when the labor market is in equilibrium. The natural rate of unemployment, U^*, is the amount of unemployment in the economy in normal times, when employment is at full employment, N^*, and GDP is equal to potential GDP, Y^*.

Potential GDP and the Labor Market

1. Potential GDP is the level of real GDP when labor is fully employed. Prices and wages have moved so that markets are in balance.

2. The determinants of potential GDP are the labor force and its willingness to work as expressed by the labor supply schedule, the capital stock, and the technology of the economy.

3. In the labor market, the real wage adjusts as needed to keep the market in balance. Full employment is the common value of labor supply and labor demand after the real wage has made the two equal.

From Potential GDP to Economic Growth

Using the production function, labor supply, and labor demand, we have seen how full employment and potential GDP are determined. While this analysis abstracts from short-run fluctuations around potential GDP, it still describes the economy at a point in time. In the rest of the chapter, we study how the economy moves over time. We first consider how GDP per capita can remain constant over long periods of time, then study how GDP per capita can grow over time.

4.3 | MALTHUSIAN STAGNATION AND THE DEMOGRAPHIC TRANSITION

For most of recorded history, there was no economic growth. Per-capita GDP was unchanged in Europe between 500 AD and 1500 AD, and real wages in ancient Greece and Rome were comparable to England and France in 1800. Writing in 1798, Thomas Malthus proposed a model that accounted for the long-run stability in living standards. Designed for consistency with the lack of economic growth over the previous two millennia, the **Malthusian model** proved to be a spectacular failure in predicting economic growth over the next two centuries. We first analyze the process of Malthusian stagnation, then describe the demographic transition to modern growth.[3]

Malthusian Stagnation

The first building block of the Malthusian model is diminishing marginal product of labor. Think of an agricultural society where land, capital and technology are unchanged. This is, at first glance, not a bad model for 18th century England. The amount of available farmland could be increased only by clearing forests, and farming methods had not changed much for thousands of years. Given a fixed plot of land, increasing employment from one to two workers would raise food production more than increasing employment from 101 to 102 workers, which in turn would raise food production more than increasing employment from 1001 to 1002 workers. This is illustrated by the shape of the production function in Figure 4.1.

The second building block is a theory of fertility and mortality. Malthus postulated that the population needed a minimum level of output to avoid starvation. This level is depicted as the **subsistence line** in Figure 4.6. Note

---

[3] See Robert E. Lucas, "The Industrial Revolution: Past and Future," in Robert E. Lucas, ed., *Lectures on Economic Growth* (Cambridge, MA: Harvard University Press, 2002), pp. 109–188; Oded Galor and David N. Weil, "From Malthusian Stagnation to Modern Growth," *American Economic Review*, Vol. 89 No 2 (May 1999), pp. 150–154; and Charles I. Jones, "Was an Industrial Revolution Inevitable? Economic Growth over the Very Long Run," *Advances in Macroeconomics*, Vol. 1, No. 2, Article 1 (2001), at www.bepress.com/bejm/advances/vol1/iss2/art1.

that this is drawn as a 45-degree line through the origin. Along the subsistence line, output per worker, Y/N, is constant. Above the subsistence line, output per worker is greater than needed for subsistence. Birth rates increase because families can support more children and death rates decrease because of better nutrition, both leading to population growth. Below the subsistence line, output per worker is less than needed for subsistence. With output below the subsistence level, death rates increase as people begin to die of disease and starvation. Birth rates decrease because, with such low levels of output, families avoid having children they cannot feed. Both factors lead to declines in population.

The combination of fertility and mortality moves the economy toward the subsistence line in Figure 4.6. Above the subsistence line, population increases, moving employment to the right. Below the subsistence line, population decreases, moving employment to the left.

The outcome of combining the production function with diminishing marginal product of labor and the subsistence line is illustrated in Figure 4.7. The economy is always on the production function, which depicts how much output is produced by the labor input. Suppose the economy is at a point on the production function above and to the left of the subsistence line. Output per worker is above the subsistence level, the population increases, and the economy moves up and to the right over time to the intersection of the two lines. Now, suppose the economy is at a point on the production function below and to the right of the subsistence line. Output per worker is below the subsistence level, the population decreases, and the economy moves down and to the left over time to the intersection of the two lines. Wherever the economy starts, the outcome is **Malthusian stagnation.** Output per worker is just sufficient to sustain life, and the population is constant. With no output growth and no population growth, there is no economic growth.

An important prediction of the Malthusian model is that technological change does not allow an economy to escape from Malthusian stagnation. While output increases, it is matched by a population increase that leaves output per worker unchanged. This is depicted in Figure 4.8, which shows the effect of an increase in total factor productivity. Technological change shifts up the production function, raising output at the initial level of population from point A to point B. The improvement in living standards, however, raises birth rates and lowers death rates, increasing population. The process continues until Malthusian equilibrium is restored along the subsistence line at point C. Output per worker, Y/N, is unchanged by technological progress.

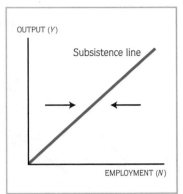

FIGURE 4.6   THE SUBSISTENCE LINE

Along the subsistence line, output per worker, Y/N, is constant. Above the subsistence line, population and employment rise. Below the subsistence line, population and employment fall.

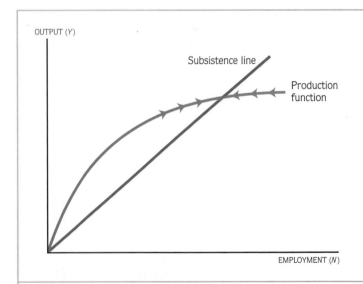

FIGURE 4.7   MALTHUSIAN STAGNATION

In the Malthusian model, output and employment are determined by the intersection of the subsistence line and the production function.

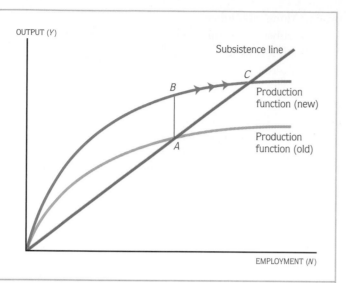

OUTPUT (Y)

Subsistence line

B

C

Production
function (new)

A

Production
function (old)

EMPLOYMENT (N)

**FIGURE 4.8   TECHNOLOGICAL CHANGE
IN THE MALTHUSIAN MODEL**

Technological change shifts up the production function, increasing
both output and employment. The output per worker, however, does
not change.

Was Malthus Correct?

Malthusian stagnation depicts an extremely pessimistic picture. How well does it accord with the facts? This can be divided into two questions. How well does Malthusian stagnation accord with the facts before Malthus wrote his theory and how well does it accord with the facts afterward?

World GDP and population from 1000 AD to 2000 AD are illustrated in Figure 4.9. While population data is available as far back as 1 million BC, GDP data goes back only to 1750 AD. The figure is drawn using a logarithmic scale, so that constant growth of either GDP or population is depicted by a straight line. It is assumed that per-capita GDP was unchanged until 1750, which accounts for the constant vertical distance between the two lines until that time.

Malthus's theory predicts constant per-capita GDP in the long run. Figure 4.9 shows that, prior to 1800, the theory works well. While GDP per capita was unchanged, there was population growth. For GDP per capita to remain unchanged with a growing population, either the amount of land under cultivation must have increased or there must have been technological progress. In fact, both occurred, but there was no economic growth. Another piece of evidence is that, prior to 1800, there was much disparity in technology among countries and among regions within countries. The disparity in technology caused differences in population density but not differences in GDP per capita.

The evidence after 1800 is dramatically different. Growth rates of both GDP and population rose sharply in the 19th and 20th centuries. More important, GDP grew much faster than population, causing per-capita GDP to rise sharply. Furthermore, this economic growth was higher in the 20th than in the 19th century, and much higher after 1960 than in the first part of the 20th century. Between 1960 and 2000, world GDP grew at 4.0 percent per year while world population grew at 1.8 percent per year. Subtracting the latter from the former, world GDP per capita, or the rate of economic growth, was 2.2 percent per year. This is for the world as a whole. The growth rate for industrialized countries was even faster.

The Industrial Revolution
and the Demographic Transition

What happened after 1800? The *industrial revolution* in Western Europe caused the pace of technological change to increase. According to the Malthusian model, this should have caused fertility rates to increase, leaving GDP per

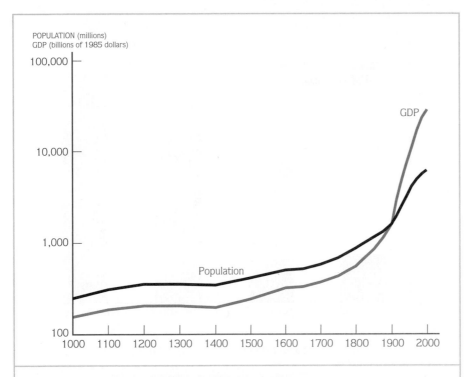

FIGURE 4.9   WORLD POPULATION AND PRODUCTION

World GDP and population grew at approximately the same rate until 1750, so that GDP per capita was unchanged. Between 1750 and 1900, GDP grew faster than population, causing a rise in GDP per capita. After 1900, GDP grew much faster than population, causing a sharp rise in GDP per capita.

SOURCE: Lucas, *Lectures on Economic Growth.*

capita unchanged. While fertility rates did increase between 1800 and 1870, technology grew faster than population, causing GDP per capita to increase. The slow progress from Malthusian stagnation is called the *post-Malthusian regime*, illustrated in Figure 4.10. While GDP per capita increased, it grew much more slowly than total GDP.

The *demographic transition* dealt the final blow to Malthusian stagnation. As income continued to rise, fertility rates did not increase, but rather declined sharply in Western Europe around the turn of the century. Continued technological progress combined with slower population growth implied much higher growth rates in GDP per capita starting in the 1920s. This is also shown in Figure 4.10. What distinguishes the *modern growth regime* of the last 85 years is not technological progress by itself or even the acceleration in the rate of growth of technological progress. The distinguishing feature is that, for the first time in recorded history, technological progress was associated with fertility reductions rather than fertility increases.

The discussion of growth proceeds in two directions. In the remainder of this chapter and in Chapter 5, we focus on the growth experiences of those

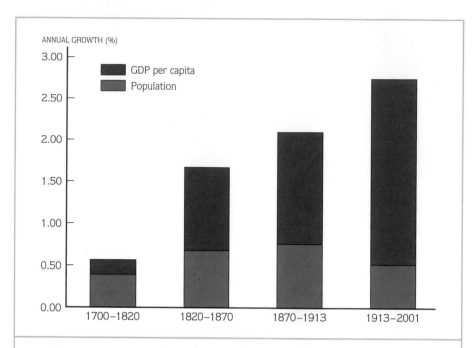

ANNUAL GROWTH (%)

FIGURE 4.10   POPULATION AND GDP PER CAPITA GROWTH RATES FOR WESTERN EUROPE

During the 19th century, GDP grew faster than population, causing growth in GDP per capita. During the 20th century, GDP growth increased further while population growth slowed, causing even higher growth rates of GDP per capita.

SOURCE: Maddison, *The World Economy: Historical Statistics*

countries that have passed through the demographic transition to the modern growth regime: the United States, Western Europe, Canada, Japan, and Australia. In Chapter 6, we return to those countries, primarily in Africa and Asia, where the demographic transition is still ongoing.

From Malthus to Modern Growth

1. Malthusian stagnation characterized most of history. Although there was some technological progress and population growth, GDP per capita was constant and there was no economic growth.

2. The industrial revolution increased the pace of technological progress. Fertility rates also increased, and so GDP per capita grew slowly at first.

3. The demographic transition, the decrease in fertility rates in Western Europe following the industrial revolution, is the key to understanding the evolution of the modern growth regime. With technological progress rising and population growth slowing, economic growth increased sharply.

4. Not all countries have yet gone through the demographic transition. Many countries in Africa and Asia still have high birth rates and stagnant growth.

4.4 | THE SOLOW GROWTH MODEL

Having defined the production function and studied the transition from Malthusian stagnation to the modern growth regime, we are now prepared to explore the behavior of the economy as it steadily grows through time. In particular, we want to look at the relationship between labor growth, capital growth, and technological growth and examine whether the growth process has any inherent tendencies to slow down. We focus on a particular real-world example: the growth path of the United States economy in the first two decades of the twenty-first century.

The growth of the labor force is predicted by the Bureau of Labor Statistics to average around 1 percent per year through the year 2020. The forecast is very reliable, because the people who will be in the labor force, which is limited to those who are 16 years of age and over, during this time have already been born. Projecting the labor force much beyond 2020 is more difficult because it requires forecasting future birthrates.

Now consider the growth of the capital stock over the same period. Capital growth depends on how much investment there is each year, which in turn depends on how much Americans save and how much foreigners invest in the United States. Forecasting future saving and foreign investment is much more difficult than forecasting the growth of the labor force. Saving depends not only on what private individuals do, but also on whether the federal government succeeds in reducing the budget deficit. Instead of trying to forecast future capital growth, we consider the implications of a future in which the growth rate of capital exactly equals the growth rate of labor, so that the amount of capital available for each worker neither rises nor falls. Such a steady growth path, called a **balanced growth path** because the growth rates of capital and labor are balanced, would be a useful baseline from which to make judgments about how alternative economic policies would affect the future. But first we need to check whether the economy tends to follow a balanced growth path.

Robert Solow of M.I.T., who won the Nobel Prize in 1987, wrote a paper in 1956 on balanced growth paths such as the one hypothesized.[4] In fact, the long-run growth model was introduced for the first time in that paper. Solow's model is sometimes called the *neoclassical growth model* because it built on the classical models used by economists before Keynes. The **Solow growth model** makes extensive use of the production function, the identities we discussed in Chapter 2, and a simple assumption about saving.

[4] R. M. Solow, "A Contribution to the Theory of Economic Growth," *Quarterly Journal of Economics*, Vol. 70 (February 1956), pp. 65–94.

Saving and Balanced Growth

In the simplest version of Solow's neoclassical growth model, the economy is closed (so domestic saving equals investment) and there is no technological change (the term A is constant over time). Both assumptions can be modified, but they make it easier to see what is going on. In the next chapter, we allow A to increase over time and even be determined endogenously within the growth model. Labor force growth is assumed to be at a constant rate, n. Each year the labor force increases by n times N, the level at the start of the year. Currently, growth of the labor force in the United States is about 1 percent per year, so $n = 0.01$.

We saw in Chapter 2 that the change in the capital stock equals net investment. If capital is to grow at the rate n, then each year capital must rise by the amount nK. In order to stay on a growth path where the capital stock grows at rate n, net investment must be nK each year. We can think of nK as *balanced growth* investment. For example, if the capital stock is $10 trillion and n is 1 percent, then net investment must equal $100 billion (0.01 times $10,000 billion) if the capital stock is to grow at the same 1 percent rate as labor. To summarize, we have derived the first key condition for balanced growth:

$$\text{Net investment} = nK. \tag{4.3}$$

The second major element of Solow's analysis deals with saving. Saving depends on (1) the fraction of national income saved and (2) the level of national income. Let s be the fraction of income that is saved; s is called the *saving rate*. Saving in the economy is equal to s times income. We know from Chapter 2 that income equals output, Y. Hence,

$$\text{Saving} = sY. \tag{4.4}$$

For example, if income Y is $5 trillion and the saving rate is 0.02, then saving would be $100 billion. Since saving equals net investment, we see that sY equals the *actual* amount of net investment in the economy.

A subsidiary assumption of Solow's growth analysis is that the production function has *constant returns to scale*. Under constant returns and with unchanging technology, if there are equal proportional changes in labor and capital, output changes by the same proportion. Recall that the production function is

$$Y = F(K, N, A). \tag{4.5}$$

We could divide K, N, and Y by any number and the production function would still apply, with constant returns. We choose to divide by N. This has the effect of stating output as output per worker, Y/N, and capital as capital per worker, K/N:

$$Y/N = F(K/N, 1, A). \tag{4.6}$$

EXAMPLE Suppose $Y = F(K, N, A) = K^{1/3}N^{2/3}A$. Divide by N to get

$$Y = \left(\frac{K}{N}\right)^{1/3} \cdot \left(\frac{N}{N}\right)^{2/3} \cdot A = \left(\frac{K}{N}\right)^{1/3} \cdot 1 \cdot A = F(K/N, 1, A);$$

in other words, we replace K with (K/N) and N with 1 in the production function. Output per worker depends just on capital per worker, since we are assuming that technology, A, is constant over time.

In the absence of technological change, there is no growth of output per worker in the Solow growth model. This can be seen from Equation 4.6. Along a balanced growth path, the growth rates of labor and capital are equal, so K/N is constant. With A constant, output per worker Y/N does not change. Output can grow, but only at the rate of population growth. In contrast to the Malthusian model, however, the Solow model can explain economic growth. The engine of growth in per-capita GDP is technological progress. Along a balanced growth path, the growth rate of output per worker is equal to the growth rate of technology. In the next chapter, we focus on technology and economic growth.

Actual investment can be either greater or less than balanced growth investment. Solow developed a famous diagram to explain what happens in the two cases. The diagram is shown in Figure 4.11.

The straight line in Figure 4.11 expresses our conclusion about the amount of net investment needed to keep capital growing at the same rate as labor. The total amount of net investment is nK, so the amount per worker is nK/N. Because the horizontal axis is capital per worker, K/N, the amount of net investment—n times (K/N)—is a straight line with slope n. The curving line expresses our conclusion about saving per worker. Total saving is $sF(K, N, A)$, so saving per worker is $sF(K, N, A)/N$, which we can also write as $sF(K/N, 1, A)$; the line is curved because it is a constant (s) times the curved production function.

The intersection of the investment line and the saving curve in Figure 4.11 is the *steady-state point*. At this point, the actual amount of investment, determined by saving, is just the amount needed to keep the capital stock growing at the same rate as labor input is growing. If the economy starts at the steady state, it will stay there.

What happens if the economy starts with less capital per worker? This would correspond to a point to the left of the steady-state point in Figure 4.11. Saving per worker, and therefore actual investment, *exceeds* the amount needed to keep capital

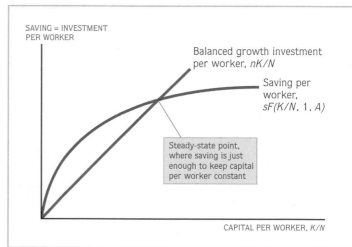

FIGURE 4.11 SOLOW'S GROWTH ANALYSIS

Solow's growth diagram shows the amount the economy saves per worker (the curving line) and the amount of investment per worker needed to keep the capital stock growing at the same rate as the labor force (the straight line). The steady state occurs at the intersection, where saving generates just the right amount of investment to stay on the balanced growth path. If capital per worker is less than the steady-state level, investment exceeds the amount needed for balanced growth and the amount of capital per worker rises. Hence, the economy tends toward its steady state.

per worker constant. Each year, capital per worker increases. The economy gradually approaches the steady-state point. Similarly, if the economy starts with more capital per worker than the steady-state amount, capital per worker declines each year and the economy approaches the steady state.

Solow showed that the growth process is *stable*. No matter where the economy starts, it converges over time to the same steady state, with the capital stock growing at the same rate as the labor force.

The Effect of Saving on Growth

Another important conclusion from Solow's work is that, in the long run, the growth rate does not depend on the saving rate. In the steady state, the capital stock and output both grow at the same rate as the labor force. The only factor that matters for the rate of growth of the economy is the growth of labor input. Economies that save more do not grow faster in the long run.

What then is the impact of increasing the saving rate in the Solow analysis? Suppose that the saving rate suddenly rises from 0.02 to 0.04 and stays there. Then the balanced growth condition is violated with $K/Y = 2 < s/n = 4$. According to Solow's stability argument, capital increases more rapidly than labor, and because of diminishing returns to capital, the capital-output ratio increases. The ratio continues to increase until it reaches 4 and the economy returns to the balanced growth rate of 1 percent. There is a **transition period,** however, during which the growth rate of the economy is greater than the balanced growth rate. This is illustrated in Figure 4.12, which shows how the level of output rises as a result of the increase in saving, but the growth rate of the economy returns to the balanced growth rate after the transition period. Hence, greater saving benefits the economy by raising future GDP per capita, but not by increasing the long-term growth rate.

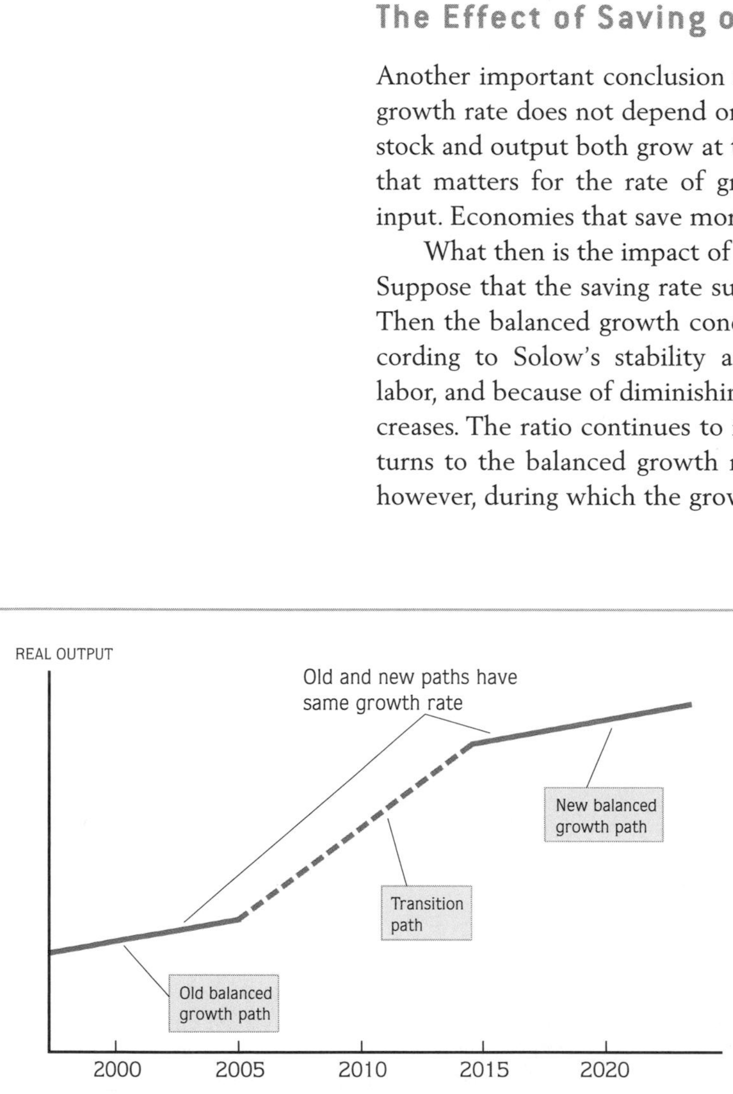

The same reasoning can be used to analyze the effect of changes in population growth. Suppose that, starting from a balanced growth path, population growth (assumed to equal the growth of the labor force, n) increases. Then, the balanced growth condition is violated, with actual investment (equal to saving sY) less than balanced growth investment nK. Put differently, the capital-output ratio $K/Y > s/n$. According to the Solow model, the growth rate of the

FIGURE 4.12   TRANSITION BETWEEN BALANCED GROWTH PATHS

A higher saving rate starting in the year 2005 leads to a higher level of real output. During a transition period, growth is higher. The growth rates in the old and new balanced growth paths are the same.

THE MIRACLE OF COMPOUND GROWTH

The concept of *compound growth* can be used to explain why seemingly small differences in growth rates lead to very large differences in GDP per capita over time. If real GDP per capita grows by 4 percent per year, how long does it take for it to double? Your first thought might be 25 years, since adding 4 percent per year for 25 years would add up to 100 percent. But you would be wrong; compound growth makes the process faster.

Suppose the real GDP per capita of a country is $100 billion in the year 2000 and grows at 4 percent per year. In the year 2001, real GDP per capita is $104 billion. In 2002, adding 4 percent to the $104 billion gives $108.16 billion. In 2003, adding 4 percent to $108.16 billion gives $112.49 billion. In 2004, adding 4 percent to $112.49 billion gives $116.99 billion. In 2005, adding 4 percent to $116.99 billion gives $121.67 billion. Because of compounding, each 4 percent increase is more than the $4 billion that you would get without compounding.

The formula for compound growth is

$$(\text{Initial level}) \times (1 + g)^x = \text{Level at end of } x \text{ years},$$

where g is the annual growth rate stated as a fraction. In this example, the 4 percent growth rate g stated as a fraction is 0.04 and the number of years x is 5, so that

$$\$100 \times (1.04)^5 = \$100 \times 1.2167 = \$121.67 \text{ billion}.$$

The formula can be inverted to calculate growth rates from initial to final levels:

$$g = [(\text{Level at end of } x \text{ years})/(\text{Initial level})]^{1/x} - 1.$$

According to the *rule of 70*, a country growing at g percent per year doubles its GDP per capital approximately every $70/g$ years. The concept of *compound growth* can be used to illustrate the rule of 70. According to the rule of 70, a country growing at 4 percent per year doubles its GDP per capita approximately every 17.5 years. From the formula for compound growth, a country growing at the rate of g percent per year doubles its GDP per capita in x years if $(1 + g)^x = 2$. If $g = 0.04$, then $(1.04)^{17.5} = 1.99$, approximately doubling.

economy during the transition period is less than the balanced growth rate. After the transition period, the growth rate of the economy returns to the balanced growth rate. The higher-population growth rate lowers the level of GDP per capita, but does not affect the growth rate.

Balanced Growth and the Solow Analysis

1. Balanced growth occurs when the labor force, capital stock, and real output all grow at the same rate.

2. Along a balanced growth path, the ratio of capital to output equals the ratio of the saving rate to the labor force growth rate.

3. Solow showed that the balanced growth path is stable: if the economy is off a balanced growth path, it will naturally tend to return to that path.

4. A higher saving rate will raise GDP per capita in Solow's analysis of the long-run growth model, but it will not permanently raise the growth rate.

5. A higher population growth rate will lower GDP per capita in the Solow growth model, but it will not permanently lower the growth rate.

REVIEW AND PRACTICE

Major Points

1. In the long-run growth model, the economy is always operating at full employment. Output is determined by the labor force, the capital stock, and technology.

2. Even when the economy is operating at its potential, there is some unemployment. The rate of unemployment when the labor market is in equilibrium is called the *natural rate*.

3. At any one time, the capital stock and technology are predetermined. Therefore, output is determined in the labor market. Employment is given by the equality of labor demand and labor supply.

4. Potential GDP is the amount of output predicted by the long-run growth model. It is the amount of output the economy would produce if it were at full employment.

5. In the Malthusian model, there is no economic growth.

6. The Malthusian prediction of no growth had not been fulfilled. Starting around 1800, the combination of the industrial revolution and demographic transition led to sustained economic growth.

7. Balanced growth occurs when labor and capital grow at the same rate.

8. In the Solow growth model, the growth process is stable.

9. In the Solow growth model an increase in saving does not permanently raise the growth rate.

10. In the Solow growth model, an increase in saving can temporarily increase the growth rate during a transition period.

Key Terms and Concepts

long-run economic growth

long-run growth model

labor force participation rate

production function

marginal product of labor

real wage

full employment

potential GDP

full-employment level of output

Malthusian model

subsistence line

Malthusian stagnation

balanced growth path

Solow growth model

transition period

Questions for Discussion and Review

1. What are the three basic determinants of long-run growth?

2. What is the unemployment rate when the economy is in equilibrium?

3. Why is the demand for labor a negative function of the real wage?

4. Explain why microeconomic theory predicts that, for labor supply, the income effect is negative and the substitution effect is positive. What do empirical studies indicate about the sum of these two effects?

5. Explain why the long-run growth model predicts that the level of real GDP in any one year is determined solely in the labor market.

6. What is meant by *Malthusian stagnation?*

7. What is meant by the *demographic transition?*

8. What happened in the 19th and 20th centuries to cause Malthus's prediction of no growth to become such a spectacular failure?

9. Why doesn't a higher saving rate increase growth in the neoclassical growth model?

10. What is the transitory impact of increasing the saving rate in the Solow growth model?

Problems

NUMERICAL

1. (a) The labor supply function is given by $N = 1,000 + 12 \, (W/P)$ and labor demand is $N = 2,000 - 8 \, (W/P)$. Draw a diagram showing these schedules. Find the equipment level of employment and the real wage.

   (b) Given existing technology and the capital stock, output is given by the function $Y = 100 \sqrt{N}$. Graph the production function. Does the production function exhibit diminishing marginal product of labor?

   (c) Using the labor market from part a and the production function from part b, determine the equilibrium level of output for this economy.

2. Suppose that the production function is $Y = K^{1/2}N^{1/2}A$.

   (a) If capital $K = 900$, labor $N = 400$, and technology $A = 1$, what is output Y and output per worker Y/N?

   (b) If capital and labor are increased by 50 percent while technology is held constant, how are output Y and output per worker Y/N affected?

   (c) If capital is increased by 50 percent, labor is increased by 25 percent, and technology is held constant, how are output Y and output per worker Y/N affected?

3. Suppose that the production function (written in terms of output per worker) is $Y/N = (K/N)^{1/2}A$.

   (a) Show how to derive this production function from the production function in problem 2.

   (b) If capital per worker K/N is $2,250,000 ($2.25 million) and technology $A = 10$, what is output per worker Y/N?

   (c) If the growth of the labor force is 1 percent per year, so $n = 0.01$, what is the saving rate s on the balanced growth path?

4. Suppose that an economy with GDP per capita of $2,000 grows at a rate of 3 percent per year.

   (a) Using the rule of 70, approximately how long would it take for GDP per capita to double?

   (b) Using the formula for compound growth, what would GDP per capita be at the end of 10 years?

5. Suppose that GDP per capita is $100 billion in 2000 and $164 billion in 2025 and the growth rate is constant. What is the annual growth rate?

ANALYTICAL

1. Explain the relationship between the following terms: equilibrium employment, the natural rate of unemployment, and potential GDP.

2. Using the production function, the labor demand schedule, and the labor supply schedule, show how full employment and potential output are determined.

3. In the Malthusian model, what is represented by the intersection of the production function and the subsistence line? Show that technological change does not affect output per worker in the long run.

4. In the 14th century, the Black Death killed as much as one-third of the population of Europe. According to the Malthusian model, what is the effect per worker in the long run?

5. In the Solow growth model, what is the relation between labor force growth n and saving s along the balanced growth path?

6. Show that the growth process is stable in the Solow growth model.

TECHNOLOGY AND ECONOMIC GROWTH

When we discussed the transition from Malthusian stagnation to the modern growth regime, we showed how the acceleration of technological change during the industrial revolution, together with the demographic transition, was a key factor in the advent of sustained economic growth.

Our analysis of the modern growth regime, however, put technology in the background. The Solow neoclassical growth model describes how an economy evolves along a balanced growth path, where the growth rates of labor and capital are equal. We saw how the growth process is stable. Wherever the economy starts, it converges over time to the same steady state. We also saw how an increase in the saving rate increases the long-term level of GDP but does not increase the long-term growth rate.

We now focus on technology and economic growth. We first consider the sources of economic growth and show the importance of technology. In the Solow model, technological change is exogenous, determined outside the model. We then consider an important class of models, called *endogenous growth theory*, where technological change is determined within the model itself.

It is not universally agreed that endogenous technology holds the key to understanding economic growth. We study the neoclassical growth revival, which argues that, even though modeling endogenous technology is important, long-term growth in the United States is broadly consistent with the predictions of the Solow model. We consider sources of growth in the United States economy and examine productivity growth and the new economy.

5.1 | THE GROWTH ACCOUNTING FORMULA

Robert Solow also developed a framework that can be used to determine the size of the contributions of labor, capital, and technical change to economic growth.[1] His formula is used by economists throughout the world to assign credit for growth. In its simplest form, Solow's formula says the rate of growth of output equals technology growth plus the weighed rates of growth of labor and capital:

$$\frac{\Delta Y}{Y} = \frac{\Delta A}{A} + \frac{0.7 \Delta N}{N} + \frac{0.3 \Delta K}{K} \tag{5.1}$$

The derivation of this **growth accounting formula** is shown in the appendix to this chapter. The growth accounting formula shows how total growth relates to growth in the three determinants. In words, the formula says that the rate of growth of output is equal to the rate of growth of technology plus 0.7 times the rate of growth in labor input plus 0.3 times the rate of growth of capital input. What is interesting about the formula is its lack of dependence on the details of the production function. All that matters is that technology increases the productivity of both factors in a neutral way. The weight 0.3 and its complement 0.7 are derived from data on the relative shares of capital and labor in national income. In Chapter 2, we saw that these income shares are roughly 0.3 and 0.7.

Historical Growth Accounting

The growth accounting formula can be used to determine the contributions of each factor of production to long-term growth in the United States during the last 40 years. To smooth out short-run business cycles, it helps to look at averages over longer periods, such as 10-year intervals.

[1] Robert M. Solow, "Technical Change and the Aggregate Production Function," *Review of Economics and Statistics*, Vol. 39 (August 1957), pp. 312–320.

The data for the United States over 1961–1970, 1971–1980, and 1981–2000 are shown in Figure 5.1 Observe that economic growth slowed down in the 1970s, from just above 4 percent per year to just above 3 percent per year, but partly recovered in the 1980s and the 1990s. The growth accounting formula is used to determine the contributions of capital and labor growth to economic growth, with the contribution of technology estimated as a residual.

According to the growth accounting formula, as shown in Figure 5.1, the two most important reasons for the slowdown of economic growth in the 1970s were declines in the rate of technological change and in the growth of capital. Similarly, the recovery in economic growth in the 1980s and 1990s was fueled by increases in the rate of technological change and the growth of capital. Growth increased in the 1980s and 1990s despite a decline in the growth rate of labor.

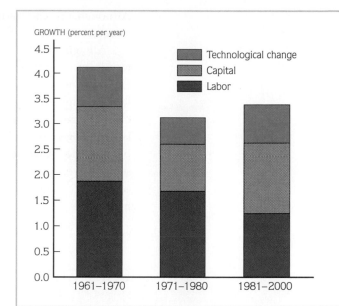

FIGURE 5.1   SOURCES OF GROWTH

The height of each bar shows the annual growth rate of the real GDP over 10-year intervals. Each bar is broken into blocks showing the contributions from labor growth, capital growth, and technological change. The contributions are calculated using Equation 5.1 in the text.

SOURCE: Data on real output growth are from the *Economic Report of the President*, 2003, Table B-51; the labor growth data are from Table B-48; and the capital stock data are calculated from investment data in Table B-2.

Exogenous Technological Change

In our discussion of balanced growth in the previous chapter, we made the simplifying assumption that there was no technology growth; that is, the term A was a constant so that $\Delta A/A = 0$. With this assumption, along a balanced growth path with labor and capital growing by 1 percent per year ($\Delta N/N = \Delta K/K = 1\%$), the growth accounting formula tells us that output growth is also 1 percent per year. That is,

$$\frac{\Delta Y}{Y} = 0 + 0.7(1) + 0.3(1) = 1.$$

with labor, capital, and output growing at the same rate, output per worker (Y/N) does not grow.

But the growth accounting formula also shows that technology growth need not be zero. For example, suppose that technology growth is 1 percent per year ($\Delta A/A = 1\%$); that is, the quantity of output that can be produced with a given level of labor and capital increases by 1 percent per year. If we maintain the assumption that capital and labor both grow by 1 percent per year, then according to the growth accounting formula (Equation 5.1) output grows by 2 percent per year:

$$\frac{\Delta Y}{Y} = 1\% + 0.7(1\%) + 0.3(1\%) = 2\%.$$

Although the capital-labor ratio (K/N) is constant, labor productivity (Y/N) increases because of the improvements in technology.

Allowing for the possibility that technology increases at a constant positive rate is an improvement over assuming that technology does not grow at all. However, we have still not explained *why* technology might increase or what factors might determine technological change. In other words, technological change—the increase in output produced with given labor and capital input—is still **exogenous** in our discussion of the neoclassical growth model. We simply assumed that technology growth was 1 percent per year. In the next section, we develop an **endogenous** growth theory in which the increase in technology is not exogenous but explained by endogenous forces within the model.

5.2 | ENDOGENOUS GROWTH THEORY

MACROSOLVE
EXERCISE

Economists typically think of the long-run growth rate of output as being *exogenous* in the neoclassical growth model. As we have shown, if there is no technological change, then the growth rate of output depends only on the growth rate of labor. And the growth rate of labor ultimately depends on the growth rate of the population, which is essentially exogenous. If the saving rate rises, the long-run growth rate does not increase; it remains equal to the growth rate of labor. True, adding technology growth to the neoclassical growth model does allow the growth rate of output to change, but if technology growth is itself treated as exogenous, as in the last section, then the growth rate of output is still exogenous to the model.

An area of macroeconomic research that has been important since the 1980s is called **endogenous growth theory.** Paul Romer of Stanford University has been one of the major contributors to this theory. Compared with the neoclassical growth model, endogenous growth theory focuses on *explaining* technological growth rather than treating technology as exogenous. In other words, *endogenous growth theory endeavors to provide an explicit theory that determines the behavior of the technology factor* (A), much as we provided a theory to determine the amount of labor (N) in Section 4.2.

A Production Function for Technology

Recall that an increase in technology (A) is anything that increases the quantity of output produced with the same amount of labor and capital. Therefore, many things can improve technology: the assembly-line method of production discussed earlier, the replacement of a horse-drawn plow with a tractor, an increase in the skills of workers (called an *increase in human capital*), and so on. Because of the wide diversity of types of technological improvements, it is difficult to develop a single simple model that includes all of these activities.

One successful approach, suggested by Paul Romer,[2] is to imagine that the ideas or inventions that represent technology are produced with labor and capital much like any other good. To see how this works, imagine that there are "invention factories" throughout the economy in which new inventions are produced by workers. In fact, research laboratories are not uncommon in the United States and many countries; the job description of the researchers who work at these research laboratories is to produce new ideas and inventions. The managers of these laboratories measure production partly by the number of new *patents* the lab produces. But the notion of an "invention factory" is more general and includes less formal although still purposeful methods of improving technology, whether in a laboratory or not.

Analogous to the production function for output (Equation 4.1), we can describe a **production function for technology** as

$$\Delta A = T(N_A, K_A, A), \tag{5.2}$$

which says that the increase in technology ΔA each year depends on the amount of labor producing the technology (N_A), the amount of capital employed in producing the technology (K_A), and the existing stock of technology (A). The function T is the production function for technology. Note that the amount of labor and capital employed in technology production (research) is only part of the total available supply of labor and capital; that is, $N_A < N$ and $K_A < K$.

Equation 5.2 readily shows how technology is endogenous. If more labor resources (i.e., researchers) are devoted to technology production, then technology increases by a larger amount. If more capital (i.e., research laboratories and equipment) is devoted to technology production, then technology production also increases by a larger amount. In the next section, we consider economic policies that might bring about such changes in labor and capital resource use.

Technology itself (A) also contributes to the production of new techology (ΔA). Technology is a good that possesses two properties not generally found in other goods. First, technology is characterized by **nonrivalry**. One person's use of technology does not limit another person's use of the same technology. If you are sitting in class with your laptop computer connected to the Internet using wireless technology, this does not affect the ability of the person sitting next to you to use the same technology. Most goods, in contrast, are *rivalrous*. The can of Coke you drink cannot also be consumed by the person sitting next to you. There are important spillover effects of technology. An idea developed in one laboratory can be used to help create ideas in other laboratories.

Technology is also characterized by **partial excludability.** The inventor or owner of the technology cannot completely prevent other people from using it. While some inventions can be patented and therefore excluded from use in

[2] Paul Romer, "Endogenous Technological Change," *Journal of Political Economy,* Vol. 98 (1990), No. 5, Pt. 2, pp. s71–s102.

the production of goods without permission, often the idea underlying the patent can be used by researchers in other laboratories. If your computer has a Windows operating system, it uses the idea of pull-down menus moved around a screen by a mouse that was originally developed for Apple computers. After hearing Apple's complaint, a court ruled, however, that the features were not so similar to preclude Microsoft from using them. Technology, as it is used in the production of new technology, is an example of *nonrivalry* and *partial excludability*—the same idea can be used over and over again and one firm cannot exclude another firm from using it.

Increasing the Long-Run Growth Rate

It is clear from Equation 5.2 that the production of new technology can be increased by investing more resources in research. But, can the growth rate of technology—and therefore the growth rate of output—be permanently increased? Or can the growth rate be increased only during a transition period, as in the neoclassical growth model?

In an interesting and important special case of the technology production function, the growth rate can be permanently increased. To see this, suppose the technology production function is

$$\Delta A = c N_A A, \tag{5.3}$$

where c is a coefficient. This implies that

$$\frac{\Delta A}{A} = c N_A \tag{5.4}$$

Equation 5.4 says that the long-run growth rate of technology depends on the number of workers in technology production; that is, the number of workers doing research. Hence, an increase in the share of workers doing research increases the growth rate of technology $\Delta A/A$. Since $\Delta A/A$ appears in the growth accounting equation, this increases the growth rate of output as well. In other words, for a technology production function like Equation 5.3, an increase in investment in research causes a permanent increase in the rate of growth, as illustrated in Figure 5.2 and not only during a transition period as in Figure 4.12.

The reason for this crucial difference between Figure 4.12 and Figure 5.2 is that technology—the stock of ideas—does not have diminishing returns in Equation 5.3. Observe that higher levels of tech-

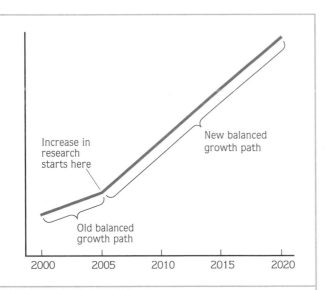

FIGURE 5.2   AN INCREASE IN THE GROWTH RATE

If technology does not have diminishing returns in the production of more technology, then an increase in the number of workers doing research increases the growth rate permanently, as shown here, in contrast to Figure 4.12, which shows only a temporary increase in growth.

nology increase researchers' productivity in producing more technology in Equation 5.3, much as higher levels of capital increase workers' productivity in producing more output in Equation 4.1. But each additional unit of capital increases output by a *smaller* amount, while each additional unit of technology increases the production of new technology by the *same* amount. If diminishing returns to technology did exist, for example, if rather than Equation 5.3 we had

$$A = cN_A\sqrt{A}, \qquad (5.5)$$

then there would be no permanent effect on long-term growth. Figure 5.3 illustrates the difference between the technology production function in Equation 5.3 without diminishing returns and the technology production function in Equation 5.5 with diminishing returns.

Endogenous Growth Theory

1. Endogenous growth theory endeavors to provide an explicit theory of technology. A production function for technology is one simple way to describe how technology depends on labor, capital, and technology inputs.

2. If technology does not have diminishing returns in producing more technology, then devoting more resources to improving technology increases the growth rate of output in the long run.

3. According to endogenous growth theory, economic policy may increase the growth rate permanently; within the neoclassical growth model, a permanent increase in the growth rate may occur only during a transition period.

5.3 | POLICIES TO STIMULATE GROWTH

The government can influence all three of the determinants of growth—technological change, capital formation, and labor input. Disappointing rates of growth in the 1970s led to a number of federal policies to stimulate growth. Under what circumstances might a free market economy deliver an inadequate rate of growth in potential output that could be improved by government intervention? In general, government intervention is justified if a market failure exists. A *market failure* exists when there is a divergence between social and private costs or benefits of a particular activity. Many activities, such as education and research, that generate growth have social benefits that exceed private benefits. Government can encourage such activities.

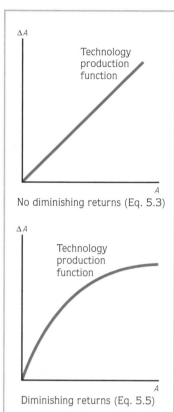

No diminishing returns (Eq. 5.3)

Diminishing returns (Eq. 5.5)

FIGURE 5.3   TWO TECHNOLOGY PRODUCTION FUNCTIONS

In both cases, higher technology leads to the creation of more technology. In one case, there are diminishing returns, in which case growth does not increase permanently when more labor is devoted to research.

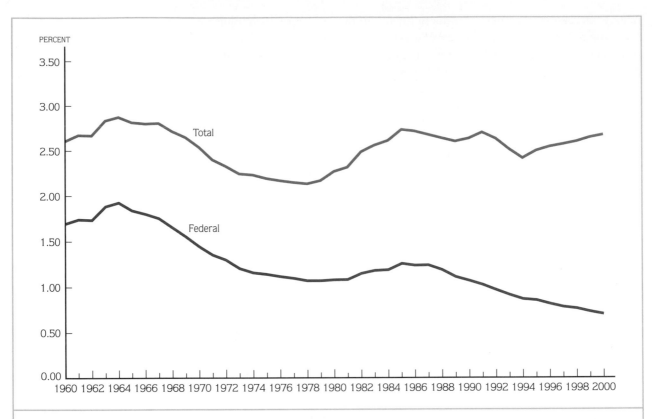

FIGURE 5.4   FEDERAL SPENDING FOR R&D AS A FRACTION OF GDP

Total R&D spending has been stable at around 2.5 percent of GDP. The federal portion has fallen and been replaced by rising private spending for R&D.

SOURCE: *Economic Report of the President, 2003.* National Science Foundation.

Policies to Improve Technological Growth and Productivity

Figure 5.1 shows that technological change fell significantly in the 1970s. Hence, the idea of stimulating technology has been attractive to policy makers.

Perhaps the most important role that the government can play in improving technology growth is in the area of education. In the United States, state and local governments provide most of the support for primary and secondary schools and universities. A highly skilled labor force is obviously a key ingredient to successful productivity growth.

As we emphasized with the technology production function, an important source of technology growth is investment in research and development (R&D). Figure 5.4 shows the total amount of R&D spending in the United States as a fraction of GDP. The fraction has been stable at around 2.5 percent.

Figure 5.4 also shows federal spending for R&D as a fraction of GDP. The federal government's contribution to the total has declined substantially—in the 1960s, the government contributed about two-thirds of the total, but by the 1990s, the fraction fell to a third.

Like education, through spillovers, discussed in the previous section, basic research may provide social benefits in excess of the private benefits that accrue to those engaged in these activities. Left to their own devices, individuals and firms choose levels of spending on education and research that fall short of the social optimum. Government may want to encourage these activities through grants and subsidies.

The Research and Experimentation Tax Credit in the United States provides tax incentives for research and development expenditures. This special tax credit allows firms to reduce their taxes by 20 percent of their research and development expenses. If R&D programs are an important source of technology growth, then tax incentives like these should improve growth. The use of public funds for this purpose, through the tax system, is justified if the sponsors of R&D are unable to capture the full benefits themselves.

Policies to Stimulate Capital Formation

Government policy to stimulate growth has historically concentrated on capital formation. A rising capital stock adds to economic growth as the growth formula in the previous section made clear. Numerically, an extra percentage point of capital growth adds about 0.3 percentage point to growth in output. To get an added 1 percent of growth in output, the capital stock would have to grow 3.3 percent per year.

Consider a numerical illustration. At the end of 2002, the capital stock was about $11,425 billion, counting plants, equipment, and software. The 3.3 percent growth in capital needed to add a point to growth of output would be

$$3.3 \text{ percent} \times \$11,425 \text{ billion} = \$377 \text{ billion in added investment.}$$

Nonresidential fixed investment in 2003 was $1,124 billion. Investment would have to rise by 377/1,124 = 34 percent to add just 1 percentage point to growth in output. Of course, 1 percent more growth would restore the growth path that the United States experienced in the mid-1960s and compound itself to an impressive increase in living standards in 20 years. Moreover, it is possible that the increase in new plants and machines would bring forth additional technical innovations, which could spur productivity growth.

Increased growth in the capital stock requires consistently high levels of investment spending. This can occur only if there are fewer competing demands on output from households and government purchases. To expand investment, we need to reduce consumption, government purchases, or net exports.

Under the right combination of economic conditions, a large increase in investment is possible. For example, investment was at depressed levels in 1962 when President Kennedy sponsored the first investment tax credit. The new investment incentive plus generally expansive conditions caused investment to rise from 306 billion 1987 dollars in 1962 to $401 billion in 1966, an increase of about 30 percent.

Although an increase in investment of 30 percent is feasible, it does not appear to be sustainable. Output growth can be raised by a percentage point for a few years, but then investment tends to decline to more normal levels. For example, the annual growth of the capital stock reached its peak from the Kennedy stimulus at 7 percent per year in 1966 but then subsided to about 5 percent through 1974. During most of this period, the investment tax credit was in effect. Between 1975 and 1982, the growth of the capital stock fluctuated between 1 and 4 percent per year. The investment credit was in effect at a higher rate throughout these disappointing years.

Growth Through Capital Formation

1. Because the coefficient of capital growth in the growth formula is about 0.3, it takes about 3.3 percent of growth in capital to add 1 percent to output growth.

2. In 2003, it would have taken a 34 percent increase in the amount of investment to raise the growth of the capital stock by 3.3 percent.

3. Increases of this magnitude in investment have occurred in the past, but only when special incentives were combined with other favorable conditions. Even then, the high levels of investment were sustained for only a few years.

Policies to Increase Labor Supply

In the growth equation, employment growth has more than twice the leverage of capital growth. Each percentage point of extra growth of employment adds 0.7 percent to output growth. To put it the other way around, it takes 1.4 percent of added employment growth to increase output growth by 1 percent per year. Reductions in income tax rates are one way to stimulate work effort by improving incentives.

The income tax depresses the incentive to work by reducing the wage that workers receive for their work. On this account, one might expect that a cut in income taxes would stimulate work by improving incentives. A prime selling point of the tax cuts put into place in 1981 and 1986 was precisely this incentive argument. But, a cut in income taxes also makes people better off, which depresses labor supply. The net effect of a simple tax cut could therefore be quite small. This is illustrated in Figure 5.5. If the labor supply curve is steep, as statistical evidence seems to suggest, the intersection of supply and demand occurs at almost the same level of employment. A prediction of large stimulus to employment and output from tax cuts would be contrary to the evidence.

Growth policies need not take the exclusive form of tax cuts. In fact, the federal government's need for revenue makes it impossible to improve work incentives dramatically by cutting taxes. Another type of policy is *tax reform*. A tax reform keeps revenue the same although tax rates are cut. This can be done by reducing deductions and lowering tax rates on earned income. Because revenue is the same, the typical taxpayer pays the same amount of tax and there is no income effect. The cut in taxes due to the lower tax rate is off-set by the increase in taxes due to the lower deductions. This type of reform necessarily involves a reduction in the progressivity of the income tax. What matters for work incentives is the *marginal* tax rate, the rate applied to the last dollar of earnings. For example, a flat tax system that puts roughly the same tax rate on all dollars of earnings above the first few thousand dollars of income could raise the same amount of revenue with lower marginal rates. This type of tax reform has no income effect to depress work. The labor supply schedule shifts by the full amount of the substitution effect.

Growth Through Increased Work Effort

1. Because the labor supply schedule is nearly vertical, even a large tax cut has only a small effect on employment. The substitution effect of lower tax rates raises incentives to work, but the higher level of income depresses work.

2. If the tax change is a tax *reform*, which keeps tax receipts constant, rather than a tax *cut*, it improves incentives without changing average income. Then, the substitution effects are not offset by income effects.

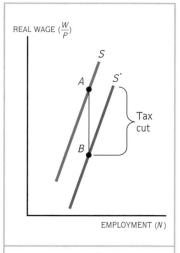

FIGURE 5.5   SHIFT IN LABOR SUPPLY FROM A TAX CUT

A tax cut shifts the labor supply function downward in proportion to the cut. S is the labor supply schedule before the tax rate cut; A is an arbitrary point on it. S' is the supply schedule after the cut. B is a point on S' where the real wage after tax is the same as the real wage after tax on S at A. B is below A by the amount of the tax cut. The amount of labor supplied at B is the same as at A because the real wage received by workers is the same at B as at A. A downward shift in a schedule that is nearly vertical has almost no substantive effect on employment.

5.4 | THE NEOCLASSICAL GROWTH REVIVAL

Sustained technological progress is the key to economic growth in both the Solow neoclassical growth model and the endogenous growth model. The central insight of endogenous growth theory is to explain technological change through a production function for technology (endogenous) rather than leave it unexplained as in the Solow model (exogenous). This leads to the most compelling result of endogenous growth theory: the possibility of using government policy to increase the long-run growth rate. In contrast with the Solow model, increased investment in research permanently increases the growth

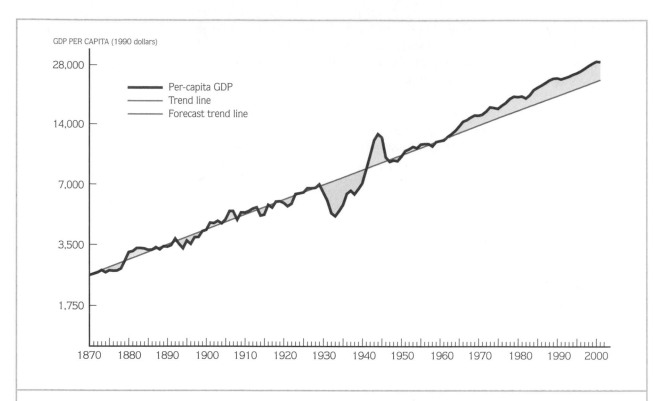

GDP PER CAPITA (1990 dollars)

FIGURE 5.6   ACTUAL AND FORECASTED GDP PER CAPITA FOR THE UNITED STATES

Suppose you were an economist in 1929 trying to predict GDP per capita for the United States in 2001. Your prediction would have been fairly accurate, being under by 19 percent. The reason for the accuracy of your prediction is that growth rates for the United States were only slightly higher after 1929 than they were before 1929.

SOURCE: Angus Maddison, *The World Economy: Historical Statistics* (Paris, OECD, 2003).

rate. In Figure 5.1, we showed that growth rates increased in the 1980s and 1990s compared with the 1970s and the sources of this increased growth are increases in the rate of technological change and growth of capital. As we saw in the previous section, a number of government policies have been used to stimulate growth. Can we interpret the increased growth in the past two decades as evidence in favor of endogenous growth models?

The **neoclassical growth revival,** led by N. Gregory Mankiw of Harvard University and Charles Jones of the University of California at Berkeley, argues that long-term growth in the United States is consistent with the Solow growth model.[3] GDP per capita for the United States from 1870 to 2001 is shown in Figure 5.6. A logarithmic scale is used so that constant growth is depicted by a straight line. Growth rates were fairly steady until the stock market

---

[3] N. Gregory Mankiw, "The Growth of Nations," *Brookings Papers on Economic Activity*, No. 1 (1995), pp. 275–310, and Charles I. Jones, "Times Series Tests of Endogenous Growth Models," *Quarterly Journal of Economics*, Vol. 110, No. 2 (May 1995), pp. 495–525.

crash of 1929. The Great Depression of the 1930s saw a sharp fall in the level of GDP per capita but an increase in the growth rate, especially as World War II approached. Following the end of World War II, growth rates returned to about their values before 1929.

Consider this thought experiment. Using data from 1870 to 1929, draw the straight line that provides the closest fit for the actual data. (More technically, you would choose the straight line that minimized the sum of the squared distance between the line and the data.) You now have a long-run growth rate for 1870 to 1929. Suppose you were an economist in 1929 trying to predict GDP per capita in 2001. Assuming that growth rates between 1929 and 2001 would be the same as between 1870 and 1929, extrapolate the same straight line to 2001. This is also shown in Figure 5.6. Your prediction would be fairly accurate. Using data only through 1929, your prediction of GDP per capita for 2001 would be off by only 19 percent.

An implication of the endogenous growth models described in Section 5.2 is that an increase in the number of workers doing research increases the long-run growth rate. These **scale effects** can be seen in Equation 5.4, where an increase in the amount of labor producing the technology, N_A, raises the growth rate of technology and thus the growth rate of output. Between 1950 and 1990, the number of scientists and engineers engaged in research and development in the United States increased more than fivefold, from less than 200,000 to almost 1 million. During the same time period, neither the growth rate of technology nor the growth rate of output increased comparably.

An important feature of endogenous growth models is the possibility of using government policy to produce permanent changes in long-run growth rates. The evidence for the United States, however, seems to be broadly consistent with the constant long-run growth prediction of the Solow model. Moreover, there seems to be no evidence of scale effects. This does not mean that we should discard endogenous growth models. Technological change is crucially important for growth in both models, and the sustained technological progress in the United States over the last century must come from somewhere. Attempts to explain technological progress, as in the production function for technology, are important and continue to provide fruitful areas for research.

Evidence for Endogenous and Neoclassical Growth Models

1. The long-run growth experience for the United States appears to be broadly consistent with the constant growth predictions of the Solow model.

2. There seems to be no evidence of scale effects. The large increase in the number of scientists and engineers engaged in R&D in the United States has not produced a large increase in growth.

5.5 | REAL WAGES AND LABOR PRODUCTIVITY

Because the real wage is equal to the marginal product of labor in the growth model, we should be able to learn about growth by looking at the movements of the real wage over time. Remember that the income side of the national income and product accounts reports the total earnings of workers. Total annual earnings divided by total annual hours of work gives a measure of the average hourly wage paid to workers in the United States. The Bureau of Labor Statistics calls this *compensation per hour.* Compensation per hour includes the value of fringe benefits as well as cash wages. Wages are the most important component of the cost of production.

Wages and prices generally moved together throughout the swings in inflation in the 1970s. Dividing the hourly average wage by the cost of living gives us the real wage. From the point of view of workers, the real wage measures the purchasing power of the wage—the amount of goods and services that can be bought with one hour of work. From the point of view of employers, it measures the real costs of labor input. The real wage does not fluctuate in any systematic way during recessions or booms. Its most noticeable property is growth over time. The real wage since 1960 is shown in Figure 5.7.

After steady growth in the 1960s, the upward path of the real wage was interrupted in the early 1970s. Between 1973 and 1997, real wage growth was much lower than in the 1960s and the slowdown in real wage growth was one of the most pressing problems facing the U.S. economy. Between 1997 and 2002, real wage growth increased to levels not seen since the 1960s. It remains to be seen, however, how long this real wage growth increase will last.

Labor Productivity

Productivity is the amount of output produced per unit of input. Because labor is the most important input, the most popular measure of productivity is **labor productivity,** or output per hour of labor. When economists talk about productivity, they usually mean labor productivity. A broader measure of productivity, called **total factor productivity,** is output per generalized unit of input (*factor* is a general term for an input like labor or capital). The generalized unit counts capital, energy, and materials as inputs in addition to labor. However, output per unit of labor and total factor productivity for the United States as a whole tell about the same story in recent years.

The recent history of labor productivity is shown in Figure 5.8. Productivity has generally been increasing as workers have become more efficient and have had more and better machines to work with. This increase in productivity underlies the growth in real wages we saw in the previous section. But productivity is also procyclical: It rises in booms and falls in recessions. Firms tend to keep skilled workers on the payroll and let them produce fewer items in slack times, rather than lay them off and run the risk that they find jobs elsewhere.

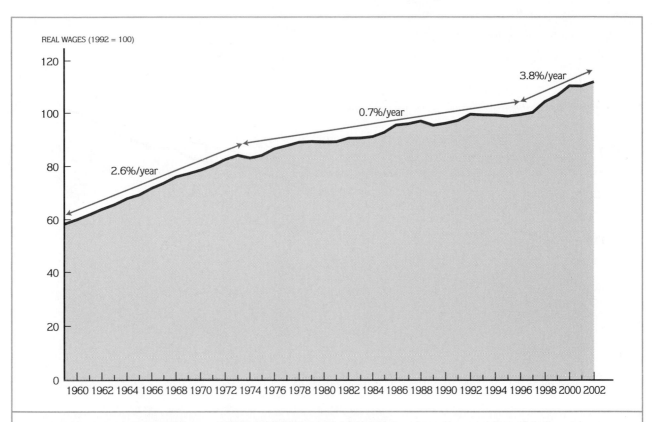

FIGURE 5.7   THE SLOWDOWN AND RECOVERY IN REAL WAGE GROWTH

The real wage is the ratio of the dollar wage (compensation per hour) to the cost of living (the consumer price index). Real wage growth slowed down significantly in the early 1970s and rose in the late 1990s.

SOURCE: *Economic Report of the President*, 2003, Table B-49.

They make up for their low productivity in bad times with higher productivity in good times.

Productivity growth slowed down in the early 1970s, and this is the main reason why real wage growth slowed down. Economists disagree about the reasons for the productivity slowdown. Some stress the role of the increases in oil prices, but the real price of crude oil was not much different in the 1990s from what it was in the 1950s and 1960s. Others point to a reduction in expenditures on research and development and say that technical innovation slowed down as a result. Still others say that we are not investing enough in new machines and factories. Of all the puzzles about the recent performance of the U.S. economy, the slowdown in productivity growth is perhaps the most difficult for economists to solve. Starting in 1995, labor productivity returned to the levels of the 1960s, mirroring the increase in real wage growth. We now turn to an analysis of the factors causing this productivity growth recovery.

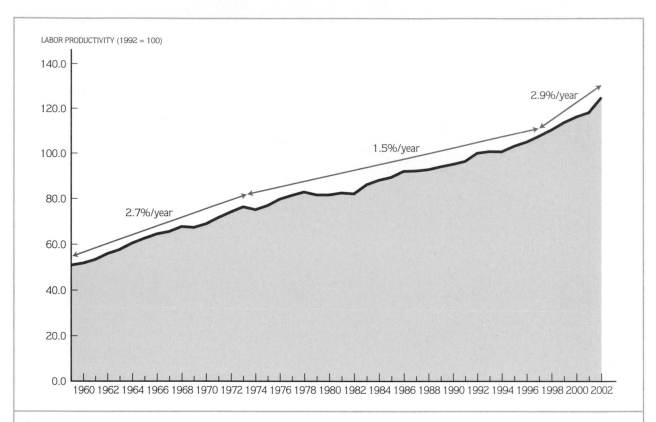

FIGURE 5.8   THE SLOWDOWN AND RECOVERY IN LABOR PRODUCTIVITY GROWTH

Productivity is the amount of output produced per hour of work. The general trend in productivity has been upward, but growth slowed down in the early 1970s and rose again starting in the mid-1990s. Productivity also fluctuates during recessions and booms.

SOURCE: *Economic Report of the President,* 2003, Table B-49.

Real Wages and Productivity

1. The real wage measures the purchasing power of the wage payment. The real wage grew steadily in the United States until the early 1970s, when its growth slowed down.

2. *Labor productivity* is defined as output per unit of labor input. Labor productivity has been growing for a long time, although with fluctuations during business cycles.

3. In the United States, productivity growth slowed down in the early 1970s. Growth of productivity permits the real wage to grow, and the slowdown in productivity is the main reason for the slowdown in real wage growth in the United States.

4. At the end of the 1990s, both productivity growth and real wage growth returned to their levels in the 1960s.

5.6 | PRODUCTIVITY AND THE NEW ECONOMY

The post-1995 acceleration in productivity growth coincided with what many commentators heralded as the birth of a "new economy," dominated by high-technology industries. While stock prices in the high-technology sector collapsed starting in March 2000 and the economy entered a recession in 2001, the high productivity growth continued. In this section, we take a longer-run perspective and examine the sources of the productivity growth recovery.

Productivity growth can be understood in the context of the growth accounting formula. Remember that productivity is output per hour of labor, so that productivity growth is the increase in output per hour of labor. Using a framework similar to that of Equation 5.1, productivity growth can be divided into **capital deepening;** growth of capital per hour of labor, **labor quality;** improvements in the measurable skills of the workforce; and technological change or total factor productivity.

The sources of productivity growth from 1973 to 1995 and from 1996 to 2000 are shown in Figure 5.9. A major source of the post-1995 increase in productivity growth is investment in information technology. The contribution of capital deepening to the post-1995 productivity increase was entirely caused by the buildup in information technology capital. The buildup of capital outside of information technology and the increase in labor quality were not much different before and after 1995, so did not contribute to the acceleration in productivity growth.

The largest source of the post-1995 productivity increase is technological change, or total factor productivity (TFP). This, in turn, can be divided into TFP growth in computer-producing industries and TFP growth in other industries. Quantifying this division, however, is very difficult. Estimates of the contribution of TFP growth in computer-producing industries to total TFP growth range from under 25 percent to over 75 percent. Part of the difficulty is that TFP growth in computer producing industries is fueled by the rapid decline in computer prices, which are notoriously hard to measure. For example, a $1,500 desktop computer purchased in 2003 was about twice as fast as a $1,500 computer purchased in 2001. For some numerically intensive applications, this represents a doubling of productivity. For others, such as word processing or surfing the Internet, the change is not even noticeable.

The final contribution to the post-1995 productivity increase is TFP growth in other industries. Total TFP growth is estimated as a residual after the

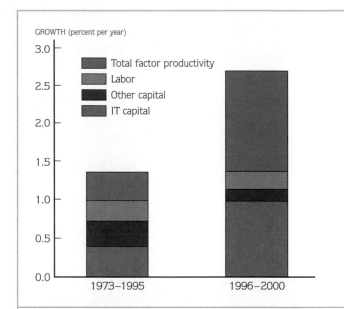

FIGURE 5.9   PRODUCTIVITY GROWTH IN THE 1990S

Labor productivity growth in the United States was very high in the second half of the 1990s. The two largest sources of the post-1995 increase in labor productivity growth were increases in technological change, or total factor productivity, and information technology capital.

SOURCE: *Economic Report of the President,* 2002, Table 1-3.

contributions of capital deepening and labor quality to productivity growth are calculated. TFP growth in other industries is then estimated as a residual after the contribution of TFP growth in computer-producing industries is calculated. Since estimates of TFP growth in computer-producing industries are subject to much uncertainty, so are the estimates of TFP growth in other industries. This uncertainty illustrates the limits of our ability to quantify the sources of the past-1995 productivity acceleration.

Growth Accounting and Increased Security Spending

In the wake of the September 11 terrorist attacks, spending on security increased. This decreased economic growth because labor and capital are diverted away from production of final goods towards production of an intermediate product—security. How large is this decrease in growth? The Council of Economic Advisors uses the economic growth formula to estimate the magnitude of the decreased growth.[4]

Private business spends about $55 billion on security, or 0.53 percent of GDP. Assume that security spending doubles to $110 billion and one-third of the additional spending goes to security capital and two-thirds to security labor. The diversion lowers the "productive" capital stock by 0.10 percent and lowers labor input by 0.69 percent in the first year.

Using the growth accounting formula, the decrease in output in the first year is about two-thirds of the decrease in labor growth of 0.69 percent, or 0.46 percent, plus about one-third of the decrease in capital growth of 0.10 percent, or 0.03 percent, for a total of 0.49 percent. Calculations for subsequent years are complicated by secondary effects from the decrease in lower output on future saving and investment and by depreciation of capital.

The Council of Economic Advisors estimates that, by the fifth year, output will be about 0.6 percent lower, with 85 percent of the fall occurring in the first two years. Productivity growth decreases by 0.25 percentage point during the first two years but is only slightly affected afterward.

REVIEW AND PRACTICE

Major Points

1. GDP growth can be divided into three sources: growth in labor input, growth in capital stock, and technological change.

2. In the endogenous growth model, technology growth is endogenous and the growth rate can be permanently increased.

---

[4] *Economic Report of the President*, 2002, p. 56.

3. The 1970s and 1980s had reduced rates of growth in output. The slow-down is attributed primarily to slower growth in technology.

4. Government policies can improve economic growth through increased expenditures on education and basic research or through tax incentives to encourage labor supply or capital accumulation.

5. Tax reform can improve incentives without reducing the tax revenue collected by government. Such a reform usually requires flattening marginal tax rates on income.

6. Evidence for long-run growth in the United States appears to be broadly consistent with the predictions of the neoclassical Solow growth model.

Key Terms and Concepts

growth accounting formula

endogenous growth theory

production function for technology

nonrivalry

partial excludability

neoclassical growth revival

scale effects

labor productivity

total factor productivity

capital deepening

labor quality

Questions for Discussion and Review

1. Identify the components of the growth accounting formula. Discuss the weights of each of these components and the different effect that each weight has on output and each other. How is the importance of technology expressed in the growth accounting formula?

2. Does an increase in the rate of growth of labor add more or less to the growth rate of output than the same size increase in the rate of growth of capital? Explain why.

3. Describe three different policies that could be used to increase the growth rate of the potential GDP. Identify whether the policy is aimed at technology, capital formation, or labor supply.

4. Explain what is meant by *endogenous growth theory*.

5. What is the fundamental difference between the Solow growth model discussed in the last chapter and the endogenous growth theory? Be sure to comment on the treatment and expression of technology in the two models.

6. What effect does nonrivalry and partial excludability have on growth in the long run? What would be the negative consequence of a rival or excludable technology in terms of long-run growth?

7. Describe the evidence that led to a revival of the neoclassical growth model.

8. How might the U.S. government improve technology growth, capital formation, and labor productivity? Identify a few possible trade-offs associated with attempting to stimulate these. For instance, what effect do policies to stimulate capital formation have on consumption? Why do we, as consumers, care about this?

9. What is the real wage? What does it measure from both the employee's and the employer's point of view?

10. Describe what has led to the recovery of real wage growth in the latter half of the 1990s.

11. Explain what is meant by *total factor productivity.*

12. Explain whether the increased spending on security in the United States since the September 11 terrorist attacks will permanently reduce the growth rate of the economy.

Problems

NUMERICAL

1. Assume that, over a 10-year period, the growth rate of capital is 4 percent, the growth rate of employment is 2 percent, and the growth rate of real output is 5 percent. Calculate the growth rate of technology. Suppose that a permanent cut in the budget deficit increases investment and the growth rate of capital rises by 1 percent. How much does the growth rate of output increase? Suppose that a tax reduction increases the supply of labor by 1 percent in one year. What happens to the growth rate of real output?

2. Suppose that the production function takes the special form $Y = AN^{0.7}K^{0.3}$. By taking the logarithms and first differences of this production function, show that the growth formula is satisfied. (If you have had calculus, calculate the marginal products of labor and capital. Derive the labor demand function. Calculate the labor share and the capital share.)

3. Assume that the technology production function takes the form $\Delta A = 1 + N_A \sqrt{A}$. Trace out the effects of an increase in researchers' N_A on technology growth over time. Now do the same for a change in N_A if $A = cN_A A$. What is the difference between the two, and how does it affect long-run growth?

ANALYTICAL

1. Suppose the target rate of long-run equilibrium per-capita GDP growth is 1 percent per year. Labor input and population are expected to grow at 1 percent.

   a. What rate of GDP growth is required to achieve the target for per-capita GDP growth?

b. Using the growth accounting formula, what is the required growth in the capital stock necessary to achieve the target assuming technology growth of 0.5 percent? What is the required growth in the capital stock if there is no growth in technology?

2. Using the growth accounting formula, show how technology growth is necessary to produce an increase in output per worker along a balanced growth path.

3. Suppose the numbers of workers doing research increases by 10 percent. How would this affect economic growth in the Solow and the endogenous growth models? Which prediction seems to be more in accord with the evidence for the United States?

4. Explain how increased spending on education would promote economic growth.

5. The unification of Germany created a nation with a much lower capital-to-labor ratio relative to what previously existed in West Germany. What impact do you think unification had on the level of productivity compared with what existed in West Germany alone? What impact did unification have on the growth rate of labor productivity after the initial shock? Explain.

APPENDIX: Deriving the Growth Formula

Suppose that A, N, and K grow by rates $\Delta A/A$, $\Delta N/N$, and $\Delta K/K$. We derive a formula for the growth rate of output, $\Delta Y/Y$. First, with neutral technological change we can write the production function as $F(N, K, A) = Af(N, K)$. Then, the growth rate of output is approximately

$$\Delta Y/Y = \Delta A/A + \Delta f(N, K)/f(N, K). \qquad (5.6)$$

In other words, the growth rate of the *product* of A and $f(N, K)$ is the *sum* of the growth rates of A and $f(N, K)$.

Second, the part of the change in output that comes from changes in employment and capital can be further broken down using the marginal products of the two. Let M_N be the marginal product of labor and M_K be the marginal product of capital. Then,

$$\Delta f(N, K)/f(N, K) = M_N \, \Delta N/Y + M_K \Delta K/Y. \qquad (5.7)$$

In words, this expression states that the proportional change in f can be divided into two components that measure the contributions of the proportional changes in N and K. (If you have had calculus, this formula can be derived by taking the total derivative of f and dividing by Y.) Putting this into the formula for $\Delta Y/Y$, we get

$$\Delta Y/Y = \Delta A/A + M_N \Delta N/Y + M_K \Delta K/Y. \qquad (5.8)$$

If firms use labor and capital up to the points where their marginal products are equal to the real wage and real rental prices, then

$$M_N = W/P \text{ and } M_K = R^K/P. \qquad (5.9)$$

Now, the formula is

$$\Delta Y/Y = \Delta A/A + (W/P)\Delta N/Y + (R^K/P)\Delta K/Y. \qquad (5.10)$$

We can rewrite this as

$$\Delta Y/Y = \Delta A/A + (WN/PY)\Delta N/N + (R^K K/PY)\Delta K/K. \qquad (5.11)$$

WN/PY is the fraction of revenue, PY, paid out to labor in the form of compensation, WN. Similarly, $R^K K/PY$ is the fraction of revenue earned by capital. From the national income and product accounts, we find that these fractions are about 0.7 and 0.3. Therefore,

$$\Delta Y/Y = \Delta A/A + 0.7\Delta N/N + 0.3\Delta K/K, \qquad (5.12)$$

which is the growth formula (Equation 5.1).

Observe also that the growth accounting formula can be written simply in terms of labor productivity, or output per unit of labor (Y/N). The growth rate of labor productivity is $\Delta Y/Y - \Delta N/N$. By subtracting $\Delta N/N$ from both sides of Equation 5.12, we get

$$\begin{pmatrix} \text{Growth rate of} \\ \text{labor productivity} \end{pmatrix} = \frac{\Delta A}{A} + 0.3 \begin{pmatrix} \text{Growth rate of} \\ \text{capital per unit of labor} \end{pmatrix}$$

GROWTH AND THE WORLD ECONOMY

When Robert Solow's theory of growth was published, he was thinking in terms of the United States, where the key fact was constant long-run growth. He was not thinking about growth differences among countries and never applied the model to any country except the United States. The Solow model, however, has a striking prediction regarding growth among countries. Assuming that all countries have the same production function and access to technology, those countries that start our poor should grow faster than those countries that start out rich. The gap between rich and poor should narrow over time.

There is one big problem with this prediction—it is contradicted by the facts. Since 1960, when the vast majority of former colonies achieved independence, income differences between rich and poor nations have not diminished

131

at all. Taking a longer run perspective, income inequality has increased over time. While there is evidence that income inequality has declined among industrialized countries, especially among those countries that have reduced barriers to trade, the evidence does not extend to the world as a whole.

Two strands of growth theory developed in response to these facts. First, endogenous growth theory attempts to explain the continuing, or even increasing, gap between rich and poor nations through endogenous technological change. Empirical implementation of endogenous growth theory, however, has not been an unqualified success. Second, the neoclassical growth revival argues that the gap between rich and poor countries is indeed narrowing once differences in saving and population growth rates are accounted for.

The purpose of studying economic growth is to both understand and remedy the gap between rich and poor countries. Tropical underdevelopment, the large gap between countries in tropical and temperate climates, remains an unsolved problem in both dimensions. We study the role of geography and institutions in creating the gap, and how understanding of incentives can help close the gap.

6.1 | CONVERGENCE

MACROSOLVE
EXERCISE

In 1900, income per capita in the United States was 3.5 times as large as income per capita in Japan and 6.6 times as large as income per capita in India. A century later, the per capita income ratio between the United States and Japan narrowed to 1.3, or almost parity. The data for the United States and India tell a very different story, as the per capita income ratio widened to 14.7. Why did the first gap narrow and the second gap widen?

Convergence in the Solow Growth Model

The Solow growth model relates output per worker, Y/N, to capital per worker, K/N, and technology, A, by the production function in Equation 4.6:

$$Y/N = F(K/N, 1, A) \tag{6.1}$$

Assuming that all countries have the same production function and access to technology, countries with low levels of capital per worker have low levels of income per worker and countries with high levels of capital per worker have high levels of income per worker. Since income and capital per worker are closely related to income and capital per person, countries with low levels of capital per worker are poorer, or have lower levels of income per capita, than countries with high levels of capital per worker.

This is illustrated in Figure 6.1, which uses Solow's growth analysis from Figure 4.11. The figure is a stylized depiction of Japan and the United States in

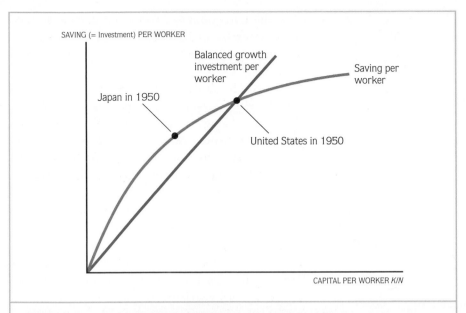

SAVING (= Investment) PER WORKER

Balanced growth
investment per
worker

Saving per
worker

Japan in 1950

United States in 1950

CAPITAL PER WORKER *K/N*

FIGURE 6.1   SOLOW'S GROWTH DIAGRAM FOR TWO COUNTRIES

Japan and the United States have the same steady-state point. In the year 1950, however, only
the United States attained the steady state. Over time, investment and saving per worker is
higher in Japan than in the United States, until capital per worker is equal in the two countries.

1950, with capital per worker lower for Japan than for the United States. What
does the figure tell us about the subsequent growth rates of the two countries?
The United States is assumed to be at the steady-state point, where saving is
just sufficient to keep capital per worker constant. Growth after 1950 equals
the exogenous growth rate of technology. The situation is different for Japan.
Since the two countries share the same production function and technology
and *K/N* is lower for Japan than for the United States, Japan must be to the
left of the balanced growth line.

This situation is not sustainable. The rate of return on capital is higher for
Japan than for the United States. To see this, think of two farms, each with 100
acres of land and employing 100 equally skilled workers. The only difference
between them is that Farm A has 1 tractor and Farm B has 100 tractors. Investment in one additional tractor, so that Farm A has 2 tractors and Farm B has
101, brings a much higher return for Farm A than Farm B. The rate of return
on capital is higher for the farm (A) or the country (Japan) with lower capital
per worker than for the farm (B) or the country (United States) with higher
capital per worker.

Over time, capital per worker increases for Japan relative to the United
States. The equilibrium for Japan moves along the saving per worker line until
it intersects the balanced growth investment per worker line at the same
steady-state point as for the United States. At that point, income per capita is

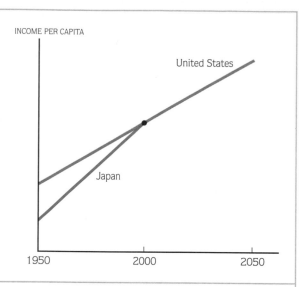

INCOME PER CAPITA

United States

Japan

1950   2000   2050

FIGURE 6.2   CONVERGENCE IN THE SOLOW GROWTH MODEL

Japan starts with lower income per capita than the United States. Along the transition path, Japan grows faster than the United States. Once income per capita is equal in the two countries, they grow at the same rate along the same balanced growth path.

equal in the two countries. Following the steady-state point, growth rates in Japan and the United States are equal both to each other and to the growth rate of technology.

These results are illustrated in Figure 6.2. Japan starts out with lower income per capita than the United States. Along the transition path, Japan grows faster than the United States until the per capita incomes are equal. The **convergence hypothesis** of the Solow model is that, over time, gaps in per capita income among countries narrow. If the steady-state point is reached and the gap is eliminated, the initially poorer country is said to **catch up** to the initially richer country. Following the steady-state point, the growth rates are equal to each other and the lines are identical.

How well does the convergence hypothesis describe the actual experience of Japan and the United States? In 1950, income per capita in the United States was 5.0 times per-capita income in Japan. By 2000, income per capita in the United States was only 1.3 times per capita income in Japan. While Japan has not yet caught up to the United States, the gap has narrowed tremendously.

Testing the Convergence Hypothesis

The convergence hypothesis states that the growth rate of GDP per capita should be negatively related to the initial level of GDP per capita. Countries with low levels of income per capita should have higher growth rates. Suppose you have data on GDP per capita for 100 countries from 1960 to 2000. For each country, compute the initial level and the annual growth rate of GDP per capita. The convergence hypothesis can be tested with the following equation:

$$\Delta(Y/N)/(Y/N) = a + c(Y/N)(1960), \qquad (6.2)$$

where $\Delta(Y/N)/(Y/N)$ is the annual growth rate of GDP per capita, (Y/N) (1960) is the initial level of GDP per capita, and a is a coefficient. The convergence hypothesis implies that the coefficient c is negative. Countries with low GDP per capita in 1960 should grow faster than countries with high GDP per capita in 1960.

How well does the convergence hypothesis work? The data most often used to test convergence comes from the Penn World Tables, a painstaking research project of Alan Heston, the late Irving Kravis, and Robert Summers of the University of Pennsylvania to make internationally valid comparisons of real quantities and price parities.[1] The initial year is usually 1960 because most African countries did not achieve independence before that date.

The results of the convergence hypothesis are summarized in Figure 6.3. Panel A pertains to the more advanced countries in the world, including those in Europe, Japan, and the United States. Panel B pertains to all countries in the world, including countries such as China and India as well as the countries in the top graph. On the horizontal axis of each of the panels is a measure of income per capita in 1960; on the vertical axis is a measure of the average growth rate during the years since 1960.

According to the model, there should be a negative relationship between the level and the growth rate; that is, countries with low levels of income per capita should have higher growth rates. Panel A of Figure 6.3 shows a strong negative correlation for the advanced countries, just as the model predicts. The coefficient c in Equation 6.2 is negative. Countries with low income per capita in 1960, such as Austria and Japan, grew faster than countries, such as Australia and the United States, with high income per capita in 1960.

The picture is very different when all the countries are included. Panel B of Figure 6.3 shows virtually no relation between income per capita in 1960 and subsequent growth. In contrast with the predictions of the model, coefficient c in Equation 6.2 is close to zero. Despite evidence of convergence *among* advanced countries, the evidence does not extend to the world as a whole. The reason is that many countries with very low levels of per-capita income have very low growth rates. The Philippines, Chile, and the United States all grew at about 3 percent per year, but GDP per capita in 1960 was about $1,000 for the Philippines, $3,000 for Chile, and $10,000 for the United States. This pattern is repeated over and over again. There is no evidence of catch-up behavior for most countries.

Returns to Investment in Rich and Poor Countries

The large disparity in GDP per capita between rich and poor countries was an important motivation in the development of endogenous growth theory. Robert Lucas pointed out another important problem in the Solow growth model.[2] Suppose that the average capital share in India and the United States is 0.40, so that the production function is

$$Y = K^{0.4}N^{0.6}A \qquad (6.3)$$

Divide both sides by N to get

$$Y/N = A(K/N)^{0.4}. \qquad (6.4)$$

[1] Robert Summers and Alan Heston, "The Penn World Table (Mark 5): An Expanded Set of International Comparisons, 1950–1988," *Quarterly Journal of Economics*, Vol. 106 (May 1991), pp. 327–368.
[2] Robert E. Lucas, "Why Doesn't Capital Flow from Rich to Poor Countries?" *American Economic Review*, Vol. 80, No. 2 (May 1990), pp. 92–96.

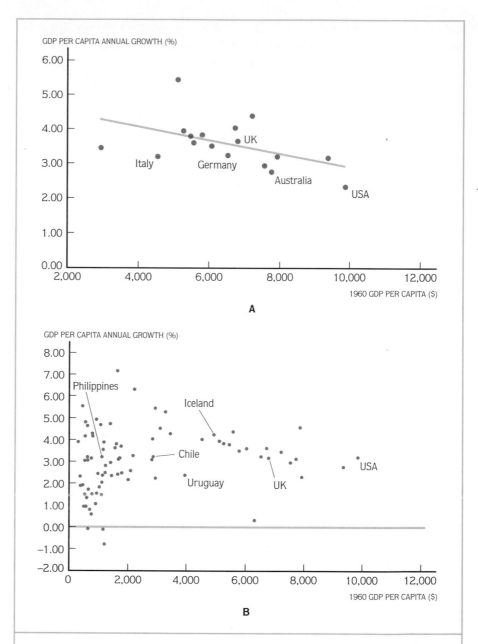

FIGURE 6.3   CONVERGENCE AND LACK OF CONVERGENCE AMONG COUNTRIES, 1960–2000

Panel A depicts convergence of GDP per capita for advanced countries from 1960 to 2000. The negative slope of the line shows that those countries that were initially poorer grew faster than those countries that were initially richer. Panel B depicts the lack of convergence for the world for the same period. There is no relation between GDP per capita in 1960 and subsequent growth rates.

SOURCE: *Penn World Tables*, Mark 6.1.

If income per worker, (Y/N), is 15 times larger in the United States than in India, what is capital per worker, (K/N), if the two countries have the same technology? Because capital is a relatively small share of production, the answer is almost 900. While it is true that American workers use more machines than Indian workers, the difference in capital per worker ratios is about 20, a long way from 900. Furthermore, because Indian machines are so much scarcer, the returns to investment in India should be 58 times higher than the returns to investment in the United States. Even allowing for more political risk in India than in the United States, the question posed by Lucas, "Why doesn't capital flow from rich to poor countries?" is difficult for the Solow model to answer.

Evidence of Convergence

1. The convergence hypothesis of the Solow neoclassical growth model states that, over time, gaps in per capita income among countries narrow.

2. The convergence hypothesis implies a negative relation between the growth rate of GDP per capita and the initial level of GDP per capita.

3. There is strong evidence of convergence among industrial countries since 1960.

4. The evidence of convergence since 1960 does not extend to the world as a whole.

6.2 | CROSS-COUNTRY GROWTH IN THE LONG RUN

The period since 1960 represents a very small part of recorded history. Data on GDP per capita is available as far back as 1820, and we would like to see whether the post-1960 evidence of convergence for advanced countries and lack of convergence for the world as a whole extends further back. Unfortunately, most of the countries for which we have data in 1820 are now classified as advanced. This is partly because many of today's poorest countries did not exist as countries in 1820, but also because poor countries lack the resources and the records to construct long series of income statistics. Testing for convergence among countries that have become rich over the period under study presupposes the answer. Whatever their income in 1820, all are advanced now and so "converge." For example, income per capita for Argentina was more than 50 percent higher than for Japan in 1870, but it is not included in the advanced countries. This is not a problem when we use the post-1960 data because the classification of some countries as advanced has not changed between 1960 and today.

Divergence in the Long Run

We can make some progress toward a longer-term perspective by using data since 1900. In addition to countries now classified as advanced, data are available for some Eastern European, Latin American, Asian, and African countries. Figure 6.4 depicts the relation between income per capita in 1900 and subsequent growth rates for 17 advanced countries. The evidence of convergence in the form of a negative relationship is similar to that found in the post-1960 data, although this result should be interpreted with caution because of the reasons described previously. Figure 6.4 also depicts the relation between income per capita in 1900 and subsequent growth rates for all countries for which data are available. The picture is one of **divergence,** not convergence. Those countries that were relatively poor in 1900 have grown slower than those countries that were relatively rich in 1900. **Income inequality,** the gap between rich and poor, has increased in the last century.[3]

The evidence of divergence presented here is based on data for very few nonindustrialized countries. Although data on GDP for most countries is not available before 1960, a thought experiment can provide some insight on divergence over the long run. The poorest countries today have levels of income per capita just above subsistence. Their levels of income per capita in 1800 or 1900 must also have been just above subsistence. They could not have been below subsistence, for that would mean mass starvation and the countries would have ceased to exist; and they could not have been much above subsistence, for there is no evidence of rich African and Asian countries becoming poorer. The rich countries today, in contrast, did exhibit substantial growth over the same period. The combination of substantial growth for rich nations and little to no growth for poor nations means that worldwide income inequality has increased over the past two centuries. Divergence has been the rule, not the exception.

Will the rise of income inequality during the nineteenth and twentieth centuries continue indefinitely? The concept of the demographic transition in Chapter 4 suggests that the gap between rich and poor will eventually narrow. Today's advanced countries have progressed from Malthusian stagnation through the post-Malthusian regime to the modern growth regime. Figure 6.5 shows annual growth rates of GDP per capita and population for Africa from 1820 to 2001. We showed in Figure 4.10 that the demographic transition has been completed for Europe. Population increased rapidly in the nineteenth century and leveled off in the twentieth century. The demographic transition is still in progress for Africa, with no leveling off of population. Africa today is in the post-Malthusian regime that Western Europe was in the early nineteenth century. Income per capita is growing, but the population is growing faster. We can hope that a forthcoming demographic transition for Africa will raise

---

[3] See Lant Pritchett, "Divergence, Big Time," *Journal of Economic Perspectives*, Vol 11, No. 3, (Summer 1997), pp. 3–17.

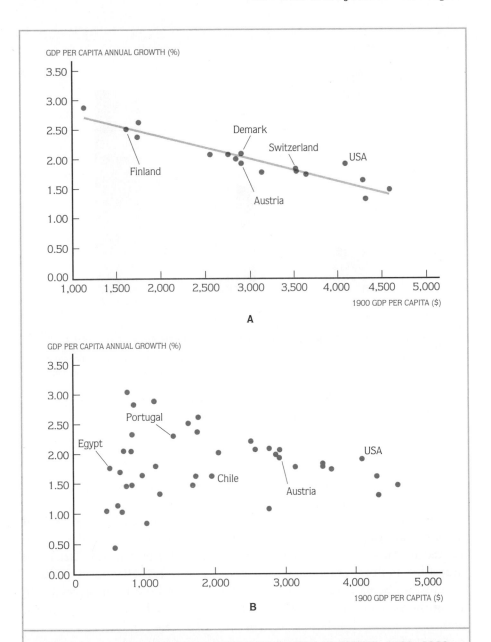

FIGURE 6.4   CONVERGENCE AND DIVERGENCE AMONG COUNTRIES, 1900–2000

Panel A depicts convergence of GDP per capita for advanced countries from 1900 to 2000. Panel B depicts divergence for the world during the same period.

SOURCE: Angus Maddison, *The World Economy: Historical Statistics* (Paris: Organization for Economic Cooperation and Development, 2003).

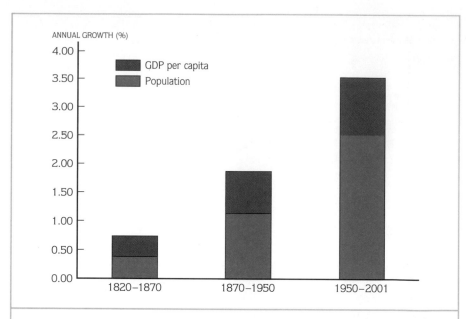

FIGURE 6.5   POPULATION AND GDP PER CAPITA GROWTH RATES FOR AFRICA

Between 1870 and 1950, GDP grew faster than population, causing growth in GDP per capita. After 1950, GDP and population growth both increased, leaving growth rates of GDP per capita unchanged.

SOURCE: Maddison, *The World Economy: Historical Statistics*.

twenty-first-century growth rates as its post-Malthusian regime ends and its modern growth regime begins.

These relatively optimistic projections for future economic growth in Africa are mitigated by the AIDS epidemic. Over 90 percent of the people infected by HIV live in developing countries, with Sub-Saharan Africa the hardest hit. In Botswana, one out of every three adults is HIV-positive. While attempts are being made to spread treatments that have been successful in raising the survival rate for HIV patients in developed countries to African countries, it is not clear how successful these attempts will be. The AIDs epidemic destroys human capital, lowers physical capital, and reduces population growth. Because of the AIDS epidemic, the United Nations recently lowered its projection for world population for the year 2050 by 300 million people. Combining these effects, the World Bank estimates that AIDS has lowered the growth of GDP per capita in Africa by 0.5 percent per year.[4] While this may seem like a small number, remember that small changes in economic growth cause large differences in GDP per capita over long periods

---

[4] See Peter Wehrwein, "The Economic Impact of AIDS in Africa," *Harvard AIDS Review*, (Fall/Winter 1999/2000).

of time. With economic growth rates already low, the impact of the AIDS epidemic has profound implications for income per capita in Africa over the twenty-first century.

Steady-State Growth

Another prediction of the Solow growth model is constant steady-state growth. We illustrated this in Chapter 5 for the United States by asking what level of GDP per capita an economist in 1929 would have predicted for 2001 by extrapolating data from 1870 to 1929. The year 1929 where the extrapolation begins is called a **break date** because growth rates were fairly steady until that date. The answer was that the prediction was fairly accurate. The economist in 1929, predicting GDP per capita 72 years later, would only have been off by 19 percent.

Does this long-run predictability extend beyond the United States? Figure 6.6 illustrates the same thought experiment for Japan and the United Kingdom. For Japan, which was relatively unaffected by the Great Depression but tremendously affected by World War II, the break date where the extrapolation begins is 1944. For the United Kingdom, which was most affected by World War I, the break date where the extrapolation begins is 1918. The picture looks very different for Japan and the United Kingdom than for the United States. The economist in 1918 predicting GDP per capita in 2001 for the United Kingdom would have been off by 39 percent. The economist in 1944 predicting GDP per capita in 2001 for Japan would have been even further off, by 64 percent.

The simplest way to evaluate the **constant steady-state growth hypothesis** of the Solow model is to compare growth rates before and after the break date. The hypothesis works very well for the United States. The growth rates are nearly identical, 1.8 percent before 1929 and 2 percent after 1929. The hypothesis does not work as well for the United Kingdom. The growth rate after 1918 is 1.4 times the growth rates before 1918, 1.5 percent compared to 1.1 percent. The hypothesis fares even worse for Japan, where the growth rate after 1944 is 2 times the growth rates before 1944, 3.8 percent compared to 1.9 percent.

This naïve comparison overstates the differences among the countries. Following wars where part of a country's capital stock is destroyed and the level of GDP per capita falls, it would be expected for growth rates to be higher while factories and machinery are rebuilt. To avoid counting growth following a war as steady-state growth, we call the *postwar transition period*, the time between the break date and the year, 1958 for Japan and 1940 for the United Kingdom, where the extrapolated growth line intersects the actual growth data in Figure 6.6. We test the steady-state growth hypothesis by comparing the growth rates before the break date and after the postwar transition period. The growth rate after 1940 is 1.6 times the growth rate before 1918 for the United Kingdom, and the growth rate after 1958 is 2.4 times the growth rate before 1944 for Japan. Even after allowing for postwar transitions, we do not find support for constant steady-state growth.

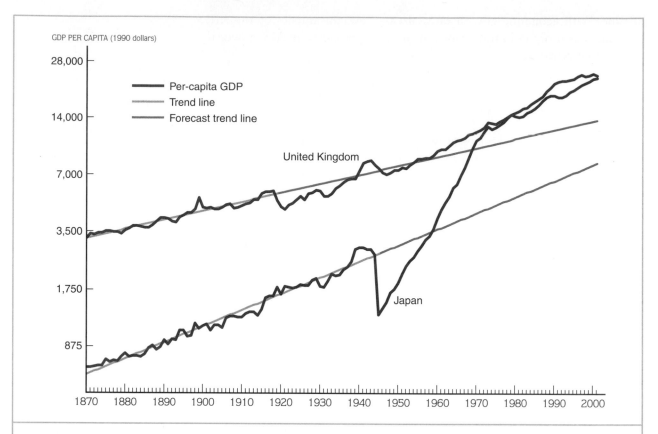

GDP PER CAPITA (1990 dollars)

FIGURE 6.6   ACTUAL AND FORECASTED GDP PER CAPITA FOR JAPAN AND THE UNITED KINGDOM

Suppose you were an economist in 1918 trying to predict GDP per capita for the United Kingdom in 2001, or an economist in 1944 trying to predict GDP per capita for Japan in 2001. Your predictions would not have been very accurate, being under by 39 and 64 percent, respectively. The reason for the under-predictions is that growth rates for the United Kingdom and (especially) Japan increased sharply after the break dates.

SOURCE: Maddison, *The World Economy: Historical Statistics.*

We can extend the analysis for Japan one step further. Looking at Figure 6.6, post-World War II growth rates decreased beginning in 1973, not in the posttransition year of 1958. We conduct another test of the constant steady-state growth hypothesis by comparing growth rates after 1973 with growth rates before 1944. We still find no support for constant steady-state growth. The annual post-1973 growth rate is 2.3 percent, 1.2 times the pre-1944 growth rate of 1.9 percent.

This analysis extends beyond Japan, the United Kingdom, and the United States.[5] Canada is a country that was relatively unaffected by either world war.

[5] Dan Ben-David and David H. Papell, "The Great Wars, the Great Crash, and Steady-State Growth: Some New Evidence about an Old Stylized Fact," *Journal of Monetary Economics,* Vol. 36 (December 1995), pp. 453–475.

The slow growth experienced by most developing countries over the last 40 years is a topic of great importance. Economists in international financial institutions, such as the World Bank, have used the Solow growth model and, more recently, the endogenous growth model to formulate growth-promoting policy advice. In a recent book, William Easterly of New York University argues that most of these policies have failed.* In a series of provocatively titled chapters, he argues that the growth-promoting strategies inspired by both the augmented Solow model and the endogenous growth model have not succeeded in practice. Here are a few examples:

• *Educated for what?* There has been a tremendous expansion of schooling in the past four decades. According to the augmented Solow model, the growth of schooling should increase GDP by raising human capital, and we reported evidence that secondary school enrollment rates are positively related to growth. Easterly argues that, because human capital, like physical capital, is a relatively minor aspect of production, explaining income differences through differences in human capital implies counterfactual predictions about rates of return. If a poor country is poor because of lack of human capital, the few skilled workers in the poor country should earn high salaries. For similar reasons, skilled workers in poor countries should earn more than skilled workers in rich countries. Neither of these predictions accord with data from India and the United States.

• *Cash for condoms?* A prediction of the Solow model is that countries with higher population growth have lower income per capita. Does this mean that subsidizing contraception raises income per capita? Easterly says no. He presents evidence that, in high-fertility countries, about 90 percent of the differences in fertility across countries are explained by actual fertility. Since the cost of contraception is miniscule compared with the cost of having a child, lowering the cost of contraception does not affect fertility. The evidence from the demographic transition is that as income per capita rises, fertility decreases.

• *Forgive us our debts.* Many of the world's poorest countries use a substantial fraction of their tax revenues to pay interest on their debt. Bono from the rock group U2, Jeffrey Sachs, the Dali Lama, and the Pope have supported debt forgiveness, canceling all of the debt of poor countries. Does debt forgiveness benefit poor countries? Again, Easterly says no. He reviews the past two decades' history of debt relief and finds that highly indebted poor countries are more likely to have irresponsible governments than less indebted countries that are equally poor. Unless there has been a change from a government with bad policies to a government with good policies, debt forgiveness will not improve economic development, and there will be another cycle of bad policy and high indebtedness.

The common theme in Easterly's examples is incentives. If policies provide incentives for governments, individuals, and aid donors to take actions that promote growth, they succeed. If not, they fail. Easterly describes how governments distort markets and create incentives that destroy growth. Corruption, a high black-market premium on foreign exchange, and restrictions on trade are some of the ways that governments create perverse incentives. The history of failed policies and slow growth of poor, mostly tropical countries over the past 40 years ensures a pessimistic message of far fewer successes than failures. The optimistic message is that the same need not hold in the future.

* William Easterly, *The Elusive Quest for Growth: Economists' Adventures and Misadventures in the Tropics* (Cambridge, MA: M.I.T. Press, 2001).

Using 1929 as a break date, the extrapolation is very accurate and the pre- and postbreak growth rates are nearly identical. Canada and the United States are the two countries that provide the most support for the steady-state growth hypothesis. The other countries most affected by World War I, Finland and Sweden, behave much like the United Kingdom. The ratio of their postwar transition period to their prebreak growth rates is about 1.85. The countries most affected by World War II, such as France and Germany, look more like Japan. The ratio of their postwar transition period to their prebreak growth rates is, on average, much higher, about 2.60.

While the steady-state growth hypothesis holds for Canada and the United States, we do not find evidence that it holds for other advanced countries. This does *not* mean that we should throw out the neoclassical growth model in favor of the endogenous growth model. World wars are about the most exogenous event possible, and they seem to be associated with the largest changes in long-run growth. What the analysis *does* suggest is that we need to be careful about assuming constant steady-state growth across time. The next section suggests that we also need to be careful about assuming common steady-state growth across countries.

Long-Run Convergence and Steady-State Growth

1. Convergence among advanced countries is not just a post-1960 phenomenon. The gap in GDP per capita has narrowed over the past two centuries.

2. When extended to the world as a whole, the picture is one of divergence, not convergence. The long-term gap between rich and poor countries has widened.

3. While the constant steady-state growth hypothesis holds for Canada and the United States, this does not generalize to other advanced countries.

6.3 | THE AUGMENTED SOLOW MODEL

Why is there convergence in GDP per capita among advanced countries but not for the world as a whole? Why are the differences in income between rich and poor countries so large? Why aren't the rates of return to capital much larger in poor than in rich countries? The neoclassical growth revival, discussed in Chapter 5 in conjunction with long-term growth in the United States, argues that these questions can be better answered by an augmented Solow growth model than by endogenous growth theory.

Conditional Convergence

We begin by revisiting the argument for convergence in the Solow model. Suppose two countries differ by only their initial levels of capital per worker, K/N. Since the return on capital is higher for the initially poor country than for the initially rich country, over time, the initially poor country saves more, accumulates capital faster, and grows faster than the initially rich country. Since the two countries are moving toward the same steady state, their incomes per capita will converge.

The key assumption for the convergence hypothesis is that the two countries are moving toward the *same steady state*. Suppose the two countries have different steady states. How could this occur in the Solow growth model? In Chapter 4, we showed how an increase in the saving rate s increases growth during a transition period, increasing the steady-state *level* of income, but leaves the steady-state *growth rate* unchanged. We also showed how an increase in the labor force growth rate n decreases growth during a transition period, decreasing the steady-state *level* of income, but leaves the steady-state *growth rate* unchanged. While the steady-state *rate of growth* of income per capita depends only on the rate of growth of technological progress, the steady-state *level* of income per capita also depends on the saving rate and labor force growth rate.

While two countries with the same saving and labor force growth rates move toward the same steady-state levels of income per capita, two countries with different saving and labor force growth rates move toward different steady-state levels of income per capita. This is shown in Figure 6.7. Countries A and B start at the same steady-state, so their initial balanced growth paths are identical. If the saving rate increases for country A but not country B in the year 1800, country A will have a higher growth rate along the transition path. Once the new steady state is reached in 1900, the two countries grow at the same rate but the level of income per worker is higher for country A.

What does this example tell us about testing for convergence? Suppose you had data for the two countries from 1900 to 2000. Using Equation 6.2 and 1900 as the year for the initial level of GDP per capita, you would not find evidence of convergence. Although country B had lower per capita income in 1900 than country A, they grew at the same rate. With data going back to 1800, you would find divergence. The two countries have the same initial level of income per capita, but country A has higher income per capita in 2000.

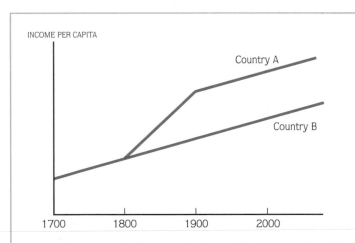

**FIGURE 6.7   CONDITIONAL CONVERGENCE
IN THE AUGMENTED SOLOW MODEL**

Country A and country B start on the same balanced growth path. Then, the saving rate rises for country A but not for country B. The two countries end up with the same steady-state growth rate, but income per capita is higher in country A than in country B.

How well does the Solow model work when countries are not constrained to have the same steady-state levels of per-capita income? N. Gregory Mankiw of Harvard University, David Romer of the University of California at Berkeley, and David Weil of Brown University find that, for a sample of 98 advanced and developing countries, saving rates and population growth rates explain 59 percent of the cross-country variation in income per capita.[6] Even though saving rates and population growth rates do not affect steady-state growth, they explain a substantial fraction of the variation in steady-state levels of income per capita across countries.

Mankiw, Romer, and Weil also test for **conditional convergence,** the hypothesis that income per capita in a given country converges to that country's steady-state value. Conditional convergence implies that the initial level of income per capita is negatively related to the growth rate of income per capita after controlling for the variables, saving rates and population growth rates, that determine the steady state. This is accomplished by adding saving and population growth rates to the right-hand side of Equation 6.2:

$$\Delta(Y/N)/(Y/N) = a + c(Y/N)(1960)$$
$$+ \text{ (saving and population growth rates)}. \qquad (6.5)$$

When saving and population growth rates are included for the sample of 98 countries, coefficient c becomes negative. Recall that, in Equation 6.2, the coefficient c was close to zero for the same sample of 98 countries. The only difference between the equations is that, in Equation 6.5, saving and population growth rates are included while, in Equation 6.2, saving and population growth rates did not appear. The negative value of the coefficient c in Equation 6.5 provides evidence of conditional convergence for the world as a whole. It is important to remember that, since the determinants of the steady state are controlled for, conditional convergence means only that countries converge to their own steady states. It does not mean that the gap between rich and poor countries narrows.

The Solow growth model predicts convergence among countries with the same saving rates and population growth rates. This can explain why convergence (without controlling for the determinants of the steady state) occurs among advanced countries but not for the world as a whole. Saving and population growth rates are much more similar among advanced countries than between advanced and developing countries. Robert Barro of Harvard University and Xavier Sala-i-Martin of Columbia University provide additional evidence of convergence across states in the United States and prefectures in Japan.[7] This is in accord with the predictions of the Solow model, for you would expect less variation in saving rates and population growth rates within a country than among even similar countries.

---

[6] N. Gregory Mankiw, David Romer, and David N. Weil, "A Contribution to the Empirics of Economic Growth," *Quarterly Journal of Economics*, Vol. 107 (May 1992), pp. 407–437.

[7] Robert J. Barro and Xavier Sala-i-Martin, *Economic Growth* (New York: McGraw-Hill, 1995).

TESTING FOR CONVERGENCE AND CONDITIONAL CONVERGENCE

The concept of *convergence* is central to understanding economic growth. The idea of convergence is intuitive. If the difference in GDP per capita among countries is narrowing over time, they are converging. If the difference in GDP per capita among countries is widening over time, they are diverging.

Testing for convergence is straightforward. Suppose you have data on GDP per capita in 1960 and 2000 for a group of countries. Calculate the average annual growth rate for each country. (Use the formula for compound growth from Chapter 4). If the countries are converging, the relation between the initial level of GDP per capita in 1960 and the subsequent growth rates is negative. Countries are converging if those countries that are initially poorer grow faster than those that are initially richer.

There are two ways to test for convergence. The first is shown in Figure 6.3. Plot the average annual growth rate of GDP per capita on the vertical axis and GDP per capita in 1960 on the horizontal axis for each country. Then draw the straight line through the points that provides the best fit for the actual data. (More technically, choose the straight line that minimizes the sum of the squared distance between the line and the data.) This line is called a *regression line*. If the slope of the regression line is negative, as in panel A of Figure 6.3, countries that are initially poorer are growing faster than those that are initially richer and there is evidence of convergence.

The second way to test for convergence is to estimate a *regression equation*, described in Equation 6.2. If those countries that are initially poorer in 1960 grow faster than those countries that are initially richer in 1960, the coefficient c in Equation 6.2 is negative and there is evidence of convergence. The figure and the equation depict the same information. The coefficient c in the regression equation (6.2) is the slope of the regression line in Figure 6.3.

The concept of *conditional convergence* is also central to understanding economic growth. Conditional convergence means that GDP per capita in an individual country converges to that country's steady-state value but different countries can have different steady-state values. It is important to understand that, because countries are converging to different steady-state values, conditional convergence does not mean that the gap between rich and poor countries is narrowing over time.

As shown in Chapter 4, saving rates and population growth rates affect the steady-state level of GDP per capita in the Solow model but do not affect the growth rate of GDP per capita. The key to testing for conditional convergence is that, if countries converge to their own steady states, the relation between initial GDP per capita and subsequent growth rates is negative, but only after taking out, or controlling for, the influence of those variables (saving rates and population growth rates) that affect the steady-state level of GDP per capita but do not affect the growth rate in the Solow model.

Testing for conditional convergence is more complicated and less intuitive than testing for convergence. Suppose you have data on GDP per capita growth rates, saving rates, and population growth rates for 1960 to 2000 as well as GDP per capita in 1960 for a group of countries. Conditional convergence implies a negative relation between GDP per capita in 1960 and subsequent growth rates *after controlling for the effects of different saving rates and population growth rates*. The way to control for the effects of one or more variables in a regression is to include them on the right-hand side. Consider Equation 6.5, which augments Equation 6.2 by including savings rates and population growth rates on the right-hand side. Equation 6.5 depicts a relation, described by the coefficient c, between real GDP per capita in 1960 and subsequent growth rates *after controlling for the effects of different savings rates and population growth rates*. If the coefficient c is negative, there is conditional convergence.

Human Capital

While allowing countries to be in different steady states helps understand the nature of convergence, it does not eliminate all of the problems of the Solow growth model. First, the differences in income per capita between rich and poor countries are too large to be explained by the Solow model. Second, the speed of conditional convergence predicted by the Solow model is about twice the rate that actually occurs. Third, the Solow model predicts very large differences in rates of return to investment between rich and poor countries.

These problems with the Solow growth model led Robert Lucas to focus on human capital in the development of endogenous growth theory. The same problems led N. Gregory Mankiw, David Romer, and David Weil to focus on human capital in the **augmented Solow model.** We defined capital K as equipment, structures, and other productive facilities, also called **physical capital.** More generally, we accumulate capital when we forgo consumption to produce more income in the future. An important aspect of capital formation is **human capital,** schooling and on-the-job training. When you attend school, you forgo current income to receive greater income in the future. We use the letter H to denote human capital.

A production function that includes labor, technology, physical capital, and human capital is

$$Y = F(K, H, N, L) = K^{1/3}H^{1/3}N^{1/3}A, \tag{6.6}$$

where K is physical capital, H is human capital, L is labor, and A is technology. Divide by N to get

$$Y/N = (K/N)^{1/3}(H/N)^{1/3}A. \tag{6.7}$$

Mankiw, Romer, and Weil use a measure of secondary school enrollment as a proxy for human capital accumulation. In many developing countries, where enrollment in secondary school is much lower than in advanced countries, the choice of whether to attend school or work is typically made in secondary, or even primary, school. In advanced countries, the choice is typically made in college or even in graduate school. The researchers find that saving rates, population growth rates, and human capital accumulation explain 78 percent of the differences in income per capita among the 98 countries in their sample. This is considerably higher than the 59 percent explained by saving and population growth rates alone and provides evidence of the importance of human capital accumulation in understanding differences in income per capita.

The augmented Solow model can also be used to investigate conditional convergence. Mankiw, Romer, and Weil test whether the initial level of income per capita is negatively related to the growth rate of income per capita after controlling for the variables—saving rates, population growth rates, and human capital accumulation—that determine the steady state. This is accomplished by adding human capital accumulation to the right-hand side of Equation 6.5:

$$\Delta(Y/N)/(Y/N) = a + c(Y/N)(1960) +$$
(saving rates, population growth rates,
and human capital accumulation).   (6.8)

When human capital accumulation, as well as saving and population growth rates, are included for the sample of 98 countries, the coefficient c becomes more negative. This implies a faster rate of convergence for the augmented Solow model than for the Solow model without human capital.

The share of physical and human capital in the augmented Solow model is greater than the share of capital in the original Solow model. This can help explain why the difference in capital per worker between rich and poor countries is not as large as would be predicted by the Solow model. Suppose that the average share of physical and human capital in India and the United States is 0.80, so that the production function is

$$Y = K^{0.8}N^{0.2}A,   (6.9)$$

where K denotes both physical and human capital. Divide both sides by N to get

$$Y/N = A(K/N)^{0.8}.   (6.10)$$

We ask the question posed by Robert Lucas: If income per worker, (Y/N), is 15 times larger in the United States than in India, what is physical and human capital per worker, (K/N), if the two countries have the same technology? The answer is about 30. While this is larger than the capital per worker ratios actually observed, which are around 20, it is much smaller than the capital per worker ratio, 900, predicted by the original Solow model.

Cross-Country Growth

What determines differences in economic growth across countries? A large literature has evolved that tests what variables affect income per capita across the countries in the Heston-Summers data set. We focused on conditional convergence. Countries with low levels of initial income per capita grow faster than countries with high levels of initial income per capita.

Conditional convergence can be seen by the negative value of the coefficient c in equations such as

$$\Delta(Y/N)/(Y/N) = a + c(Y/N)(1960) +$$
(saving rates, population growth rates, and other variables).   (6.11)

These equations are called **cross-country growth regressions.** Variations in saving rates, population growth rates, and other variables are used to explain variation of growth rates across countries.

According to the augmented Solow model, variables that are proxies for physical capital and human capital should affect the steady-state level of income per capita but not its steady-state growth rate. Robert Hall of Stanford University and Charles Jones of the University of California at Berkeley argue that many of the predictions of growth theory should be studied by examining the levels of income across countries.[8] Consider the following equation:

$$Y/N = a + \text{(saving rates, population}$$
$$\text{growth rates, and other variables).} \qquad (6.12)$$

These equations are called **cross-country level regressions.** The variables that enter cross-country growth regressions, including saving rates and population growth rates, are used to explain variation of levels of income per capita across countries.

How do economists explain cross-country growth since 1960? While different studies arrive at different conclusions, some variables consistently help explain differences in growth rates of income per capita among countries in cross-country growth regressions and differences in levels of income per capita among countries in cross-country level regressions.[9]

- *Saving rates* are positively related to growth. Since saving equals net investment, countries with a high ratio of investment to output have higher growth rates.

- *Population growth rates* are negatively related to growth in income per capita.

- *Measures of human capital*, such as secondary school enrollment rates, are positively related to growth.

- *Political variables* affect growth. Rule of law, political rights, and civil liberties are positively related to growth. Revolutions, military coups, and wars are negatively related to growth.

- *Openness to trade* is positively related to growth. Countries with free trade grow faster than countries that restrict trade.

- *Market distortions* are negatively related to growth. Countries with real exchange rate distortions and large black market premiums have lower growth rates.

---

[8] Robert E. Hall and Charles I. Jones, "Why Do Some Countries Produce So Much More Output per Worker than Others?" *Quarterly Journal of Economics*, Vol. 114 (February 1999), pp. 83–116.

[9] Xavier Sala-i-Martin, "I Just Ran Two Million Regressions," *American Economic Review*, Vol. 87, No. 2 (May 1997), pp. 178–183.

- *The fraction of primary products in total exports* is negatively related to growth, while *the fraction of GDP in mining* is positively related to growth.

- *Geographic variables* affect growth. *Absolute latitude*, the distance from the equator, is positively related to growth.

Convergence and the Augmented Solow Model

1. The evidence of convergence for the world as a whole is for conditional convergence. Countries move toward their own steady states, but the gap between rich and poor countries does not narrow.

2. The augmented Solow model incorporates human capital in the Solow model.

3. The augmented Solow model provides a better explanation of the cross-country variation in income per capita, the speed of conditional convergence, and the differences in capital per worker ratios between rich and poor countries than the original Solow model.

4. Cross-country growth regressions explain variations in growth among countries. Variables that affect growth include savings rates, population growth rates, schooling, openness to trade, market distortions, political variables, and geographic variables.

6.4 | GEOGRAPHY, INSTITUTIONS, AND GROWTH

One of the clearest patterns of cross-country growth across countries is the relation between *distance from the equator*, measured by latitude, and income per capita. Countries far away from the equator, such as the United States, Western Europe, Canada, Australia, and New Zealand have much higher income per capita than the tropical countries of Africa, Asia, and Latin America. This is illustrated in Figure 6.8. What causes the relation between geography and income? Does geography affect growth directly, or does the effect operate through social institutions? The interplay between geography, institutions, and growth is the subject of some very interesting recent research.

Social Infrastructure

Hall and Jones begin by showing that, using cross-country level regressions such as Equation 6.12, much of the variation of levels of income per capita across countries remains unexplained once the effects of physical capital and

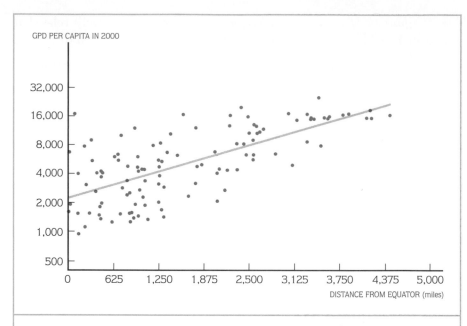

FIGURE 6.8   PER CAPITA GDP AND LATITUDE

There is a positive relationship between GDP per capita and latitude. Countries further from the equator (North or South) are richer than countries closer to the equator.

SOURCE: Hall and Jones, "Why Do Some Countries Produce So Much More Output per Worker than Others?"; Penn World Tables, Mark 6.1.

human capital are accounted for. They focus on **social infrastructure,** which they define as "the institutions and government policies that determine the economic environment within which individuals accumulate skills, and firms accumulate capital and produce output." They form a measure of social infrastructure by combining two indexes. The first quantifies the role of the government by combining law and order and bureaucratic quality (positive) with corruption, risk of expropriation, and government repudiation of contracts (negative). The second measures the openness of a country to trade with other countries. Figure 6.9 shows that their measure of social infrastructure is positively related to output per worker. Differences in social infrastructure cause large differences in income across countries through physical capital accumulation, human capital accumulation, and productivity.

What does social infrastructure have to do with geography? Hall and Jones conjecture that distance from the equator is a proxy for the influence of Western Europe, the first region to implement a social infrastructure favorable to production, on the rest of the world. Countries far from the equator that were sparsely settled in 1500, such as Australia and the United States, were highly influenced by Western European institutions and have developed social infrastructures favorable to production. Tropical countries that were more densely populated in 1500 were conquered by European countries for natural

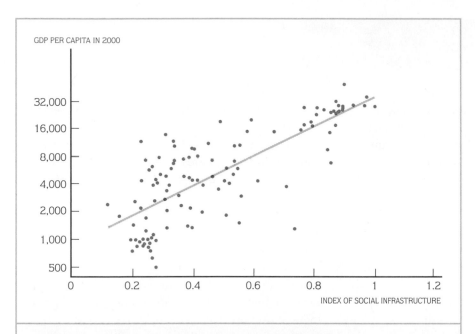

FIGURE 6.9   SOCIAL INFRASTRUCTURE AND GDP PER CAPITA

There is a positive relationship between social infrastructure and GDP per capita. Countries with good institutions that are more open to foreign trade are richer than countries with bad institutions that are more closed to foreign trade.

SOURCE: Hall and Jones, "Why Do Some Countries Produce So Much More Output per Worker than Others?"; Penn World Tables, Mark 6.1.

resources and commodities but were influenced much less by Western European institutions and have not developed social infrastructures favorable to production.

Geography

The **geography hypothesis** is that most of the differences in income per capita can be explained by geographic, climatic, and ecological differences across countries. Jeffrey Sachs of Columbia University postulates that geography has direct effects on production, as well as indirect effects through institutions such as those measured by social infrastructure.[10] *Tropical regions* are centered on the equator and include the area between 23.5 degrees North latitude (Tropic of Cancer) and 23.5 degrees South latitude (Tropic of Capricorn). *Temperate regions* are those north or south of the tropics.

---

[10] Jeffrey D. Sachs, "Tropical Underdevelopment," National Bureau of Economic Research Working Paper 8119, February 2001.

RESEARCH IN PRACTICE
The Millennium Challenge Account

New research on economic growth is already having an impact on public policy, as a whole new approach to international development assistance is being implemented. The centerpiece of the new approach to aid is the Millennium Challenge Account, proposed by President George W. Bush in March 2002. The United States pledged to increase foreign aid by $5 billion annually by 2006 to strong-performing poor countries, an increase of core development assistance of 50 percent, with the potential for half of the new aid going to African countries that "govern justly, invest in their own people, and promote economic freedom."

A novel feature of the Millennium Challenge Account is the link between increased development assistance and specific performance indicators. The indicators include civil liberties and political rights (governing justly), public primary education spending and public expenditures on health as percent of GDP (investing in people), and country credit rating and trade policy (promoting economic freedom). These indicators are highly correlated with the variables, discussed in Section 6.3, that are under the control of governments and positively related to growth. The Millennium Challenge Account is putting into practice what economists have learned from research on economic growth.

Similarly, the annual summit of the Group of Eight (G-8) leading industrialized countries in June 2002 focused on a "New Partnership for African Development," which ties aid for African countries to economic and political reforms. The G-8 Africa Action Plan included an increase by $1 billion of support for debt relief for the heavily indebted poor countries. It also endorsed an increase in the use of grants, rather than loans, for those countries. By avoiding making more loans to already heavily indebted poor countries, the hope is the cycle where new debt follows debt forgiveness will not repeat itself.

Yet another well publicized event in 2002 brought attention to these issues. Treasury Secretary Paul O'Neill and rock star Bono, of U2 fame, joined together for a 12-day tour of four Sub-Saharan African countries—Ghana, South Africa, Uganda, and Ethiopia—in May 2002. The highly publicized tour of one of the poorest regions of the world included, in addition to meetings with government officials, firsthand observation of living conditions in each country through visits to villages and development projects.

There was much commonality in the views expressed by the self-described "odd couple." Both focused on the importance of three factors—clean water, primary education, and health. In the area of health, a particular focus was on preventing further HIV contagion, especially infant HIV infection, to fight the AIDS epidemic.

They also had some significantly different views. Bono stressed the necessity for additional spending on development assistance. Treasury Secretary O'Neill, while agreeing with the need for increased spending, stressed the importance of incentives, leadership, and governments that enforce laws and contracts, respect human rights and property, fight corruption, and remove barriers to trade.

One area of discussion was debt forgiveness. Bono has been, and continues to be, a strong proponent of debt forgiveness. Treasury Secretary O'Neill, while agreeing on debt forgiveness, stressed the importance of new grants rather than new loans, as proposed by President Bush in 2001: "Many extol debt forgiveness as the path to African development. I would agree that debt forgiveness may help, but it alone is not the solution. Debt forgiveness solves nothing if we allow new debt to create the next generation of heavily indebted poor countries a decade from now." The focus on incentives and skepticism about debt forgiveness echo the factors highlighted by William Easterly in his analysis of the failures of development programs.

The long-term performance of tropical and temperate regions illustrates how seemingly small differences in growth rates produce very large differences in income per capita over time. In 1820, income per capita in tropical regions was two-thirds of income per capita in temperate regions. Over the following 150 years, the average annual growth of income per capita was 1.4 percent in temperate regions and 0.9 percent in tropical regions. By 1992, income per capita in tropical regions was only one-fourth of income per capita in temperate regions.

Why were tropical regions poorer than temperate regions at the start of the modern growth regime, and why did tropical regions grow slower than temperate regions? Sachs argues that technologies for food production, health, and energy are ecologically specific in ways that favor temperate over tropical regions. There are substantial differences between temperate and tropical regions in soil formation and erosion, pests and parasites, water availability and control (food production), types of infectious diseases (health), and endowments of coal, oil, and gas (energy).

These factors can potentially explain the difference in income per capita between temperate and tropical regions in 1820. Since climate has been relatively stable, something more is needed to explain the subsequent differences in growth. According to endogenous growth theory, the absence of diminishing returns to technology is the key to sustained steady-state growth. Technological innovation was much higher in temperate regions than in tropical regions in the nineteenth and twentieth centuries. This alone cannot explain the growth differences, because *technological diffusion*, the spread of technology from innovating to noninnovating countries, can spread economic growth across countries. Sachs argues that the *ecological divide*, the differences in ecological conditions between temperate and tropical countries, limits the diffusion of technological innovation. This causes convergence among temperate countries but divergence between temperate and tropical countries.

The demographic transition, studied in Chapter 4, is the transition from the post-Malthusian regime of high fertility and low growth to the modern growth regime of low fertility and high growth. Ecological factors can help explain why the demographic transition has progressed much further in temperate than in tropical countries. Poor food production in tropical countries slows the shift of population from rural to urban areas, keeping fertility rates high. Poor public health causes high child mortality, which slows the demographic transition since households compensate for high child mortality through high fertility.

Institutions

The **institutions hypothesis** is that differences in economic performance are caused by the organization of society. In this view, geography does not affect growth directly or through technological factors. Instead, geography influences growth through differences in institutions among countries. An example of the institutions hypothesis is the argument of Hall and Jones that distance from the equator is a proxy for the influence of Western Europe on social infrastructure favorable to production.

Daron Acemoglu and Simon Johnson of M.I.T. and James Robinson of the University of California at Berkeley argue that the effects of institutions on income per capita of former European colonies are both large and persistent.[11] There were two types of European colonies. In some places, such as Australia, Canada, and the United States, settlers created *neo-Europes*. These colonies attempted to replicate European institutions with protection of private property and checks against government expropriation. In other places, including most of Africa and Latin America, European countries set up *extractive states* to transfer resources from the colony to the colonizer. These colonies did not create institutions to protect private property or provide checks against government expropriation.

The decision whether to create neo-Europes or extractive states was determined by settler mortality. In regions where Europeans faced low mortality rates, settlement was possible and settlers created neo-Europes. In regions where Europeans faced high mortality rates, settlement was not possible and European countries set up *extractive states*. How does mortality in the seventeenth, eighteenth, and nineteenth centuries affect per-capita income today? According to the institutions hypothesis, these early institutions persisted and have an important effect on institutions today. Differences in institutions explain about three-quarters of the differences in income per capita among former colonies.

According to the geography hypothesis, differences in income per capita should be highly persistent, since geographic factors are stable. The evidence presented by Sachs supports this view. Tropical countries that were poor relative to temperate countries in 1820 are still relatively poor. In contrast, Acemoglu, Johnson, and Robinson argue that, among regions colonized by European powers, there has been a **reversal of fortune.** Those regions that were relatively rich in 1500 are now relatively poor. Although data for income per capita in 1500 is not available, the degree of urbanization and population density can be used as a proxy. This is illustrated in Figure 6.10. Regions that were more densely populated in 1500, such as Africa, are now poorer than regions that were more sparsely populated in 1500, such as the United States.

Why did the reversal of fortune occur? Their argument is that European colonization caused an *institutional reversal*. Regions that were densely populated and relatively rich prior to colonization were more likely to become ex-

---

[11] Daron Acemoglu, Simon Johnson, and James Robinson, "The Colonial Origins of Comparative Development: An Empirical Investigation," *American Economic Review*, Vol. 91 (December 2001), pp. 1369–1401; "Reversal of Fortune: Geography and Institutions in the Making of the Modern World Income Distribution," *Quarterly Journal of Economics* 117, (November 2002), pp. 1231–1294.

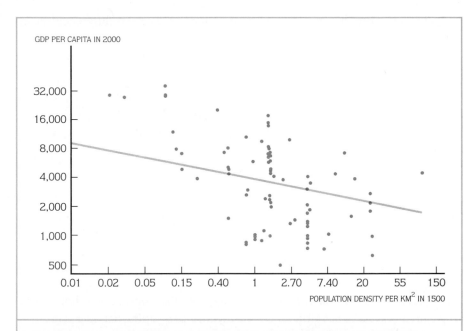

FIGURE 6.10   GDP PER CAPITA IN 2000 AND POPULATION DENSITY IN 1500

Over the last 500 years, there has been a *reversal of fortune* in GDP per capita. Regions that were more densely populated in 1500, and therefore relatively rich, such as parts of Africa, are now poorer than regions that were less densely populated in 1500, and therefore relatively poor, such as the United States.

SOURCE: Acemoglu, Johnson and Robinson, "Reversal of Fortune"; Penn World Tables, Mark 6.1.

tractive states with bad institutions, and regions that were sparsely populated and relatively poor prior to colonization were more likely to become neo-Europes with good institutions. The institutional reversal, in turn, led to the reversal of fortune. The spread of industrial technology in the nineteenth century favored societies with good institutions that could take advantage of growth opportunities.

Geography and Institutions

1. Distance from the equator is highly related to income per capita. Countries far from the equator are relatively rich, and countries close to the equator are relatively poor.

2. Differences in social infrastructure can explain much of the variation of levels of income per capita across countries beyond what can be accounted for by physical capital and human capital.

3. The geography hypothesis conjectures that most of the differences in income per capita across countries can be explained by geographic, climatic, and ecological differences.

4. The institutions hypothesis conjectures that differences in social infrastructure and institutions are the main determinant of differences in income per capita across countries. To the extent that geography matters, the institutions hypothesis suggests that this is because it has influenced institutions in the past.

REVIEW AND PRACTICE

Major Points

1. Evidence from advanced countries supports the convergence hypothesis, which predicts that differences in income per capita between countries narrow with time. Evidence from the world as a whole, however, does not support this hypothesis.

2. The gap in income per capita between rich and poor countries has widened over time.

3. While the constant steady-state growth hypothesis holds for Canada and the United States, this does not generalize to other advanced countries.

4. The conditional convergence hypothesis is that countries converge to their own steady states, not to a common steady state.

5. The augmented Solow model provides a better explanation of the cross-country variation in per capita income, the speed of conditional convergence, and the differences in capital per worker ratios between rich and poor than the original Solow model.

6. Distance from the equator is highly related to income per capita. Countries far from the equator are relatively rich, and countries close to the equator are relatively poor.

7. Differences in social infrastructure explain a significant proportion of the variation in income per capita across countries that are not explained by physical capital and human capital.

8. The geography hypothesis states that most of the differences in income per capita across countries can be explained by geographic, climatic, and ecological factors.

9. The institutions hypothesis states that geography influences growth through differences in institutional frameworks.

Key Terms and Concepts

convergence hypothesis
catch up
divergence
income inequality
constant steady-state growth
    hypothesis
conditional convergence
augmented Solow model

physical capital
human capital
cross-country growth regressions
cross-country level regressions
social infrastructure
geography hypothesis
institutions hypothesis
reversal of fortune

Questions for Discussion and Review

1. What assumptions are necessary for convergence to be a prediction of the Solow model?

2. What are the major differences between the Solow growth model and the augmented Solow model?

3. What is the evidence for convergence in income per capita among advanced countries since 1960?

4. Discuss the evidence of whether or not the gap in GDP per capita has narrowed between rich and poor countries.

5. How does the augmented Solow model deal with the issue of convergence?

6. Describe what is meant by the *geography hypothesis*.

7. What is the *institutions hypothesis*?

Problems

NUMERICAL

1. Use the following data:

COUNTRY	GDP PER WORKER IN 1960	AVERAGE ANNUAL GROWTH RATE OF GDP PER WORKER, 1960–1990
United States	$24,500	1.4 percent
Japan	$ 4,900	5.0 percent
Belgium	$14,200	2.7 percent
Spain	$ 8,300	3.9 percent
Netherlands	$17,100	2.0 percent

(a) Using a graph like Figure 6.3, plot the average annual growth rate of GDP per worker from 1960 to 1990 on the vertical axis and the GDP per worker in 1960 on the horizontal axis.

(b) Draw the straight line that provides the closest fit for the actual data. Is its slope positive, negative, or zero? Would the coefficient c in Equation 6.2 be positive or negative? Does this provide evidence of convergence, divergence, or neither?

2. Suppose that the production function for both India and the United States is $Y/N = A(K/N)^{1/2}$. If capital per worker K/N is \$2,250,000 (\$2.25 million) in the United States, technology $A = 10$ in both countries, and output per worker Y/N is 15 times as large in the United States as in India, what would be the capital per worker in India?

ANALYTICAL

1. Discuss briefly how each of the following changes would affect the steady-state growth rate of an economy.

   (a) A government policy designed to increase investment

   (b) A new free trade agreement

   (c) An increase in secondary school enrollment rates

   (d) An increase in the population growth rate.

2. The Solow model predicts that countries with less capital per worker will see increased investment in capital until they catch up to countries with higher initial levels of capital per worker. Evidence does not always support this prediction. Explain what factors might cause this prediction to fail.

3. Distance from the equator is positively related to growth. How can this finding be explained by the geography and the institutions hypotheses?

4. Suppose you are given annual data on per-capita GDP from 1960 to 2000 for a number of countries. How would you use this data to test the convergence hypothesis?

5. According to the book by William Easterly, describe how well growth promoting policies have worked in practice?

6. Describe how you could use the augmented Solow model to test for conditional convergence.

7. If countries in Africa experience the same demographic transition in the twenty-first century that Western European countries experienced in the nineteenth century, how would their GDP-per-capita growth rates and population growth rates be affected?

ECONOMIC FLUCTUATIONS

SHORT-RUN

FLUCTUATIONS

The long-run growth model of Chapters 4, 5, and 6 is an important part of modern macroeconomics. But it does not explain recessions, such as those that occurred in 1981–1982, 1990–1991, and 2001, when the economy deviated from its long-run path. Therefore, we now shift gears and focus on economic fluctuations in the short run, in an attempt to explain questions not addressed by the long-run growth model.

Why does it take several years for the economy to return to potential GDP after a shock? What forces push output away from its potential? In this chapter and the next two chapters, we answer these two key questions by developing the economic fluctuations model, which addresses these questions by allowing demand to affect output in a manner not considered in the long-run growth model.

In this chapter, we first explain why changes in spending, or demand, can cause real GDP to depart from its potential. We then examine an important determinant of spending—people's income. The relationship between income and spending gives rise to the concept of spending balance. While the material covered in this chapter is an important component of the economic fluctuations model, it does not tell the whole story. In Chapter 8, we introduce interest rates and add financial markets to our model. In Chapter 9, we study price adjustment and see how the economy returns to equilibrium following shocks and disturbances.

7.1 | FORCES THAT PUSH THE ECONOMY OFF ITS GROWTH PATH

In Chapter 3, we concluded that the economy can deviate from full employment and the forces pushing it back to full employment take time. What kinds of forces are responsible for departures from full employment? To answer this question, macroeconomists have to take a stand on which relationships in the economy hold in both the short and long runs and which hold only in the long run. The view that we take is that prices are unresponsive to current developments; they move only gradually over time. On the other hand, certain key relationships involving spending hold even in the short run. Accordingly, the complete model we develop considers spending relationships. It takes prices, and therefore the average price level, as given for now from the past history of the economy. In the short run unemployment can be above the natural rate.

In the short run, we assume that firms stand ready to supply whatever output their customers want, given existing prices. When firms let their customers determine their level of output and employment, demand becomes the ruling force. If demand is strong, real GDP exceeds potential. In a recession, when demand is weak, real GDP drops below potential. Firms then adjust their prices gradually to get back toward equilibrium. Price adjustment eventually takes the economy back to its long-run growth path. Chapter 9 considers this transition process of price adjustment.

To preview how we use these ideas to explain economic fluctuations, we introduce the diagram in Figure 7.1, with the price level on the vertical axis and real GDP on the horizontal axis. This basic diagram is called the **aggregate demand (AD) curve.** This chapter and Chapters 8 and 9 develop the details of the aggregate demand curve. Figure 7.1 illustrates its basic use. Given a price level on the vertical axis, we can find the amount of output generated by the spending process by moving across, on a horizontal line, to the aggregate demand curve.

Any event that shifts the aggregate demand curve moves the economy away from potential. Figure 7.2 illustrates the effect of a leftward (inward) shift of aggregate demand. The shift leaves output below potential. In accord

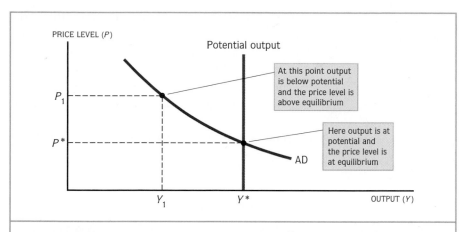

FIGURE 7.1   THE AGGREGATE DEMAND (AD) CURVE

Given a price level on the vertical axis, the AD curve tells us the amount of output demanded in the economy. A higher price level corresponds to lower output, and a lower price level corresponds to higher output.

with our assumption that the price level does not respond immediately to this type of shift, the price level remains unchanged. In the next two chapters, we consider the types of changes that shift the aggregate demand curve. They include changes in the government's tax and spending policies, spontaneous changes in consumption and investment, and changes in purchases of U.S. goods by foreigners. Changes in monetary policy and financial markets also shift the AD curve.

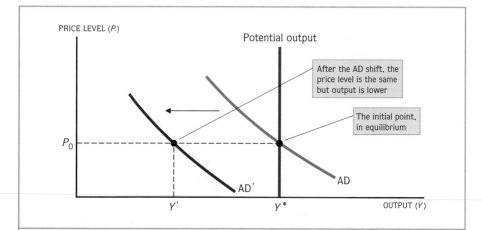

FIGURE 7.2   OUTPUT DECLINES WHEN AD SHIFTS INWARD

A shock moves the AD curve and pushes the economy away from potential. The economy starts in equilibrium at output Y^* and price level P_0. Because of a negative shock, the AD curve shifts to the left, to AD'. The price level stays at P_0. The new level of output is Y', which is below Y^*.

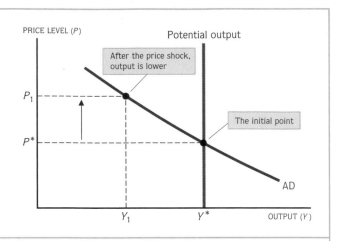

PRICE LEVEL (*P*)

Potential output

After the price shock, output is lower

P_1

The initial point

P^*

AD

Y_1 Y^* OUTPUT (*Y*)

FIGURE 7.3   A PRICE SHOCK

A price increase moves the economy to a point on the AD curve with lower output.

A second event that could move the economy away from potential is a shift in the price level. Changes in world prices, especially oil prices, are the most common source of price shocks. Figure 7.3 shows the effect of a price increase. From an initial position, the economy moves to a lower level of output. Again, the AD schedule tells how a price increase leads to a decline in output.

The Aggregate Demand Curve

1. In the short-run, demand determines output; firms provide the level of output their customers demand at existing prices.

2. The aggregate demand curve shows the level of output corresponding to alternative price levels, including the existing price level.

3. Any event that shifts the AD curve pushes the economy away from potential. Fiscal and monetary policy, consumption, investment, and foreign purchases can all shift the AD curve.

7.2 | AGGREGATE DEMAND AND THE SPENDING DECISION

Firms produce goods because they expect that people will buy them. Aggregate demand theory starts by examining people's decisions to buy goods, or their spending decisions. Many factors influence spending. If a personal tax cut occurs, then the demand for consumption goods by households rises. If interest rates rise because of a change in monetary policy, then investment demand from firms is likely to fall. If there is a cut in defense spending, then government demand falls. By adding up the spending demands of the various sectors of the economy, we obtain an estimate of aggregate spending. But, a crucial next step is to see if this aggregate spending is consistent with the income that the public bases its spending decisions on. The explanation of how spending is consistent with income is the topic of this chapter. Because total spending is an aggregation of demand in all sectors of the economy, we refer to the total as **aggregate demand.**

Our discussion of the short run sets aside, temporarily, the question of whether the economy has the resources to produce the volume of output demanded. We make the assumption that aggregate demand determines the amount of goods produced in the economy. This assumption is central to our analysis of economic fluctuations. In Chapter 9, we bring back the resource constraints described by the long-run growth model. In the complete model developed there, fluctuations in demand have effects on output in the short run, but the growth model, with its emphasis on resources, takes over in the longer run.

To see why the assumption that aggregate demand determines output is usually a reasonable assumption, we need to consider the typical behavior of business firms at the microeconomic level. Under normal conditions most business firms operate with some excess capacity and respond to increases in demand by producing more goods. In the United States, the average level of capacity utilization in manufacturing industries is about 80 percent. Some machines are left idle on standby; others are run for only two out of three shifts. Hence, firms have considerable leeway to produce more by increasing capacity utilization when demand increases. If additional labor is necessary to operate the equipment more intensively, it is usually possible to have some workers increase their hours per week, recall some workers from layoff status, or even hire additional workers. The natural rate of unemployment is between 5 and 6 percent; this indicates that additional workers can be hired in the short run, even at full employment. Therefore, for both capital and labor inputs to production, there is considerable short-run flexibility for firms to meet an increase in the demand for their products. And though we have been speaking entirely in terms of increases in demand, the same response occurs for declines in demand. A firm produces less when the demand for its product declines.

In sum, both increases and decreases in demand for a firm's product get translated into increases and decreases in production. In the economy as a whole, short-run fluctuations in aggregate demand result in similar fluctuations in GDP. In this sense, the assumption that "demand determines output" is reasonable for analyzing most short-run fluctuations of GDP from its long-run growth path.

The Unresponsiveness of the Price Level

Firms not only adjust their production in response to changes in demand, they also adjust their prices. When an increase in demand results in a firm producing at above-average operating levels, it usually increases its prices as well. Similarly, a decline in demand that brings a firm to below-normal operating levels results in a price adjustment below what would have been appropriate otherwise. By adjusting its price in this way, a firm can usually both increase its profits in the short run and encourage a change in quantity demanded to a more desirable level from the firm's point of view.

There is a crucial difference, however, between the adjustment of production and the adjustment of prices in response to a change in demand: Prices appear to be "sticky" compared with production. The adjustment of prices occurs gradually, whereas the adjustment of production and employment occurs almost instantaneously. In fact, in the very short run, it is usually a good approximation to ignore price adjustment and focus on the changes in production.

We have left out one important aspect of firms' behavior in our discussion so far. Many firms maintain a stock or inventory of their finished products, so that when there is an increase in demand, the immediate response is usually to meet the demand out of the inventory. Conversely, a drop in demand can be matched by an accumulation of inventory. Clearly, changes in demand that are exactly matched by changes in inventory do not affect production or GDP. However, for the economy as a whole, increases in sales are met with increases in production. Therefore, as an approximation, it is possible to ignore inventory adjustments and assume that changes in demand are directly translated into changes in production. A full treatment of the process of inventory adjustment is given in Chapter 11.

An Example: General Motors

Production in the automobile industry rises and falls by large magnitudes in response to changes in demand, and automobile purchases are a very large part of total spending, so this is an important example. During the large downturn from 1929 to 1933, for instance, annual production of automobiles in the United States fell from about 5 million to about 1 million cars. In the downturn from 1988 to 1991, production of cars at General Motors plants in the United States fell from 5.6 million to 4.3 million cars per year.

Consider what happens at GM when there is a change in the demand for automobiles. For example, suppose that there is an increase in demand for automobiles, as there typically is in a recovery period following a recession like the one that ended in 1991. In the short run, this increase in demand results in more automobiles being produced; some workers are asked to work more hours, others are recalled from layoff, some new workers are hired, plants are worked an extra shift, and plants that were closed earlier are reopened. Employment and capacity utilization in the automobile industry are increased to correspond to the increase in demand.

7.3 | THE POINT OF BALANCE OF INCOME AND SPENDING

MACROSOLVE
EXERCISE
The first step in studying spending behavior is to take account of the effects of income on spending. Recall that both income and spending are measured by GDP: When we add up total spending in the economy to get GDP, we also calculate total income. **Spending balance** occurs when the level of income used by consumers and other spenders in making their spending decisions is the same as the sum of the spending of all spenders.

It is important to distinguish spending balance from the concept of equilibrium used in the long-run growth model and many other parts of economics. In equilibrium, supply equals demand; firms and workers cannot make changes that will make both better off. The long-run growth model portrays the economy as being in equilibrium. Spending balance is a narrower concept. The consistency of total spending and individual incomes is just one requirement of equilibrium. As we will see, an economy can be in spending balance yet the quantity of labor supplied can exceed the quantity of labor demanded. In other words, the situation depicted in Figure 3.6 can occur when an economy is in spending balance.

To show how the principle of spending balance works, we start with the simple case where investment, government purchases, and net exports all are fixed and do not depend on income or the interest rate.

The Income Identity

We already looked at the income identity in Chapter 2. It says that

$$Y = C + I + G + X,$$ The Income Identity (7.1)

where Y is GDP, C is consumption, I is investment, G is government purchases, and X is net exports. GDP, consumption, investment, government purchases, and net exports in this identity are measured in real terms, as discussed in Chapter 2.

We now consider the components of spending. We start with consumption.

The Consumption Function

How do consumers make their spending decisions? The **consumption function** is a description of the total consumption demand of all families in the economy. It states that consumption depends on disposable income. *Disposable income*, as we saw in Chapter 2, is income less taxes. The consumption function is based on the simple idea that the larger is a family's disposable income, the larger that family's consumption is. Therefore, total consumption for all families in the economy is larger if disposable income in the economy is larger.

The consumption function should be viewed as a simple approximation of actual consumption. Clearly, consumption depends on other things in addition to current income: wealth, expected future income, and the price of goods today compared with tomorrow. We discuss these and other factors that affect consumption in Chapter 10. The more elementary consumption function used in this chapter was first introduced to the study of macroeconomics by John Maynard Keynes. Despite its simplicity, it has proven remarkably versatile as a macroeconomic tool.

When studying algebraic relationships like the consumption function in macroeconomics, it is very important to distinguish between the constants and the variables. Sometimes, constants are called *coefficients*. The consumption function contains both constants and variables. These elements are distinguished by the fact that variables move around and constants stay fixed. To highlight this important distinction, we use lowercase letters for constants and uppercase letters for variables. This convention is applied to the consumption function and for the remainder of this text, as you will see in the next chapter, when we discuss the money demand function.

The consumption function can be written algebraically as

$$C = a + bY_d.$$ The Consumption Function   (7.2)

Specifically, this algebraic formula says that consumption C is equal to some constant a plus another constant b times disposable income Y_d. Both constants (a and b) are positive and b is less than 1. The coefficient b is called the **marginal propensity to consume.** It measures how much of an additional dollar of disposable income is spent on consumption. The constant a is the intercept of the consumption function. The two coefficients work together to describe the relationship between income and consumption. Remember the distinction between the constants and the variables. In this consumption function the variables are C and Y_d. The constants, or coefficients, are a and b.

EXAMPLE.   If coefficient $a = 220$ and coefficient $b = 0.9$, then the consumption function looks like this:

$$C = 220 + 0.9Y_d.$$

If disposable income is $4,000 billion, then consumption is $220 billion + 0.9 · $4,000 billion, or $3,820 billion. If disposable income rises to $5,000 billion, then consumption rises to $220 billion + 0.9 · $5,000 billion, or $4,720 billion. If disposable income increases by $1,000 billion, consumption increases by $900 billion. Note how the variables, consumption and disposable income, change in this calculation but the coefficients stay fixed. The marginal propensity to consume in this example is 0.9—90 percent of each additional dollar of income is spent on consumption.

We can also represent the consumption function graphically, as in Figure 7.4. The vertical axis measures consumption. The horizontal axis measures disposable income. The consumption function is shown as a straight, upward-sloping line. It indicates that, as disposable income increases, so does consumption.

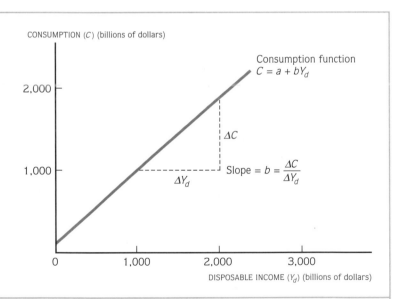

FIGURE 7.4   **THE CONSUMPTION FUNCTION**

Consumption depends on income. The upward-sloping line shows that higher levels of disposable income correspond to higher levels of consumption. The slope of the line tells us how much consumption changes when disposable income changes. The slope of the line equals the marginal propensity to consume.

The Consumption Function

1. Disposable income is the amount of income people have available to spend after taxes.

2. The consumption function says that there is a predictable relationship between disposable income and consumption. The higher is disposable income, the higher is consumption.

3. The marginal propensity to consume is the fraction of an increase in disposable income that is consumed.

We can also write the consumption function in terms of income rather than disposable income. Disposable income is obtained by subtracting income taxes from income. If the tax *rate* is given by the constant t, then total tax payments are tY. Disposable income Y_d equals income Y minus taxes tY. Therefore, we can write disposable income as $Y_d = (1 - t)Y$. For example, if the tax rate t is 0.3 and income Y is \$6,000 billion, then taxes are \$1,800 billion and disposable income is \$4,200 billion. By replacing disposable income Y_d with $(1 - t)Y$, the consumption function can be written

$$C = a + b(1 - t)Y. \qquad\qquad (7.3)$$

This says that consumption depends positively on income. For example, if the marginal propensity to consume b is 0.9 and the tax rate t is 0.3, then $b(1 - t) = 0.63$. An increase in income of \$100 billion increases consumption by \$63 billion. This alternative way to write the consumption function is useful because it has the same income variable Y that appears in the income identity.

So far we discussed the determinants of only one of the components of spending—consumption—but we already have the ingredients of an elementary theory of income or GDP determination. Before considering the determinants of the other components of spending—investment I, government G, and net exports X—we illustrate how this theory works. To do this, the values for investment, government spending, and net exports must be taken from *outside* the model. Variables determined outside a model are called *exogenous variables*. Of the five variables we discussed so far (income Y, consumption C, investment I, government spending G, and net exports X), this leaves two, consumption C and income Y, to be determined *inside* the model. Variables determined inside a model are called *endogenous variables*.

This basic idea that the endogenous variables must simultaneously satisfy a number of relationships is central to macroeconomic analysis. In the chapters that follow, we elaborate on this simple theory by adding more endogenous variables and more relationships that they must satisfy.

The elementary model consists of two basic relationships: the income identity, summarized algebraically in Equation 7.1, and the consumption function, summarized algebraically in Equation 7.3. These two relationships can be used to determine values for the two endogenous variables of the model:

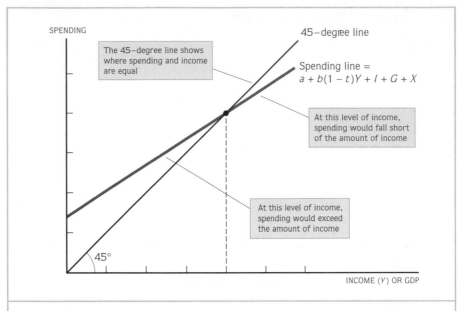

SPENDING

45−degree line

The 45−degree line shows
where spending and income
are equal

Spending line =
$a + b(1 - t)Y + I + G + X$

At this level of income,
spending would fall short
of the amount of income

At this level of income,
spending would exceed
the amount of income

45°

INCOME (Y) OR GDP

FIGURE 7.5   SPENDING BALANCE

The intersection of the two lines shows where consumption and income satisfy both the consumption function and the income identity. The point of intersection is the solution to the model consisting of Equations 7.1 and 7.3.

consumption C and income Y. *The values for C and Y are determined by requiring that both the consumption function and the income identity are satisfied simultaneously.*

Once we determine income and consumption in this way, we will have also determined GDP, of course, because income equals GDP. We illustrate the determination of income and consumption first using graphs and then using algebra.

Graphical Analysis of Spending Balance

In Figure 7.5 spending is measured on the vertical axis and income on the horizontal axis. Two intersecting straight lines are shown, a **spending line** and a **45-degree line.**

The spending line (the flatter of the two) shows how total spending depends on income. Total spending is the sum of consumption, investment, government spending, and net exports. In this model, only consumption depends on income, through the consumption function. Investment, government spending, and net exports are exogenous. The spending line is obtained by adding the consumption function in Equation 7.3 to investment, government spending, and net exports. The equation corresponding to the spending line is

$$\text{Spending} = \underbrace{a + b(1 - t)Y}_{\substack{\text{Consumption} \\ \text{from} \\ \text{Equation 7.3}}} + \underbrace{I}_{\substack{\text{Exogenous} \\ \text{investment}}} + \underbrace{G}_{\substack{\text{Exogenous} \\ \text{government} \\ \text{spending}}} + \underbrace{X.}_{\substack{\text{Exogenous} \\ \text{net exports}}}$$

The spending line thus incorporates the consumption function. The spending line is flatter than the 45-degree line because consumers spend only part of each added dollar of income. They save the rest.

The 45-degree line is drawn halfway between the vertical spending axis and the horizontal income axis. For any point on the 45-degree line, income equals spending. This line thus represents the income identity. The line makes a 45-degree angle with the horizontal axis; hence its name. Sometimes Figure 7.5 is called a *Keynesian 45-degree diagram*, or a *Keynesian cross* diagram, because of its early use to illustrate this simple model with a Keynesian consumption function.

The point of intersection of the spending line and the 45-degree line is the point where consumption and income satisfy both relationships of the model. On the 45-degree line, the income identity is satisfied. On the spending line, the consumption function is satisfied. The intersection of the two lines therefore gives the value of income we are looking for. At this point, total spending in the economy equals total income and consumption spending satisfies the consumption function. Income and spending are in balance.

The 45-degree line is steeper than the spending line. The 45-degree line has a slope of 1. The consumption function has a slope $b(1 - t)$, which is less than 1. For example, if $b = 0.9$ and $t = 0.3$, then $b(1 - t) = 0.63$. Because the lines have different slopes, they always intersect.[1]

Spending Balance

1. The simple model of income determination consists of two relationships, the consumption function and the income identity. The model determines two endogenous variables: consumption and income. Three exogenous variables—investment, government spending, and net exports—are determined outside the model.

2. Spending balance occurs when consumers choose their consumption levels, C, on the basis of a level of income that is the same as the level $Y = C + I + G + X$.

3. In terms of the equations, spending balance occurs at levels of consumption C and income Y that obey both the consumption function and the income identity.

---

[1] See the box on p. 175 for a review of the concept of slope.

Algebraic Solution

The levels of consumption and income can also be found algebraically. Substitute the consumption function, Equation 7.3, into Equation 7.1. The result is

$$Y = \underbrace{a + b(1 - t)Y}_{C} + I + G + X. \tag{7.4}$$

The brace below Equation 7.4 shows where C in the income identity has been replaced by the consumption function. Equation 7.4 has one endogenous variable, Y. Recall that I, G, and X are exogenous variables. The variable Y appears on both sides of Equation 7.4. To solve the equation for Y, we gather together both terms involving Y on the left-hand side of the equation. Doing so, we see that the value of Y that solves Equation 7.4 is given by

$$Y = \frac{a + I + G + X}{1 - b(1 - t)}. \tag{7.5}$$

This is the solution of the model and corresponds exactly to the value of Y, which is at the point of intersection in Figure 7.5. The solution value for consumption can then be obtained by plugging this value into the consumption function (Equation 7.3). That is,

$$C = a + b(1 - t)Y,$$

where Y comes from Equation 7.5.

EXAMPLE.   Suppose that investment equals $900 billion, government spending equals $1,200 billion, and net exports equal −$100 billion. Suppose, as in previous examples, the marginal propensity to consume b equals 0.9, the constant a equals 220, and the tax rate t equals 0.3. Then, according to the formula in Equation 7.5, income equals

$$\frac{220 + 900 + 1,200 - 100}{1 - .9(1 - .3)} = \frac{2,220}{.37},$$

or $6,000 billion. GDP also equals $6,000 billion. Using the consumption function (Equation 7.3), we find that consumption equals

$$220 + 0.9(1 - 0.3)(6,000),$$

or $4,000 billion.

How Spending Balance Is Maintained

It is important to understand the logic of finding the values of consumption and income that satisfy both the consumption function and the income identity. When people buy more in stores, firms will produce more. As we discussed

GRAPHS, SLOPES, AND INTERCEPTS VERSUS ALGEBRA AND COEFFICIENTS

Figure 7.4 and Equation 7.2 express exactly the same idea—that consumption depends positively on disposable income—in two different ways, graphically and algebraically. A third way is *verbal* presentation and analysis, which, although sometimes less precise, is necessary if you want to explain your economic ideas to those without economic training.

In general, a graph is a diagram with a line or lines showing the relationship between two variables. The lines can be straight, as with the consumption line, or bending, as with the aggregate demand curve (Figure 7.1). Relationships shown by straight lines are called *linear* relationships to distinguish them from those represented by bending lines. Sometimes, lines are called *schedules*, a term that derives from the presentation of the relationship numerically as two columns of numbers that look like a train schedule. Graphs provide a more intuitive understanding, and because visual images are sometimes easier to recall, graphs are good memory aids.

Algebra frequently provides more accurate and direct answers and is needed in more complex problems. Sometimes, only a rough sketch is needed for a graphical analysis, but it is important to know that there is a precise connection between a graphical and an algebraic representation of an economic relationship. The variable on the vertical axis of a graph is usually the one on the left-hand side of the equal sign in the algebraic expression. For the consumption function, the variable on the left-hand side is consumption. The variable on the horizontal axis is usually the one on the right-hand side of the equal sign in the algebraic expression. For the consumption function, the variable on the right-hand side is disposable income. The place where the vertical axis and horizontal axis cross sometimes represents the zero value for both variables, but this is not necessary. It is important to look carefully at the scale of a diagram. For diagrams that are simply rough illustrations, no numerical scale appears.

The place where the consumption line crosses the vertical axis in Figure 7.4 is called the *intercept*. It equals the coefficient a in the algebraic expression Equation 7.2. It gives the value of consumption when disposable income is zero. More generally, the intercept of any line is the place where the line crosses the vertical axis.

The steepness of the consumption line is measured by its *slope*. The slope tells us how much consumption increases when income increases by one unit. The slope of the line is the coefficient b in the algebraic expression. Hence, if disposable income increases by an amount ΔY_d, then consumption increases by an amount ΔC given by b times ΔY_d. On the graph, we move to the right by ΔY_d and up by b times ΔY_d. In general, a perfectly flat horizontal line has a slope of zero, and a perfectly vertical line has a slope of infinity. If the slope is positive, then we say that the line slopes *upward* as we move from left to right; if the slope is negative, then the line slopes *downward* as we move from left to right. The slope of the consumption function is positive (b is greater than zero), and clearly the consumption line slopes upward.

in the microeconomic example, firms then employ more workers or have their existing workers spend more time on the job. Their added production increases the wage incomes of their existing and new workers and adds to the profits of the owners of the firms. This added income, in turn, stimulates more consumption. When spending is in balance, the income consumers receive is the same as the income generated by their spending.

TABLE 7.1			

EXAMPLE OF THE MULTIPLIER PROCESS
(BILLIONS OF DOLLARS)

	REDUCTION IN GDP		
	THIS ROUND	SUM TO DATE	CALCULATION
Round 1	10.000	10.000	Exogenous drop in investment
Round 2	6.300	16.300	$b(1-t)(10) = (0.6300)(10)$
Round 3	3.969	20.269	$[b(1-t)]^2(10) = (0.3969)(10)$
Round 4	2.500	22.769	$[b(1-t)]^3(10) = (0.2500)(10)$
Round 5	1.575	24.344	$[b(1-t)]^4(10) = (0.1575)(10)$
Round 6	0.992	25.336	$[b(1-t)]^5(10) = (0.0992)(10)$

What happens if spending is not in balance? Suppose consumers spend too much relative to their incomes. The economy is in an untenable situation. Consumers notice that they are spending too much and contract their consumption. Then, firms produce less and workers' incomes fall. The process of contraction continues until consumption falls to a point of balance with income.

How do we know that the contraction of income and consumption ultimately reaches a point of balance rather than continues to a complete collapse of the economy? When families contract their consumption because their incomes fall, the contraction in consumption is less than the fall in income. Some of the fall in income results in reduced taxes, so that disposable income does not fall as much as national income. Moreover, the marginal propensity to consume is less than 1, so that the fall in disposable income results in a smaller reduction in consumption. The smaller reduction in consumption thus generates a smaller drop in income on the second round. So the process of consumption and income contraction converges to a new lower point of balance. A numerical example of this type of convergence is presented in Table 7.1.

We do not present a formal model of the detailed process by which the economy reaches a spending balance. The reason is that the process seems to operate quickly—more quickly than the business cycle or price adjustment. Our model assumes that the economy has already reached spending balance over each period of observation. Balance is not achieved by magic. But, it is a useful simplification to talk about the economy after it has gone through the process.[2]

---

[2] Some elementary texts describe the adjustment process by focusing on inventories: If output is greater than spending, inventories begin to rise and this leads firms to cut back on output. Output and spending are thus brought into equality. We prefer not to introduce inventories at this stage of the analysis. We feel that the description in the text is a close approximation to reality. Many types of businesses—medical services, education—do not hold inventories of finished products, yet their production responds to changes in demand.

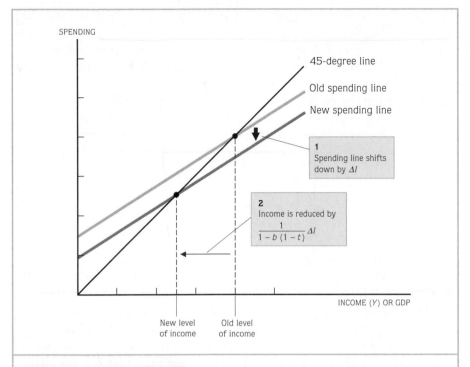

FIGURE 7.6   THE MULTIPLIER

A decrease in investment demand shifts the spending line down. The new point of intersection is at a lower level of GDP. The decline in GDP is larger than the decline in investment; this illustrates the multiplier mechanism. (Note that the drop in investment shown in the diagram is much larger than would be possible in the U.S. economy. The drop is exaggerated here so that it can be easily seen in the diagram.)

The Multiplier

To show how the elementary model can be used to analyze the short-run fluctuations in the economy, we consider what happens to income when there is a change in one of the exogenous variables. Suppose, for example, there is a *decrease* in investment I. The exact reasons for the decrease are not important at this time, but for concreteness you may think of a sudden decline in expected profitability that reduces firms' desire to invest. What are the implications of this decline in investment demand?

We first consider the situation graphically using the spending line and the 45-degree line in Figure 7.5 reproduced in Figure 7.6. The new diagram shows the impact of a decline in exogenous investment. It *shifts* the spending line downward by the amount of the decline in investment. If investment falls by $1 billion, then the spending line shifts down by $1 billion. To see this, note that the intercept of the spending line is $a + I + G + X$. Hence, the change in the intercept is the same as the change in investment; government spending and net exports do not change and a is constant. Figure 7.6 shows that income is lower as a result of the downward shift in the spending line.

Note that the decline in income is larger than the shift in the spending line, because the slope of the spending line is greater than zero. The economy thus "multiplies" the decline in investment into an even larger decline in income and GDP. This mechanism is called the **multiplier.** The steeper is the spending line, the larger the decline in income.

The effect of the decline in investment on income can be calculated algebraically. Looking back to Equation 7.5, if we change investment by an amount ΔI, then the change in income is given by

$$\Delta Y = \underbrace{\frac{1}{1 - b(1 - t)}}_{\text{The Multiplier}} \Delta I. \tag{7.6}$$

This is obtained by writing Equation 7.5 in terms of the changes in the variables and noting that neither government spending, net exports, nor the coefficient changes. All that is left is the change in investment.

The term $1/[1 - b(1 - t)]$, which multiplies the change in investment in Equation 7.6, is the multiplier. It is a general expression for the change in income associated with a change in investment. Since $1 - b(1 - t)$ is less than 1, the value of the multiplier in Equation 7.6 is greater than 1. Hence, the change in GDP is greater than the change in investment, just as we found using the graphical analysis. Note that the larger the marginal propensity to consume b, the larger the multiplier.

EXAMPLE.   If the marginal propensity to consume b is equal to 0.9 and the tax rate t is 0.3, then the multiplier is equal to 1/0.37, or about 2.7. A $10 billion *decrease* in investment results in a $27 billion decrease in income or GDP. Similarly, a $10 billion *increase* in investment results in a $27 billion increase in income or GDP.

This example can be used to illustrate the explicit actions of consumers and firms that result in the multiplier process. Suppose a $10 billion decrease in investment occurs because Hertz, Avis, and several other large car-rental companies in the United States suddenly get pessimistic about future profitability and stop buying new cars from General Motors and Ford. Initially, the decreased purchases of new cars decrease income and GDP by $10 billion. But the reduced automobile production means that the incomes of workers in those companies are reduced, as they work fewer hours or are laid off. The income of shareholders of GM and Ford is also reduced, because of the decline in profits. In this example, the income of workers and shareholders falls by the full $10 billion. If the workers and shareholders have a marginal propensity to consume of 0.9 and pay taxes equal to 30 percent of their income, then they reduce their consumption by $6.3 billion. Hence, GDP is cut by another $6.3 billion. The total reduction in GDP is now $16.3 billion.

But this is not the end. There is a third round. The workers and owners of the firms where the owners and employees of GM and Ford cut their purchases by $6.3 billion have a reduction in their income of this same amount. With the same taxes and marginal propensity to consume, they cut their consumption by 0.63 times $6.3 billion, or $3.969 billion. The total reduction in GDP is now $20.269 billion. The process continues for a fourth and fifth round and so on, but by this time, the reduction in income is diversified across many different firms in the economy. Some of the reduced consumption demand certainly gets back to GM and Ford.

If we keep summing the reduction in GDP at all these rounds, we eventually get a $27 billion reduction in GDP—the same as the direct computation using the multiplier. The total effect of these spending reductions on GDP usually occurs in a fairly short period, certainly less than a year. The different rounds of production are summarized in Table 7.1. Note how the eventual $27 billion reduction of GDP that we calculated directly through the multiplier is almost reached after just a few rounds. Note also how convenient it is to use the multiplier rather than go through all these tedious calculations.[3]

Fluctuations in investment have always been associated with cyclical fluctuations in GDP. Such fluctuations in investment were emphasized by Keynes as an essential source of business cycle fluctuations. One of Keynes's main contributions was to show that relatively small fluctuations in investment could lead to large fluctuations in GDP. The mechanism underlying Keynes's theory was the multiplier; our example of a decline in investment leading to a large decline in GDP provides a simple illustration of Keynes's theory.

Changes in the other exogenous variables—government spending and net exports—also result in changes in income. The analysis is exactly the same as the analysis of investment. For example, an increase in government spending raises income and GDP by a greater amount. The same multiplier process is at work. In fact, the formula for the government spending multiplier (the amount that income increases when government spending increases) is exactly the same as the investment multiplier.

The government spending multiplier can be derived in the same way that the investment multiplier was derived. To show this, we again reproduce the 45-degree line and the spending line from Figure 7.5 in Figure 7.7. An increase in government spending *raises* the spending line in Figure 7.7. This has an even

---

[3] The formulas for the calculations in the far right column of Table 7.1 add up to the formula for the multiplier: that is,

$$\frac{1}{1 - b(1 - t)} = 1 + b(1 - t) + [b(1 - t)]^2 + [b(1 - t)]^3 + \cdots.$$

This result can be shown using the formula for a geometric series. A formal algebraic model of the adjustment process could come from putting *past* income rather than current income in the consumption function. This leads to a dynamic model, called the *dynamic multiplier*, that describes how consumption adjusts over time after a sudden change in investment.

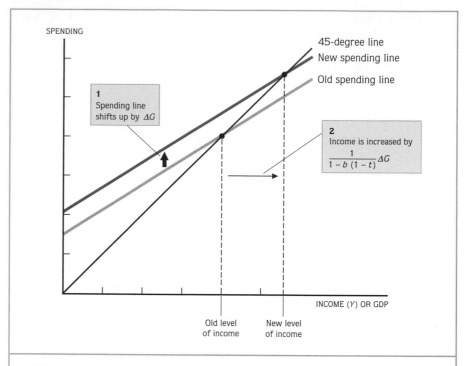

SPENDING

1
Spending line
shifts up by ΔG

45-degree line
New spending line
Old spending line

2
Income is increased by
$$\frac{1}{1 - b\,(1 - t)}\,\Delta G$$

INCOME (Y) OR GDP

Old level
of income

New level
of income

FIGURE 7.7   THE GOVERNMENT SPENDING MULTIPLIER

An increase in government spending shifts the spending line up. Income or GDP expands by the multiplier times the increase in government spending.

larger effect on income, because of the multiplier process. Knowing the size of the government spending multiplier is important for assessing the impact of a change in government policy on the economy.

The Multiplier

1. When investment rises, GDP rises; investment is part of total GDP.

2. As GDP rises, disposable income also rises, so consumption rises.

3. The increase in GDP is larger than the increase in investment, because of the increase in consumption. The multiplier measures the amount of GDP stimulated by an increase in investment or other categories of spending that are not themselves sensitive to income.

4. The formula for the multiplier is $1/[1 - b(1 - t)]$.

5. The government spending multiplier is exactly the same as the investment multiplier. When government spending increases, GDP increases by a larger amount.

Spending Balance When Net Exports Depend on Income

The next step is to drop the assumption that net exports are exogenous. We need to consider the influence of foreign trade and the value of the dollar on the macroeconomy. It is time to bring these crucial variables into the model—to consider the subject of *open-economy macroeconomics.*

As we saw in Chapter 2, foreign trade is divided into exports, sales of goods and services to the rest of the world, and imports, purchases of goods and services from the rest of the world. **Net exports** are simply exports less imports. When exports are greater than imports, there is a **trade surplus;** conversely, when exports are less than imports, there is a **trade deficit.**

Recall the income identity, Equation 7.1:

$$Y = C + I + G + \underbrace{}_{\substack{\text{Domestic} \\ \text{purchases}}} \underbrace{X}_{\substack{\text{Net exports} = \\ \text{Exports} - \text{Imports}}}$$

This income identity tells us two things: (1) Income and GDP are the same thing, and (2) aggregate demand, as measured by total spending, determines GDP. In thinking about how imports and exports affect the aggregate demand for goods produced in the United States, keep in mind that consumption C, investment I, and government spending G by Americans include some purchases of goods and services abroad. To get a measure of how much of American demand is for U.S.-produced goods, we need to subtract imports. For example, if Americans buy 1 million more cars, then consumption rises by 1 million cars. But, if all these cars are imported from abroad, then imports increase by 1 million cars and aggregate demand for U.S. goods (Y) does not change. The reason we add exports to the identity is straightforward: When foreigners increase their purchases of U.S.-produced goods, aggregate demand increases.

For this reason, we develop a relation between net exports and the level of U.S. income. The relation is negative. There is no reason to think that U.S. exports are affected by U.S. income; they are affected instead by incomes in the countries purchasing the exports. But imports are affected by U.S. income. When U.S. income rises, consumers increase their spending on imported as well as domestic goods.

We can summarize the relation between income and net exports in a **net export function:**

$$X = g - mY. \tag{7.7}$$

Here g is a constant and m is a coefficient. For each dollar that GDP rises, imports rise by m dollars. Exports remain unchanged, so net exports fall by the same m dollars.

Compare the net export function with the consumption function, discussed earlier in this chapter. Net exports, like consumption, depend on income. But net exports *decline* by *m* dollars for each dollar increase in income, whereas consumption *rises* by *b* dollars for each dollar increase in income (*b* is the marginal propensity to consume). The reason that net exports decline with income is that imports rise by *m* dollars for each dollar increase in income. For this reason, the coefficient *m* is sometimes called the **marginal propensity to import.** The dependence of net exports on income means that we need to take account of the response of net exports to income when we calculate the effects of monetary and fiscal policy, much as we took account of the response of consumption earlier in this chapter.

Now we can proceed exactly as we did before to develop an equation for spending balance by putting the net export function and the consumption function into the income identity. We did that before to get Equation 7.4. The corresponding equation is

$$Y = a + b(1 - t)Y + I + G + g - mY. \tag{7.8}$$

Again, we can solve for the value of *Y* at the point of spending balance. Previously, we got Equation 7.5. Now we get

$$Y = \frac{a + I + G + g}{1 - b(1 - t) + m} \tag{7.9}$$

Note how the impact of a change in government spending on output is

$$\frac{1}{1 - b(1 - t) + m}$$

This is the **open-economy multiplier.** Note that the multiplier is smaller when the marginal propensity to import is larger. By setting *m* equal to zero, the multiplier is the same as the multiplier for a closed economy. For example, if the marginal propensity to consume *b* is 0.9, the tax rate *t* is 0.3, and the marginal propensity to import *m* is 0.1, then the multiplier is 1/0.47 = 2.1, compared with a multiplier of 1/0.37 = 2.7 for the closed economy.

At this point, we can begin to analyze how policy or other economic forces affect the trade deficit. Recall from Chapter 2 that the trade deficit, as measured in the national income accounts, is just the negative of net exports. Anything that lowers net exports raises the deficit. Looking at the net export function, Equation 7.7, we can see that net exports, in turn, respond negatively to the level of GDP. Combining the two, we can say that forces that raise GDP also raise the trade deficit. In particular, an increase in government spending G raises GDP according to the multiplier derived in Equation 7.9. Therefore, increases in G raise the trade deficit. Since increases in G also raise the fiscal deficit, we can see that the two deficits are related; when the government takes an action that raises its own deficit, it causes the trade deficit to rise as well.

In Chapter 2, we noted that the trade deficit is also the total amount Americans are borrowing from overseas. An increase in the trade deficit means an increase in borrowing. Therefore, we can express the relation between fiscal

THE DECLINE OF THE MULTIPLIER

At your first exposure to the multiplier, you may be very impressed. If the marginal propensity to spend b is 0.9 and there are no taxes, then the multiplier is 10! But, when you consider the role of taxes in reducing disposable income, you get the multiplier in Equation 7.6, which we said would be about 2.7. When we consider that some of the purchasing power stimulated by growth in demand would go into imports rather than domestic spending, the multiplier drops some more, to about 2.1.

Other factors, which we study in later chapters, further reduce the multiplier. In the next chapter, we consider that higher demand raises interest rates, and these in turn discourage investment and net exports. Then the multiplier in our standard example will be only 1.1.

and trade deficits in the following way: When some force, such as higher government spending, raises government borrowing, part of the borrowing is done overseas. Instead of obtaining all the resources to be devoted to government spending from the domestic economy, some of them come from foreign economies.

In the rest of the book, the models we develop consider net exports as endogenous.

Spending Balance in an Open Economy

1. The net export function describes the negative relation between income and net exports. It arises because higher U.S. income causes higher U.S. imports from other countries.

2. The multiplier is smaller in an open economy than a closed economy.

3. Events that raise GDP, such as higher government spending, cause net exports to fall and the trade deficit to rise. Part of an increase in the fiscal deficit is financed overseas through a higher trade deficit.

REVIEW AND PRACTICE

Major Points

1. In the short run, output is determined by the aggregate demand for goods and services in the economy.

2. In the short run, firms respond to an increase in demand by producing more output rather than by raising prices.

3. The consumption function expresses the positive relation between income and consumption.

4. Spending balance occurs when consumption plus investment plus government purchases plus net exports add up to the level of GDP on which the consumers make their consumption plan.

5. The investment multiplier expresses the relation between investment and GDP. When investment rises by $1 billion, GDP rises by more than $1 billion because consumption rises as GDP rises.

6. Spending balance in an open economy occurs when the sum of all spending, including net exports, equals GDP.

7. The multiplier for an open economy is less than the multiplier for a closed economy.

8. An increase in government spending increases both the fiscal deficit and the trade deficit.

Key Terms and Concepts

aggregate demand	trade deficit
spending balance	trade surplus
consumption function	net export function
marginal propensity to consume	marginal propensity to import
multiplier	open-economy multiplier
net exports	

Questions for Discussion and Review

1. What factors can push the economy out of equilibrium in the short run?

2. How is the level of employment determined in short-run disequilibrium situations?

3. What does the aggregate demand schedule measure?

4. How do firms typically respond to an increase in demand in the short run?

5. What happens to consumption if income rises? If taxes are cut?

6. What is true at the point of spending balance? What happens if the economy is not at a point of spending balance?

7. What happens to GDP if consumers change their behavior in such a way that the constant *a* in the consumption function increases?

8. Why does an increase in investment or government purchases bring about a large increase in GDP?

9. Explain why the open-economy multiplier is smaller than the closed-economy multiplier.

10. How does an increase in government spending affect the trade deficit?

Problems

NUMERICAL

1. Suppose that the model of the economy is given by

$$Y = C + I + G + X$$
$$C = a + bY_d$$
$$Y_d = (1 - t)Y$$
$$X = g - mY,$$

where $I = \$900$ billion, $G = \$1,200$ billion, and the constants take the following values: $a = 220$, $b = 0.9$, $t = 0.3$, $g = 500$, and $m = 0.1$.

a. Show that the value of GDP at the point of spending balance is $\$6,000$ billion. Compared with the example on page 178 with exogenous net exports, is the multiplier larger or smaller?

b. What proportion of investment is private saving? Government saving? Saving by the rest of the world?

c. Now, suppose that I increases by $\$100$ billion. By what proportion of the increase in investment do each of the three categories of saving increase?

2. Consider a closed-economy model given by the following equations:

$$Y = C + I + G$$
$$C = 160 + 0.8Y_d$$
$$Y_d = (1 - t)Y - Z$$

Investment and government spending are exogenous and each equals 200. The tax system has two components: a lump-sum tax denoted by Z and an income tax of rate t.

a. Assume Z equals 200 and t is 0.25. Find the level of income that satisfies spending balance. How much does the government collect in taxes at that level of income? What is the level of government saving?

b. Suppose the lump-sum tax is reduced to 100. Find the new level of income consistent with spending balance. What is the lump-sum tax multiplier? What are the new levels of tax collections and government saving?

c. Comparing your answers in parts a and b, does the tax cut increase or decrease tax receipts? By how much? Explain why tax receipts do not simply fall by 100 with the cut in lump-sum taxes.

d. One of the arguments of "supply-side" economists in the early 1980s was that a tax cut could actually reduce the budget deficit. Can that happen with a lump-sum tax cut in the model used in this problem? Does the spending balance model ignore factors that the "supply-siders" think are important for this problem? If so, name them.

ANALYTICAL

1. Imagine that you operate an economic forecasting firm. Your stock in trade is that you know the true model of the U.S. economy. It is given by the formula

$$Y = C + I + G + X$$
$$C = a + bY_d$$
$$Y_d = (1 - t)Y$$
$$X = g - mY,$$

where I and G are exogenous, and it is assumed that you have numerical values for all of the constants in the model.

a. Of the four spending components, which must you forecast before arriving at a forecast for the U.S. GDP? Explain.

b. Now suppose that you are trying to forecast GDP for a centrally planned economy in which the production schedules for all goods are determined a year in advance. Would forecasting C, I, G, and X be a very good way of forecasting GDP?

2. For the model given in problem 1, explain why private saving, government saving and saving by the rest of the world are all endogenous variables.

3. Suppose the economy is described by the following simple model:

$$Y = C + G$$
$$C = a + bY_d$$
$$Y_d = (1 - t)Y$$

a. Give an expression that relates private saving S_p to disposable income. This is called the *saving function*.

b. What must the relationship be between private saving and the government budget deficit? (Hint: Refer back to the discussion in Chapter 2 concerning the relationship between saving and investment.)

c. Solve for the values of S_p and the budget deficit; that is, derive an expression for each that is a function only of the exogenous variable G

and the constants in the model. Are your expressions consistent with your answer to part b?

4. Consider the following simple model with investment and government spending exogenous:

$$Y = C + I + G$$
$$C = a + bY_d$$

Disposable income Y_d is given by $Y - T$, where T is total taxes. Suppose that taxes are not directly related to income, so that T can be increased or decreased independent of income.

  a. Derive the change in Y associated with an increase in taxes T. Show the results graphically and algebraically. What is the tax multiplier? That is, what is $\Delta Y / \Delta T$?

  b. Compare the tax multiplier with the government spending multiplier derived in the text. Aside from the difference in signs, which is larger? Why?

  c. Now increase government spending G and taxes T by the same amount. For this change, the government budget deficit $G - T$ does not change. If the budget was balanced before, it will still be balanced. What happens to income Y in this case? Perhaps surprisingly, it increases. Calculate by how much. That is, using algebra, calculate $\Delta Y / \Delta G$; $\Delta G = \Delta T$. The result is called the *balanced budget multiplier.*

5. For the model given in problem 1, which of the following statements are true?

  a. An exogenous increase in net exports (i.e., an increase in g) lowers the trade deficit and the government budget deficit.

  b. An increase in investment lowers the government budget deficit but raises the trade deficit.

  c. An increase in government spending and taxes of the same amount leaves both the government budget deficit and the trade deficit unchanged.

6. Imagine an economy in which the government spent all its tax revenues but was prevented (by a balanced budget amendment) from spending any more; hence, $G = tY$, where t is the tax rate.

  a. Explain why government spending is endogenous in the model.

  b. Is the multiplier larger or smaller than the case in which government spending is exogenous?

  c. When t increases, does Y increase, decrease, or stay the same?

FINANCIAL MARKETS AND AGGREGATE DEMAND

Spending balance, as discussed in the last chapter, involves finding the level of GDP that makes the spending plans of consumers and others consistent with their actual levels of income. In this chapter, we complete the discussion of spending balance by bringing in another key variable, the interest rate. Spending depends on the interest rate because of the sensitivity of investment and net exports to the interest rate. To tell the full story of the interest rate, we have to consider the money market. We introduce the IS-LM framework to help develop the story. The IS-LM framework combines the money market and the spending process. We use the IS-LM approach in the rest of the book to describe the determination of output and interest rates in the short run. At the end of this chapter, we use the IS-LM framework to derive the aggregate demand curve.

8.1 | INVESTMENT AND THE INTEREST RATE

In the description of spending balance in Chapter 7, two exogenous forces could affect the level of GDP corresponding to spending balance—investment and government spending. In this section, we introduce **financial variables**—interest rates and the supply of money—into the model. We show that investment depends on these financial variables. Investment is no longer determined outside the model; it becomes an endogenous variable. The addition of financial variables to the model means that we are concerned with the effects of changes in the money supply and interest rates, as well as with government spending.

The Investment Demand Function

When we change investment from an exogenous variable to an endogenous variable, we need to specify a behavioral relationship to explain how investment is determined within the model. The relationship we use to describe investment is a simple but fundamental one. It states that investment depends negatively on the interest rate. This means that the demand for investment goods—the new factories, offices, and equipment used by business firms, as well as the new houses built for residential use—is low when interest rates are high and vice versa.

The major reason for this negative relationship is that business firms and consumers finance many of their investment purchases by borrowing. When borrowing costs are high because of high interest rates, firms and consumers tend to make fewer investment purchases. High borrowing costs effectively make investment goods more costly. Note that, even if borrowing is not the source of funds for investment (such as when the funds come from selling financial securities), the interest rate still matters. If interest rates are high, then not holding those securities represents a larger loss of income on those securities than if interest rates are low. Hence, if interest rates are high, people are reluctant to sell those securities to purchase physical investment goods.

In algebraic terms the relationship for investment demand, called the **investment function,** can be represented as

$$I = e - dR.$$ (8.1)

As before, I is investment, R is the interest rate, and e and d are constants. Investment is measured in billions of dollars, and the interest rate is measured in percentage points. Equation 8.1 says that investment demand is equal to a constant e minus another constant d times the interest rate. The coefficient d measures how much investment falls when the interest rate increases by 1 percentage point. Note that we keep the convention that lowercase letters represent constant coefficients, while uppercase letters represent variables. The investment function is shown graphically in Figure 8.1. It is a downward-sloping line.

EXAMPLE   Suppose e equals 1,000 and d equals 2,000; then Equation 8.1 looks like

$$I = 1,000 - 2,000\,R.$$

When the interest rate is 5 percent, investment I is $1,000 - 2,000(0.05)$, or \$900 billion. An increase in the interest rate of 1 percent reduces investment by \$20 billion. Note that we speak about the interest rate R as a percent, but use decimals in algebraic formulas: "The interest rate is 5 percent" means $R = 0.05$. This convention is used throughout the book.

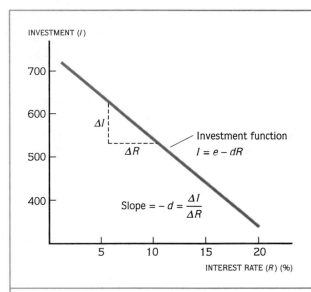

FIGURE 8.1   THE INVESTMENT FUNCTION
When the interest rate rises, the demand for investment falls. A higher interest rate means that the cost of funds required for investment is higher; only those investment projects that are particularly profitable are undertaken.

The Meaning and Interpretation of R

Note that, in changing investment from an exogenous variable to an endogenous variable, we introduced a new endogenous variable into the model: the interest rate, R. There are, of course, many different interest rates in a modern economy: rates on *long*-term securities, rates on *short*-term securities, rates on *risky* securities, and rates on *safe* securities. When we use the term "*the* interest rate," we therefore simplify the financial structure of the economy. In thinking about this simplification—that is, in trying to relate R to something you can read about or look up in a newspaper—it is useful to imagine an average or representative interest rate that represents the behavior of all the different types of rates. For many purposes, this abstraction is not too bad; interest rates on different types of securities, while not equal, tend to move in the same direction. That is, when interest rates on risk-free Treasury bills are abnormally high, so are interest rates on more risky corporate bonds. Of course, there are sometimes differences between short- and long-term interest-rate behavior. Long-term interest rates depend on expectations of future short-term rates. However, we focus on the average representative interest rate, R.

It is also important to distinguish between the real interest rate and the nominal interest rate. As noted in Chapter 1, the nominal interest rate is simply the rate you read about in the newspaper or that banks place in their windows to indicate what they will pay for different types of deposits. The real interest rate corrects the nominal rate for expected changes in the price level. Specifically, the real interest rate is the nominal interest rate minus the expected rate of inflation. For example, if your bank is paying 10 percent on deposits for a year and you expect inflation to be 6 percent for the year, then the real rate of interest for you is 4 percent. The real rate of interest measures how much you earn on your deposit after taking account of the fact that inflation increases the price of goods that you might purchase in a year. We usually mean the real interest rate when we use the symbol R in this book, but we do not generally add the adjective *real*, unless the meaning is ambiguous or we want to point out a particular reason to distinguish between the real and the nominal rates. For low rates of inflation, the real rate and the nominal rate are very close.

The Investment Function

1. Investment demand is negatively related to the interest rate. When funds are more expensive, less investment takes place. The investment function describes this negative relationship.

2. The interest rate R in the investment function is an average of the many interest rates we observe at banks and in the financial markets.

8.2 | NET EXPORTS AND THE INTEREST RATE

Another factor we want to consider in building a model of aggregate demand is that net exports depend negatively on the interest rate. In Chapter 12, we consider the reasons for this important relation in more detail. For now, we look at the relation in the following way: When the U.S. interest rate is higher than interest rates in other countries, it becomes attractive for people in those countries to put their funds in *dollars*, that is, to lend funds to businesses in the United States and the U.S. government. By the same token, it is less attractive for people in the United States to put their funds in other currencies, that is, to lend overseas, where returns are lower. This means that dollars become more attractive, and this drives up the price of dollars; that is, the exchange rate rises. But, a higher exchange rate makes U.S. goods more expensive to foreigners and foreign goods less expensive to U.S. residents. Less-expensive foreign goods make U.S. imports rise. Similarly, more expensive U.S. goods make U.S. exports fall. On both accounts, *net exports (exports minus imports) fall when the U.S. interest rate rises,* because the exchange rate rises.

How do we incorporate this negative relationship between net exports and the interest rate into our model of aggregate demand? We must add another term to the net export function of Equation 7.7 to incorporate the negative effect of the interest rate R on net exports:

$$X = g - mY - nR. \qquad (8.2)$$

The new coefficient n measures the decrease in net exports that occurs when the interest rate rises by 1 percentage point.

EXAMPLE   Suppose g is 525, m is 0.1, and n is 500. Then the net export function is

$$X = 525 - 0.1Y - 500R.$$

8.3 | THE DEMAND FOR AND SUPPLY OF MONEY

When we speak of **money**, we have a rather special meaning in mind. Money is the currency issued by the Federal Reserve (for example, coins and dollar bills) together with the checking account balances held by the public in banks. Money is used to facilitate the purchase and sale of goods. When we buy goods, we usually pay with currency or a check. Money does not include the much larger amounts of wealth held in mutual funds, bonds, corporate stock, and other forms, even though these forms of wealth are measured in dollars, because they are not usually used to pay for goods.

The Demand for Money

Three basic propositions about the demand for money are important for macroeconomics:

1. *People want to hold less money when the interest rate is high and, conversely, hold more money when the interest rate is low.* This means that there is a negative relation between the demand for money and the interest rate R. People hold money for transactions purposes, to pay daily expenses and monthly bills. But they could obtain higher earnings by keeping their wealth in other forms, such as savings accounts or bonds. Currency pays no interest. And, even though many checking deposits pay interest, the rate is less than on other forms of wealth. Because of this, people tend to economize on the use of money for transaction purposes. A common way to do this is to go to the ATM or bank more often to withdraw money from a high-interest savings account to obtain currency, or simply to transfer funds to a lower-interest checking account. With more frequent trips, a smaller amount can be withdrawn each time from savings accounts. This means that, on average, a smaller amount of currency or

checking balances are held by the individual. For example, you could go to the ATM every week, rather than every month, to obtain currency and thereby hold a smaller amount of currency on average.

How much economizing occurs depends on the interest rate. The interest rate R represents how much a consumer or firm could earn by holding more wealth in forms that pay full interest instead of in currency, which pays no interest, or checking deposits, which pay less than full interest. Clearly, the more that can be earned by holding those other forms—the higher R is—the less money an individual or firm wants to hold.

2. ***People want to hold more money when income is higher and, conversely, less money when income is lower.*** The more a family receives as income, the more the family normally spends, and the more money the family needs for transaction purposes. When income increases, the transaction demand for money increases. More money is needed to buy and sell goods.

   This means that there is a positive relationship between income Y and the demand for money. As income in the economy increases, on average, each family's income increases and the demand for money in the entire economy increases.

3. ***People want to hold more money when the price level is higher and, conversely, less money when the price level is lower.*** If the price level rises, people need more dollars to carry out their transactions, even if their real income does not increase. At a higher price level, goods and services are more expensive; more currency is needed to pay for them and checks are written for larger amounts. This means that the demand for money is an increasing function of the price level.

To summarize these three basic ideas, the demand for money depends negatively on the interest rate R, positively on income Y, and positively on the price level P. An algebraic relationship that summarizes the effect of these three variables on the demand for money is presented in the following equation:

$$M = (kY - hR)P. \tag{8.3}$$

Here, M represents the amount of money demanded by firms and consumers. The other variables in Equation 8.3 have already been defined: P is the price level, R is the interest rate, and Y is income or GDP. The lowercase symbols k and h are positive coefficients: The coefficient k measures how much money demand increases when income increases; the coefficient h measures how much money demand declines when the interest rate increases.[1] Equation 8.3

---

[1] Note that the appropriate interest rate for the money demand function is the nominal rate. Most alternatives to holding currency, such as bonds, pay a nominal interest rate. To keep our analysis simple, we place the real interest rate R in the money demand function. If inflation is low, this is a very good approximation.

is called the **money demand function.** It is a more complicated algebraic expression than the equation used previously for consumption and investment demand. The money demand function shows that money demand depends on three variables (the interest rate R, income Y, and the price level P), whereas consumption demand and investment demand each depend on only one variable.

As we discussed in the last chapter, when studying algebraic relationships like the money demand function in macroeconomics, it is very important to distinguish between the constants, or coefficients, and the variables. In the money demand function, the variables are M, Y, R, and P. The coefficients are k and h. Variables move around; constants stay fixed. We use lowercase letters for constants and uppercase letters for variables.

EXAMPLE   If k equals 0.1583 and h equals 1,000, then Equation 8.3 looks like this:

$$M = (0.1583Y - 1,000R)P.$$

If income Y is \$6,000 billion, the interest rate is 5 percent ($R = 0.05$), and the price level P is 1, then the demand for money equals \$900 billion. An increase in income of \$10 billion increases the demand for money by \$1.583 billion. An increase in the interest rate of 1 percentage point decreases the demand for money by \$10 billion.

The Supply of Money

The Federal Reserve System determines the level of the **money supply.** In Chapter 14, we study the interesting question of how the Fed goes about setting the money supply. For now, we assume that the Fed has picked a certain level for the money supply.

We also assume that the demand for money and the supply of money are equal. For this reason, we do not introduce a new symbol to represent the money supply; the variable M means both money supply and money demand. Since these are always equal, this should cause little confusion. (Recall that the symbol Y also refers to two variables: income and GDP.)

How does the demand for money become equal to the supply of money? Suppose that the demand is greater than the supply. Since the supply of money is fixed by the Fed, the demand for money must fall if the two are to be equal. The demand for money can adjust down by an increase in the interest rate, a decline in the level of income, or a decline in the price level. For example, an increase in the interest rate causes people to demand less money. In principle, all three variables could move, but in the economic fluctuations model, the price level is predetermined. Thus, income and the interest rate can move to equilibrate the money market.

Money and the Interest Rate

1. Money is currency plus the balances in checking accounts.

2. The demand for money falls if the interest rate rises, income falls, or the price level falls.

3. The Federal Reserve determines the money supply.

8.4 | THE IS CURVE AND THE LM CURVE

MACROSOLVE
EXERCISE

Now that we have developed all the economic relationships needed to understand short-run spending behavior, we can tackle the problem of short-run output and interest-rate determination. Recall that this is a challenging problem because output and the interest rate are determined simultaneously.

KEY MACRO RELATIONSHIPS

Macro Variables

Endogenous Variables:		*Exogenous* Variables:	
Income	Y	Government purchases	G
Consumption	C	Money supply	M
Investment	I		
Net exports	X		
Interest rate	R		

Predetermined Variable:

Price level P

Five Relationships (how the variables interact with each other)

Algebra		Name	Numerical Example
$Y = C + I + G + X$	(7.1)	Income identity	
$C = a + b(1 - t)Y$	(7.3)	Consumption function	$C = 220 + 0.63Y$
$I = e - dR$	(8.1)	Investment function	$I = 1,000 - 2,000R$
$X = g - mY - nR$	(8.2)	Net export function	$X = 525 - 0.1Y - 500R$
$M = (kY - hR)P$	(8.3)	Money demand	$M = (0.1583Y - 1,000R)P$

The IS and LM curves are convenient ways to describe the solution to the problem.

In the short-run model, we take the price level as given or predetermined. Five economic relationships must be considered: the income identity, the consumption function, the investment demand function, the net export function, and the money demand function. The theory implies that all five relationships must hold at the same time.

The analysis proceeds as follows: We take as given the values for the variables determined outside our model in any year, for example, 2005. These are the exogenous variables: the money supply M and government spending G. They are determined by the Federal Reserve, the President, and Congress. We want to find values for income, consumption, investment, net exports, the interest rate, and the price level that are implied by the model and by the values of the money supply and government spending for that year. We also want to find out what happens if the money supply or government spending changes. Will interest rates and output rise or fall, and by how much? The economic relationships and the key macroeconomic variables are summarized in the box on key macro relationships.

Suppose that $P = 1$. Then the five macro relationships determine values for the five remaining endogenous variables. The situation is analogous to that in Chapter 7 where we had to find values for two variables to satisfy two relationships. We first use graphs and then algebra.

Because graphs allow for only two variables, we need to reduce the five relationships to two relationships. A way to do this was originally proposed in 1937 by J. R. Hicks, the British economist who won the Nobel Prize in 1972. Hick's graphical approach, called the IS-LM approach, is still used widely today because of its great intuitive appeal.[2]

The IS Curve

The **IS curve** is shown in Figure 8.2. *The IS curve shows all the combinations of the interest rate R and income Y that satisfy the income identity, the consumption function, the investment function, and the net export function.* In other words, it is the <u>set of points for which spending balance occurs</u>. The left-hand panel of Figure 8.2 shows how higher levels of the interest rate are associated with lower levels of GDP along the IS curve.

SLOPE   The first thing to remember about the IS curve is that it slopes downward. Understanding the intuitive economic reason for this downward slope is very important. *The IS curve slopes downward because a higher interest rate reduces*

---

[2] See J. R. Hicks, "Mr. Keynes and the Classics: A Suggested Interpretation," *Econometrica*, Vol. 6 (1937), pp. 147–159. The IS curve gets its name because, when all relationships are satisfied, investment demand, I, must equal income less consumption demand, or saving, S. The M in the LM curve stands for the money supply and the L stands for liquidity preference, which is a synonym for money demand. (Money is more liquid—easier to exchange for goods and other items—than bonds or corporate stock.)

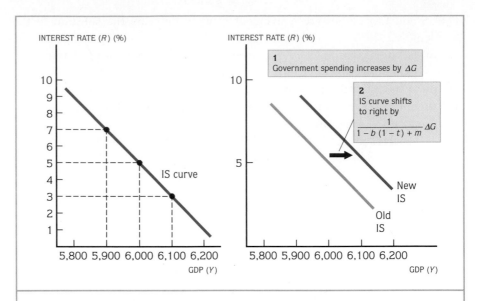

FIGURE 8.2   THE IS CURVE

The IS curve shows all the combinations of the interest rate R and income Y that satisfy the consumption, investment, and net export functions and the income identity. As shown in the left-hand panel, it is downward sloping; an increase in the interest rate reduces investment and net exports. Through the multiplier, GDP falls. The right-hand panel illustrates how the IS curve shifts to the right when government spending increases.

investment and net exports and thereby reduces GDP through the multiplier process. To find a specific point on the IS curve, choose an interest rate and calculate how much investment and net exports result using the investment function and the net export function. The higher is the rate of interest, the lower the level of investment and net exports. Pass this level of spending through the multiplier process to find out how much GDP results. The less there are of both, the less GDP. The interest rate and this level of GDP are a point on the IS curve. A self-contained explicit graphical derivation of the IS curve is shown in Figure 8.3

SHIFTS   The second thing to remember about the IS curve is that *an increase in government spending shifts the IS curve to the right*. An increase in government spending increases GDP through the multiplier; as GDP increases, we move the IS curve to the right. Note that, conversely, a decrease in government spending pushes the IS curve to the left.

To find how much the IS curve shifts, pick an interest rate R and calculate a corresponding level of investment and net exports. Now increase government spending. Through the multiplier process, output increases by the multiplier times the increase in government spending. Holding the interest rate constant, the IS curve shifts to the right along the horizontal GDP axis by the amount of

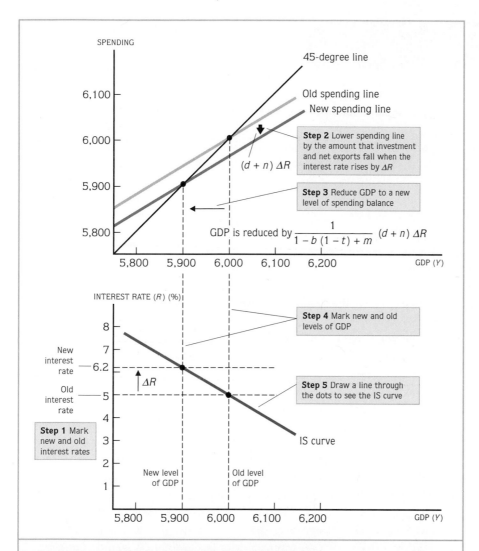

FIGURE 8.3   GRAPHICAL DERIVATION OF THE IS CURVE

The upper part of the diagram shows the 45-degree line and spending line. The lower part of the diagram is the graph where the IS curve is to be drawn. The lower diagram has the interest rate on the vertical axis and GDP on the horizontal axis. Points on the graph are obtained as described in the instructions placed in boxes on the diagram. Start with an interest rate and find the position of the spending line for that interest rate. (Higher interest rates lower the spending line because they reduce investment and net exports.) Then find the resulting level of GDP that satisfies the requirements of spending balance. Note how the slope of the IS curve depends on the marginal propensity to consume b, the tax rate t, and the marginal propensity to import m, because these affect the multiplier. Note also that the slope depends on the sensitivity of investment and net exports to changes in the interest rate, controlled by the coefficients d and n.

RESEARCH IN PRACTICE
The Stock Market

In this book, the interest rate plays a fundamental role. When the interest rate is high, firms have an incentive to defer investment; households have an incentive to defer purchases, especially of cars and other durable goods; and the United States draws on the resources of other countries by importing more than it exports. For simplicity, we consider a single interest rate. In fact, not only are there many different interest rates, but the stock market is just as important as the bond market in channeling resources from sectors whose incomes exceed their purchases to sectors where resources are needed. The financial pages of the newspaper spend more space on the stock market than on the bond market. What have we left out by concentrating on the interest rate and not discussing the returns on stocks?

The Nobel Prize in economics was awarded to Harry Markowitz, Merton Miller, and William Sharpe in 1991 for their development of the theory of the relation between interest rates and returns in the stock market. Their work has not remained a theoretical abstraction. The capital asset pricing model (CAPM) they developed is used on Wall Street to make decisions about trillion-dollar portfolios. The ideas behind the CAPM help explain not only the prices of stocks, but also the prices of derivatives—securities such as options whose payoffs depend on the prices of stocks or bonds.*

The CAPM focuses on one interest rate, called the *risk-free rate*, usually measured as the interest rate on Treasury bills (short-term bonds issued by the federal government). The CAPM, along with almost all modern finance theory, relies on the idea of *arbitrage* to explain the prices of stocks and other securities. Arbitrage occurs when an organization takes on an obligation and buys some other securities that offset the risk that it would otherwise face from the obligation. The CAPM assumes the absence of arbitrage profits to arrive at formulas for predicting the prices of stocks and other securities.

The most basic principle of the CAPM is that there is one portfolio—containing all stocks in proportion to their presence in the market—with a unique role in finance. It is called the *market portfolio*. Investors get the best combination of risk and return by holding a fraction of their wealth in Treasury bills and the rest in the market portfolio. A risk-averse investor holds mostly Treasury bills; a risk-tolerant investor holds mostly the market portfolio. The return expected from the market portfolio is 5 to 7 percentage points higher than the risk-free rate, so the investor willing to take on risk generally earns a higher return.

Instead of having to think about the returns to each of thousands of different stocks and bonds, according to the CAPM, we have to think about only the risk-free rate and the expected return on the market portfolio. All other rates or returns are weighted averages of these two, with weights that depend on risk. Moreover, there are good reasons to think that the premium between the expected return on the market portfolio and the risk-free rate (the equity or risk premium) is reasonably stable over time. Then all rates move up and down along with the Treasury bill rate. In that case, the approach we take in this book, considering just one interest rate, is completely sound. One rate can stand in for all interest rates and expected returns on all stocks.

Of course, the world may be more complex than this model suggests. With the huge increase in stock prices in the 1980s and 1990s, the equity premium may have declined—it is possible that investors today are not going to earn 5 to 7 percentage points more than on Treasury bills. And cutting-edge versions of the CAPM used on Wall Street today do not use a single market portfolio— they use models with multiple aggregate influences.

*See Richard A. Brealey and Stewart C. Myers, *Principles of Corporate Finance*, 7th ed. (New York: McGraw-Hill, 2003).

the multiplier times the increase in government spending. This is shown in the right-hand panel of Figure 8.2.

The LM Curve

The **LM curve** is shown in Figure 8.4. *The LM curve shows all combinations of the interest rate R and income Y that satisfy the money demand relationship for a fixed level of the money supply and a predetermined value of the price level.* The left-hand panel of Figure 8.4 shows that higher levels of the interest rate are associated with higher levels of GDP along the LM curve.

SLOPE   The first thing to remember about the LM curve is that it slopes upward. The reason for this is somewhat involved, but important to keep in mind. Imagine that the interest rate increases. What must happen to income if money demand is to remain equal to money supply? An increase in the interest rate R reduces the demand for money. But the money supply is fixed. Hence, income must adjust to bring money demand back up. A rise in income is what is required. A rise in income increases the demand for money and offsets the decline in money demand brought about by the rise in the interest rate. In sum, the increase in the interest rate is associated with an increase in income. Therefore, the LM curve slopes upward.

To understand better the derivation of the LM curve, it is helpful to recall the concept of **real money** introduced in Chapter 1. *Real money is defined as*

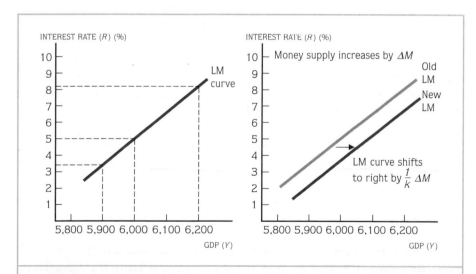

FIGURE 8.4   THE LM CURVE

The LM curve shows the values for the interest rate and income such that the supply of money is equal to the demand for money. As shown in the left-hand panel, the LM curve slopes upward. The right-hand panel shows how an increase in the money supply shifts the LM curve to the right.

the money supply *M* divided by the price level *P*. Because the term *real money* is used so much in macroeconomics, we sometimes use the term **nominal money** when we mean just plain money *M*. Real money *M/P* is a convenient measure of money that corrects for changes in the price level. For example, if the money supply increases by 10 percent and the price level increases by 10 percent, then real money does not change. The money demand function from Equation 8.3 can be written in terms of real money if we simply divide both sides by the price level. That is,

$$M/P = kY - hR. \tag{8.4}$$

This says that the demand for *real* money depends positively on real GDP and negatively on the interest rate. The real money demand equation is an attractive way to think about money demand because it depends on two rather than three variables. Looking at Equation 8.4, we see that real money demand consists of two parts: one part, *kY*, increases with income, while the other part, −*hR*, decreases with the interest rate. Of course the same economic principles apply whether we write the money demand function in terms of real money or nominal money.

Looking at Equation 8.4, we see clearly why the LM curve slopes up. If the Fed holds nominal money constant and the price level does not move, then the real money supply is also constant. If the real money supply is constant, then an increase in the interest rate *R*, which reduces money demand by *hR*, must be offset by an increase in *Y*, which increases money demand by *kY*. Hence, when the interest rate *R* increases, income *Y* increases.

A self-contained graphical derivation of the LM curve, based on this line of reasoning, is shown in Figure 8.5. The left-hand panel of Figure 8.5 is a graph of the demand for real money as a function of the interest rate. Real money demand decreases with the interest rate. But note that an increase in GDP increases money demand and this shifts the money demand line to the right. If money demand is to stay equal to money supply, then the interest rate must increase, as shown in the diagram.

SHIFTS   The second thing to remember about the LM curve is that *an increase in the money supply shifts the LM curve to the right*. Conversely, a decrease in the money supply shifts the LM curve to the left. Looking again at Equation 8.4, we can get an economic understanding for this. An increase in the money supply increases the variable on the left-hand side, *M/P*. If money demand is to remain equal to money supply, then either output *Y* must rise or the interest rate *R* must fall. If we hold the interest on the LM diagram at a particular value, then output *Y* must increase as the LM curve shifts to the right. This is shown in the right-hand panel of Figure 8.4.

Changes in the price level also shift the LM curve. Again, look at the symbols in Equation 8.4 to keep track of what is going on. An increase in the price level reduces real balances. Hence, an increase in the price level does exactly the same thing to the LM curve as a decrease in the money supply. *An increase*

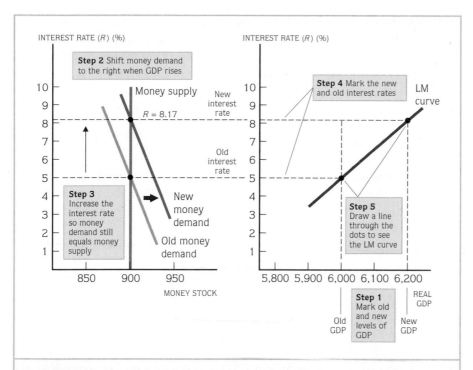

FIGURE 8.5 GRAPHICAL DERIVATION OF THE LM CURVE

The left-hand panel shows the demand for real money as a function of the interest rate. The demand schedule slopes downward because higher interest rates make the public conserve on money holdings. Money demand shifts to the right if real GDP rises. A higher GDP causes the public to hold more real money at a given interest rate. The LM curve is constructed in the right-hand panel. The instructions show how to get points on the curve. Start with a level of GDP and find the money demand suitable for that level. Then, find the interest rate that equates money demand and money supply. The LM curve traces out the market-clearing interest rate for different levels of GDP.

in the price level shifts the LM curve to the left. The rationale is this: An increase in the price level means that less real money is available for transactions purposes. This means that either the interest rate must rise or real income must fall to reduce money demand. Either way the LM curve shifts to the left. Conversely, a decrease in the price level shifts the LM curve to the right, just like an increase in the money supply.

Algebraic Derivation of the IS and LM Curves

The algebraic statement that defines the IS curve is the expression of spending balance; that is, the GDP, Y, generated as total spending, is equal to the level of income Y, assumed by consumers and importers in making their spending decisions:

$$Y = a + e + g + [b(1 - t) - m]Y - (d + n)R + G. \qquad (8.5)$$

Note that the right-hand side is just the consumption function plus the investment function plus the net export function plus government spending. We want to express the IS curve as an equation giving the value of R that gives spending balance at a specified level of Y. We solve Equation 8.5 for R by moving the R term to the left-hand side and dividing by $d + n$:

$$R = \frac{a + e + g}{d + n} - \frac{1 - b(1 - t) + m}{d + n}Y + \frac{1}{d + n}G. \quad \text{IS Curve} \quad (8.6)$$

Government spending G increases the interest rate for a given level of income. Graphically, this looks like a shift of the IS curve to the right, a result that we saw in Figure 8.2. A higher value of G raises the IS curve or, equivalently, shifts the IS curve to the right.

The coefficient

$$\boxed{\frac{1 - b(1 - t) + m}{d + n}}$$

that multiplies Y in Equation 8.6 is the slope of the IS curve. Note that the slope of the IS curve depends on the sensitivity of investment to the interest rate, represented by the coefficient d. The algebraic formula shows that the slope of the IS curve is small—this means that the IS curve is fairly flat—if investment is very responsive to the interest rate. Then, small changes in the interest rate result in large changes in investment and hence large fluctuations in GDP. Similarly, the IS curve is flat if net exports are highly sensitive to the interest rate, that is, if the coefficient n is large. What matters is the sum of the two interest-rate coefficients, $d + n$. Note that the IS curve is flat if the marginal propensity to consume b is large, if the tax rate t is small, or if the marginal propensity to import m is small. In these cases, the multiplier is large and changes in the interest rate have large effects on GDP.

AN EXAMPLE OF AN IS CURVE   With the numerical values summarized in the key macro relationships box, the IS curve is

$$R = \frac{1,745}{2,500} - \frac{1 - 0.53}{2,500}Y + \frac{1}{2,500}G$$

or

$$R = 0.698 - 0.000188Y + 0.0004G. \quad \text{Numerical Example of IS Curve} \quad (8.7)$$

The slope of the IS curve is -0.000188: Along the IS curve, when GDP rises by \$100 billion, the interest rate falls by 1.88 percentage points. The IS curve that appears in Figure 8.2 is drawn accurately to scale for this numerical example. The IS curve on the left is drawn for government spending G equal to

$1,200 billion. The shift in the IS curve to the right in Figure 8.2 is due to an increase in government spending of $40 billion.

The algebraic expression for the LM curve is obtained simply by moving R to the left-hand side of the money demand equation (8.3) and dividing by the coefficient h. That is,

$$R = \frac{k}{h}Y - \frac{1}{h}\frac{M}{P}. \quad \text{LM Curve} \qquad\qquad (8.8)$$

Equation 8.8 says that an increase in real money balances M/P lowers the interest rate for a given level of income. This means that the LM curve shifts to the right, a result that corresponds to the graph in Figure 8.4. The slope of the LM curve is k/h. Note that the slope of the LM curve k/h is small—meaning that the LM curve is fairly flat—if the sensitivity of money demand to the interest rate is large, that is, if the coefficient h is large. Then, a small decline in the interest rate raises the demand for money by a large amount and requires a large offsetting increase in income. The small change in the interest rate combined with the large change in income trace out a flat LM curve. Note also that the LM curve is flat if the sensitivity of money demand to income k is small.

AN EXAMPLE OF AN LM CURVE   With the numerical values summarized in the key macro relationships box, the LM curve is

$$R = \frac{0.1583}{1.000}Y - \frac{1}{1,000}\frac{M}{P}$$

or

$$R = 0.0001583Y - 0.001\frac{M}{P}. \quad \text{Numerical Example of LM Curve} \qquad (8.9)$$

This LM curve is drawn to scale in Figure 8.4. The shift of the LM curve for an initial money stock of 900 in the right-hand side of Figure 8.4 corresponds to an increase in the money supply of $40 billion.

Finding Income Y and the Interest Rate R

Finally, we are ready to find the values of the interest rate and income predicted by the theory. We first proceed graphically. To satisfy all five relationships of the model, the values of R and Y must be on both the LM curve and the IS curve, that is, at the intersection of the LM curve and the IS curve. The IS curve incorporates the consumption, investment, and net export functions, as well as the income identity, while the LM curve incorporates the equality of money demand and money supply. The values of the interest rate and income that we look for are therefore at the intersection of the LM curve and the IS curve. The intersection is shown graphically in Figure 8.6.

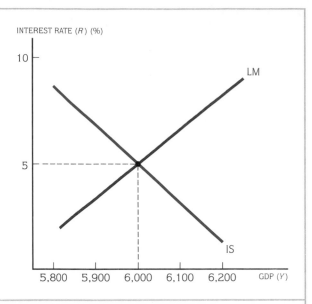

INTEREST RATE (*R*) (%)

FIGURE 8.6   THE INTERSECTION OF THE IS CURVE AND THE LM CURVE

The values of the interest rate and income predicted by the macro model occur at the intersection of the IS curve and the LM curve. For these values, all five relationships of the model are satisfied. Along the IS curve consumption demand, investment demand, net export demand, and the income identity are satisfied. Along the LM curve, money demand equals money supply.

Once we have determined the levels of income *Y* and the interest rate *R*, we can determine consumption C, investment I, and net exports X. Consumption is obtained by putting the value of income into the consumption function, investment is obtained by putting the value of the interest rate into the investment function, and net exports are obtained by putting income and the interest rate into the net export function.

Recall that all these predictions of the model are made with the price level fixed, on the "back burner." This is fine for the short run—for about a year or so—but for no longer. We look at what happens to the price level in the next chapter.

The IS-LM Framework

1. The IS curve shows all combinations of the interest rate and income that satisfy spending balance.

2. The LM curve shows all combinations of the interest rate and income that satisfy money market equilibrium.

3. Given the price level, the IS-LM diagram tells the levels of GDP and the interest rate at the intersection of the IS and LM curves. This is the only combination of *Y* and *R* that satisfies both spending balance and money market equilibrium.

8.5 | POLICY ANALYSIS WITH IS-LM

Monetary Policy

MACROSOLVE
EXERCISE

We are now ready to make the IS-LM approach go to work. Consider **monetary policy**. What happens if the Fed increases the money supply? We now know that an increase in the money supply shifts the LM curve to the right. The effect of such a change on the interest rate and income is shown in Figure 8.7. As the left-hand panel indicates, the theory predicts that, *when the money supply increases, the interest rate falls and GDP rises*. This increase in GDP may put upward pressure on prices, but we are saving the details for the next chapter.

What actually happens in the economy when the Fed increases the money supply? Immediately after the increase, more money is in the economy than

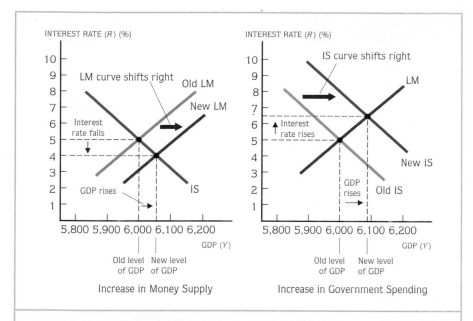

FIGURE 8.7   EFFECTS OF MONETARY AND FISCAL POLICIES
In the left-hand panel, an increase in the money supply shifts the LM curve to the right; this raises GDP and lowers the interest rate. In the right-hand panel, an increase in government spending shifts the IS curve to the right; this raises GDP and raises the interest rate. A comparison of the two panels illustrates a fundamental difference between monetary policy and fiscal policy: An expansionary monetary policy lowers interest rates, and an expansionary fiscal policy raises interest rates.

people demand. This makes the interest rate fall, so the demand for money increases. The lower interest rate then stimulates investment and net exports; this raises GDP through the multiplier process. In sum, <u>GDP rises and the interest rate falls</u>.

Fiscal Policy

Suppose Congress passes a bill that increases defense spending. This is an example of **fiscal policy**, the use of tax rates and government spending to influence the economy. We now know that an increase in government spending pushes the IS curve to the right. Figure 8.7 shows what happens to interest rates and GDP. In the right-hand panel, _an increase in government spending increases the interest rate and increases income_.

What goes on in the economy when the government purchases more goods? First, the increase in government demand increases GDP through the multiplier. But the increase in GDP increases the demand for money: More money is needed for transactions purposes. Since the Fed does not change the money supply, we know that interest rates must rise to offset the increase

IS-LM IN THE BUSINESS PAGES

Not many reporters are versed in the IS-LM model. It is not surprising to find statements like this one in the financial pages:

> A new recession is feared because higher government spending for business bailouts is raising interest rates. Those higher rates are discouraging housing purchases and plant and equipment investment.

More bailout spending shifts the IS curve outward. The economy moves up and to the right along the LM curve. It is true that interest rates are higher, but this is a symptom of a higher GDP, not something that causes a decline in GDP.

How about

> There is concern about declining sales and employment because of the collapse of the dollar. That collapse will

be accompanied by higher interest rates, which will lead to lower investment and total spending.

Same error. The lower dollar leads to a diversion of demand to domestic products, which shifts the IS curve outward. GDP and the interest rates rise as the economy moves up the LM curve.

And,

> The only way to head off the impending recession is to bring the government's deficit under control. Otherwise, high interest rates will choke off economic activity.

It is true that an antideficit move (lower spending or higher taxes) lower interest rates by moving the IS curve inward, but the result is to worsen, not head off, an incipient recession.

in money demand that came from the increase in GDP. This increase in the interest rate reduces investment demand and net exports, offsetting some of the stimulus to GDP caused by government spending. The offsetting negative effect is called **crowding out.**

NUMERICAL EXAMPLE Explicit numerical values for the effect of changes in the money supply and government spending can be obtained from the numerical IS-LM curves in Equations 8.7 and 8.9. By setting the right-hand side of Equation 8.7 equal to the right-hand side of Equation 8.9 and solving for Y, the level of income that satisfies the IS-LM model can be written as a function of constants, the real money supply, and government purchases:

$$Y = 2{,}015 + 2.887 \frac{M}{P} + 1.155G. \qquad (8.10)$$

Suppose that the money supply M is $900 billion, government spending G is $1,200 billion, and the price level is 1. Then Equation 8.10 says that GDP equals $6,000 billion. Plugging this value for Y into either the equation for the IS curve or the equation for the LM curve, we find that the interest rate is 5 percent. Figure 8.6 is drawn accurately to scale for these values. Equation 8.10 says that an increase in government spending of $1 billion increases real GDP by $1.155 billion, for a ratio of 1.155. Compare this effect with the government spending multiplier of 2.1 that we found in Chapter 7 in the model where investment is exogenous and net exports depend only on income. The effect is smaller when we take account of the financial system, because interest rates rise and crowd out investment and net exports. As for monetary policy, if the price level is 1, then an increase in the money supply of $1 billion increases GDP by $2.887 billion.

Policy Analysis with the IS-LM Framework

1. An increase in the money supply increases GDP and decreases the interest rate.

2. An increase in government spending increases GDP and increases the interest rate.

3. These are short-run results with the price level predetermined. When the time frame is lengthened in the next chapter, so that the price level can adjust, these results will have to be modified.

8.6 | THE AGGREGATE DEMAND CURVE

With the IS-LM diagrams, we are in a position to derive formally the aggregate demand curve previewed in Chapter 7. The **aggregate demand curve,** shown in Figure 8.8, tells how much people will demand at a given level of prices. The higher is the price level, the less aggregate demand. Hence, like most demand curves in microeconomics, the aggregate demand curve slopes downward.

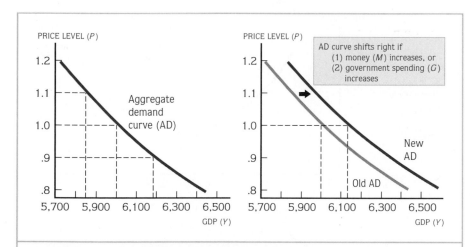

FIGURE 8.8   THE AGGREGATE DEMAND CURVE

On the left is the aggregate demand curve (AD). It shows that aggregate demand is a declining function of the price level. On the right, the aggregate demand curve shifts to the right if either monetary or fiscal policy is expansionary.

Except as a mnemonic device to remember which way the aggregate demand curve is sloped, the analogy between the standard microeconomic demand curve and the aggregate demand curve of macroeconomics is a weak one and should not be emphasized. The ideas behind the aggregate demand curve are much different from those that underlie the typical demand curve of microeconomics. In particular, it is important to keep in mind that the financial system—the demand and supply for money—lies behind the aggregate demand curve.

Figure 8.9 is a graphical derivation of the aggregate demand curve. In the top part of Figure 8.9 is an IS-LM diagram. Recall that changes in the price level shift the LM curve. Higher prices shift the LM curve to the left, and lower prices shift the LM curve to the right.

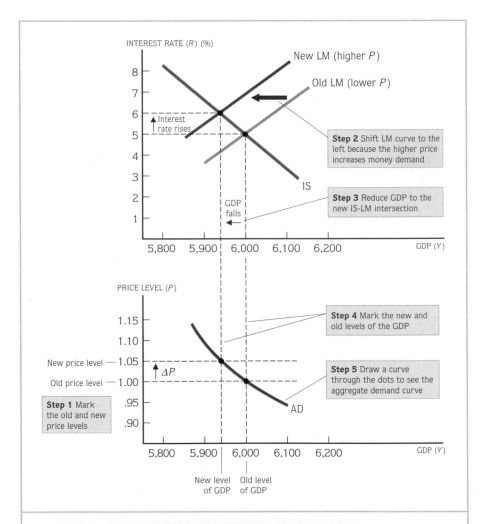

FIGURE 8.9   DERIVATION OF THE AGGREGATE DEMAND CURVE

An increase in the price level shifts the LM curve to the left. This raises interest rates and reduces output. The resulting negative relationship between the price level and GDP is summarized in the aggregate demand curve.

Now suppose that the price level rises. The LM curve shifts to the left; this raises the interest rate, lowers investment and net exports, and ultimately lowers GDP. Therefore, a higher price level reduces GDP because it increases the demand for money. The increase in demand causes interest rates to rise and GDP to fall. The different values for the price level and GDP constitute the aggregate demand curve.

Derivation of Aggregate Demand Curve

The Aggregate Demand Curve

1. The aggregate demand curve shows what level of GDP is demanded given a particular price level.

2. The two economic principles governing the aggregate demand curve are spending balance and the equality of the demand and supply of money.

3. The aggregate demand curve slopes downward. A higher price level means that real money balances are lower and therefore the real interest rate is higher. This means that investment, net exports, and GDP are lower.

4. An increase in government spending or the money supply shifts the aggregate demand curve to the right.

Monetary and Fiscal Policies

Changes in the money supply and in government spending both shift the aggregate demand curve. This is shown in the right-hand panel of Figure 8.8. Suppose that the money supply increases. At a given price level, aggregate demand rises. More money means that a lower interest rate equates money demand with money supply. A lower interest rate stimulates more investment and net exports, which in turn require a higher level of GDP for spending balance. In sum, the aggregate demand curve shifts to the right when the money supply increases.

monetary policy

Fiscal policy also shifts the aggregate demand curve. An increase in government spending shifts the aggregate demand curve to the right. At a given price level, more government spending means more aggregate demand. Conversely, a decrease in government spending shifts the aggregate demand curve to the left.

The effects of fiscal and monetary policies are easily seen by using Equation 8.10. Recall that this equation gives the level of income that satisfies spending balance and money market equilibrium. But that is precisely the aggregate demand curve. All combinations of Y and P that satisfy Equation 8.9 for given values of G and M represent points on the aggregate demand curve. Inspection of this equation shows clearly that increases in M or G will increase Y for a given P; they shift the curve outward.

8.7 | DETERMINATION OF OUTPUT AND UNEMPLOYMENT IN THE SHORT RUN

Recall from Chapter 7 that prices are sticky in the sense that they are not adjusted quickly by firms in response to demand conditions. Firms wait a while before adjusting their prices. For some period of time, therefore, the price level is stuck at a predetermined level. During this time, sellers wait to see how demand conditions change before they adjust their prices again. Prices eventually adjust, of course, but not until the next time period—a year or quarter later, for example. For the time being, the price level is predetermined.

price adjusts slowly →

Determination of Output

Figure 8.10 shows how aggregate demand determines output at a predetermined price. The aggregate demand curve is the same one derived in the previous section. The predetermined price is shown by the horizontal line drawn at P_0. GDP is determined by the point of intersection of the aggregate demand curve and the flat predetermined-price line.

Shifts in the aggregate demand curve—caused perhaps by changes in the money supply or government spending—result in increases or decreases in output. A rightward shift in the aggregate demand curve results in an expansion of output; a leftward shift in the aggregate demand curve results in a contraction of output.

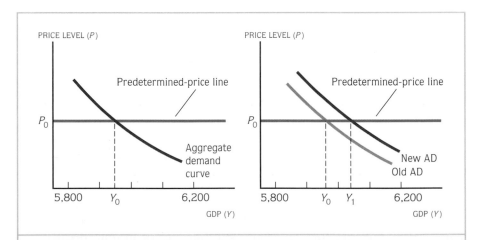

FIGURE 8.10   DETERMINATION OF OUTPUT WITH A PREDETERMINED PRICE

The horizontal line shows the price level predetermined for this year at level P_0. This year's output is at the intersection of the aggregate demand schedule and the horizontal line. In the left-hand panel, the intersection occurs at the level of output marked Y_0. In the right-hand panel, the aggregate demand curve shifts right and output expands from Y_0 to Y_1.

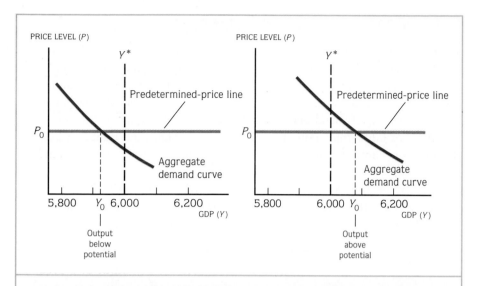

FIGURE 8.11   GDP CAN BE ABOVE OR BELOW POTENTIAL GDP

On the left, the level of output is below potential. On the right, the level of output is above potential. Both positions exert pressure on firms to change prices. On the left, the pressure is to lower prices. On the right, the pressure is to raise prices.

The price level inherited from last year, when combined with the aggregate demand curve, determines the level of output this year. Output can be below potential output. Then, we observe unemployment and other unused resources. Or output can exceed potential output. These two possibilities are shown in Figure 8.11, where we superimpose the vertical potential GDP line to indicate potential. In the left-hand panel of Figure 8.11, output is below potential. In the right-hand panel, output is above potential.

Although the price level does not change immediately when firms find themselves producing above or below equilibrium, there is an incentive to move back to equilibrium, as we discussed in Chapter 7. The incentive is to lower prices when output is below potential and raise prices when output is above potential. A price cut raises output and a price increase lowers output, so these moves take the firm and the economy back toward equilibrium.

These adjustments lead to a changed price level for the *next year* or period—not this year. For example, if output is above potential in the year 2011, then the price level will be higher in 2012. When the aggregate demand curve is drawn to determine output for the year 2012, the predetermined price is drawn at a higher level. If the intersection of the aggregate demand curve for the year 2012 and this new price line is still not at an output level equal to potential, then there is a further adjustment in prices, but this does not occur until the year 2013. The process continues this way until aggregate demand equals potential output, at which point the desire for firms to adjust their prices no longer is present. How the process converges depends on the explicit price-adjustment process, which we consider in the next chapter.

Determination of Unemployment

We noted in Chapter 3 that Okun's law establishes a close relation between real GDP and unemployment. <u>When an adverse shock shifts the aggregate demand curve inward, real GDP falls</u>. Figure 8.12 starts with that shift and shows how it generates an increase in unemployment as well. From the decline in real GDP, the lower left-hand diagram converts it into a change in the percentage deviation of GDP from potential, $(Y - Y^*)/Y^*$. Then, the right-hand part of the diagram computes the resulting increase in unemployment by applying Okun's law.

A number of important mechanisms are at work in the process described in Figure 8.12. If GDP declines, employers need a smaller amount of labor input. They cut the length of the workweek, reduce the intensity of work, and cut the size of the workforce. Most workers who are laid off become unemployed. In addition, people who are looking for work find it harder to lo-

> OKUN'S LAW:
> For each %
> the unemployment
> rate is above the
> natural rate, real
> GDP is 3% below
> potential GDP
> (GDP Gap)
> $$\frac{(Y - Y^*)}{Y^*} = -3(u - u^*)$$

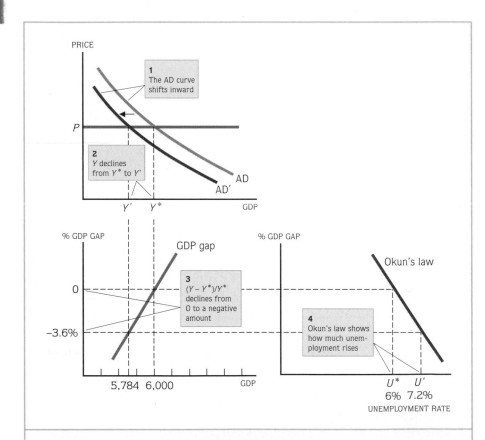

FIGURE 8.12   DETERMINATION OF UNEMPLOYMENT

The upper left-hand diagram shows the aggregate demand curve in its original position and after it shifts inward. Output declines from Y^* to Y'. The lower left-hand diagram translates the GDP decline into percentage terms. The right-hand diagram uses Okun's law to show the amount of increase in unemployment that occurs as a result of the decline in GDP.

cate jobs. Because of the importance of hours reductions and the common pattern of retaining workers during temporary declines in demand (called *labor hoarding*), a 3 percent decline in GDP is associated with only a 1 percentage point increase in unemployment. This close negative relation is one of the most reliable generalizations that macroeconomists have found. Whenever some force causes GDP to decline, you can be confident that unemployment will rise.

Determination of Output and Unemployment in the Short Run

1. In the short run, the price level is predetermined. It can change over time, but in a given year, the events of that year have almost no impact on the price level.

2. The level of output is predetermined by the point on the aggregate demand schedule corresponding to the price level.

3. In the short run, output can be below or above its potential level.

4. Okun's Law describes the relation between real GDP and unemployment.

REVIEW AND PRACTICE

Major Points

1. Investment depends on the interest rate. A higher interest rate discourages some investment projects and lowers total investment.

2. Net exports also depend negatively on the interest rate. A higher interest rate attracts capital from other countries; this drives up the exchange rate and lowers net exports.

3. The IS-LM model determines output, the interest rate, and each of the spending components in the short run. It does not require that the economy operate at its long-run equilibrium.

4. The IS curve shows the level of GDP that brings spending balance for each interest rate. It slopes downward.

5. The LM curve shows the interest rate that brings equality of supply and demand in the money market for each level of GDP. It slopes upward.

6. The IS-LM model answers questions about the effect of policy over the period when it is reasonable to consider prices fixed. Monetary expansion

raises output and lowers the interest rate. Fiscal expansion raises output and raises the interest rate.

7. The intersection of the IS and LM curves tells the levels of GDP and the interest rate for a given price level and fiscal-monetary policies. It corresponds to a point on the aggregate demand schedule.

8. The aggregate demand curve shows all combinations of GDP and the price level that satisfy spending balance and money market equilibrium for given fiscal and monetary policies. Fiscal and monetary expansions shift the aggregate demand curve out.

9. In the short run, the price level is predetermined. GDP is determined by aggregate demand at the predetermined-price level and can be above or below potential GDP.

Key Terms and Concepts

financial variables	real money
investment function	nominal money
money	monetary policy
money demand function	fiscal policy
money supply	crowding out
IS curve	aggregate demand curve
LM curve	

Questions for Discussion and Review

1. What are the important determinants of aggregate demand? For each one, trace out what happens if it changes.

2. What are the determinants of the demand for money? For each one, trace out what happens if it changes.

3. How is the supply of money determined?

4. What is the difference between the nominal interest rate and the real interest rate?

5. Explain why the IS curve slopes downward.

6. Explain why the LM curve slopes upward.

7. Explain why the aggregate demand curve slopes downward.

8. Why does a decrease in government spending reduce interest rates?

9. Why does an increase in the money supply reduce interest rates?

Problems

NUMERICAL

1. This problem pertains to the numerical example in the box on key macro relationships. Set the price level equal to 1.

   a. Use the algebraic form of the aggregate demand curve to find the leval of GDP that occurs when the money supply is $900 billion and government spending is $1,200 billion.

   b. Use the IS curve and the LM curve to find the interest rate that occurs in this situation. Explain why you get the same answer in each case.

   c. Use the consumption function to find the level of consumption, the investment function to find the level of investment, and the net export function to find the level of net exports for this situation.

   d. Show that the sum of your answers for consumption, investment, government spending, and net exports equals GDP.

   e. Repeat all the previous calculations if government spending increased to $1,300 billion. How much investment is crowded out as a result of the increase in government spending? How much are net exports crowded out?

2. For savings and budget deficits, the problem pertains to the numerical example in the box on macro relationships and uses the answers to problem 1.

   a. Set government spending at $1,200 billion and the money supply at $900 billion. Calculate government saving (the budget surplus). Calculate the level of private saving, and show that private saving plus government saving plus rest of world saving equals investment.

   b. Now repeat the calculations for a level of government spending equal to $1,300 billion. Does private saving plus government saving plus rest of the world saving still equal investment? How does each element in the identity change?

   c. Explain why private saving increases as a result of government spending. In light of these calculations, evaluate the statement: "Government budget deficits absorb private saving that would otherwise be used for investment purposes."

3. Compare the IS curve in the numerical example on page 204 with the IS curve you get by increasing the coefficient d to 4,000.

   a. What is the slope of each IS curve? Explain in words why the second IS curve is flatter.

   b. Derive the aggregate demand curve in each case. Which has a larger coefficient for M/P?

4. Compare the LM curve in the numerical example on page 205 with the LM curve you get by increasing the coefficient h to 2,000.

   a. What is the slope of each LM curve? Explain why the slopes are different.

   b. Derive the aggregate demand curve in each case. Which has a larger coefficient for M/P?

5. Using the numerical example of the chapter, calculate values for the money supply and government spending that increase GDP from $6,000 billion to $6,100 billion *without changing the interest rate at all*.

6. The following relationships describe the imaginary economy of Nineland:

$$Y = C + I \qquad \text{(Income identity)}$$
$$C = 90 + 0.9Y \qquad \text{(Consumption)}$$
$$I = 900 - 900R \qquad \text{(Investment)}$$
$$M = (0.9Y - 900R)P \qquad \text{(Money demand)}$$

   Y is output, C is consumption, I is investment, R is the interest rate, M is the money supply, and P is the price level. There are no taxes, government spending, or foreign trade in Nineland.

   The year is 1999 in Nineland. The price level is 1. The money supply is 900 in 1999.

   a. Sketch the IS curve and the LM curve for the year 1999 on a diagram and show the point where the interest rate and output are determined. Show what happens in the diagram if the money supply is *increased* above 900 in 1999.

   b. Sketch the aggregate demand curve. Show what happens in the diagram if the money supply is *decreased* below 900 in 1999.

   c. Derive an algebraic expression for the aggregate demand curve in which P is on the left-hand side and Y is on the right-hand side.

   d. What are the values of output and the interest rate in 1999 when the money supply is 900?

ANALYTICAL

1. Higher interest rates reduce investment and increase foreign saving. What then must happen to the combination of private and government saving after a rise in interest rates? If neither private nor government saving depends directly on the interest rate, how can this change come about?

2. Graphically derive the LM curve, as in Figure 8.4, using instead a graph that relates money demand to income. (Hint: Put the stock of money on the vertical axis and income on the horizontal axis and set this diagram above the LM diagram.)

3. Suppose that money demand depended only on income and not on interest rates.

   a. What does the LM curve look like in this case?

   b. Show graphically that G has no effect on the level of output Y. What does G affect?

   c. Show the same thing algebraically. Explain why the LM equation becomes the aggregate demand equation.

4. Show how the IS curve and the LM curve can be shifted to get an increase in output without a change in interest rates. What kind of mix of monetary and fiscal policy is needed to do this? Will a reduction in interest rates, while holding output constant, do this?

5. Suppose that two administrations, one Democratic and the other Republican, both use fiscal and monetary policy to keep output at its potential level, but the Democratic administration raises more in taxes and maintains a larger money supply than the Republican administration.

   a. On a single graph, show how the IS and LM curves of these two administrations differ.

   b. Indicate whether the following variables are higher under the Democratic or Republican administration or whether they are unchanged: consumption, investment, net exports, government saving, and private saving.

   c. Under which administration will foreign holdings of U.S. financial assets grow more slowly?

THE ECONOMIC FLUCTUATIONS MODEL

The aggregate demand curve developed in Chapter 8 is one of the basic components of the economic fluctuations model. In this chapter, we develop the second major component—the adjustment process that takes the economy from a position where GDP is either above or below potential GDP back to potential. We consider shocks to the economy and see how monetary and fiscal policy can be used to respond to these shocks. We also study the long-run effects of monetary and fiscal policy.

9.1 | PRICE ADJUSTMENT

Decisions about prices are made by individual firms. But moving from the level of the firm to the macro level is tricky. Finding a good way to model aggregate price adjustment has occupied much of the research time of macroeconomics during the last 35 years.

Firms adjust their prices in response to conditions in their markets. If demand has been strong and they are producing more than they think is appropriate given their current prices, they raise their prices. If demand has been weak and they are producing less than is appropriate, they lower their prices. When we look at the process in terms of aggregate variables (GDP and the price level) prices tend to rise when GDP has been above potential and fall when it has been below potential. We have already mentioned this aspect of price adjustment in illustrating the dynamic analysis in the previous chapter.

Specifically, if demand in the previous period Y_{-1} is greater than Y^*, then the price level P in this period is raised (the subscript -1 indicates the previous period). Conversely, if demand in the previous period Y_{-1} is below Y^*, then the price level P is bid down. The percentage difference $(Y_{-1} - Y^*)/Y^*$ measures the pressure on prices to change. Note that because P depends on Y_{-1}, it is *predetermined*, or set, according to demand conditions prevailing in the recent past.

Firms make their price decisions with the prices of their inputs in mind. The most important input is labor. Hence, the behavior of the wage rate is a major determinant of price adjustment. Wages tend to rise when conditions in the labor market are strong. Remember that, when real GDP is high relative to potential, unemployment is low and employment is high. These conditions are likely to lead to rising wages. Wage pressure comes at the same time as the direct pressure on prices, and these two pressures combine to form a relation between the deviation of GDP from potential and inflation.

Both economic intuition and historical experience support the notion that market pressure, as measured by $(Y_{-1} - Y^*)/Y^*$, and inflation are related. There is a different way to think about the relationship. Suppose a firm and its workers realize that it is in their mutual interest to raise the level of employment. In terms of Figure 3.7, they find themselves at a level of employment below equilibrium, where the value of the workers' time (measured by the labor supply schedule) is below the value of what they produce (measured by the labor demand schedule). The firm decides to produce more output. How can the firm get its customers to buy the additional output? By setting or accepting a lower price. Thus, even firms that have little control over their own prices obey the positive relation between the output gap, $(Y_{-1} - Y^*)/Y^*$, and price change.

A second factor in the rate of change of prices is inflationary momentum. In times when prices have risen consistently in past years, they will rise this year even if there is no pressure from the market. For example, in 1989, prices rose by almost 5 percent even though the economy was not much above full employment. Inflation in 1987 and 1988 was also close to 5 percent, so it appears that the continuation of inflation at about the same level was the result of momentum. Macroeconomists usually explain the momentum in terms of expectations: When firms and workers expect a particular level of inflation, that level occurs even without pressure from the output or labor market.

The relation between the change in the price level and its determinants is called the **Philips curve,** after A. W. Phillips, the British economist who first studied it.[1] We let the Greek letter π stand for the rate of inflation, $(P - P_{-1})/P_{-1}$, and let π^e stand for the expected rate of inflation. The Phillips curve is

$$\pi = \pi^e + f\frac{Y_{-1} - Y^*}{Y^*}$$ The Phillips Curve   (9.1)

The coefficient f controls the slope of the Phillips curve. If f is large, inflation responds quickly and the economy moves back to equilibrium rapidly. If f is small, a difference between output and potential persists for many years. Figure 9.1 shows the Phillips curve as a graph. When inflation becomes expected at the rate π^e, it shifts the Phillips curve upward.

The Phillips curve with the expectation term has an important property: If real GDP is above potential GDP on a permanent basis, then the rate of inflation never stops increasing. As actual inflation rises, expected inflation π^e also begins to rise; as firms see actual inflation increasing, they begin to expect higher inflation. Then, actual inflation must be even higher, because GDP can exceed potential only if actual inflation exceeds expected inflation. This property of the price adjustment equation is called the **natural rate property.** The terminology comes from the property that, if real GDP is brought above its potential level Y^*, then the inflation rate rises and the price level accelerates. There is no way for real GDP to be held constantly above its natural level without inflation constantly rising with no limit. In an economy with reasonably stable prices, the level of real GDP tends to be near potential on average.

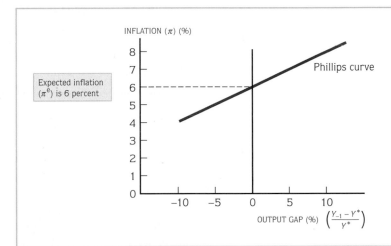

FIGURE 9.1   THE PHILLIPS CURVE

The higher GDP is relative to potential, the higher is the rate of inflation. When GDP is below potential, the Phillips curve predicts that inflation will be below the expected rate of inflation. In booms, when GDP is above potential, actual inflation exceeds expected inflation. The higher is the expected rate of inflation, the higher is actual inflation. The expectational shift is important in explaining persistent inflationary periods, like the 1970s, in the United States.

---

[1] Phillips fit this type of relationship to data for the United Kingdom from 1861 to 1957. The fit was very good. Phillips actually related percentage changes in wages to the unemployment rate. See "The Relationship between the Unemployment Rate and the Rate of Change in Money Wage Rates in the United Kingdom, 1861–1957," *Economica* (November 1957) pp. 283–299.

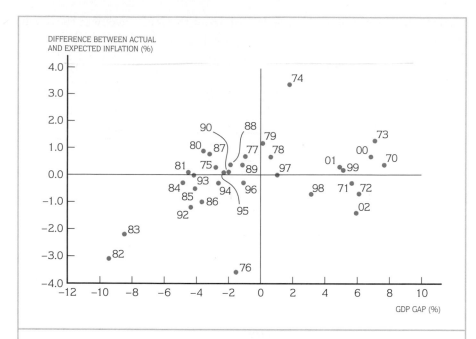

FIGURE 9.2   PRICE ADJUSTMENT IN THE UNITED STATES SINCE 1970

The horizontal axis shows the percentage departure of GDP from potential. The vertical axis shows the amount of inflation relative to the expected amount. Years in the upper right are ones when output was above potential and inflation exceeded expectations. Years in the lower left are recession years, when output was low and inflation subsided. Most, but not all, years fit into the general pattern predicted by the price adjustment relationship. In this diagram, the expected inflation rate is measured as the inflation rate in the year before.

SOURCE: *Economic Report of the President*, 2003, Tables B-63 and B-2.

This relationship between expectations and price adjustment was developed in the late 1960s by Edmund Phelps of Columbia University and independently by Milton Friedman of the University of Chicago and Stanford University. At the time they developed the relationship, most economists had not considered the role of expectations in the Phillips curve. Friedman presented his controversial theory at a large convention of economists in his presidential address to the American Economic Association in 1967.[2] At that time, inflation in the United States was pretty low and many economists were skeptical of the Friedman-Phelps theory. As it turned out, data that became available in the 1970s showed that Friedman and Phelps were right.

Figure 9.2 shows that there has been a stable Phillips curve price-adjustment relationship of the type proposed by Phelps and Friedman for the period since

[2] Friedman's presidential address is found in Milton Friedman, "The Role of Monetary Policy," *American Economic Review* (March 1968) pp. 1–17. Phelps's results were first published in Edmund S. Phelps, "Money Wage Dynamics and Labor Market Equilibrium," *Journal of Political Economy* (July–August 1967), pp. 678–711.

1970. The vertical axis measures the amount by which inflation exceeds expectations and the horizontal axis measures the gap between actual and potential GDP. According to the theory, this relationship should be stable over time and upward sloping. Although there are exceptions, the general positive slope is evident. Note in particular the reduction in inflation during the recessions of the mid-1970s and early 1980s.

What Determines Expected Inflation?

So far we have said nothing about what determines the expected inflation term π^e in the price adjustment equation. The simplest idea is that π^e depends on past inflation. Suppose, for example, that GM thinks the price of Fords will increase at last year's inflation rate. Suppose that all firms forecast inflation in the same way. Then, the expectation π^e would be set to π_{-1}. Equation 9.1 would then become

$$\pi = \pi_{-1} + f\frac{Y_{-1} - Y^*}{Y^*}, \quad \text{Expected Inflation} \qquad (9.2)$$

This Phillips curve is based on a particularly simple model of inflation. It is a rational way for firms to forecast in an economy where inflation has been low for an extended period of time. For example, inflation in the United States was between 1.0 and 2.5 percent per year for every year between 1992 and 2003. With low and stable inflation, it would be rational for firms in 2004 to use the inflation rate in 2003 as their expected inflation for 2004.

With a different inflationary environment, the determination of expected inflation would change. Inflation in the United States was relatively low in the 1950s and 1960s but, between 1971 and 1982, inflation fluctuated from a low of 4.5 percent to a high of 9.5 percent, with upward and downward movements of as large as 4 percentage points in one year. With such high and unstable inflation, it would have been rational for firms to forecast that abnormally high inflation does not persist year after year but eventually returns to lower inflation. The best guess of inflation would be a fraction (like 0.6) of past inflation. Firms would then set expected inflation $\pi^e = 0.6\pi_{-1}$. Once inflation has been brought down to a low level, as by the mid-1990s, firms would no longer expect further decreases in inflation, and expected inflation would be last year's inflation.

On the other hand, if high inflation tended to last a long time, then people would expect inflation to come down only a little each year, if at all. They might simply extrapolate from the past and set $\pi^e = \pi_{-1}$. The process of expectations formation is the same with high and stable inflation as with low and stable inflation: Firms set expected inflation equal to last year's inflation. Only when inflation is abnormally high is it rational for firms to set expected inflation as a fraction of last year's inflation. In more complex inflationary environments, expected inflation would also be more complex, perhaps depending on inflation in the previous two years. Or, firms might attempt to guess where inflation was heading based on what they expect the Fed to do with the money supply: If they expect the Fed to start fighting inflation, they might forecast less inflation.

But even if firms attempt to bring future policy changes into their calculations, the past rate of inflation has some influence on expected inflation. Firms know that some prices will continue to rise for a while, even if they suspect that the Fed would start fighting inflation right away. Some price increases would already have been announced by other firms, and these will take place in any case. Wage setting is also a factor in price decisions, and wage increases negotiated in earlier years would continue. For unionized workers, such as the United Automobile Workers, the contractual nature of wage setting is conspicuous. Contracts frequently set wages for as much as three years in advance. The contracts of different unions are set at different times. When wage contracts are renegotiated, they are influenced by the wages currently paid to workers under contracts settled in previous years and what other workers are likely to get in upcoming years. The expected rate of increase in prevailing wages is thus influenced by past wage decisions, as well as by upcoming wage decisions. Overlapping contracts mean that expected inflation is related to past inflation, even if forecasters are perfectly rational and forward looking.

We will come back to alternative ideas about expected inflation in Chapter 15. For now, we use Equation 9.2 as our Phillips curve.

CHANGE in inflation

Note that the larger is the difference between real GDP and potential GDP, the faster is the change in inflation. Suppose, for example, that the coefficient f in the price adjustment equation is equal to 0.2. This value implies that a 5 percent gap between real GDP and potential GDP, which lasts for one year, reduces the rate of inflation by 1 percent. When output is 10 percent below normal for one period, the rate of inflation is reduced by 2 percent. Of course, the price adjustment equation works the other way around as well. If real GDP is above potential GDP, then there is an increase in inflation.

Price Adjustment

1. The process of price adjustment moves the economy toward potential GDP. When the price level is too high, GDP is less than potential, prices fall, demand rises, and eventually full employment is restored.

2. If no inflation is expected, the price adjustment equation relates the rate of inflation to the deviation of GDP from potential.

3. Under conditions of expected inflation, the price adjustment relation is shifted upward by the amount of the expected inflation. When output exceeds potential, inflation exceeds expected inflation.

4. A simple model of expected inflation is that expected inflation is given by last year's inflation.

9.2 | COMBINING AGGREGATE DEMAND AND PRICE ADJUSTMENT

The aggregate demand curve, in combination with price adjustment, governs the dynamic response of the economy to a change in economic conditions. We look first at what happens to the economy when the money supply is increased, then at what happens with an increase in government spending.

MACROSOLVE
EXERCISE

Response to Monetary Stimulus

We assume that the economy starts out with zero inflation and GDP equals potential GDP. The increase in money initially pushes the aggregate demand curve to the right and increases output. Gradually prices rise to bring the economy back into equilibrium at potential GDP. We now trace out the path of GDP as it returns to potential.

On the left in Figure 9.3 we show the aggregate demand curve intersecting the predetermined-price line. The intersection occurs where output equals potential GDP. Suppose that this is the situation in the year 2010 but that,

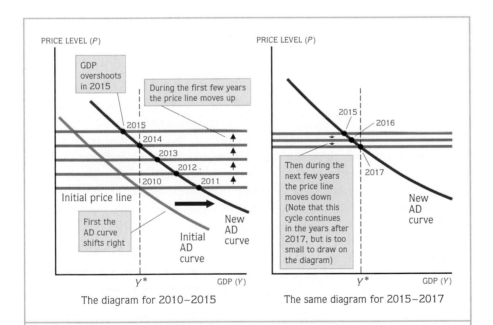

FIGURE 9.3   AGGREGATE DEMAND AND PRICE ADJUSTMENT

The diagram on the left shows the aggregate demand curve intersecting the predetermined-price line at potential GDP (Y^*). After an increase in the money supply, the aggregate demand curve shifts to the right. Then the price line begins to shift up and output declines. GDP falls below potential GDP, but then there is downward pressure on prices and the price line begins to fall. This is shown in the diagram on the right, where we see the same aggregate demand curve during the years after 2015.

starting in 2011, the Fed increases the money supply. The aggregate demand curve shifts to the right, and GDP expands. The economy goes into a boom during 2011, and GDP is above potential GDP. Since the stimulus to aggregate demand comes from monetary policy, we know from the IS-LM model of the last chapter that the interest rate falls, and this stimulates investment and net export spending. Then, GDP expands via the multiplier. All this occurs during the year that the money supply increased.

With firms now operating above potential, they adjust their prices upward. The price line shifts up. We can easily calculate the exact size of the price adjustment in 2012 using the price adjustment equation (9.2): Calculate the inflation rate $(P - P_{-1})/P_{-1}$ associated with the level of GDP for 2011. Multiply this inflation rate by the previous price level P_{-1} to get the absolute change in the price level, $P - P_{-1}$, and hence the price level P for 2012. We shift the price line in Figure 9.3 upward by the amount of this price increase. Assuming the Fed does not increase the money supply again, the same aggregate demand curve continues to apply in 2012. Therefore, the new point of intersection of aggregate demand and the price line occurs at a lower level of output compared with 2011. The economy moves up and to the left along the aggregate demand curve.

What is happening in the economy? At a higher price level more money is demanded by people for transactions purposes. But, since the Fed does not increase the money supply again, this puts upward pressure on the interest rate. The higher interest rate reduces investment and net exports below what they were in 2011, and this reduction has multiplier effects throughout the economy. Hence, GDP falls.

According to Figure 9.3, GDP is still above potential in 2012. Hence, there will be another upward adjustment in the price level. This time the price adjustment is the sum of two effects, which correspond to the two terms on the right-hand side of the price adjustment equation (9.2). Because there was inflation the year before, there are expectations of continuing inflation in 2012. This factor adds to inflation. On the other hand, output is no longer so far above potential. The contribution from that term in the Phillips curve is smaller. In the scenario in Figure 9.3, the price rises by about the same amount in 2013 as it did in 2012. Again, the aggregate demand curve does not move, so output falls again in 2013. As before, the interest rate rises because of the increased demand for money, and this reduces investment and net exports.

If output is still above potential or if inflation is still above where it started in 2010, there is another price adjustment. Hence, GDP continues to fall. Note that GDP falls below—overshoots—potential because expected inflation keeps the price line moving up.

This overshooting is shown in Figure 9.3, where GDP falls below potential GDP in the year 2015. But this overshooting creates forces that reverse the decline in GDP and bring it back to potential GDP. When actual GDP is below potential GDP, the depressed economic conditions place downward pressure on prices. As firms bid down their prices, the price line begins to shift down, as shown in the right-hand panel of Figure 9.3. As the price line reverses its previous movement and begins to shift down, GDP starts to rise. The process continues, period after period, until GDP eventually returns to potential. In Figure 9.3, we show GDP getting very close to potential in the year 2016, although there are tiny movements (too small to see on the diagram) after that. By 2017, inflation has returned to zero, where it began in 2010, although the price level has permanently increased. The price level increases by the same proportion as the increase in money supply.

Note how the graphical analysis in Figure 9.3 is divided into different phases. In the first phase (on the left), the price line is moving up. In the second phase (on the right), the price line is moving down. The graphs are divided into phases because it is confusing to draw in the new price lines for 2016 and 2017 on top of the previous ones for 2010 to 2015. Rather, the new diagram on the right has simply omitted the previous price lines. The important thing to imagine visually is that the price line moves up and then reverses direction and moves down. Getting out a pencil and paper and shifting the price lines yourself will convince you of the dynamic nature of this adjustment process. Alternatively, this movement can be shown very nicely with computer graphics in which you can see the price line moving gradually over time.

The fact that the economy returns to potential GDP, as shown in Figure 9.3, is a key result in macroeconomic theory. In the long run, an increase in money does not increase GDP. The increase in money eventually leads to an increase in the price level of the same proportion. This raises interest rates back to where they were before the monetary expansion and eventually reduces investment and net exports back to their original levels. Note that all other variables—except the price level—are also back to where they were before the increase in the money supply. In the long run, the increase in money has no effect on real variables. Therefore, our complete model has the property of monetary neutrality in the long run. But money is not neutral in the short run. It has a powerful effect on output in the short run, before prices have had a chance to adjust. The same analysis holds in reverse for a decline in the money supply.

Figure 9.4 is a summary of how GDP and the price level move over time according to the calculations just given. The upper panel shows GDP and the lower panel shows the price level. Note how GDP returns to potential after overshooting and how the price level permanently rises to a new level.

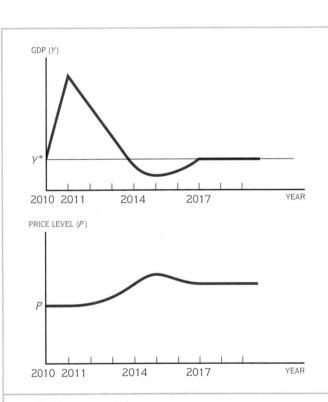

FIGURE 9.4   GDP AND THE PRICE LEVEL AFTER AN INCREASE IN MONEY

The top panel shows GDP and the bottom panel shows the price level. Time (years) is measured on the horizontal axis of both diagrams. The money supply is increased in the year 2011, which is marked on both graphs. At first, GDP increases and the price level does not move. In 2012, the level of GDP begins to fall, and the price level begins to rise. The movements continue in 2013 and so on until GDP returns to potential GDP, and the price level rises by the full proportion that the money supply increases.

Algebraic Derivation

The response of the economy to a change in the money supply can also be analyzed with algebra. Suppose the aggregate demand curve is

$$Y = 3{,}401 + 2.887 \, \frac{M}{P} \qquad (9.3)$$

where we have set government spending to $1,200 billion. We combine this aggregate demand curve with the price adjustment equation (9.2) to describe the evolution of the economy. We then use Equation 9.2 along with Equation 9.3. The algebraic calculations proceed in flip-flop fashion, just like the graphical analysis: Take the price level as given, use Equation 9.3 to find output Y, and plug the value of output into Equation 9.2. Calculate the inflation rate π and the price level P for the next year. Then go back to Equation 9.3 with the new price level, determine a new output level, and so on.

Response to Fiscal Stimulus

Fiscal policy works a little differently from monetary policy. Suppose that, in the same circumstances, government spending, rather than the money supply, is increased in 2011. Again, the aggregate demand curve shifts to the right just as in Figure 9.3, and GDP rises. But now, from IS-LM results of the previous chapter, we know that interest rates rise during the first year and thus crowd out investment and net exports and partly offset the stimulus to demand from government spending. Consumption also falls because spending on consumer durables, such as automobiles, depends negatively on the interest rate. As the price level begins to rise, interest rates rise further, and more investment and net exports are crowded out.

In the long run, GDP returns to potential GDP, even though government spending has been increased. As a result, we know that, in the long run, investment spending, net exports, and consumption must have been reduced by the same amount that government spending was raised. Otherwise, the income identity would be violated. In the long run, fiscal policy completely crowds out investment spending, net exports, and consumption. The rise in the price level increases the demand for money; this leads to higher interest rates and less investment spending, net exports, and consumption. Again, note that, in the long run, our complete model preserves the policy implications of the long-run growth model. But, since shifts in demand cause employment to diverge from its equilibrium level in the short run, both fiscal and monetary policy can influence real output in the short run.

We have now completed our first description of the complete macroeconomic model. In the short run, the price level inherited from the previous year, together with the current aggregate demand schedule, determines the level of output. In the medium run, the process of price adjustment moves the economy closer to potential GDP. Eventually, the economy reaches potential GDP.

The Movement to Potential GDP

1. The aggregate demand curve and the price adjustment line govern the movement to potential GDP. After being pushed away from potential GDP by monetary policy or fiscal policy—whether toward slack or overfull employment—the economy eventually reaches potential GDP.

2. Because expected inflation responds to past inflation, the economy overshoots potential GDP. However, it still eventually reaches potential GDP.

3. An increase in the money supply increases GDP in the short run, but eventually this effect wears off as the price level rises. In the long run, an increase in the money supply has no effect on GDP.

4. An increase in government spending also increases GDP in the short run, although there is some reduction in the other components of spending: investment, net exports, and consumption. In the long run, the stimulus to GDP is completely offset by a decline in the other components as interest rates rise. In the long run, fiscal policy completely crowds out the other components.

9.3 | SHOCKS TO THE ECONOMY

Economic shocks move real GDP away from potential GDP. Different types of shocks affect the aggregate demand curve and the price adjustment line. An important question in macroeconomics is how the economy moves back to potential GDP following the different types of shocks.

Shocks to Aggregate Demand

An **aggregate demand shock** is some event other than a change in policy that shifts the aggregate demand curve. Consider two examples of shocks to the behavioral relationships of the extended model of aggregate demand:

1. Foreign demand suddenly shifts away from U.S. goods. Net export demand falls.

2. A new type of credit card makes it easier to get by with less cash. The money demand schedule shifts inward.

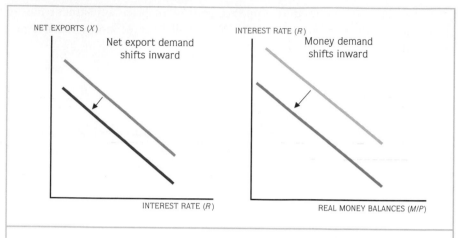

FIGURE 9.5   SHOCKS: INWARD SHIFTS IN NET EXPORTS AND MONEY DEMAND

On the left, a shift in foreign demand away from U.S. goods shifts the net export schedule inward. On the right, technological change reduces money demand. The money demand function shifts inward.

These two examples are illustrated graphically in Figure 9.5. The reduction in the demand for exports shifts net exports inward for each interest rate. The decline in money demand shifts the demand for money inward for each interest rate.

Shocks can be distinguished according to whether they are temporary or permanent. This distinction is important for policy makers: A temporary disturbance might be ignored because its effects disappear soon anyway. In practice, it is difficult to distinguish between temporary and permanent shocks when they occur. In the following examples, we assume that the shocks are permanent.

Analyzing the Effects of Aggregate Demand Shocks

We look at the effects of different kinds of shocks on the aggregate demand curve. Before we start, we need to clarify one point. Monetary and fiscal policies are important determinants of the shape and position of the aggregate demand curve; the curve is not just a property of the economy itself. To talk about the effect of a shock on the curve, we need to take a position on how monetary and fiscal policy react to the disturbance. To start the discussion, we assume that monetary policy keeps the money stock the same no matter what kind of disturbance hits the economy. We also assume that fiscal policy—taxes and spending—does not respond to the disturbance. Both assumptions are arbitrary and unrealistic, but they are a good place to start. In Section 9.4 and Chapter 16, we turn to more-realistic assumptions about the Fed's response to disturbances.

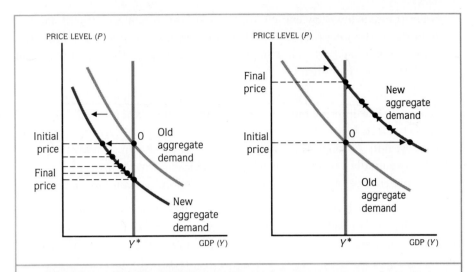

FIGURE 9.6   AGGREGATE DEMAND SHOCKS
On the left, aggregate demand has shifted inward because of the decline in the net export schedule. On the right, aggregate demand has shifted outward because of the decline in money demand. On the left, GDP falls at first. Then, the economy moves down and to the right along the AD schedule until it reaches equilibrium again at a lower price level. On the right, GDP rises at first. Then, the economy moves up and to the left along the AD schedule until it reaches equilibrium again at a higher price level.

Under our assumptions about monetary and fiscal policies, shocks to both spending and money demand, the two major components of our model of aggregate demand, shift the aggregate demand curve: The downward shift in net export demand pushes the aggregate demand curve to the left. The downward shift in money demand has the same effect as an increase in the money supply, which we know shifts the aggregate demand curve to the right.

These shifts in the aggregate demand curve have immediate impacts on real GDP, as shown in Figure 9.6. From the analysis used in the previous section, we can trace out the full dynamic movement of the economy in response to the aggregate demand shocks.

1. With real GDP below potential GDP after the drop in net exports, the price level begins to fall. Firms find that the demand for their products has fallen off and start to cut their prices. This drop in the price level is shown in Figure 9.6 as a movement down and to the right along the aggregate demand (AD) schedule. The lower price level causes the interest rate to fall. With a lower interest rate, investment spending and net exports increase. The increase in investment and net exports tend to offset the original decline in net exports. This process of gradual price adjustment continues as long as real GDP is below potential GDP. By the time real GDP has recovered and returned to potential GDP, investment and net exports have increased by just the amount that net exports fell in the first place. The

interest rate is lower by enough to stimulate this much investment and net exports. In the long run, real GDP will be back to normal, but during the period of gradual price adjustment, the economy goes through a recession with an increase in unemployment.

2. When the demand for money drops, the aggregate demand curve shifts outward. The interest rate drops; investment, net exports, and consumption rise. But, higher GDP causes prices to rise, and this tends to raise the interest rate. Through this process of gradual price adjustment, the economy eventually returns to normal. In the meantime, however, the economy experiences a period of inflation and a boom in economic activity.

To summarize the examples, in both cases, there is a shock to aggregate demand that temporarily moves the economy away from potential GDP and sends the economy into either a boom or a recession. Through gradual adjustment of the price level, the economy eventually returns to normal.

Shocks to the Price Level

The shocks considered so far had the effect of shifting the aggregate demand curve. A **price shock** is some event that shifts the price adjustment relationship. There are several reasons why this might occur.

1. The price of an input to the economy might suddenly rise; the best example is an increase in the price of oil, such as occurred in the 1970s, in 1990, and in 2004. Suppose crude oil production is cut back, and as a result, the price of crude oil increases. This tends to increase the price of all petroleum-related products. Moreover, prices in other energy industries also tend to increase. Unless there is a fall in the price of other goods, when the price of crude oil rises there is an increase in the overall price level.

2. A large group of workers—perhaps, during a union negotiation—gets a wage increase that is abnormally high. When firms pass on the wage increase in the form of higher prices, there is an upward shift in the price level—a price shock.

3. Firms might simply make a mistake and increase their prices, perhaps because they mistakenly expect an increase in inflation.

A price shock is shown in Figure 9.7. If monetary and fiscal policies do not change, then real GDP falls below potential GDP. After the initial price shock, the economy operates below its full-employment level at Y_1. With no increase in the money supply, this in turn causes prices to fall as firms try to cut prices to increase sales. The fall in prices corresponds with a downward movement in the price adjustment curve, which continues until real GDP equals potential GDP. Eventually, therefore, the economy returns to normal

demand for $ (M) positively correlated with GDP (Y)

operating levels. In the meantime, the price shock causes a recession. The period of recession puts downward pressure on prices and offsets the original price shock.

Economic Shocks

1. There can be <u>unexpected shifts in spending</u>; for example, the amount of investment undertaken by businesses at any given interest rate might rise or fall.

2. There can be <u>unexpected shifts in the money market</u>; for example, the amount of money demanded by the public at any given interest rate might rise or fall.

3. Spending or money market shifts in turn <u>shift the aggregate demand curve</u>. At first, real GDP rises or falls. Later, as price adjustment occurs, real GDP returns to equilibrium and the price level moves to a permanently different level.

4. Prices may shift <u>unexpectedly as well</u>. When that occurs, <u>real GDP changes at first</u>. Then, price adjustment returns the economy to its original equilibrium. <u>Neither the price level nor GDP changes in the long run</u>.

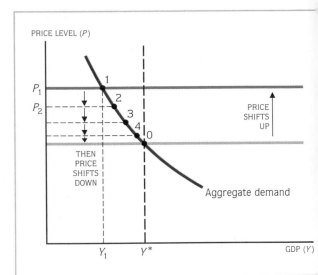

FIGURE 9.7   AN UPWARD SHOCK TO THE PRICE LEVEL

Real GDP is reduced when the price level jumps up; the economy moves to point 1, up and to the left along the aggregate demand curve. Then, the process of price adjustment causes the economy to return gradually to its original equilibrium as the price level falls.

9.4 | RESPONDING TO AGGREGATE DEMAND AND PRICE SHOCKS

To analyze the effects of aggregate demand and price shocks in the previous section, we made the unrealistic assumption that monetary and fiscal policy did not respond to the shocks. To see just how unrealistic that assumption is, consider the effects of a decrease in net exports, shown in Figure 9.6. To return to potential GDP after the shock, the price level has to fall. But there have not been falling prices, or deflation, in the United States during the last 50 years. Clearly, something is missing from the analysis.

The response of monetary and fiscal policy to aggregate demand and price shocks is a very important part of macroeconomics. In this section, we analyze **discretionary policy,** one-time changes in monetary and fiscal policy in response to a specific shock or combination of shocks. In Chapter 16, we consider *monetary policy rules,* the systematic response of monetary policy to economic conditions.

Aggregate Demand Shocks

In March 2001, the U.S. economy entered a recession, a period when real GDP declined, after a decade of uninterrupted expansion. While part of the slowdown in economic activity was simply moderation of the very rapid growth from 1995 through 1999, the decline in stock market wealth starting in early 2000, collapse of the high-technology sector in 2000, increase in energy prices starting in 1999, higher interest rates in 2000, and fall in investment spending starting in 2000 following the surge in investment spending in anticipation of and in response to the Y2K event all contributed to the recession. With the economy already in a recession, the situation worsened after the terrorist attacks of September 11.

This combination of events can be described as a negative aggregate demand shock, shown in Figure 9.8 as a shift of the aggregate demand curve to the left. Decreases in consumption, nonresidential fixed investment, and inventory investment were the primary reasons that the aggregate demand curve shifted to the left during 2000 and 2001. Residential fixed investment remained strong, and net exports did not change much between 2000 and 2001.

Fiscal policy responded to the aggregate demand shock. The Economic Growth and Tax Relief Reconciliation Act of 2001 reduced marginal tax rates and provided rebate checks totaling $36 billion to 85 million taxpayers during

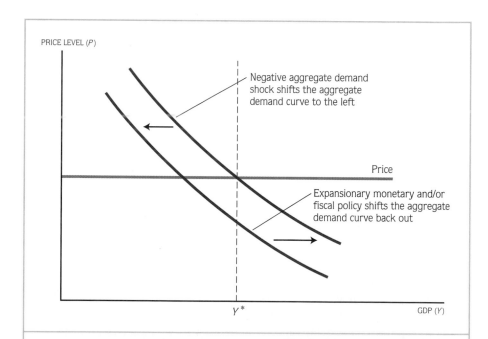

FIGURE 9.8   RESPONDING TO AGGREGATE DEMAND SHOCKS

The aggregate demand curve can shift to the left because of a decrease in demand for consumption, investment, or net exports or an increase in money demand. Real GDP falls. Timely action by the Fed to increase the money supply (and therefore lower interest rates) or by the president and Congress to increase government spending or lower taxes could offset the reduction in GDP.

the second half of 2001. Further tax reductions were enacted in 2002 and 2003. Government spending increased in 2001–2003 because of spending on victim assistance and homeland security following the terrorist attacks, as well as military spending in Afghanistan and Iraq.

Monetary policy also responded to the aggregate demand shock. Starting in January 2001, the Fed began aggressively pursuing a more expansionary monetary policy, increasing the money supply and cutting the overnight interest rate (more precisely, the target level of the federal funds rate), from 6.5 percent at the start of the year to 1.75 percent at the end of the year, its lowest level in 40 years. The Fed continued to keep interest rates low during the slow recovery from the recession, reducing the overnight interest rate to 1 percent during the second half of 2003.

Figure 9.8 also shows how monetary and fiscal policy can be used to counter the effects of an aggregate demand shock. Following the negative shock, expansionary monetary and fiscal policy both contributed to shifting the aggregate demand curve back to the right, mitigating the length and severity of the recession.

The type of aggregate demand policy outlined in this example is called **countercyclical stabilization policy,** because it attempts to counter those shocks to the economy that otherwise would cause cyclical fluctuations in real GDP and the price level. Such a policy is also sometimes called *activist*, because the policy makers actively manipulate the instruments of monetary and fiscal policies.

9.5 | PRICE SHOCKS

The response to a price shock raises more difficult issues than the response to a demand shock. Even under the best of circumstances—no lags or uncertainty in the conduct of policy—such a shock inevitably affects either the price level or real GDP.

Suppose, for example, that there is a price shock of the type illustrated in Figure 9.9. As we discussed, with no policy response, such a price shock tends to reduce real GDP and raise the price level. This is shown in the left-hand panel of Figure 9.9.

Now, suppose that the monetary authorities increase the money supply permanently in response to the price shock. As shown in the right-hand panel of Figure 9.9, this shifts the aggregate demand curve outward and tends to mitigate the downward fluctuation in real GDP. However, the increase in the money supply accommodates the temporary increase in the price level. If output does not fall much below potential, there is little downward pressure on the price level. The price level stays high and never returns to its previous level. As shown in the right-hand panel of Figure 9.9, the price line remains at a higher level if the aggregate demand curve remains at its new, higher position. In the sense that there is less downward pressure on the price level so that it never returns to its previous level, there is therefore less long-run price stability with the policy that tries to offset the fluctuation

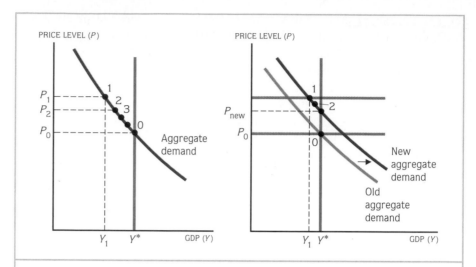

FIGURE 9.9   MONETARY RESPONSE TO A PRICE SHOCK

On the left, monetary policy does not respond to the price shock. The shock raises the price level from P_0 to P_1. Output falls from Y^* to Y_1. Then the price adjustment process starts. In the next year, the price level drops to P_2. Eventually prices fall back to normal and output returns to potential output. On the right, monetary policy responds to the price shock. The money supply is increased and the aggregate demand curve moves outward. At the new intersection of the price line (point 1), there is less downward pressure on the price level because output at Y_1 is closer to potential than in the panel on the left. Assuming that the new aggregate demand curve is maintained, eventually the price level falls to the level marked P_{new}.

in real GDP. In other words, <u>with a price shock there is a trade-off between the stability of real GDP and the stability of the price level</u>.

Policies that increase the money supply in response to positive price shocks are called **accommodative policies**. A policy that holds the money supply constant is called **nonaccommodative**. Figure 9.10 summarizes, for the two policies, the behavior of GDP and the price level after a price shock. The plots show the results of the calculations of GDP and the price level from Figure 9.9. The accommodative policy is better in terms of GDP performance but worse in terms of price level performance.

Policy Response to Aggregate Demand and Price Shocks

1. When an aggregate demand shock occurs, monetary or fiscal policy can offset it. Whatever inward or outward shift of the aggregate demand curve has taken place can be reversed through a policy move in the opposite direction.

2. In the absence of a policy response (that is, with a nonaccommodative monetary policy), a positive price shock causes a rise in the price level and a sustained period of economic slack.

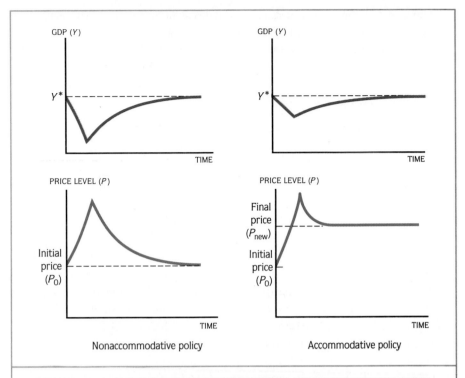

FIGURE 9.10   THE RESPONSE OF THE PRICE LEVEL AND GDP TO PRICE SHOCKS FOR ACCOMMODATIVE AND NONACCOMMODATIVE POLICIES

These charts summarize the calculations from Figure 9.9. The nonaccommodative policy is shown on the left and the accommodative policy is shown on the right. Output is more stable with the accommodative policy, but the price level is less stable.

3. Price shocks create a serious problem for policy. If policy tries to limit the decline in GDP from a positive price shock, it makes the price level less stable. If it tries to head off the inflation, it deepens the recession.

9.6 | HOW FISCAL POLICY AFFECTS THE SHARES OF OUTPUT IN THE LONG RUN

In Section 9.2 we looked at the long-run effects of fiscal policy on the *total amount* of real GDP. In this section, we look at the effects on the *components*, or *shares*, of GDP. Recall that, in Chapter 2, we presented the components of GDP using the simple accounting identity

$$Y = \underbrace{C + I + X}_{\substack{\text{Nongovernment} \\ \text{purchases}}} + \underbrace{G,}_{\substack{\text{Government} \\ \text{purchases}}} \quad \text{The Income Identity} \qquad (9.4)$$

where Y is GDP, C is consumption, I is investment, X is net exports, and G is government purchases.

Many of the long-run questions about fiscal policy involve the effects of changes in government spending as a *share* of output. For example, we might want to know what would happen if government purchases in the year 2010 are 20 percent rather than 15 percent of GDP. Equation 9.4 can be rewritten and interpreted in terms of shares of GDP if we simply divide both sides of the equation by *Y*. This gives

$$1 = \frac{C}{Y} + \frac{I}{Y} + \frac{X}{Y} + \frac{G}{Y}. \tag{9.5}$$

In other words, the shares of the different components of spending must sum to 1.

We now want to use Equation 9.5 to determine what happens to the components of output when fiscal policy changes. A quick glance at the equation shows that *a change in government purchases as a share of GDP must bring about a change in nongovernment purchases as a share of GDP by the same amount but in the opposite direction.* For example, a decrease in government purchases of 3 percent of GDP must bring about an increase in nongovernment purchases of 3 percent of GDP. An increase in government purchases of 3 percent of GDP implies that nongovernment purchases must fall by 3 percent of GDP. This is straightforward arithmetic. It is also straightforward logic.

How much do consumption, investment, and net exports individually rise? Would consumption *C*, income *I*, and net exports *X* each rise by 1 percent of GDP in the case of a cut in government purchases of 3 percent of GDP? Or, would some other combination of percentages occur? The answer depends on how sensitive each of these items is to interest rates.

Interest-Rate Sensitivity of Consumption, Investment, and Net Exports

What brings about a change in consumption, investment, and net exports in the long-term growth model? We have simply used arithmetic and logic to show that such a change must take place. The economic mechanism involves interest rates. An increase in interest rates tends to reduce investment, net exports, and consumption. A decrease in interest rates has the opposite effect. These changes in interest rates, which accompany changes in fiscal policy, are what bring about the changes in the nongovernment components of output.

We discussed why investment and net exports depend negatively on the interest rate in Chapter 8. We now also consider consumption. Consumption is expenditure by households. Higher interest rates mean that consumers have to pay more to finance consumption of automobiles and other durables. These higher finance costs discourage consumption. For example, higher required payments on a car loan discourage purchases of cars.

Figure 9.11 shows the three negative relationships between the interest rate and (1) consumption, (2) investment, and (3) net exports. Note that, in

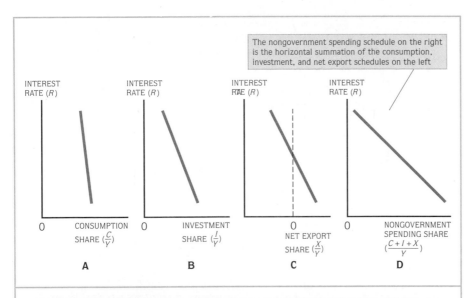

The nongovernment spending schedule on the right is the horizontal summation of the consumption, investment, and net export schedules on the left

FIGURE 9.11   INTEREST-RATE SENSITIVITY OF CONSUMPTION, INVESTMENT, AND NET EXPORTS

Consumption, investment, and net exports shares all depend negatively on the interest rate R. Therefore, the sum of the shares depends negatively on the interest rate. Panel D is the sum of the shares in the other panels at each interest rate.

the diagram, the slope of the consumption relationship is less steep than that of investment and net exports. This reflects historical observations that the sensitivity of consumption to interest rates is smaller than that of investment and net exports. Note also that the fourth panel on the far right in Figure 9.11 is the sum of consumption, investment, and net exports shares. This illustrates how the total nongovernment share $(C + I + X)/Y$ depends negatively on the interest rate. Having derived the interest-rate sensitivities of the major components of output, we can proceed to derive the impact of a change in government purchases and other fiscal actions on the composition of output.

Government Purchases

When government purchases fall, we know that nongovernment purchases rise. Figure 9.12 shows how a decrease in interest rates brings about this increase in consumption, investment, and net exports. First look at Panel D, which shows that lower interest rates must be associated with higher spending on nongovernment purchases. This panel also tells us how much interest rates must fall. Panels A, B, and C can then be used to determine by how much consumption, investment, and net exports individually rise. According to Figure 9.12, consumption rises by a smaller amount than investment because consumption is less sensitive to interest rates than investment. Net exports rise because the lower interest rates cause a decline in the exchange rate.

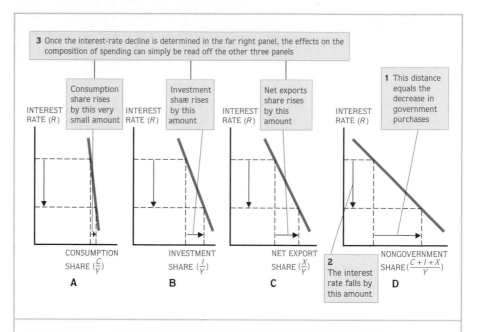

FIGURE 9.12   EFFECTS OF A DECREASE IN GOVERNMENT PURCHASES
The nongovernment share of GDP must rise by the same amount as the fall in the government share of GDP. This rise is brought about by a decline in interest rate *R*. The decline in the interest rate also causes the exchange rate to fall.

The Budget Deficit and the Trade Deficit

Note that this analysis illustrates the close connection between the budget deficit and the trade deficit. The cut in government purchases as a share of GDP reduces the budget deficit as a share of GDP. But, as we have seen, the cut in government purchases also reduces the trade deficit (net exports rise). That is, the government's attempt to reduce the budget deficit has reduced the trade deficit.

Other Fiscal Policy Changes

The analysis of other types of fiscal policy changes in the long run is very similar to the analysis of a decline in government purchases. The analysis of an increase in government purchases is just the reverse of the analysis of a decline in government purchases. In this case, the interest rate rises to depress the demand for investment and net exports to make room for a greater government use of resources. The term **crowding out** is used to describe this process—higher government spending crowds out investment and net exports. A dollar of government purchases crowds out almost a dollar of investment and net exports and a small amount of consumption.

Changes in taxes affect consumption. For example, higher taxes on consumption will reduce consumption because people have less to spend. But the reduction in consumption does not immediately affect potential GDP because the supply of the three productive factors does not change. Hence, the decline in consumption must result in an increase in net exports and investment. The effects can be illustrated in a diagram similar to Figure 9.12.

Figure 9.13 illustrates how well the model works in predicting the effects of policy changes. It compares GDP shares in 1961–1969 and 1982–1990 with those in 1991–2000. Two major policy changes occurred during these periods. First, taxes on income were lowered. Families had more resources at their disposal, and they consumed more. Second, government use of resources, as measured by the share of government purchases in GDP, fell dramatically. The large fall in the share of government purchases caused a large rise in the share of investment. The increase in the consumption and investment shares was larger than the decrease in the government purchases share. The difference was made up by a fall in net exports.

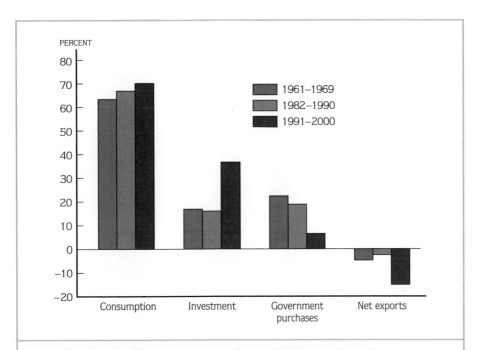

FIGURE 9.13   CHANGES IN GDP SHARES FOR THREE EXPANSIONS

During the 1990s, the consumption and investment shares of GDP rose, while the government purchases and net exports shares of GDP fell.

SOURCE: Bureau of Economic Analysis.

Importance of the Long-Run Assumption

Where does the assumption about the long run fit into these calculations? Clearly, the shares of output add up to 1 in both the long run and the short run. The answer is that the long-run assumption makes sure that other things in addition to interest rates do not affect the shares of spending in GDP.

For example, if we cut government spending by 3 percent of GDP in one fell swoop, real GDP falls in the short run, possibly by more than 3 percent. A fall in real GDP results in an even sharper decline in investment as businesses see their sales falling. The share of investment in GDP falls rather than rises. The results in this section would be all wrong and terribly misleading to policy makers if applied in the very short run. The long-run assumption allows us to view the economy on its long-run potential growth path. Hence, there are no sharp movements in GDP.

Fiscal Policy and the Composition of Output

1. In the long run, an increase in government purchases raises interest rates and reduces (crowds out) investment and net exports. The exchange rate also rises.

2. The budget deficit and the trade deficit are closely related. A decrease in government spending that lowers the budget deficit also lowers the trade deficit.

3. The interest rate is a key factor in the analysis of fiscal policy. Consumption and especially investment and net exports are negatively affected by higher interest rates.

9.7 | MONEY AND INFLATION IN THE LONG RUN

In the previous section, we discussed how the real interest rate divides output among consumption, investment, government, and net exports. We showed how fiscal policy affects these variables. Now, we consider the long-run behavior of another important macroeconomic variable, the inflation rate. In the long run, the price level is determined by equating money demand to money supply. Monetary policy determines the money supply.

Equilibrium in the Money Market

We continue to assume that the economy is on the long-run growth path; GDP is at potential Y^*, and the interest rate is at the value R^* determined in Figure 9.12. Money demand is

$$M = (kY^* - hR^*)P. \tag{9.6}$$

Money demand is proportional to the price level; if P rises by 10 percent, people want to hold 10 percent more money. Money supply is fixed by the Fed. The price level equates money demand to money supply, as shown in Figure 9.14. The algebraic expression for the price level that brings the amount of money demanded into equality with the amount of money supplied is

$$P = \frac{M}{kY^* - hR^*}. \tag{9.7}$$

When the Fed raises the money supply M by 10 percent, the price level rises by the same 10 percent. With money more plentiful, its purchasing power falls and the price level rises. If potential GDP rises and the money stock remains the same, the price level falls; money becomes more valuable when the economy produces a higher volume of goods and services. If government spending

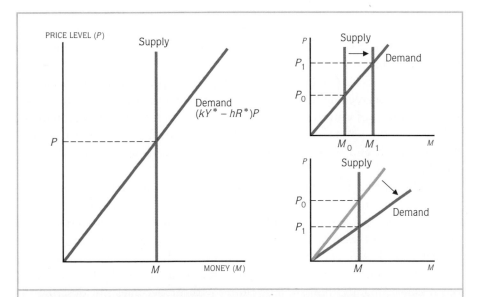

FIGURE 9.14   DETERMINATION OF THE PRICE LEVEL IN THE MONEY MARKET

On the left, the demand for money depends positively on the price level. The supply of money is fixed by the Fed. Equilibrium occurs at the intersection of supply and demand. On the top right, if the money supply rises, the price level rises in the same proportion. On the bottom right, if potential GDP is higher, the price level is lower.

or some other determinant of demand falls, the equilibrium interest rate R^* falls, and the price level also falls, to offset the rise in money demand.

In the long run, monetary policy is a very simple matter. The price level is proportional to the money stock. The money supply has no influence on output or the interest rate. This property is known as the **neutrality of money**. Another term for the independence of real variables like output from the money stock is the **classical dichotomy**, because the real variables are determined *separately* from the money variables. We can think first about the determination of employment and output and then, separately, about the price level.

Inflation

Recall that *inflation* is the rate of increase of the price level. In an economy where GDP does not change, our model of the money market implies that the price level is proportional to the money supply (see Equation 9.7). More money simply raises prices. The Fed can choose whatever rate of inflation it wants just by raising the money supply by that percentage each year. For price stability, the Fed should keep the money supply constant from one year to the next. For 5 percent inflation, it should raise M by 5 percent each year.

In a growing economy, the rate of inflation is less than the rate of money growth. If Y^* is growing over time, some money growth is needed just to keep the price level from falling from one year to the next.

Figure 9.15 shows the relationship between money growth and inflation in a group of six countries. Money growth is measured over a 30-year period, so the long-run analysis should apply even if recessions or booms are important over a three- or five-year period. If the relationship were as simple as 1 percent of inflation for each percent of money growth, all the observations would lie along the 45-degree line that equates inflation and money growth in the figure. Because growth of output also affects the relation between money growth and inflation, all the points lie above the 45-degree line. But it remains clear that money growth and inflation have a close relationship over a period of this length.

In the United States and all other economies, monetary policy and inflation are contentious issues. The United States has had episodes of inflation at rates of 10 percent and more, and some countries suffer hyperinflations, with rates of price increase of thousands of percent. Why does this happen if the central bank has direct control over inflation? There are two reasons why central banks do not deliver an inflation-free economy. In the United States, the reason is mainly that the long-run growth model does not describe the year-to-year movements of the economy. Instead, the economy can move away from potential. A monetary contraction is one force that may cause a recession, a period when GDP is below potential. The fear of setting off a recession may prevent the Fed from cutting money growth, even though the reduced growth is just what the long-run growth model says is needed to end inflation.

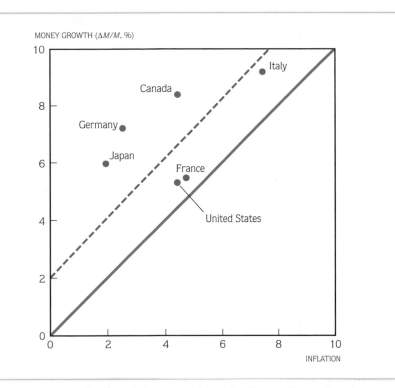

FIGURE 9.15   MONEY GROWTH AND INFLATION IN SIX COUNTRIES, 1973–2002

The vertical axis shows the average annual growth rate of money supply over a 30-year period. The horizontal axis shows the average annual rate of inflation. Generally, the observations appear to lie about 2 percent above the 45-degree line, clustered around the dashed line. Growth in real output absorbs about 2 percent of annual money growth, and the remaining money growth leads to inflation.

SOURCE: International Monetary Fund, *International Financial Statistics.*

In some smaller countries with less efficient tax systems, the second reason for inflation is important. The central bank, an arm of the government, issues large amounts of new money each year because the government spends more than it takes in as taxes or from issuing bonds. The deliberate creation of high rates of inflation is one way of financing government, although not a very good way. Severe deliberate inflation has not been part of U.S. economic policy since the Civil War.

9.8 | THE CLASSICAL DICHOTOMY

The analysis of fiscal and monetary policies in this chapter illustrates an important property of the economic fluctuations model in the long run. Real variables like the interest rate and the composition of spending in the long run can be analyzed solely by looking at other real variables, like government purchases. Nominal variables such as the money supply do not influence the level of GDP, the composition of GDP, or the level of interest rates. The diagrams in Figure 9.13 enabled us to determine the interest rate and the composition of output without considering monetary policy. In other words, to study the real economy, we could conveniently restrict ourselves to real variables in the economy. Once we know the stance of fiscal policy, we know all we need to know to determine the interest rate. Information about the money supply would not tell us anything else about the interest rate. Monetary variables such as the money supply affect only other nominal variables like the price level.

REVIEW AND PRACTICE

Major Points

1. The process of price adjustment takes the economy to potential GDP over time. When output is above potential, prices rise; when output is below potential, prices fall.

2. If the public expects inflation, the price adjustment schedule shifts upward by the amount of the expected inflation.

3. The economy reaches potential GDP through the repetition of price adjustment year after year. Each year, conditions in the previous year determine the price level coming into the year. Then, the aggregate demand curve determines GDP.

4. Because expected inflation fluctuates according to recent actual inflation, the economy overshoots its potential on the way to its final resting point at potential.

5. One important type of macroeconomic shock shifts the aggregate demand curve. Such a shock can originate anywhere in the spending and financial parts of the economy.

6. The other important type of shock shifts the price level.

7. Monetary and fiscal policy can be used to offset shifts in aggregate demand, so that the shifts have little effect on GDP or the price level.

8. Price shocks create a much more serious problem for policy. Without a policy response, shocks bring lower GDP and higher inflation. Policy can limit the GDP decline only by permanently increasing the price level.

9. A decrease in government purchases as a share of GDP causes an equal increase in nongovernment purchases as a share of GDP.

10. The price level is proportional to the money supply in the long run.

11. The Fed chooses the long-run rate of inflation by choosing the rate of money growth.

Key Terms and Concepts

Phillips curve	countercyclical stabilization policy
natural rate property	accommodative policies
economic shocks	nonaccommodative policies
aggregate demand shock	crowding out
price shock	neutrality of money
discretionary policy	classical dichotomy

Questions for Discussion and Review

1. Explain how the Phillips curve is derived from a model of relative price setting. What happens to the Phillips curve if firms expect inflation?

2. Explain why money is neutral in the long run but not in the short run.

3. Does government spending completely crowd out private investment and net exports in the long run? What about the short run? Why?

4. Why does the economy overshoot potential GDP when expectations of inflation depend on last year's inflation?

5. What would happen to inflation if policy makers attempted to hold unemployment below the natural rate year after year?

6. If firms expect the Fed to start fighting inflation with an aim of bringing it to zero, will their expectations of inflation suddenly drop to zero? Why?

7. What are some possible reactions of the economy in the short run to an event that causes an aggregate demand shift? To an event that causes a price shock? What about in the long run? What if both types of shocks occur at the same time?

8. Explain how the economy would respond to a negative price shock if there were no policy response.

9. Explain why an increase in government purchases decreases nongovernment purchases by the same amount.

Problems

NUMERICAL

1. Suppose the economy has the aggregate demand curve

$$Y = 3,401 + 2.888 \frac{M}{P}$$

and the price adjustment schedule

$$\pi = 1.2 \left(\frac{Y_{-1} - 6,000}{6,000} \right)$$

The money supply is $900 billion.

a. Plot the aggregate demand curve and the potential GDP line. Explain why the *aggregate demand curve is not a straight line.*

b. If $P_0 = 0.5$, what is Y_0? Does this place upward or downward pressure on prices?

c. Compute the path of the economy—that is, calculate GDP, the price level, and inflation—for each year until GDP is within 1 percent of potential.

d. Diagram the economy's path on the demand curve plotted in part a. Then, draw your own version of Figures 9.3 and 9.4. (You may assume that inflation was initially zero). From these graphs, does the economy overshoot or converge directly to equilibrium?

e. Assume now that inflation is given by $\pi = \pi_{-1} + 1.2\,[(Y_{-1} - 6,000)/6,000]$. Compute the path of the economy for the first five years, and diagram the economy's path as in part d. Now is there overshooting?

f. What does the π_{-1} term in the price adjustment equation in part e represent? Explain the relationship between this term and overshooting.

2. Suppose the economy is initially described by the following equations:

$$Y = C + I + G$$
$$C = 220 + 0.63Y$$
$$I = 1,000 - 2,000R$$
$$X = 525 - 0.1Y - 500R$$
$$M = 0.1583Y - 1,000R$$
$$\pi = 1.2\,[(Y_{-1} - 6,000)/6,000]$$

The money supply is equal to $900 billion, government spending is $1,200 billion, and output is at its potential level of $6,000 billion with a price level of 1. Then, there is a money demand shock. The new money demand equation is given by

$$M = 0.1583Y - 2,000R.$$

a. In the year of the shock, compute the value of GDP, the price level, interest rates, and the real money supply.
b. Using aggregate demand curves, illustrate the economy's path in the year of the shock and in subsequent years.
c. Calculate the new long-run equilibrium values for income, prices, interest rates, and the real money supply.
d. Could the Fed have done something to avert the adjustment process? If no, why not? If yes, describe exactly what it could have done.

3. Repeat Problem 2, parts a to c, assuming now that the shock is to investment. The new investment equation is given by

$$I = 800 - 2,000R.$$

What change in fiscal policy would offset the shock?

4. Suppose the economy has the aggregate demand schedule

$$Y = 3,401 + 2.888 \frac{M}{P}$$

and a price adjustment schedule

$$\pi = \pi_{-1} + 1.2[(Y_{-1} - Y^*)/Y^*] + Z,$$

where Z is an exogenous price shock; potential GDP is $Y^* = 6,000$.

a. Graph the aggregate demand schedule for $M = 900$. Graph the price adjustment schedule. Find the price level for $Z = 0$.

b. Suppose the economy starts with a price level of 1.0 and zero expected inflation. A price shock of 5 percent occurs in the first year ($Z = 0.05$). No further price shocks occur ($Z = 0$ in all future years). Trace the path of the economy back to potential by computing the values of the price level, GDP, unemployment, and expected inflation in each year for five years.

c. Repeat the calculations for the following monetary accommodation: The money supply is 5 percent higher starting in the second year. Compare this new path for inflation and unemployment with the original path.

d. Suppose, instead, that monetary policy tries to limit inflation by contracting the money stock by 5 percent starting in the second year. Repeat the calculations and compare with the original path.

e. Now suppose that there is no price shock ($Z = 0$ in all years) but the economy starts with expected inflation of 3 percent. Compute the path to potential. How much excess unemployment (over the natural rate of 6 percent) occurs in the process of returning to potential? Use Okun's law.

5. Consider a closed economy in which net exports $X = 0$. Suppose that consumption is insensitive to the interest rate but the share of investment in GDP rises by 2 percent for every 1 percent decline in the interest rate.

   a. By how much does investment rise as a share of GDP if government purchases decrease by 4 percent of GDP?

   b. By how much does the interest rate change?

   c. Using the growth accounting formula from Chapter 5, calculate how much more real GDP there would be if the capital-output ratio starts at 2.

6. Suppose that output is equal to potential at 4,000 and the equilibrium interest rate is 0.05. Money demand is given by

$$M = (0.3Y - 4{,}000R)P.$$

Money supply is set at 1,000 by the Fed.

   a. What price level is required for equilibrium in the money market?

   b. Suppose the Fed increases the money supply by 100. What is the new price level? What is the percentage change in the money supply? In the price level?

   c. Starting with a money supply of 1,000 and price level of 1.0, how does an increase in the interest rate from 0.05 to 0.10 affect the equilibrium price level? What could cause such an increase in the real interest rate?

   d. Starting again with $M = 1{,}000$ and $P = 1.0$, what effect does an increase in output from 4,000 to 4,500 have on the equilibrium price level?

ANALYTICAL

1. Using the Phillips curve, explain what happens when the unemployment rate decreases for one year and then returns to the natural rate. Next, describe what happens when the unemployment rate stays below the natural rate year after year.

2. From a position of potential GDP and zero inflation, the government increases defense spending. Describe qualitatively, using words and graphs but no algebra, what happens to GDP, the price level, interest rates, con-

sumption, investment, and net exports. Assume at first that expectations of inflation remain at zero. Then, describe how your answers change if expectations of inflation depend on last year's inflation.

3. From a position of potential GDP and zero inflation, suppose there is a sudden and permanent decline in potential GDP. Describe the behavior of prices, output, interest rates, consumption, investment, and net exports.

4. Suppose output is below potential output in year 0. Prices that year are given by P_0. In year 1 (with the level of potential output unchanged), the Fed stimulates the economy by shifting the aggregate demand curve until it intersects the point (P_0, Y^*).

   a. Sketch the aggregate demand curve for years 0 and 1. Describe the action taken by the Fed.

   b. Assume that the price adjustment process is given by Equation 9.2. If inflation in year 0 was zero, how do prices behave in year 1? Sketch the price adjustment curve for year 1.

   c. Explain why output in year 1 is above potential.

   d. In which direction should the Fed have shifted the aggregate demand curve to set $Y_1 = Y^*$? Is it possible to say?

   e. Given the Fed's action, is it possible to say whether prices will increase or decrease in year 2? Why or why not?

5. The Phillips curve originally described a relationship between inflation and unemployment. In this problem, we look at some of the properties of the Phillips curve.

   a. Use Okun's law and the price adjustment equation (9.1) to derive a relationship between inflation and unemployment. Is inflation related to current or past values of unemployment? Sketch a graph of this relationship with inflation on the vertical axis and unemployment on the horizontal axis.

   b. How would a change in Y^* shift the curve? How about a change in U^*?

   c. How would a change in π^e shift the curve?

   d. In view of your answers to parts b and c, how might the Phillips curve have actually shifted in the 1970s and again in the 1990s? Explain.

6. When thinking about the adjustment process, remember that underlying the aggregate demand curve are the IS and LM curves.

   a. During the adjustment process, does the IS or LM curve move? Why does it move?

   b. Assume that the economy is initially in equilibrium, then the IS curve is shifted out. Using the IS and LM graphs, show the adjustment process (i) for the case when the economy returns directly to equilibrium and (ii) for the overshooting case.

c. Repeat part b for the case where the LM curve is initially shifted out.

7. Suppose that the economy is initially in equilibrium and there is a permanent increase in money demand. The following year, the money supply is increased so that, at the old equilibrium level of prices, income, and interest rates, money supply equals money demand.

a. Illustrate the shock and the Fed's reaction to it with an aggregate demand graph. Using arrows, as in Figure 9.6, sketch the economy's path.

b. What happens to prices, income, and interest rates in the year of the shock, the year immediately following the shock, and all subsequent years?

8. Evaluate the following statement: It is price changes, not higher prices, that bother people so much. Therefore, the best response to a price shock is full accommodation. This prevents output from falling below potential, as well as avoiding any additional price changes.

9. Explain the following statement: The reason why price shocks pose a dilemma for policy makers is that they cannot directly control the price level. Contrast this situation to the case of aggregate demand shocks.

10. Suppose the Fed fully accommodates a price shock, shifting out the aggregate demand curve until aggregate demand equals Y^* at the higher price level. The behavior of income and the price level are given by the following graphs:

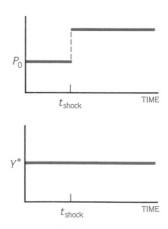

a. Assuming that aggregate demand is given by the usual relationship, which of the following equations must describe the adjustment of prices?

$$\pi = f[(Y_{-1} - Y^*)/Y^*] \qquad \pi = 0.6\pi_{-1} + f[(Y_{-1} - Y^*)/Y^*]$$

   b. Assume now that there is the same policy response but prices are gov-
       erned by the other equation. Describe the path followed by output
       and prices.

11. Suppose the Fed used monetary policy to keep the interest rate at 4 per-
    cent no matter what else happened in the economy.

   a. When would such a policy be inflationary? How would the nominal
       money stock and output behave in this instance?

   b. When would such a policy be deflationary? How would the nominal
       money stock and output behave in this instance?

   c. What other policy is available for targeting the interest rate? What are
       its advantages?

12. *Stagflation* was a term coined in the 1970s to describe a sustained period
    of high inflation and unemployment. Using graphs, describe how stagfla-
    tion may come about in the wake of a price shock.

MICROFOUNDATIONS
OF MACROECONOMICS

PART

CONSUMPTION DEMAND

Consumer behavior—what, how much, and when individuals consume—has been a lifetime study of thousands of economists. This is not surprising, for in economics, the consumer occupies center stage. A first principle of microeconomics is that consumers choose their consumption plans to maximize their satisfaction or utility. And ever since Adam Smith, the performance of an economic system has been judged by how efficiently it allocates scarce resources to satisfy the wants of consumers. So it is natural to start with consumers in our examination of the microfoundations of macroeconomics.

Traditionally, macroeconomists have been concerned with consumption because consumption is such a large and important component of aggregate demand. In Part 1 we saw that consumption is about two-thirds of all spending and the response of consumption to changes in income—the consumption function—is a crucial ingredient in macroeconomic analysis. In the first section of this chapter, we look at the empirical evidence on consumption. We show that this evidence raises questions about the simple consumption function, and then we show how consumption theory has been reconstructed in light of this empirical evidence. We also examine the response of consumption to interest rates.

10.1 | FLUCTUATIONS IN GDP CONSUMPTION, AND INCOME

As the overall economy grows and fluctuates, so does consumption. Figure 10.1 shows how real GDP and personal consumption expenditures have grown and passed through cycles together during the period 1959 to 2002.

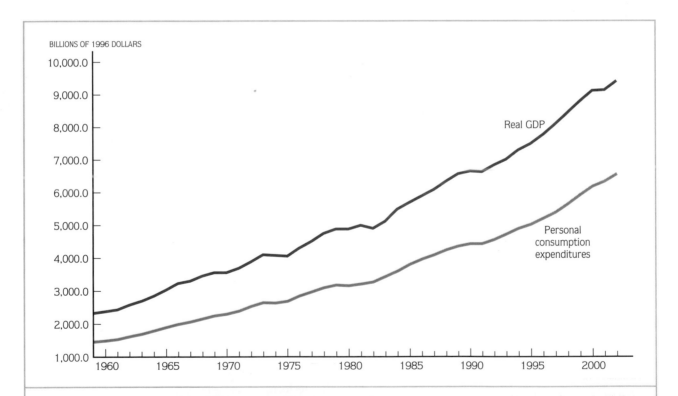

FIGURE 10.1   CONSUMPTION EXPENDITURES AND GDP

Real GDP and real personal consumption expenditures grow at about the same rate over long periods of time so that, on average, consumption expenditures maintain roughly a two-thirds share of GDP. However, over the business cycle, consumption expenditures fluctuate much less than GDP. Consumption expenditure is less volatile than the other components of GDP.

SOURCE: *Economic Report of the President,* 2003, Table B-2.

Note that, *over the long run, consumption expenditures and GDP grow at about the same rate, but over short-run business cycles, consumption expenditures fluctuate less than GDP*.[1] The smoother path for consumption expenditures is particularly evident during the period 1980 to 1984, when real GDP fell and rose sharply, while consumption expenditures slowed down only slightly before returning to a more normal pace. This relatively smooth behavior of consumption expenditures compared with GDP is one of the most important facts of the business cycle.

short-run: consumption fluctuates less than GDP

consumption = "smooth"

The smoothness of consumption differs greatly by type of consumption. Figure 10.2 shows the breakdown of personal consumption expenditures into its three components: durables, nondurables, and services. Note that the

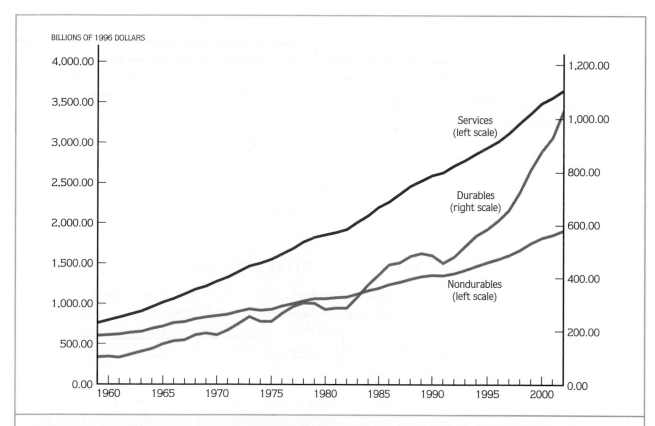

FIGURE 10.2   FLUCTUATIONS IN THE COMPONENTS OF REAL PERSONAL CONSUMPTION EXPENDITURES

Expenditures on services grow smoothly with little cyclical fluctuation. Expenditures on durables are the most volatile component of consumption.

SOURCE: *Economic Report of the President*, 2003, Tables B-3 and B-4.

[1]Note that the increasing gap between real GDP and real consumption in Figure 10.1 is not inconsistent with the fact that the *ratio* of real consumption to real GDP remains constant. The gap gets larger as the level of the two series increases.

relatively smooth behavior of consumption expenditures is most striking for services, which grow steadily regardless of the fluctuations in the economy. Nondurables fluctuate a bit more, but most of the business cycle fluctuations in consumption expenditures are due to durables. When recessions occur, people reduce their purchases of durable items such as furniture and automobiles much more than their purchases of nondurable items, such as food; service items, such as medical care, hardly fluctuate at all. Note, too, that services now represent the largest component of consumption. As services become more important, we might expect overall consumption expenditures to become less volatile.

Overall consumption behavior would show even smaller fluctuations if we looked at the true economic measure of **consumption** rather than *consumption expenditures*. The distinction between consumption and consumption expenditures is a subtle one, but takes on special importance in the case of durables. Consider a car, for example. Expenditure on a car occurs at the time that we buy the car and bring it home from the car dealer, even if we finance it by borrowing. Consumption of the car is then spread out over several years as we drive the car and it gradually deteriorates through normal wear and tear. Expenditure occurs when the car is acquired; consumption occurs as the car is used up. Consumption of durables is more spread out over time and is smoother than expenditure on them. For services and nondurable items, there is no meaningful distinction between consumption and expenditure: When we purchase a haircut, we consume it at the same time. Because consumption of durables fluctuates less than expenditure on durables, it is clear that total consumption has smaller fluctuations than total consumption expenditures.

consumption fluctuates less than expenditure

GDP and Personal Disposable Income

Why does consumption fluctuate less than GDP? Part of the answer can be found in the behavior of disposable personal income. As we saw in Chapter 7, according to the simplest theory, consumption depends on personal disposable income: When fluctuations in disposable income are small, fluctuations in consumption are small as well. We stressed in Chapter 2 that GDP is very different from the personal disposable income available to consumers for spending. GDP is about 40 percent greater than personal disposable income. Part of GDP is not really income at all, because it includes the depreciation of machines, factories, and housing. An important part of GDP is unavailable to consumers because it is paid to the various levels of government in the form of taxes. Still another part is plowed back into corporations in the form of retained earnings rather than paid out to consumers. On the other hand, some people receive transfers from the government, such as unemployment compensation or social security, that are not related to current production.

Although the difference between GDP and disposable income is large on average, what is more important for our purposes is that the difference shrinks during recessions and expands during booms. <u>Taxes fall during recessions, and</u> <u>transfers increase</u> because more people collect unemployment insurance and social security. Therefore, disposable income does not fall as much as GDP. These changes in taxes and transfers are called **automatic stabilizers** because of their stabilizing effect on disposable income; we study them in more detail in Chapter 13. Retained earnings also fall during recessions, because corporations do not cut their dividends very much and thus further mitigate the effect on disposable income. The sum of these effects is shown in Figure 10.3, where real GDP and real disposable income are plotted for the years 1959 to 2002.

⌉ automatic stabilizers keep Yd from changing as much as GDP during booms/recessions ⌋

Figure 10.3 shows that personal disposable income fluctuates less than GDP. On average, when GDP falls during a recession, disposable income does not fall as much. There are exceptions to this general rule, but again, on average,

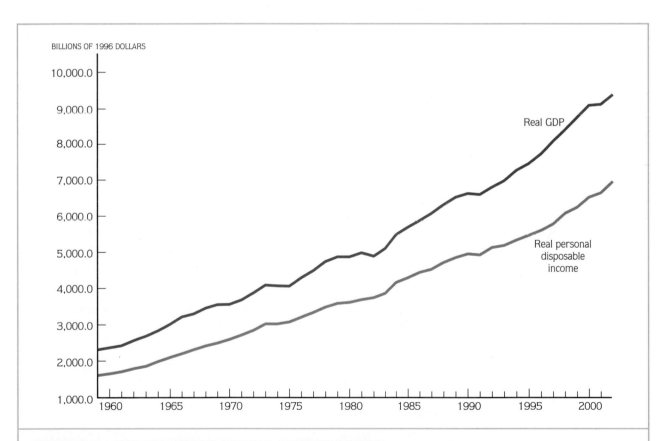

FIGURE 10.3   REAL GDP AND REAL PERSONAL DISPOSABLE INCOME

Disposable income fluctuates much less than real GDP. The automatic stabilizers, taxes and transfers, as well as the dividend policies of corporations prevent disposable income from falling as far as GDP during recessions.

SOURCE: *Economic Report of the President*, 2003, Tables B-2 and B-31.

over this period a fall in real GDP of $10 billion reduced real disposable income by only $5.3 billion.[2]

The Relation between Real Disposable Income and Consumption

As we just saw, part of the reason why consumption fluctuates less than real GDP is that disposable income fluctuates less than GDP. But, can all consumption behavior be explained by current personal disposable income, as the simplest consumption function would suggest? In Figure 10.4, we examine the

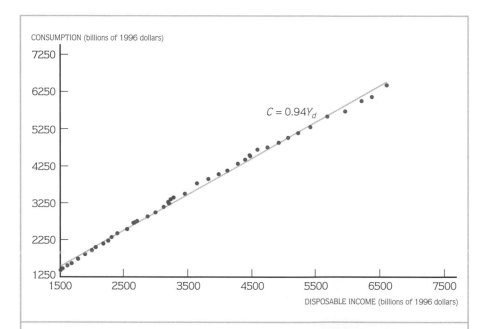

FIGURE 10.4   THE RELATION BETWEEN REAL DISPOSABLE INCOME AND REAL CONSUMPTION EXPENDITURES

The horizontal position of each dot shows real disposable income in that year and the vertical position shows real consumption in that year. The straight line is a simple consumption function fit through the scatter of dots. The vertical distances between the line and the dots measure the error in the consumption function.

SOURCE: *Economic Report of the President*, 2003, Table B-31.

[2]The relationship was estimated by comparing real disposable income and real GDP in the United States each year during the 1959–2002 period. The least-squares relation between the *change* in real disposable income and the *change* in real GDP has a slope coefficient of 5.3. The least-squares line is the straight line that minimizes the sum of squared vertical distances between the dots and the line.

relationship between personal consumption expenditures and personal disposable income for the period from 1959 through 2002. Each dot in Figure 10.4 represents real consumption and real disposable income in the United States for one year. We can summarize the relationship by drawing a straight line through the dots.[3] The straight line gives the relationship

$$C = 0.94Y_d \tag{10.1}$$

which is in the form of the simple consumption function; the **marginal propensity to consume (MPC)** is 0.94. On average, the U.S. public spends about 94 percent of its disposable income on consumption goods and saves 6 percent. Figure 10.4 indicates that consumption is sometimes less and sometimes greater than predicted by the simple consumption function. The errors are given by the equation

MPC = .94 on avg

$$\boxed{\text{Error} = C - 0.94Y_d} \tag{10.2}$$

and are measured by the vertical distances between the line and the dots in Figure 10.4. The errors appear to be small. The simple consumption function seems to give a surprisingly good description of consumption.

10.2 | DEFECTS IN THE SIMPLE KEYNESIAN CONSUMPTION FUNCTION

Unfortunately, Figure 10.4 paints too rosy a picture about the reliability of the simple consumption function. Although the errors in Figure 10.4 appear small to the naked eye, for some purposes (such as forecasting or policy analysis) they are actually quite large. A more revealing picture of the errors is found in Figure 10.5, where the error in the simple consumption function (as calculated in Equation 10.2) is plotted for each year. The vertical scale in Figure 10.5 is much finer than the vertical scale in Figure 10.4. This magnifies the errors, much like a photographic enlargement, and makes them easier to analyze.

Very large negative errors occurred in the 1980s and early 1990s. People consumed much less than normal given their disposable incomes; they acted as if they distrusted their income figures in those years. High inflation rates and

---

[3]We estimated this relationship by finding the straight line that minimizes the sum of the squared vertical distances between the dots and the line (that is, the least-squares line) for the years 1959 through 2002. This line has a negligible intercept or constant term, which is therefore omitted from Equation 10.1.

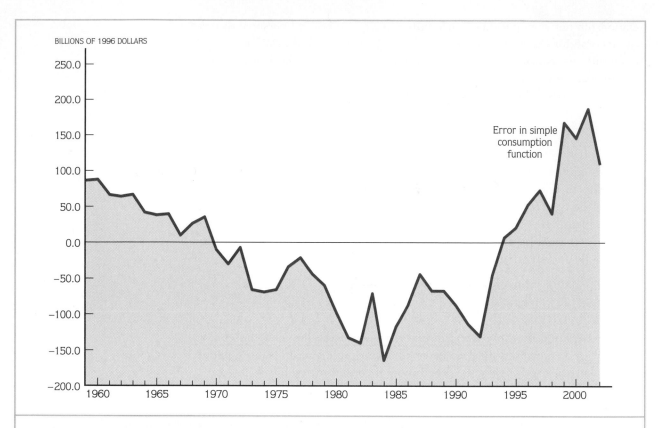

FIGURE 10.5   ERROR ANALYSIS IN THE SIMPLE CONSUMPTION FUNCTION

This diagram gives a microscopic view of the errors in the simple consumption function that are barely visible in Figure 10.4. It blows up the distances between the actual consumption-income dots and the simple consumption-income line in Figure 10.4. The distances are then plotted for each year from 1959 through 2002.

SOURCE: The errors are computed from Equation 10.2 with consumption and income data from Figure 10.4.

two recessions in the early 1980s and stock market gyrations in the late 1980s might have led to a feeling of uncertainty about future income.

At the other extreme, consumption rose well above its normal relationship to disposable income in the 1990s expansion. The economy was on a consumption binge. The bull market in stocks from 1995 through 1999 may have led consumers to feel wealthier. A similar buying binge occurred just after World War II.

Note that these informal but plausible explanations of the errors in the simple theory imply a much more sophisticated consumer than the one that simply looks at current income, as the Keynesian model postulates. Expected future income and wealth also enter the decision. The main contribution of the newer theories of consumption described in the next section is to bring expectations of the future explicitly into account.

future expectations

Short-Run versus Long-Run Marginal Propensity to Consume

There is one systematic feature of the errors in the simple consumption function that is difficult to see in the charts with a naked eye but nonetheless has provided a crucial insight and stimulus to advanced research on consumption: _On average, consumption is smoothed out compared with disposable income; consumption fluctuates less than disposable income._ This phenomenon can be detected and illustrated by using the concept of the long-run and short-run marginal propensity to consume. Figure 10.6 shows how the long-run and the short-run marginal propensities to consume differ for total consumption. The **long-run marginal propensity to consume** tells us how much consumption increases over the long haul when personal disposable income rises. For total consumption, the long-run marginal propensity to consume is 0.94, as we have already seen in Equation 10.1.

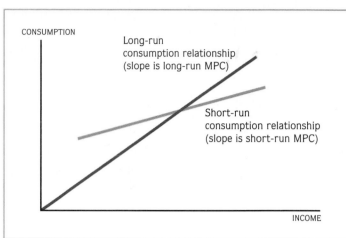

FIGURE 10.6   THE MARGINAL PROPENSITY TO CONSUME IN THE SHORT RUN AND LONG RUN

The steeper line shows how consumption rises with income in the long run. Its slope is the long-run marginal propensity to consume (MPC). The flatter line shows how consumption rises with income in the short run. Its slope is the short-run MPC.

The **short-run marginal propensity to consume** tells us how much consumption rises over the short run (during one year or one business cycle) when disposable income rises. As Figure 10.6 illustrates, the short-run marginal propensity to consume is less than the long-run marginal propensity to consume.

SR-MPC < LR-MPC

Table 10.1 shows the actual difference between the short-run and long-run marginal propensity to consume in the United States from 1959 to 2002 for total consumption and two of its components. The short-run marginal

TABLE 10.1

SHORT-RUN AND LONG-RUN MARGINAL PROPENSITY TO CONSUME 1959–2002

	TOTAL CONSUMPTION	NONDURABLES PLUS SERVICES	DURABLES
Long-run MPC	0.94	0.80	0.15
Short-run MPC	0.77	0.47	0.29

NOTE: The long-run MPCs are based on the least-squares fit of the annual *levels* of real consumption and real disposable income. The short-run MPCs are based on the fit of the year-to-year *changes* in the same two variables.

propensity to consume can be calculated statistically by noting how much consumption changes from one year to the next when disposable income changes. For total consumption, the short-run MPC is 0.72, compared with 0.94 for the long-run MPC. The difference is even more pronounced for consumption of nondurables plus services: For each dollar decrease in disposable income, nondurables and services consumption falls by 47 cents in the short run, but the fall is 80 cents over the long run if that dollar shortfall in income persists. Note that the difference between the long-run and short-run MPC is reversed for durable expenditures; unlike the other components of consumption, durables are more sensitive to income in the short run than in the long run. A complete theory of consumption has to come to grips with these empirical observations.

GDP, Consumption, and Income

1. Consumption fluctuates much less than GDP. The least stable component of consumption expenditures is durables consumption. Services and nondurables consumption grow more smoothly.

2. The main reason that consumption fluctuates less than GDP is that disposable income fluctuates less than GDP. Consumption is financed out of disposable income.

3. Over the past few decades in the United States, consumption has more or less tracked income, according to a simple Keynesian consumption function, with a marginal propensity to consume of 0.94. Of each incremental dollar of disposable income, 94 cents has been spent on consumption goods and 6 cents has been saved.

4. There have been significant deviations from the simple consumption function. Just after World War II, consumers spent more than the simple function predicted. In the 1980s, they spent quite a bit less. And in the late 1990s, they again consumed much more than the simple function predicted.

5. A systematic feature of consumption behavior is that the short-run marginal propensity to consume is less than the long-run marginal propensity to consume. The change in consumption that results from a change in income is apparently spread over a number of years.

10.3 | THE FORWARD-LOOKING THEORY OF CONSUMPTION

MACROSOLVE
EXERCISE

A number of different theories of consumption have been developed in response to the deficiencies in the simple consumption function. The most durable and widely accepted today are the **permanent-income theory** developed in the 1950s by Milton Friedman and the **life-cycle theory** developed independently at about the same time by Franco Modigliani of the Massachusetts Institute of Technology.[4] The two theories are closely related, and together they have served as a foundation for most of the rational expectations research on consumption in macroeconomics in recent years. We refer to them jointly as the **forward-looking theory of consumption.** The theory embodies the basic idea that individual consumers are forward-looking decision makers. The life-cycle theory gets its name from its emphasis on a family looking ahead over its entire lifetime. The permanent-income theory is named for its distinction between permanent income, which a family expects to be long lasting, and transitory income, which a family expects to disappear shortly. In practice, the theories differ primarily in the types of equations used to express the basic idea of forward-looking consumers and to implement this idea empirically.

permanent vs. transitory incomes

Like the simple consumption function, the forward-looking theory of consumption assumes that families or individuals base their consumption decisions on their disposable incomes. To simplify matters, we begin by ignoring factors other than disposable income that might also influence consumption, such as interest rates. The forward-looking theory breaks ranks with the simple consumption function by saying that consumers do not concentrate exclusively on this year's disposable income. Instead, it also looks ahead to their likely future disposable income, which depends on their future earnings from working, their future income from wealth they have accumulated, and how high taxes will be in the future. Based on their current income and expected future disposable income, they decide how much to consume this year after taking account of their likely consumption in future years as well.

Forward-Looking Theory

The consumption decision is thus much like a plan; this year's consumption is the first year of a plan that covers, perhaps, the next 50 years. Next year, the plan can be adjusted to take account of new information that becomes available, but if everything works out as expected, the plan is followed. Although few consumers actually sit down and work out formal forward-looking plans in great detail, it is likely that a significant fraction do some informal planning when they borrow to buy now and plan to pay off the loan later with future anticipated earnings or when they save for retirement. We talk about a very self-conscious plan, of the sort that an economist might make, but we recognize that most families are much more informal in their planning.

[4]Friedman's findings were published in 1957 in a famous book, *A Theory of the Consumption Function* (Princeton, NJ: Princeton University Press); the findings on the life-cycle theory were published in a series of papers, the most important of which are F. Modigliani and R. E. Brumberg's "Utility Analysis and the Consumption Function: An Interpretation of Cross-Section Data," in K. K. Kurihara, ed., *Post-Keynesian Economics* (New Brunswick, NJ: Rutgers University Press), pp. 388–436, and A. Ando and F. Modigliani, "The 'Life-Cycle' Hypothesis of Saving: Aggregate Implication and Tests," *American Economic Review*, Vol. 53 (March 1963), pp. 55–84.

The Intertemporal Budget Constraint

To describe how such a planning process results in a consumption decision, we focus on a single family. The family could be a single individual, a couple, a single-parent household, or two parents and their children. The first aspect we look at is the budget constraint the family faces. The budget constraint applies not to a single year but to many future years taken together. The constraint is more flexible in any one year than over time; in any one year, a family can consume more than its disposable income by borrowing or drawing down some of its financial assets. But a family can not go on forever consuming more than its disposable income; eventually, it runs out of assets or places to borrow. The family faces an **intertemporal budget constraint** that limits its consumption over the years. In some years, a family consumes less than its income; the excess of income over consumption (saving) is then added to the family's financial assets and can be used for consumption in later years. Consumption this year is therefore reduced so that consumption in later years can be increased. The budget constraint incorporates the accumulation of assets that results from savings.

[margin note: shorter period of time = more flexibility]

The intertemporal budget constraint can be described in words as follows:

Assets at the beginning of next year
= Assets at the beginning of this year
    + Income on assets this year
    + Income from work this year ⎱ Disposable
    − Taxes paid this year ⎰ income ⎱ Saving
    − Consumption this year ⎰

Assets include items such as bank deposits, bonds, corporate stock, and pension funds. There are two types of income: (1) income on assets, such as interest payments from the bank where the family holds its deposits, and (2) income from work. If a family adds to its assets, then it also adds to its future income on those assets. Hence, it is important to distinguish between the two types of income.

[margin note: Income]

Disposable income is, of course, income on assets plus income from work minus taxes. Note that the budget constraint simply states that each year's saving (disposable income less consumption) is added to assets.

To give a clearer picture of the intertemporal budget, we introduce the following symbols:

$$A_t = \text{Assets at the beginning of year } t$$
$$R = \text{Interest rate on assets}$$
$$E_t = \text{Income from work during year } t$$
$$T_t = \text{Taxes during year } t$$
$$C_t = \text{Consumption during year } t.$$

The small subscript indicates the year. The interest rate R tells us how much income a given amount of assets earns. For example, if the interest rate is 5 percent and assets A_t equal \$1,000 in year t, then income on assets is \$50 in year t. (The interest rate R is the *real* interest rate, that is, the nominal interest rate less the expected rate of inflation).

Using these symbols, the intertemporal budget constraint can be written as follows:

Assets next year = Assets this year

$$A_{t+1} = A_t + RA_t + E_t - T_t - C_t. \qquad (10.3)$$

The six algebraic terms in Equation 10.3 correspond one for one with the six items listed in the budget constraint written in words. The subscript $t + 1$ indicates assets at the beginning of year $t + 1$. (For example, if year t is 2002, then year $t + 1$ is 2003.) The budget constraint, Equation 10.3, applies to all years of the family's future—working years and retirement years. By applying this equation year after year, the family can figure out what its asset position will be many years in the future, given expectations about the interest rate, income from work, and taxes. By reducing consumption this year, the family can increase its assets in future years. The increased assets—plus the interest earned on these assets—could be used for consumption on timely items such as the children's education, retirement, or a bequest. (The interest rate R is measured in fractions in this formula: If the interest rate is 5 percent, then set R equal to 0.05 in Equation 10.3. Then, R times A, for example, equals \$50 if A equals \$1,000.)

$C \downarrow = A_{t+1} \uparrow$

A consumption plan is feasible if it does not involve an impractical asset position at any time in the future. Any positive amount of assets is practical, since it means the family is lending to others rather than borrowing. For most people, it is impractical to have their assets drop significantly below zero. Our concept of assets is *net* across all borrowing and ownership of the family; if a family buys a house with a 20 percent down payment and takes on a mortgage for the remaining 80 percent, its net asset position is positive. The value of the house as an asset exceeds the liability of the mortgage. Borrowing from a positive net asset position is perfectly practical, almost everybody does it. But it is difficult to borrow when there is a negative net asset position. An exception might be medical or business school students who borrow because their expected future incomes are so favorable.

Preferences: Steady Rather than Erratic Consumption

Many different consumption plans are feasible. As long as the family is careful not to consume too much, it has a wide choice about when to schedule its consumption. It could consume very little in the early years and build up significant assets by middle age. Or it could consume as much as possible and keep its assets only barely positive. Which of the feasible plans will the family choose? The forward-looking theory of consumption assumes that *most people prefer to keep their consumption fairly steady from year to year.* Given the choice between consuming \$10,000 this year and \$10,000 next year, as against

$5,000 this year and $15,000 next year, people generally choose the even split. There are exceptions, but it seems that most people prefer not to have ups and downs in their standard of living.

Figure 10.7 shows a typical path for income for a family with a steady consumption plan. Income from employment is low in the early years and gradually rises until retirement, as job experience and seniority increase. During retirement, income from work is zero. Note how consumption is relatively large compared with income in the early years of work; young families tend to borrow when they can in anticipation of greater future income in later years. During the years immediately before retirement, consumption is relatively low as the family saves more in anticipation of retirement. Finally, during retirement, consumption is much greater than income as the family draws down its assets.

Preferences: How Large an Inheritance for the Next Generation?

Figure 10.7 illustrates the important features of a typical smooth consumption path. But the assumption that families prefer a smooth consumption path is not sufficient to pin down one consumption path among all feasible alternatives. The family can choose a high smooth consumption plan or a low smooth

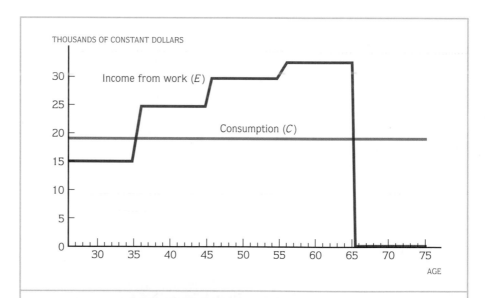

FIGURE 10.7   ILLUSTRATION OF STEADY CONSUMPTION COMPARED WITH INCOME GROWTH AND DECLINE

Income from work is assumed to grow as experience and seniority increase and then drop to zero during retirement. Forward-looking consumers who prefer a smooth consumption path tend to borrow during their early years, save in their middle years, and draw down their assets during retirement.

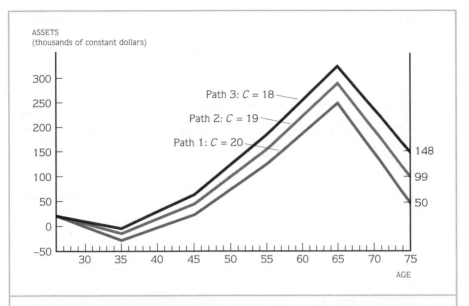

FIGURE 10.8   ASSETS AND BEQUESTS UNDER SMOOTH CONSUMPTION PATHS, STARTING WITH $15,000

If consumption follows Path 1 over the family's lifetime, assets will follow the path marked 1, with little left for the next generation. If consumption follows Path 2, more assets are accumulated to leave more for the next generation. Along Path 3, consumption is even lower and assets left for inheritance are even higher.

consumption plan. Different smooth paths of consumption will leave the family with different levels of assets at the end of the parents' lifetimes. Figure 10.8 shows the path of assets for the smooth consumption path already shown in Figure 10.7 (Path 2) along with asset paths for higher (Path 1) and lower (Path 3) consumption paths.

different paths of "smooth consumption"

A higher consumption path leaves fewer assets at the end of the lifetime. To pin down the consumption path completely, we need to make an assumption about what the parents' preferences are for assets at the end of their lifetimes. How much do they want to leave to the next generation as inheritance? If parents are convinced that their children can make it on their own, they may prefer to consume most of their assets during retirement. Or they might want to reward their children for doing well by giving a large bequest. There is little agreement among economists on what motivates bequests.[5] Fortunately, however, many of the important empirical predictions of the life-cycle and the permanent-income hypotheses hold regardless of what assumption we make about inheritance.

[5]Douglas Bernheim, Andrei Shleifer, and Lawrence Summers argue that parents use bequests to influence their children's actions in "The Strategic Bequest Motive," *Journal of Political Economy*, Vol. 93 (December 1985), pp. 1045–1076.

The Marginal Propensity to Consume out of Temporary versus Permanent Changes in Income

It should already be apparent from Figure 10.7 that there is a relation between the family's current assets plus its expectations about future earnings from work and its consumption decisions. If news comes along that the family is better off, either because it has higher assets today or because it expects higher earnings in the future, the family adjusts its consumption upward. Moreover, it adjusts its future consumption plans upward by about the same amount. If the family reacted to good news by changing only current consumption and not future planned consumption, it would be planning a consumption path that would not be smooth.

$\Delta I \uparrow = \Delta C \uparrow$

By how much does consumption change when disposable income changes? For forward-looking consumers, the answer depends on how long the change in income will last; in particular, whether the change is viewed as *temporary* or *permanent*.

Consider first the case where income increases permanently. An interesting and important example is a permanent cut in taxes, although any other change, such as the winning of a state lottery that pays the family a yearly payment for life, would serve just as well. Suppose that the family learns that its taxes will be lower by a certain amount (say, $1,000) this year, next year, and every year in the future. Disposable income increases in the first year by $1,000, and the increase is viewed as permanent. Assume that the tax cut was unexpected, so that the family could not have planned for it in advance. If the family did not change its consumption plans, future assets would pile up quickly. Next year, assets would be higher by $1,000. In later years, this would grow as interest compounded. But next year, there would be another increment to assets in the amount of $1,000, and in later years this too would earn compound interest. Moreover, if the family raised its consumption, assets would still pile up unless the increase in consumption were equal to the decrease in taxes, $1,000. The family's exact plan would depend on how much of the income improvement it wanted to pass on to the next generation. Assuming that the amount of the improvement passed on is zero, we get a simple conclusion: *The marginal propensity to consume from the increase in disposable income is 1*. *Consumption rises by the full amount of the increase in income when the increase is viewed as permanent*. If the family wanted to pass on some of the increased income as a bequest, then the marginal propensity to consume would be smaller.

MPC from ↑ of permanent y = 1

Now consider a temporary tax cut of $1,000 that will last only one year; taxes are then expected to return to their normal level in the remaining years. Again assume that the tax cut was unexpected, so that the family could not have adjusted its plans in advance. If the family raises its consumption by $1,000 in the year of the tax cut, then it will finish the year with nothing extra saved. At the end of the year, it has to reduce its consumption to the level previously planned; this goes against the rule that consumption should be smooth. The family can achieve a better consumption plan by raising consumption less than the tax cut and accumulating some assets. Hence, the marginal propensity to consume is less than 1. But how much less?

Temporary ΔY

We can determine the amount by using the forward-looking model. If the family did not change its consumption plans at all, the $1,000 would be added to the family's assets and start earning interest at rate R. Suppose that the interest rate is 5 percent. As the years passed, the increment to assets, including compound interest, would become quite large. After 50 years, $1,000 left to compound at 5 percent interest becomes $12,000. But rather than leave this much more for the next generation, the typical family probably raises its planned consumption. If it raises planned consumption by the amount of the interest, $50 per year, then after 50 years, the family has just the additional $1,000, not the extra $11,000 in compound interest. Therefore, one option for the family is to plan to consume an extra $50 per year and leave an extra $1,000 to the next generation. Or, the family could consume just a bit more and leave nothing extra to the next generation. The intertemporal budget constraint, Equation 10.3, can be used to figure out how much more than $50 the increase in consumption would have to be to exhaust the $1,000 windfall after 50 years.

The forward-looking theory predicts the following consumption rule from this planning process: *If a family receives an unexpected temporary increment to its disposable income, it will raise its consumption by the interest earned by the increment, plus a bit more if it does not want to pass the full amount on to the next generation.* If the tax cut is $1,000, then the rise in consumption is $50, or a little more if not all of the $1,000 is passed on. The marginal propensity to consume from the one-year temporary tax cut, or any other temporary increase in income, is the same as, or a little greater than, the interest rate, or about 0.05 in this example. It is far, far less than the marginal propensity to consume arising from a permanent increase in income, which is close to 1. It is also much less than that suggested by the simple consumption function we looked at earlier in the chapter. The difference between the marginal propensity to consume out of a temporary change in income and the marginal propensity to consume out of a permanent change in income is the single most important feature of the newer theories of consumption based on a forward-looking consumer.

consumption $\uparrow$ = *Interest earned from Y increase*

Permanent vs. Temporary

Anticipated versus Unanticipated Changes in Income

In each of the preceding examples, we assumed that the change in income was unanticipated. If the change were anticipated, then the family would adjust its plans in advance. How? If the family learns about the temporary tax cut of $1,000 one year in advance, then it would increase its consumption before the tax cut actually takes place. Postponing the increase in consumption to the year of the tax cut would mean that the planned consumption path would not be smooth, and this would violate the steady consumption rule. The increase in the consumption path would be slightly less than in the case where the tax cut was unanticipated, simply because there is one more year of consumption over which to spread the improved income. If the family wants to leave the full $1,000 to the next generation, then the increase in consumption would be slightly less than the interest rate times the tax cut. If the tax cut occurs with 50 years on the planning horizon, then consumption would be spread over 51 years. The increase in consumption would therefore be about $48.

Note that the marginal propensity to consume in the year that the tax cut is anticipated is astronomical. The change in income is zero in that year and consumption increases by about $48. The marginal propensity to consume is literally infinite. But the important point is that, with forward-looking consumers, the marginal propensity to consume depends not only on whether the change in income is temporary or permanent but also on whether it is anticipated or unanticipated.

The Forward-Looking Model

1. The forward-looking model of consumption assumes that households choose current consumption as part of a lifetime consumption plan.

2. The intertemporal budget constraint implies that total planned consumption cannot exceed total household resources (the sum of current wealth and expected future income). If the household plans to leave a bequest, total planned consumption is less than total resources.

3. Although the forward-looking model can accommodate any pattern of preferences, it is typically assumed that households prefer smooth consumption profiles.

4. The theory predicts that the marginal propensity to consume out of permanent changes in income is close to 1. The marginal propensity to consume out of temporary changes in income approximately equals the rate of interest.

5. Another important insight that comes from the theory is that current consumption responds not only to changes in current income but also to changes in expected future income.

10.4 | HOW WELL DOES THE FORWARD-LOOKING THEORY WORK?

The key point of the forward-looking theory of consumption is that the marginal propensity to consume from new funds depends on whether the new funds are a onetime increment or will recur in future years. The marginal propensity to consume from temporary increases is low, only a little above the interest rate. The marginal propensity to consume from permanent increases in earnings is high, close to 1.

Consumption in the economy as a whole is the aggregation of the consumption decisions of millions of families. Some tests of the forward-looking model focus on aggregate consumption. Many of the events that matter a great deal for an individual family—births and deaths, promotions, winning big at the racetrack—do not matter at all in the aggregate. The "law of large numbers" guarantees that purely random individual experiences do not influence the total. But some of the influences affecting individual families are common across all families, as for example, when the economy goes into recession.

The Short-Run and Long-Run MPC: A Rough Check of the Theory

Before looking at the particular methods that Friedman, Modigliani, and other economic researchers have used to test this theory formally, let us see how well it explains the facts of aggregate consumption presented in Section 10.3. The most important statistical regularity that the simple consumption function misses is that the short-run marginal propensity to consume is less than the long-run marginal propensity to consume; that is, consumption does not increase as much with income over short-run business cycle periods as over long-run growth periods. If consumers usually expect short-run business cycle fluctuations in their income to be temporary, then the forward-looking consumption theory provides an explanation for this finding. If they expect the drop in income they experience during a recession to be temporary, then they do not cut their consumption as much as if they thought the drop were more lasting. Similarly, they do not increase their consumption so much during the boom stage of a cycle. Is it plausible that many consumers tend to view recessions and booms as temporary? Throughout U.S. history, recessions and booms have in fact been temporary. If consumers can remember this experience, then an expectation that recessions are temporary seems reasonable. Moreover, economic forecasters usually predict a return to a steady growth path following a recession—they, at least, remember what happened in the last cycle—and their forecasts are covered on television, in newspapers, and on the Internet.

An important exception seems to prove the rule: In the recession that followed 1973, the dramatic increase in the price of oil and other energy sources made many consumers feel that the drop in real income they were experiencing was unlike a typical recession and likely to be permanent. According to the forward-looking consumption model, consumers therefore would have cut their expenditures by more than the decreased consumption of a typical recession. This is just what happened in 1973 through 1975. (See Figure 10.5, which shows that consumption was well below normal during that period.) Overall the forward-looking theory of consumption seems to pass this rough check pretty well.

S-R MPC < L-R MPC
(S-R fluctuates less)

Ando and Modigliani: Do Assets Matter for Consumption?

One of the earliest formal statistical tests of the forward-looking theory was done by Albert Ando of the University of Pennsylvania in collaboration with Franco Modigliani. Ando and Modigliani formulated consumption as depending on two factors: (1) current income from work and (2) total assets. In their formulation, a change in income, given the value of assets, is assumed to be indicative of a permanent change in income (the current level of income would be representative of all future income). Hence, the marginal propensity to consume from a change in income from work—holding constant the level of assets—would be close to 1. The equation would have to be made more complicated if current income was known to be different from likely future income. On the other hand, their formulation assumes that a change in the value of total assets, given the level of income, would tend to be a temporary change—an example would be a onetime increase in the value of corporate stock. Hence, the marginal propensity to consume from a change in the value of total assets would be close to the interest rate. Algebraically, the Ando-Modigliani consumption function takes the form

$$C = b_1 Y_d + b_2 A, \qquad\qquad (10.4)$$

where Y_d is disposable income, A is assets, and b_1 and b_2 are coefficients. Note that Equation 10.4 is a modification of the simple Keynesian consumption function: Assets have been added as a second factor to income. When Ando and Modigliani fit this simple equation to data in the United States during the period after World War II, they found that b_1 was close to 0.7 and b_2 was close to 0.06; this provided striking confirmation for their ideas about consumption.

The addition of total assets to the equation could eliminate some of the errors in the simple Keynesian consumption function that we noted earlier. For example, the bulge of consumption relative to income in the years just after World War II could be explained by the high level of consumer assets from wartime savings. The decline in consumption starting in 1973 could be explained by the drop in the stock market and other asset valuations. Fluctuations in asset values are also helpful in explaining the fluctuations of consumption in recent years. The bull market in stocks from 1995 through 1999 added about 0.5 percentage point to consumption growth in 1995 and 1996 and about 1 percentage point from 1997 through 1999, while the bear market subtracted about 1 percentage point from consumption growth in 2001 and 2002.

Friedman: Does Past Income Matter for Consumption?

Friedman expressed the ideas about forward-looking consumers in a slightly different way. He defined permanent income as that constant level of annual income that has a present value equivalent to the family's assets and expected future income. All other changes in income are then viewed as transitory. Friedman argued that the marginal propensity to consume from permanent income should be close to 1, and the marginal propensity to consume from transitory income should be close to zero. Algebraically, he formulated the consumption function as

$$C = b_p Y_p,$$ (10.5)

where Y_p is permanent disposable income and b_p is a coefficient. According to Friedman's formulation b_p should be close to 1.

    An important part of Friedman's formulation was his assumption that permanent income is an average of income over the last several years. Therefore, if current income suddenly increased, there would be only a small increase in permanent income; income would have to increase for several years in a row before people would expect that permanent income had increased. To test the theory, he substituted an average of current income and previous income over the past several years for permanent income in Equation 10.5. Effectively, therefore, consumption should depend on past income as well as current income. Past income should matter for consumption because it helps people forecast future income. Although it is an admittedly simple model of people's expectations, Friedman found that his formulation of the consumption function fit the facts better than the simple Keynesian function with current income.

Y_p = avg over past years

Where Do We Stand Now?

The empirical work of Ando, Modigliani, and Friedman is now more than 40 years old. Economic research in recent years has led to more revealing tests of the forward-looking theory and raised puzzling new questions. Three strands of the new research are particularly important: the use of rational expectations to measure future income prospects, the analysis of data on the histories of thousands of individual families, and case studies of particular economic policy "experiments."

RATIONAL EXPECTATIONS   The hypothesis of consumers as forward-looking decision makers already postulates a considerable degree of rationality to consumers. The hypothesis of rational expectations postulates more, but not necessarily less plausible, rationality. Recall that Ando, Modigliani, and Friedman postulated rather naive assumptions about what people expected about their future income: that it would tend to stay where it was recently. The rational expectations approach attempts to look at the actual historical behavior of income and use this to describe statistically how people expect income to behave in the future.

    The approach is a statistical formalization and a much finer version of the rough check on the theory we described at the start of this section. Rather than just saying that people expect business cycles to be temporary, the approach

RESEARCH IN PRACTICE
Locked-Up Savings

The life-cycle theory of consumption says that families should gradually accumulate assets to finance retirement. It does not say how families might hold their savings—these could be in savings accounts, mutual funds, or individual stocks and bonds. The theory says that families should treat their savings as a pool—it does not predict that families would have separate funds earmarked for retirement.

In fact, most families hold virtually all their savings in locked-up form. Even among families close to retirement, only a minority have assets in accounts where they are free to withdraw. Most families have the great bulk of their assets tied up in home equity, retirement plans, and life insurance. They follow the life-cycle principle but keep their savings locked away. It appears that they do not trust themselves not to dip into savings if the savings were not locked away.

David Laibson of Harvard University developed a theory of locked-up saving. He hypothesizes *hyperbolic discounting of future satisfaction*—consumption this month delivers much more satisfaction than you foresee from consumption in future months and years. As a result, you plan to consume as much as you can this month, by drawing down all available assets.

Hyperbolic preferences are evenhanded in their weighting of the near future and the distant future—you think about spreading consumption in just the way the life-cycle model describes. In particular, you would like to plan to save for retirement. But you can see that your propensity to spend everything you can on current consumption would defeat a saving plan. In the first place, the plan you make today would not include any saving today. You plan to start saving next month. When next month rolls around, though, you defer the onset of savings. You never start your saving program.

Now suppose someone offers you a contract. After signing it today, you are obligated to pay into an account each month starting next month. You cannot withdraw from the account until you are 65. You will sign the contract enthusiastically. It solves the problem of providing for retirement by locking your savings up.

The three main forms of locked-up saving are retirement programs, mortgages, and life insurance. These account for a large fraction of the saving of all but the richest families.

Financing retirement is not the only objective of locked-up savings. Some people join Christmas clubs, where their savings are locked up until the next Christmas.

Some forms of locked-up saving (life insurance and Christmas clubs) offer poor returns compared to ordinary investments, yet remain popular.

Laibson's theory of locked-up saving seems to explain some of the features of the way families save. And it may explain the political popularity of the single biggest locked-up fund, the social security system.

Although hyperbolic preferences are different from the preferences that underlie the life-cycle model, as long as families can make full use of locked-up accounts, their actual behavior will be almost the same as predicted by the life-cycle model.

assumes that people act as if they have a little model of the behavior of income over the business cycle in their heads and use this model when guessing their future income. Of course, nobody would actually use such a model in their personal family planning: The idea is that, by watching television, reading the newspaper, or just talking with friends, people get a view of future economic developments that is not much different from that of the average professional economist who actually uses such a model.

The rational expectations approach is used by many economists engaged in macroeconomic research.[6] The most straightforward version of this approach is to substitute the forecasts of income from such a model into the permanent-income equation (10.5) for consumption. More technical versions substitute forecasts of future income into the intertemporal budget constraint, Equation 10.3, and calculate the optimal plan for consumption directly without the intermediate step of Friedman's permanent-income equation. Using rational expectations this way clearly requires advanced mathematical skills, and understandably the approach has attracted economists who specialize in such skills.

It is clear now from this research that the forward-looking consumption theory does not fare as well as when people are assumed to forecast rationally. One problem is that consumption is too responsive to temporary changes in income, although clearly not as responsive as in the simple Keynesian consumption theory. In other words, the forward-looking theory with rational expectations suggests that the short-run marginal propensity to consume should be even smaller than is observed in the United States data summarized in Table 10.1.

INDIVIDUAL FAMILY HISTORIES | One of the most important improvements in our knowledge of the economy in recent years is the availability of data on the economic histories of individuals and families over a span of several years. At the University of Michigan, for example, a survey called the Panel of Study on Income Dynamics has kept tabs on the major economic and personal events of thousands of families since 1969. Such surveys that collect information on individuals over a number of years are typically called *panel* or *longitudinal surveys*. They are useful to macroeconomists because they tell how families experience recessions and booms individually. Aggregate data tell us only about all families in the economy added together. One study looked at how well the forward-looking consumption model performs in describing the consumption behavior of about 2,000 families in the Michigan panel data set.[7] The results show an excess sensitivity of consumption to temporary changes in disposable income. The marginal propensity to consume from temporary income was about 30 percent of the marginal propensity to consume from permanent income. This is higher than the 5 to 10 percent ratio the pure forward-looking model suggests. The results seem to say that about 80 percent of the families behaved according to the forward-looking model, while about 20 percent

---

[6]See Robert Hall, "Stochastic Implications of the Life Cycle–Permanent Income Hypothesis: Theory and Evidence," *Journal of Political Economy*, Vol. 86 (December 1978), pp. 971–988; and Marjorie Flavin, "The Adjustment of Consumption to Changing Expectations about Future Income," *Journal of Political Economy*, Vol. 89 (October 1981), pp. 974–1009.

[7]Robert Hall and Fredric Mishkin, "The Sensitivity of Consumption to Transitory Income: Estimates from Panel Data on Households," *Econometrica*, Vol. 50 (March 1982), pp. 461–481.

behaved according to a simple model in which consumption is proportional to disposable income.

POLICY EXPERIMENTS In 1968, during President Johnson's administration, Congress passed a temporary surcharge on the personal income tax; the surcharge raised taxes by 10 percent. One purpose was to restrict consumption temporarily and thereby reduce aggregate demand in an economy overheated by Vietnam War expenditures. A similar temporary tax change occurred during President Ford's administration but in the reverse direction. When the economy was in the trough of the 1974–75 recession, a tax rebate and social security bonus of $9.4 billion was paid out. The hope was to stimulate the economy by increasing aggregate demand. According to the forward-looking theory of consumption, families who realized that these tax changes were temporary would adjust their consumer expenditures by only a small amount; if so, the policy changes would not have their desired effect of restricting demand in 1968 or stimulating demand in 1975. On the other hand, according to the simple consumption function, these tax changes would be translated into large changes in consumption and thereby in aggregate demand.

Although clearly not conceived as experiments, these two changes in policy gave economists a rare opportunity to test the predictions of the forward-looking theory of consumption. It is probably as close as macroeconomics will ever get to a laboratory experiment. As it turned out, the response of consumption to the change in disposable income was small in both cases. After the increase in taxes in 1968, consumers simply saved less of their reduced income and thereby reduced their spending only slightly. In the second quarter of 1975, the rate of saving as a fraction of disposable income rose to almost 10 percent, from about 6 percent in the first quarter. Almost all the increase in disposable income was saved, evidently because people knew the temporary nature of the income changes. In addition to providing evidence in favor of the forward-looking theory of consumption, the lesson from these two policy experiments has been to make policy makers much more reluctant to use such temporary tax changes to affect aggregate demand. Economists in the Ford administration wrote in the 1977 *Economic Report of the President:* "Consumers normally adjust expenditures to their 'permanent' or long-run income." In 1977, President Carter came into office proposing another rebate to stimulate the economy out of an apparent slowdown in the recovery, but the proposal was criticized by many economists and was not passed by Congress.

In 1992, President George H. W. Bush proposed to reduce the amount of taxes withheld from workers' paychecks to speed the recovery from the 1990–91 recession. However, the reduction in withholding in 1992 implied a smaller refund for taxpayers in 1993. This proposal was much like the temporary tax cuts of the 1970s. As predicted by the forward-looking consumption model, the effect on consumption was small.

The Economic Growth and Taxpayer Relief and Reconciliation Act of 2001 lowered the tax rate to 10 percent at the bottom of the previous 15 percent bracket. In anticipation of the likely tax savings from this reduction, advance rebate checks ($300 for single taxpayers, $600 for married couples) were mailed in the summer of 2001. This increased disposable income by $36 billion in the short run, helped keep consumption relatively high, and contributed towards making the 2001 recession mild by historical standards.

Statistical research on temporary tax experiments indicates that the marginal propensity to consume from a temporary tax change is about half the marginal propensity to consume from a permanent tax change. This ratio is a bit above that found in the Michigan panel data (0.3). In other words, the world is split about 50–50 between forward-looking consumers and those who consume a constant proportion of their current disposable income. Perhaps the most important lesson from these experiments is that the response of the economy to a temporary income tax change is not the sure, predictable stimulus predicted by the simple consumption function.[8]

Tax Cuts of the 2000s: Temporary or Permanent?

The most striking implication of the forward-looking model of consumption is that the marginal propensity to consume out of temporary tax changes is much smaller than the marginal propensity to consume out of permanent tax changes. The second most striking implication is that the impact of tax changes on consumption also depends crucially on whether they are anticipated or unanticipated. One difficulty in predicting the effects of the tax cuts of the early 2000s is that they contain, on the one hand, temporary and permanent components and, on the other hand, anticipated and unanticipated components.

tax change MPC: temporary vs. permanent

The two major tax cuts of the early 2000s were the Economic Growth and Taxpayer Relief and Reconciliation Act of 2001 and the Jobs and Growth Tax Relief Reconciliation Act of 2003. Both acts contain provisions scheduled to expire in several years and other provisions not fully phased in for several years. It is not at all clear whether tax cuts that are scheduled to expire will be interpreted by consumers as temporary or permanent. If consumers expect them to expire, they will adjust their consumption in accord with the relatively small effects of temporary tax changes. If, however, they expect the tax cuts to be extended by a future Congress, they will adjust their consumption in accord with the larger effects of permanent tax changes.

Refinements to the Forward-Looking Model

Overall, the empirical research just discussed indicates that the forward-looking model works fairly well: The marginal propensity to consume from temporary income is always less than the marginal propensity to consume from permanent

[8]Alan Blinder, "Temporary Income Taxes and Consumer Spending," *Journal of Political Economy*, Vol. 89 (February 1981), pp. 26–53.

income, as the theory predicts. But why doesn't it work better? Why does consumption respond as much as it does to temporary income? One reason is that the tests might be incorrectly estimating expectations of future income. In the case of temporary tax changes, for example, families may not be so aware of the machinations of the government. Perhaps, they pay no attention to the news about tax changes. If they see the benefits of a tax cut in the form of reduced withholding deductions from their paychecks, they may mistakenly assume that this cut in deductions is permanent. Then, they will apply their regular marginal propensity to consume from income. Moreover, when they find their deductions back up to the old level, they will reduce consumption accordingly.

Or suppose the family pays close attention to the economic news and believes that a temporary tax cut will accomplish its purpose of stimulating the economy. The family will benefit in the next year or two from the more favorable performance of the economy. According to the life-cycle and permanent-income hypotheses, the family should immediately increase its consumption because of its expected increase in economic well-being. Even though such a family would spend only a little of its tax rebate, it might raise its total consumption level because of the improved national economy.

When making consumption decisions, people do not know with certainty what their income will be over their lifetime. Uncertainty leads to impatience; consumers discount expected future income by more than the interest rate. **Precautionary savings** is the idea that, with *uncertain future labor income* and *impatience*, consumers put more weight on what is happening today than on their expectations of what will happen in the future. People set their consumption to approximately the average value of current income and expected income over the next few years, not over expected income far into the future.[9]

immediate future

Precautionary savings can explain why the marginal propensity to consume out of temporary changes in income is higher than predicted by the forward-looking theory. Suppose you have a temporary increase in income of $1,000. According to the forward-looking theory, if the interest rate is 5 percent you will consume $50 per year (plus a little more if you do not want to add the full $1,000 to your bequest.) With precautionary savings, you will make consumption decisions by looking over the next few years, not over your lifetime. Suppose you adopt a five-year planning horizon. Then you will spend the $1,000 in five increments of $200 (plus a little more for interest income on the unspent balance) for a marginal propensity to consume out of temporary income of 20 percent, not 5 percent.

Precautionary saving can also explain why the marginal propensity to consume out of permanent changes in income, while high, does not quite equal 1. Prudent consumers are reluctant to spend on the basis of expected future income that might not actually materialize. Any permanent increase in income

[9]See Christopher Carroll, "A Theory of the Consumption Function with and without Liquidity Constraints," *Journal of Economic Perspectives*, Vol. 5, No. 3 (Summer 2001), pp. 23–45.

is, by definition, an increase in lifetime expected income. With uncertainty, you cannot be sure that the "permanent" change in income will really materialize. Consumers will not spend all of the expected "permanent" change, causing the marginal propensity to consume out of permanent changes in income to be less than 1.

Another possibility is that consumers cannot borrow as easily as the forward-looking model suggests. Especially during recessions, they cannot obtain the funds to maintain their consumption. Economists call such consumers **liquidity constrained.**[10] Such consumers might be described very well by the simple Keynesian model; they increase their expenditures as they receive more income regardless of whether it is permanent or temporary.

The refinements to the forward-looking model suggested by precautionary savings and liquidity constraints have much in common. With liquidity constraints, consumers cannot borrow against future income to finance current consumption. With precautionary savings, consumers choose not to borrow against future income to finance current consumption because the future income is uncertain. These commonalities make it difficult to categorize departures from the predictions of the forward-looking model as being caused by one or the other.

Restrict current consumption

In concluding this discussion of the forward-looking model of consumption, it is important not to lose sight of the central ideas by focusing too much on the particular equations or tests that express them. The basic point is that families are thoughtful about consumption decisions. The way they react to a change in economic circumstances depends on the context of the change. If the change is transitory—if it involves a windfall gain or loss—consumption is likely to respond relatively little. If the change in income will sustain itself for the foreseeable future, consumption changes almost by the full amount of the change in income.

Empirical Evidence on the Forward-Looking Model of Consumption

1. Verification of the forward-looking model with aggregate data confirms its main implications.
2. More-detailed tests with data on individual families reveal some shortcomings. Precautionary savings and liquidity constraints help explain the discrepancies between the theoretical predictions of the forward-looking model and actual behavior.

[10]See Fumio Hayashi, "Tests for Liquidity Constraints: A Critical Survey and Some New Observations," in Truman Bewley, ed., *Advances in Econometrics*, Vol. 2 (Cambridge, England: Cambridge University Press, 1987), pp. 91–120.

10.5 | REAL INTEREST RATES, CONSUMPTION, AND SAVING

Thus far, we have assumed that consumers want a steady consumption path. They would like to consume about the same amount this year as next year and every year thereafter. This is a reasonable assumption if the price of future consumption goods is neither too low nor too high relative to present consumption goods. But suppose that the price of future consumption goods is suddenly expected to fall; suppose, for example, that sales taxes will be repealed starting next year. Clearly, people would postpone their consumption expenditures until next year to take advantage of the lower price. They would do this as long as they were not so impatient that they could not get along without the goods this year. Consumption today would fall and consumption next year would rise.

real interest rate

The interest rate becomes a factor in consumption because it affects the price of future consumption relative to current consumption. In fact, the *real* interest rate is the relative price between present consumption and future consumption. It thus directly affects the choice of whether to consume more today or tomorrow. Recall that the interest rate quoted in the newspaper, the *nominal* interest rate, does not correct for changes in purchasing power. The real interest rate R equals the nominal interest rate minus the expected rate of inflation π^e. For example, if the nominal interest rate is 7 percent but prices are expected to rise at 3 percent per year, then the real interest rate is 4 percent. If you postpone one unit of consumption this year, you can consume 1.04 units next year by investing at a 7 percent nominal rate and losing 3 percent to inflation.

If the real interest rate is positive, as it generally is, people face an incentive to defer spending: A dollar saved today buys more than a dollar's worth of goods tomorrow. Hence, people tend to defer consumption unless they are too impatient. Economists have a measure of impatience called the **rate of time preference.** If the real interest rate is higher than the rate of time preference, then people tend to shift their consumption a bit toward the next year. If the real rate of interest is high, today's consumption tends to be low. This factor makes consumption negatively related to the real rate of interest. Saving, which is simply the difference between disposable income and consumption, is therefore positively related to the real rate of interest.

Changes in the interest rate do something in addition to changing tomorrow's price of goods relative to today's. They change income. If interest rates rise, for example, a family can earn a higher real return from its accumulated assets. This makes the family better off. On this account, planned consumption is higher. This increase in consumption might offset the reduced consumption that comes from the incentive to defer consumption from today to tomorrow. Hence, we can not say unambiguously whether consumption in the first year falls or rises; the *income* effect makes it rise, while the incentive to make a *substitution* of future consumption for present consumption makes it fall. Similarly, the effect of change in the real interest rate on saving is also ambiguous.

Of course, this offsetting tendency of the income effect and the substitution effect is common to many relative price changes in economics, not only to interest-rate changes.

It is a controversial matter whether or not consumption is negatively related to the interest rate in the U.S. economy.[11] The most difficult problem in interpreting the data is that consumption depends on disposable income as well as on the interest rate, and during the business cycle, income and the interest rate tend to move together. It is difficult to separate out the effect of just the interest rate.

Another complication in examining the relation between real interest and consumption is that the real interest rate is not observed directly. What we observe is the nominal interest rate. To convert it to a real rate, we must subtract the expected rate of inflation. Measuring the expected rate of inflation is difficult.

Effect of Real Interest Rates on Work

There is one last complication in our analysis of consumption. For this whole chapter, we have assumed that individuals do not or cannot change how much they work. Income from work was taken as exogenous. But some people are free to vary how much they work. In particular, if real interest rates rise, the value of income from working today relative to tomorrow rises. People could gain from working harder and longer hours now and taking time off to spend the earnings later. Hence, in principle, income from work is a positive function of the real interest rate. Because saving is the difference between disposable income and consumption, this positive effect of real interest rates on income from working reinforces the negative effect of real interest rates on consumption to make saving positively related to income.

Detecting the effect of real interest rates on work effort has proven even more elusive than detecting the effect of real interest rates on consumption. It appears that most people cannot or do not adjust their work effort very much in response to interest-rate changes. This corresponds with casual observation.

from work

$$Y = f(R)$$

Consumption, Saving, and the Interest Rate

1. The consumption planning process should take the interest rate into account. The real interest rate (the nominal interest rate less the expected rate of inflation) is the trade-off facing the consumer between current and future consumption. When real interest rates are high, future consumption becomes cheaper relative to consumption this year.

---

[11]One attempt to measure the substitution effect alone is Robert E. Hall, "Intertemporal Substitution in Consumption," *Journal of Political Economy*, Vol. 96 (April 1988), pp. 971–987.

2. It is difficult to isolate the effect of interest rates on consumption in actual data. There is no strong empirical confirmation of the theoretical possibility that saving responds positively to real interest rates, at least for the variation in real interest rates observed in the United States.

3. In principle, interest-rate changes may cause people to reallocate labor supply over time. Higher interest rates today increase the return to current labor effort measured in units of future consumption. Evidence suggests this effect is very weak.

10.6 | CONSUMPTION AND THE IS CURVE

In Chapter 8 we introduced the IS curve. It shows all the combinations of real GDP and interest rates where spending balance occurs. To find a point on the IS curve, we consider a particular interest rate. Then, we find the level of GDP that gives spending balance at that rate. The IS curve slopes downward in the IS-LM diagram, with the interest rate R on the vertical axis and output Y on the horizontal axis. The slope of the IS curve and how much it is shifted by fiscal policy are crucial for evaluating the effects of monetary and fiscal policy.

Recall that the simple Keynesian consumption function was used in the derivation of the IS curve in Chapter 8. How is the IS curve affected by the factors considered in this chapter?

The Slope of the IS Curve

Consider first the slope of the IS curve. The smaller the marginal propensity to consume, the steeper is the slope of the IS curve. A small MPC means that the multiplier is small and changes in interest rates thereby have a small effect on output. The results considered in this chapter make us scale down the MPC. In our complete model, departures of output from potential are best thought of as temporary changes in income. Therefore, the variation in income along the IS curve is a variation in temporary income, for which the marginal propensity to consume is likely to be quite small. On this account, the IS curve is steeper than it seemed in Chapter 8, because output is less sensitive to the interest rate.

However, the interest-rate effects on consumption considered in the preceding section have an opposite effect on the IS curve. If consumption depends negatively on the interest rate, then a higher interest rate shifts the consumption function down, in which case the level of GDP corresponding to spending balance is lower. On that account, the IS curve is flatter than it seemed in Chapter 8, because output is more sensitive to the interest rate.

On balance, it is an empirical question whether the true IS curve that incorporates the issues raised in this chapter is flatter or steeper than the IS curve derived in Chapter 8.

Shifts in the IS Curve Due to Tax Changes

The IS curve in Chapter 8 did not distinguish between temporary and permanent changes in taxes. A cut in tax payments of any kind would shift the IS curve to the right by the same amount and thereby stimulate output by the same amount. The forward-looking theory of consumption says that the shift in the IS curve should be much larger if the tax cut is permanent rather than temporary. A purely temporary tax cut, such as the 1975 tax rebate, would have a very small effect on the IS curve.

Because it is sometimes difficult to tell whether people think a tax cut is permanent or temporary, the forward-looking theory points to an element of uncertainty in our ability to determine how much the IS curve shifts in response to tax changes.

Finally, the forward-looking theory says that the IS curve shifts to the right in response to an *expectation* of future tax cuts. Future tax cuts stimulate consumption today because lifetime disposable income has increased.

REVIEW AND PRACTICE

Major Points

1. Consumers finance their consumption from their incomes, and consumption has tracked income reasonably closely in U.S. history.

2. There have been significant deviations, however, from the simple consumption function.

3. The forward-looking consumption theory relates consumption to current and expected future income rather than to just current income.

4. In this view, the marginal propensity to consume from transitory changes in income is much lower than that from permanent changes in income.

5. The forward-looking model passes empirical tests with aggregate data quite well, but still has some defects, which have been revealed mainly by studies of individual family behavior.

6. Precautionary savings and liquidity constraints are refinements that help explain departures from the forward-looking model.

7. Although higher real interest rates ought to stimulate saving by making consumers defer consumption, this hypothesis has not been firmly established by the data.

8. The marginal propensity to consume is one of the determinants of the slope of the IS curve. Because of automatic stabilizers and the low short-run marginal propensity to consume of forward-looking consumers, the IS curve may be steeper than the one derived in Chapter 8.

Key Terms and Concepts

consumption

consumption expenditures

automatic stabilizers

marginal propensity to consume
(MPC)

long-run marginal propensity
to consume

short-run marginal propensity
to consume

permanent-income theory

life-cycle theory

forward-looking theory of consumption

intertemporal budget constraint

panel surveys

longitudinal surveys

precautionary savings

liquidity constraints

rate of time preference

Questions for Discussion and Review

1. List some of the reasons why disposable income is less than GDP. What factors tend to raise disposable income even though they are not part of GDP?

2. How can you tell if a simple consumption function governs the relation of consumption and income?

3. What is an estimate of the marginal propensity to consume from the historical relation of consumption to income? Why is this estimate probably an overstatement of the reaction of consumption to a temporary tax cut? What is an estimate of the short-run marginal propensity to consume?

4. Outline the way that a family might plan its consumption. How would it react to learning that tax rates are going to rise in the future?

5. Why is the marginal propensity to consume out of temporary income above what would be predicted by the forward-looking theory?

6. List some of the reasons why a tax cut has an uncertain effect on consumption.

7. Review all the steps involved in constructing the IS curve, including the possibility that consumption responds to the interest rate.

Problems

NUMERICAL

1. Use the intertemporal budget constraint for this problem. To make the calculations easy, assume that a family lives for five years with four years of work and one year of retirement. (A more realistic assumption would be a 50-year horizon with 40 years of work and 10 years of retirement.) Consider a family that wishes to consume the same amount each year. Assume earnings of $25,000 per year and an interest rate of 5 percent. Assume initial assets of zero.

a. Find the level of consumption such that the assets at the end of five years are roughly zero, say, within $100. What is the level of assets at the beginning of retirement?

b. Repeat the calculation of consumption but with initial assets of $1,000. By how much does consumption rise? Compare this with the interest earnings on $1,000 at 5 percent, namely, $50 per year. Would the increase be closer to $50 if the family lived for 50 years?

c. Repeat the calculation of consumption, with initial assets of zero, but with earnings of $26,000 per year. By how much does consumption rise? Explain why the increase in consumption is larger than in part b.

2. Suppose that we have a consumption function of the form

$$C = 220 + 0.9Y_p,$$

where Y_p is permanent disposable income. Suppose that consumers estimate their permanent disposable income by a simple average of disposable income in the present and previous years:

$$Y_p = 0.5(Y_d + Y_{d-1}),$$

where Y is actual disposable income.

a. Suppose that disposable income Y_d is equal to $4,000 in year 1 and is also equal to $4,000 in year 2. What is consumption in year 2?

b. Suppose that disposable income increases to $5,000 in year 3 and then remains at $5,000 in all future years. What is consumption in years 3 and 4 and all remaining years? Explain why consumption responds the way it does to an increase in income.

c. What is the short-run marginal propensity to consume? What is the long-run marginal propensity to consume?

d. Explain why this formulation of consumption may provide a more accurate description of consumption than the simple consumption function that depends only on current income.

3. Suppose that consumption is given by the same equation as in problem 2 but consumers set their permanent income Y_p equal to the average of their expected income in all future years.

a. Suppose that, as in the previous problem, disposable income is $4,000 in years 1 and 2, but suppose also that, in year 2, consumers expect disposable income to be $4,000 in all future years. What is consumption in year 2?

b. Suppose that, in year 3, disposable income rises to $5,000 and consumers expect the $5,000 level to remain in all future years. What is consumption in year 3?

c. Explain why consumption in year 3 is different from that in problem 2 even though the disposable income is the same.

4. Suppose again that consumption is given by the same equation as in problem 2 and permanent income is estimated in the same way as in problem 2. Place this consumption function into a simple macro model like the one in Chapter 8. That is, disposable income Y_d is equal to income Y less taxes T, where taxes equal $0.3Y$, and the income identity is $Y = C + I + G$.

a. Suppose that, in year 2, investment I is $650 and government spending G is $750. Suppose that disposable income Y_d in year 1 was $2,800. What are consumption, income, and disposable income in year 2?

b. Suppose that, in year 3, government spending increases to $800 and then remains at $800 for all future years. What are consumption, income, and disposable income in year 3? (Make sure to use your calculation from part a of disposable income in year 2 when you calculate consumption in year 3.)

c. Calculate income and consumption for years 4, 5, and 6. Do you see a pattern developing?

d. Where do you think income will end up after it stops changing? Compare your answer with the simple case where consumption depends on current disposable income only, so that the multiplier formulas of Chapter 7 apply.

5. Suppose that the consumption function is given by

$$C = 270 + 0.63Y - 1,000R$$

rather than by the consumption function in Chapter 8. Add this consumption function to the other four equations of the macro model:

$$Y = C + I + G + X$$
$$M = (0.1583\ Y - 1,000R)P$$
$$I = 1,000 - 2,000R$$
$$X = 525 - 0.1Y - 500R.$$

Treat the price level as predetermined at 1.0 and let government spending be $1,200 and the money supply be $900.

a. Derive an algebraic expression for the IS curve for this model and plot it to scale. Compare it with the IS curve in the examples in Chapter 8. Which is steeper? Why?

b. Derive the aggregate demand curve and plot it to scale. How does it compare with the aggregate demand curve in the example in Chapter 8?

c. Calculate the effect of an increase in government spending on GDP. Is the effect larger or smaller than in the case where consumption does not depend on the interest rate? Describe the process of crowding out in this case.

d. Calculate the effect of an increase in the money supply on GDP. Is the impact larger or smaller than in the case where consumption does not depend on the interest rate? Explain.

ANALYTICAL

1. Which of the following facts are consistent with forward-looking theories of consumption? Which are not? Justify your answer in each case. Where the facts are not consistent with the theory, can you suggest some alternative explanations?

   a. The marginal propensity to consume out of current income is less for old people than for middle-aged people.

   b. The marginal propensity to consume out of current income is less for farmers than for most other occupations.

   c. The saving rate for the United States fell in the late 1990s.

   d. The marginal propensity to consume out of temporary tax cuts is around 0.3 to 0.5.

   e. Across the population as a whole, people with lower incomes have lower saving rates than people with higher incomes.

   f. The amount of wealth in the economy is far greater than what current wage earners will consume in their retirement.

2. Suppose that actual GDP is below potential GDP, inflation is low, and the president and Congress want to cut taxes to increase aggregate demand and bring the economy back to its potential.

   a. Describe the situation using an IS-LM diagram. Show where you want the IS curve to move to reach potential.

   b. In light of the forward-looking theory of consumption, describe some of the problems that might arise with the tax cut plan.

3. Draw a sketch of an IS-LM diagram. Compare two cases, one where the consumption function depends on the interest rate and the other where the consumption function does not depend on the interest rate. Compare the relative effectiveness of monetary and fiscal policy in the two situations.

4. Explain the following puzzle: Saving depends positively on the interest rate, investment depends negatively on the interest rate, and saving equals investment. How does an increase in the money supply that lowers the

interest rate and thereby increases investment also increase saving? It would seem that, with the lower interest rate, saving would be lower. What's going on?

5. An important implication of the permanent-income hypothesis is that fiscal policy operates with a lag.

   a. Explain why a permanent increase in government spending may cause the IS curve to shift out slowly over time rather than all at once.

   b. If permanent income is a weighted average of last period's and this period's income, what determines the speed at which the IS curve shifts out over time?

6. Suppose a family wants a smooth consumption profile and does not wish to leave a bequest. Indicate how each of the following factors would affect the magnitude of the marginal propensity to consume out of a temporary change in income.

   a. The size of the temporary income change.

   b. The length of the family's planning horizon.

   c. The rate of interest.

7. Suppose that you know the true magnitudes of the marginal propensities to consume out of temporary and permanent changes in income and that they are stable over time. Explain what can be learned about households' perceptions of the nature of changes in income from observations on the short-run marginal propensity to consume. In particular, what is implied by unusually large changes in consumption relative to income in a given year? What about unusually small changes?

INVESTMENT DEMAND

Investment is the most volatile component of GDP. While smaller in magnitude than consumption, it fluctuates more. Keynes argued that investment is the primary driving force in the business cycle, it fluctuates erratically because of capricious shifts in business expectations, whereas consumption responds passively according to the simple consumption function.

In looking at the microeconomic underpinnings of investment, we will see that this distinction between investment and consumption is not so pronounced. For one thing, investment, much like consumption, responds to income and output in a systematic way. When investment rises, it may be the result, not the cause, of an increase in spending elsewhere in the economy. Moreover, while investment decisions depend on business expectations, these expectations are based on calculated estimates of future changes in demand and prices that businesses are likely to face. In making their investment decisions, business firms are at least as forward-looking as the consumers described in Chapter 10.

11.1 | FLUCTUATIONS IN INVESTMENT SPENDING

We saw in Chapter 2 that investment spending is divided into three categories:

1. <u>Nonresidential fixed investment</u>—business purchases of new plant and equipment.

2. <u>Residential fixed investment</u>—construction of new houses and apartments.

3. <u>Inventory investment</u>—increases in stocks of goods produced but not yet sold.

Nonresidential fixed investment was 10.6 percent of GDP in 2002. Residential investment was 4.5 percent of GDP in the same year. But the shares of the different types of investment in GDP are not good measures of their importance in economic fluctuations. Although plant and equipment investment is the dominant component of total investment, it is the most stable over time. Since inventory investment is negative as stocks of unsold goods fall and positive when stocks of goods rise, its share of GDP is not a very meaningful statistic. Yet <u>inventory investment is particularly volatile and plays a major role in recessions</u>. Finally, <u>residential investment is important because housing construction drops when mortgage interest rates go up</u>.

Figure 11.1 shows how tightly fixed investment is linked to overall economic activity. <u>Reductions in investment frequently occur at about the same time as the economy goes into a recession</u>. Recoveries from recessions, as in the years following the 1990–91 recession, are usually periods when investment rises rapidly. <u>The fluctuations of investment are larger in percentage terms than the fluctuations in real GDP</u>. Sometimes, fluctuations in investment occur without fluctuations in GDP, when consumption, government spending, or net exports move in the opposite direction. Note that investment slowed down in 2002, although there was no slowdown in real GDP growth in 2002.

The behavior of the two components of fixed investment—business (nonresidential) and residential—is shown in Figure 11.2. In some recessions, residential investment turns down before business investment turns down. This was true of the downturn in 1990. We show later that <u>rising interest rates have large negative effects on residential investment and the start of most recessions is accompanied by rising interest rates</u>. Note that, in 1986, business fixed investment declined even though residential investment continued to grow. As we will see, this decline may have been due to the increase in taxes on business capital passed into law in 1986.

I↑ rapidly during recoveries

R↑ and recessions (correlation)

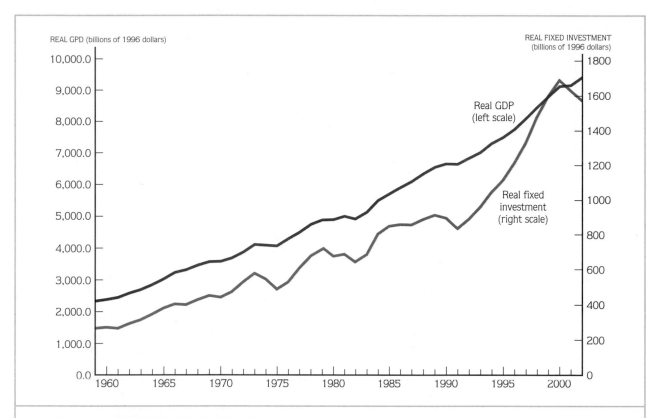

FIGURE 11.1   FIXED INVESTMENT AND GDP

Real fixed investment and real GDP fluctuate together. Investment and GDP rose together in the great expansion of the 1960s, fell together in the recession beginning in 1974, rose again in the late 1970s, fell together in the recessions of the early 1980s, 1990–91,
and 2001. Investment has risen faster since 1991. The fluctuations in fixed investment are larger, as percentages, than the fluctuations in total GDP.

SOURCE: *Economic Report of the President,* 2003, Table B-2.

Real GDP and *business* fixed investment move together almost in tandem.
We cannot tell from the data whether movements in GDP induce movements
in business investment or movements in business investment induce movements in GDP. Another mechanism to be considered is that both GDP and
business investment respond to the same underlying stimulus, which causes
both to move together.

In the economy as a whole, the volume of investment observed is the joint
outcome of three factors: (1) **investment demand,** decisions made by businesses about the amount of investment to undertake; (2) **saving supply,** decisions made by consumers about the amount to save; and (3) **investment
supply,** decisions made by producers of investment goods about how much to
supply.

This chapter focuses on investment demand. A complete model of the
economy that combines saving behavior as described in Chapter 10 and the

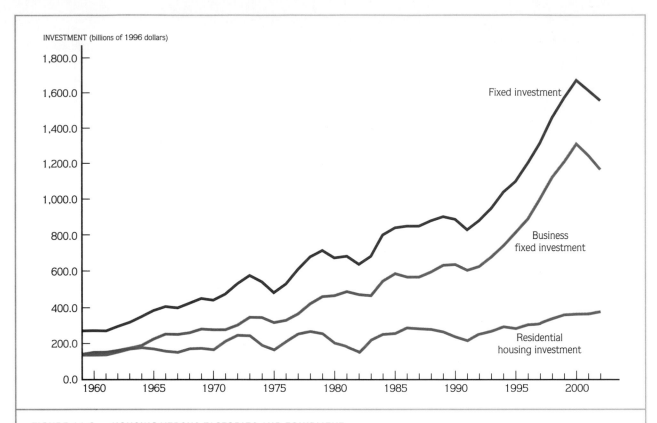

INVESTMENT (billions of 1996 dollars)

FIGURE 11.2   HOUSING VERSUS FACTORIES AND EQUIPMENT

Separating housing investment from business investment reveals some important timing differences. Both business investment and housing investment fluctuate widely during recessions and booms. But housing investment leads real GDP while business investment moves together with real GDP.

SOURCE: *Economic Report of the President*, 2003, Table B-2 and Table B-6.

supply side of the economy is necessary to give a complete picture of investment. The economy reconciles the decisions of the various groups with the interest rate and the price of capital goods. If businesses want to invest more than consumers are willing to lend, the interest rate rises enough to depress investment and stimulate saving to the point of equality. If businesses want to invest more than the producers of investment goods want to produce, the price of capital goods rises. Then investment demand falls and the supply of capital goods rises, again to the point of equality.

economy reconciled with fluctuating R

Investment Analysis

1. Investment is the flow of newly produced capital goods. It consists of plant and equipment investment, residential investment, and inventory investment.

2. Investment is much more volatile than consumption. Declines in business fixed investment are closely timed with declines in the overall economy. Declines in housing investment lead the declines in the overall economy.

3. The overall level of investment depends on three elements: the investment demand of firms and households, the funds available for investment, and the amount of investment goods produced. Interest rates and the prices of investment goods move to equate the three elements. In this chapter, we focus on investment demand.

11.2 HOW FIRMS MAKE INVESTMENT DECISIONS

In examining the micro foundations of investment demand, we start with business fixed investment and look at the decision process of a typical business firm. From a firm's perspective two decisions can be distinguished. The first thing for the managers to decide is how many factories and machines they want. That is, what is the firm's desired **capital stock?** The second question is how fast to build the factories and when to order the machines that they want. That is, what is the *flow of investment*? We start with the question of the desired capital stock and derive the flow demand subsequently.

It is helpful to pose the typical firm's problem in the following rather abstract way: Suppose a firm has already figured out how much output it plans to produce during the upcoming year. Further, suppose that whatever capital it will use it will *rent* from another firm in the equipment rental business. For example, a firm in the business of offering typing services to its customers would rent word-processing equipment from a computer-leasing firm. (Many firms own most of their capital, but we look at that case a little later.) The idea of thinking about a firm's investment decision as a choice about how much capital to rent was developed through models by Dale Jorgenson of Harvard University in the early 1960s.[1] It is a useful abstraction because it makes the capital decision much like the decision to employ other factors used in production, such as labor and raw materials.

How much capital will the firm choose to rent? Microeconomics tells us the answer: the amount that equates the marginal benefit to the marginal cost. MR = MC The *marginal benefit* is the amount of dollars saved by using fewer of the other factors of production when more capital is employed. A firm with more capital needs fewer workers, less energy, or fewer materials to produce the same amount of output. For example, with a word processor, a firm offering typing services might require fewer hours from proofreaders and typists and perhaps fewer correction materials. Note that the firm must look ahead to determine

[1]Dale Jorgenson, "Capital Theory and Investment Behavior," *American Economic Review*, Vol. 53 (May 1963), pp. 247–259.

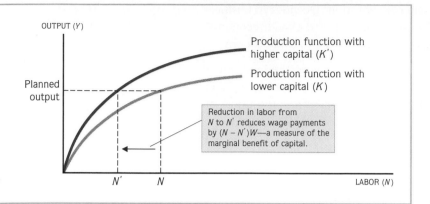

FIGURE 11.3   THE PRODUCTION FUNCTION AND THE MARGINAL BENEFIT OF CAPITAL

The production function shows the amount of output produced from different amounts of labor. The lower production function describes the situation with the existing capital of the firm. To produce the planned output, the firm must employ N workers. The upper production function applies if the firm decides to rent some extra capital. In that case, to produce the planned output, only N' workers need to be employed. The marginal benefit of capital is the reduced wage payments, $(N - N')W$.

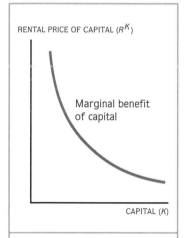

FIGURE 11.4   THE MARGINAL BENEFIT OF CAPITAL SCHEDULE

The marginal benefit of capital is a declining function of the amount of capital because of the diminishing marginal product of capital. The position of the schedule depends on the level of planned output and the wage rate.

the marginal benefit of employing more capital during the period that it rents the capital. Firms are thus assumed to be *forward-looking* in this theory of investment.

The **marginal cost of capital** is just the rental cost charged by the renting firm. For example, it is the amount that the computer-leasing firm charges each year for word-processing equipment.

The firm's decision can be illustrated graphically. The most important input to production is labor, so consider the case where the input displaced by capital is labor. The production function relating labor input to output produced is shown in Figure 11.3. When there is more labor input, there is more output. For example, for the typing-services firm, when typists and proofreaders work more hours, more typed pages are produced. When there is more capital in the firm, the production function relating labor input to output produced is shifted upward, as shown in Figure 11.3. In this case, fewer hours worked by typists and proofreaders result in the same number of typed pages. In Figure 11.3, N is the level of employment needed to produce planned output with the existing capital stock, and N' is the reduced level of employment needed to produce planned output if extra capital is rented. If the wage per worker is W, the marginal benefit of the extra capital is $(N - N')W$.

We assume that capital has a *diminishing marginal product*, which means that the amount of the upward shift in the production function and the corresponding decrease in labor requirements decline as the amount of capital grows. For example, if the typing-services firm began with one full-time typist and one half-time proofreader, the first word processor would result in more labor saved than a second word processor. The third and fourth word processors would displace essentially no labor. We can describe the relationship between capital and the marginal benefit of additional capital in a **marginal benefit of capital** schedule, as shown in Figure 11.4.

The marginal benefit of capital schedule is the firm's *demand curve for rented capital* as well. To choose its level of capital, the firm simply finds the amount of capital that equates the marginal benefit of capital to the marginal cost of capital, which is the rental price. We call the rental price of capital R^K. The superscript K is a mnemonic for capital. Figure 11.5 illustrates the process.

What happens if the firm decides to produce more output? Looking back at Figure 11.3, you can see that producing more output with the same capital stock requires more labor. That, in turn, raises the marginal benefit of capital. To equate the marginal benefit to an unchanged rental price of capital, the firm must rent more capital. Figure 11.6 shows how the firm responds to an increase in output.

We have not said anything yet about investment, only about the firm's decision to rent capital. A firm could rent more capital without bringing about any investment in the economy as a whole. The firm might just rent some existing capital that another firm had decided not to rent anymore. The relation between the decisions of individual firms and total investment in new capital goods is the subject of Section 11.3.

Determination of the Rental Price of Capital

How would the market set the rental price of capital? We can answer this by looking at the costs faced by a rental firm, like a computer-leasing firm, that is in the business of owning machines and renting them out. We use the following terms and assumptions:

P^K is the price for purchasing a new machine from a producer of machines. The price is assumed to be unchanging for now. The price is measured in "real" terms, that is, relative to the price of other noncapital goods, like haircuts or typing services.

R is the real interest rate.

d is the rate of depreciation. At the end of each year, the rental firm has to spend an amount d times the original amount spent on the machine P^K to make up for wear and tear on the machine.

R^K is the rental price of the equipment. This is the amount received by the rental firm for renting out the machine for one year.

First, consider the cost side of the rental operation. Suppose the rental firm decides to sell the machine after one year in the rental market. At the beginning of the year, it borrows P^K to buy the machine at an interest rate of R and incurs an interest cost of RP^K. It has to pay dP^K to make up for depreciation. Total rental costs are therefore

Rental costs: $\boxed{(R + d)P^K.}$ (11.1)

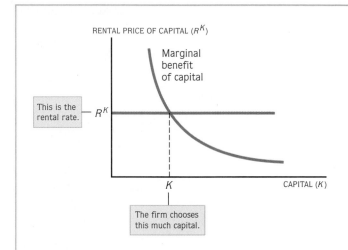

FIGURE 11.5   CHOOSING THE CAPITAL STOCK

The marginal benefit of capital schedule is the firm's demand function for rented capital. The firm chooses its capital stock by equating the marginal benefit of capital to its rental price. With planned output and the wage rate held constant, the firm chooses to rent more capital and employ less labor if the rental price falls.

P^K = price of purchase

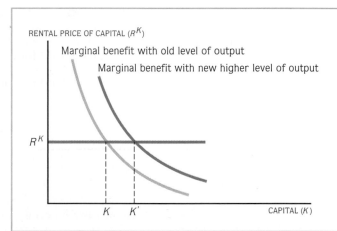

FIGURE 11.6   EFFECT OF HIGHER OUTPUT

When planned output rises and the rental price of capital and the wage remain the same, the firm's demand for capital rises. Higher planned output shifts the marginal benefit for capital schedule to the right. The firm's demand for rented capital rises from K to K'.

In words, Equation 11.1 states:

> The cost of renting out one machine for one year
> = (The rate of interest + The rate of depreciation)
> × The price of a new machine.

For example, if the price of a word processor is $1,000, the interest rate $R = 0.05$, and the depreciation rate $d = 0.15$, then the rental price is $200 per year.

What is the market rental price? If the renter does not have a monopoly in the rental market, the market rental price exactly equals the cost of renting. If it were any higher, new firms would enter the rental business and bid down the rent. If the rent were below cost, some rental firms would go out of business and rents would rise. Thus, the rental price of a machine for a year is just as spelled out: the interest rate plus the rate of depreciation times the price of a new machine. Algebraically, we have

$$R^K = (R + d)P^K. \tag{11.2}$$

Now we can go back to Figure 11.5 and relate the demand for capital by the firm that uses capital to the underlying determinants of the rental price of capital. Remember that the firm's demand for capital is a declining function of the rental price, so that the demand for capital is a declining function of the price of new equipment and a declining function of the real interest rate.

Demand for Capital and Rental Price

1. The demand for capital declines if the rental price of capital rises. The rental price rises if the price of new equipment or the interest rate rises.

2. The demand for capital rises if planned output rises.

3. The demand for capital rises if the wage rises.

The Rental Price and the Decision to Buy New Capital Goods

Much of the capital equipment in U.S. industry is in fact rented, so the analysis we just presented is more than an abstraction. But the bulk of capital is owned by the firm that uses it in production. Moreover, the one-year perspective we used to solve for the rental price of capital is not representative. Most firms purchase capital for the long run. Their concern is not just with the payoff in the first year, but with the financial success of the project over a decade or more. They must look ahead and estimate the benefits of a new capital project under the assumption that it will operate for quite a number of years.

Jorgenson's approach determines the desired capital stock in terms of the rental price of capital. He showed that the same formula for the desired capital stock applies in the more common case where a firm owns the capital instead of renting it. Firms constantly formulate and evaluate investment projects. An investment project that consistently earns more than the rental price of capital is worth undertaking. The project is a winner because the firm earns more than it would have to pay to borrow money to finance the project plus pay to cover the depreciation of the capital required for the project. Similarly, an investment project that consistently earns less than the rental price of capital is not worth undertaking. It is a loser.

Because of the diminishing marginal product of capital, as the winning projects are put into effect, they depress the earnings of future projects. Eventually, the last winning project earns just the borderline revenue, namely, the rental price of the capital. On the margin, the firm taking a long-term view and purchasing its own capital reaches just the same point it would if it chose to rent capital and made a year-by-year decision about the amount of capital to use. Both the capital budgeting approach and the rental approach arrive at the same conclusion: *The firm uses capital up to the point where the marginal benefit of capital equals the rental price of capital.*

Not all investment decisions fit neatly into this analysis. If the firm's technology requires that investments take place in large lumps, like building blast furnaces or power plants, it may not be able to find a combination of projects with the property that the marginal benefit of investment in each year is just equal to the rental price of capital. It may have to settle for a situation where the marginal benefit is higher in some years and lower in others. The basic criterion for selecting winning investment projects remains the same for these lumpy investments. On the average, the marginal benefit of capital equals the rental price even in those cases. An investment theory based on the equality of marginal benefit and rental price seems a reasonable approximation by which to deal with the aggregate economy, even when some of the thousands of firms in the aggregate are making decisions about lumpy investments.

[handwritten margin note: Marginal Benefit = rental price (when owning)]

Expected Changes in the Future Price of Capital

So far we have assumed that the relative price of capital, P^K, does not change, and is therefore not expected to change. What happens if the relative price of capital goods is expected to change? The forward-looking aspects of the firm's investment decision now become important. Consider first the rental firm. Suppose that the price of capital is *expected* to *decrease* during the period that the capital equipment is rented out. On this account, the rental firm stands to take a loss. It purchased the capital for P^K, and the capital will be worth less than that, say, P_1^K, next year when the equipment is returned. The rental firm expects to lose $P^K - P_1^K$. Recall that a competitive firm in the rental market must break even in equilibrium. Therefore, the rental rate must increase. For example, if the price is expected to fall from $P^K = \$1,000$ to $P_1^K = \$950$ next year, then it would increase the rental price by $50. Conversely, if the rental firm expected an increase in the price of capital, it would stand to gain. It could cover its costs by charging a lower rental price. In general, the rental price is decreased by the amount of the *expected* increase in the price of capital, ΔP^K.

With capital goods prices expected to change, the formula for the rental price becomes the old formula in Equation 11.1 less the expected change in the price of capital equipment:

$$R^K = (R + d)P^K - \Delta P^K.$$

The same thing can be written a bit more compactly as

$\pi^k =$ expected % change in price of capital

$$R^K = (R - \pi^K + d)P^K,$$

where π^K is the expected percentage change in the relative price of capital equipment: $\pi^K = \Delta P^K/P^K$.

This modification of the earlier rental price formula becomes very important when the price of capital is expected to change by a large amount relative to the price of other goods. As we will see, for example, changes in taxes can alter the effective price of capital. If these changes in taxes are *anticipated* by firms, then the rental price of capital will change. Since firms increase their desired capital stock when the rental rate falls, a decline in the rental rate due to an expected change in taxes increases capital spending.

11.3 | THE INVESTMENT FUNCTION

MACROSOLVE
EXERCISE

To keep things simple in our derivation of the investment function, we assume that firms purchase all their capital. As we have just seen, the rental price of capital is the central economic variable for investment decisions.

The firm's **investment demand function** tells how much capital equipment the firm will purchase given its planned level of output and the rental price of capital. If the firm has been in business for a while, it will have an existing stock of capital at the beginning of the year. After examining the planned level of output and the rental price of capital, it will decide on a level of capital to use during the year. Finally, it will purchase enough new capital to make up the difference. In a nutshell, this is the theory of investment.

Earlier we showed that the firm chooses the amount of capital it uses by equating the marginal benefit of capital to the rental price of capital. When the amount of capital is high, the marginal benefit of further capital is low. By adjusting the amount of capital, the marginal benefit can be brought into equality with the rental price. The result of this process is the firm's **desired capital stock,** which we call K^*.

An example of an algebraic formula describing the desired capital stock is

Desired capital stock

$$K^* = 0.5(W/R^K)Y.$$

(11.3)

In this formula, W is the wage rate, Y is the firm's level of output, and R^K is the rental price of capital. The formula says that the desired capital stock equals 0.5 times the ratio of the wage to the rental price of capital, times the level of output. Hence, the firm wants to increase its use of capital whenever the wage to rental price ratio rises. When labor becomes more expensive relative to capital, the firm substitutes toward capital. Whenever planned output Y rises, the firm also wants to use more capital.

Now, consider how the **actual capital stock** changes. Suppose that the firm finishes the last year with a capital stock of K_{-1} (the subscript -1 means last year) that is not equal to the desired capital stock for this year, K^*. If there is no depreciation, then the level of investment increases the capital stock by the amount of the investment. That is, investment equals the change in the capital stock:

$$I = K - K_{-1}. \tag{11.4}$$

If the firm wants its capital stock K to equal the desired capital stock K^*, then its investment demand I during the year is obtained by substituting $K = K^*$ into Equation 11.4. That is,

$$I = K^* - K_{-1}. \tag{11.5}$$

This much investment added to its existing capital gives the firm its desired level of capital for this year. This formula is the firm's **investment function.** The investment function for the example formula for the desired capital stock K^* in Equation 11.3 can be written out as

$$I = 0.5(W/R^K)Y - K_{-1}. \tag{11.6}$$

Then, it is apparent that *investment depends positively on the wage rate, negatively on the rental price of capital, and positively on output.*

The effect of output on investment is called the **accelerator.** To simplify the notation, set $0.5(W/R^K)$ equal to the simple expression v. Then, Equation 11.3 states that $K^* = vY$. If the firm always adjusts its capital stock each year so that it equals the desired stock, then

$$K = vY \quad \text{and} \quad K_{-1} = vY_{-1}. \tag{11.7}$$

This year   Last year

Investment, which is the change in the capital stock, therefore must be given by the difference between the two expressions in Equation 11.7. That is,

$$I = vY - vY_{-1} = v\Delta Y. \tag{11.8}$$

In words, the *level* of investment I depends on the *change* in output ΔY. When output accelerates, that is, when its change gets bigger, investment is stimulated. A rise in output from one level to another causes a burst of investment, but if output remains at its higher level, investment subsides. This accelerator process seems to explain a large fraction of the movements in investment.[2] It certainly is part of the reason for the close association between investment and GDP that we noted at the beginning of the chapter.

Depreciation and Gross Investment

If the capital stock depreciates, as of course it does in reality, then the investment equations derived so far are only for net investment; recall that net investment is the change in the capital stock. A gross investment equation can be easily derived by adding a term to Equation 11.6 that measures the part of investment that goes for replacing worn-out capital. One assumption is that a constant fraction d of the existing capital stock wears out each period.[3] Then d times K_{-1} is added to Equation 11.6 and all the related forms of the investment demand function in this chapter. Depreciation accounts for a very large part of gross investment. In 2002, for example, gross private domestic investment was $1,597.3 billion, while depreciation was $1,174.8 billion. Net investment was therefore $422.5 billion.

Properties of the Investment Function

1. When the growth of output Y is high, investment is high.

2. When the rental price of capital (R^K) is high, investment is low. In particular:

   (a) When the real interest rate is high, investment is low.

   (b) When the price of new capital goods is high, investment is low.

3. When wages are high, investment is high.

4. The amount of replacement investment due to depreciation is a large fraction of investment in a typical year. This large fraction of investment is closely related to the level of the capital stock and thus to the level of output.

Lags in the Investment Process

A somewhat unrealistic element in the investment function just derived is that the capital stock is adjusted to its desired level immediately. The investment function in Equation 11.6 assumes that the firm puts new capital in place as

[2]See Peter K. Clark, "Investment in the 1970s: Theory, Performance and Prediction," *Brookings Papers on Economic Activity*, Vol. 1 (1970), pp. 73–113.
[3]There has been relatively little research on replacement investment. A good but somewhat mathematical discussion is in Martin S. Feldstein and Michael Rothschild, "Towards an Economic Theory of Replacement Investment," *Econometrica*, Vol. 42 (March 1974), pp. 393–423.

soon as it becomes aware that the level of output, the rental price of capital, and the wage warrant the new capital. For some kinds of equipment, this assumption is reasonable. But for many projects, there is a **lag** of several years between the firm's realization that new capital is needed and the completion of the capital installation. To put it another way, much of the investment occurring this year is the result of decisions made last year, the year before, and even the year before that. The decisions were governed by the expectations prevailing in those years about economic conditions this year. New information about this year's conditions that became available after the launching of the projects cannot affect this year's investment in those projects. Much of this year's investment was predetermined by earlier decisions.

To set down an algebraic expression of lags in the investment process, we assume that firms invest so that their capital stock is adjusted *slowly* toward the desired capital stock. Suppose that firms change their capital stock by a fraction s of the difference between the desired capital stock and the capital stock at the end of the last year. That is, — *slower adjustment = smaller s*

$$I = s(K^* - K_{-1}).$$ (11.9)

Comparing this equation with Equation 11.5, we see how the investment function is modified to take account of lags in the investment process. The investment demand function in Equation 11.9 has all the properties of the original investment demand function plus one more: The more slowly the capital stock is adjusted (the smaller s is), the weaker is the reaction of investment demand to any of its determinants: planned output, the rental price of capital, or the wage rate.

Economic researchers have reached the conclusion that the responsiveness of investment to its determinants is very much attenuated by lags.[4] Only certain types of investment can take place in the year that economic changes make it apparent to firms that more capital is needed. Investment in this category includes tools, trucks, computers, and other portable items that can be produced quickly or are not produced to order. Major investments like whole plants or new custom-made equipment take one or more years to put in place.

The Aggregate Investment Demand Function

The discussion has looked at investment in the firm. We need to go from the firm to the economy as a whole. We assume that total investment in plant and equipment is governed by Equation 11.9, with the wage to rental ratio taken as an economywide average and output taken as total real GDP. Of course, going from the firm to the total economy involves an element of approximation, because not all of the firms we add together have the same investment functions. Still, an aggregate investment demand function is a reasonable

[4]See Clark, "Investment in the 1970s," pp. 73–113.

THE STOCK MARKET AND INVESTMENT

The stock market closely tracked nonresidential investment during 1995–2002, both in the 1995–2000 stock market boom and the 2000–2002 stock market bust. Why is there a link between the stock market and investment? In Chapter 10, we discussed how the stock market and consumption are linked because of wealth effects. The link between the stock market and investment, in contrast, is caused because both are forward-looking variables.

Firms undertake investment projects because they hope to increase future profits. A firm with strong investment projects sees its stock price rise as market participants, hoping to share in the future profits generated by the firm, bid up the stock price. Firms with a high stock price can fund additional investment projects either by issuing more equity or by debt financing, borrowing in the capital markets. As long as the projects turn out to be profitable, investment and stock prices can move upward together.

The link between investment and stock prices is complicated by several factors. One factor is that the managers of the firm are better informed of the profitability of the firm's investment prospects than outsiders, who are unable to accurately access the firm's prospects. This informational asymmetry can break the close link between stock prices and investment. A second factor is that dividend income is subject to double taxation, at both the corporate and individual levels. This makes equity financing less attractive to firms than debt financing.

These factors can explain the movements of stock prices and investment in the late 1990s and early 2000s. During the late 1990s, market participants overestimated the value of installed capital in many industries, driving stock prices to unsustainable levels and encouraging overinvestment by firms. During the stock market boom, most investment, influenced by the bias built into the tax code, was financed by issuing debt rather than equity.

Between the first quarter of 2000 and the third quarter of 2002, stockholders lost nearly $7 trillion in equity wealth. The decline in the stock market can be attributed to both a decline in expectations of future corporate earnings and an increase in the risk premium required to hold equities. Many observers have characterized the run-up in stock prices in the late 1990s, especially in technology stocks, as a "bubble" and, when the bubble burst, there was an inevitable fall. There is clear evidence that the risk premium increased after September 11, 2001. There is also evidence that issues of corporate governance, in the form of corporate wrongdoing and questionable accounting practices, most notably by Enron and Arthur Anderson, contributed to the sustained fall in stock prices by calling into question the reported profitability of firms in general.

Just as an increase in stock prices raises investment, a decrease in stock prices lowers investment. Firms are less optimistic about future corporate earnings and, even with unchanged optimism, are less able to raise funds for investment projects by equity or debt financing. There is also some evidence that overinvestment in the late 1990s led to a capital overhang, too much capital for the economy's output, by the recession of 2001, further depressing investment in 2001 and 2002. For this variety of reasons, both stock prices and nonresidential investment fell precipitously in the early 2000s.

In January 2003, President George W. Bush proposed, as part of the Jobs and Growth Tax Relief Reconciliation Act of 2003, to eliminate the double taxation of corporate income by excluding dividends from individual's taxable income. The plan finally approved by Congress and signed by the president in May 2003 cut the maximum tax rate on dividends from 38.6 percent to 15 percent. It also lowered the maximum capital gains tax from 20 to 15 percent. While not as far-reaching as the president's original plan, it eliminates much of the advantage of debt financing over equity financing.

approximation. Even if firms are diverse, the basic properties of the investment process still hold: Investment responds positively to planned output and negatively to the rental price of capital. The strength of the response depends on how quickly investment plans can be carried out.

The Investment Function

1. The firm's investment demand function tells how much investment it needs to make this year in order to raise its capital stock to the desired level. Investment demand depends negatively on the rental price of capital and positively on the planned increase in output and on the wage.

2. Lags in putting new investment in place limit the response of investment to changes in its determinants. Only certain types of investment are put in place in the first year.

11.4 | TAXES AND INVESTMENT

Taxation of capital tends to discourage investment by reducing the earnings the firm receives from its investment. This effect of taxation can readily be incorporated into the rental price formula.[5] We first consider the effect of permanent tax changes.

Permanent Tax Changes

Consider again our derivation of the rental price of capital. Suppose the rental firm has to pay a tax rate of u on rental income. In addition, suppose the rental firm receives a payment of z dollars as an investment incentive from the government for each dollar of capital purchased. We derived the formula for the rental price by equating the rental income of the rental firm to the costs of renting. We can modify that analysis to take account of taxes by equating the after-tax rental income to the after-tax costs of renting. After-tax rental income is $(1 - u)R^K$. The effect of the investment incentives is to make the cost of purchasing a machine equal to $(1 - z)P^K$. Equating after-tax rental income to after-tax costs gives

$$(1 - u)R^K = (R + d)(1 - z)P^K. \qquad (11.10)$$

---

[5]This method of incorporating taxes into the rental price of capital is based on the work of Robert E. Hall and Dale W. Jorgenson, "Tax Policy and Investment Behavior," *American Economic Review*, Vol. 57 (June 1967), pp. 391–414.

Dividing by $1 - u$ gives

Rental
cost

$$R^K = \frac{(R + d)(1 - z)P^K}{1 - u}$$

(11.11)

The net effect of taxation and investment incentives is to multiply the rental cost by $(1 - z)/(1 - u)$.

For example, suppose the marginal tax rate applied to the revenue from capital is 50 percent. That is, $u = 0.5$. This by itself would double the rental price of capital. If rental firms lose half their revenue to taxation, they must double their earnings to cover the costs of holding capital.

Suppose further that there is an investment incentive of 10 percent and tax deductions for depreciation on investment are worth 30 cents of current benefits for each dollar of investment. The combined effect of the two makes z equal 0.4. In this example, the tax multiplier in the rental price of capital, $(1 - z)/(1 - u)$, is 0.6/0.5, or 1.2. The tax system adds 20 percent to the rental price of capital.

For investments financed by issuing debt or taking on mortgages, the tax system gives further incentives to invest because firms can deduct their interest costs as well. Suppose that borrowing adds another 20 cents in current tax benefits for each dollar of investment. In that case, z would be 0.6 and the tax multiplier would be 0.4/0.5, or 0.8. Tax incentives then outweigh the direct effect of taxes, and the net effect of the tax system is to subsidize investment.

Changes in taxes and tax incentives for investment have powerful effects on investment spending. One of the largest recent tax changes affecting investment occurred in the mid-1980s. The Tax Reform Act of 1986 raised the rental price of capital by as much as 10 percent. An elimination of the investment tax credit, a lower depreciation allowance, and a reduction in the value of deductions for interest payments were the main factors raising the rental price.

Suppose the desired capital stock falls by 0.75 percent for each percentage point that the rental price of capital is increased (that is, the elasticity is -0.75). Then, the desired capital stock would fall by 7.5 percent as a result of this legislation. If the capital stock of plants and equipment in the United States is about $4,000 billion, then this reduction would amount to a fall in investment of $300 billion. Even if it were spread over 10 years, the effect on aggregate demand in each year could be substantial.

Anticipated Tax Changes

The previous calculations assume that the tax rates are always in effect and tax changes are not anticipated by firms. If firms are forward looking, as we argue, then anticipations of future tax changes can also affect investment. The effects are tricky to calculate and can go in a direction opposite from unanticipated changes.

Investment is the key component of spending that usually falls the most in recessions. Therefore, recessions create the desire for tax policies to increase investment. Moreover, higher investment would lead to higher productivity in the long run. Three types of tax policies would increase investment.

The Investment Tax Credit

The investment tax credit first came into being in 1962, just after the recession of 1960–61. The credit is essentially a percentage subsidy on investment. As it applied in the United States from 1962 through 1986, it subsidized investment in equipment only. The investment tax credit is part of the variable z in Equation 11.11 for the rental price of capital. A 10 percent investment credit adds 0.1 to z. A permanent investment credit creates an incentive for a permanently higher capital stock, so it stimulates a burst of net investment as the economy makes the transition to the higher stock.

But there are pitfalls in the systematic use of changes in the investment credit to stabilize the economy. If firms anticipate that an investment tax credit will be enacted during a recession, then a forecast of a recession could lead firms to hold back on investment and help bring on the recession. These are the findings of Lawrence Christiano of Northwestern University, whose work shows that the anticipation of changes in the investment tax credit can actually increase the volatility of investment.*

Write-Offs

A permanent feature of tax laws is write-offs (depreciation deductions) for fixed investment. The present discounted value of these write-offs is another factor increasing the variable z in Equation 11.11. When write-offs can be made faster (accelerated depreciation), their present discounted value is higher and the rental price of capital is lower. Write-offs were dramatically reduced in the 1986 tax bill, which passed during a period of strength in the economy. The recession of 2001 brought forth proposals for speeding up write-offs as a way to get investment moving again. Both the Job Creation and Worker Assistance Act of 2002 and the Jobs and Growth Tax Relief Reconciliation Act of 2003 include provisions for accelerated depreciation that increased write-offs.

Capital Gains Taxes

It stands to reason that lower capital gains taxes should stimulate investment. Essentially, the capital gains tax rate is one of the determinants of the interest rate R, which appears in Equation 11.11. Many firms invest their shareholders' funds—most commonly by keeping the funds within the firm rather than paying them out as dividends. The tax rate that matters in that case is the tax that shareholders pay when the investment generates added profit for the firm. Part of the tax is the personal income tax on capital gains. Thus a lower capital gains rate stimulates investment. The maximum tax rate on capital gains was lowered from 28 to 20 percent in 1997, contributing to the investment boom of the late 1990s. The Jobs and Growth Tax Relief Reconciliation Act of 2003 further lowered the maximum capital gains tax rate from 20 to 15 percent. This can be expected to stimulate investment in the future.

How Large is the Effect?

Recent empirical research that examines the behavior of individual firms has found the incentive effect of tax policies to be quite large. A change in tax policy that lowers the rental price of capital by 1 percent would raise investment by about 1 percent over several years, according to one study.[†]

*See "A Re-examination of the Theory of Automatic Stabilizers," *Carnegie-Rochester Conference Series on Public Policy*, 1984, Vol. 20. (Amsterdam: North Holland, 1984) pp. 147–206.
[†]J. Cummins, K. Hasset, and R. G. Hubbard, "Tax Reforms and Investment: A Cross-Country Comparison," *Journal of Public Economics*, Vol. 62 (1996), pp. 237–273.

Suppose, for example, that U.S. firms anticipated in 1985 that the 10 percent investment tax credit would be repealed starting in 1986. In fact, this is a very realistic example, because such a repeal was proposed by the Reagan administration and widely discussed in 1985. The repeal occurred as part of the Tax Reform Act of 1986 and was made effective on January 1, 1986.

Firms that anticipated such a change would realize that they would have to pay 10 percent more for capital goods starting in January 1986 than in 1985. Accordingly, they would want to buy capital in 1985 before the effective price rise. If possible, they would shift their purchases of equipment from 1986 to 1985.

Rental firms would also cut their rental price in 1985 in anticipation of the repeal of the investment tax credit. With the effective price of capital goods expected to increase, rental firms could charge less for rent because of the expected capital gain on the capital that they owned. With a decrease in the rental price there would be more investment in 1985. Hence, an *anticipated* elimination of the investment tax credit would increase investment in the year that the elimination was anticipated.

The behavior of investment in the United States in 1985 and 1986 provides dramatic confirmation of this forward-looking anticipatory behavior of firms. Investment in business equipment grew by 19 percent at an annual rate in the last quarter of 1985 and then fell by about the same amount in the first quarter of 1986. Evidently firms bunched their capital purchases in the last months of 1985, right before the effective date of the repeal. Investment remained rather low throughout 1986, as we discussed previously.

These same anticipatory effects can work in the opposite direction. If firms anticipated a reenactment of the investment tax credit, perhaps because of a prolonged economic slump, then the rental price of capital would increase at the time of anticipation, and investment would actually fall.[6]

Tax Incentives

1. The government can influence the level of investment through tax policy. Heavier taxation raises the rental price of capital and discourages investment.

2. Tax incentives such as investment tax credits and depreciation deductions lower the rental price of capital and stimulate investment.

3. Anticipated increases in tax incentives can reduce investment today, because firms postpone their capital purchases until they can take advantage of the incentives.

---

[6]For rational expectations approaches to consequences of anticipated changes in investment incentives, see Lawrence H. Summers, "Taxation and Corporate Investment: A q-Theory Approach," *Brookings Papers on Economic Activity*, Vol. 1 (1981), pp. 67–140; and John B. Taylor, "The Swedish Investment System as a Stabilization Policy Rule," *Brookings Papers on Economic Activity*, Vol. 1 (1982), pp. 57–97.

11.5 | RESIDENTIAL INVESTMENT

The economic theory of residential investment can be approached in much the same way as the theory of business investment. We can start again with the concept of the rental price. Because a significant amount of housing of all kinds is rented in the open market, there is nothing unfamiliar about the idea of a rental price of housing. Even though many American families own their houses rather than rent them, we can examine their decision about how large a house to own by looking at the rental price they pay implicitly when they own. Let R^H represent the rental price for houses. As before, the rental price is the interest rate plus a rate of depreciation times the price of houses (P^H):

$$R^H = (R + d)P^H. \qquad (11.12)$$

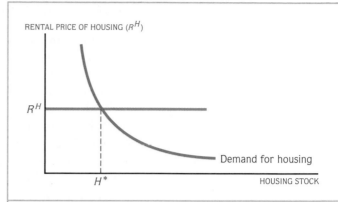

FIGURE 11.7   DETERMINATION OF THE DESIRED HOUSING STOCK

The desired stock of housing, H^*, is found at the point on the demand curve for housing where the rental price of housing, R^H, has the value determined by the real interest rate and the price of houses.

An important quantitative difference is the rate of depreciation, d. The equipment that makes up the bulk of business investment depreciates at around 10 percent per year, so d is 0.10 in the formula for R^K. Houses hardly depreciate at all. A reasonable value for d in the formula for R^H is 0.02. Consequently, the real interest rate is a much larger fraction of the rental cost of housing than the rental cost of business investment. As we will see, residential investment is much more sensitive to interest rates than business investment.

[handwritten: real interest rate = large % of cost in residential investment]

The public has a demand function for housing just as it has a demand function for any good. When the rental price of housing is high, the public demands less rental housing. We can find the public's **desired stock of housing** by finding where the rental price of housing intersects the demand curve, as in Figure 11.7.

Lags in housing construction are not nearly as long as lags in business investment. It is reasonable to suppose that the bulk of housing can be put in place within a year after a change in demand. The investment demand function for housing is just

$$I = H^* - H_{-1}. \qquad (11.13)$$

where H_{-1} is the stock of houses in the previous year and H^* is the desired stock of houses.

The accelerator principle operates for housing investment as well as for business investment. The stock of housing is related to the level of real income. Therefore, investment, which is the change in the stock, is related to the change in real income.

Housing Investment and Monetary Policy

Of all the components of aggregate demand, housing investment is the most sensitive to real interest rates. We already noted one reason for the sensitivity: Because housing depreciates at a low rate, the real interest rate is the dominant element in the rental price of housing. Most of what you pay your landlord is compensation for the capital tied up in your apartment. If you own a house, most of your annual cost is mortgage interest. Therefore, when a monetary contraction or other influences raise interest rates, housing investment declines the most. When interst rates fall, housing investment rises. The interest rate on new fixed-rate 30-year mortgages fell to an average of 5.75 percent in 2003, the lowest in a generation, and housing investment boomed.

Housing Investment

1. Housing investment is negatively related to the interest rate R. A higher interest rate makes housing more expensive by raising the rental price. A higher rental price depresses investment demand.

2. Housing investment is positively related to real GDP. Higher incomes raise the demand for housing and so raise investment demand.

3. Housing is the component of investment most sensitive to monetary policy through interest rates. Because housing depreciates so slowly, its rental price is dominated by interest cost.

11.6 | INVENTORY INVESTMENT

Inventories are stocks of goods in the process of production and also finished goods waiting to be sold. In 2002, total inventories were $1,446.9 billion. Gross domestic product was $10,506.2 billion, so about 14 cents' worth of inventories were held for each dollar in annual GDP. A significant amount of capital is tied up in inventories in the U.S. economy.

Inventories fit into the general framework for analyzing investment set up at the beginning of this chapter. Inventories have a rental price, equal to the real interest rate times the price of goods held in inventory.

Firms choose a desired level of inventories by equating the marginal benefit of inventories to the rental price. What benefits do inventories provide the firm? We can distinguish two basic functions. First and quantitatively most important, inventories are an intrinsic part of the physical production process. We call this the **pipeline function** of inventories. In the oil industry, large amounts of oil are unavoidably in transit in pipelines at any moment. The pipeline function also includes goods in process. Inside an auto plant, you find stocks of parts ready to be made into cars together with a large number of cars partway through the assembly process. The manufacturer has made a basic decision about the design of the production process that balances the advantages of inventories against their holding cost. About two-thirds of all inventories seem to be held because of the pipeline function.

The other third of inventories are finished goods. Auto plants have cars sitting in parking lots ready for shipment to dealers. The dealers themselves also keep quite a number of cars in their lots and showrooms. As a general matter, substantial inventories of finished goods ready for sale are held at the wholesale and retail level. One reason for holding these inventories is to maintain a **buffer stock** to accommodate unexpected changes in demand. The buffer stock is the second major function of inventories. The grocery store keeps dozens of bottles of ketchup on the shelves because there is always a chance that an unusual number of people will buy ketchup on any given day.

Buffer-stock inventories are held at a certain average level that equates the marginal benefit to the rental cost. When sales surge, the inventories decline to below the desired stock. The firm then adjusts its purchases to replenish the stock. When sales fall short of expectations, inventories build up. The firm then decreases its purchases to run inventories down to their desired level.

Occasionally, unintended disinvestment and investment in buffer-stock inventories show up in the aggregate amount of inventory investment throughout the economy. For example, in 1989, aggregate final sales of goods in the U.S. economy slowed. The production of goods continued to rise despite slowing sales. As a result, inventory investment bulged. Inventory investment was 30 billion 1987 dollars in 1989.

We can get an idea of the relative importance of the pipeline and buffer-stock influences on inventory investment by looking at the relationship between the *change* in real GDP and the *level* of inventory investment in the U.S. economy. Figure 11.8 shows this relationship for the years 1959 to 2002.

We can draw two important conclusions about inventory investment from Figure 11.8. First, inventory investment tends to be closely related to changes in production. When higher levels of output are being produced, more goods are in the pipeline. Filling up the pipeline to the higher level requires more inventory investment. Consequently, years of rapid GDP growth tend to be years of high inventory investment. This is the third important place where the accelerator principle is in operation. The accelerator effect is particularly strong for inventory investment, because lags are less important for inventories than for any other component of investment.

Second, occasional episodes occur when businesses are caught by surprise and inventories pile up or are depleted unintentionally. In these episodes, inventory investment departs from its usual relation to the change in real GDP. In Figure 11.8, the small number of dots away from the prevailing upward-sloping line are years when unintended accumulation or depletion of inventories occurred. There is no systematic tendency for buffer stocks to absorb every change in real GDP. Instead, big movements of buffer stocks are a rare

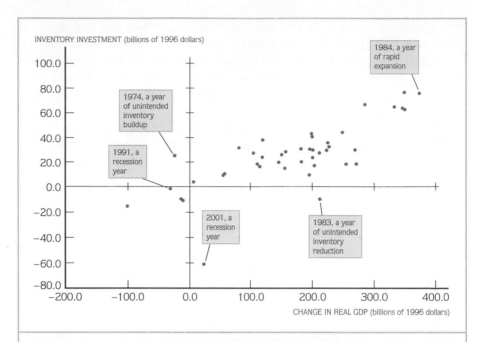

FIGURE 11.8   INVENTORY INVESTMENT AND THE CHANGE IN GDP

The amount of inventory investment tends to be closely related to the change in real GDP. Each dot corresponds to a year in the period from 1960 through 2001. The horizontal axis shows the change in real GDP and the vertical axis shows the real amount of inventory investment. As a rule, inventory investment is high when real GDP is growing and low when it is contracting. By far the largest contraction in inventories occurred in 2001. There are two large exceptions, 1974 and 1983, when unintended changes in inventory stocks dominated intended changes. As a general matter, intended changes in inventory stocks dominate unintended changes. Years of high GDP growth are years of high inventory investment and vice versa.

SOURCE: *Economic Report of the President*, 2003, Table B-9.

surprise. Research on inventory behavior has confirmed the general proposition that relatively few important movements of inventories can be traced to surprises in sales.[7]

Inventory Investment

1. Inventories provide two benefits to firms. The production process involves a pipeline of partly produced goods. When the level of output is high, the stock of goods in the pipeline is high. Inventories of finished goods also function as a buffer stock against unexpected changes in sales.

---

[7]See Albert A. Hirsch and Michael Lovell, *Sales Anticipations and Inventory Behavior* (New York: John Wiley & Sons, 1969). For a formal treatment of the pipeline function of inventories, see Valerie A. Ramey, "Inventories as Factors of Production and Economic Fluctuations," *American Economic Review*, Vol. 79 (June 1989), pp. 338–354.

2. The pipeline function of inventories dominates inventory investment in most years, but occasionally economywide surprises in sales are large enough for changes in buffer stocks to contribute an important component to inventory investment.

3. The increase in pipeline inventories when output rises is a major part of the accelerator in the short run.

11.7 | THE INVESTMENT FUNCTION AND THE IS CURVE

Total investment is the sum of investment in plant and equipment, residential housing, and inventory. We can summarize the ideas of this chapter in an overall investment function. Investment depends positively on real GDP and negatively on the real interest rate R.

The accelerator principle is important in investment. Higher output requires firms to invest in new plant and equipment, it causes families to want to increase their stock of housing, and it calls for higher pipeline stocks of inventories. For all three reasons, an increase in GDP stimulates added investment. However, the stimulus is stronger in the short run than in the long run. If the economy moves once and for all to a higher level of GDP, there will be a bulge of investment as the economy moves to the new, higher stock of plant, equipment, housing, and inventories desired at the new level of GDP. Once the new stock is reached, investment will subside to normal levels.

GDP↑ = more investment stimulus stronger in short run

Investment depends negatively on the real interest rate. When the real rental cost of plant and equipment rises, firms substitute toward other inputs, especially labor. When the real rental price of housing rises, families substitute toward other forms of consumption. When the real cost of holding inventories rises, firms reduce their stocks of inventories, although this effect appears to be small. But the influence of higher real interest rates in depressing total investment is unmistakable.

Investment is central to the IS curve—in fact, as mentioned in Chapter 7, the I in IS stands for investment. Recall that the IS curve can be defined as the set of combinations of real GDP and the interest rate where investment and saving are equal.

As a general matter, the IS curve slopes downward because it takes a lower interest rate to stimulate spending enough to achieve spending balance at a higher level of GDP. The investment function is a key part of that process. Lower interest rates stimulate investment—the effect is most important for housing and least important for inventories. The interest sensitivity of investment is an important determinant of the slope of the IS curve. If investment is highly responsive to the interest rate, the IS curve is flat; small changes in the interest rate cause large changes in investment and thus large changes in the level of GDP. If investment is not very responsive to interest rates, and other components are also unresponsive, the IS curve is steep. Because investment

If investment is unresponsive to ΔR, IS curve = steep

IS Curve = vertical
in short run

and other categories of spending are unable to respond in the very short run (say, one month) to changes in interest rates, the IS curve is close to vertical in the very short run.

REVIEW AND PRACTICE

Major Points

1. There are three types of investment: business purchases of new plant and equipment, construction of new housing, and addition to inventories.

2. A business determines its desired capital stock by equating the marginal benefit of capital to the rental price of capital. A household determines its desired stock of housing in the same way.

3. The desired capital stock falls if the rental price of capital rises. It also rises if output or income rises. A business's desired capital stock rises if the wage rises, because it will substitute away from labor and toward capital.

4. The rental price of capital depends on the real interest rate and the price of capital goods.

5. The investment function tells how much investment will occur in a given year, depending on conditions in that year. Although firms would like to invest up to the point where actual capital equals desired capital, they generally cannot do so. Only a fraction of the move to the new level can occur in the first year.

6. Because of the lag in investment, a large fraction of the investment that occurs in one year is actually the result of investment projects initiated in earlier years. This part of investment is predetermined in the current year and does not respond to current economic conditions.

7. For plant and equipment, it is a good approximation to say that suppliers supply whatever amount of new investment goods businesses demand.

8. Tax incentives, including depreciation deductions and interest deductions, have an important influence on investment. A higher investment credit lowers the rental price of capital and stimulates investment.

9. Inventory investment contributes an important part of the fluctuations in total investment. The stock of inventories tends to be proportional to real GDP, so an increase in GDP is accompanied by a period of inventory investment.

10. Overall, investment responds positively to both the level of and the change in real GDP. The relationship with the level of GDP is due to re-

placement investment. The relationship with the change in GDP, called the *accelerator*, is due to the need to increase the capital stock in order to maintain output at higher levels and because desired inventories grow when output increases.

11. Investment is negatively related to the interest rate. The effect is most important for housing and least important for inventories. If the relationship is strong, the IS curve is relatively flat.

Key Terms and Concepts

investment demand	desired capital stock
saving supply	actual capital stock
investment supply	investment function
capital stock	accelerator
marginal cost of capital	lag
marginal benefit of capital	desired stock of housing
rate of depreciation	pipeline function
investment demand function	buffer stock

Questions for Discussion and Review

1. What variables adjust so that the level of investment chosen by firms and households is equal to the amount of funds available for investment?

2. Why do investment and GDP move so closely together?

3. Suppose a firm can reduce its energy bill by adding some capital. How does this enter the marginal benefit of capital schedule?

4. Why does the marginal benefit of capital schedule shift upward when output rises?

5. Explain the various predetermined elements in the investment function.

6. What are the effects of tax policy on investment in the long run?

7. Why is housing especially important in the economy's response to a low-interest-rate policy?

8. Explain exactly what happens to the three categories of investment as you move down the IS curve.

9. Explain how announcements of future changes in tax policy can affect current investment demand.

10. Describe the relation between the stock market and investment.

Problems

NUMERICAL

1. Suppose that the demand for investment is given by the model

$$I = s(K^* - K_{-1}),$$

where K^* is the desired stock of capital given by

$$K^* = 0.1Y/R,$$

where Y is output and R is the interest rate. Assume that there is no depreciation and $R = 0.05$. Let $s = 0.25$ to start.

   a. Calculate the desired capital stock in year 1 if output is 200. Calculate the level of investment in the first year if the capital stock was 400 at the beginning of the first year.

   b. Suppose now that output rises from 200 to 250 in year 2 and remains at this new level forever. Calculate the level of investment and the capital stock in years 2, 3, and 4. What are the new long-run levels of investment and capital? Explain why investment reacts with a lag to the increase in output.

   c. Repeat the calculations in parts a and b for $s = 1$ and comment on the difference between your answers.

2. Repeat problem 1 for the case where investment is given by

$$I = s(K^* - K_{-1}) + 0.1K_{-1}.$$

   The last term on the right is replacement investment. Explain the reason for the differences between the answers to problems 1 and 2.

3. Suppose that the investment function is given by

$$I = 400 - 2{,}000R + 0.1Y$$

   rather than by the investment function given in Chapter 8. Add this investment function to the other four equations of the IS-LM model:

$$Y = C + I + G + X$$
$$C = 220 + 0.63Y$$
$$X = 525 - 0.1Y - 500R$$
$$M = (0.1583Y - 1{,}000R)P$$

   Treat the price level as predetermined at 1.0, and let government spending be 1,200 and the money supply be 900.

a. Derive an algebraic expression for the IS curve for this model and plot it to scale. Compare it with the IS curve in the examples of Chapter 8. Which is steeper? Why?

b. Derive the aggregate demand curve and plot it to scale. How does it compare with the aggregate demand curve in the example of Chapter 8?

c. Calculate the effect of an increase in government spending on GDP. Is the effect larger or smaller than in the case where investment does not depend on output Y? Describe what is going on.

d. Calculate the effect of an increase in the money supply on GDP. How does the impact compare with the situation where investment does not depend on output?

4. Multiplier-accelerator interaction: Consider a macro model that has both a consumption function that depends on lagged income (like Friedman's permanent-income equation) and an investment equation that depends, with a lag, on changes in income. Ignore interest-rate effects. In particular, assume that the following equations describe the economy:

$$Y = C + I + G$$
$$C = 220 + 0.63Y_p, \quad \text{with } Y_p = 0.5(Y + Y_{-1})$$
$$I = 900 + 0.2(Y_{-1} - Y_{-2})$$
$$G = 1{,}200$$

a. By algebraic substitution of C and I into the income identity, obtain a single expression for output Y in terms of output in the previous years (Y_{-1} and Y_{-2}).

b. Calculate the constant level of output Y that satisfies all the relationships in the model. (Hint: Set $Y_{-1} = Y$ and $Y_{-2} = Y$ in the equation from part a and solve for Y using algebra.)

c. Suppose that Y is equal to the value you calculated in part b for the past two years (years 1 and 2). Now, suppose that government spending increases by $50 billion (in year 3). Calculate the effect on output in year 3. Calculate the effect on output in years 4 through 10. Be sure to use the relationship you derived in part a and substitute the values for Y_{-1} and Y_{-2} you calculated in the previous two steps.

d. Plot the values of Y on a diagram with the years on the horizontal axis. Do you notice any cyclical behavior in Y? Explain what is going on. (This algebraic model was originally developed by Paul Samuelson of M.I.T. while he was a student at Harvard in the 1930s.)

ANALYTICAL

1. What theory of inventory investment predicts that inventory investment is negative when GDP suddenly rises? What theory predicts the opposite? For both theories explain what happens at firms during a sudden *decline* in GDP.

2. Consider a firm whose capital stock is initially equal to its desired capital stock, where $R = 0.05$, $d = 0.1$, $P^K = 100$, and P^K is initially not expected to change in the future.

   a. Suppose P^K suddenly rises to 110. Ignoring taxes, what must the firm expect P^K to be next year in order for its desired capital stock to remain unchanged?

   b. Suppose now that P^K is expected to return to 100 the following year and remain at 100 in all future years. Assume that this in fact happens. Describe the behavior of investment in the year of the price increase and all future years. Consider both the case where the capital stock adjusts immediately to its desired level and the case where it adjusts with a lag.

3. In this problem, we consider an economy in which the price of *new* capital goods never changes. It is always equal to 100.

   a. Assuming $R = 0.05$, $d = 0.1$, and the corporate income tax is 50 percent, what is the rental cost of capital?

   b. The government is considering an investment tax credit (ITC), where 10 percent of the purchase price of a new capital good can be subtracted from a firm's taxes. Under such a proposal, what is the rental cost of capital? Assuming that the ITC is unanticipated, describe the behavior of I and K^* in the year that it is implemented.

   c. Assuming that the old capital goods are perfect substitutes in production for new capital goods, what is the price of old capital goods under the ITC? If the value of a firm's capital stock changes in the year the ITC is implemented, does this change directly affect the firm's investment decision?

   d. Assume now that such a proposal is announced a year ahead of time. What will the rental cost of capital be in the year in which firms learn about the ITC? Compare your answer with the rental cost calculated in parts a and b. Explain any differences.

   e. Compare the level of investment in the year in which the ITC is announced with what it would be without the ITC. Compare the level of investment in the following year, when the ITC is implemented, with what it would be if the ITC was implemented *unannounced* that year.

4. How sensitive would you expect automobile production to be to the interest rate? In answering this question, consider (i) the sensitivity of the desired stock of automobiles to the interest rate, (ii) the lags in the adjustment of the automobile stock to its desired level, and (iii) the impact of changes in final automobile sales on inventory investment in automobile manufacturing.

5. *Paradox of thrift:* Assume a closed-economy model with $Y = C + I + G$. Suppose that investment demand depends on the level of income but not on the interest rate, according to the formula

$$I = e + dY$$

and that consumption also depends on income according to the consumption function

$$C = a + b(1 - t)Y.$$

a. Sketch the spending line for the economy that shows how total spending increases with income Y. (Put spending on the vertical axis and income on the horizontal axis.) Draw a 45-degree line and indicate where spending balance is.

b. Suppose that consumers decide to be more thrifty, to save more. They do this by reducing a once and for all. Show the new point of balance in the diagram.

c. What happens to investment as a result of consumers' attempts to save more? Explain.

d. Explain the paradox of thrift, that the attempt to save more may result in a reduction in private saving. What happens to total saving?

e. Explain why the paradox of thrift is a short-run phenomenon. Introduce interest rates into the investment function, and add a money demand function and price adjustment equation to the model. If the economy is operating at potential GDP before the reduction in a, will it eventually return to potential after the reduction in a? What happens to saving and investment when prices have fully adjusted?

6. Suppose the desired capital stock is given by the expression

$$K^* = vY/R^K,$$

where v is a constant and R^K is the rental cost of capital.

a. Assuming that output in the economy is fixed at Y^*, will a permanent increase in the interest rate have a permanent or a temporary effect on the level of investment?

b. Is your answer to part a consistent with the investment function incorporated in the IS curve?

c. Suppose now that output in the economy is growing each period so that $\Delta Y = g$. Assuming that the actual capital stock adjusts immediately to its desired level, answer part a.

7. Sketch an IS-LM diagram. Compare two cases, one in which the investment demand function depends on income and the other in which it is independent of income. In which case are both monetary and fiscal policy more effective? Explain.

8. Suppose that GDP is below potential GDP and inflation is low. The president and Congress are talking about reducing taxes on investment to get the economy back to potential.

   a. Sketch the situation on an IS-LM diagram. Show where you want to move the IS curve to get back to potential.

   b. In light of lags in the investment process and the forward-looking nature of firms' investment decisions, describe some of the problems that the policymakers need to worry about in enacting the tax legislation.

9. The 1986 Tax Reform Act called for an increase in taxes on businesses and a decrease in taxes on consumers, with total revenue remaining about the same. Describe the effects the tax had on *investment demand*. Be explicit: Did these effects occur immediately or did they occur with a lag? Distinguish between the effects that work through the rental rate on capital and the effects that work through the accelerator. Which of these two effects was likely to have been larger in the long run?

10. Countercyclical policy in recessions has typically involved increases in incentives for investment, often through increases in the investment tax credit. How might firms' behavior at the beginning of future recessions be affected by beliefs that government may take actions to reduce the cost of investment? What effect would this have on the behavior of real GDP?

FOREIGN TRADE AND THE EXCHANGE RATE

Foreign trade is a central issue in U.S. economic policy. International trade contributes to long-term economic growth. Equally, trade is a factor in economic fluctuations. When consumers decide to purchase foreign rather than American cars, the demand for U.S.-made goods declines. The immediate effect is a decline in GDP and employment in the United States.

The international value of the dollar affects foreign trade and thereby influences aggregate demand, GDP, and employment. Fluctuations in the dollar have been common since the 1970s. Against other major currencies, the dollar rose to extreme heights in the first half of the 1980s, fell precipitously to reach new lows in the early and mid-1990s, and then rose again in the late 1990s, before falling in 2003.

Many commentators have called for policies to reduce the U.S. trade deficit. Some think that restrictions on imports from China, Japan, and other countries with trade surpluses would be appropriate. Others call for a correction of the fiscal budget deficit to reduce borrowing from foreigners. Some economists feel that the volatility of the value of the dollar in relation to other currencies needs to be controlled by intervention in the foreign exchange market or even by pegging exchange rates at fixed levels. Proposals for policy intervention are founded on the belief that something is wrong with a trade deficit or a volatile currency. A contrary view, held by many economists, is that the trade deficit and the value of the dollar should be set in international markets, free from intervention by the United States or other governments. In this chapter, we study the determinants of net exports and exchange rates. We look at the ways that changes in trade affect the domestic economy and how policy can respond. We also look at policies aimed at influencing the trade deficit and the international value of the dollar.

12.1 | FOREIGN TRADE AND AGGREGATE DEMAND

Figure 12.1 shows what happened to the flows of goods and services into and out of the United States between 1959 and 2002. The top panel, which depicts exports and imports separately, shows an excess of imports over exports in almost every year since 1959 and in every year since 1983. In other words, net exports, defined as exports minus imports, have been negative in almost every year since 1959. The bottom panel, which depicts net exports as a percentage of GDP, shows the fluctuations in net exports. While net exports are almost always negative, there are sharp decreases in net exports in the late 1960s through the early 1970s, mid-1980s and especially the late 1990s and early 2000s.

The sharp decrease in net exports in the late 1990s and early 2000s has been accompanied by a major change in its composition. Figure 12.2 shows the contribution of China and Japan to the U.S. trade deficit since 1985. During the 1980s, the large trade deficit with Japan was a major concern of policy makers, while the trade deficit with China was miniscule in comparison. Over time, the trade deficit with China has grown steadily, while the trade deficit with Japan has fluctuated while increasing relatively slowly. Starting in 2000, the trade deficit with China exceeded the trade deficit with Japan.

The quantity of goods and services flowing into and out of the United States is not the only important dimension of trade. It matters how much we have to pay for imports and how much we can get for our exports. In this respect, nominal or dollar flows are important in foreign trade, whereas real flows concern us in considering domestic production. If imports become more expensive, it is costly to the United States even if net exports in real terms do

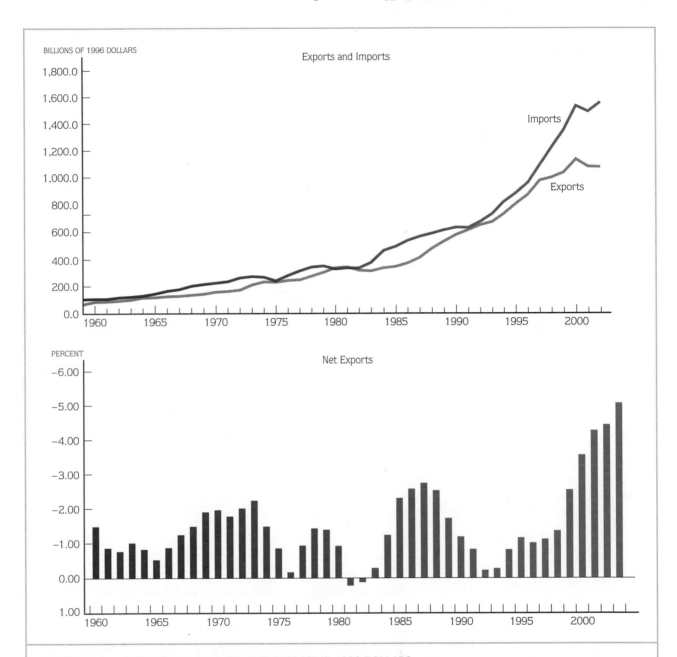

FIGURE 12.1   EXPORTS, IMPORTS, AND NET EXPORTS IN 1996 DOLLARS

The top panel shows the quantities of goods exported out of and imported into the United States in constant 1996 dollars. The difference between the two is net exports, shown separately in the bottom panel as a percentage of GDP. Imports grew much more rapidly than exports in the late 1990s and early 2000s. Net exports turned sharply negative.

SOURCE: *Economic Report of the President,* 2003, Table B-2.

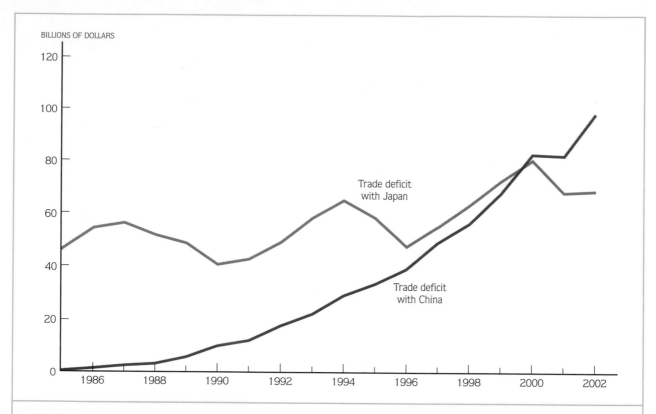

FIGURE 12.2   UNITED STATES TRADE DEFICIT WITH JAPAN AND CHINA

The United States trade deficit with Japan has fluctuated and grown relatively slowly since the mid-1980s. The U.S. trade deficit with China grew steadily in the 1990s, surpassing the U.S. trade deficit with Japan in 2000.

SOURCE: U.S. Department of Commerce.

not change. The **terms of trade** is the ratio of the price of exports to the price of imports. When the prices of imports rise, we say there has been an adverse shift in the terms of trade.

Borrowing abroad = "capital inflow"

When the value of American imports exceeds the value of exports, because of either a high quantity of imports or a high price of imports, the United States must borrow enough from foreigners to pay for the difference. As we saw in Chapter 2, U.S. borrowing from abroad is called a *capital inflow.* For example, in 2002 net exports were −$448 billion; the United States had to borrow in order to finance the excess of imports over exports. Actually, total borrowing was even larger because the United States also paid transfers to people outside the country of about $52 billion.

The capital inflows since the mid-1980s have been large by historical standards. They brought the United States from a net creditor position with the rest of the world to a net debtor position. In other words, Americans now owe more to foreigners than foreigners owe to Americans.

Foreign Trade and Aggregate Demand

1. Foreign trade influences U.S. aggregate demand in two ways. First, Americans can purchase their goods from abroad instead of from U.S. producers. When they do, their imports contribute to aggregate demand in the rest of the world instead of to U.S. aggregate demand. Second, foreigners can purchase goods produced in the United States. These exports enter U.S. aggregate demand.

2. When exports are less than imports, Americans must finance the difference plus any other expenditures abroad by borrowing. This borrowing— or, equivalently, investment by foreigners in the United States—is called *capital inflow from abroad.*

[margin note:] Imports DON'T contribute to US —AD (Exports do)

12.2 | THE EXCHANGE RATE

The **exchange rate** is the amount of foreign currency that can be bought with 1 U.S. dollar. For example, on August 19, 2003, the exchange rate between the Japanese yen and the dollar was 119 yen per dollar. If you went to a bank with $100 on that day you could have obtained 11,900 yen. Like other prices, the exchange rate can change: On August 18, 1995, the exchange rate between the yen and the dollar was 97 yen per dollar. The exchange rates between the dollar and foreign currencies are listed in the financial pages of most newspapers.

[margin note:] yen/dollar exchange rate = 97 yen/dollar

The exchange rate is determined in the **foreign exchange market,** where dollars and other currencies are traded freely. The foreign exchange market is not in one location; it is a global market. Banks all over the world actively buy and sell dollars and other foreign currencies for their customers. The banks are linked by a network of telecommunications that allows instantaneous contact around the globe. Because of different time zones, the foreign exchange market is open 24 hours a day.

In today's monetary system the dollar exchange rate is allowed to *float* against the currencies of other large countries. For this reason, the system is called a *floating* or **flexible exchange-rate system.** The United States and other major Western countries permit a free market in foreign exchange. Neither the United States nor other major countries tries to fix the exchange rate with the dollar within narrow bands, as done prior to the early 1970s. This does not mean that the United States is powerless to affect the exchange rate or must ignore the exchange rate when it sets its macro policy. As we will see, changes in monetary and fiscal policy have strong influences on the exchange rate, and these influences must be considered when setting macro policy.

[margin note:] "floats" = not fixed

Since there are many countries in the world, there are many exchange rates for the dollar. A convenient single measure of the dollar exchange rate is the **trade-weighted exchange rate,** which we denote by the symbol E. This is an average of several different exchange rates, each one weighted according to

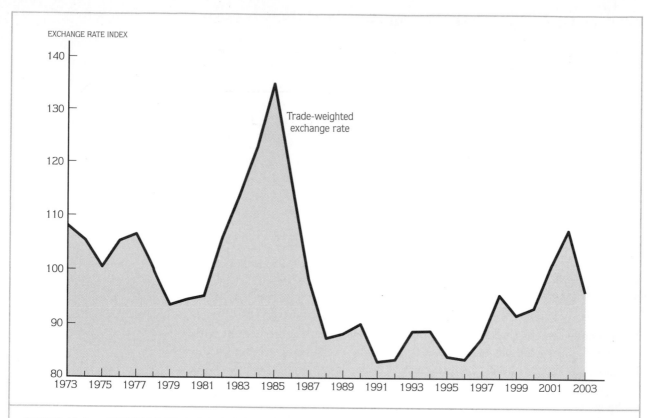

FIGURE 12.3   THE TRADE-WEIGHTED EXCHANGE RATE

The trade-weighted exchange rate is the best overall measure of the dollar exchange rate. It is an average of exchange rates with many different currencies, including the Canadian dollar, the French franc, the euro, the Japanese yen, and the British pound. The exchange rate fluctuates by large amounts. It was very high in the mid 1980s. The dollar was low in the late 1970s and early 1990s.

SOURCE: Board of Governors, Federal Reserve System.

the amount of trade with the United States. Figure 12.3 shows the trade-weighted exchange rate E for the United States for the years 1973 to 2003. The dollar fluctuated widely during this period. **Depreciation of the dollar** occurs when the exchange rate E falls. **Appreciation of the dollar** occurs when the exchange rate E rises. The dollar depreciated steadily by 17 percent from 1976 to 1980. The dollar then turned around and appreciated by over 60 percent through 1985. From 1985 to 1987, it fell by over 30 percent, reversing the appreciation. The dollar fluctuated in a relatively tranquil period until 1996, appreciated through 2002, and depreciated again in 2003.

The Exchange Rate and Relative Prices

In discussing the role of the exchange rate in foreign trade, we speak of the rest of the world (ROW) as if it were a single country with a single monetary unit, a single price level P_w, and a single level of GDP. Then, the trade-weighted exchange rate E is simply the exchange rate between the U.S. dollar and the foreign monetary unit. Like the exchange rate, the price level in the rest of the world P_w is measured by taking an average of the price levels in the countries that trade with the United States.

The **real exchange rate** is a measure of the exchange rate adjusted for differences in price levels between the United States and the ROW. It is a measure of the relative price of goods produced in the United States compared with goods produced in the ROW. If P is the U.S. price level, the real exchange rate can be written in symbols as

$$\text{Real exchange rate} = \frac{\text{Foreign price of U.S. goods}}{\text{Foreign price of ROW goods}} = \frac{E \times P}{P_w}.$$

When the real exchange rate is high, foreigners have to pay more for goods produced in the United States compared with the price of goods produced in the rest of the world. For example, when the yen-dollar exchange rate rises from 115 to 120 yen per dollar, the price of a $2,000 computer produced in the United States rises from 230,000 yen to 240,000 yen in Japan. Note that the exchange rate for the individual item is multiplied by its price in the United States to get the price outside the United States; similarly, we multiply E times P in the numerator of the real exchange rate to get a measure of the average price of U.S. goods in the ROW.

Recall our basic assumption that prices set by U.S. producers are fixed in the short run. Aggregate demand in this period, domestic or foreign, does not influence the dollar price level P in this period. We make the same assumption about the ROW. The price level P_w set by ROW producers is fixed in the short run.

The exchange rate E, on the other hand, varies minute by minute. Hence, the real exchange rate (EP/P_w) varies minute by minute. The price of U.S. products in the ROW is flexible in the short run because the exchange rate is flexible. By the same token, the dollar price of ROW products is flexible in the short run.

When the dollar appreciates, ROW products become cheaper to Americans. At the same time, U.S. products become more expensive in the ROW. If the United States and the ROW produced identical, readily transportable products, the exchange rate would not fluctuate in the short run. We would always buy from the cheapest producer. The exchange rate would always have the single value that equated the dollar prices of U.S. and ROW products. The real exchange rate would never change. If the United States and the ROW produced all the same products, the exchange rate could not fluctuate in the short run and would change in the longer run only by as much as prices in the ROW rose by more than prices in the United States. This theory of exchange-rate fluctuations is called **purchasing power parity.** The theory does not work for short-run fluctuations. Exchange rates fluctuate far more than the theory predicts. We can see this easily. According to the theory, the *real* exchange rate ought to be constant over time. The real exchange rate between the U.S. dollar and the currencies of the rest of the world is shown in Figure 12.4. The real exchange rate is not at all constant.

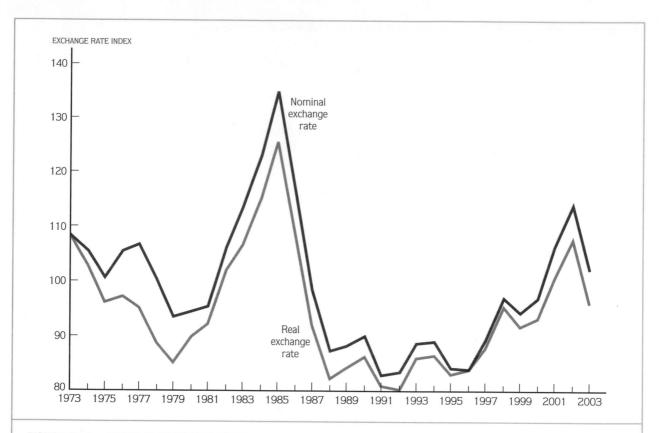

EXCHANGE RATE INDEX

Nominal exchange rate

Real exchange rate

FIGURE 12.4   THE REAL TRADE-WEIGHTED EXCHANGE RATE

The real exchange rate between the United States and the ROW is the nominal exchange rate adjusted for changes in the domestic purchasing power of the dollar and the currencies of the ROW. When the real exchange rate falls, it means that Americans find foreign goods more expensive. Through much of the 1970s, the real exchange rate fell. In the early 1980s, the relative price of American goods rose dramatically; then it fell sharply in 1986. The relative price of American goods rose again from 1996 to 2002, but fell sharply in 2003.

SOURCE: *Economic Report on the President*, 2003, Table B-110.

Purchasing power parity works well in the long run. The theory of *long-run purchasing power parity* is that there is a constant long-run level of the real exchange rate. Looking again at Figure 12.4, there is no obvious upward or downward trend in the real exchange rate. The rise in the dollar from 1980 to 1985 was followed by an equally large fall from 1985 to 1988. More recently, the dollar rose from 2000 to 2002, follow by a fall in 2003. While the real exchange rate has fluctuated a lot over the last 30 years, the value of the real exchange rate was not much different in 2003 from its value in 1973.[1]

Clearly, purchasing power parity is not a good theory of the determination of the exchange rate in the short run. On the other hand, the theory has a

[1] See David H. Papell, "Searching for Stationarity: Purchasing Power Parity under the Current Float," *Journal of International Economics*, Vol. 43 (1997), pp. 313–332.

powerful economic logic. How can we reconcile the fact of wide variations in the real exchange rate with the principle that people buy at the lowest possible price?

One answer is that different countries produce different products. Japanese cars are not identical to American cars, for example. When the dollar appreciates, Japanese cars become cheaper, but the U.S. public does not stop buying American cars altogether. Instead, the new price advantage of Japanese cars raises Japanese sales in the United States somewhat and depresses sales of American cars somewhat. The same thing occurs in hundreds of other markets. Appreciation of the dollar makes it more difficult for U.S. producers to sell their output, but it does not wipe them out. The exchange rate has room to vary. It is not locked in place by purchasing power parity.

The Exchange Rate and Purchasing Power Parity

1. The exchange rate is the number of units of foreign currency that a dollar is worth. An increase in the exchange rate is an appreciation of the dollar.

   E↑ = $ appreciation

2. The real exchange rate measures the relative purchasing power of the dollar by adjusting the nominal exchange rate by the price levels in the respective countries. When the real exchange rate is high, U.S. goods are expensive for foreigners and foreign goods are inexpensive for U.S. buyers.

3. Purchasing power parity asserts that the nominal exchange rate must equate the prices of tradable goods across countries. This implies a constant real exchange rate, which is inconsistent with the empirical evidence. Nonetheless, purchasing power parity exerts some influence on the exchange rate and works well in the long run.

   PPP = constant real exchange rate

* "strong" dollar = high exchange rate

12.3 | THE DETERMINANTS OF NET EXPORTS

The Effect of the Exchange Rate

As we have just seen, fluctuations in the exchange rate change the relative price of U.S. and ROW goods and thereby affect the demand for imports and exports. Imports depend positively on the exchange rate. If the dollar is strong, it buys a lot of foreign currency, and the goods sold by the ROW are correspondingly cheaper. Exports, too, are sensitive to the exchange rate. A strong dollar—that is, a high exchange rate—makes U.S. goods more expensive in the ROW. In the period of the strong dollar in the early 1980s, U.S. export industries like construction equipment suffered from the increase in their prices as perceived by the ROW, even though dollar price increases were moderate.

The Effect of Income

In Chapter 7, we noted that net exports depend on U.S. income. Higher incomes make consumers spend more on imported products; this relation is particularly sensitive because many types of products that consumers spend extra income on, such as electronics and cars, are frequently imported. In addition, some investment goods are imported, such as machine tools from Germany. When GDP rises and investment strengthens, part of the increase in investment goods comes from overseas. In general, imports respond positively to GDP. On the other hand, there is little connection between U.S. exports and U.S. GDP. Hence, net exports depend negatively on GDP.

Imports respond (+)
to GDP

Exports depend (−)
on GDP

The Net Export Function

As we have seen, we can combine imports and exports into a single measure, net exports X, defined as exports less imports. Our conclusions about the determinants of net exports are as follows:

1. Net exports depend negatively on the real exchange rate. When the dollar is strong, exports are lower and imports are higher. Net exports are lower on both counts.

2. Net exports depend negatively on real income in the United States. This dependence comes from subtracting imports, which depend positively on real income.

We can summarize these ideas in a simple algebraic formula:

$$ X = g - mY - n\frac{EP}{P_w}. \qquad \text{The Net Export Function} \qquad (12.1) $$

Equation 12.1 is the net export function. It says that net exports equal a constant g minus a coefficient m times income Y, minus a coefficient n times the real exchange rate. The net export function summarizes how net exports depend negatively on both income Y and the real exchange rate (EP/P_w).

How well does the net export function work? Figure 12.5 shows the relation between net exports and the real exchange rate since 1973. The negative relation is quite evident; note especially that the increases in the dollar exchange rate in the mid-1980s, late 1990s, and early 2000s were accompanied by a decline in net exports. The effect of the other determinant of net exports (real income in the United States) is not so evident in Figure 12.5 because exports rose as income in the ROW increased in this period. However, in the early 1980s, the economy of the United States grew more rapidly than the economies of many European countries and this added to the trade deficit. The weakening of the dollar in the late 1980s was the dominant factor in the increase in net exports.

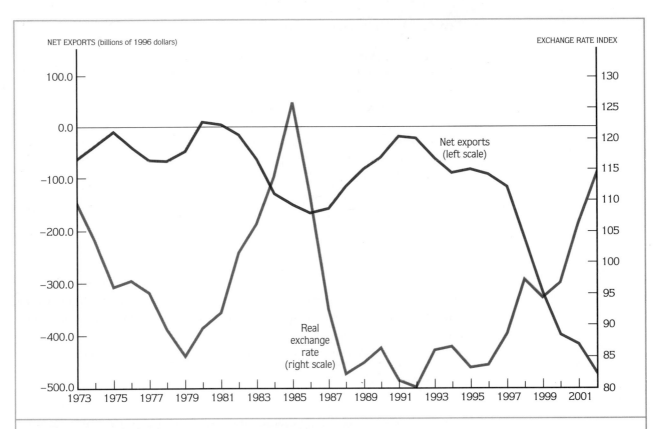

FIGURE 12.5   NET EXPORTS AND THE REAL EXCHANGE RATE

The real exchange rate and net exports move at the same time but in opposite directions. When the real exchange rate rises, net exports fall; conversely, when the real exchange rate falls, net exports rise.

SOURCE: *Economic Report of the President*, 2003, Tables B-2 and B-110.

EXAMPLE   A numerical example of the net export function can be written:

$$X = 600 - 0.1Y - 100\,\frac{EP}{P_w}. \quad \substack{\text{Numerical Example of the}\\ \text{Net Export Function}} \qquad (12.2)$$

Suppose that the price level in both the United States and the ROW are predetermined at the value of 1.0. If output Y is $5,000 billion and the exchange rate E is 1.0, then net exports X equal zero. If output Y rises by $100 billion, then net exports fall by $10 billion, because imports rise by this amount. If the exchange rate falls from 1.0 to 0.6, about as much as it did from 1985 to 1992, then net exports would rise by $40 billion.

Trade Deficits with China

In Figure 12.2, we showed how, starting in the late 1990s, China has replaced Japan as the country with the largest trade surplus with the United States. In contrast with the United States' other major trading partners, China keeps its currency, the yuan, rigidly fixed to the value of the U.S. dollar. If China deliberately keeps the yuan weak, it will promote its exports. The effect of such a policy can be seen from Equation 12.1, the net export function. When the yuan is weak, the dollar is strong, causing trade surpluses for China and trade deficits for the United States. These persistent and growing surpluses led in 2003 to pressure by U.S. policy makers on China to let the yuan float and allow the normal adjustment mechanism to take place. During Treasury Secretary John Snow's visit to China in September 2003, China stated that it would eventually let the value of the yuan be more flexible and be determined in international markets, but no timetable was set.

While allowing the yuan to float, in conjunction with reductions in barriers to trade and capital flows, would be an important step in integrating China into the world economy, it would not eliminate the U.S. trade deficit. Although the U.S. bilateral trade deficit with China is the largest of any single country, it accounted for less that 25 percent of the overall U.S. trade deficit in 2002. Many imports from China are goods from other Asian countries processed or finished off in China before shipping to the United States. If the yuan were to float, the price of Chinese goods in the United States would not rise by as much as the exchange rate, because only a portion of exports from China are entirely produced in China. Moreover, if the price of Chinese goods in the United States were to rise, substitutes for Chinese products would likely come from other countries.

Net exports is an endogenous variable that depends on the exchange rate. To complete our theory, we therefore need to explain what determines the exchange rate. As we have just seen, purchasing power parity does not work very well in the short run. We now develop a theory that relates the exchange rate to the interest rate.

12.4 | A MODEL OF THE REAL EXCHANGE RATE

Fluctuations in the exchange rate are closely related to interest rates in the United States and the ROW. In particular, policies in the United States that raise interest rates tend to cause the dollar to appreciate. The appreciation of the dollar in the early 1980s, for example, was related to the monetary and fiscal policies that brought extraordinarily high interest rates. Why are interest rates and the exchange rate positively related?

The financial markets of the major developed countries are closely linked. Investors are constantly comparing the returns they make by investing in Ger-

R↑ causes $ appreciation

many (in stocks and bonds that pay in euros), in Japan, in Britain, and in many other countries. There are billions of dollars and euros and trillions of yen of "hot money" that migrate almost instantly to the place where it earns the highest return.

As we stressed in Chapter 2, when the dust settles, trade flows and capital flows have to equal each other, except for measurement error. The net exports of the United States must be equal to the amount of U.S. capital flowing to the rest of the world less the amount of foreign capital coming into the United States. It is not possible for a large U.S. trade deficit to exist at the same time that large amounts of capital are flowing out of the United States to seek a higher return in other countries. The exchange rate and interest rates fluctuate minute by minute to keep trade flows and capital flows equal to each other.

Net Exports = (US capital → ROW) − (ROW capital → US)

When the U.S. interest rate is high in comparison with foreign interest rates, capital is attracted to the United States.[2] Even a fraction of a percentage point of extra return could bring hundreds of billions of dollars of wealth to be invested in the United States. To prevent such a large flow, something else must happen at the same time that the U.S. interest rate rises. What happens is an appreciation of the dollar. When foreign investors see the combination of attractive U.S. interest rates and a strong dollar, they reason in the following way: On the one hand, I like the high return I can earn in dollars. But on the other hand, I am not so sure that the return I will earn in my own currency is any better than at home. The dollar is strong today, but it is likely to come back to normal over the next year or two, as it always has in the past. As the dollar depreciates, I will lose some of my capital when I convert it back to my own currency. *appreciates simultaneously THEN depreciates*

The more the dollar rises when the U.S. interest rate rises, the more powerful is the second part of that logic. Hence, some degree of appreciation of the dollar will block the huge capital inflow that would otherwise accompany a higher U.S. interest rate. Figure 12.6 shows the relation between the U.S. interest rate and the exchange rate that is needed to stave off the capital inflow.

In algebra, we can express the positive relation between the real exchange rate and the U.S. interest rate as

$$\frac{EP}{P_w} = q + vR,$$

(12.3)

where R is the U.S. interest rate and q and v are constants. Recall that the rise in the U.S. interest rate relative to foreign interest rates brings about the rise in the exchange rate. In Equation 12.3, we suppress the foreign interest rate under the assumption that it does not move as much as the U.S. interest rate.

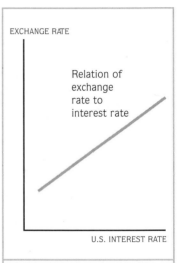

EXCHANGE RATE

Relation of exchange rate to interest rate

U.S. INTEREST RATE

FIGURE 12.6   RELATION BETWEEN THE U.S. INTEREST RATE AND THE EXCHANGE RATE

A higher U.S. interest rate requires a stronger dollar. If not, huge capital inflows would occur, which would be inconsistent with trade flows. The stronger dollar discourages the capital inflow that would otherwise occur by creating expectations of a subsequent depreciation of the dollar, which would offset the advantage of the higher U.S. interest rate.

---

[2]Just as in the case of consumption and investment, the interest rate that matters for the foreign exchange market is the real interest rate. If the U.S. nominal interest rate is high only because expected U.S. inflation is high, foreigners are not attracted to U.S. investments. They anticipate that the value of the dollar and so the value of dollar-denominated bonds will decline in the future at the expected rate of inflation.

EXAMPLE   If prices are measured in such a way that the real exchange rate EP/P_w is equal to 1 when purchasing power parity holds, then the relation between the U.S. interest rate and the real exchange rate might be

$$\frac{EP}{P_w} = 0.75 + 5R. \quad \text{Numerical Example of the Exchange Rate–Interest Rate Relation} \quad (12.4)$$

When the net export function, Equation 12.2, is combined with this relation, we get the numerical example of the net export relation used in Chapter 8:

$$X = 525 - 0.1Y - 500R.$$

The Interest Rate and the Exchange Rate

1. The exchange rate and the interest rate are positively related. When the real interest rate rises, say because of an increase in government spending, the exchange rate also rises.

2. The relationship between the interest rate and the exchange rate comes about as investors shift their funds between different countries to obtain the best return. When the interest rate rises in the United States, investors buy dollar-denominated bonds and this drives up the exchange rate.

3. When U.S. interest rates are high relative to the rest of the world, it must be the case that investors expect the dollar to depreciate at an annual rate equal to the interest-rate differential. Expectations of future depreciation require a strong dollar today. Hence, there is a positive relation between the interest rate and the exchange rate.

12.5 | THE IS CURVE AND ECONOMIC POLICY IN AN OPEN ECONOMY

Recall that the IS curve describes the combinations of interest rates R and incomes Y that satisfy the income identity and the equations for spending: consumption, investment, and net exports. *Without* net exports in the income identity, the IS curve slopes downward because higher interest rates reduce investment and, through the multiplier, reduce GDP. *With* net exports, more things happen to spending when the interest rate rises. An increase in the interest rate raises the exchange rate and thereby reduces net exports; this tends to augment the effect of the interest rate on investment and makes the IS curve flatter than it would be in a closed economy. Not only do high interest rates cause firms to invest less, they also cause Americans to meet their needs with imported goods and foreigners to divert their demand away from U.S. products.

But the presence of net exports also reduces the size of the multiplier, and this tends to make the IS curve steeper. Net exports depend negatively on GDP. As GDP rises, part of the increase in spending goes overseas and does not enter domestic aggregate demand. This spillover abroad, sometimes called **leakage,** reduces the size of the multiplier.

ΔX depends $(-)$ on Y

In Chapter 8, we derived the open-economy IS curve graphically and algebraically. The next section adds some more details in the process of deriving it algebraically.

Algebraic Derivation of the Open-Economy IS Curve

The IS curve is derived algebraically by substituting the functions for consumption C, investment I, and net exports X into the income identity. That is,

$$Y = \underbrace{a + b(1 - t)\,Y}_{C} + \underbrace{e - dR}_{I} + G + \underbrace{g - mY - n(EP/P_w)}_{X}. \quad (12.5)$$

Putting the interest rate on the left-hand side gives

$$R = \frac{a + e + g}{d} - \frac{1 - b(1-t) + m}{d}\,Y - \frac{n}{d}\frac{EP}{P_w} + \frac{1}{d}\,G. \quad (12.6)$$

This equation relates the interest rate R to output Y, the real exchange rate EP/P_w, and government spending G. It shows that the interest rate is negatively related to the real exchange rate. Appreciation of the dollar shifts the IS curve downward; depreciation raises the curve. To get the IS curve, substitute Equation 12.3 into Equation 12.6 to eliminate the real exchange rate:

$$R = \frac{a + e + g - nq}{d + nv} - \frac{1 - b(1 - t) + m}{d + nv}\,Y + \frac{1}{d + nv}\,G. \quad (12.7)$$

The coefficient on Y shows that the IS curve slopes downward for two reasons: the negative response of investment to the interest rate, described by d, and the negative response of net exports, described by nv.

The IS curve of Equation 12.7 is the one we discussed in Chapter 8.

Effects of Monetary and Fiscal Policy on Trade in the Short Run

Monetary and fiscal policy have important effects on trade and the exchange rate. Suppose the Fed increases the money supply. This shifts the LM curve to the right; that is, it lowers interest rates and stimulates investment. The decline in interest rates depreciates the exchange rate; net exports rise. Because of the

$M_s \uparrow$

E depreciates

$\Delta X \uparrow$

rise in investment and net exports, GDP rises. However, the increase in GDP tends to decrease net exports because imports rise. There are thus two offsetting effects of an increase in the money supply on net exports. Exports definitely rise, but imports may rise by a greater amount. In any case, interest rates fall, the dollar depreciates, and GDP rises. Conversely, when the money supply is decreased, interest rates rise, the dollar appreciates, and GDP falls.

Now suppose that government spending is increased. The IS curve is pushed to the right and interest rates rise. The rise in interest rates reduces investment spending but also causes the exchange rate to appreciate. The higher exchange rate reduces exports as U.S. goods become relatively expensive compared with foreign goods. Hence, the increase in government spending crowds out export industries as well as investment. Imports also rise because of the increase in the dollar and GDP. Thus, an increase in government spending increases the trade deficit or reduces the trade surplus as it stimulates the economy.

Price Adjustment

What happens in these alternative policy scenarios when firms begin to adjust their prices? In the case of the increase in the money supply, if output is equal to potential output, the price level begins to rise because output increases above potential. The increase in prices lowers real money balances and the interest rate begins to rise. As it does, the real exchange rate begins to rise. These adjustments continue until the economy has returned to potential. Eventually the price level will increase by the amount of the original increase in the money supply. The real exchange rate will return to normal so that the nominal exchange rate E will depreciate by the amount of the increase in the price level. In the long run, money is neutral.

An increase in government spending also eventually brings about an upward adjustment in prices. The reduction in real balances raises interest rates and further reduces investment and net exports. Eventually, output returns to potential output, and the sum of investment and net exports declines by exactly the amount of the increase in government spending. The real exchange rate and the real interest rate are permanently higher after the process is complete.

The theory of long-run purchasing power parity, discussed earlier in the chapter, is that there is a constant long-run level of the real exchange rate. The long-run effects of an increase in the money supply (the nominal exchange rate depreciates by the increase in the price level so that the real exchange rate is constant) are consistent with long-run purchasing power parity. The long-run effects of an increase in government purchases (a permanently higher real interest rate and real exchange rate) are not consistent with long-run purchasing power parity. The evidence that long-run purchasing power parity has worked well between the United States and its major trading partners over the last 30 years, as shown in Figure 12.4, implies that differences in fiscal policy between the United States and its major trading partners have not been sufficient to cause a long-run appreciation or depreciation of the U.S. real exchange rate.

Open-Economy IS Curve and Policy

1. The downward slope of the IS curve in an open economy comes in part from the positive relation between the interest rates and the exchange rate. Net exports decline when the interest rate rises.

   $\Delta X \downarrow$ when $R \uparrow$

2. The offset to fiscal expansion through crowding out is stronger in an open economy. Fiscal expansion raises the interest rate and depresses net exports.

3. Monetary policy has an enhanced effect through the interest rate in an open economy. A monetary expansion lowers the interest rate and stimulates net exports as well as investment in the short run.

4. In the long run, money remains neutral with respect to all real variables. The price level increases and the nominal exchange rate depreciates in proportion to the increase in the money supply. This is an example of long-run purchasing parity.

12.6 | THE EXCHANGE RATE AND THE PRICE LEVEL

One macroeconomic principle we stress in this book is that the price level is very unresponsive to most economic events in the short run. For example, a sudden contraction in monetary policy does not seem to have any measurable impact on the price level within the first year, even though its eventual effect is to lower prices considerably. An important exception is that prices respond quickly to changes in costs of imports, such as oil. The dramatic price rises of 1974–75, 1979–80, and 1990 and the sudden slowing of inflation in 1986 can be linked directly to events in the world oil market. To a certain extent, fluctuations in the exchange rate can influence the price level in a similar way. A rise in the dollar is like a decline in world oil prices. It makes imports cheaper. A collapse of the dollar, as in 1986–87, is an adverse price shock.

In a small economy, the domestic price level is closely tied to the exchange rate. Many consumption and investment goods are imported; those that are not compete with imports. A small country's exports trade in large world markets and are usually constrained to sell at home for essentially the world price. Hence, changes in a small country's exchange rate bring immediate and important changes in that country's price level.

In the large U.S. economy, the situation is quite the reverse. For Japanese cars, for example, the U.S. market is over half the total market worldwide. The setting of the U.S. dollar price for foreign products is a major business decision for the makers of those products. Frequently, the outcome of that decision is to keep the dollar price of foreign products unchanged in the United States, even though the exchange rate has risen or fallen sharply. For example, when the dollar rose dramatically against the German mark in 1983, German auto companies raised the mark price of cars to stabilize their dollar prices in the United States. They might have chosen to let the dollar price fall to sell more cars. Similarly, when the dollar fell sharply relative to the mark after 1985, the mark price of cars shipped to the United States fell. Again, the dollar price was stable. German car makers maintained a stable share of the U.S. market and kept their cars at stable prices relative to other cars in the market. Many other foreign sellers of products with well-known brands in the United States behaved in the same way.

From its peak in early 1985 until late 1986, the real exchange rate declined by over 15 percent. The real price of imports to the United States rose by only about 1 percent over the same period. All the rest of the change in the exchange rate was absorbed by a decline in profit margins by importers. For Japan, the numbers are particularly striking: Stated in yen, the cost of producing products in Japan rose by about 6 percent from the beginning of 1985 to the middle of 1986. But the number of yen received by the Japanese for their typical exported product declined by 23 percent over the same period.[3] Costs and profit margins of U.S. exporters appear to be much less sensitive to exchange-rate fluctuations. Dollar prices of U.S. exports are largely unaffected by exchange-rate changes; this implies that foreign-currency prices of U.S. goods change roughly in proportion to the exchange rate.[4]

Because importers tend not to adjust their U.S. prices quickly in response to changes in the exchange rate, large movements in the exchange rate do not create price shocks in the U.S. economy. The price adjustment process described in Chapter 9 applies reasonably well to the prices of imported goods as well as those made in the United States. We do not stress the immediate impact of the exchange rate on the U.S. price level. That impact would be large in a small, highly open economy but appears to be quite small in the U.S. economy.

12.7 | PROTECTIONISM VERSUS FREE TRADE

All industries in the United States that produce products that can be shipped from one country to another face foreign competition. These industries make up the tradables sector. Only industries like services, communications, and utilities are insulated from that competition. If foreign competition could be eliminated or discouraged, domestic producers would enjoy increased profits. The losers would be U.S. consumers, who would pay higher prices as a result of lessened competition.

---

[3]The data are from Paul Krugman and Richard Baldwin, "The Persistence of the U.S. Trade Deficit," *Brookings Papers on Economic Activity*, Vol. 1 (1987), pp. 1–43.
[4]See the comparative study by Michael Knetter, "Price Discrimination by U.S. and German Exporters," *American Economic Review*, Vol. 79 (March 1989), pp. 198–210.

Industries in the tradables sector push constantly in favor of protectionist measures. These measures include

1. Tariffs, which are a tax on imports

2. Quotas, which limit the quantity of imports

3. Outright bans of certain imports.

The incentive to seek protection exists all the time. However, the likelihood of convincing Congress to enact protectionist legislation rises dramatically when imports are high and domestic industries are suffering from diminished sales and high unemployment.

The history of protection in the United States can be characterized in the following way. In normal times, under the leadership of the president, trade barriers are gradually reduced. Consumer interests predominate in the long run; purchasers in the United States are generally free to take advantage of bargains that foreigners make available. But, in times of recession or large trade deficits, strong pressures develop for protectionist legislation. Tariffs and quotas are tightened in those times. When the emergency is over, protectionism lingers for some years but eventually is reduced.

Macroeconomic Effects of Protectionism

A tariff or quota has the effect of shifting the net exports schedule in the direction of higher net exports given the exchange rate. That shift enters the spending process just like any other shift in a spending schedule or an increase in government purchases. The IS curve shifts to the right. The interest rate and GDP increase along the LM curve, which remains unchanged. All the usual accompaniments to a spending stimulus occur. In particular, the higher interest rate makes the dollar appreciate.

Because a tariff makes the dollar appreciate, the actual effect on prices and trade is smaller than it might appear at first. Although a tariff makes imports more expensive, a stronger dollar offsets this to some extent. In other words, the exporting country pays part of the tariff, rather than the U.S. consumer. Moreover, to the extent that the exporter tends to stabilize its dollar price in the United States, as we discussed in the previous section, it is even more true that the exporter, not the consumer, pays the tariff. At the same time, the macroeconomic stimulus becomes smaller, because if U.S. consumers see no price change, they will not cut their imports. Note that this effect cannot apply to quotas. If a quota forces the quantity of imports to decline, it must cause an increase in the prices paid by U.S. purchasers.

Our analysis assumes foreign countries do not respond to trade restrictions with similar sanctions against U.S. products. Retaliation would certainly undo whatever short-run benefits protection might bring. In fact, the infamous Smoot-Hawley tariff touched off a trade war in the 1930s that contributed to the Great Depression.

Protectionism

1. Protectionist policies lessen foreign competition faced by domestic producers. They generally help domestic producers and hurt domestic consumers. They include tariffs on imports, quotas on the quantities of imports, and bans on some imports.

2. Protectionist measures stimulate net exports. They shift the IS curve outward, raise the interest rate, and raise GDP.

3. Protectionism raises the exchange rate; this discourages net exports and offsets some of the effects of protection.

4. Protection runs the risk of retaliation by our trading partners. A trade war would certainly undo any temporary benefits protectionism might bring and reduce the welfare of the nations involved.

12.8 | STABILIZING THE EXCHANGE RATE

MACROSOLVE
EXERCISE

The wild swings in the exchange rate shown in Figure 12.3 have been of concern to both Americans and foreigners. When the dollar was strong, U.S. producers of tradables suffered, while U.S. purchasers of imports had the advantage of bargains. The collapse of the dollar in the mid-1980s reversed the situation. Many observers have suggested that the world would have been better off with more stable exchange rates, although no detailed analysis has tried to add up the benefits and costs of both consumers and producers. Most discussions consider only the interests of producers and fail to give weight to the benefits that consumers receive when the rest of the world is making bargains available to the United States.

How might U.S. policy be changed to stabilize the exchange rate? Recall that there is a simple relation between the exchange rate and the U.S. interest rate, holding constant economic conditions in the rest of the world. When the rest of the world is quiescent, the United States would have to hold its own interest rate constant in order to keep the exchange rate constant. Figure 12.7, panel A, illustrates the necessary policy in terms of the LM curve. A commitment on the part of the Fed to keep the interest rate constant means that the LM curve is perfectly flat. A shock in spending—say, unexpectedly strong investment—shifts the IS curve to the right, as shown in the figure. GDP rises by the full amount of the spending shift together with the resulting multiplier effects. The normal offset from higher interest rates does not occur. Therefore, GDP would be highly vulnerable to spending disturbances under a policy that kept the exchange rate constant.

Note that the flat LM curve also indicates that fiscal policy is more powerful when the central bank stabilizes the exchange rate. An increase in government spending pushes the IS curve to the right. With floating exchange rates, we saw that the increase in government spending partially crowds out private

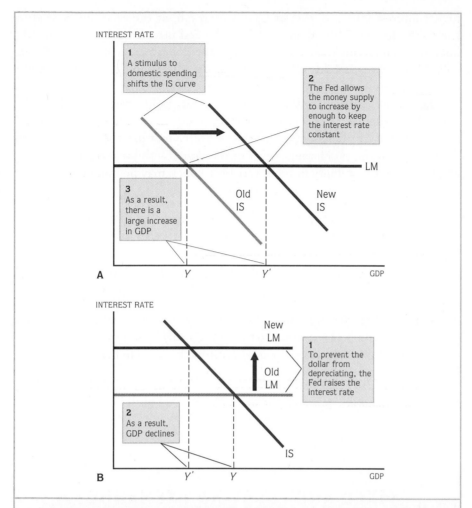

INTEREST RATE

1
A stimulus to domestic spending shifts the IS curve

2
The Fed allows the money supply to increase by enough to keep the interest rate constant

LM

3
As a result, there is a large increase in GDP

Old IS

New IS

A Y Y' GDP

INTEREST RATE

New LM

1
To prevent the dollar from depreciating, the Fed raises the interest rate

Old LM

2
As a result, GDP declines

IS

B Y' Y GDP

FIGURE 12.7   EFFECT OF A SPENDING SHOCK AND A FOREIGN SHOCK UNDER EXCHANGE-RATE STABILIZATION

(A) When the Fed is operating monetary policy under the principle of keeping the exchange rate stable, it must keep the interest rate constant. That is, the LM curve is a horizontal line. When the IS curve shifts, it causes large changes in output. (B) When a change occurs in the rest of the world, such as a monetary contraction in a major foreign country, the Fed must raise the interest rate to prevent depreciation of the dollar if it has a policy of stabilizing the exchange rate. Such a move contracts output in the United States.

investment *and* net exports, because interest rates rise and the exchange rate appreciates. With the exchange rate stabilized, there is no appreciation of the currency and the interest rate does not rise. Hence, there is no crowding out. Production increases by the full amount of the shift in the IS curve. This is illustrated in Figure 12.7, panel A.

Figure 12.7, panel B, shows what would happen if there were a shock in the rest of the world that would normally have made the dollar depreciate (such as an increase in interest rates in other countries). The Fed has to shift the LM curve upward by enough to prevent the depreciation. As a result of the

Defending the Dollar

higher interest rate, the level of GDP would fall, as the economy moved up and to the left along the IS curve. When the Fed takes an action like this (deliberately contracting the economy to raise the dollar), it is called *defending the dollar*. It sacrifices stability of employment and output in the United States to stabilize the exchange rate.

The important point is that making monetary policy responsible for stabilizing the exchange rate prevents monetary policy from achieving other goals, such as stability of employment or prices. We cannot ask the Fed to prevent fluctuations in the purchasing power of the dollar without recognizing that it must sacrifice the stability of other variables, which may be more important.

Stabilizing the Exchange Rate

1. To stabilize the exchange rate, the Fed would have to set a horizontal LM curve.

2. With a stable exchange rate, a domestic spending shock would have a large effect on GDP. The normal cushioning through interest-rate fluctuations would not occur, because it would cause exchange-rate fluctuations.

3. With a stable exchange rate, the Fed would have to change the U.S. interest rate in response to each foreign shock. It could not insulate GDP and employment from those shocks as it could with a floating rate.

12.9 | FIXED AND FLOATING EXCHANGE RATES IN THE LONG RUN

The exchange rate, price level, and monetary policy for an economy in the long run are related by

$$PE = P_w. \qquad \text{Long-Run} \qquad (12.8)$$

That is, the domestic price level P times the exchange rate E equals the foreign or world price P_w. Equation 12.8 says that *purchasing power parity* holds in the long run.

Recall from Chapter 9 that the price level P is simply proportional to the money supply in the long run. Given an exchange-rate target E, we can solve Equation 12.8 for the price level needed to achieve that exchange rate:

$$P = P_w/E. \qquad (12.9)$$

Thus, to fix the exchange rate E, the money supply has to be held proportional to the level P_w/E. If the world price rises by 50 percent over a decade, the money stock must also rise by 50 percent. A fixed exchange rate locks monetary policy to the price level in the country whose currency is the basis for the fixed rate.

With a floating exchange rate, Equation 12.8 has a different interpretation. We can solve it for the exchange rate:

$$E = P_w/P. \qquad \text{Floating Exchange Rate} \qquad (12.10)$$

Monetary policy uses whatever principles it wants to set the money supply and thus set the domestic price level P. If the central bank chooses to raise the price level by expanding the money supply, it lowers the exchange rate in the same proportion.

World Inflation with Floating Exchange Rates

Yet another use of Equation 12.8 is to study rates of change in prices and exchange rates over time periods of a decade or longer. Stated in terms of rates of change, Equation 12.8 says

$$\pi + \frac{\Delta E}{E} = \pi_w. \qquad (12.11)$$

domestic rate of inflation → | rate of appreciation ↓ | forelgn rate of inflation ←

The domestic rate of inflation π plus the rate of appreciation $\Delta E/E$ equals the foreign rate of inflation π_w. Another way to express the same relationship is to observe that the excess of the foreign rate of inflation over the domestic rate of inflation is equal to the rate of appreciation of the domestic currency:

$$\pi_w - \pi = \frac{\Delta E}{E}. \qquad (12.12)$$

How accurate is this equation as a description of the long-run behavior? Figure 12.8 shows the inflation differentials and exchange-rate appreciations between six economies and the United States. The difference between inflation in each country (π_w) and inflation in the United States (π) is shown on the vertical axis. The rate of appreciation ($\Delta E/E$) of the dollar against each of the corresponding currencies is on the horizontal axis. The 45-degree line is then the relation between inflation differentials and exchange-rate depreciation implied by Equation 12.12. The actual inflation rates and exchange-rate behavior come very close to the theoretical prediction. Japan has had the strongest currency and the lowest inflation rate compared with the United States. Italy, in contrast, has had a comparatively weak currency and a high inflation rate compared with the United States. This relation between inflation and exchange-rate behavior is even more striking for countries with very high inflation rates. For example, during the period from 1973 to 2002, the difference between the inflation rate in Mexico and that in the United States was almost 25 percent per year. The Mexican peso depreciated by nearly 25 percent per year against the dollar during that period.

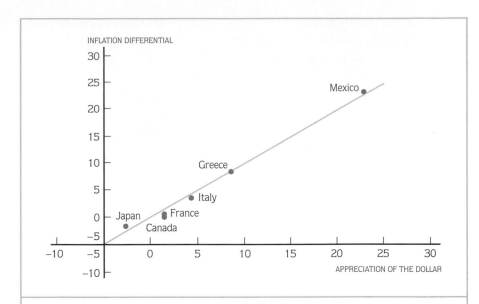

FIGURE 12.8   INFLATION DIFFERENTIALS AND APPRECIATION OF THE DOLLAR RELATIVE TO SIX COUNTRIES, 1973–2002

The inflation rates are measured by the consumer price index in each country. The rates of inflation and appreciation are annual averages for the 30-year period. When the inflation differential is high, appreciation of the dollar against that country's currency is high.

SOURCE: Office of Economic Cooperation and Development.

The freedom that a floating exchange rate gives to countries in determining their own inflation rates is a mixed blessing, according to some economists. They feel that discipline rather than freedom is needed because of the tendency for many countries' political systems to generate too much inflation. For a small country, it might be better to peg its currency to one of its trading partners that has a relatively low inflation rate. As long as the exchange rate is maintained, the small country will eventually also have a low inflation rate.

Macro Policy and Exchange Rates

1. Under a fixed-rate regime, the central bank must keep the domestic price level in step with the price level of the country whose currency forms the base of the system. The center country thus establishes monetary policy for the group.

2. Under floating rates, each country is free to choose its own inflation rate. Inflation differentials then determine the long-run behavior of exchange rates.

REVIEW AND PRACTICE

Major Points

1. The long-run value of the exchange rate is determined by purchasing power parity. In the short run, expectations and conditions in financial markets create large deviations from purchasing power parity.

2. The interest-rate differential between two countries is equal to the expected rate of depreciation.

3. When the U.S. interest rate is relatively high, the exchange rate must be high also, so that interest-rate parity holds in the short run and purchasing power parity holds in the long run.

4. The net export function depends negatively on income and the real exchange rate.

5. The multiplier is smaller in an open economy than in a closed economy. This makes the IS curve steeper.

6. In an open economy, an increase in the interest rate has a larger first-round effect on spending because it reduces net exports as well as investment. This makes the IS curve flatter.

7. An expansionary monetary policy lowers the interest rate and the exchange rate. Investment and exports are stimulated in the short run. In the long run, money is neutral.

8. An expansionary fiscal policy raises the interest rate and the exchange rate. The policy crowds out the investment industries and export industries.

9. Changes in the exchange rate do not have large immediate effects on the price level. The U.S. price of imported products is sticky.

10. Protectionist policies such as tariffs and quotas reduce the trade deficit and stimulate GDP in the short run. They also tend to make the dollar appreciate, which offsets some of their effects. Protectionism is harmful to consumers because it raises prices of foreign products and is likely to lead to retaliation by foreign governments.

11. If the Fed sets a policy of stabilizing the exchange rate, it must give up other goals, such as employment stability. When the exchange rate is held constant, domestic spending shocks have large effects on GDP. In addition, the policy makes GDP vulnerable to shocks occurring in foreign countries.

12. Starting in 2000, the trade deficit with China surpassed the trade deficit with Japan as the largest U.S. bilateral trade deficit. This led to pressure by U.S. policy makers on China to let its currency, the yuan, be determined in international markets.

Key Terms and Concepts

terms of trade

exchange rate

foreign exchange market

flexible exchange-rate system

real exchange rate

trade-weighted exchange rate

appreciation

depreciation

purchasing power parity

leakage

Questions for Discussion and Review

1. Explain how you would compare the return on a Japanese bond with the return on a U.S. bond.

2. What happens to the exchange rate between the U.S. dollar and the Italian lira when chronic inflation in Italy is well above inflation in the United States?

3. Why is it rational for investors to expect that the exchange rate will depreciate when it is above normal? Under what circumstances would it not be rational to expect this?

4. Summarize the steps and assumptions that link the exchange rate and the interest rate. What would happen to the relationship if the ROW decided to use a more expansionary policy?

5. Describe what happens to consumption, investment, and net exports when you move down the IS curve.

6. What happens to net exports, investment, and consumption when government spending is decreased? Distinguish the long run from the short run.

7. What happens to net exports, investment, and consumption when the money supply is decreased? Why is monetary policy neutral in the long run but not in the short run?

8. Describe the changes in the short run to the U.S. price of Japanese cars when the yen appreciates.

9. What would happen to the interest rate, GDP, exchange rate, and trade deficit if a uniform 10 percent tariff were placed on all imports? What would happen to these variables if foreign countries retaliated with an equal tariff on U.S. goods?

10. What must the Fed do to keep the exchange rate constant if interest rates in Europe rise because of monetary contraction there?

11. Suppose that the Chinese currency, the yuan, were allowed to float. Why wouldn't the U.S. trade deficit be eliminated?

Problems

NUMERICAL

1. Consider a macro model consisting of the following relationships:

$$Y = C + I + G + X$$
$$C = 220 + 0.63Y$$
$$I = 400 - 2{,}000R + 0.1Y$$
$$M = (0.1583Y - 1{,}000R)P$$
$$X = 600 - 0.1Y - 100 \, EP/P_w$$
$$EP/P_w = 0.75 + 5R$$

where government spending G equals 1,200 and the money supply M equals 900. Suppose that the ROW price level P_w is always equal to 1.0 and the U.S. price level is predetermined at 1.0.

a. Which are the endogenous variables and which are the exogenous variables in this relationship?

b. Find the values of Y, R, C, I, X, and E predicted by the model.

c. Derive an algebraic expression for the aggregate demand curve in which the money supply M, government spending G, and price level P explicitly appear. For $M = 900$ and $G = 1{,}200$ draw the aggregate demand curve accurately to scale.

d. Keeping the price level P at 1.0, calculate the effect a decrease in government spending of $10 billion has on output, the interest rate, consumption, investment, net exports, and the exchange rate. Do the same thing for an increase in the money supply of $20 billion.

2. Using the same numerical example as in problem 1, calculate private saving, the government budget surplus, and the capital inflow from abroad for the case where $G = 1{,}200$ and $M = 900$. Show that the sum of these three equals investment. Repeat your calculation for $G = 1{,}190$ and $M = 920$. Comment on what happens to the three components of saving.

3. For the same numerical example as in problem 1, calculate a change in the mix of monetary and fiscal policy that leaves output equal to the level it is when $M = 900$ and $G = 1{,}200$ but in which the interest rate is 3 percent rather than 5 percent. Describe what happens to the value of the dollar, net exports, the government budget deficit, and investment for this change in policy.

4. Now assume that prices adjust according to the price adjustment equation

$$\pi = 1.2(Y_{-1} - Y^*)/Y^*,$$

where π is the rate of inflation and potential output Y^* is equal to $6,000 billion. Continuing where you left off in problem 1d, calculate the effect on the endogenous variables in the second, third, and fourth years after the increase in the money supply of $20 billion. Do the same for the decline in government spending of $10 billion. Describe the economy after prices have fully adjusted.

5. Consider a small economy that is much more open than the one in the previous examples. Its net export function is

$$X = 900 - 0.1Y - 400\ EP/P_w$$

and the relationship between the interest rate and the exchange rate is

$$EP/P_w = 10R + 0.5.$$

The other equations are the same.

a. Explain why this economy is more open.

b. Calculate what happens in the first year and in the long run when the money supply increases by $10 billion. Calculate what happens when government spending increases by $10 billion.

ANALYTICAL

1. Suppose it was agreed that the United States would spend less on defense and that Japan would spend more.

a. How would a reduction in defense spending affect the U.S. trade balance?

b. How would an increase in Japan's defense spending affect the U.S. trade balance?

c. To the extent that the United States and Japan purchase defense goods from each other, how does this affect your answer?

2. Purchasing power parity (PPP) is a theory of exchange-rate behavior described in Section 12.2.

a. Explain why the real exchange rate never changes under the theory of purchasing power parity.

b. What governs the behavior of nominal exchange rates under PPP? Under what conditions are nominal exchange rates sticky?

c. Suppose that inflation in the United States is 4 percent while in the rest of the world it is 7 percent. Under PPP, how does E change over time? Does the dollar appreciate or depreciate?

d. PPP clearly does not hold up in the short run; see Figure 12.4, where the real exchange rate is calculated using the GDP deflators for the United States and the ROW. If the real exchange rate was calculated using price indexes for manufactured goods, would you expect it to vary by more or less than it does in Figure 12.4?

3. On any given day, interest rates will differ from country to country. For example, U.S. government securities may pay 10 percent interest while comparable Japanese securities pay 5 percent interest.

  a. Assume Japanese investors have access to U.S. securities. Why would any of them invest in Japanese securities when they could earn a higher interest rate on U.S. securities? Be specific.

  b. Is it likely that any American investors would want to hold the Japanese securities?

  c. Suppose that PPP (see problem 2) holds exactly; interest rates in the United States and Japan are 10 percent and 5 percent, respectively; and the U.S. inflation rate is 5 percent. If international investors are to be indifferent between holding U.S. and Japanese securities, what must the Japanese inflation rate be?

4. Given the net export function developed in this chapter, explain why the effect of fiscal policy on the trade balance is unambiguous, whereas the effect of monetary policy is ambiguous.

5. In Chapter 8 we developed a model in which net exports were a function of the interest rate. In this chapter, we described in more detail why net exports depend on the interest rate.

  a. What factors determine the sensitivity of net exports to the interest rate?

  b. Consider the cases where net exports are very sensitive to the interest rate and where they are very insensitive. Compare the effect that an increase in the money supply has on output, the interest rate, investment, and the trade balance for each case.

  c. Suppose foreign manufacturers maintain a fixed dollar price for their goods regardless of the exchange rate. Does this result in net exports' being more or less sensitive to the interest rate?

  d. Given this behavior, explain why the only way the monetary authorities could act to reduce the trade deficit is by inducing a recession.

6. Suppose that the economy is at potential but the trade deficit is thought to be too large and the dollar is overvalued. Describe a change in monetary and fiscal policy that keeps the economy at potential but lowers both the dollar and the trade deficit. Explain intuitively how the change in policy brings about the desired results. Illustrate your answer using an IS-LM diagram.

7. Suppose that the economy is operating at potential but inflation is thought to be too high. Macro policy therefore must turn contractionary to reduce inflation. Describe the pros and cons of using monetary policy or fiscal policy to bring about the contraction, paying attention to the international factors.

SPENDING, TAXES, AND THE BUDGET DEFICIT

The budget of the U.S. federal government was in deficit every year between 1970 and 1997. Starting in 1998, the deficits turned to surpluses, but in 2002 and 2003, the surpluses turned back to deficits. How does the budget deficit affect the economy? First, government purchases contribute directly to demand. Second, transfer payments such as social security and unemployment compensation augment income. Third, interest paid on the national debt also augments income. Fourth, personal and business income taxes reduce income. In the last three cases, demand is indirectly influenced because incomes change. The effect of the budget deficit is best analyzed in terms of these components of the deficit: purchases plus transfers plus interest on the national debt less taxes. In this chapter, we examine in detail the effects of these components on the economy.

Traditionally in macroeconomics, government purchases have been considered exogenous—not explained in the model. This was so, for example, in the economic fluctuations model of Part 3, where government purchases G were taken as an exogenous variable. Empirically speaking, however, the government sector reacts to the state of the economy, partly because of conscious attempts to affect the economy. Transfers and taxes react to the state of the economy even more than purchases. The equation describing government behavior is typically called a **reaction function.** Sometimes, it is called a **policy rule,** because government actions are policy in one way or another, and if the behavior is systematic, it is like a rule. For example, generally, taxes decline in recessions.

13.1 | GOVERNMENT BUDGETS

Because the United States has a federal system of government, we need to distinguish between the different types of government: federal, state, and local. In 2003, federal government purchases were 38 percent of total government purchases, and state and local purchases were 62 percent.

The Federal Government Budget and Deficit

The best place to start looking at the budget deficit's effect on the economy is with the federal **budget.** The federal government budget summarizes all three of the types of effects on aggregate demand: purchases, transfers, and taxes. The overall budget totals do not distinguish between purchases and transfers. Rather, purchases of goods and services and transfers are lumped together as government **outlays.** The federal government's budget for 2003 is shown in Table 13.1.

Government outlays consist of purchases and transfers. Purchases involve the use of goods and services by the government, whereas transfers move funds to people outside the government. Less than a third of federal outlays take the form of purchases of goods and services. National defense accounts for about two-thirds of federal purchases. Federal purchases in 2003 were $664 billion, out of which $452 billion went for defense. Clearly, a major direct contribution of the government to aggregate demand is military spending. In 2002, total federal purchases of goods and services were about 6.6 percent of GDP.

Note that a substantial part of the government's expenditures is interest on the debt. As the debt has risen with high deficits in recent years, these interest payments have also risen. In 2003, interest payments on the debt represented about $1,400 for each person in the labor force on average. The government can do little to change interest payments in a given year. The payments depend on past deficits and the interest rate on past borrowing.

TABLE 13.1

THE 2003 BUDGET OF THE UNITED STATES GOVERNMENT (BILLIONS OF DOLLARS DURING THE CALENDAR YEAR)

RECEIPTS	1876
Individual income taxes	809
Corporate income taxes	196
Social security taxes	759
Other taxes and receipts	112
OUTLAYS	2259
Purchases	
National defense	453
Other purchases	212
Transfer payments	989
Grants to local governments	351
Interest on the debt	195
Subsidies less enterprise profits	59
DEFICIT	383

SOURCE: Bureau of Economic Analysis, *National Income and Product Accounts*, Second Quarter 2004.

Aside from national defense, the major role of the federal government is to take in funds through taxes and pay them out as transfers. Most of the transfer takes the form of taxing families through the personal income tax and the social security tax and then paying out the proceeds as family benefits. The great bulk of these benefits are social security payments for retirement, disability, and medical needs.

The $383 billion deficit at the bottom of Table 13.1 is simply expenditures less receipts. The federal government spent more than it received in every year between 1970 and 1997, with the largest deficit, $298 billion, occurring in 1992. The deficits steadily declined in the 1990s and, in 1998, the federal budget surplus was $44 billion. The surpluses peaked at $207 billion in 2000 and, starting in 2002, the deficits returned. The three major causes of the return of the deficits in 2002 were the effects of the 2001 recession, the fall in the stock market, and increased federal spending on the war on terrorism and homeland security. The tax cuts passed in 2001–2003 were not a major cause of the return of the deficits in 2002, but added to the deficit in the next few years.

State and Local Government Budgets

A major development in the 1980s and 1990s has been to shift responsibility away from the federal government to the local level, especially state governments. If this decentralization process continues, the state and local governments will play an increasingly important role in the economy in the future.

Table 13.2 shows the receipts and outlay figures in 2003 for all state and local governments combined in the United States. Compared with the federal government, a much larger percentage of state and local government outlays are purchases of goods and services that add directly to demand. The largest single purchase item for state and local governments is education, about one-third of total purchases. Much as defense dominates federal government purchases, education dominates state and local government purchases.

Like the federal government, the state and local government ran a combined budget deficit in 2003. A combined budget surplus at the state and local level, however, has been more typical except for years following recessions. Between 1959 and 2000, state and local governments ran combined budget deficits only in 1987 and 1991–1992. This state and local surplus tends to offset the federal government deficit. Many municipal governments have laws

TABLE 13.2

THE 2003 COMBINED BUDGETS OF STATE AND LOCAL GOVERNMENTS (BILLIONS OF DOLLARS)

RECEIPTS	1396
Personal tax	277
Corporate tax	38
Sales and property taxes	628
Payroll and other taxes	102
Grants from federal government	351
OUTLAYS	1412
Purchases (goods and services)	1068
Transfer payments	359
Net interest paid	−2
Subsidies less enterprise profits	−13
DEFICIT	16

SOURCE: Bureau of Economic Analysis, *National Income and Product Accounts*, Second Quarter, 2004.

that prevent their operating budgets from going into large deficits. In recent years, balanced budget laws have been enacted in many states. Of course, some local governments run serious deficits even though there is a general surplus.

A large percentage of state and local government receipts—about 45 percent—comes from property taxes and sales taxes. The federal government raises only a negligible part of its revenues from these sources. This means that the economy has different effects on state and local governments' budgets than on the federal government's budget.

13.2 | FLUCTUATIONS IN THE DEFICIT: PURCHASES, TRANSFERS, AND TAXES

From the point of view of macroeconomic *fluctuations*, what matters most about the government budget deficit is not its average level, but the way the budget responds to conditions in the economy. How large is this response? How do the fluctuations in the government deficit compare with the fluctuations in the economy as a whole? We try to answer these questions separately for purchases, transfers, and taxes. We do not consider changes in the fourth component of the deficit, interest on the national debt; the federal government has no immediate separate control over that component, because the amount of debt is determined by past deficits, and the interest rate is determined by monetary policy as well as fiscal policy and other factors.

MACROSOLVE
EXERCISE

First, federal purchases of goods and services do not seem to change much as real activity in the private economy fluctuates. This is shown in Figure 13.1. During the post–World War II period, federal spending has fluctuated mostly because of defense spending. Federal spending rose during the Vietnam War, when unemployment was low, and during the defense buildup of the early 1980s. Except possibly for the early 1980s, when defense spending increased as the Fed tightened monetary policy and there was a recession, federal spending has not increased during recessions. Federal purchases were flat during the recession starting in 1990.

Following the recession of 2001, federal purchases in real terms increased by 6.4 percent in 2002. Most of this spending was for the war on terrorism, with more than half going to the Department of Defense and various intelligence agencies. Most of the rest went to homeland security and the emergency response and recovery efforts in New York City.

Every recession brings programs to raise spending and provide added government employment. In fact, however, spending programs have been small and taken several years to get into gear. Programs launched in the depths of a recession frequently do not generate a significant contribution to aggregate demand until several years later. By then, the economy might be approaching boom conditions.

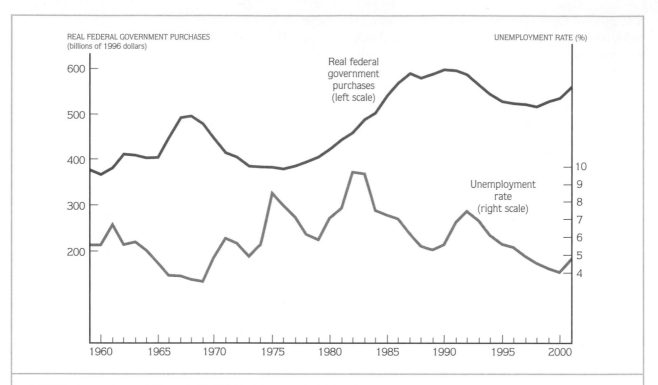

FIGURE 13.1   REAL FEDERAL GOVERNMENT PURCHASES AND UNEMPLOYMENT

Federal purchases of goods and services have not responded in any systematic way to the state of the economy, as measured by the unemployment rate. There was a big increase in federal spending in the late 1960s and again in the early 1980s. Except possibly for the 1980s, spending has not cranked up the economy during recessions by increasing relative to aggregate demand.

SOURCE: *Economic Report of the President*, 2003, Tables B-1, B-7, and B-35.

On the other hand, the federal government's transfers usually fluctuate in the right direction and offset other movements in the economy. Government transfers rise when unemployment rises, as can be seen clearly in Figure 13.2.

Government transfers rise in recessions and fall in booms largely through the normal operation of benefit programs. No discretionary intervention on the part of government officials is required. As discussed in Chapter 10, when unemployment rises and incomes fall, a number of government programs automatically increase their income transfers to families. For this reason, they sometimes are called *automatic stabilizers*. These programs are listed in Table 13.3.

Taxes also rise and fall with the level of economic activity. The data are summarized in Figure 13.3. In each recession since 1959, federal government tax receipts dropped sharply. This behavior was particularly dramatic in the 1969–70, the 1974–75, the 1981–82, and the 2001 recessions. On the other hand, the decline in the 1990–91 recession was small. The drop in tax receipts in these periods was larger in percentage terms than the drop in real GDP. The

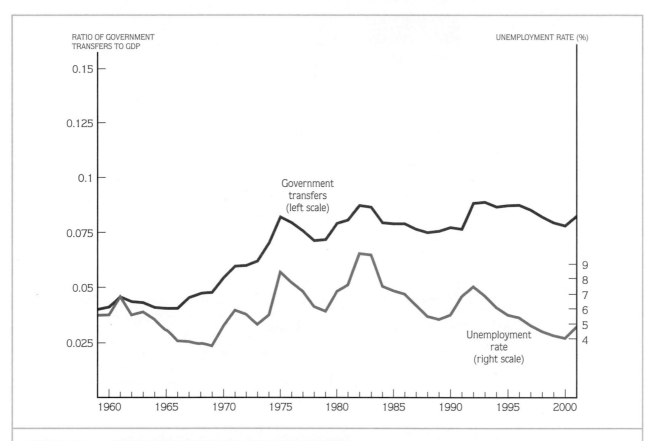

FIGURE 13.2   GOVERNMENT TRANSFERS AND UNEMPLOYMENT

Government transfer payments tend to rise in years of high unemployment and fall in years of low unemployment. This has been especially true in recent years. The synchronization is achieved mainly through unemployment insurance and other programs that make the rise in transfers during recessions automatic.

SOURCE: *Economic Report of the President,* 2003, Tables B-1, B-35, and B-84.

elasticity of year-to-year changes in real tax receipts with respect to changes in real GDP was above 1 (an elasticity is the percentage change in one variable induced by a 1 percent change in another variable). This can be seen directly in Figure 13.3 as a decline in the tax receipts–GDP ratio in each recession.

One reason that tax receipts fall by more than real GDP—why the elasticity is greater than 1—is that the items that are not taxed do not fluctuate much compared with the items that are taxed. Depreciation, which is not taxed, hardly fluctuates at all. Corporate profits, on the other hand, fluctuate widely. Another reason that the elasticity is greater than 1 is that average tax *rates* rise and fall with income. Some of the fluctuations in tax rates occur automatically because of the progressive tax system in the United States. As incomes fall in a recession some people fall into lower tax brackets, or even fall

TABLE 13.3

AUTOMATIC STABILIZERS: GOVERNMENT TRANSFER PROGRAMS THAT RESPOND TO THE STATE OF THE ECONOMY

PROGRAM	DESCRIPTION
Unemployment insurance	A combined federal-state program that pays benefits to workers who have lost their jobs.
Food stamps	A federal program that pays benefits to any family with an income below a certain threshold; in recessions, additional families become eligible.
Welfare programs	A combined federal-state program that pays benefits to poor families with dependent children; as incomes fall during recessions, payments increase.
Medicaid	A combined federal-state program that assists poor families with medical benefits; the number drawing these benefits rises during recessions.
Social security	A federal program that supports people in retirement; some people who are eligible for benefits choose to work instead, but their number declines in a recession and the volume of benefits rises.

into the region in which no taxes are paid. Hence, the proportion of their income paid in taxes goes down as income falls. Conversely, the proportion goes up as income rises.

Some of the reductions in tax rates in recessions have occurred because the tax law was changed by Congress to mitigate the drop in aggregate demand. These are *discretionary changes* rather than automatic changes, but they have been fairly regular and should be included as part of our behavioral description of the reaction of government to the economy. Proposals to cut taxes to stimulate the economy out of a recession in the early 1960s were made by President Kennedy, and most of these changes were enacted into law by Congress. Proposals to cut taxes were made by President Reagan during the depressed economic conditions of the early 1980s. Although the rationale for these tax cuts was not the conventional countercyclical one—some in the Reagan administration argued that the tax cuts would greatly increase supply, others argued that they were necessary to offset the effect of inflation on tax rates—in retrospect they fit right into the general story that tax rates are usually cut during periods of high unemployment. The most recent example is the tax cut of 2001, which helped keep the recession of 2001 mild by historical standards. Discretionary policies are summarized in Table 13.4.

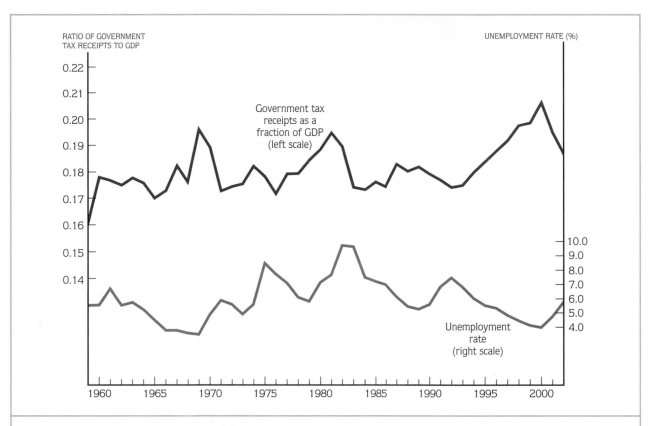

FIGURE 13.3   GOVERNMENT TAX RECEIPTS AND UNEMPLOYMENT

As the economy fluctuates in and out of recessions and booms, government tax receipts also fluctuate. Tax receipts tend to fall in years of high unemployment and rise in years of low unemployment. The decline in tax receipts mitigates the drop in demand and helps stabilize the economy.

SOURCE: *Economic Report of the President,* 2003, Tables B-35 and B-74.

In Chapter 7, we wrote tax receipts *T* as a constant proportion of income *Y*:

$$T = tY \qquad\qquad (13.1)$$

where *t* is the constant tax rate. The discussion of the previous two paragraphs means that it is incorrect to treat the tax rate *t* as a constant. The tax rate *t* actually falls when income *Y* falls and rises when income rises.

Much of the overall impact of the government's influence through taxes and transfers eventually shows up in personal disposable income. Recall that, in Chapter 10, we looked at the relation between disposable income and GDP and found that the fluctuations in disposable income were much smaller (look back to Figure 10.3 for a review). Disposable income changes by only about 40 percent as much as total income. Consumers see only about 40 percent of the

TABLE 13.4

DISCRETIONARY STABILIZATION MEASURES: WAYS THE FEDERAL GOVERNMENT CAN AFFECT DEMAND THROUGH FISCAL POLICY

MEASURE	DESCRIPTION
Temporary income tax change	A temporary cut in personal income taxes stimulates consumption and offsets a recession; a temporary surcharge discourages consumption and cools off a boom.
Investment tax credit	A subsidy to investment through the tax system stimulates investment for the period when the credit is in effect and discourages investment before it takes effect and after it is removed.
Home purchase credit	A subsidy for home purchases by individuals has the same effect as an investment credit but on residential investment.
Public works	An increase or speedup in highway construction and other government purchases adds directly to demand.

total loss in the economy's income when a recession hits. Automatic stabilizers and discretionary changes in taxes and transfers soak up much of the other 60 percent. (Recall that a bit of the 60 percent is due to the fact that corporations try to maintain their dividend payouts when corporate profits fall during recessions.)

Note that the effect of such countercyclical movements in taxes and transfers is to reduce the multiplier of the IS-LM model. When there is an increase in investment spending, for example, the increase in GDP leads to a smaller increase in disposable income and hence a smaller effect on consumption. The multiplier effect is smaller due to the automatic stabilizers.

13.3 | THE EFFECTS OF THE GOVERNMENT DEFICIT

Why is the government deficit so controversial and mysterious? Part of the reason is that the deficit is just a summary statistic that reflects the behavior of many other variables. It is really just the tip of an iceberg. We emphasized that the budget deficit is simply the difference between government *expenditures* (purchases and transfers) and *receipts*. Moreover, from the government accounting identity discussed in Chapter 2, we know that deficits must be financed by issuing *bonds* or *money* to the pubic. The overall impact of the

FIGURE 13.4   THE CYCLICAL BEHAVIOR OF THE DEFICIT

The chart shows the budget deficit, as a percentage of GDP, and the unemployment rate. The latter is a measure of the state of the economic cycle. The deficit is strongly cyclical.

SOURCE: *Economic Report of the President*, 2003, Tables B-1, B-35, and B-84.

budget on the economy can therefore be pieced together by looking at the effects of receipts, expenditures, bonds, and money.

In this section, we examine the cyclical behavior of the deficit, the empirical relation between deficits and interest rates, and the implications of the simple fact that the government must borrow to finance its deficits.

Cyclical versus Structural Deficits

The government budget deficit always goes deep in the red during recessions. We know the reasons for this from the last section: Expenditures rise and receipts fall during recessions. The automatic stabilizers exacerbate the swing of the deficit during a recession.

Figure 13.4 shows the relationship between the deficit and the cyclical fluctuations in unemployment for the years 1959 to 2003. When the economy is below potential, the budget deficit is large. When the economy is above potential, the budget is in surplus, or at least less in the red. Economists have developed the concept of the **full-employment deficit** to adjust for cyclical effects.[1] The full-employment deficit is the deficit that would occur if the economy were at full employment. The full-employment deficit takes out the cyclical effects on the deficit. This is done by estimating reaction functions for expenditures and receipts and calculating what expenditures and receipts would occur at potential GDP and full employment.

In more recent years, the concept of the full-employment deficit has usually been discussed by distinguishing between the structural and cyclical parts of the deficit. The **structural deficit** is the same thing as the full-employment deficit, and the **cyclical deficit** is the difference between the actual deficit and the structural deficit.

Have Deficits Been Related to Interest Rates in Recent U.S. History?

The relation between the deficit and interest rates is one of the most important issues with respect to the government's role in aggregate demand. In Chapter 8, we showed that the IS-LM model implies that an increase in the government's budget deficit, brought about by either an increase in expenditures or a cut in taxes, would raise interest rates and expand output by shifting the IS curve to the right. How does that theory fit the facts? Here, we look at some of the relevant facts. Figure 13.5 shows the historical relation between a measure of the real interest rate and the budget deficit. Two things are important from the chart.

First, over short-run periods and for much of the last 40 years, it appears that the real interest rate falls when the government budget goes into the red. This is particularly evident in the early 2000s. Deficits do not appear to cause high real interest rates. Before you jump to any conclusions, recall the previous discussion, which pointed to the cyclical behavior of the deficit. Deficits occur when the economy is in a slump. Now, there are many reasons for interest rates to be low during a slump: The demand for money is low and investment demand is low. It is thus likely that much of the relation between interest rates and the deficit during the last 40 years is due to other factors in the economy.

Second, there is some evidence of a positive relation between the budget deficit and interest rates during the 1982–90 period. Real interest rates were higher than normal rates during this period and the budget deficit reached a high-water mark as well. Perhaps the very large deficits—and prospects for future deficits—raised interest rates. This would be the prediction of both the long-run and short-run models we developed. But real interest rates fell in 1991 and 1992 even though deficits continued.

---

[1]The idea of the full-employment deficit was used by E. Cary Brown in "Fiscal Policy in the Thirties: A Reappraisal," *American Economic Review*, Vol. 46 (December 1956), pp. 857–879. He showed that the actual deficits observed in the early 1930s were large surpluses in the full-employment deficit.

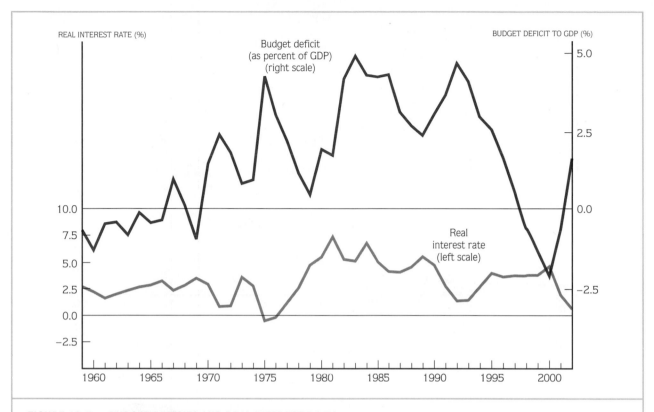

FIGURE 13.5 BUDGET DEFICITS AND REAL INTEREST RATES

During much of the past 40 years, interest rates fell during periods when the federal government was running a deficit. However, this does not mean that deficits cause lower interest rates. Falling interest rates and deficits are both largely the result of recessions. The 1980s was one of the few periods when high budget deficits and high interest rates occurred at the same time. Note: The real interest rate is the three-month Treasury bill less the average of the rate of change in the GDP deflator during the previous three years.

SOURCE: *Economic Report of the President,* 2003, Tables B-1, B-3, B-73, and B-83.

The Deficit and the Explosion of Government Debt

When the government runs a deficit, it must borrow from the public. The top panel of Figure 13.6 shows how budget deficits have led to an explosion of outstanding national debt since the 1960s. Most of the debt consists of interest-bearing bonds, but part is non-interest-bearing money. As we will see in the next chapter, the Federal Reserve System *monetizes* part of the government debt when it purchases it and issues currency and non-interest-bearing deposits. In the United States, the Fed has monetized only a small amount of the debt. It monetizes the debt primarily to provide sufficient money for the economy to work efficiently, rather than to raise revenues.

During World War II, the government also ran a large deficit, as is typical of most wars. Government expenditures were, of course, abnormally high in the war years; rather than raise taxes temporarily to pay for the war, the government

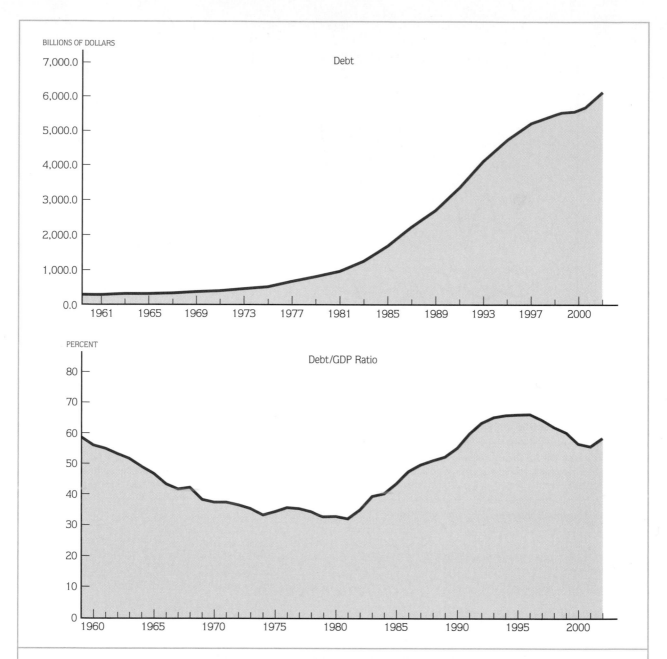

FIGURE 13.6   THE NATIONAL DEBT

The national debt grew rapidly between 1981 and 1993. Between 1959 and 1981 and again between 1997 and 2001, the debt dropped as a ratio of GDP.

SOURCE: *Economic Report of the President,* 2003, Tables B-1 and B-78.

borrowed the money. This shifted some of the burden of the war to future generations, who would have to pay the interest on the borrowings. After the war years until the 1960s, the federal government ran a surplus in its budget, with some exceptions during recessions. The debt fell slightly during the surplus years, but was relatively unchanged compared with the increase during World War II.

Scaling the debt by nominal GDP gives a better perspective of the importance of the debt for the whole economy, as shown in the lower panel of Figure 13.6. At the end of World War II, the government debt relative to GDP reached an all-time high of a bit over 100 percent. Since World War II, the public debt divided by GDP fell steadily until the mid-1970s. Then the stock of outstanding debt began to grow relative to GDP as we had a big deficit in the recession of 1974–75 and even bigger deficits in the 1980s and early 1990s. The ratio of the debt to GDP fell with the budget surpluses of 1998–2001 but rose again with the deficits of 2002 and 2003. It is now about 60 percent, well below the levels reached at the end of World War II.

We can express the relation between the deficit and the accumulation of debt formally as

> Debt at the start of next year
> = Debt at the start of this year
>   + Purchases this year
>   + Transfers this year ⎫ Deficit
>   + Interest on the debt this year
>   − Receipts this year

Using the notation D for debt, G for purchases, F for transfers, T for receipts, and R for the interest rate, we can write this as

$$D_{t+1} = D_t + G_t + F_t + RD_t - T_t. \qquad (13.2)$$

Each of the terms in Equation 13.2 corresponds with the verbal description of the relation between the deficit and debt accumulation. Note that Equation 13.2 is nothing more than an **intertemporal government budget constraint** faced by government officials. It corresponds exactly to the intertemporal budget constraint for the households in our analysis of forward-looking consumption (Chapter 10). The only difference is that the government is usually a net debtor; hence, we call its outstanding financial stock D. The household's asset stock was simply called A; we assumed that the household was usually a net lender.

Economic Significance of the National Debt

The growth of the U.S. national debt has attracted a lot of attention from economists and other commentators. The debt exists because the federal government sold bonds to finance spending in excess of current revenue. Historically, the U.S. debt has grown mainly in wartime. The decline in the debt to GDP ratio through 1974, shown in Figure 13.6, is typical of earlier U.S. experience except during major wars and typical of the peacetime experience of other countries. The massive accumulation of debt since 1981 is an unusual event. Similar buildups occurred in many other advanced industrial countries during the same period.

During the 1990s, federal purchases of goods and services declined as a fraction of GDP, from 8.8 percent to 6 percent. But growth in transfer payments made up the difference. The ratio of transfers to the GDP was 7.8 percent in 1990 and rose to 8.1 percent in 1999. Interest on the debt fell slightly, from 3.6 percent of GDP in 1990 to 2.8 percent in 1999.

The federal debt appears to be an important element in the political process for making spending decisions. When relatively little debt is outstanding, spending on goods and services and income maintenance tends to rise above revenue. Those in Congress have trouble saying no to their constituents' spending demands when the budget is in balance or close to it. A deficit develops and debt builds up. Rising interest on the debt adds to spending growth. As the deficit grows, political opposition to spending rises. The economy reaches a sustainable path where spending growth is held down to the rate of growth of the economy. Debt also grows at the rate of growth of the economy, so the path can be sustained year after year.

Economists are divided on the question of the purely economic significance of the national debt. A good way to think about the issue is to ask how the 1980s and early 1990s would have been different if the government had spent the same amount but had not financed any of the spending by borrowing. There are two differences between what actually happened and the hypothetical zero-deficit case. First, consumers had more disposable income because they paid lower taxes. Borrowing made up for the taxes that would have been levied in the zero-deficit case. Families felt better off and consumed more than they would have in the hypothetical case. Second, taxpayers are worse off because they now have to pay higher future taxes to finance the interest on the debt. Their consumption is lower than in the zero-deficit case because of this factor.

Which effect is larger? Economists have usually emphasized the first effect. The increase in current disposable income is immediate and concrete; the increase in future taxes is distant and theoretical. Deficit spending makes families think they are better off than they really are. They consume too much and the economy has fewer resources for investment. There is a *burden of the national debt*. Debt displaces productive capital in portfolios.[2] But one analysis reaches the conclusion that the two effects offset each other precisely; it asserts that there is no burden of the debt. This analysis, called **Ricardian equivalence,** was put forward in its modern form by Robert Barro, currently at Harvard University.[3] (David Ricardo, a 19th-century British economist, was the originator of the analysis.)

[2]See Peter Diamond, "National Debt in a Neoclassical Growth Model," *American Economic Review,* Vol. 32 (June 1965), pp. 161–168.
[3]See Robert Barro, "Are Government Bonds Net Wealth?" *Journal of Political Economy,* Vol. 82 (November–December 1974), pp. 1095–1117.

Ricardian equivalence holds if consumption is independent of the timing of taxation. When the government defers taxation by building up debt, as it did in the 1980s and 1990s, consumption is just the same as it would have been with the same amount of government spending financed by current taxes. Moreover, income taxes affect other macro variables through consumption. Looking at the economic fluctuations model of Chapters 7–9, we can see that a change in income taxes that has no effect on consumption has no effect on interest rates, investment, trade, GDP, or inflation. On the other hand, if there is a burden of the debt—if deficit spending encourages consumption—all variables are affected. Higher consumption means a higher real interest rate, less investment, a larger trade deficit, and a lower potential GDP in the longer run. Figure 13.5 shows the evidence on the real interest rate. There is little overall relation between deficits and real interest rates.

Two assumptions are critical to Ricardian equivalence. First is that families think about the future when they make consumption plans. The forward-looking theory of consumption, based on the idea of rational expectations and rational behavior, supports this assumption. Second is that families look as far into the future as the taxes will be levied. If the government never pays off the debt from the 1980s, but simply continues paying interest on it forever, then strict Ricardian equivalence would require that families look into the indefinite future. One of Barro's important contributions to the theory of Ricardian equivalence was to point out that families may look into the indefinite future even though individual lifetimes are limited. Families may be linked across generations through gifts and bequests. When the government defers taxes to future generations, the current generation may respond by saving more to make gifts to future generations. These gifts would spread the burden of taxation evenly across generations.

Ricardian equivalence takes the path of government spending as exogenous. If, on the contrary, spending responds to the conditions of the budget, the analysis becomes more complex. Some of the supporters of tax cuts see lower revenue as a way to force down government spending. They consider most government spending as wasteful. To them, the buildup of debt following a tax cut is just part of the process of scaling back government. On the other hand, lower revenue may cut into government investment. Then, the burden of the debt includes the displacement of public as well as private capital.

Although the business press accepts the burden of the debt as absolute economic truth, with the support of many prominent economists (such as Martin Feldstein of Harvard University), the burden has been hard to quantify. The bulge of consumption during the 1980s may have been a response to artificially high disposable income, or it may have been the result of great consumer optimism. High real interest rates in the 1980s may have been the result of huge amounts of federal borrowing, or they may just have reflected the combined effect of optimistic consumers, strong government purchases of goods and services, and favorable investment opportunities in the United States in comparison with the rest of the world. There is no strong consensus among macroeconomists that the federal debt is either a large or a small burden on the economy.

13.4 | THE GOVERNMENT AND THE IS CURVE

Fiscal policy can shift the IS curve in two ways. First, government purchases of goods and services G enters spending directly. In Chapters 7 and 8, we looked at how changes in G shift the IS curve through the multiplier process. We noted in this chapter that the federal government rarely offsets fluctuations in aggregate demand by altering its purchases of goods and services. Historically, government purchases do not appear to be an effective instrument to control aggregate demand but rather another shock or disturbance to aggregate demand. Recent experience with large deficits does not indicate that this situation is likely to change soon.

Second, policies on taxes and transfers can influence consumption. A tax cut increases income and stimulates consumption and so shifts the IS curve to the right. However, the magnitude of this shift is highly uncertain because of people's uncertainty about how permanent the tax cut will be. Moreover, there is a possibility that some people may increase their saving because they figure that taxes will rise in the future to pay the interest on the increased government debt.

Fiscal policy also influences the *slope* of the IS curve. We noted in this chapter that the automatic stabilizers operating through taxes and transfers reduce the multiplier. Because of the automatic stabilizers, an increase in interest rates along the IS curve brings about a smaller decline in consumption and GDP. Therefore, the IS curve is steeper as a result of the automatic stabilizers.

REVIEW AND PRACTICE

Major Points

1. Government purchases, transfers, and receipts are not exogenous. They respond to the state of the economy.

2. Expenditures rise and receipts fall in recessions. Real tax receipts fall by a greater percentage than real GDP during recessions. This is mainly because of the progressive tax system.

3. The deficit fluctuates countercyclically with GDP.

4. The structural or full-employment deficit has had these cyclical effects removed.

5. Public debt is the cumulation of past deficits.

6. The debt fell relative to GDP during the 1960s and 1970s. It rose in the 1980s and early 1990s, but fell again in the late 1990s.

7. Higher government purchases of goods and services shift the IS curve to the right, although the federal government has not used this policy instrument to try to stabilize the economy in the past few decades.

8. Taxes influence both the position and the slope of the IS curve. A tax cut shifts the IS curve to the right, although the magnitude of the shift is uncertain. Automatic stabilizers make the IS curve steeper.

Key Terms and Concepts

reaction function	full-employment deficit
policy rule	structural deficit
budget	cyclical deficit
outlays	intertemporal
elasticity	government budget constraint
discretionary changes	Ricardian equivalence

Questions for Discussion and Review

1. Explain the difference between government purchases and government transfers. Which is larger for the federal government? For state and local governments? Which fluctuates more with the business cycle? In which direction?

2. What are the major automatic stabilizers? What is their significance for economic fluctuations?

3. Why is the budget typically in deficit during periods when the unemployment rate is high? What is the full-employment budget deficit? Does the full-employment deficit fluctuate with the state of the economy?

4. Explain why a progressive tax structure leads to an increase in the tax revenue–GDP ratio when the economy is growing rapidly in a boom.

5. Why has the deficit usually been large when interest rates have been low? Does this mean that the deficit does not cause interest rates to rise as predicted by the IS-LM model?

6. Describe the behavior of the government debt since World War II. Why did the debt decline as a fraction of GDP until 1981?

Problems

NUMERICAL

1. Use the following example of a progressive tax schedule to compute what happens to average tax rates in the economy during a typical recession:

INCOME BRACKET	MARGINAL TAX RATE
0–9,999	0
10,000–29,999	0.2
30,000–49,999	0.4
50,000 and above	0.6

To make it easy, suppose that there are just three income groups of taxpayers. Just before the recession there are 200,000 taxpayers making $20,000, 700,000 making $40,000, and 100,000 making $60,000.

a. Compute the average tax rate for the whole economy before and just after the recession if everybody's income drops by $10,000 during the recession. Has anyone moved to a different tax bracket?

b. What happens to the average tax rate if everybody's income is reduced by $20,000?

c. Suppose that the government introduces a flat tax, whereby everyone making equal to or more than $10,000 pays the same proportional tax of 25 percent. For this new tax system recalculate your answers to parts a and b.

d. Comment on the effect on stabilization policy of a move from a progressive tax-rate system to a flat tax-rate system.

2. Suppose federal tax receipts, transfers, and purchases are given by $T = 0.25YP$, $F = 0.075YP$, and $G = 2,000$, all in billions of current dollars. Suppose that at the start of 2004 the federal debt D was $6,000 billion, the interest rate R was 2.0 percent, real GDP was $10,000 billion, and the price level P was 1.00.

a. Calculate the actual and full-employment budget deficit for 2004 in current dollars assuming that real potential output is $10,200 billion. Include interest payments in your calculation of the deficit using Equation 13.2. How would your answers change if real potential output was $9,800 billion?

b. What is the federal debt at the start of 2005?

3. Assume that government outlays and taxes are initially zero, as is the stock of government debt. In year 1, the government begins to spend $50 billion per year, in real terms, on environmental protection. Each year the government issues enough debt to finance this program, as well as to repay the interest on the previous stock of debt. The stock of government debt and the deficit, measured in current dollars, obeys the equations

$$D_t = (D_{t-1} + G_{t-1})(1 + R)$$
$$DEF_{t-1} = D_t - D_{t-1}$$

where G is measured in current dollars. The initial price level is 1.

a. For an interest rate of 5 percent and an inflation rate of zero, calculate the real and nominal values of government debt and the deficit for each of the first five years.

b. Now suppose prices rise at an annual rate of 5 percent. Assuming that the interest rate remains at 5 percent, repeat your calculations for part a.

c. Finally, assume an inflation rate of 5 percent and an interest rate of 10.25 percent. Again, repeat your calculations for part a.

d. Compare the path of real debt under parts a, b, and c. Explain any differences.

e. Comparing parts a and c, you should find that the real debt stock is the same for part c but the real deficit each year is higher. Why doesn't a higher deficit lead to a higher stock of debt?

f. In which case was inflation anticipated by financial markets? Explain your answer.

4. Suppose that instead of G being exogenous, it is given by the formula

$$G = 1,200 - 0.1(Y - Y^*),$$

where Y^* is potential GDP and equals \$6,000 billion. Suppose that the other relationships in the economy are given by the example considered in Chapter 8:

$$C = 220 + 0.63Y$$
$$I = 1,000 - 2,000R$$
$$M = (0.1583Y - 1,000R)P$$
$$X = 525 - 0.1Y - 500R$$

where the price level is predetermined at $P = 1$ and the money supply is 900.

a. Derive an algebraic expression for the IS curve for this model. Plot it to scale. Compare it with the IS curve of Chapter 8, in which government purchases are exogenous. Which is steeper? Why?

b. Derive the aggregate demand curve and plot it to scale. How does it compare with the aggregate demand curve when government spending is exogenous?

c. Calculate the effect on GDP of an increase in the money supply of \$10 billion. Is the effect larger or smaller than the case where government spending is exogenous? Explain in words what is going on.

d. Is this equation an accurate description of government purchases in the United States? If not, what other components of the government budget act as automatic stabilizers? How is the impact of aggregate demand and price shocks affected by such stabilizers?

5. Simple proof of the Ricardian equivalence: Consider the intertemporal budget constraint for families that we introduced in Chapter 10 and the intertemporal budget constraint for the government that we introduced in this chapter. Suppose that taxes are cut by $1,000 in year 1 and the government debt increases.

   a. If the interest rate is 5 percent, by how much will taxes have to increase next year if the government debt is to come back to normal by the end of next year?

   b. What is the effect of this decrease and subsequent increase in taxes on the intertemporal budget constraint for consumers? How would you expect this change to affect consumption?

ANALYTICAL

1. Suppose our model of the economy is the simple spending balance model of Chapter 7. The equations of the model are

$$Y = C + I + G + X$$
$$C = 100 + 0.9Y_d$$
$$Y_d = Y + F$$

   where $I = 750$, $X = 0$, and F stands for government transfer payments.

   a. You are told that government outlays equal 500, and there are no taxes. With this information can you calculate the point of spending balance?

   b. What is the maximum value of income for which there could be spending balance? What is the minimum value?

   c. Explain why government transfers and spending affect aggregate demand differently. Be specific.

2. Explain why imports act as automatic stabilizers. Compare the case in which imports consist mainly of necessities with the case in which they consist mainly of luxury goods.

3. Suppose it is 2009, and the newly elected president, in order to win, promised not to raise taxes and not to tamper with social security and other transfer programs. At 6 percent unemployment, output is very close to potential. There still, however, are the two nagging problems of the government, budget deficit and the trade deficit.

   a. In the short run, how can the administration reduce the budget deficit without breaking any of its campaign promises? Be specific about the policy. What effect will the policy have on output and interest rates? How will this policy reduce the budget deficit? Describe the effect of this policy on the trade deficit. Is it unambiguous?

b. Will this policy reduce the budget deficit in the long run? Again, be specific. What are its long-run effects on the trade deficit?

c. What will the effects of such a policy be, in the short run and in the long run, on the real value of government debt outstanding?

d. Recall the relationship between nominal interest rates and expected inflation discussed in Chapter 8. How might the expectations of such a policy affect long-term nominal interest rates?

4. Suppose that government spending is increased when the economy is below potential GDP. Why doesn't the decrease in government saving lead to an equal decline in total saving and investment?

5. Sketch an IS-LM diagram. Compare two cases, one in which government spending is exogenous, and the other in which government spending declines when the economy rises above potential GDP and increases when the economy is below potential GDP. Which curve is steeper? For which curve is monetary policy more powerful?

6. Suppose that the president and the Congress agreed to raise personal income taxes by $100 billion per year starting in 2005 in an attempt to reduce the budget deficit by 2008. However, the legislation actually increased taxes only until 2008; starting in 2009, taxes would automatically be lowered back down by $100 billion. What would be the effect of this tax increase on *consumption demand*? Use the forward-looking theory of consumption to explain what the impact of the tax increase would be.

7. Consider once again the simple spending balance model of Chapter 7. Suppose now that the model is

$$Y = C + I + G + X$$
$$C = 100 + 0.9Y_d$$
$$Y_d = Y + F - T$$

where $I = 750$, $X = 0$, and G, T, and F are initially zero.

a. Calculate the initial point of spending balance.

b. Suppose that the country goes to war for a year—requiring government expenditures of 100—and that taxes are temporarily raised to 100 in that same year. Calculate consumption and the point of spending balance in the war year and all future years.

c. Now suppose that the government issues war bonds instead of raising taxes. The war bonds are 5 percent consoles. Consoles are bonds on which interest is paid forever and the principal is never repaid. Again, calculate consumption and the point of spending balance in the war year and in all future years.

d.   What is the net effect of the government's running a deficit in the war year instead of raising taxes? Is your result consistent with the idea of Ricardian equivalence? If not, how can you explain the difference?

8. In deriving the aggregate demand curve, we have implicitly assumed that the government announces a budget in real terms. In practice, the budget is announced in nominal terms for the coming fiscal year before the price level is known with certainty. This practice of not indexing public-expenditure plans to the price level has implications for the shape of the aggregate demand schedule. Relative to an aggregate demand schedule with constant real government expenditures, will a schedule with constant nominal government expenditures be flatter or steeper? Is the policy rule of nominal budgeting stabilizing or destabilizing with respect to GDP in the presence of unanticipated price shocks?

9. In an attempt to stimulate the economy, the government announces that it will drastically reduce taxes for one year with no change in government spending. Describe the effect of the temporary tax cut on output, consumption, investment, and net exports for each of the following assumptions about household consumption behavior.

a.   Households obey the simple Keynesian consumption function.

b.   Households are forward-looking but do not anticipate future tax increases to offset the current reduction.

c.   Households are forward-looking and anticipate future tax increases to offset the current reduction.

THE MONETARY SYSTEM

A monetary system is an arrangement through which people express economic values and carry out transactions with each other. A well-developed monetary system is essential to a smoothly operating economy. History has shown that poorly developed monetary systems have been responsible for severe recessions and inflations. But even normal, everyday economic life is greatly facilitated by an efficient monetary system.

The monetary system is just one of many social arrangements that exist in any civilization. Language is another. Weights and measures are a third. Some of these arrangements have evolved without formal or conscious social agreements; others have been the result of organized planning and formal agreement. Although monetary systems originally evolved informally in primitive cultures, in modern times most countries have enacted laws and institutions that define their monetary systems. One of the concerns of macroeconomics is whether certain revisions to these laws and institutions might improve macroeconomic performance.

In Chapter 8 we saw how changes in the money supply affect real GDP in the short run and prices in the long run. The central bank carries out monetary policy through actions that change the money supply. A country's monetary institutions—its central bank and the powers of the central bank over the rest of banking—together with its monetary policy make up the country's monetary system.

Because changes in the money supply have such powerful effects on the economy, monetary policy is often in the news. When the chair of the Federal Reserve testifies before a congressional committee, hoards of reporters crowd the room. Each sentence uttered by the Fed chair is dissected for clues about whether the Fed might increase or decrease interest rates. News about changes in the Fed's policies influences financial markets instantaneously around the world. Guessing right about the Fed's next move means big profits for those involved in financial markets.

In this chapter, we first look at the microeconomic foundations of money supply and money demand. We then examine how the Fed makes decisions about monetary policy and consider the implications of lags in the effect of monetary policy.

14.1 | ELEMENTS OF A MONETARY SYSTEM

A monetary system must specify two things: first, the way that payments are to be made; second, the meaning of the numbers that merchants put on goods and the numbers that appear in contracts. The first is called the **means of payment,** and the second the **unit of account.**

In most monetary systems, one item is designated a universally acceptable means of payment. Traditionally, it was a precious metal, gold or silver. With gold or silver serving as the means of payment, it was natural for merchants to price their goods with numbers that corresponded to units of these precious metals; horse traders would find it natural to charge a certain number of gold pieces for a horse. Hence, designated amounts of precious metals became units of account as well as means of payment. For example, in England at the time of William the Conqueror, silver was the universally accepted means of payment and the pound of silver became the unit of account. Ever since, the English unit of account has been called the *pound*, even though its purchasing power has become much less than the value of a pound of silver.

As financial systems developed, means of payment came into use that were different from the underlying unit of account. For example, in the United States before the Civil War, the unit of account was 0.04838 of an ounce of gold, but the most common means of payment was paper money issued by private banks. A dollar bill from a bank carried a promise that it could be re-deemed for gold at any time.

In the twentieth century, governments became more involved in the mon-etary system. In the United States, banks are not allowed to issue dollar bills; only the Federal Reserve has that power. Moreover, the unit of account no longer has anything to do with gold. Instead, the unit is the government's dol-lar bill. Although dollar bills are widely used as means of payment, other means of payment are even more important, such as checks and credit cards.

Although there is no law in the United States that requires prices to be quoted in dollars, nobody would choose to quote prices in another unit, such as euros. The public is familiar with dollar prices and reluctant to think in any other terms. Even if you are good at doing arithmetic in your head, it is a lot more convenient to do all your financial thinking in one set of units.

Together, the government's paper money and coins are called **currency**. Until the nineteenth century, currency was virtually the only means of pay-ment. As monetary systems evolved during the nineteenth and twentieth cen-turies, currency began to be replaced by other means of payment in the great majority of transactions. Nevertheless, all transactions continue to be denomi-nated in the units of the government's currency. By law, if you owe somebody a dollar debt, that person can require you to pay in currency. For larger debts, this right is rarely exercised. Instead, the person's right to receive currency sets up a situation where the two of you agree on some alternative, more conve-nient way to settle the debt. The other person may agree to accept a personal check from you. A check is an instruction to the banking system to make ac-counting entries to transfer wealth from you to the other person.

A great many customs exist about what means of payment are acceptable besides currency. In prisoner-of-war camps during World War II, prisoners used cigarettes as a means of payment. In modern times, credit cards are frequently an acceptable means of payment. Credit cards are another way to issue instruc-tions to the banking system to transfer funds from one person to another. Like accepting checks, the acceptance of a credit card in place of currency is volun-tary. When you buy a house, neither a personal check nor a credit card is likely to be accepted. You will be expected to present a bank check, which is a promise by the bank itself to pay from its own funds and a guarantee that the funds actually exist. Customs differ by country as well. In Japan, for example, currency rather than a personal check is a much more common means of pay-ment than it is in the United States.

As discussed in Chapter 8, we use the term *money* to mean currency plus the deposits in checking accounts. Checking accounts are held usually at banks, but sometimes at other financial institutions, such as savings and loan associa-tions. Some checking accounts pay interest, but usually at rates below market interest rates. The Federal Reserve monitors the sum of currency and checking accounts in the United States, which they call M_1. In September 2004, M_1 was $1,300 billion, of which $688 billion was currency. Another measure of money is M_2. Savings deposits or small time deposits against which checks cannot be directly written are included in M_2. M_2 includes everything that is in M_1 as well). Money market mutual funds and money market deposit accounts at banks that can be used for checking are also included in M_2. In September 2004, M_2 was $6,359 billion.

The Monetary System

1. A monetary system includes a unit of account and various means of payment. Usually, one of the means of payment (in the United States, the dollar bill) defines the unit of account.

2. Various means of payment make up the money supply. The money supply includes the means that are close substitutes for currency. These are primarily balances in checking accounts.

14.2 │ HOW THE FED CONTROLS THE MONEY SUPPLY

MACROSOLVE
EXERCISE

We now consider how the Fed controls the money supply. The money supply consists of currency (CU) and checking deposits (D) that individuals and firms hold at banks. We do not distinguish at this point between M_1 and M_2 by distinguishing between different types of deposits. Rather, we let the symbol D represent all deposits at banks (or private financial institutions more generally) and M be the resulting money supply. The money supply M is therefore defined as

$$M = CU + D. \tag{14.1}$$

Because deposits at banks are part of the money supply, we must consider how the Fed's actions affect these deposits. Table 14.1 shows a set of balance sheets for four sectors of the economy: the private nonfinancial sector (consumers and businesses), the banks, the Federal Reserve, and the government. This balance sheet shows how the sectors are related financially.

In the balance sheet, assets are shown on the left and liabilities on the right. Assets are the things owned by the individual or organization, and liabilities are the amounts owed to others. For example, loans are assets for banks and liabilities for borrowers. Note that all the things listed in these accounts appear at least twice; once in somebody's assets and again in somebody else's liabilities.

The Banks column of the balance sheet includes all depository institutions that accept checking deposits and that hold reserves at the Fed. Therefore "banks" include not only commercial banks but also those savings and loan associations and mutual savings banks that provide checking services to their

TABLE 14.1

FINANCIAL RELATIONSHIPS (BALANCE SHEETS) BETWEEN
THE BANKS, THE FED, THE GOVERNMENT,
AND THE PRIVATE SECTOR

Liabilities = owed
Assets = owned

Consumers/
Businesses

PRIVATE NONFINANCIAL		BANKS		FED		GOVERNMENT	
ASSETS	LIABILITIES	ASSETS	LIABILITIES	ASSETS	LIABILITIES	ASSETS	LIABILITIES
Currency (CU)					Currency (CU)		
Deposits (D)			Deposits (D)				
Bonds (B)		Bonds (B)		Bonds (B)			Bonds (B)
		Reserves (RE)			Reserves (RE)		
	Loans	Loans					

customers. The Fed column of the balance sheet includes the assets and liabilities of all 12 district banks of the Federal Reserve System.[1]

   Note where the major assets and liabilities appear on the balance sheets of each sector.

CURRENCY (CU) AND DEPOSITS (D)   The private sector holds currency issued by the Fed.[2] As we will discuss, the Fed's job is to supply the currency that the private sector demands. The private sector also holds deposits at the banks. These are assets of the account holders and liabilities of the banks.

GOVERNMENT BONDS (B)   Government bonds are shown as a liability of the government. The private sector, the banks, and the Fed hold bonds as assets.

ALL sectors (other than gvt) hold BONDS

RESERVES (RE)   These are what the banks hold on deposit at the Fed. The Fed acts as a banker's bank by accepting deposits from banks. By law, these reserves must be held at a fixed fraction of the checking deposits that the banks have as liabilities.

---

[1]The 12 District Federal Reserve Banks are in Atlanta, Boston, Chicago, Cleveland, Dallas, Kansas City, Minneapolis, New York, Philadelphia, Richmond, St. Louis, and San Francisco. Open-market operations take place at the New York Fed.
[2]Part of the reserves held by the banks is in the form of paper money in the vaults of the bank. The term *currency* in the text always means paper money and coin *outside* banks. Vault cash is essentially equivalent to bank reserves held on deposit at the Fed.

LOANS (L) The last line in the balance sheet shows the loans of the banks to the private sector. A main reason that banks are in business is to issue loans to their customers. They take deposits from some individuals and make loans to others. This is the **intermediation role** of the banks. They intermediate between individuals.

The Fed controls the money supply by selling bonds to, or by purchasing bonds from, the banks, and the public. These purchases or sales of government bonds by the Fed are called **open-market operations.** To see how these open-market operations affect the money supply, we first define the **monetary base** (M_B). The monetary base is defined as currency plus reserves.[3] That is,

$$M_B = CU + RE. \tag{14.2}$$

The Fed does not try to exercise separate control of reserves and currency. Instead, it controls only the total of the two. The Fed lets the banks and the private sector decide how much of the monetary base is currency and how much is reserves. Any bank can withdraw currency from its reserve account whenever it wants, and any bank can put currency into its reserve account and receive credit dollar for dollar.

Fed buys bonds to expand M_B

Using open-market operations, the Fed can add to or subtract from the total amount of bank reserves plus currency whenever it chooses. An open-market operation to expand the monetary base involves a purchase by the Fed of government bonds from the banks. Look again at the balance sheet in Table 14.1. When a bank sells a bond to the Fed, the bank receives a credit in its reserve account that adds to the total amount of reserves. The simple fact that assets must equal liabilities in the Fed's balance sheet indicates that any purchase of bonds must lead to an increase in the sum of currency and reserves, that is, an increase in the monetary base. Whenever a bank transfers funds to another bank, nothing happens to total reserves; one bank's reserves rise by the exact amount that the other bank's fall. But a purchase of bonds by the Fed must raise the monetary base. Similarly, a sale of bonds by the Fed must reduce the monetary base.

There is a direct relationship between the monetary base and the money supply, and this is how the Fed achieves its control of the money supply. The relationship between the monetary base and the money supply is due to two factors.

1. *Reserve requirements.* Banks are required to hold a certain ratio of their checking deposits on reserve at the Fed. This ratio is called the **reserve ratio** (r). For example, r might equal 0.1 (or 10 percent). Reserves (RE) are then given by the formula

$$RE = rD. \tag{14.3}$$

2. *Currency demand.* Most people want to hold some of their money in the form of currency. We discuss the determinants of currency demand in Sec-

[3]The monetary base is also called *high-powered money*.

tion 14.3. For now, we can describe this demand in terms of a simple ratio. The **currency ratio** (c) measures how much currency people want to hold as a ratio of their deposits. For example, the currency ratio c might equal 0.2. Currency demand is therefore given by

$$CU = cD. \tag{14.4}$$

Now we can derive the relationship between the monetary base and the money supply. From the definition of the money supply,

$$M = CU + D = cD + D = (1 + c)D,$$
$$M_B = CU + RE = cD + rD = (c + r)D.$$

Dividing M by M_B, we get

$$M = \frac{1 + c}{r + c} M_B. \tag{14.5}$$

The coefficient that multiplies M_B is called the **money multiplier,** which we call m. If $r = 0.1$ and $c = 0.2$, then the money multiplier is 4. Open-market operations that increase the monetary base by \$1 billion would then increase M by \$4 billion. Here, the reserve ratio and the currency ratio are assumed fixed, so the Fed can control the money supply as accurately as it wants by controlling the monetary base. In practice, the reserve ratio and currency ratio are not constant, which makes the money supply difficult to control in the short run.

[handwritten margin note: $m = \frac{1+c}{r+c}$; m is not usually constant]

Excess Reserves and Borrowed Reserves

In the United States, the reserve requirement for banks is 10 percent. Since banks are penalized if their reserves fall below their reserve requirements, they always keep some **excess reserves.** The amount of excess reserves is small because banks receive no interest on their reserve balances at the Fed. They prefer to keep reserves close to the minimum required amount and invest the rest of their funds in loans or bonds.

Banks can also increase their reserves by borrowing reserves from the Fed. The part of bank reserves borrowed from the Fed is called **borrowed reserves.** One traditional function of the Fed has been to provide loans to troubled banks. This tradition developed because of the frequent bank failures and bank panics in the late nineteenth and early twentieth centuries. The Fed was created to serve as "lender of last resort" to the banks.

The Fed usually makes loans to banks at the borrowing "window" of one of the 12 District Federal Reserve Banks. The interest rate on the borrowings is called the **discount rate.** In the past, changes in the discount rate have signaled movements in the Fed's monetary policy. In recent years, the discount rate has been adjusted to follow market interest rates, although usually with a time lag.

In recent years, the discount rate has been adjusted to be slightly under the short-term market interest rate. Starting in 2003, the discount rate is now set

FINANCING GOVERNMENT THROUGH THE PRINTING PRESS

How much does the United States resort to the printing press to raise revenues to pay for government expenditures? The monetary base gives a good measure of this. Suppose, for example, that Congress passes a bill authorizing highway construction for an amount of $2 billion. But Congress does not raise taxes to pay for the highways. To pay for the construction, the government issues bonds. But, rather than selling the bonds to the public, it sells the bonds to the Fed in exchange for currency, which it then pays out to the construction workers and firms that build the highways. In effect, the increase in government expenditures was financed by printing more currency. Note that the monetary base increased by $2 billion.

Just as in this example, the increase in the monetary base is a measure of the amount of government revenue raised each year through the printing press rather than through taxes or borrowing. In 2003, the monetary base increased by $39 billion. Compared with the $2,158 billion of government expenditures during 2003, this is a trivial amount, only about 2 percent of government expenditures were financed by the printing press in 2003. This small percentage is typical in recent U.S. history. Hence, the printing presses are not a very important source of revenue for the United States in modern times. But this was not always true. About 80 percent of American Revolutionary War expenditures were financed by printing paper money called *continentals*. So much money was printed that a serious inflation occurred: prices rose by over 300 percent from 1776 to 1778 and by 1,000 percent from 1778 to 1780; hence the phrase "not worth a continental." The printing press set off even worse inflations in Germany and several other European countries in the 1920s and in Argentina, Brazil, and other South American countries in the 1970s and 1980s.

to be 1 percentage point above Fed's target for the short-term nominal interest rate (the federal funds rate). The policy change was designed to remove any stigma associated with borrowing from the Fed.

What happens to the monetary base when a bank borrows reserves from the Fed? Because bank reserves increase, the monetary base increases, just as with an open-market operation. However, if the Fed wants to insulate the monetary base from changes due to an increase in borrowings, then all it needs to do is make an offsetting open-market sale. Even when banks are borrowing heavily at the discount window, the Fed can set the monetary base at any level it chooses. Hence, the existence of borrowed reserves does not change the basic principle of money-supply analysis that the Fed can control the monetary base.

Distinguishing between Monetary and Fiscal Policies

Our analysis of the money supply and the monetary base raises some definitional questions about monetary and fiscal policy. The government budget identity implies a relationship between the monetary base, government bonds, and government expenditures that must be kept in mind when distinguishing between monetary and fiscal policies. The monetary base, government bonds, and the deficit are related to each other by the following government budget identity:

F = transfers
Q = interest payments

$$G + F + Q - T = \Delta M_B + \Delta B, \qquad\qquad (14.6)$$

where ΔM_B is the change in the monetary base and ΔB is the change in government bonds. As defined in Chapter 2, G is government purchases, F is transfers, Q is interest payments, and T is taxes. Equation 14.6 says that the government budget deficit is financed by increasing either the monetary base or government bonds. Note that the base as well as government expenditures and taxes appear in this equation, so there is a link between monetary policy and fiscal policy.

To separate monetary policy changes from fiscal policy changes, we therefore need to specify what is happening to budget financing.

Fiscal policy is defined as bond-financed changes in government expenditures and taxes. That is, the monetary base and the money supply remain unchanged, and bonds are issued if government spending increases or taxes are reduced.

Monetary policy is defined as a change in the monetary base matched by a change in government bonds in the opposite direction. This exchange of money for bonds is an *open-market operation*. Note that open-market operations do not affect government purchases (G), transfers (F), interest payments (Q), or taxes (T). Hence, open-market operations do not affect fiscal policy.

open market operation:

$$\Delta M_B = \Delta B$$

The Monetary System and the Fed

1. The monetary system in the United States is based on the dollar, which is the unit of account. The Fed and other institutions provide means of payment denominated in dollars.

2. The institutions most prominent in providing the means of payment are the Federal Reserve System and banks. The liabilities of the Fed (currency and reserves) make up the monetary base.

3. The money supply consists of currency and deposits at banks and other financial intermediaries. The supply of money is directly related to the monetary base.

4. The Fed controls the monetary base by buying and selling bonds. In doing so, it controls the supply of money. The control over the supply of base money is the fundamental source of the Fed's leverage over the economy.

14.3 | THE DEMAND FOR MONEY: CURRENCY AND CHECKING DEPOSITS

Having considered the determination of the supply of money, we now explore the demand for money. John Maynard Keynes distinguished three motives in people's demand for money: a **transactions motive,** a **precautionary motive,** and a **speculative motive.** More recent research has refined these categories, and Keynes's classification scheme has been revised somewhat. However, our discussion of money demand touches on all three of these elements.

What Are the Opportunity Costs of Holding Funds as Money?

Before discussing the different motives for holding money, we need to consider the costs of holding money. When you put funds in a checking account, you give the bank the use of the funds. The bank earns the interest you would have earned had you invested the funds. In exchange, the bank may pay you some interest, but less than what the bank is earning. In addition, if you have a sufficiently high balance, the bank may excuse you from service charges you would otherwise have to pay. Your opportunity cost per dollar in your checking account is the interest you forgo (the rate you might have received elsewhere less the amount you receive from the bank) less the avoided service charges. As usual in economics, what matters precisely is the *marginal* opportunity cost— the interest forgone on the last amount added to your balance less the reduction in service charges if you took it out. For example, suppose you would earn 7 percent elsewhere and your bank pays 3 percent interest on checking accounts. Suppose that, over the year, it excuses you from $2 in service charges if you raise your average balance by $100, so you earn 2 percent on the $100. Then, your opportunity cost for the $100 of funds placed in your checking account is

$$7\% - 3\% - 2\% = 2\%.$$

We call the opportunity cost of holding money R_o, the subscript o standing for "opportunity." When you think about the added convenience of having another $100 in your account on the average over the year, keep in mind that you are sacrificing 2 percentage points of annual return on the funds.

Whatever complicated system the bank has for paying you interest on the one hand and charging you for services on the other, you can boil it down to an annual net opportunity cost of the account. This is the price we have in mind for checking deposits as one of the many financial services available to you.

For currency, the computation of the opportunity cost is easy. There are no service changes at all. Currency pays no interest. Therefore, the cost of holding currency is just the forgone interest. If you are contemplating meeting your needs by holding an average amount of currency of $500 and you could earn 7 percent on the funds elsewhere, then the cost is just 7 percent of $500, or $35 per year.

Another hypothetical way of handling your finances might be to avoid money altogether. You could open a special savings account and obtain a credit card. The savings account would allow you to write three checks a month, one of which could pay for your credit card charges. You would pay for everything with the credit card. Suppose the special savings account pays you 6 percent interest (1 percent less than the 7 percent that you could get outside the bank) and the credit card has no finance charges if you pay the bill on time. If you keep an average balance of $2,500 in the account, your only cost would be the opportunity cost of 1 percent of $2,500, or $25 per year.

By now it should be clear that each type of financial service has its own opportunity cost. But consumers do not simply pick the cheapest service on the market. Different services have different characteristics. Choosing among them is like choosing laundry detergent at the grocery store.

✕ The Transactions Demand for Money: An Inventory Theory

One reason that families and businesses hold currency and keep funds in their checking accounts is the same as the reason stores keep inventories of goods for sale. Because income is received periodically and expenditures occur every day, it is necessary to hold a stock of currency and checking deposits. This inventory theory of the demand for money falls into Keynes's category of **transactions motive.**[4]

We first illustrate the inventory theory of money demand with a simple case. Suppose a family earns an amount W every month. The family consumes W over the month, in equal amounts each day. If the family draws down its money to zero just before being paid, then its money balance starts at W and declines smoothly to zero over the month. Panel A of Figure 14.1 illustrates how the family's money holdings decline smoothly each day during the month. Its average level of money balances M is $W/2$. This family has a demand for money ($W/2$) proportional to its income W and does not respond to the prices of financial services. For one reason or another, the family has rejected ways other than money to hold its funds.

Next, take the same family with one additional financial option. It can have its paychecks deposited for free in a savings account. It can transfer any amount of funds to its checking account. The cost of each transfer is k. The cost k includes the value of the time of the family members who make the transfer—it might involve a trip to the bank. The checking account has an

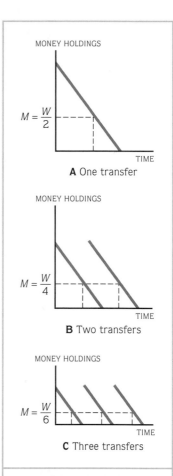

FIGURE 14.1   THREE ALTERNATIVE MONEY MANAGEMENT STRATEGIES

In A, the family puts all its money into its checking account at the start of the month. Average money holdings are large. In B, the family leaves half its income in a savings account at the start of the month and withdraws the rest at the middle of the month. Average money holdings are less than in A. In C, the family makes three withdrawals and money holdings are even lower. Hence, when there are more withdrawals, the family's average money balance is lower.

---

[4]The inventory theory of the demand for money was first worked out by William Baumol in "The Transactions Demand for Cash: An Inventory Theoretic Approach," *Quarterly Journal of Economics*, Vol. 56 (November 1952), pp. 545–556; and James Tobin, "The Interest Rate Elasticity of the Transactions Demand for Cash," *Review of Economics and Statistics*, Vol. 38 (September 1956), pp. 241–247.

opportunity cost R_o. The family chooses an average balance to hold in its checking account. With a higher average balance, fewer transfers have to be made from the savings account. But the higher the average balance, the larger the opportunity cost. The family wants to balance one cost against the other. For example, if the family makes one transfer at the beginning of the month, its money balance is the same as in panel A. If the family makes two transfers to checking, one at the start of the month and one halfway through, as in panel B, the average money balance is half as much as when it makes one transfer. If three transfers are made, as in panel C, the average money holdings are lower still.

In general, the average money balance M is half the amount transferred from savings to checking on each transfer. The total number of transfers is the size of each transfer, 2 times M, divided into the total amount of consumption planned over the month, W. That is, the family makes $W/2M$ transfers during the month. The total cost of the transfers is k times $W/2M$ (remember that k is the cost of one transfer). The opportunity cost over the month is just R_o times the average balance, that is, $R_o M$. The family wants to choose its average balance to minimize the sum of the two costs. Algebraically, it wants to find M to minimize total cost:

$$\frac{kW}{2M} + R_o M. \qquad (14.7)$$

A famous theorem from management theory is the **square-root rule** for inventories. The square-root rule says that stores should hold inventories proportional to the square root of sales. The same square-root rule applies to the demand for money. Specifically, the theorem says that the value of the average checking balance M that minimizes total cost is given by[5]

$$M = \sqrt{\frac{kW}{2R_o}}. \qquad (14.8)$$

[5]Calculus is not necessary to derive the square-root rule. Rather, one can use a "complete the square" approach as follows. The total cost is

$$kW/2M + R_o M = \sqrt{(kW)/2M + R_o M)^2}$$
$$= \sqrt{(kW/2M)^2 + kWR_o + (R_o M)^2}$$
$$= \sqrt{(kW/2M)^2 - kWR_o + (R_o M)^2 + 2kWR_o}$$
$$= \sqrt{(kW/2M - R_o M)^2 + 2kWR_o}.$$

The second term under the last square-root sign does not depend on M. Thus, costs are minimized when the first term under the square-root sign is at its smallest value, which is zero. This term is equal to zero when

$$M = \sqrt{kW/2R_o}$$

which is the square-root rule. Alternatively, if you have had calculus you can differentiate Equation 14.7 with respect to M.

The square-root rule gives the family's transactions demand for cash. Note that the formula would be the same if they chose to keep their transactions balance in the form of currency instead of in a checking account. In that case, because currency earns no interest, the opportunity cost of currency would be the interest rate paid on their savings account.

According to the square-root rule, the family holds less money if the opportunity cost R_o of holding money increases. The services of money are just like anything else the family consumes; they make do with less when the price rises. The square-root rule also says something about the relation between total spending and income W and the family's demand for money: Demand depends on the square root of total income. In comparing two families, one with double the income of the other, we should find that the second family has a transactions balance only 41 percent higher (the square root of 2 is 1.41). ✗

The Demand for Money as a Store of Wealth

Some families hold their wealth in the form of money; if they completely distrust all financial institutions, they might accumulate dollar bills under a mattress. Criminal activities generate wealth that is held as currency to avoid detection. People who are not thinking very hard about their affairs sometimes leave large amounts idle in their checking accounts at zero or low interest rates.

Keynes's notions of precautionary and speculative demand for money fit into this store-of-wealth category. Under the precautionary motive, individuals save some wealth in the form of money in case of an emergency need for funds. Since currency and checking deposits are the easiest funds to obtain, it might seem natural to hold money in this form. However, in the United States, other interest-bearing assets serve the precautionary demand perfectly well. In politically unstable countries or in countries without a well-developed financial system, this motive for holding money would be more important.

Keynes's speculative motive captures the idea that changes in market interest rates change the value of bonds. For individuals, bonds paying fixed interest rates are one of the main alternatives to holding the money in financial institutions. But when interest rates rise, the price of these bonds falls.[6] Keynes argued that, when interest rates are high, more people would expect them to fall or, equivalently, expect bond prices to rise and therefore want to hold more bonds and less money. Therefore, the demand for money declines as interest rates rise. Changes in bond prices also add risk to holding bonds. People are assumed to be averse to risk; hence, they do not put all their wealth in a risky asset. Some of their wealth is held as relatively riskless money. Unless they are unwilling to take on any risk, they balance their wealth between money and bonds. This balancing gives rise to a demand for money as an aversion to risk.

balance btw $ (no risk) and bonds (risk)

[6] Interest rates and prices of existing bonds have an inverse relation. When the interest rate falls, the market price of a bond issued earlier rises. The bond continues to pay its interest payments, but new bonds have smaller payments. Hence, the old bond has a higher market price.

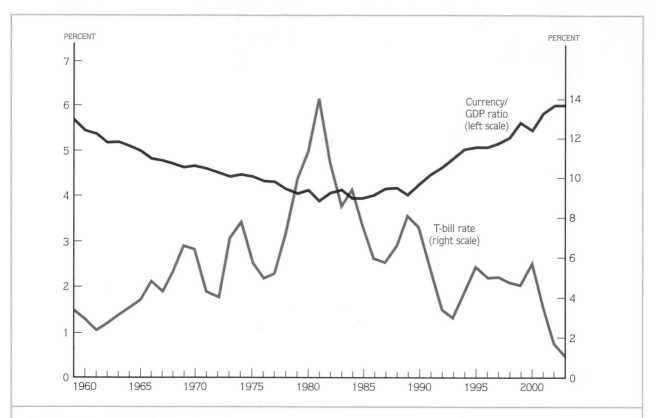

FIGURE 14.2   CURRENCY DIVIDED BY GDP

Holdings of currency have increased in recent years. The upper line is the total amount of currency in circulation, divided by nominal GDP. The interest rate on T-bills is also shown in the diagram. Higher interest rates are associated with less currency as a percentage of GDP.

SOURCE: *Economic Report of the President,* 2003, Tables B-1, B-70, and B-73.

Recent Trends in Currency and Deposits

Currency holdings have increased relative to GDP in recent years after many previous years of gradual decline. This is shown in Figure 14.2. Even though credit cards are used much more widely today and checking accounts have more favorable terms than they used to, the public has increased the amount of currency it holds per dollar of production. The sustained level of demand for currency may be due to an "underground economy"—activities not reported to the Internal Revenue Service and not part of GDP, such as "under-the-table" wages or illicit drug sales. There also is substantial holdings of U.S. currency in some foreign countries.

We would expect that periods of low income and high interest rates would be periods of low holdings of currency. Currency holdings drop a little during recessions and seem to be inversely related to interest-rate trends. With the extremely high interest rates of the late 1970s and early 1980s, currency fell quite a bit, but it has increased with low interest rates more recently.

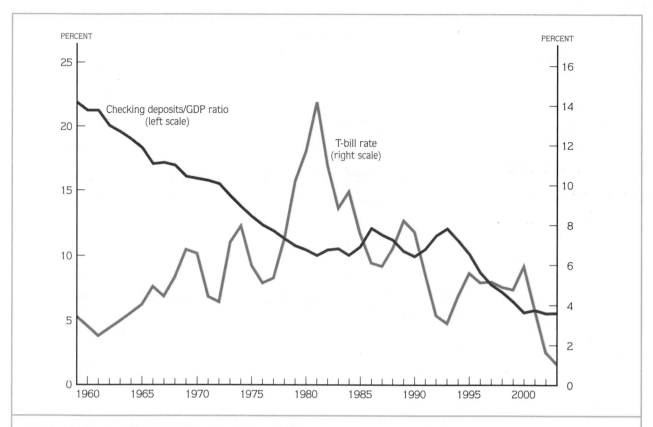

FIGURE 14.3   CHECKING DEPOSITS DIVIDED BY GDP

Checking deposits divided by nominal GDP declined steadily in the 1960s and 1970s, stabilized in the 1980s and early 1990s, and declined again in the mid-1990s to early 2000s. The interest rate on T-bills is also shown in the diagram. Higher interest rates are associated with lower checking deposits.

SOURCE: *Economic Report of the President,* 2003, Tables B-1, B-70, and B-73.

The behavior of checking deposits is shown in Figure 14.3. There was a downward trend in checking deposits until the early 1980s. After interest rates reached a peak around 1980, the decline in demand deposits in relation to GDP stabilized. With the low interest rates since the early 1990s, the downward trend in checking deposits resumed.   *Checking Deposits ↓*

The Demand Function for Money

We can summarize the previous discussion about the demand for currency and checking deposits in two demand functions,

Currency

$$CU = CU(R, PY) \qquad\qquad (14.9)$$

Checking Deposits

$$D = D(R, PY), \qquad\qquad (14.10)$$

where CU is currency and D is checking deposits. The equations show that the demand for currency and the demand for checking deposits are functions of the market interest rate R and nominal income PY (the price level P times real income Y). Total **money demand** is the sum of these two demands; that is,

$$\text{Money demand} = CU(R, PY) + D(R, PY). \tag{14.11}$$

Our discussion implies the following characteristics for total money demand:

1. Money demand depends negatively on the costs of holding currency and checking balances. These costs depend on the interest rate R.

2. Money demand is positively related to the price level P.

3. Money demand is positively related to real income or output Y.

Why does the opportunity cost of checking balances depend on the interest rate R? Banks pay some interest on checking deposits. When interest rates rise, banks pay somewhat higher interest on checking accounts. However, the account holder does not get the full benefit of an increase in interest rates. For one thing, the bank has to hold 10 percent of the account holder's funds as reserves at the Fed, and these reserves do not pay any interest. The bank therefore cannot be expected to pass along any more than 90 percent of any increase in interest rates. Another reason why the opportunity cost of checking balances rises with interest rates is that the rate banks pay on checking accounts has proven to be quite sticky. The rate may stay at 2 percent per year as the market rate rises from 5 to 7 percent. In that case, the opportunity cost rises by the full 2 percentage points of the increase in the market rate.

Knowing that the opportunity cost of checking balances depends on the market interest rate, we can write the demand function for checking balances using R rather than R_o. When the interest rate R rises, it raises the opportunity cost of checking balances and so depresses the demand for checking balances. The strength of this effect is greater if checking-account interest rates are sticky and if account holders conserve aggressively on balances when the opportunity cost rises.

The Demand for Money

1. The demand for currency depends negatively on the interest rate and positively on income and the price level.

2. The demand for checking deposits depends negatively on the difference between the interest rate and the rate that banks pay on checking deposits and positively on income and the price level.

3. The demand for money is the sum of the demand for currency and the demand for checking deposits.

Money Demand depends on R & positive related to P and Y

14.4 | HOW THE FED CONDUCTS MONETARY POLICY

We saw in Section 14.2 how the Fed can use open-market operations to change the monetary base and the money supply by any amount that it wants. And we know from the IS-LM price adjustment analysis of Chapters 8 and 9 that changes in the money supply have effects on real GDP in the short run and prices in the long run. Therefore, by undertaking open-market operations, the Fed has great power to affect the economy. The central question for monetary policy is this: How should the Fed use this power to achieve its objectives of keeping inflation low and economic fluctuations small?

Decisions about monetary policy in the United States are made by the *Federal Open Market Committee* (FOMC). The FOMC consists of the seven members of the Board of Governors of the Federal Reserve System plus the presidents of the district Federal Reserve Banks around the country. The FOMC meets about eight times each year in Washington, DC. At any one meeting there are 12 voting members of the FOMC, including the chair of the Fed, the other 6 members of the board, and 5 of the 12 presidents of the district banks. The chair of the Fed serves as chair of the FOMC and the president of the New York district Federal Reserve Bank serves as vice chair. The New York district is particularly important for monetary policy because the open-market operations of the Fed are conducted in Wall Street financial markets by bond traders who work at the New York Fed. The other presidents rotate their voting responsibilities on the FOMC.

> *FOMC =*
> *Federal open Market*
> *committee*

Setting Interest Rates or Money Growth

How does the FOMC make its decisions? What issues does the FOMC vote on? FOMC decisions can be specified in one of the following two alternative ways.

1. **Set the growth rate of the money supply.** With this approach, the FOMC votes on what the growth rate of the money supply should be. For example, the FOMC might vote to set money supply growth at 5 percent per year for the next year. Milton Friedman and other monetarist economists have long recommended that the FOMC set the growth rate of the money supply, and the Fed made use of such a procedure in the late 1970s and early 1980s, although it does not do so now. Under a money-supply procedure, the FOMC communicates its decision to the bond traders at the New York Fed, and they make the appropriate open-market purchases or sales to set the FOMC's money-supply growth. To determine the correct amount of open-market purchases or sales, the bond traders use the equation $M = mM_B$ relating the monetary base (M_B) to the money supply (M) through the money multiplier (m); see Equation 14.5. For example, if the money multiplier m is 4 and the FOMC instructions call for an increase in the money supply M by \$8 billion, then the traders make open-market

> *money supply* ↓   *monetary base* ↙
> $$M = m\, M_B$$
> ↓
> *money multiplier*

Open Market
Opperations affect
monetary base

purchases to increase the monetary base M_B by \$2 billion. Then, the money supply increases by $2 \times 4 = 8$ billion dollars as instructed by the FOMC.

2. **Set the short-term interest rate.** With this alternative approach, the FOMC decides at its meetings whether to raise or lower the short-term interest rate. The short-term interest rate the FOMC looks at is the federal funds rate, which is the one-day interest rate on loans between banks. For example, the members of the FOMC might vote to raise the federal funds rate from 1.50 percent to 1.75 percent as they did at their September 21, 2004 meeting. The FOMC has been using this approach to monetary policy since the mid-1980s and now explicitly announces its decision about interest rates after each FOMC meeting. Once a decision is made, the FOMC instructs the bond traders at the New York Fed to make open-market purchases or sales to bring about the desired change in the interest rate. If the FOMC calls for a reduction in the interest rate, then the bond traders buy bonds, which increases the money supply and reduces interest rates. If the FOMC calls for an increase in the interest rate, then the bond traders sell bonds, which decreases the money supply and raises the interest rate. The bond traders then keep the interest rate at the new level until they are given a new set of instructions from the FOMC to change the interest rate. For example, suppose the instruction from the FOMC is to set the interest rate at 5 percent. Then, if the interest rate starts to rise above 5 percent, the bond traders buy bonds; if the interest rate starts to fall below 5 percent, the bond traders sell bonds.

Buy Bonds: $R \downarrow$
Sell Bonds: $R \uparrow$

Which of these two approaches—setting the money supply or setting the interest rate—is better? In either case the Fed must decide what levels to set and what factors to consider when setting them. For example, if the FOMC is setting interest rates, it might decide to raise the short-term interest rate if inflation or GDP starts to rise. Alternatively, if the FOMC is setting money growth, it may decide to lower money growth if inflation or GDP starts to rise.

The choice between interest-rate setting and money-supply setting usually boils down to practical questions about which variable is easier to measure and interpret. As discussed earlier in this chapter, the money supply is difficult to measure—for example, should it be M_1 or M_2?—and there appeared to be changes in the behavior of M_1 in the early 1980s. If we do not know how to measure money, then the money-demand function and the LM curve, which are the bases for our assessment of the effects of money on the economy, are not reliable. A situation where money demand is difficult to measure or interpret is illustrated in Figure 14.4. The location of the

SET INTEREST RATE HERE

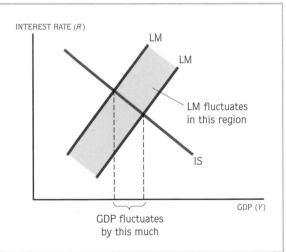

FIGURE 14.4   SHIFTS IN THE LM CURVE

If there are large shifts in the LM curve, it is better for the Fed to set interest rates. Then, GDP would not fluctuate as much.

LM curve is shown to be uncertain and shifting around because of uncertainty about how to measure money. For example, if the Fed's demand for money function shifts down because the Fed is mismeasuring the money supply, then the LM curve shifts to the right (recall from Chapter 9 that a downward shift in money demand has the same effects as an increase in the money supply). Or, if the demand for money increases, the LM curve shifts to the left. As shown in Figure 14.4, such shifts in the LM curve cause interest rates to fluctuate and undesirable fluctuations in real GDP; the fluctuations in real GDP also cause fluctuations in inflation and are therefore doubly harmful to the economy. With such uncertainty about money and the LM curve, interest-rate setting is a more appropriate policy for the Fed because it reduces these fluctuations. The difficulty with measuring money is an important reason why the FOMC now concentrates on interest-rate setting rather than money-supply setting. Another problem with money-supply setting is that, since the money multiplier is not constant, the Fed can have difficulty hitting its short-run target.

Shifts in LM curve cause interest rates, GDP to fluctuate

However, interest rates have their own measurement problems. The *real* interest rate affects spending in the economy. Measuring the real interest rate requires a good measure of the expected rate of inflation (recall that the real interest rate is the nominal interest rate, which the Fed sets, minus the expected rate of inflation). It is especially difficult to measure people's expectation of inflation during periods when inflation is very high and fluctuating. Unobserved fluctuations in the real interest rate affect investment spending and thereby cause the IS curve to fluctuate as shown in Figure 14.5. To emphasize a situation where the Fed sets the nominal interest rate, the vertical axis in Figure 14.5 is the nominal interest rate. If the real interest rate shifts in such a situation, the IS curve in Figure 14.5 shifts; thus uncertainty about the real interest rate causes real GDP (and therefore inflation) to be volatile. More generally, if the IS curve fluctuates as in Figure 14.5, then interest-rate setting is a poor policy. With such uncertainty about the IS curve, money-supply setting is a more appropriate policy for the Fed.[7] This explains why, in the late 1970s, when the inflation rate was high and the real interest rate was uncertain, the FOMC shifted away from interest-rate setting toward money-supply setting in its policy deliberations. By 1982, when inflation declined and the real interest-rate fluctuations apparently became less uncertain, the FOMC moved back to the interest rate.

Inflation = difficult to measure

Over the past 20 years, inflation in the United States has been relatively low. Since uncertainty in the

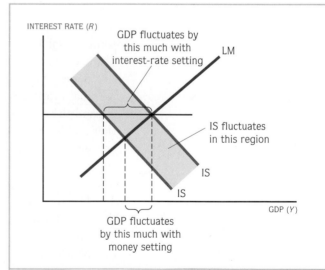

FIGURE 14.5   SHIFTS IN THE IS CURVE

The band around the IS curve illustrates the shifts perhaps due to unobserved changes in the real interest rate. If such shifts are large, money-supply setting results in smaller GDP fluctuations than interest-rate setting.

[7]See William Poole, "The Optimal Choice of Monetary Policy in a Simple Stochastic Macro Model," *Quarterly Journal of Economics,* Vol. 84, pp. 197–216.

w/ low inflation,
FOMC sets
nominal interest rate

real interest rate and shifts in the IS curve have not been a major problem, it makes sense for the FOMC to set the nominal interest rate rather than money supply growth. In Chapter 16, we study macroeconomic policy by using a monetary policy rule that describes the behavior of the Fed since the mid-1980s. This policy rule is specified in terms of the nominal interest rate rather than money supply growth.

The Zero Bound on Nominal Interest Rates

During the early 2000s, the FOMC aggressively lowered nominal interest rates. The federal funds rate declined from 6.5 percent in the fall of 2000 to 1 percent in the summer and fall of 2003, and three-month Treasury bills were at their lowest levels in 45 years. This echoed the experience of Japan, where the overnight call rate, the Japanese equivalent of the U.S. federal funds rate, decreased from 8 percent in 1991 to zero during most of 1999–2003. The values of the two short-term interest rates since 1989 are shown in Figure 14.6. What are the implications for the conduct of monetary policy when nominal interest rates approach or equal zero? We focus on the United States here and study the experience of Japan in Chapter 18.[8]

When we studied countercyclical stabilization policy in Chapter 9, we showed how monetary policy could be used to counteract the effects of aggregate demand disturbances. The basic idea is that, if an aggregate demand disturbance decreases GDP below potential GDP, the Fed can expand the money supply to counteract the disturbance. More specifically, the Fed conducts an open market purchase and lowers the nominal interest rate. With sticky prices, this decreases the real interest rate, raising investment, net exports, and consumer durables. The higher investment and net exports counteract the effects of the disturbance, stimulating the economy back toward potential GDP.

A monetary policy based on interest rates loses its effectiveness once the nominal interest rate hits zero. At that point, for monetary policy to further expand the economy, the nominal interest rate would have to be lowered further and become negative. But it is impossible for the nominal interest rate to be negative. Why would anyone hold a negative interest bearing asset if you could hold cash at a zero return? The constraint of a *zero bound* on the nominal interest rate limits the scope of monetary policy.

The zero bound on the nominal interest rate can pose a serious problem in the case of *deflation*—negative inflation or, equivalently, falling prices. Remember that the real interest rate, the nominal interest rate minus the expected rate of inflation, is the interest rate that influences investment, net exports, and consumer durables. In the usual case, low but positive inflation, a zero nominal

---

[8]A nontechnical analysis of these issues can be found in Evan Koenig and Jim Dolmas, "Monetary Policy in a Zero-Interest-Rate Economy," *Southwest Economy* (July/August 2003), Federal Reserve Bank of Dallas.

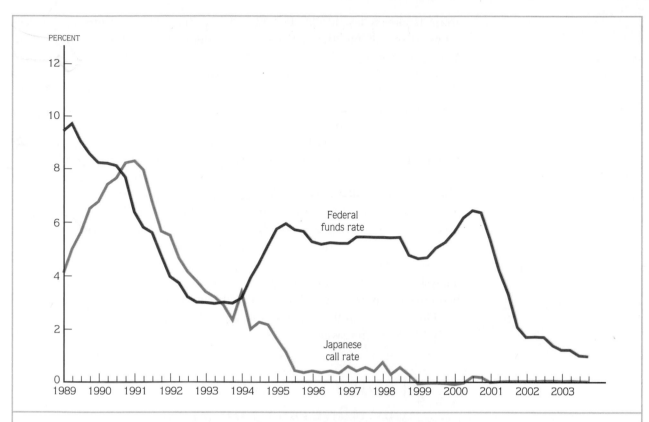

FIGURE 14.6   SHORT-TERM INTEREST RATES IN JAPAN AND THE UNITED STATES

The overnight call rate in Japan has been zero during most of 1999–2003. The U.S. federal funds rate, which was considerably higher from 1995 to 2001, decreased to 1 percent in 2003.

SOURCE: Bank of Japan, Federal Reserve Board.

interest rate produces a negative real interest rate. Now, suppose there is deflation. In that case, even a zero nominal interest rate produces a positive real interest rate, which may be too high to stimulate the economy.

The Great Depression of the 1930s illustrates the potential magnitude of
the problem. While the Federal Reserve cut the short-term nominal interest
rate from 5.0 percent in 1929 to 0.5 percent in 1932, inflation fell even faster,
from (positive) 1.5 percent in 1929 to (negative) 14.5 percent in 1932. Despite the cut in the nominal interest rate, the real interest rate increased from
3.5 percent in 1929 to 15 percent in 1932. Monetary policy became tighter
during the early 1930s even though the Fed, by cutting the nominal interest
rate, tried to stimulate the economy.

Concern about deflation clearly influenced monetary policy making in the
United States during 2003. In June, the FOMC lowered the federal funds rate
from 1.25 percent to 1.0 percent, citing that "the probability, though minor, of
an unwelcome substantial fall in inflation exceeds that of a pickup in inflation

from its already low level."[9] In July, Fed Governor Ben Bernanke, in a widely reported speech, mentioned that inflation could fall from 1.2 percent in 2003 to 0.7 percent in 2004. While he stated that inflation in the range of 0.5 percent was considerably more likely than deflation in the range of 0.5 percent for the next few years, he advocated that, if necessary to support the economy in the future, the federal funds rate should be cut to zero.

A number of proposals have been made for conducting monetary policy once the zero bound constraint on the nominal interest rate becomes binding. One proposal is for the Fed to depreciate the U.S. dollar by buying substantial amounts of foreign currency. The dollar depreciation would stimulate net exports and, eventually, increase inflation. A second proposal is for the Fed to buy long-term, 10- and 30-year Treasury bonds. Other proposals are for the Fed to buy corporate and mortgage bonds, or even real goods and services, although these proposals currently violate the Federal Reserve Act.

Attempting to evaluate these proposals involves more speculation than analysis. Conducting monetary policy once the zero interest rate bound has been reached puts the economy into uncharted waters, and the experiences of the United States in the 1930s and Japan in the late 1990s and early 2000s do not provide much reassurance.

14.5 | LAGS IN THE EFFECT OF MONETARY POLICY

Monetary policy affects real GDP and prices with a lag. In Chapter 11, we stressed the lags in the investment process. Businesses take months to get almost any investment plan into effect; those involving the construction of new plants or orders of special equipment can take years. Housing investment takes six months or a year to respond strongly to a change in the interest rate.

Less is known about the lags in the response of net exports to dollar depreciation. Exchange rates respond immediately to changes in the interest rate. But buyers in the United States and overseas do not switch their purchases immediately when U.S. goods become cheaper. Americans who have learned that Japanese cars offer good value do not immediately reconsider U.S.-produced alternatives when the value of the dollar declines and causes the dollar price of Japanese cars to rise. It takes time for foreigners to discover the advantage of American products as well.

Despite many uncertainties about the lag in the effect of monetary policy, the peak effect on GDP probably occurs between one and two years after the expansion. The effect on prices takes much longer. At first, a monetary expansion drives down the interest rate without much effect on GDP. After a year or so, the response of spending to the interest rate is stronger and GDP expands.

[9]Federal Reserve Board press release, FOMC statement, June 25, 2003.

The lag in the economy's response to monetary expansion greatly complicates the conduct of monetary policy. The Fed can step on the gas to try to head off a recession, but the peak effect of the stimulus may occur well after the worst part of the recession is over. In fact, if the recession is brief and followed by a brisk recovery, the monetary stimulus may hit hardest when it is least needed; in the worst case, it can worsen the boom that follows the recession and cause inflation to rise.

Because the main effect of monetary expansion occurs in the year after the expansion is launched, when formulating monetary policy the Fed must always think about the likely conditions in the economy a year in the future. Even if the economy is in bad shape this year, the Fed will not expand if it anticipates that the economy will recover on its own by next year. There is little the Fed can do to help the economy this year; any stimulus it adds now will only create problems next year, if a recovery is impending.

The recovery from the 2001 recession provides an example of the lags in the effect of monetary policy. As you can see from Figure 14.6, the federal funds rate was lowered by 4.75 percentage points, from 6.5 percent to 1.75 percent in 2001. While the recession officially lasted only eight months, from March 2001 to November 2001, a period of economic underperformance began with the end of the stock market boom in mid-2000 and continued until mid-2003. Unemployment remained high and growth remained sluggish during 2002 and the first half of 2003, and the Fed responded by lowering the federal funds rate still further, bringing it down to 1 percent by June 2003, its lowest level in 45 years. Fiscal policy, in the form of the tax cuts of 2001–2003, was also expansionary. Economic growth finally picked up in the last half of 2003 and 2004.

The Fed never knows with confidence what will happen in the future. As a general matter, the more uncertain the Fed is about conditions next year, the more cautious it will be about policy actions this year. The response of the Fed to developments in the economy must take account of the lags and uncertainty. After examining the effects of monetary policy on prices more closely in the next chapter, we consider how different monetary policies deal with the lags and uncertainties.

Lags in Monetary Policy

1. Monetary policy operates through interest rates. Consequently, there is a lag before the policy influences GDP.

2. The evidence suggests that the peak effect of monetary policy on GDP occurs after a lag of between one and two years.

3. Today's monetary policy has to be formulated with the state of the economy a year from now in mind. Even if GDP is well below potential, it may not be desirable to launch a monetary expansion.

4. Uncertainty about the future state of the economy adds to the caution of monetary policy makers.

REVIEW AND PRACTICE

Major Points

1. A monetary system is an agreement on the way to quote prices and convey purchasing power.

2. In the United States, the Fed issues currency and also reserves. Reserves are accounts at the Fed equivalent to currency. The sum of currency and reserves is the monetary base.

3. According to the square-root rule, the transactions demand for money depends on the square root of total income.

4. The demand for money is the sum of the demand for currency and the demand for checking deposits. It depends negatively on the interest rate and positively on income and the price level.

5. An interest-rate target for monetary policy cushions the economy against the effects of shifts in money demand, while a money-supply target provides greater stability against shifts in spending.

6. There is a zero bound on nominal interest rates; the nominal interest rate cannot fall below zero. This constraint causes serious problems for the conduct of monetary policy if the economy is experiencing deflation.

7. Monetary policy influences GDP with a lag. The immediate effect of monetary stimulus is to lower interest rates. After the lags in investment and foreign trade work themselves out, the stimulus raises GDP. Because of the lag and the Fed's uncertainty about the future, monetary policy needs to be used with caution.

Key Terms and Concepts

means of payment	excess reserves
unit of account	borrowed reserves
currency	discount rate
intermediation role	transactions motive
open-market operation	precautionary motive
monetary base	speculative motive
reserve ratio	square-root rule
currency ratio	money demand
money multiplier	

Questions for Discussion and Review

1. Why is the dollar the unit of account and the medium of exchange in the United States?
2. In what sense do commercial banks play a role as financial intermediaries? What other role do they play in determining the nation's money supply?
3. Why doesn't the Fed have separate control over the quantities of both reserves and currency?
4. Why do some banks borrow reserves from the Fed? How does the Fed decide on the discount rate on these borrowings?
5. How does the Fed control the monetary base? What types of open-market operations increase the monetary base?
6. Does the demand for currency depend on the real rate of interest or the nominal rate of interest?
7. How does the Fed set interest rates?
8. Why might the Fed want to set interest rates?

Problems

NUMERICAL

1. Suppose that money demand is given by an expression similar to Equation 14.8,

$$M = \sqrt{\frac{kY}{2R_o}}$$

where Y is income, the opportunity cost of holding money is given by

$$R_o = q_1R - q_o,$$

and the transaction cost k equals 2.

   a. Assuming $q_1 = 1$ and $q_o = 0.06$, what is the level of money demand at $Y = 2,500$ and $R = 0.08$? Suppose the money supply is set equal to this value. Find the interest rate at which money supply equals money demand for $Y = 1,000$ and $Y = 4,000$. Plot the points to scale on a graph.

   b. Now let $q_1 = 0.25$ and $q_o = 0$. Find the level of money demand at $Y = 2,500$ and $R = 0.08$. Again, supposing that the money supply is set equal to this value, find the interest rate at which money supply equals money demand for the values of Y given in part a. Plot these points on the same graph.

2. In this problem, we consider the relationship between monetary policy and the financing of the deficit.

   a. Suppose that the reserve ratio r is equal to 0.1, and the currency ratio c is equal to 0.2. Assume that $G - T + F = \$200$ billion. By how much would the money supply, the monetary base, currency, and bank reserves have to change if the Fed were to finance the entire budget deficit?

b. Suppose now that the money supply is initially equal to $600 billion, with output equal to potential. Suppose further that potential output is increasing by 2 percent per year, prices are expected to grow by 3 percent, and monetary velocity ($V = PY/M$) is expected to remain constant. If the Fed wishes to keep output at potential, what percentage of the deficit does it have to finance?

3. Suppose that the required reserve ratio is 0.12 for deposits and there are no excess reserves. Suppose also that the total demand for currency is equal to 0.3 times deposits.

a. If total reserves are $40 billion, what is the level of the money supply?

b. By how much does the money supply change if the Fed increases the required reserve ratio to 0.20? Assume that total reserves are unchanged at $40 billion.

c. By how much does the money supply change if the Fed buys $1 billion of government bonds in the open market? (Keep the required reserve ratio at 0.12.)

ANALYTICAL

1. Suppose that, as a result of recent tax cuts, the amount of activity in the underground economy is significantly reduced.

a. What effect would this have on the demand for currency?

b. Explain why such a change would have an expansionary effect on the economy (holding the Fed's open-market operations fixed).

c. Describe the Fed's response to such a change if it sets the short-term interest rate.

2. Use Equation 14.8 to write an expression for real money demand as a function of real income and real transactions costs. Assuming that nominal income and nominal transactions costs increase proportionately with changes in the price level, describe how real money demand is affected by a change in prices. How is the nominal demand for money affected?

3. Consider the following cash management problem. A college student earns $400 a month which she uses to meet personal expenses. All expenses are paid for in cash. She maintains a savings account at a local bank which pays 1 percent per month (12 percent annually) in interest. At the beginning of each month she deposits her $400 paycheck in her savings account and makes periodic cash withdrawals throughout the month. Cash withdrawals are made through an automatic teller at a service charge of 25 cents each.

a. Calculate the student's average currency holdings and the number of withdrawals made each month.

b. Suppose it's observed that the student always withdraws $40. There are several possible explanations. Perhaps she doesn't wish to risk losing larger amounts of cash. Protection against such loss is one of the benefits of a savings account. In addition, she may wish to avoid the temptation of spending more money than she can really afford. Call this the "piggy bank" value of savings accounts. What must the value of such benefits be, expressed as a rate of return, for her withdrawals of $40 to be optimal?

4. Suppose that competition in the credit card industry drives down the cost of using credit cards.

   a. How is that likely to affect money demand? Illustrate the macroeconomic impact using an IS-LM diagram.

   b. If the Fed is aware of such a trend but cannot be certain of its timing, should it set the money supply or the interest rate?

5. Suppose that banks began both to pay market rates of interest on all checking accounts and to charge the full costs of providing such accounts. These costs would not be waived, regardless of one's average balance. Describe the possible effects of such a change on money demand.

6. The velocity of money V is defined by the expression

$$V = PY/M.$$

One way the Fed can set the money supply is described as follows. First, it is assumed that the velocity of money remains roughly constant from year to year. Next, the Fed forecasts this year's rate of inflation (which is viewed as being predetermined and thus beyond its control). Finally, the Fed chooses its target rate of growth for real output. This results in a target rate of growth for the money stock.

   a. Suppose that inflation for the current year is forecasted to be 5 percent and that the Fed's target rate of growth for output is 2 percent. By how much should it increase the money stock this year?

   b. Suppose now that money demand is given by the expression

$$M/P = kY - hR.$$

   Derive an expression for the velocity of money V. On what does V depend?

   c. What kinds of changes in the economy could affect V? Consider both the cases where $h > 0$ and $h = 0$.

7. Suppose the U.S. government budget deficit is reduced through a cut in government purchases. Assume that the Fed sets the *interest rate* according to the policy rule in Equation 14.12. What happens to the inflation rate in the long run?

8. Monetary policy is one of the most hotly debated issues in macroeconomics. Yet the policy implications of the IS-LM model would seem to be rather clear: Assuming that the Fed wishes to maintain output at potential, simply set the LM curve to intersect the IS curve at Y^*. Provide a brief explanation of why monetary policy is not so simple a matter.

9. There is reason to believe that money demand may be more closely related to consumption than to total output. Suppose this is indeed the case. The money-demand function takes the form

$$M = (sC - hR)P, \qquad s > 0,$$

where the rest of the economy is described by the usual spending equations:

$$C = a + b(Y - T)$$
$$I = e - dR$$
$$X = g - mY - nR.$$

a.   What is the slope of the LM curve for this model?

b.   Suppose taxes T are lump-sum rather than proportional to income. Show the short-run effect of a tax cut in this modified model using an IS-LM diagram. Comment on the qualitative effect on interest rates and income in relation to the model in which money demand depends on income rather than on consumption.

THE MICROECONOMIC FOUNDATIONS OF PRICE RIGIDITY

Why does an increase in the money supply have a positive effect on real GDP in the short run? The most common reason given by economists—from the first monetary economist, David Hume, in the 18th century, to John Maynard Keynes, Milton Friedman, and Robert Lucas in the 20th—is that, in the short run, the price level does not increase as much as the money supply. Thus, real money—the money supply divided by the price level—increases, causing the interest rate to decline and directly stimulating spending and production. The short run is different from the long run: In the long run, the price level does fully increase by the same percentage as the money supply, real money docs not change, and real GDP is therefore unaffected.

This chapter delves into the reasons why the price level does not increase by as much as the money supply, a phenomenon we refer to as **price rigidity.** We review several different microeconomic explanations for price rigidity. The explanations can be classified into two broad groups: those based on *imperfect information* and those based on *sticky prices* or *nominal wage contracts*. Both kinds of explanation are necessary for a complete understanding of price rigidity in the real world, as the 1995 Nobel price winner Robert Lucas emphasized in his Nobel address ("The Neutrality of Money"). Moreover, understanding the microeconomic foundations of price rigidity clarifies how macroeconomists view the effects of monetary policy. While macroeconomists disagree about the size and timing of the effects, they agree that the efficacy of monetary policy depends on price rigidity.

15.1 | THE IMPERFECT INFORMATION THEORY

We first consider explanations of price rigidity based on imperfect information. Explanations based on imperfect information start from the premise that prices at individual firms are perfectly flexible, just as in the long-run neoclassical growth model. But because of imperfect information about whether a change in the money supply or some other factor is the source of the shift to a firm's demand curve, prices change by less than they would if the firms were fully informed. Robert Lucas did the original research on this imperfect information theory.[1]

The role of information is very important in Lucas's theory. According to basic microeconomics, a firm produces up to the point where its *price equals marginal cost*. Marginal cost depends on the price of the firm's inputs to production. If the price of the firm's output rises *relative* to the price of other goods in the economy, including its inputs, then the firm produces more. However, if all other prices rise by the same amount that the firm's output price rises, there is no incentive for the firm to produce more. In other words, the firm produces more only if the price of its output rises relative to some other prices in the economy—in particular, its input prices.

Firms are assumed to have difficulty getting information about prices in the economy other than their own output price. There are temporary information barriers through which firms cannot see what is going on in other markets. Put another way, firms specialize in monitoring conditions in their own mar-

---

[1] The two main references for the work of Lucas on this topic are Robert Lucas, "Expectations and the Neutrality of Money," *Journal of Economic Theory*, Vol 4. (April 1972), pp. 103–124, and "Some International Evidence on Output-Inflation Tradeoffs," *American Economic Review*, Vol. 63 (June 1973), pp. 326–334. These papers, especially the first, had a major impact on macroeconomics because of the use of rational expectations and microeconomic principles to deal with key macroeconomic problems for the first time. The second paper is less technical and our discussion follows that paper.

ket. They know very quickly when demand drops off and prices begin to fall. On the other hand, they are relatively uninformed about developments in other markets and learn relatively slowly what is happening in them.

Derivation of the Lucas Supply Curve

To explain how this works, we start with the supply curves of individual firms and show how we can derive a supply curve for the whole economy from these individual curves. We use the subscript i to represent an individual firm. The representative firm's supply curve is given by

$$Y_i = h(P_i - P) + Y_i^*, \tag{15.1}$$

where Y_i is the firm's production, P_i is the firm's price, P is the aggregate price, and Y_i^* is the firm's potential or normal production. In words, the equation says that the firm's output Y_i is greater than the normal Y_i^* by an amount equal to a constant h times the difference between the firm's price P_i and the general price level P. We enter the general price level into the supply curve as an indicator of the prices in all other markets. The firm supplies more output only if its price rises relative to these other prices. The supply curve slopes upward ($h > 0$) in terms of the difference between P_i and P and is shown graphically in Figure 15.1.

Note that, if the price of the firm's product rises by the same amount as the overall price level, there is no change in the firm's supply, according to the supply equation. The firm sees that, although it can receive more for its output, the prices of all other items in the economy have increased by the same amount. Hence, in relative terms, there has been no change.

Suppose, however, that the firm does not know what is going on in other markets in the economy. The information about the rest of the economy may arrive late, or the firm's managers may not have the time to monitor economic conditions throughout the economy. When information is restricted in this way, firms do not know the prices of other commodities in the economy. Hence, they do not know the aggregate price level; they have to guess it. We therefore rewrite Equation 15.1 to reflect this fact:

$$Y_i = h(P_i - P^e) + Y_i^*. \tag{15.2}$$

The superscript e on the P indicates the firm's *estimate* of the overall price level.

Now consider again the case where all prices in the economy rise by the same amount. Each firm observes only the increase in price of its own product and must guess about all the other prices as summarized in the index P. If the firm does not adjust its guess of P, then it clearly produces more. The firm thinks that its own relative price has increased. If the other firms in the economy behave the same way, then they all produce more as a result of the general increase in prices. In this way, all the firms in the economy mistake

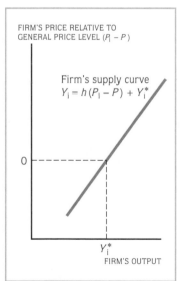

FIRM'S PRICE RELATIVE TO
GENERAL PRICE LEVEL $(P_i - P)$

Firm's supply curve
$Y_i = h(P_i - P) + Y_i^*$

0

Y_i^*
FIRM'S OUTPUT

FIGURE 15.1   THE FIRM'S SUPPLY CURVE

The firm's supply decision depends on its own price relative to the general level of prices in the economy. If P_i and P rise in the same proportion, then Y_i does not change.

the general price rise for an increase in their own price. With all firms producing more than their potential Y_i^*, output in the economy as a whole is above potential.

In an economic environment where there is a close relationship between economic activity in different industries, a firm would be naive not to guess that other firms in the economy are having the same type of experience. In other words, the observation that the price is high in one firm's market is an indication to that firm that prices are likely to be high in other markets. This is especially true in a highly inflationary economy, where an increase in the price of one commodity is usually an indication that inflation is continuing: The price of everything else is going up, too.

Consider, first, an extreme case, where economic conditions are such that relative prices of different products never change; that is, all the fluctuations in prices are due to general inflation where all prices move together. If relative prices never change, then firms would realize that any change in their own price simply represents an equal change in all prices. The firms would instantaneously adjust their expectations of other prices by the same amount that their own price increased. In Equation 15.2, P^e increases by exactly the amount that P_i increases. Hence, the firm's production does not change. In this example, the information-based explanation for the departure of real GDP from potential disappears. Although this example is extreme, even in a less extreme situation we expect firms to use information available in their own market when guessing economic conditions elsewhere. More specifically, when a firm observes the price of its own product, it adjusts its expectation of prices elsewhere. This adjustment is based on the relationship between the firm's price and the general price level that the firm experiences over time.

A simple way to describe the adjustment of the firm's expectation is through the equation

$$P^e = \hat{P} + b(P_i - \hat{P}). \tag{15.3}$$

In words, this means that the firm's guess P^e of the general price is greater than what was forecast $\hat{P}$ at the start of the year by an amount equal to a constant b times the difference between the firm's own price P_i and the forecast of the general price $\hat{P}$. For example, if the coefficient b is 0.3, the forecast of the general price $\hat{P}$ is 1.0, and the firm observes a price P_i in its own market equal to 1.1, then the best guess of the general price is $1.0 + 0.3(1.1 - 1.0) = 1.03$. In the example, the firm observes a price 10 percent higher in its own market and its guess is that the general price is 3 percent higher than originally forecast.

Note that if $b = 0$, the firm's own price does not influence its estimate of the general price level. At the other extreme is the case where $b = 1$. Then the firm increases its estimate of the general price level by exactly the amount that its own price increases. This case corresponds to the extreme example considered earlier, where there are never any changes in relative prices.

In general, however, the coefficient b is less than 1 and greater than zero. The size of b depends on whether the relative price variability is large compared with the general price variability. The larger the general price variability, the more the firm changes its estimate of the general price level when it sees its own price increase. For example, in a typical high-inflation economy, the general price variability is high. Firms usually guess that their own price increase is a signal for another increase in inflation.

If we substitute the firm's best guess (Equation 15.3) into the firm's supply equation (15.1), we get

$$Y_i = h[P_i - \hat{P} - b(P_i - \hat{P})] + Y_i^*, \qquad (15.4)$$

or

$$Y_i = h(1 - b)(P_i - \hat{P}) + Y_i^* \qquad (15.5)$$

Equation 15.5 shows how the representative firm produces more when its own price is greater than the forecast of the general price level. It has the same form as the firm's supply function except that the supply coefficient is related to the coefficient b. If b is near 1, then $h(1 - b)$ is near zero and the firm does not supply much additional output. At the other extreme, when b is near zero the supply coefficient is larger.

The supply curve for the entire economy is obtained by adding up all the representative firms' supply curves. Real GDP, or Y, is the sum of all the individual firms' Y_i. The aggregate price level P is simply the sum of the individual firms' prices P_i divided by n, the number of firms.

If we add up Equation 15.5 for all the firms in the economy, we get

$$Y = nh(1 - b)(P - \hat{P}) + Y^*, \qquad (15.6)$$

which is called the **Lucas supply curve.** It shows that, if the price level P rises above the forecast of P, then real GDP rises above potential GDP. To graph the Lucas supply curve with P on the vertical axis, we must rewrite it with the price level P on the right-hand side. The Lucas supply curve then looks like

$$P = \hat{P} + c(Y - Y^*), \qquad (15.7)$$

where $c = 1/[nh(1 - b)]$. Equation 15.7 is plotted in Figure 15.2.

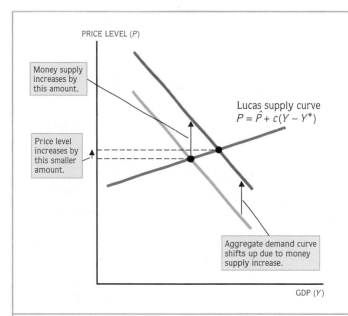

PRICE LEVEL (P)

Money supply increases by this amount.

Lucas supply curve
$P = \hat{P} + c(Y - Y^*)$

Price level increases by this smaller amount.

Aggregate demand curve shifts up due to money supply increase.

GDP (Y)

FIGURE 15.2   THE LUCAS SUPPLY CURVE

The upward-sloping line is a plot of Equation 15.7, or the Lucas supply curve. Price rigidity is revealed when the aggregate demand curve shifts up by the amount that the money supply increases but the price level rises by a smaller amount. If firms were fully informed, the price level would rise by the same amount as the price increase, because the Lucas supply curve would be vertical.

The Appearance of Price Rigidity

How does the Lucas supply curve generate price rigidity? Suppose that the aggregate demand curve is given by

$$Y = k_0 + k_1 (M - P), \tag{15.8}$$

where M is the money supply. We plot the aggregate demand curve in Figure 15.2 along with the Lucas supply curve. If the Fed increases the money supply, then the aggregate demand curve shifts up by the amount of the money-supply increase, as shown in Figure 15.2. This leads to a new intersection with the Lucas supply curve. However, note that, as long as the Lucas supply curve is not perfectly vertical, the price level rises by less than the increase in the money supply. This explains why real GDP rises when the money supply increases.

Thus, we have shown that price rigidity can occur as a result of the limited information firms have about what is going on in other markets. If they were fully informed (that is, if $b = 1$), then the Lucas supply curve would be perfectly vertical and the price would increase by the same amount as the increase in money. Price rigidity would not appear.

In the long run, of course, firms will become informed about what is happening in other markets and their *estimate* of the price level $\hat{P}$ rises as much as the *actual* price level P. Then, the Lucas supply curve shifts up by the amount that prices have risen and the actual price rise is the same amount as the money supply increase. In the long run, there is no impact on real GDP.

Policy Ineffectiveness Theorem

The Lucas supply curve has an interesting implication that has fascinated macroeconomists since it was first pointed out in a paper by Thomas Sargent and Neil Wallace.[2] Suppose that the Fed announces that it is increasing the money supply. Suppose also that people believe the Fed's announcement and they have rational expectations about the future, in other words, they act as if they understand the implications of the theory in Equations 15.7 and 15.8 or Figure 15.2. Looking closely at Equation 15.7, we can see that the price level P, or output Y, must increase. Since people are rational in forming their expectations of P, they also are looking at Equations 15.7 and 15.8 trying to figure out what is going to happen to Y and P when the money supply goes up. They further anticipate the money-supply increase and therefore *expect* the price level to rise. That is, their rational expectation of the price level $\hat{P}$ increases.

[2]Thomas Sargent and Neil Wallace, "Rational Expectations, the Optimal Monetary Instrument, and the Optimal Money Supply Rule," *Journal of Political Economy*, Vol. 83 (1975), pp. 241–254.

But note from the Lucas supply function shown in Equation 15.8 that this means that Y does not rise at all: P and $\hat{P}$ rise in the same proportion when an increase in M is anticipated. Now, looking back at Equation 15.7, it is clear that if Y does not change then P must rise by the same amount that M increases. Graphically, the Lucas supply curve in Figure 15.2 shifts up immediately and real GDP does not change.

In summary, with rational expectations, an *anticipated* increase in the money supply does not increase real output. It causes an increase in the price level that matches the increase in money. *Anticipated monetary policy is ineffective.* This result is called the **policy ineffectiveness theorem.**

Sargent and Wallace's starting point was the premise that the central bank has essentially the same information about the economy as people have. When the Fed uses information—say, about real GDP—to make monetary policy, then people can use the same information to take account of the Fed's policy when forming their expectation P_t^e. The Fed affects employment only by surprising people. But it cannot surprise people by expanding the money stock every time real GDP rises, because people know the real GDP data. Put differently, people with rational expectations cannot be surprised by systematic policy. According to this theory, surprise monetary expansions have an important influence on employment, but expansions based on observed conditions affect only the price level. The policy ineffectiveness theorem has profoundly influenced economists since the 1970s and has had an impact on thinking in the government and the Federal Reserve.

Critique of the Imperfect Information Theory

Although the idea that surprises about monetary policy are an important driving force in fluctuations had a profound impact on macroeconomists, the policy ineffectiveness theorem receives less attention today than in past decades. First, early evidence supporting the theory[3] is now seen as showing only that monetary changes precede employment and output fluctuations. It does not show that imperfect information, rather than some other channel of influence, is at work. Second, recent evidence shows the importance of other types of shocks in macro fluctuations. Monetary variables explain only part of the total variability of real GDP. The economics profession has moved to the more general view that a variety of forces (technological shocks and changes in preferences) are at least as important as monetary developments. The diminishing importance of monetary shocks is partly a reflection of the stability of monetary policy in the United States and other major economies from the mid-1980s to the present.

---

[3]Robert Barro, "Unanticipated Money Growth and Unemployment in the U.S.," *American Economic Review*, Vol. 67 (March 1977), pp. 101–115.

The Lucas Supply Curve

1. An important explanation of the effects of changes in money on real GDP is the imperfect information theory developed by Robert Lucas. According to this theory, people are not perfectly informed about what is going on in other parts of the economy.

2. Therefore, when firms see an increase in prices—whether due to a shift in their demand curve or to changes in other parts of the economy—they respond by producing more. This response is the Lucas supply curve.

3. Price rigidity is an implication of the Lucas imperfect information theory: When the money supply increases, the aggregate price level increases by a relatively small amount. Hence, real money balances rise and real GDP rises above potential GDP.

15.2 | STICKY PRICES AND NOMINAL WAGE CONTRACTS

In Lucas's theory, imperfect information produces a type of price rigidity. Now we consider another explanation of price rigidity. We find that firms and workers have incentives to keep prices and wages from changing too much or too rapidly. Price change may be costly, giving rise to sticky prices. Or firms and workers may have agreed in a contract not to change wages by more or less than a certain prespecified amount.

Sticky Prices

Firms' prices are set in dollars. Studies show that the dollar amount appears "stuck" at one value for long periods; in other words, prices are sticky. We could imagine a world where prices were sticky but not in dollar terms. For example, firms could set their prices relative to the price of some standard commodity. Instead of setting the price of a six-pack of Coke at $2.50, Coca-Cola bottlers could set the price at the level of six pounds of sugar. Someone buying a six-pack would have to find out how much a pound of sugar currently costs to know how much they would have to pay. Under the hypothetical sugar reference point for prices, there would be stickiness in the relative prices of goods compared with sugar, but not in their dollar prices. Sugar policy would be an important determinant of overall economic activity, whereas monetary policy would have little impact on output and employment. It is important for macroeconomists to explain why price stickiness takes the particular form of setting prices in dollars rather than in sugar or some other relative price.

Not every economy follows the price-setting conventions that are familiar in the United States. In countries with histories of extreme inflation, prices are sometimes set in terms other than those countries' monetary units. Macroeconomic analysis for these countries cannot make the same type of sticky-price assumptions that are appropriate for the United States. Other countries have found other alternatives to their own monetary units for quoting prices. One of the most common is to use the U.S. dollar. In countries where this "dollarization" has reached an advanced stage, domestic monetary policy has less impact and U.S. monetary policy is correspondingly more important.

In the United States and other countries that have avoided extreme inflation, prices are almost invariably set in terms of the country's own currency unit, not in commodity units or another country's currency unit. For this reason, the assumption that prices are sticky in terms of the nominal currency unit makes sense in the U.S. economy and similar economies.

Studies of nominal stickiness have found enormous variations in the length of time over which prices remain the same in nominal terms. Stickiness tends to be most extreme in cases where there are significant hardware costs for change in the price: Pay telephone calls cost a dime for decades before jumping to 25 cents. Magazine prices remain the same for several years then jump up by 25 cents.[4] A study by Dennis Carlton of the University of Chicago showed that businesses tend to keep the same price for a given customer for a year or more even when they have set new prices for new customers.[5]

Prices printed in catalogs, on price sheets, and on menus can be sticky simply because it is costly to print new versions with new prices. These **menu costs** are a possible contributor to overall price stickiness, although it is not known what fraction of total transactions occur under this type of pricing.[6]

Not every price is sticky. Many agricultural and industrial commodities trade in open markets where prices change every few seconds. In addition, many prices paid in transactions between businesses are linked to these open-market prices. Among businesses, and, to a lesser extent, between businesses and consumers, many prices are set on the spot by negotiations. There is no reason to expect stickiness of negotiated prices. However, if the retailer pays a sticky price at wholesale, stickiness is passed on at retail. Even though you negotiate a price for a car from a dealer, the result of that negotiation is sticky if the car manufacturer sets a dollar price in advance that the dealer pays at wholesale.

---

[4]Stephen G. Cechetti, "The Frequency of Price Adjustment," *Journal of Econometrics*, Vol. 20 (April 1986), pp. 255–274.

[5]Dennis Carlton, "The Rigidity of Prices," *American Economic Review*, Vol. 76 (September 1986), pp. 637–658.

[6]N. Gregory Mankiw, "Small Menu Costs and Large Business Cycles: A Macroeconomic Model of Monopoly," *Quarterly Journal of Economics*, Vol. 100 (May 1985), pp. 529–539.

Sticky Nominal Wages

In the next section, we show that an important reason why prices are sticky is that wages are sticky. But we first need to show why wages are sticky. One of the most important principles of macroeconomics, dating back to Keynes, is that *the wage bargain is made in money terms*. Wages are not set in pounds of sugar or foreign currency units. Even though the importance of the fact that wages are set in dollars has been evident to macroeconomists for over 50 years, the reasons for nominal wage stickiness are still imperfectly understood and controversial. Many economists feel that we should simply accept the fact that wages are predetermined in money terms and build it into our macro models. In the next section, we discuss more of the institutional detail about how wages are set in the U.S. labor market. All the details support the basic idea of nominal wage stickiness.

As we will see in the next section, many wage-setting institutions link wages at one firm to the general level of wages. But it is difficult to measure wages in general and complicated to update wages at one firm based on whatever measures are available. Keeping wages on a predetermined nominal track between occasional rebargaining seems to be a workable approximation of the goal of setting wages at one firm in line with wages elsewhere in the economy. And the reason we discussed earlier for the use of the currency unit rather than other units of purchasing power in the case of price setting applies equally to wage setting.

The Relation of Wage Stickiness to Price Stickiness

For a competitive firm, price equals marginal cost. For a firm with market power, price is a fixed markup over marginal cost where the market depends on the elasticity of demand. In either case, price moves directly with marginal cost. Marginal cost depends on the wage and the prices of inputs the firm buys. If the wage and input prices are sticky in nominal terms, then the firm's price is sticky in nominal terms as well. This conclusion holds even if the firm carefully sets its price and output at exactly the optimum. And this leads to an important conclusion: *Prices can be sticky in nominal terms because firms have limited incentives to set their prices at the exact optimum and they find it convenient to stay with existing prices. A second, independent cause of sticky nominal prices is that wages are sticky in nominal terms, and this makes prices sticky even if firms price at the exact optimum.*

Research has not succeeded in determining which source of nominal price stickiness is the more important. For pay telephone calls, magazines, and many other goods and services, straight price stickiness is probably the most important factor. For basic industrial goods sold by businesses to one another, price rigidity probably derives mainly from wage stickiness. And, of course, for some products (such as precious metals or commodities) price stickiness is not a significant factor at all.

Nominal Price and Wage Stickiness

1. In the United States and in other countries with relatively low inflation, prices tend to be sticky in terms of the domestic currency unit. In inflation-prone economies, prices are set in terms of some other unit that has stable purchasing power.

2. Nominal price stickiness can arise in a number of ways. Because of menu costs, firms may have little incentive to change their prices when conditions change. If wages are sticky in nominal terms, prices will be sticky because costs are sticky.

Wage Determination in the United States

Most workers in large labor unions change their contracts less often than every year. Contracts are unsynchronized; not all workers sign contracts at the same time. Wage negotiations are staggered over the contract cycle. At any one time, only a small fraction of the workers sign contracts; the remaining workers either have recently signed their contracts or will sign their contracts in the future. The period in which one contract is in force overlaps the period in which other contracts are in force.

What factors determine the size of the wage adjustment when it does occur? Wage and salary decisions are made in collective-bargaining meetings for which both management and labor leaders spend extensive time preparing. While the outcome of any one bargaining situation cannot be predicted with much certainty, a number of factors clearly influence the outcome in particular directions.

The first and perhaps most important is the state of the labor market. If unemployment is high, labor is in a relatively weak bargaining position. Conversely, if unemployment is low, workers can bargain for larger wage increases. The threat of a strike is more credible in good times than in bad. Moreover, firms are likely to settle for larger wage increases in tight market conditions, because they are better able to pass on their costs in the form of higher prices.

A second factor influencing wage bargaining is the wage paid to comparable workers in other industries. Because contract negotiations are not synchronized, there are two components of this comparison wage: the wage settlements of workers who have recently signed contracts and the expected wage settlements of workers who will sign their contracts in the near future. Looking back at the wage settlements in recently signed contracts makes sense in a current negotiation because those settlements will be in force during part of the contract period under consideration. This backward-looking behavior tends to give some built-in inertia to the wage-determination process. If one union group gets a big increase, then the next group of workers in the wage-determination cycle also tends to get a big increase. But looking forward to future settlements also makes sense, because the current contract will be in force when these changes take place. In other words, wage determination generally combines elements of forward-looking and back-ward-looking behavior.

A third factor that influences wage decisions is the expected rate of inflation. If inflation is expected to be high, workers ask for larger wage increases and management is willing to pay them because their own prices are expected to rise. As with the effect of comparable wage increases, the effect of expected inflation has both a backward-looking element and a forward-looking element.

It is very common for workers who are not in unions to receive wage and salary adjustments once each year. Although no formal contract is involved, it is unlikely that this wage decision will be changed before the next scheduled adjustment period. Hence, the nominal wage stickiness is very similar to that in the union contracts.

For example, our universities adjust our salaries once each year. We get a letter from the dean in July giving our salary for the 12-month period beginning September 1. This nominal wage rate is rarely changed before the next salary adjustment period the following year. This type of annual wage setting is common in many sectors of the economy.

In preparation for a wage adjustment, the management of nonunion firms must obtain information very similar to that obtained by the management of unionized firms preparing for a collective-bargaining meeting. A large nonunion firm usually has specialists, called *wage and salary administrators*, who must make a wage decision. They obtain information about the current labor-market situation. They conduct wage surveys or subscribe to a wage survey performed by an outside group. They also attempt to forecast the rate of inflation.

Although the wage decision usually is made under more competitive conditions than exist in a collective-bargaining situation, the same factors (the state of the labor market and wage and price inflation) influence the final outcome in similar directions. If unemployment is very low and expected to remain low for the next year, management will try to pay a relatively high wage compared with other firms employing similarly skilled workers. An attractive wage prevents workers from quitting and helps lure workers from other firms if necessary for expansion. On the other hand, if unemployment is high, there is less worry that workers will quit to look for jobs elsewhere. Moreover, if the year is expected to be bad for sales, an expansion of production requiring more workers is unlikely.

Although there is little direct evidence on when most nonunion firms have their scheduled wage increases, it is unlikely that they all occur at the same time. Hence, there is a type of nonsynchronization that we observe also for the union sector. Figure 15.3 illustrates the simple situation where there are four wage adjustment periods through the year: January 1, April 1, July 1, and October 1. It is clear from this illustration that staggered wage setting gives rise to overlapping wage decisions.

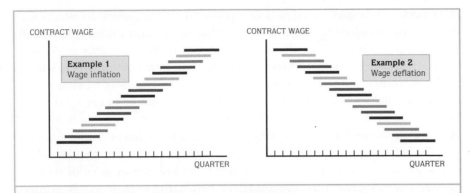

FIGURE 15.3 STAGGERED ANNUAL WAGE-SETTING WITH FOUR WAGE-ADJUSTMENT PERIODS THROUGHOUT THE YEAR

There are four groups of workers in each example. The contract wage of each worker group is denoted by a different color shade, from very dark to very light. Because all wages are not set at the same time (that is, they are not synchronized), the contract wage of one group overlaps that of all the other groups. This is shown in the diagram as flat contract wage lines on top or below each other. In the left panel, there is a general inflation: Each group attempts to get above the previous group. In the right panel, there is a general deflation: Each group tries to get below the previous group.

Why Are Wages Set for Long Periods with Few Contingencies?

We have just seen that workers generally have their wages predetermined in contracts. Only a fraction of these contracts are contingent on the cost of living and none, to our knowledge, is contingent on any other economic variable.

ADJUSTMENT COSTS The costs of adjusting wages and salaries may be high. Consider the situation where wage rates are determined in collective-bargaining negotiations between large corporations and labor unions. In preparation for these negotiations management spends months surveying wages in other industries, estimating changes in labor productivity, forecasting changes in the firm's own profits, and obtaining estimates of the general inflation during the upcoming contract period. To be adequately informed during the collective-bargaining sessions, labor leaders must be equally and independently prepared; hence, they must also spend months preparing for negotiations. Moreover, almost every collective-bargaining situation contains the threat of a strike. An actual strike obviously is costly for both sides, but the mere preparation for a possible strike is also costly. The firm must accumulate and finance additional inventories to be used if a strike occurs. Hence, production is abnormally high before negotiations and abnormally low after negotiations as firms draw down inventories when a strike does not occur. These swings in production raise average costs to the firm.

INDEXING   Why aren't contracts negotiated to be contingent on events that that may occur before the next renewal? While some contracts include cost-of-living adjustments, whereby the wage is indexed to the consumer price level, these clauses rarely involve 100 percent protection from cost-of-living changes, and most contracts have no such clauses. Moreover, cost-of-living clauses represent only one of many possible contingency clauses. For example, the contracts could be directly linked to the unemployment rate, GDP, or more local measures of the performance of the economy and the value of workers' time.

The primary reason why more contracts are not indexed to the cost of living is that such indexing can be harmful if there are import price or technology shocks. Suppose that the marginal productivity of labor is reduced because of a shift in the production function. Such a shift eventually requires a reduction of the real wage; that is, W/P must decline so that it is equal to the marginal productivity of labor. But a 100 percent indexed contract prevents such a decline. The escalator clause calls for an increase in W in the same proportion as the increase in P. Hence, W/P remains constant and too high. It is understandable that many firms and workers are reluctant to institute an arrangement that rules out any adjustments in the real wage if prices should rise suddenly during the contract period. Of course, if the reason for the increase in prices is a general monetary-induced inflation, then there is no need for a reduction in the real wage. Unfortunately, there is usually no way to tell in advance whether the price rise is due to monetary effects or shifts in the production process.

Why not index wages to unemployment, GDP, or other indexes that might indicate whether the shocks are to money or productivity? Part of an answer is similar to the reason we gave for caution in indexing to the cost of living. For instance, some of the shifts in overall unemployment are not relevant for the productivity of a particular group of workers. When a special event, not a recession, makes unemployment zoom for autoworkers, the unemployment rate may not reveal much about the jobs available to computer workers.

A final reason why contracts have few indexing clauses is that they add complexity. There are good reasons to have a straightforward contract that the rank and file can easily understand and vote on. Similarly, contingency clauses appear to add uncertainty about the wage that the workers actually get. Many workers would object to this added uncertainty, even though the economic theorist might argue that the uncertainty would make the worker better off.

Why Is Wage Setting Staggered?

In a decentralized economy like that of the United States, firms and workers decide by themselves when their wages and salaries are adjusted. The fact that these decisions are not synchronized therefore seems natural; one would be surprised to see a coordinated wage (or price) adjustment without some centralized orchestration of such a move. Historical accident would be enough to explain why the autoworkers always negotiate just before the machinists.

Imagine what would happen if all wages and prices were set *at the same time* and without a central planner to tell workers and firms what to do. A firm which thought that a relative wage increase was appropriate for its workers would not know what other wages were; hence, it could not achieve that relative increase.

Staggered wage setting provides information to firms and workers about wages and prices elsewhere. Even though other wages will be adjusted before the current contract expires, there is a period of time when the desired relative wage is in force. Nonsynchronized wage and price setting thus seems desirable in a decentralized economy.[7]

Moreover, staggered wage setting adds some stability to wages. Without staggering, all wages and prices would be up for grabs each period; there would be no base for setting each wage. Tremendous variability would be introduced into the price system.

Wage Contracts

1. Workers typically have wage adjustments infrequently, about once per year or less often. These adjustments are staggered over time. Since the wage is rarely changed within the year, this wage-setting process creates wage stickiness.

2. Wages are set for long periods because collective bargaining, threats of strikes, or simply careful reviews of worker performance make adjusting the wage costly. Wages are rarely indexed in the United States because supply shocks as well as demand shocks occur. With indexing, the real wage does not adjust enough after supply shocks. Moreover, extensive contingency clauses add complexity and apparent uncertainty to wage contracts.

15.3 | A MODEL WITH STAGGERED WAGE SETTING

In this section, we present a simple stylized model of staggered wage setting to illustrate the ideas about wage and price stickiness discussed in the previous section. In the model, wage setting is nonsynchronized, prices are given by a markup over costs, and expectations are rational.

---

[7]See Gary Fethke and Andrew Policano, "Will Wage Setters Ever Stagger Decisions?" *Quarterly Journal of Economics,* Vol. 101 (November 1986), for further discussion of the rationale for nonsynchronized wage setting.

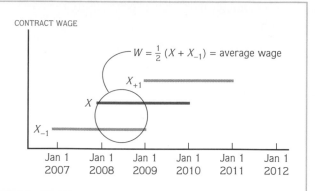

CONTRACT WAGE

$W = \frac{1}{2}(X + X_{-1})$ = average wage

FIGURE 15.4   CONFIGURATION OF WAGE SETTING IN THE SIMPLE MODEL

There are two groups of workers in the economy. One group has a wage adjustment January 1 of the even years and the other group has a wage adjustment January 1 of the odd years. The average wage W is shown to be equal to the average of this period's contract wage X and last period's contract wage X_{-1}. In the figure, the average wage for 2008 is shown. It is the average of the contract wage set in 2007 and the contract wage set in 2008.

Suppose that all wage contracts last two years, all wage adjustments occur at the beginning of each year, and there is no indexing. Half the workers sign contracts at the start of even-numbered years and half at the start of odd-numbered years. This configuration of assumptions is shown in Figure 15.4, where X represents the contract wage and W the average wage. Since we need to distinguish between past and future variables, we let the subscript -1 represent the *previous* year and the subscript $+1$ represent the *next* year. Of course, events in the next year are not known; people must form expectations of them. The average wage is given by

$$W = \frac{1}{2}(X + X_{-1}). \qquad (15.9)$$

In words, the wage W *this year* is the simple average of the contract wage signed *last year* X_{-1}, which is still outstanding, and the contract wage signed *this year* X. For example, suppose that the contract wage is 10 in 2007 and 8 in 2008. Then the average wage is 9 in 2008.

An algebraic relationship that describes how the contract wage is set each period might be given by

$$X = \underbrace{\frac{1}{2}(W + W_{+1})}_{\substack{\text{Effect of} \\ \text{expected} \\ \text{average wage}}} - \underbrace{\frac{d}{2}[(U - U^*) + (U_{+1} - U^*)]}_{\substack{\text{Effect of} \\ \text{current and} \\ \text{future unemployment}}}, \qquad (15.10)$$

where U is the unemployment rate, U^* is the natural rate of unemployment, and d is a coefficient describing the response of wages to unemployment.

Equation 15.10 leads to an interesting observation. Rewrite Equation 15.10 with W and W_{+1} replaced by the expressions in Equation 15.9. That is,

$$X = \frac{1}{2}\left[\underbrace{\frac{1}{2}(X + X_{-1})}_{\substack{W \text{ from} \\ \text{Equation 15.9}}} + \underbrace{\frac{1}{2}(X_{+1} + X)}_{\substack{W_{+1} \text{ from} \\ \text{Equation 15.10}}}\right] - \frac{d}{2}[(U - U^*) + (U_{+1} - U^*)]. \quad (15.11)$$

Now gather together the X terms (without the subscripts) and put them on the left-hand side of the equation. After some cancellation, we get the simpler expression:

$$X = \frac{1}{2}\underbrace{(X_{-1}}_{\substack{\text{Backward-}\\\text{looking}\\\text{component}}} + \underbrace{X_{+1})}_{\substack{\text{Forward-}\\\text{looking}\\\text{component}}} - d[(U - U^*) + \underbrace{(U_{+1} - U^*)]}_{\substack{\text{Expected future}\\\text{unemployment}\\\text{is also a factor}}}. \qquad (15.12)$$

Equation 15.12 shows how wage determination has a backward-looking component X_{-1} and a forward-looking component X_{+1}. The backward-looking component is what makes inflation persist from year to year. Workers base their wage decisions partly on what previous wage decisions were. The forward-looking component, also discussed previously in words, is what makes expectations of the future so important. Expectations of moderate wage settlements next year tend to moderate wage settlements this year. For example, if wage settlements next year are expected to be 10 percent lower, then, according to Equation 15.12, actual settlements this year are 5 percent lower. The coefficient on X_{+1} is 1/2.

Equation 15.12 also shows how expected future unemployment conditions next year can affect wage settlements this year. If the unemployment rate is expected to rise next year by 2 percent, then wage settlements this year are 2 times d percent lower. For example, if d equals 0.5, then wage settlements this year will be 1 percent lower. The expectation of a slump in the future with its accompanying increase in unemployment has a simple effect: It decreases wage inflation today.

With prices given by a constant markup over costs, all these effects on wages are passed through to prices. The policy implications are therefore clear. Expectations of a monetary policy that is noninflationary in the future and lets unemployment rise if necessary, should inflation rise, has favorable effects on inflation today. These favorable effects on inflation can actually work with little or no adverse effects on unemployment. The expectation of a credible stance against inflation in the future should therefore have a favorable effect on the trade-off between inflation and unemployment.

Consider, finally, the operations of the model in a steady inflation. Say the contract wage X increases by the same amount each year. For example, let the amount of increase be 10. In a steady inflation the *change* in the contract wage this year, $X - X_{-1}$, and the change in the contract wage next year, $X_{+1} - X$, is the same, namely, 10. Equation 15.12 can then be written as

$$\underbrace{\frac{1}{2}(X - X_{-1})}_{5} = \underbrace{\frac{1}{2}(X_{+1} - X)}_{5} - \underbrace{d[(U - U^*) + (U_{+1} - U^*)]}_{0} \qquad (15.13)$$

Note that there is $10/2 = 5$ on the left-hand side and $10/2 = 5$ on the right-hand side. The two cancel out. The term involving unemployment must equal zero. This implies that $U = U^*$ and $U_{+1} = U^*$. In other words, the unemployment rate is always equal to the natural rate. The same result holds, of course, for any steady change in prices, not just 10. Regardless of the rate of inflation, as long as it is steady and anticipated, there is no trade-off between inflation and unemployment in the long run.

The simple model consisting of Equations 15.9, 15.10, and 15.11 can be viewed as an alternative, more-microeconomic-based representation of the price adjustment equation that we introduced in Chapter 9, Equation 9.2. As such, it can be combined with a model of aggregate demand that tells how the money supply and government spending shift demand when prices are predetermined. Simulating such a model requires a large computer and sophisticated computer programs. Fortunately, most of the results can be conveyed in a more intuitive and less complex way by introducing some simple approximations to capture the essence of forward-looking and rational expectations behavior. We turn to this in the next section.

Staggered Wage Contracts

1. Wage determination has backward-looking and forward-looking elements when contract negotiations are staggered over time.

2. The backward-looking component reflects the influence of last year's contracts on this year's prices. This influence of the past on the present gives inflation persistence.

3. The forward-looking component reflects the impact of next year's contracts on this year's prices. This influence of the future on the present makes expectations about policy important. The more accommodative policy has been to price shocks in the past, the more inflation may be expected in the future.

15.4 | PRICE ADJUSTMENT

MACROSOLVE
EXERCISE

Our basic theory of price adjustment indicates that inflation rises when demand conditions are tight, when expectations of inflation rise, or when there are price shocks. A simple algebraic summary of this theory can be written as follows:

$$\pi = \underbrace{f\hat{Y}_{-1}}_{\substack{\text{Market} \\ \text{conditions} \\ \text{(slack or} \\ \text{tight)}}} + \underbrace{\pi^e}_{\substack{\text{Expecta-} \\ \text{tions of} \\ \text{inflation}}} + \underbrace{Z.}_{\substack{\text{Price} \\ \text{shocks}}} \qquad (15.14)$$

Here $\hat{Y}_{-1} = (Y_{-1} - Y^*)/Y^*$, the percentage deviation of real GDP from potential GDP. The subscript -1 indicates that current inflation is related to market pressure in the previous period, reflecting the lags in price and wage adjustment. The last term, Z, representing price shocks, describes the upward or downward effect of a change in world oil prices or other factors that affect inflation through channels other than market conditions or expectations. In most years, Z is close to zero, but occasionally sharp movements in oil, grain, or other markets create noticeable shocks in the process of inflation.

One of the most important properties of Equation 15.14 is that there is no long-run trade-off between inflation and the level of GDP. A country with a high average inflation rate has no higher output than a country with a low inflation rate that is generally expected to continue. That there is no trade-off follows from Equation 15.14: On average, the effect of price shocks are zero ($Z = 0$), and expected inflation π^e equals actual inflation π in the long run regardless of the level of actual inflation. Hence, according to Equation 15.14, the market conditions term $\hat{Y}_{-1}$ equals zero, or, equivalently, actual output equals potential output. The proposition that there is no long-run trade-off between output and inflation is sometimes called the **natural-rate property**, because the unemployment rate equals the natural rate regardless of the rate of inflation; it is also sometimes called the **accelerationist property** because attempts to keep output above normal result in accelerating prices.

The theories of price rigidity discussed in this chapter indicate that there are several alternative interpretations of Equation 15.14. For example, both the imperfect information theory (Section 15.1) and the staggered-wage-setting model (Section 15.3) can explain the positive relationship between the rate of change in prices and real GDP in Equation 15.14. This equation is an approximation that explains the basic facts of inflation and is consistent with these theories; but in using it for policy, we must be careful how we interpret the coefficients. In particular, the sensitivity of inflation to recent market conditions (f) is likely to change when the economic environment changes. Here, we consider three important examples of changes in the economic environment: an increase in the amount of indexing, a reduction in the average size and length of business cycles, and changes in the average rate of inflation.

The Effect of Wage Indexing

As we saw in Section 15.2, there is little indexing in the United States of labor contracts (cost-of-living adjustment provisions). Indexing is more prevalent in countries with high inflation, such as Colombia. With indexing, each time the price level rises by 1 percent, wages rise by a fraction of a percent a, automatically. The indexing coefficient is greater than zero and can be as high as 1. How would indexing affect the price adjustment relationship? Indexing means that the wage responds to the current rate of inflation as well as to the lagged rate of inflation. The effect of this is to speed up the overall response f of inflation to changes in unemployment. To see this, suppose there is an increase in output that initially increases wage inflation by 1 percent. This quickly has an upward influence of 1 percent on prices. But, if wages are indexed, the upward adjustment of price inflation means a further upward adjustment of wage inflation of the amount a. This in turn increases price inflation by a, through the markup process. Again indexing raises wage inflation, now by an amount a times a, or a^2. And the process continues for a third round, where inflation increases by another multiple of a (a^3). The whole process is called a **wage-price spiral.** As long as indexing is less than 100 percent (that is, as long as $a < 1$), the process eventually settles down, but the result has been to make wages adjust more to the increase in output than if there had not been any indexing. The total effect is

$$1 + a + a^2 + a^3 + \cdots = \frac{1}{1 - a}$$

using the formula for the geometric series. Note that the total effect is much like the formula for the multiplier. For example, if a equals 0.5, then the effect of market conditions on inflation is doubled: $1/(1 - 0.5) = 2$. In general, indexing makes inflation more responsive to market conditions, as represented by a higher value for the coefficient f in Equation 15.14.

For the same reasons, indexing also increases the response of inflation to price shocks Z. When the cost of materials rises, firms increase their prices. But because of indexing, this price increase raises wages. In turn, the increase in wages increases prices again. The wage-price spiral thus multiplies the effect of a raw materials price on inflation. If there is no indexing, so that the wage does not respond at all to prices, other costs go directly into prices with a coefficient of 1. But, because wages rise when prices rise, there is a feedback effect—the wage-price spiral. The feedback effect can more than double the impact of a price shock.

Length and Severity of Business Cycles

In Section 15.2, we looked at the implications of forward-looking behavior: Workers and firms look ahead to future labor market conditions and price and wage inflation. If workers expect a recession to be short, then they are more reluctant to accept lower wages than if they expect the recession to last for a number of years. In the price adjustment equation, the market conditions term $\hat{Y}_{-1}$ represents not only current conditions but also future excess supply or demand. Usually business cycles last for a number of years, so if output is below potential this year, that is an indication that output will probably be below normal for a few more years.

But suppose departures of output from potential become less persistent; for example, suppose that the average length of business cycles is reduced from four to two years. Then, if GDP is below potential today, there is no implication that GDP will be below potential two years from now. The best guess is that GDP will be back to potential two years from now. As a result, inflation is less responsive to recessions. Algebraically, the coefficient f in Equation 15.14 is smaller when recessions are expected to be less prolonged.

Models of the Expected Inflation Term

One of the most difficult issues in the price adjustment equation is how to determine the measure of expected inflation π^e. There are two important factors to consider.

1. **Forward-looking forecasts.** The expectation that prices and other wages will rise in the future influences the process of wage setting between the worker and the employer and the wage that emerges from it. The amount of inflation forecast to occur in the future is therefore part of the expected inflation term. If workers and unions are informed about the economy, these forward-looking forecasts match the rational expectations theory.

2. **Staggered contracts and backward-looking wage behavior.** The influence of today's expectations on the expected inflation term is only part of the story, however. Because of wage contracts and staggered wage setting, the expectations term involves inertia that cannot be changed overnight. Workers and firms take account of the wages that will be paid to other workers in the economy. Since wage setting is staggered over time, some wages are set by looking back at the previous wage decisions of other workers; once these wages are set, they are not changed during the contract period unless economic conditions change drastically. Wage inflation has a momentum due to contracts and relative wage setting. The expectations term must take account of this momentum as well as of the pure expectational influence.

Our description of expected inflation must be consistent with the actual behavior of inflation as observed over a number of years. If inflation typically tends to have momentum, then the public's model of expected inflation also has momentum. But, if inflation tends to be temporary, because of a policy to stabilize prices, for example, then people's view of expected inflation incorporates the belief that a burst of inflation will probably not be followed by continued inflation.

For these reasons, any model of expected inflation is itself endogenous to the type of economy or type of policy in operation. If policy changes, the model of expected inflation should change.[8] For example, if the Fed announces that it is switching to a new policy that puts more weight on controlling inflation and the public believes it, the model of expected inflation changes. If, on the other hand, people are highly skeptical about promised changes in government programs, then it may take an actual change in inflation to convince them that expected inflation has changed. In that case, a simple backward-looking model of

---

[8]Robert Lucas made this point forcefully in his critique of macroeconomic models as they existed in the early 1970s. He pointed out that these models failed to consider that rational individuals change their behavior when policy rules change. Fixed models of expected inflation in the Phillips curves were a particular target of his criticism. See Robert Lucas, "Econometric Policy Evaluation: A Critique," in Karl Brunner and Allan Meltzer, eds., *The Phillips Curve and Labor Markets*, Carnegie-Rochester Conference Series on Public Policy, Vol. 1 (Amsterdam: North-Holland, 1976), pp. 19–46.

the expected inflation term is closer to the truth—at least for the period of time that it takes the government to convince people that it means business.

The simplest model says that this year's expected inflation depends on actual inflation last year:

$$\pi^e = \pi_{-1}. \qquad (15.15)$$

This description of expected inflation is not satisfactory in all situations. Suppose monetary policy tried to keep GDP above potential GDP ($Y > Y^*$) year after year. Because of the lag in forming expected inflation, it appears that this policy would be feasible, although it would mean that inflation would rise each year. In reality, a policy that increased inflation each year would not keep output above potential indefinitely. Eventually, the public would catch on and build the steady increase in inflation into its expectations of inflation. Then, actual and expected inflation would be equal, and from Equation 15.14, output would be at potential, not above.

We could look at more complicated models of expected inflation that try to keep up with the rate of change of inflation as well as its level, but the main ideas should already be clear. There is a very general point at work here: *No mechanical model of expected inflation is universally applicable.* If the public has a particular way of arriving at expected inflation, the government can design a policy that fools the public and makes actual inflation continually exceed expected inflation. But then, the public will revise its method of calculating expected inflation so that it will no longer be fooled.

If the government uses a policy that does not attempt to fool the public by making actual inflation exceed expected inflation, then there can be a stable way that the public arrives at expected inflation. In particular, if the government aims at a steady inflation rate and acts to offset occasional bursts of inflation from materials prices and elsewhere, then our simple model of expected inflation is a reasonable description of the process.

A policy that attempts to keep output above normal permanently will fail. Eventually the public will catch on to the policy and revise expected inflation by a method that makes it keep up with actual inflation.

REVIEW AND PRACTICE

Major Points

1. The imperfect information model assumes that people are unaware of the nature of changes in demand, which may represent relative price increases or pure inflation. If some probability is attached to each possibility, firms alter supply when the price level changes.

2. In the imperfect information model, unobserved changes in the money supply can affect real output. If workers can rationally anticipate the behavior of the Fed and thus the money supply, then money has no effect on output. This is known as the *policy ineffectiveness theorem*.

3. The situation in which prices are infrequently adjusted is known as *nominal price stickiness*.

4. Sticky prices may result from sticky wages. Much empirical evidence suggests that price-cost margins are quite stable over time.

5. Workers typically have their wages adjusted about once each year. The size of the wage adjustment is influenced by expectations of inflation, expectations of the wages paid to other workers, and the level of unemployment.

6. Wage setting is staggered. Not all workers obtain wage adjustments at the same time. This staggering adds to the inertia of wage movements.

7. A specific model of wage adjustment with overlapping contracts confirms that an unvarying unemployment rate is consistent with any chronic rate of inflation.

8. A model of price adjustment must incorporate the response of inflation to excess demand and to expected inflation.

9. Expected inflation has forward-looking features and backward-looking features. Expectations and contracts are both part of the micro underpinnings of the expected inflation term.

10. No simple mechanical formula is satisfactory as a model of expected inflation. Any such model would be inconsistent with actual inflation behavior if policy or the economic environment changed.

11. In the long run, unemployment equals the natural rate regardless of how high inflation is, as long as inflation is steady; this proposition is called the *natural-rate property* or the *accelerationist property*.

Key Terms and Concepts

price rigidity   natural-rate property
Lucas supply curve   accelerationist property
policy ineffectiveness theorem   wage-price spiral
menu costs

Questions for Discussion and Review

1. Which assumption of the imperfect information model is essential to generate a Lucas supply curve?

2. Suppose the money supply evolves according to a policy rule that is known by all firms and households. Would you expect movements in the money supply to have any correlation with output?

3. What factors contribute to price rigidity?

4. What is staggered wage setting? Why does it occur?

5. Describe the typical wage adjustment for workers. Are these wage-setting dates staggered? Why aren't wages adjusted more frequently?

6. Is monetary policy effective when expectations are rational? Why? Do any wages adjust when expectations of future monetary policy change?

7. What are the forward-looking and the backward-looking components of wage determination? What is their significance?

8. Why is there no long-run trade-off between inflation and unemployment, even though there is a short-run trade-off?

9. What three elements are included in the price adjustment equation?

10. How is expected inflation related to forward-looking behavior? To staggered wage setting?

Problems

NUMERICAL

1. Suppose that the Lucas supply curve is

$$Y = nh(1 - b)(P - \hat{P}) + Y^*,$$

with $nh(1 - b) = 20{,}000$ and $Y^* = 4{,}000$ (billions of dollars). For example, when the price level P is 1.01 and the expected price $\hat{P}$ is 1.0, output Y is 4,200, or 5 percent above the potential output $Y^* = 4{,}000$. Suppose that the aggregate demand curve is

$$Y = 1{,}101 + 1.288G + 3.221M/P.$$

a. Suppose that the economy has been at rest for some period with output at potential and no changes in policy are expected for the near future. The money supply M is 600 and government spending G is 750. What is the price level? (Hint: If there are no surprises, actual and expected price levels will be the same.)

b. Now suppose that the Fed announces that it will increase the money supply from 600 to 620. What are the new levels of output and price level?

c. Now suppose that the Fed announces that it will increase the money supply from 600 to 620 but actually increases it to 670. What are the new levels of output and price level?

2. Suppose that automatic stabilizers cause government purchases to rise when GDP is below potential and fall when GDP is above potential. Algebraically, we might represent this as

$$G = 750 - g(Y - Y^*),$$

where potential output Y^* is 4,000. The coefficient g measures the strength of the automatic stabilizer.

a. Substitute this expression for G in the aggregate demand function in problem 1 and solve for output Y in terms of P (M is held fixed at 600). This is the aggregate demand curve incorporating the automatic stabilizer. Describe how the slope of the aggregate demand curve depends on the coefficient g.

b. For three different values of g (0, 0.01, and 0.1) describe the effect on output of an unanticipated increase in money like the one in problem 1c. Assume that people know the value of g in each case. Do the effects on output depend on the value of the coefficient g? If they do, then does it appear that even well-understood automatic stabilizers are effective in that they influence output? Explain your results intuitively. Why might automatic government-spending stabilizers affect output while anticipated changes in money do not? (See B. T. McCallum and J. K. Whitaker, "The Effectiveness of Fiscal Feedback Rules and Automatic Stabilizers under Rational Expectations," *Journal of Monetary Economics*, Vol. 5 [1979], pp. 171–186, for a further discussion of this type of policy problem.)

3. Using a tight monetary policy, the Fed is able to bring about a deceleration of prices, so that inflation falls from 10 percent to zero. The time path of the price level is as follows:

YEAR	PRICE LEVEL
1	1.000
2	1.100
3	1.188
4	1.259
5	1.310
6 and later	1.336

There are two groups of workers, those whose wages are set in odd years and those whose wages are set in even years. When the wage is set, it equals 10 times the price level in the preceding year, raised by the amount of inflation that occurred in that year relative to the year before; that is, $W = 10P_{-1}(1 + \pi_{-1})$ and $\pi = (P - P_{-1})/P_{-1}$. In the second year of the contract, the wage is increased in proportion to the inflation that occurred in the first year relative to the year before; that is, $W_{+1} = W(1 + \pi)$. Compute the wages paid to the two groups and the average wage across the two groups starting in year 2. Compute the rate of wage inflation and the real wage. Comment on the problems that disinflation creates when there are lags in wage setting, using the numbers from this example.

4. Suppose our model of the economy is given by

$$Y = k_0 + k_1(M/P) \qquad \text{(Aggregate demand)}$$
$$Y = h \ (P - P^e) + Y^* \qquad \text{(Lucas supply)}$$

Assume further that workers have complete information about the model of the economy, including the value of the money supply. Potential output is equal to 4,000. The aggregate demand curve goes through the point (4,000, 1.5).

a. Consider three possible Lucas supply curves going through the points (4,000, 1), (4,000, 1.5), and (4,000, 2). What is the value of P^e for each curve?

b. Which of the three curves in part a is the rational expectations Lucas supply curve? In what sense would the other two curves not satisfy rational expectations?

ANALYTICAL

1. If the Lucas supply curve is written with output on the right and price surprises on the left, it looks like a Phillips curve. Explain what happens to this Phillips curve when (i) price changes are due mostly to changes in the local conditions and relative prices, and (ii) when price changes are due mostly to changes in the supply of money.

2. Discuss the relationship between Lucas's imperfect information model and the overlapping contracts model in terms of correlation between output and the price level.

3. In what way does an economy in which prices are determined by the condition that marginal revenue equals marginal cost respond differently to an aggregate demand shock than an economy in which prices are set as a markup over cost? Does it matter how wages are set in the latter case? How does each type of economy respond to a price shock?

4. Suppose that wage contracts last for three years. Each year, one-third of the economy's wage contracts are renegotiated. Contract wages are set according to

$$X = \frac{1}{3}(W + W_{+1} + W_{+2}) - \frac{d}{3}[(U - U^*) + (U_{+1} - U^*) + (U_{+2} - U^*)]$$

a. Provide an expression for the average wage rate W.

b. Derive an expression analogous to Equation 15.12. How far backward and forward looking is the wage-determination process? What determines the responsiveness of contract wages to *current* labor market conditions?

5. "If expectations are rational, monetary policy has no effect on output." Is this statement true or false? Explain your answer calling on both models with the Lucas supply function and models with wage contracts and sticky prices.

6. On a graph (3–4 inches square) sketch an aggregate demand curve and a Lucas supply curve. Label their intersection point as Y^* and P^*. Now draw two aggregate demand curves, each one $\frac{1}{4}$ inch to either side of your initial curve. Label the intersection points with the Lucas supply curve $Y+$, $P+$ and $Y-$, $P-$. Finally, draw two more aggregate demand curves, $\frac{3}{4}$ inch or so to either side of the original curve, and label the intersection points as Ys and Ps with $++$ and $--$.

a. What kinds of shocks can cause the aggregate demand curve to vary in the way shown on your graph? What is the relationship between the magnitude of those shocks and the variability in Y and P?

b. Suppose initially that shocks to the money supply cause the aggregate demand curve to vary within the narrow region. Assume that the Lucas supply curve shown in your graph is the appropriate curve given the magnitude of these shocks. In what sense is the curve "appropriate"?

c. Now suppose that shocks to the money supply cause the aggregate demand curve to vary within the wider region. How will the new Lucas supply curve appropriate to these shocks compare with your initial Lucas supply curve? Sketch the new curve. How do the swings in output and price level compare with $P--$, $P++$ and $Y--$, $Y++$?

d. Use these results to explain why output may not deviate much from potential in periods of either highly stable or highly variable prices but may deviate considerably from potential in the transition period from stable to variable prices. Relate your analysis to the experience of the U.S. economy in the late 1960s.

MACROECONOMIC POLICY

PART five

THE
MACROECONOMIC
POLICY MODEL

CHAPTER **16**

When we derived the economic fluctuations model, we assumed that the money supply was an exogenous variable. While this is useful for understanding the short- and long-run effects of one-time changes in government purchases and the money supply, it is not a good way to think about macroeconomic policy making. When the Fed and other central banks make monetary policy decisions, it is in response to the various shocks and disturbances that hit the economy, not in a one-shot vacuum. While we studied how monetary policy can respond to aggregate demand and price shocks in Chapter 9, we need to go further to understand the workings of macroeconomic policy.

Thinking about policy responses to shocks and disturbances naturally leads to thinking about monetary policy rules, the systematic response of monetary

437

policy to economic events. We focus on a particular policy rule that accurately describes the behavior of the Fed since the mid-1980s. We use this policy rule in conjunction with the IS curve and price adjustment line to construct the macroeconomic policy model, then use the model to analyze macroeconomic policy and events in the United States. In Chapter 17, we study the normative implications of the model, and in Chapter 18, we use the same model to extend the analysis to the world economy.

16.1 | MONETARY POLICY RULES

A **monetary policy rule** describes a systematic response of monetary policy to events in the economy. Many different monetary policy rules have been proposed and adopted around the world. Even if, as in the United States, policy makers do not determine policy according to a mechanical formula, they do respond to economic events. Their behavior and its impact on the economy are more accurately described by a systematic behavioral relationship than purely by discretion. If so, we can think of the behavioral relationship as a policy rule.

As we discussed in Chapter 14, monetary policy rules can be specified in two ways. The central bank can set either the growth rate of the money supply or the short-term nominal interest rate. Since almost all central banks, including the Fed, now conduct monetary policy by setting the short-term nominal interest rate, we focus on those types of rules.

The Fed does not actually set the short-term nominal interest rate. To be precise, the FOMC sets a target level of a very short-term (overnight) nominal interest rate, the federal funds rate, and then keeps the federal funds rate close to its target by increasing or decreasing the money supply through open-market operations. Since, except in unusual circumstances, the actual federal funds rate deviates little from its target level, we use the shorthand of saying that the Fed "sets" the interest rate.

Reacting to Events in the Economy

Recall from Chapter 14 that the Fed's ultimate goal is to keep inflation low and stable and the fluctuations of real GDP small. Like many other central banks, we can think of the Fed as having a **target inflation rate,** a level of inflation it would like to see on average over the long term. Let π be the inflation rate and let π^* be the target inflation rate. Then, if the central bank is successful in its inflation goals, the actual inflation rate π will fluctuate around the target π^*, with the fluctuations as small as possible. The idea of an inflation target has become increasingly accepted among central bankers. In fact, some central banks are very explicit about their target inflation rate. For instance, the European Central Bank, the ECB, sets money growth with a 2 percent target inflation rate. The Reserve Bank of New Zealand seeks a range of 0 to 2 percent inflation, with an implicit target inflation rate of 1 percent. The Bank of England also has an explicit inflation target. The Fed is less explicit about a target inflation rate, but it has emphasized the importance of a low inflation rate like other central banks.

Central banks are also concerned with the fluctuations of real GDP and unemployment. Most central bankers recognize that monetary policy has no impact on the level of real GDP or unemployment in the long run; in other words, they recognize that potential GDP (Y^*) and the natural unemployment rate (U^*) do not depend on monetary policy. But they know that monetary policy affects real GDP and unemployment in the short run. Therefore, central banks try to keep business cycle fluctuations small; in other words, they endeavor to keep the gap between real GDP and potential GDP as small as possible. To derive the implications of these endeavors for monetary policy, let $\hat{Y} = $ 100 times $(Y - Y^*)/Y^*$, or simply the percentage deviation of real GDP from potential GDP. Then, central bankers try to keep $\hat{Y}$ as close to zero as possible; alternatively stated, they try to keep the fluctuations in $\hat{Y}$ small.

How do the Fed and other central banks set the interest rate to achieve their long-run inflation and output-stability goals? A convenient way to describe the actions of a central bank is through a **monetary policy rule,** or reaction function. A monetary policy rule is simply a function that describes how the Fed, or any other central bank, sets the interest rate in response to variables in the economy. Just as a consumption function describes how aggregate consumption reacts to economic variables, such as income or wealth, a policy rule describes how the interest rate reacts to economic variables, such as real GDP or inflation. The consumption function describes the behavior of consumers, while the monetary policy rule describes the behavior of Fed policy makers. Both a consumption function and a policy rule are approximations of actual behavior. The idea of describing the behavior of central bank policy makers through a policy rule is now common among macroeconomists.

The Taylor Rule

The best known description of a monetary policy rule for the United States and other countries is called the **Taylor rule.**[1] The Taylor rule states that the central bank raises the nominal interest rate r when real GDP is greater than potential GDP, or the GDP gap $\hat{Y}$ is positive, and when inflation is greater than the target inflation rate. The Taylor rule is given by the equation

$$r = \pi + \beta\hat{Y} + \delta(\pi - \pi^*) + R^* \qquad (16.1)$$

where r is the short-term nominal interest rate set by the Fed (the federal funds rate). Both coefficients β and δ are greater than zero and indicate how much the central bank changes its setting for the interest rate r when real GDP or inflation changes. The variables $\hat{Y}$ and π have been previously defined as the percentage

[1]John B. Taylor, "Discretion versus Policy Rules in Practice," Carnegie-Rochester Conference Series on Public Policy, Vol. 39 (December 1993), pp. 195–214.

deviation of real GDP from potential GDP and the rate of inflation, respectively. Finally, π^* is the Fed's target inflation rate and R^* is the **equilibrium real interest rate,** the real interest rate when the economy is at full employment.

Suppose the economy is at its long-run equilibrium, so that real GDP is equal to potential GDP, or the GDP gap $\hat{Y}$ is zero, and the real interest rate R is equal to the equilibrium real interest rate R^*. If, in addition, the inflation rate π is equal to the target inflation rate π^*, Equation 16.1 says that the nominal interest rate r equals the real interest rate R plus the *actual* rate of inflation π. Since the nominal interest rate is defined to equal the real interest rate plus the *expected* rate of inflation, the Fed's target inflation rate determines inflation expectations at the long-run equilibrium.

An important attribute of the Taylor rule is that it is *stabilizing*. When real GDP is greater than potential GDP or when inflation is greater than the target inflation rate, following the Taylor rule smooths out fluctuations. To see this, you need to think about the difference between nominal and real interest rates. This is easier to see by rearranging Equation 16.1:

$$r = (1 + \delta)\pi + B\hat{Y} + R^* - \delta\pi^*. \qquad (16.2)$$

When inflation rises above the target inflation rate, the Fed raises the nominal interest rate by more than inflation rises. This raises the real interest rate, decreasing investment and net exports. This in turn lowers real GDP, causing inflation to fall. When real GDP is greater than potential GDP, the Fed raises the nominal interest rate. Since expected inflation has not changed, this also raises the real interest rate, lowering investment and net exports and causing real GDP to fall toward potential GDP.

The importance of raising the nominal interest rate more than one-for-one with the inflation rate, so that the real interest rate rises when inflation increases, is known as the **Taylor principle.** Because the nominal interest rate in the Taylor rule responds to both the inflation rate (one-for-one) and the difference between the inflation rate and the target inflation rate, the combined response is more than one for one and the Taylor rule automatically obeys the Taylor principle. In general, a monetary policy rule is stabilizing only if it obeys the Taylor principle. Otherwise, the real interest rate does not increase when inflation rises.

What is the rationale for the Taylor rule? One interpretation comes from the rule itself. The Fed is concerned with keeping inflation close to target and keeping output and unemployment fluctuations small, and the Taylor rule helps accomplish both objectives. Another interpretation comes from thinking about the Taylor rule in conjunction with price adjustment. Suppose that inflation is on target but the GDP gap is positive. According to the price adjustment equation, when the GDP gap is positive, inflation will rise in the future. The Fed knows this and so, even though inflation is now on target, it takes steps to prevent inflation from rising above target in the future. Under this interpretation, the Taylor rule is an example of inflation targeting, but one that targets both current and expected future inflation. A third interpretation combines elements of the first two. Again suppose that inflation is on target. When the GDP gap is negative, unemployment is high and the Fed lowers the real interest rate to stimulate the economy. When the GDP gap is positive, the Fed is concerned primarily with future inflation and raises the real interest rate to slow down the economy.

The Taylor rule when real GDP equals potential GDP is depicted in Figure 16.1. The nominal interest rate is on the vertical axis and the inflation rate is on the horizontal axis. The slope of the Taylor rule is steeper than 1 because, as discussed, it is necessary for the Fed to increase the nominal interest rate more than point for point when inflation rises above its target. The flatter dashed line shows the relationship between the nominal interest rate and the inflation rate corresponding to a given real interest rate. The real interest rate is assumed to be 2 percent for the dashed line.

An equilibrium occurs where the dashed and solid lines in Figure 16.1 intersect. At the intersection point A, the real interest rate is equal to its long-run equilibrium value of 2 percent and the Fed is following the Taylor rule. The inflation rate is also on target at 2 percent.

While the exchange rate does not appear in the Taylor rule, this does not mean that the Taylor rule should be thought of in the context of a closed economy. Changes in the exchange rate affect the interest rate implied by the Taylor rule indirectly. Suppose the dollar rises. According to the net export function, derived in Section 12.3, when the dollar is strong, net exports and real GDP are lower. In addition, inflation is lower because the price of imported goods does not increase as rapidly when the dollar appreciates. Both effects cause the Fed to lower the interest rate even though the exchange rate is not directly in the policy rule. Alternatively, suppose the dollar falls. When the dollar is weak, net exports and real GDP are higher. Inflation also is higher, because the price of imported goods increases more when the dollar appreciates. These effects cause the Fed to raise the interest rate.

The Taylor rule requires a flexible exchange rate. Recall that, in Chapter 12, we saw that, if the Fed wants to fix the exchange rate, it needs to keep the U.S. interest rate equal to the world interest rate. In that case, the Fed cannot also adjust the interest rate in response to movements in inflation and the GDP gap. Fixing the exchange rate is incompatible with conducting monetary policy according to the Taylor rule.

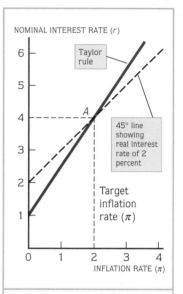

FIGURE 16.1   GRAPH OF THE TAYLOR RULE

The Taylor rule of Equation 16.1 is shown for the situation where GDP equals potential GDP ($\hat{Y} = 0$). Higher inflation causes the Fed to raise interest rates by more than the increase in inflation. Therefore, the slope of the Taylor rule is greater than 45°.

EXAMPLE   Suppose that $\beta = 0.5$, $\delta = 0.5$, $\pi^* = 0.02$, and $R^* = 0.02$. Then, the Taylor rule in Equation 16.1 becomes

$$r = \pi + 0.5\hat{Y} + 0.5(\pi - \pi^*) + 0.02$$
$$r = 1.5\pi + 0.5\hat{Y} + 0.01.$$

Hence, if real GDP rises above potential GDP by 1 percentage point, the policy rule says the Fed will raise the short-term interest rate by 0.5 percent. On the other hand, if real GDP falls below potential GDP, as it would in a recession, the Fed will cut the interest rate according to the example policy rule. Changes in inflation also cause the Fed to change interest rates. If the inflation rate rises

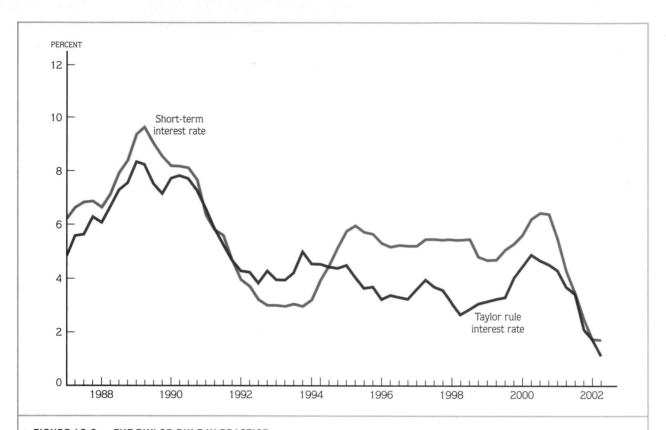

PERCENT

Short-term
interest rate

Taylor rule
interest rate

FIGURE 16.2 **THE TAYLOR RULE IN PRACTICE**

The actual short-term interest rate is compared with the interest rate predicted by the Taylor rule. The parameters are those given in the example on page 441, $B = 0.5$, $\delta = 0.5$, $\pi^* = 0.02$, and $R^* = 0.02$. While it is not a perfect fit, the rule is as accurate as many other macroeconomic relationships.

SOURCE: The Federal Reserve System and *Economic Report of the President*, 2003, Tables B-2 and B-3.

by 1 percentage point, then the Fed raises the interest rate by 1.5 percentage points. The Fed increases the nominal interest rate by more than the inflation rate to raise the real interest rate and slow down the economy. Recall that, when the real interest rate rises, net exports and investment decline, real GDP falls, and inflation eventually is reduced. When real GDP equals potential GDP ($\hat{Y} = 0$) and inflation equals its target ($\pi = 0.02$), the interest rate r equals 4 percent, which implies that the real interest rate equals 2 percent.

How accurate is the Taylor rule in Equation 16.1 as a description of Fed policy? Figure 16.2 compares the actual value of the short-term interest rate with that predicted by the Taylor rule. The graph shows that, while not a perfect predictor, the Taylor rule gives a very accurate description, as accurate as other macroeconomic relationships. For instance, the Taylor-rule-predicted interest rate tracks the actual interest rate very closely between 1987 and 1992. In 1992 and 1993, however, the Taylor rule overpredicted the actual interest rate. After the Fed raised the interest rate in 1994, the Taylor rule underpredicted the actual interest rate for the remainder of the decade. In 2001 and 2002, however, the Taylor-rule-predicted interest rate again tracks the actual interest rate very closely.

Recent developments in monetary policy can be understood in the context of the Taylor rule. In response to the recession of 2001, the Fed lowered the short-term interest rate from 5.00 percent in March 2001 to 1.75 percent in December 2001. Because of the slow recovery from the 2001 recession and continued low inflation, the Fed further decreased the short-term interest rate to 1.25 percent in November 2002 and 1.00 percent in June 2003. The economy started growing faster during the second half of 2003. In the first half of 2004, inflation began to rise, although some of the contributing factors, such as higher gasoline prices, appeared to be transitory. In response to faster growth and possible inflation, the Fed raised the short-term interest rate five times in .25 percent increments between June and December of 2004, ending the year at 2.25 percent. Since most forecasters predicted continued growth and inflationary pressures, financial markets expected the Fed to continue increasing the short-term interest rate, maybe to as high as 4.00 percent by the end of 2005.

Shifts of the Taylor rule are illustrated in Figure 16.3. Suppose the Fed raises its target inflation

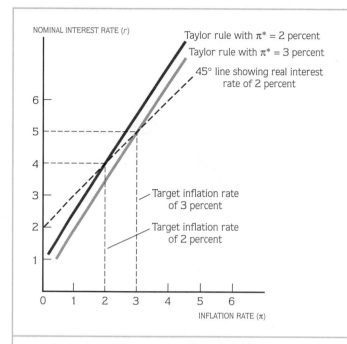

FIGURE 16.3   SHIFTS OF THE TAYLOR RULE

An increase in the target inflation rate shifts the Taylor rule to the right. The nominal interest rate rises by the amount that the target inflation rate increases.

rate from 2 percent to 3 percent. This shifts the Taylor rule to the right. When GDP equals potential GDP, the Fed raises the nominal interest rate from 4 percent to 5 percent to keep the real interest rate at 2 percent. Alternatively, if the Fed lowered its target inflation rate, the Taylor rule would shift to the left.

The Taylor rule can be used to study the interaction between monetary and fiscal policy. As we saw in Chapter 9, an increase in government purchases raises the real interest rate. Suppose that the equilibrium real interest rate rises by 1 percentage point because of a change in fiscal policy. This is represented as an upward shift in the dashed line from 2 percent to 3 percent, as shown in Figure 16.4 (the increase in the real interest rate is 1 percent, so we shift the line up by 1 percent). Since the target inflation rate has not changed, the Fed raises the nominal interest rate by the amount that the equilibrium real interest rate rises. This is shown by an upward shift in the Taylor rule in Figure 16.4 and a movement from the original equilibrium (point *A*) to the new equilibrium (point *B*). The nominal interest rate rises point for point with the equilibrium real interest rate, but the inflation rate does not change. If government purchases were reduced, lowering the equilibrium real interest rate, the Fed would respond by lowering the nominal interest rate point for point. This would leave the inflation rate unchanged.

While the example policy rule explains Fed behavior in recent years, it does not explain the behavior during the 1970s, when the inflation rate was very high. It is implausible that the Fed had a target inflation rate as low as 2 percent

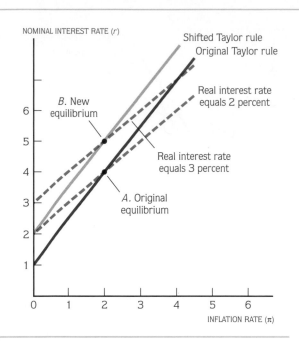

FIGURE 16.4   EFFECT OF A FISCAL POLICY CHANGE

The fiscal policy change is assumed to increase the equilibrium real interest rate by 1 percentage point. The Taylor rule shifts up, raising the nominal interest rate by 1 percentage point and leaving the inflation rate unchanged.

during that period, when inflation rose above 10 percent. It appears that, since the 1970s, the Fed policy rule has shifted to one with a lower target rate of inflation; that is, the term π^* in the policy rule Equation 16.1 changed.

Monetary Policy Rules

1. A monetary policy rule, or reaction function, describes how the Fed and other central banks set the money supply or the interest rate in response to variables in the economy.

2. The Taylor rule is a specific example of a monetary policy rule that works well for many countries. It states that the central bank raises the nominal interest rate when real GDP is greater than potential GDP and when inflation is greater than the target inflation rate.

3. The Taylor rule is stabilizing. Following the principles of the Taylor rule enables a central bank to smooth out economic fluctuations.

4. Changes in the central bank's target inflation rate shift the Taylor rule.

5. Changes in the equilibrium real interest rate, such as those caused by changes in the government budget deficit, also shift the Taylor rule.

16.2 | THE MACROECONOMIC POLICY MODEL

MACROSOLVE
EXERCISE

We derived the economic fluctuations model by first combining the IS curve and the LM curve in Chapter 8 to produce the aggregate demand curve, and then by combining aggregate demand and price adjustment in Chapter 9. While this model provides a good description of how the economy operates, it does not allow us to understand macroeconomic policy. The reason is that, in the LM curve, the money supply is fixed. Understanding macroeconomic policy requires us to incorporate monetary policy rules. We derive the macroeconomic policy curve by combining the IS curve and the Taylor rule. We then incorporate price adjustment to construct the macroeconomic policy model.

The IS Curve Revisited

The IS curve is a downward-sloping curve showing all the combinations of real GDP Y and the real interest rate R that correspond to a spending balance. The economy always operates at a point on its IS curve because the economy is always in spending balance. Monetary policy determines where the economy is on its IS curve. Before we can combine the IS curve and the Taylor rule, we need to rewrite the IS curve as a relation between the output gap and the difference between the actual and equilibrium real interest rates.

Take a look at the algebraic IS curve in Equation 8.6, page 204. To use a simpler notation, we now write the IS curve as

$$R = s_0 - s_1 Y + s_2 G, \qquad (16.3)$$

where, as before, R is the real interest rate and Y is real GDP. The coefficient s_0 is the intercept of the IS curve, s_1 is the slope coefficient showing that the IS curve slopes downward, and s_2 shows the amount of the upward shift of the IS curve when government purchases rise. Now think about the economy at the point on the IS curve corresponding to full employment, where $Y = Y^*$. We define R^* as the real interest rate at the full-employment point and call it the **equilibrium real interest rate.** It is

$$R^* = s_0 - s_1 Y^* + s_2 G. \qquad (16.4)$$

Now we can subtract Equation 16.4 from Equation 16.3 to get a relationship between the difference between the actual real interest rate and the equilibrium real interest rate, on the one hand, and the gap between actual and potential output, on the other hand:

$$R - R^* = - s_1(Y - Y^*). \qquad (16.5)$$

Note how government purchases dropped out. Fiscal policy affects the real interest rate but does not affect the difference between the actual real interest rate and the equilibrium real interest rate.

In our discussion of price adjustment, we measured the gap between actual and potential output in percentage terms, using the variable $(Y - Y^*)/Y^*$. We want our new version of the IS curve to use this variable too, so we rewrite Equation 16.5 as

$$R - R^* = - (s_1 Y^*)\left(\frac{Y - Y^*}{Y^*}\right) \qquad (16.6)$$

We let $\sigma = s_1 Y^*$, it is the slope of the IS curve, and we use the variable we defined earlier, $\hat{Y} = (Y - Y^*)/Y^*$, the percentage output gap. Then the IS curve is

$$R - R^* = - \sigma \hat{Y}. \qquad (16.7)$$

The Macroeconomic Policy Curve

Now that we have written the IS curve in terms of the difference between the actual and the equilibrium real interest rates and the output gap, we are ready to combine the IS curve with the Taylor rule. We start by writing the Taylor rule with the difference between the actual and the equilibrium real interest rates on the left-hand side. Take the Taylor rule from Equation 16.1 and subtract inflation π and the equilibrium real interest rate R^* from both sides:

$$r - \pi - R^* = B\hat{Y} + \delta(\pi - \pi^*). \tag{16.8}$$

Since the real interest rate R equals the nominal interest rate minus the expected rate of inflation, we can write Equation 16.8 as

$$R - R^* = B\hat{Y} + \delta(\pi - \pi^*). \tag{16.9}$$

Combining the IS curve, Equation 16.7, with the Taylor rule, Equation 16.8, we get

$$-\sigma Y = B\hat{Y} + \delta(\pi - \pi^*). \tag{16.10}$$

or

$$\hat{Y} = \frac{-\delta}{(B + \sigma)}(\pi - \pi^*). \tag{16.11}$$

We call Equation 16.11 the **macroeconomic policy curve.** It is a negative relation between the GDP gap, $\hat{Y}$, and the amount of inflation above target, $\pi - \pi^*$, where spending balance is attained (the economy is on its IS curve) and monetary policy is determined by the Taylor rule.

The macroeconomic policy (MP) curve is shown in Figure 16.5. The macroeconomic policy curve slopes downward. When the inflation rate π equals the target inflation rate π^*, the GDP gap $\hat{Y}$ is zero. On the upper-left part of the curve, inflation is above target and the Fed raises the real interest rate to contract the economy. On the lower-right part of the curve, inflation is below target and the Fed lowers the real interest rate to expand the economy. The slope of the MP curve is determined by the sensitivity of the nominal interest rate to the GDP gap (B) and the difference between the actual and target inflation rates (δ) in the Taylor rule, as well as to the slope of the IS curve σ. In the numerical example, where $\delta = B = 1/2$ and $\sigma > 0$, the GDP gap changes less than point for point with changes in the inflation rate.

The macroeconomic policy curve shifts when the Fed changes its policy rule to a different target

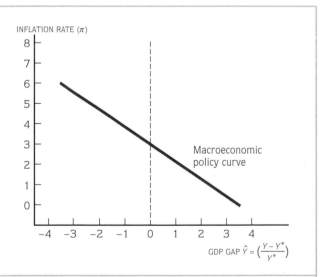

FIGURE 16.5   THE MACROECONOMIC POLICY CURVE

The curve shows a negative relationship between inflation and the GDP gap. When inflation increases, the Fed raises interest rates and this causes real GDP to fall; when inflation declines, the Fed lowers interest rates and this causes real GDP to rise; these are movements along the curve.

rate of inflation, π^*. An increase in the target rate of inflation from 3 percent to 5 percent is illustrated in Figure 16.6. The increase in the target rate of inflation shifts the macroeconomic policy curve to the right. If the Fed had decreased its target rate of inflation to 2 percent, the macroeconomic policy curve would have shifted to the left.

Price Adjustment Revisited

The price adjustment line derived in Chapter 9 is an integral part of the tool kit of practical economists and policy makers. In that chapter, we considered shocks to the price adjustment line. An equation for price adjustment that incorporates these shocks is

$$\pi = \pi_{-1} + f\hat{Y}_{-1} + Z, \qquad (16.12)$$

where π is inflation, π_{-1} is expected inflation (measured by lagged inflation), $\hat{Y}_{-1} = (Y_{-1} - Y^*)/Y^*$ is the lagged GDP gap, and Z is a price shock.

The price adjustment process is depicted in Figure 16.7 in a way useful for policy analysis. The inflation rate is on the vertical axis and the GDP gap is on the horizontal axis. Because the *lagged* GDP gap $(\hat{Y}_{-1})$ rather than the current GDP gap $(\hat{Y})$ is on the right-hand side of Equation 16.12, the inflation rate does not depend on the current level of the GDP gap. Hence, we represent Equation 16.12 as a flat line, labeled *PA* for price adjustment. According to Equation 16.12, the PA line

1. Shifts up, indicating higher inflation, if real GDP was above potential GDP last year and shifts down if real GDP was below potential GDP last year;

2. Shifts up if the expected rate of inflation π_{-1} rises and shifts down if the expected rate of inflation falls; and

3. Shifts up if there is a positive price shock (positive value of Z) and shifts down if there is a negative price shock.

Note that Figure 16.7 has the inflation rate on the vertical axis, while the diagram we used earlier

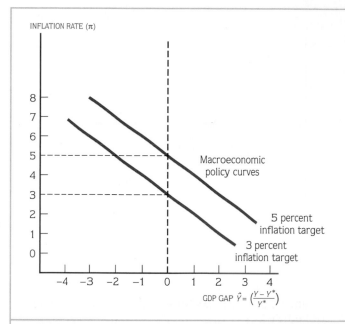

FIGURE 16.6   SHIFTS IN THE MACROECONOMIC POLICY CURVE

An increase in the target rate of inflation shifts the macroeconomic policy curve to the right.

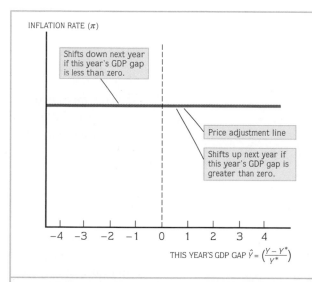

FIGURE 16.7   PRICE ADJUSTMENT LINE DETERMINING THE INFLATION RATE

In the price adjustment equation (16.12), the inflation rate is predetermined because it depends on the lagged GDP gap rather than the current GDP gap. Hence, the price adjustment line is flat in a graph with inflation on the vertical axis and the current GDP gap on the horizontal axis. Because expected inflation responds to lagged inflation, the line shifts up (or down) gradually over time when the GDP gap is positive (or negative).

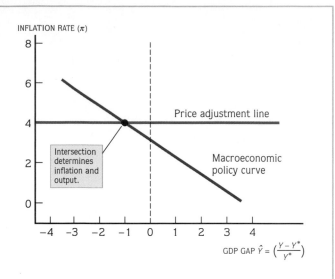

INFLATION RATE (π)

GDP GAP $\hat{Y} = \left(\frac{Y - Y^*}{Y^*} \right)$

FIGURE 16.8   SIMULTANEOUSLY DETERMINING INFLATION AND OUTPUT

The model can be represented by the macroeconomic policy curve and the price adjustment line. The solution of the model is found at the combination of inflation and output at the intersection of the two curves. When either of the curves shifts, the intersection changes and traces out patterns of inflation and the GDP gap.

had the price level on the vertical axis. We now put the inflation rate on the vertical axis to consider monetary policies, such as the Taylor rule, that focus on inflation rather than the price level. These policies typically result in low but positive rates of inflation, such as the 2 to 3 percent inflation in the United States during the 1990s and early 2000s.

Now we combine the price adjustment line of Figure 16.7 and the macroeconomic policy curve from Figure 16.5 in the same diagram, Figure 16.8. The intersection of the two curves gives the values of the GDP gap and inflation, $\hat{Y}$ and π. Figure 16.8 describes the operation of the model in a single picture. If there is a shift in either the price adjustment line or the macroeconomic policy curve, then the economy moves to a new combination of output and inflation, $\hat{Y}$ and π.

The Macroeconomic Policy Model

1. The macroeconomic policy curve is constructed from the IS curve and the Taylor rule. The macroeconomic policy curve shifts when the target inflation rate changes.

2. The macroeconomic policy model combines the macroeconomic policy curve and the price adjustment line. The model simultaneously determines inflation and output.

16.3 | MACROECONOMIC POLICY SCENARIOS

The macroeconomic policy model combines the IS curve, Taylor rule, and price adjustment. We use the macroeconomic policy model to examine four important types of macroeconomic experiences: a boom, disinflation, boom-bust cycle, and an oil price shock. We also see how well the model accords with the experience with inflation and output for the United States.

A Boom

What happens in the short, medium, and long runs when an outward shift in the macroeconomic policy curve sets off a boom? The outward shift could occur because the Fed adopted a higher inflation target. According to the Taylor rule described by Equation 16.1, an increase in the target inflation rate initially causes the Fed to lower the nominal interest rate by raising money supply growth. With inflation expectations initially unchanged, the lower nominal interest rate decreases the real interest rate, increasing aggregate demand and raising output. But higher output means inflation. In response to the higher inflation, the Fed raises interest rates and GDP falls. Eventually, the economy gets back to equilibrium, with output equal to potential and inflation at a higher level. In the new equilibrium, the only effect of the increase in aggregate demand is to raise the inflation rate. The path of the economy in response to an increase in aggregate demand is shown in Figure 16.9.

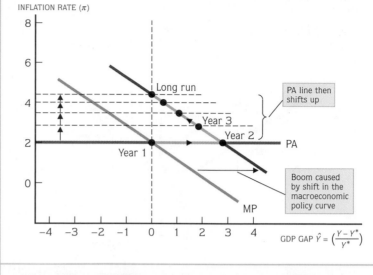

FIGURE 16.9   A BOOM

The economy starts in equilibrium in year 1, with output equal to potential (zero GDP gap) and 2 percent inflation. In year 2, the macroeconomic policy curve shifts outward. Real GDP rises immediately. Inflation then worsens. As inflation rises, aggregate demand falls and output begins to recede toward equilibrium. The GDP gap returns to zero, but the inflation rate is permanently higher.

The path starts at equilibrium in year 1. There is 2 percent inflation and output is at potential. In year 2, the outward shift in aggregate demand raises output sharply. Because the inflation rate does not respond immediately, output increases by the full amount of the shift in aggregate demand. For the next few years, a series of increases in inflation depresses aggregate demand as the Fed acts to resist the inflation. Inflation gradually stops rising because output is less and less above potential. In the long run, output returns to its potential level and inflation settles at its new level.

Disinflation

Suppose now that the inflation rate is 4 percent and the Fed decides that this is too high. Suppose the Fed decides to reduce the target rate of inflation from 4 percent to 2 percent. In this case the macroeconomic policy curve shifts to the left, as shown in Figure 16.10.

At first, real GDP falls below potential GDP as the Fed raises the interest rate, but there is little change in inflation. Eventually, however, the rate of inflation falls, and as it does, the Fed reduces the interest rate and the economy recovers gradually back to potential. Observe that this disinflation example has a path for inflation and output that is the mirror image of the boom.

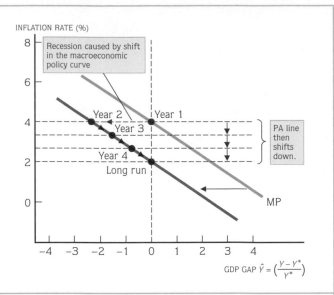

FIGURE 16.10   DISINFLATION

Here, the Fed reduces the target rate of inflation from 4 percent to 2 percent. In the short run, real GDP declines below potential GDP and inflation does not change. Eventually, inflation declines toward the new target of 2 percent and the economy returns to potential, with zero GDP gap.

A Boom-Bust Cycle

It is useful to combine the preceding examples into a single scenario. First, suppose the Fed starts on an expansionary monetary policy, as in the first example, which shifts the macroeconomic policy curve to the right, starting a boom but then leading to a higher inflation rate. Second, suppose the Fed decides that this new, higher inflation is too high and reverses itself by shifting back to a lower inflation target, as in the second example; the macroeconomic policy curve now shifts to the left, starting a recession and eventually a lower inflation rate. This is called a **boom-bust cycle.**

This combined scenario is shown in Figure 16.11, where we see a boom (real GDP above potential GDP) in the economy followed by a period of slack (real GDP below potential GDP). During the boom, inflation rises, while during the slack period, inflation falls.

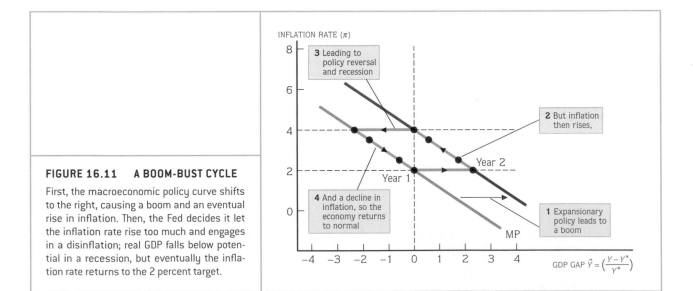

FIGURE 16.11   A BOOM-BUST CYCLE

First, the macroeconomic policy curve shifts to the right, causing a boom and an eventual rise in inflation. Then, the Fed decides it let the inflation rate rise too much and engages in a disinflation; real GDP falls below potential in a recession, but eventually the inflation rate returns to the 2 percent target.

An Oil Price Shock

In the 1970s and in 1990, the U.S. economy was battered by large and sudden increases in oil prices that sent the economy into periods of stagflation. We can trace out the reaction to a onetime price shock Z. Suppose Z increases in year 2 then returns to zero for the indefinite future. The path of inflation and output is shown in Figure 16.12.

In year 2, inflation jumps as a result of the oil price shock. Higher inflation causes the Fed to tighten, and this depresses output; the economy is in a state of stagflation. The recovery from stagflation proceeds as in Figure 16.10. As inflation subsides, aggregate demand begins to recover. The economy gradually returns to potential GDP and the original 2 percent inflation. The only effect of the price shock in the long run is a higher price level—there is no effect on real GDP or the rate of inflation.

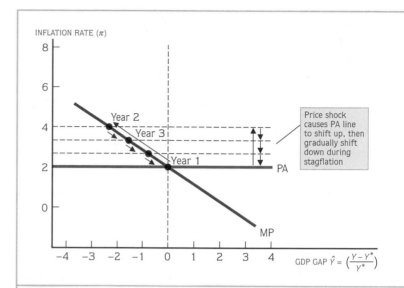

FIGURE 16.12   AN OIL PRICE SHOCK

The economy starts at equilibrium in year 1. In year 2, inflation rises because of the higher oil price. The GDP gap is negative because inflation is higher. Starting in year 3, a recovery takes place because inflation begins to fall. Output returns to potential, with zero GDP gap.

16.4 | EXPERIENCE WITH INFLATION AND OUTPUT IN THE UNITED STATES

How well does this model work as an explanation of the record of inflation and output fluctuations in modern economies? Before proceeding with policy analysis in the next chapter, it is important to check whether the theory is consistent with experience.

The inflation-output diagrams of the previous section provide a way for us to confront the theory with the facts. In the examples we considered, the model economy was displaced from its long-run potential. In each case, the return path to potential displays a striking characteristic that is clear in the diagrams: The path (shown by the arrows in the figures) is counterclockwise because the economy tends to return to potential in a counterclockwise fashion. Note in particular how Figure 16.11 shows a complete counterclockwise loop.

Do inflation and output actually behave this way? Since real-world economies are constantly being shocked by many events, it is difficult to separate out isolated

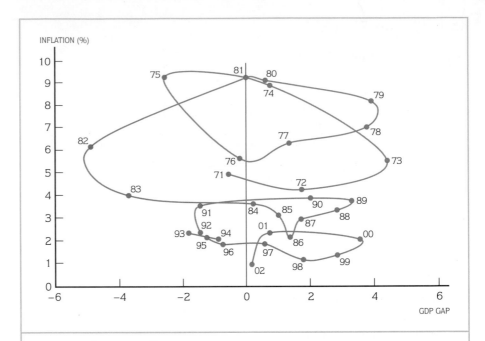

FIGURE 16.13   INFLATION–GDP GAP LOOPS IN THE UNITED STATES, 1971–2002

During the 1971–2002 period there were four loops in the United States. The second loop started from a higher rate of inflation than the first and was the largest of the three.

SOURCE: *Economic Report of the President*, 2003, Tables B-2 and B-3.

episodes like the special shocks in the model economy. Nevertheless, inflation and output fluctuations display such counterclockwise loops. They are not as smooth as in the model economy, but they are there nonetheless.

In Figure 16.13 we show inflation and GDP gap pairs in the United States for each of the years from 1971 through 2002. Four loops are evident: one from 1971 through 1976, another from 1976 through 1984, a third from 1984 to 1996, and a fourth from 1996 to 2002. The first loop starts with the monetary-induced boom of 1971–73 and continues with the recession of 1975. The second loop occurred under very similar circumstances: a boom in 1977–78, followed by a subsequent large recession in the early 1980s. Note that the second loop started at a higher rate of inflation because expected inflation was high during that period. The third loop started from a lower level of inflation in the boom of 1987–89 and had a smaller movement of GDP around potential, as the 1990–91 recession was relatively mild. A fourth loop, starting in 1996, includes the boom of 1997–2000 and the recession of 2001. This loop differs from the other three loops because inflation stayed low throughout the expansion.

Overall, the model is consistent with the dynamic movements of inflation and output. While these graphical tests focusing on loops may appear overly simplistic, they are confirmed by more accurate statistical techniques, and we believe they capture the essence of the theory and the facts.

Macroeconomic Policy Scenarios

1. The macroeconomic policy model can be used to analyze different types of macroeconomic experiences, including a boom, disinflation, and an oil price shock.

2. The macroeconomic policy model predicts that, after a shock, the path of inflation and the GDP gap follow a counterclockwise loop. The experience of the United States over the last 30 years is consistent with this prediction.

16.5 | MACROECONOMIC PERFORMANCE OF THE UNITED STATES

The inflation–GDP gaps for the United States from 1971 to 2002, as depicted in Figure 16.13, present evidence of a striking improvement in macroeconomic performance between the 1970s and today. The first piece of evidence is that inflation was much lower from 1983 to 2002 than from 1971 to 1982. The second piece of evidence is that the magnitude of GDP fluctuations has also been reduced. The third piece of evidence is the **Long Boom,** the back-to-back remarkable expansions in the 1980s and 1990s. These two expansions, the longest in peacetime history for the United States, are divided by a short recession in 1990–91 and ended by another short recession in 2001. In this section, we first document these pieces of evidence. We then relate the improvement in macroeconomic performance to changes in the Taylor rule from the 1970s to the 1980s and beyond.

GDP Fluctuations

Starting in the mid-1980s, the volatility of real GDP fluctuations has been substantially reduced. Figure 16.14 plots the quarterly real GDP growth rate from 1960 to 2002. It is clear that, beginning around 1984, the economy became much more stable. Part of this stability results from the lengthy boom experienced in the United States. The two recessions since 1984, in 1990–91 and 2001, were short and mild compared to the recessions in 1969–70, 1974–75, and 1980–82. However, the decreased volatility does not result exclusively from shorter recessions. Even if the recessions are removed, there is a clear decrease in real GDP fluctuations since about 1984.

Inflation Fluctuations

The pattern of inflation, while exhibiting some similarities to the pattern of GDP fluctuations, also shows some important differences. Figure 16.15 plots inflation in the United States from 1950 to 2002. The **Great Inflation** of the

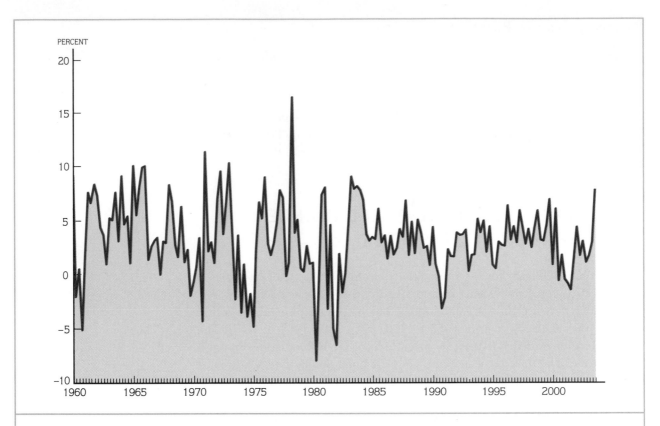

FIGURE 16.14   QUARTERLY GROWTH RATE OF REAL GDP

The volatility of real GDP fluctuations, measured by the quarterly real GDP growth rate, has decreased substantially since the mid-1980s. The economy has become more stable.

SOURCE: *Economic Report of the President*, 2003, Table B-2.

late 1960s to the early 1980s is flanked by two periods of relative price stability: the 1950s through the mid-1960s and the early 1980s to the early 2000s. Looking at GDP fluctuations and inflation fluctuations together, an interesting pattern emerges. The great inflation period of the late 1960s to the early 1980s is characterized by both high inflation and large GDP fluctuations. While inflation was low from the 1950s through the mid-1960s, GDP fluctuations were large. Only in the post-Great-Inflation period, from the early 1980s to the early 2000s, has inflation been low and GDP fluctuations small.

The Taylor Rule and Macroeconomic Performance

Changes in the conduct of monetary policy are the most probable cause of the improvement in macroeconomic performance since the early 1980s. To see this, look again at Figure 16.15. When the inflation rate rose to 4.0 percent in

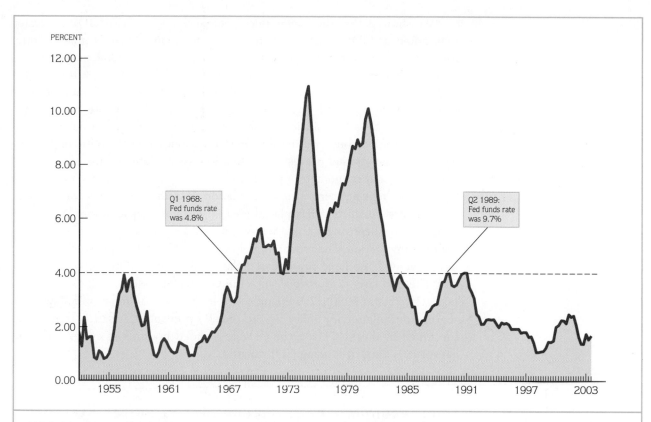

FIGURE 16.15   INFLATION

Inflation in the United States was much higher in the 1970s than in the 1960s, the 1980s, or the 1990s. One explanation is that monetary policy was much more aggressive in fighting inflation in the 1980s and 1990s than in the 1970s.

SOURCE: The Federal Reserve System.

the first quarter of 1968, the federal funds rate was 4.8 percent. When the inflation rate rose to 4.0 percent in the second quarter of 1989, the federal funds rate was 9.7 percent. This much larger policy response was accompanied by a much stronger macroeconomic performance.

These two examples are not isolated incidents. Empirical estimates of policy rules for the federal funds rate, based on Equation 16.1, find negative estimates for δ during the late 1960s and 1970s and positive estimates for δ since the mid-1980s. What does this mean for the conduct of monetary policy? Looking at Equation 16.2, a positive estimate of δ means that, when inflation rises, the response of the nominal interest rate is of a large enough magnitude that the real interest rate rises. This interest rate response reduces inflationary pressures and brings inflation back down. A negative estimate of δ, in contrast, means that, when inflation rises, the nominal interest rate does not increase enough to raise the real interest rate. Monetary policy is very accommodative and this leads to less price stability.

We showed that the Taylor rule is *stabilizing*. When real GDP is greater than potential GDP or when inflation is greater than the target inflation rate, following the Taylor rule smooths out fluctuations. This stabilizing property, however, holds only if d is positive in Equation 16.1 so that $1 + d$ is greater than 1 in Equation 16.2. It is not enough to simply raise the federal funds rate when inflation rises; it is necessary to increase the interest rate by the right amount. It is thus no coincidence that the negative value for δ describes the years of price instability during the Great Inflation, while the positive value of δ describes the years of price stability that followed. Monetary history confirms what theory and econometrics predict.

It is perhaps not surprising that inflation decreased as a result of a change in monetary policy that has placed greater emphasis on inflation. What may appear more surprising is that there was also a decrease in GDP volatility during the same period. The monetary policy with increased emphasis on inflation has prevented the large run-ups of inflation that precipitated boom-bust cycles. The two largest recessions since the Great Depression of the 1930s, during 1974–75 and 1980–82, were preceded by increases in inflation followed by sharply antiinflationary policy by the Fed. By preventing inflation from rising too much in the first place, the Fed has avoided boom-bust cycles since the early 1980s, thus decreasing GDP volatility.

Macroeconomic Performance for the United States

1. The macroeconomic performance for the United States has improved greatly since the 1970s. This can be seen in both much lower inflation and much smaller GDP fluctuations since 1984.
2. Changes in the conduct of monetary policy are the most probable cause of the improvement in macroeconomic performance. Since the mid-1980s, the Fed has increased the nominal interest rate by enough to raise the real interest rate when inflation rose. This was not true in the 1970s.
3. By keeping inflation low since the mid-1980s, the Fed has avoided the boom-bust cycle.

REVIEW AND PRACTICE

Major Points

1. A monetary policy rule describes a systematic response of monetary policy to events in the economy. The Taylor rule (that the central bank raises the nominal interest rate r when real GDP is greater than potential GDP and when inflation is greater than the target inflation rate) is the best-known description of a monetary policy rule for the United States.

2. The Taylor principle is that, when inflation rises, the nominal interest rate needs to be raised by more than one for one, so that the real interest rate rises.

3. A monetary policy rule is stabilizing if it obeys the Taylor principle.

4. An increase in the target inflation rate shifts the Taylor rule to the right.

5. While the Taylor rule is not a perfect predictor of the actual value of the short-term interest rate, it is as accurate as other macroeconomic relationships.

6. The macroeconomic policy curve gives a relation between the output gap and the deviation of inflation from the target inflation rate. It is derived from the IS curve and the Taylor rule.

7. An increase in the target inflation rate shifts the macroeconomic policy curve to the right.

8. A model that combines the macroeconomic policy curve with price adjustment implies that inflation and output fluctuate or spiral as the economy returns to potential after a shock.

9. From the 1970s to the present, the United States has experienced four economic fluctuations that displayed such spirals of counterclockwise loops.

10. Changes in the conduct of monetary policy, so that the Fed increases the real interest rate when inflation rises, are the most probable cause of the improvement in macroeconomic performance in the United States since the mid-1980s.

Key Terms and Concepts

target inflation rate	macroeconomic policy curve
Taylor rule	boom-bust cycle
equilibrium real interest rate	Long Boom
Taylor principle	Great Inflation

Questions for Discussion and Review

1. According to the Taylor rule, to what variables does the Fed react in setting the interest rate?

2. How can you determine the nominal and real interest rates from the Taylor rule?

3. What is the Taylor principle? Why is adherence to the Taylor principle necessary for the Taylor rule to be stabilizing?

4. How does the exchange rate affect the interest rate implied by the Taylor rule?

5. What relationships comprise the macroeconomic policy model?

6. Describe the effects over time of an increase in the target inflation rate.

7. Why don't increases in government purchases raise inflation if monetary policy is determined by the Taylor rule?

8. Explain why the economy approaches equilibrium in a counterclockwise loop in the inflation–GDP gap diagram.

Problems

NUMERICAL

1. Consider an economy with the IS curve

$$R - R^* = -\sigma\hat{Y}$$

and the Taylor rule

$$r = \pi + B\hat{Y} + \delta(\pi - \pi^*) + R^*,$$

where $B = 0.5$, $\delta = 0.5$, $\sigma = 0.75$, $\pi^* = 0.03$, and $R^* = 0.02$.

   a. Derive the equation for the macroeconomic policy curve. What is the GDP gap $\hat{Y}$ if inflation π equals the target rate of inflation $\pi^* = 0.03$ (3 percent)?

   b. Suppose the Fed raises the target rate of inflation π^* to 0.04 (4 percent). What is the effect of this policy on the Taylor rule and the macroeconomic policy curve?

   c. Suppose that, because of an increase in government purchases, the equilibrium real interest rate R^* rises to 0.03 (3 percent). What is the effect of this policy on the Taylor rule and the macroeconomic policy curve?

2. Consider an economy with the macroeconomic policy curve

$$\hat{Y} = -\frac{\delta}{B + \sigma}(\pi - \pi^*)$$

and the price adjustment schedule

$$\pi = \pi_{-1} + f\hat{Y}_{-1} + Z,$$

where $B = 0.5$, $\delta = 0.5$, $\sigma = 0.75$, $\pi^* = 0.02$, $R^* = 0.03$, and $f = 0.25$.

a. Suppose the economy starts with the GDP gap $\hat{Y} = 0$ and inflation π equal to the target rate of inflation $\pi^* = 0.02$ (2 percent). A price shock of 3 percent occurs in the first year ($Z = 0.03$). No further price shocks occur ($Z = 0$ in all future years). Trace the path of the economy by computing the values of inflation and the GDP gap for five years.

b. Now, suppose that there is no price shock ($Z = 0$ in all years), but the Fed raises the target rate of inflation π^* to 0.04 (4 percent). Trace the path of the economy by computing the values of inflation and the GDP gap for five years.

3. Section 16.3 looked at the inflation effects of a stimulus to output. In this problem, we show how such effects vary with different models of inflationary expectations. Consider the following alternatives to Equation 15.15 (i) $\pi^e = 0.4\pi_{-1} + 0.2\pi_{-2}$; (ii) $\pi^e = 0.9\pi_{-1}$; (iii) $\pi^e = 0.5\pi_{-1} + 0.5\pi_{-2}$; (iv) $\pi^e = 0.33\pi_{-1} + 0.33\pi_{-2} + 0.33\pi_{-3}$. Assume $f = 0.25$ and $Z = 0$.

a. For each of these expressions find the inflation effects of a permanent 3 percent stimulus to output ($\hat{Y} = 0.03$). Calculate the inflation rate for years 1 through 10.

b. Estimate the long-run rate of inflation in each case.

c. Do any of the expressions for inflationary expectations given above lead to systematic errors in forecasting inflation? If so, which ones? If not, explain the relationship between expected and actual inflation when fiscal and monetary policy are used to keep output at potential. Is one expression for expected inflation more likely to prevail than another?

4. In this problem, we consider the behavior of the economy following a recession. We look at how the recovery is influenced by the model used for inflationary expectations. Suppose the economy starts off with output at potential ($Y = Y^*$) and $\pi = 0.02$. Aggregate demand is given by Equations 16.1 and 16.7 with $\sigma = 0.1$, $\beta = 0.5$, $\delta = 0.5$, $\pi^* = 0.02$ and $R^* = 0.02$; price adjustment is given by Equation 15.14 with $f = 0.25$. In year 1, the Fed lowers its target inflation rate to zero; this creates a recession.

a. Calculate the path of inflation and output in years 1 through 6, assuming (i) $\pi^e = 0.4\pi_{-1} + 0.2\pi_{-2}$ and (ii) $\pi^e = \pi_{-1}$.

b. For which model of expectations does the return to potential output take longer?

c. We assumed here that the value taken by f in the price adjustment equation was the same for both models of inflationary expectations. Explain why in reality the value of f might differ from one model to the other.

5. In this problem, we look at how the recovery from an oil price shock is affected by the model used for inflationary expectations. Let the model of the economy and its initial conditions be the same as in problem 4. In year 1, let $Z = 0.025$.

   a. Calculate the path of inflation, the price level, and output in years 1 through 6 under each of the models for π^e given in part a of problem 4.

   b. In each case, how long does it take inflation to first return to its target level (π^*)? Analyze the factors that cause inflation to fall in each case.

   c. In which case is the fall in output greater? How do you explain this result?

ANALYTICAL

1. Consider an economy with the IS curve

$$R - R^* = -\sigma\hat{Y}$$

and the Taylor rule

$$r = \pi + B\hat{Y} + \delta(\pi - \pi^*) + R^f,$$

where R^f is a coefficient that does not necessarily equal the equilibrium real interest rate R^*.

   a. Suppose that the equilibrium real interest rate increases by 1 percentage point because of a change in fiscal policy, but the coefficient R^f does not change. Using a diagram similar to Figure 16.4, show the effect of this fiscal policy change. Why is your answer different from that in Figure 16.4?

   b. Derive the macroeconomic policy curve for the case where the coefficient R^f in the Taylor rule does not necessarily equal the equilibrium real interest rate R^*.

   c. Suppose that the price adjustment schedule is given by

$$\pi = \pi_{-1} + f\hat{Y}_{-1} + Z.$$

   What are the effects on inflation and the GDP gap of the change in fiscal policy in part a? Use the macroeconomic policy curve and the price adjustment schedule.

2. Consider an economy with the IS curve

$$R - R^* = -\sigma\hat{Y}$$

and the Taylor rule

$$r = \pi + B\hat{Y} + \delta(\pi - \pi^*) + R^*.$$

a. Suppose the coefficient δ in the Taylor rule equals zero. Does the Taylor rule obey the Taylor principle? Derive the macroeconomic policy curve. Is monetary policy stabilizing?

b. Now suppose the coefficient δ in the Taylor rule is negative. Does the Taylor rule obey the Taylor principle in this case? Derive the macroeconomic policy curve. Is monetary policy stabilizing now?

3. Describe the behavior of investment and interest rates during the boom described in the first example of Section 16.3, assuming that the boom was created by an exogenous increase in investment. How do interest rates and investment behave during and following an oil price shock?

4. Suppose the public uses all available information to make unbiased, but not error-free, forecasts of inflation. In that case, we can say that

$$\pi_1 = \pi_t^e + e_t,$$

where e_t is a forecast error whose average value is zero.

a. What does this relationship between π and π^e imply about the average value of the output gap? (Hint: Use the price adjustment equation.)

b. Suppose now that π^e was formed so that π^e always differed from π by a constant, e. Using the price adjustment equation, show that the accelerationist hypothesis does not hold.

THE NEW NORMATIVE MACROECONMICS

The previous chapter presented a positive theory of economic fluctuations in output and inflation. This chapter introduces the **new normative macroeconomics,** policy research that focuses on "what should be" rather than endeavors to explain the actual behavior of the Fed and other central banks. This chapter begins with a review of the principal features. After examining the problems of matching policy instruments to targets and uncertainty in implementing policy, we go on to apply these principles to macroeconomic policy problems in the United States. In Chapter 18, we extend this analysis to the world economy.

17.1 | GENERAL PRINCIPLES OF MACRO POLICY ANALYSIS

Much of our discussion of the recent developments in macroeconomics—rational expectations, policy rules, theories of wage and price rigidities, the nature of economic fluctuations—has been technical. It is important not to lose sight of the central ideas by focusing too much on the technical details. The central ideas are summarized in the following five propositions.

1. *When making decisions, people think about the future, and their expectations of the future can be modeled by assuming that they have a sense of economic fluctuations and use their information to make unbiased (but not error-free) forecasts.*

The notion that people make the most of the information available to them when forecasting the future was originally proposed by John Muth in 1960 for use in microeconomic applications, such as the demand and supply for agricultural commodities.[1] Farmers need to predict future prices to know how much to grow. Muth suggested that we model a farmer's expectations by simply assuming that the supply-and-demand model is known to the farmer. Robert Lucas applied rational expectations to macroeconomics, which eventually led to him receiving the Nobel Prize.

The idea has proven useful in macroeconomic applications. Many features of economic fluctuations are recurrent from one business cycle to another; there are established statistical regularities. We have documented many of these regularities. Since business cycles have been observed for hundreds of years, it makes sense to assume that people have become familiar with them. Of course, in the face of new, unprecedented events, people make significant errors in trying to look forward.

2. *Macroeconomic policy can be usefully described and evaluated as a policy rule, rather than by treating the instruments as exogenous and looking only at onetime changes in them.*

Because people are forward looking, their expectations of future policy actions affect their current behavior and the state of the economy. Hence, to evaluate the effect of policy on the economy, we need to specify not only current policy changes but also future ones. In other words, we need to specify a contingency plan that describes how policy will react to future events. Such a contingency is nothing more than a rule for policy. The contingency plan could be as specific as a constant growth rate rule for the money supply, but more generally, it establishes a range of reactions depending on the state of the economy.

---

[1]John Muth, "Rational Expectations and the Theory of Price Movements," *Econometrica*, Vol. 29 (1960), pp. 315–335.

The rational expectations approach almost forces a macroeconomic analyst to think about policy as a rule or a strategy. We see in our policy evaluation study in the latter part of this chapter that it is natural and convenient to specify policy as a rule. Note that the focus on rules does not mean that the effect of discretionary policy should never be calculated; such a calculation can be a useful exercise to help understand the workings of the model. We did this in Chapter 9 in our first look at macro policy.

In his famous critique of traditional policy evaluation, Robert Lucas argued in the early 1970s that traditional macro models, like the model of Chapter 9, could give incorrect answers to policy evaluation questions if expectations were forward looking and there was a change in the policy rule.[2] Since these traditional models were based on adaptive backward-looking expectations, their parameters would change when the policy rule changed. This was the negative part of the critique, and it has clearly made policy analysts wary of using the traditional models. But there was also a positive side. The critique provided a general framework for modifying the traditional models; stipulating policy as a rule, it is possible to calculate by how much the parameters of the traditional models would change. Later in this chapter, we see how changes in the coefficients of the Taylor rule affect the parameters of the macroeconomic policy model.

3. *For a particular policy rule to work well, it is necessary to establish a commitment to that rule.*

The possibility that policy makers will find it tempting to change their plans in the future is a reason for maintaining a commitment to a stated rule. The value of commitment was first pointed out in macroeconomics by Finn Kydland of Carnegie-Mellon University and Edward Prescott of Arizona State University, recipients of the 2004 Nobel Prize in Economics, and by Guillermo Calvo of the University of Maryland.[3]

In attempting to find optimal policies for economies where people are forward looking, these researchers found that, once policy makers began an optimal policy, there was incentive in future periods for them to change the plan—to be inconsistent. Policy makers could make things better by being inconsistent. This was true even if the policy makers had the interests of the public in mind. One example close at hand is that of a teacher giving an examination. It is tempting to call off an examination after the students have studied and learned the material in a course in anticipation of the exam. Then they

[2]Robert E. Lucas, "Econometric Policy Evaluation: A Critique," in Karl Brunner and Allan Meltzer, eds., *The Phillips Curve and Labor Markets*, Carnegie-Rochester Conference Series, Vol. 1 (Amsterdam: North-Holland, 1976), pp. 19–46.

[3]Finn Kydland and Edward Prescott, "Rules Rather than Discretion: The Inconsistency of Optimal Plans," *Journal of Political Economy*, Vol. 85 (1977), pp. 473–491, and Guillermo Calvo, "On the Time Inconsistency of Optimal Policy in a Monetary Economy," *Econometrica*, Vol. 46 (1979), pp. 1411–1428. Also see Stanley Fischer, "Dynamic Inconsistency, Cooperation, and the Benevolent Dissembling Government," *Journal of Economic Dynamics and Control*, Vol. 2 (1980), pp. 93–107.

do not have to sweat through the exam, and the teacher does not have to grade the exam papers. The government's patent laws provide a similar problem of inconsistency. Patent laws confer a temporary monopoly as a reward for inventions. Hence, they spur inventiveness. But the monopoly is undesirable: It would be tempting to remove patents when an invention is completed, so that the new product would be produced and marketed competitively. Another example from the government sphere is the construction of dams for flood plains. The government tells people not to build houses on a dangerous flood plain, because no dams for flood control will be built. But when people move in anyway, the government finds it desirable to build the flood-control project to protect them.

However, by being inconsistent, policy makers are likely to lose credibility; people begin to assume that the policy makers will change the rules and this leads to a new policy plan that is generally inferior to the original one. For example, if the students knew for sure that the exam would be called off, they probably would not study for it. The implication is that, to prevent this inferior outcome, it is better to maintain a firm commitment to a policy rule.

Returning to the patent example, a policy maker who had the discretion to award patents each year would indeed be tempted not to do so. By holding back the patent, the economic inefficiencies of a monopoly would be avoided. Fortunately, reneging on patent promises does not occur in practice because it is so clear that future inventive activity would suffer. Instead, we have patent laws that limit such discretion. The time inconsistency research suggests that discretion should be limited for similar reasons in macroeconomic policy.

It is important to distinguish between **activist policy rules** and **discretionary policy.** Activist policy rules involve *feedback* from the state of the economy to the policy instruments, but the feedback is part of the rule. Sometimes the term **passive policy rule** is used to refer to special rules without feedback, like the fixed growth rate rule for the money supply. An example of an activist policy rule is the Taylor rule discussed in Chapter 16. Discretionary policy is formulated on a case-by-case and year-by-year basis, with no attempt to commit to or even talk about future policy decisions in advance. Those in favor of discretionary policy disagree with the whole concept of a rules-of-the-game approach, whether the rule is a feedback rule or a fixed setting for the policy instruments. Activist and constant-growth-rate policy rules have much more in common with each other than do activist policy rules and discretionary policy. Both types of policy rules involve commitments and lead to the type of policy analysis suggested by the rational expectations approach.

4. *The economy is basically stable; after a shock, it will eventually return to its normal trend paths of output and employment. However, because of rigidities in the economy, this return could be slow.*

The macro models we have looked at are *dynamic* systems continually disturbed by *shocks*. After each shock, the economy has a tendency to return to the normal or natural growing level of output and employment, although there may be overshooting or a temporary cumulative movement away from normal.

A smooth return is never observed in practice, however, because new shocks always hit the system. Since the economy is viewed as always being buffeted by shocks, the equilibrium is really a random or stochastic equilibrium. The combination of the shocks and the dynamics of the model is capable of mimicking the actual behavior of business cycles surprisingly well, as we saw in the previous chapter; the properties of the random equilibrium are much like the actual behavior of business cycles.

The shocks can be due to many factors but usually have been money shocks, demand shocks, or price shocks. The dynamics are due to many possible rigidities in the economy, but price-wage rigidities and slow adjustment of capital (including inventories) have been the most important empirically.

Combined with these structural rigidities is the supposition that expectations are not restrained by similar rigidities. A shock can change expectations of inflation, exchange rates, and other variables overnight, even though rigidities cause the economy to take additional time to adjust fully to the shock. The expectations take account of the structural rigidities, since these are part of the model. The combination of rigidities in the economy with perfectly flexible expectations is an essential feature of most rational expectations models.

There has been a tendency to mix up expectations assumptions with assumptions about how markets work. Hence, the comment that expectations might be rational in flexible auction markets but not in sticky wage-labor markets is frequently heard. But there is no reason why expectations are not rational in both areas. Labor union staffs may spend more time predicting future wage and price inflation than the staffs of brokerage firms. When workers and firms set wages and prices, they look ahead to the period during which the prices or wages will be in effect—to demand conditions, the wages of other workers, and so on. This means that expectations of future policy actions affect wage and price decisions, a property quite unlike models of wage and price rigidities with purely backward-looking expectations. The view that the economy will eventually return to normal, however slowly, after a shock is also inconsistent with the view that the economy stagnates permanently below potential.

5. *The objective of macroeconomic policy is to keep inflation low and reduce the size (or the duration) of fluctuations in output, employment, and inflation after shocks hit the economy. The objective is to be achieved over a long period of time, which in general includes a larger number of business cycle experiences. Future business cycle fluctuations are not viewed as less important than the current one.*

By responding to economic shocks in a systematic fashion, economic policy can offset their impact or influence the speed at which the economy returns to normal. It thus can change the size of the fluctuations. How this should be done is a main area of disagreement among proponents of different policy rules.

From a technical standpoint, the disagreement can be addressed by inserting alternative policy rules into a rational expectations model and calculating how each rule affects the variability of output, employment, and inflation in the moving equilibrium that describes the business cycle fluctuations. We want to choose a policy that provides the best economic performance. One simple criterion is the minimization of the size of the fluctuations in output and inflation. Since, in many models with price and wage rigidities, there is a trade-off between the reduction of output and inflation variability, it usually is necessary to stipulate a welfare or loss function that reflects certain value judgments. Frequently, one policy so dominates another that the particular welfare weights do not matter much, however. This approach to policy is used later in this chapter.

The average rate of inflation can obviously be influenced by monetary policy, and it is important to choose a target rate that maximizes economic welfare. The objective of macroeconomic policy is then to keep the inflation rate close to this target rate, that is, to minimize fluctuations around the target, regardless of the actual value of the target. Alternatively, if a zero inflation target is appropriate, the objective of policy is to keep inflation near zero.

17.2 | INSTRUMENTS, TARGETS, AND UNCERTAINTY

Generally stated, the macro policy problem is one of choosing policy rules that describe how the *instruments* of policy should respond to economic conditions in order to improve the performance of the *target* variables. The instruments of macro policy are things like the monetary base and interest rates. The targets of policy are the endogenous economic variables that we care about: inflation, unemployment, capital formation, and economic growth.

To describe our objectives for the target variables, it is useful to define a **social welfare function** that summarizes the costs of having the target variables deviate from their desired levels. Such a social welfare function should reflect the values of individuals in society. If people do not like inflation, then deviations of inflation from zero should register as a loss of welfare in the social welfare function.

We can view the macro policy problem much as any other economic problem: We want to choose policy rules for the instruments to maximize the social welfare function. Analogously, in a consumption problem the consumer chooses a contingency plan for consumption—a decision rule—to maximize utility.

In most macro problems, we are faced with the typical economic problem of scarcity. Whenever there is scarcity in economics, we are faced with a *trade-off* between competing goals. In fact, scarcity is the most fundamental problem in economics. An important principle of optimal macro policy is that, whenever there is a scarcity of instruments (that is, the number of instruments is less than the number of target variables), there is a trade-off between the different target variables. Jan Tinbergen, the Dutch economist who won the

Nobel Prize for his work on macro modeling and techniques for macro policy evaluation, established this important principle relating the number of instruments to the number of targets.[4] As long as the number of instruments is less than the number of targets, society is faced with a choice between meeting one goal or another. The choice between inflation and unemployment is the best example of this type of choice in macroeconomics, and we consider it in detail later in this chapter.

It is very important to note that equality between the number of instruments and the number of targets is not sufficient for avoiding a choice. In many cases, the different instruments are not independent enough in their effects on the target variables. Again, the best example of this is the inflation-unemployment trade-off. A simple counting of instruments and targets could lead to the following type of incorrect reasoning: "We have two instruments, monetary policy and fiscal policy, and two target variables, inflation and unemployment. Hence, there is no trade-off. We can use monetary policy to control inflation and fiscal policy to control unemployment." This reasoning is wrong because it assumes that monetary and fiscal policies affect inflation and output in different and independent ways. In fact, we already know from our macro model that monetary and fiscal policies affect output and inflation in the same way, by shifting the macroeconomic policy curve. Unless one instrument can directly affect inflation without going through the GDP gap, we are left with a trade-off. For example, if monetary policy had a separate effect on expected inflation or if tax policy could affect price setting, then there would be a separate channel by which one or the other policy could affect inflation.

Uncertainty and Timing Considerations

In practice, the target-instrument approach just described is too simple. It ignores the inherent uncertainty in our understanding of the economy. If there is uncertainty about the effect of an instrument of policy on the economy, then we must be careful not to exploit that relationship too much. Very active use of an uncertain instrument can be risky. This is one of the central reasons for using less active policies in practice.

When there are many instruments and uncertainty, the theory of economic policy tells us to use a mix of the instruments in a way that minimizes the risk. William Brainard of Yale University showed how the choice of instruments under uncertainty is much like the problem of choosing an optimal portfolio of common stocks.[5] Just as an individual should attempt to diversify a portfolio of stocks—"Don't put all of your eggs in one basket"—policy makers should diversify their instruments to reduce risk.

---

[4]Jan Tinbergen, *On the Theory of Economic Policy* (Amsterdam: North-Holland, 1952).
[5]William Brainard, "Uncertainty and the Effectiveness of Policy," *American Economic Review, Papers and Proceedings*, Vol. 57 (1967), pp. 411–425.

Another reason why macroeconomic policy making is difficult is that its benefits do not occur at the same time as its costs. An expansionary monetary or fiscal policy, for example, involves balancing the short-term benefits of a stimulative move against the long-term costs of inflation the move will bring. Conversely, the costs of a contractionary policy occur in the short run and the benefits occur later and are perhaps drawn out over many years. We start with a look at the benefits and costs. Then, we set up a framework within which policy makers can make an intelligent choice between expansion and contraction.

17.3 | THE BENEFITS OF FULL EMPLOYMENT AND PRICE STABILITY

Economic analysis deals with trade-offs of many types. For example, consider a consumer who cannot afford an expensive car and an expensive home; to buy a better car, the consumer must settle for a more modest home, and vice versa. Micro theory describes the consumer's preferences in terms of indifference curves. The consumer chooses the combination of car and house on the best indifference curve within the consumer's budget. The combination is at a point of tangency of an indifference curve and the line showing all the different combinations of car and house the consumer can afford.

We can look at the nation's choice between employment and price stability in the same way. Preferences give a set of indifference curves. The behavior of the economy, as described by the model of Chapter 16, gives the set of different combinations of employment and price stability that can be achieved. We call the curve showing those combinations the **policy frontier.** The optimal policy is at the point of tangency of an indifference curve and the policy frontier.

The starting point for the analysis is to choose the two axes for the indifference curves and the policy frontier. One axis has something to do with price stability and the other has something to do with output and employment stability. For inflation, it seems clear that the desirable level is about 2 percent. Large departures above 2 percent were the problem for the United States in the 1970s. Departures below zero were the problem in the depression of the 1930s and, as we discuss in the next chapter, for Japan in the late 1990s and early 2000s. As a first approximation, the cost of a positive error is about the same as the cost of a negative error. In addition, it seems reasonable to suppose that *the marginal cost of an inflation or deflation error rises with the magnitude of the error.* A simple measure of the loss associated with these properties is the **squared error.**

This suggests that a good general summary of the economic loss caused by inflation is the average of the squared deviation of the inflation rate from its target. We will call this the **inflation loss.** If everything else is held the same, the ideal macro policy keeps the inflation loss at zero. In real life, the inflation rate cannot be kept exactly at its target, and the average inflation loss is positive.

For the output-employment-unemployment side of the economy, the situation is a little different. For a number of reasons, the *natural* unemployment rate is probably not the *optimal* unemployment rate. Because of factors including taxes and unemployment compensation that make the social cost of unemployment exceed the private cost and because of monopoly power, it is likely that social welfare rises whenever unemployment drops below the natural rate. Therefore, if it were feasible, policy should keep the average unemployment rate below the natural rate. But, in Chapter 16, we stressed that macro policy cannot influence the average rate of unemployment or the average GDP gap; it can influence only the fluctuations of unemployment around the natural rate and the GDP gap around zero. Consequently, macro policy makers should do what they can do: limit the fluctuations of output and employment. Based on this logic, we define the **output loss** as the average squared GDP gap.

Social preferences about inflation and output stability can be displayed in a family of indifference curves as shown in Figure 17.1. Note that the indifference curves bend in the opposite direction from the usual ones for the theory of the consumer. Consumer theory deals with things people like. Inflation and output losses are things the public does not like, so the indifference curves have the opposite curvature. At the upper left end of each curve, the public is willing to trade quite a bit of added output loss to reduce their inflation loss a little from its high level. At the lower end, they accept only a small added amount of output loss to reduce their inflation loss quite a bit. Curves closer to the origin are socially preferred because they involve lower amounts of both output loss and inflation loss.

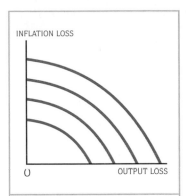

FIGURE 17.1   SOCIAL PREFERENCES ABOUT INFLATION AND OUTPUT LOSSES

Each indifference curve shows the locus of combinations of average inflation loss and average output loss that the public finds equally acceptable. The curve farthest from the origin is the worst one. The public prefers curves that are closer to the origin.

Why Is Inflation Undesirable?

The American public has made it abundantly clear that inflation is unpopular. In 1976 and 1980, two presidents—Ford and Carter—were denied reelection soon after large bursts of inflation. Stringent anti-inflation policies in the early 1980s seem to have been politically acceptable, even though they brought on a pair of recessions. Whenever inflation rises above 10 percent per year, public opinion polls show that inflation is the number-one economic problem, even when unemployment is high.

Although some specific economic costs of inflation have been identified, it is hard to quantify and assess them. The areas of economic costs include the following:

1. *"Shoe-Leather Costs" of Holding Money.* When inflation is high, currency and non-interest-bearing checking accounts are undesirable because they constantly decline in purchasing power. People wear out their shoes making extra trips to the bank to avoid holding much money. These trips involve genuine economic costs, and these costs would be avoided with stable prices. One response to inflation was the development of checking accounts that pay interest closer to market interest rates. This change in banking has reduced the cost of inflation because people do not have to spend so much time and effort transferring money between accounts.

2. *Tax Distortions.* The brackets for the personal income tax are indexed, as we discussed in Chapter 13, and they rise with the consumer price index. But many other parts of the tax system are not indexed; the presumption is that the purchasing power of the dollar is stable from one year to the next. For example, businesses take depreciation deductions based on the original dollar cost of plant and equipment investments. When inflation rages, the actual value of these deductions is much less than it should be, thanks to the declining purchasing power of the dollar. But this problem has been offset by speeding up the deductions. Even better, the tax law could be changed so that the deductions automatically rise along with the cost of living.

3. *Unfair Gains and Losses.* When inflation hits, some people gain and some lose. Retired people whose pensions are fixed in dollar terms lose. Home-owners gain because they can pay off their mortgages in less valuable dollars. In total, losses equal gains. In each transaction set in dollars, when inflation is high, somebody wins and somebody loses exactly the same amount. The social loss occurs because inflation makes long-term transactions more unreliable. There seems to be no clear tendency for inflation to favor the rich over the poor or the poor over the rich. Gains and losses from inflation are more or less randomly distributed in this respect.

4. *Nonadapting Economic Institutions.* Certain standard economic practices have not adapted readily to inflation, and the public has suffered as a result. The most important is private retirement arrangements. The typical private pension plan pays its retirees a certain number of dollars per month when they retire. The number of dollars is based on their earnings in the last few years of work. In this respect, the pension keeps up with inflation. But once retirement starts, the amount of the pension is fixed in dollars. A pension that starts out at a generous level may dwindle to inadequacy as a result of inflation. One way retirement plans could adapt would be to build in an allowance for, say, 5 percent inflation. Payments would rise by 5 percent every year. They would start at a lower level than they do now, but keep up better with inflation.

Many of these costs are avoidable by apparently simple means. Shoe-leather costs have been cut by permitting banks to pay market interest rates on checking accounts. Changing the tax system to avoid distortions from inflation is not too difficult and would be even easier if some other highly desirable tax reforms were instituted, such as immediate tax write-off for investment instead of depreciation deductions. Gains and losses could be avoided completely by linking payments and receipts to government price indexes, as many businesses do today in their transactions with other businesses. Better pension plans with cost-of-living indexation have been designed and put forward by a number of economists.

The public's negative view of inflation seems to come from sources other than these identifiable economic costs. One is the notion that the dollar is supposed to be a unit of purchasing power just as the yard is a unit of length. If the government decreased the length of the yard randomly by 5 or 10 percent each year, the public would be upset in a way that would also be out of proportion to the technical costs a changing unit of length would impose on us. It is a sign that the government is doing its job when its units of weights, measures, or purchasing power are reliable. Inflation is historically associated with the breakdown of government.

Perhaps another reason some people may be upset about inflation is that they do not take the same broad view as an economist, who sees inflation as a general rise in all prices and dollar incomes. Recall that, in a general inflation, wages and prices increase by the same amount. If wages increase less rapidly than prices, then something in addition to inflation—like a drop in productivity—is affecting the economy. Someone who does not think about the economy in that way will not associate an increase in income with the increase in prices that goes with it. Such a person may imagine that the increase in income would have occurred even without the inflation. In that case, the inflation appears to diminish the purchasing power of the income and so to be a loss. To put it another way, some people may not realize that both their incomes and the prices they pay will not rise as fast under an anti-inflation policy.

Costs of Inflation

1. There are some specific economic costs of inflation, but they are hard to quantify. These include

   - Shoe-leather costs of conserving money holdings

   - Distortions because much of the tax system is not indexed

   - Capricious losses suffered by holders of dollar claims, although offset by surprise gains enjoyed by those paying fixed-dollar debts

   - Problems caused by the failure of retirement plans and other institutions to adapt to declining purchasing power.

2. People see inflation as a breakdown of the basic government responsibility to provide a stable unit of purchasing power.

3. Some people may not understand the relation between their own incomes and rising prices. To them, higher prices represent diminished real income.

Costs of Output Loss and Unemployment

There is less mystery about output and unemployment losses, especially on the downside. As noted in Chapter 10, when real GDP falls by a billion dollars, people lose about $500 million immediately in the form of reduced disposable income. Reduced corporate retained earnings account for part of the reduction. The remainder, hundreds of millions of dollars, takes the form of reduced tax revenues for federal, state, and local governments. The public suffers from this reduction as well, in the form of either cuts in government services or future higher taxes.

In addition to the obvious economic costs of lost output, there are other serious costs of a period of low output and high unemployment. Young workers are particularly likely to become unemployed. Many of them are working in low-wage jobs where part of the benefit is the training they are receiving. When they stop work, the loss includes not just what they were producing, which is included in GDP, but also the value of the training, which is not included in GDP. The experience of unemployment itself may have social costs beyond reduced GDP. Unemployed people are more likely to turn to crime or become physically or mentally ill.

The direct costs of lost GDP are overwhelming. In a typical recession, GDP falls below potential by around 5 percent for about two years. Total lost GDP is about 10 percent of one year's GDP, or almost $1,100 billion at 2003 levels. There are about 290 million people in the United States, so the loss is about $3,800 per person. Some recessions are much deeper and involve even larger losses.

To get a full picture of the net social impact of a recession, however, we have to look at the benefits as well. If workers are able to engage in useful activities other than work in the market, or if they can store up memories of the leisure they enjoy during a recession, then there is an offset to the lost output during a recession. Data do show that people make some good use of their extra time during recessions. For example, school and college attendance rises in recessions.

Taxes are one important reason to think that the offset is far from complete. Because work in the market is taxed but leisure and most other nonmarket uses of time are not, there is a bias in the economy against market work. The social value of market work exceeds the worker's private earnings by the amount of payroll and income taxes. Any perturbation in the economy, such as a recession, that moves people from market work to nonmarket activities has a social cost even if it does not have a private cost.

The other important reason for less than full offset from the value of nonmarket activities is wage rigidity. If employers face a flat labor-supply schedule because contracts and customs require it, but workers actually have steep labor-supply schedules, then workers gain little from the extra time that becomes available during a recession. The marginal value of their time drops sharply in a recession because they quickly use up the backlog of valuable uses of time other than work in the market. With wage rigidity, there is a gap between the social value of work and the value of time to workers. As a result, recessions are socially costly.

Economists have thought less about the costs of episodes when GDP is above potential. The microeconomic argument supporting the idea that the costs are important is the following: The extra work effort needed to push GDP above potential is worth more than the extra GDP. Instead of working as many hours as they do during a boom and consuming and investing the extra output, the public would be better off with less output and more time to spend with their children, on their houses, and in recreation. Again, because of high taxes, the private value of time is well below the social value of work, so there is at least a range where a boom is socially beneficial even though it is privately costly to workers to be working longer hours.

In terms of unemployment, there is little disagreement that the marginal social costs of unemployment are higher at higher rates of unemployment. Remember that it is not the overall level of the marginal social cost that matters but the extent to which the marginal social cost of unemployment is higher in recessions than in booms. The value of the extra time at home that becomes available with higher unemployment is much lower for people who are already partly idle because of a recession than for people who are busy because of a boom. Consequently, keeping the variability of unemployment low is an important social goal.

Costs of Output Fluctuations and Unemployment

1. The marginal social cost of unemployment is higher when unemployment is high.

2. If labor supply is inelastic, the marginal value of time in other uses falls if employment falls, and rises if employment rises above normal.

3. Because of these considerations, the economy is better off with stable output at its full-employment level, as against fluctuating output and employment.

17.4 | THE POLICY TRADE-OFF BETWEEN INFLATION AND OUTPUT FLUCTUATIONS

In Chapter 9, we saw that, when aggregate demand shifts for some reason not related to macro policy, the shift can be offset through a policy that moves aggregate demand back to its original position. Then, output and inflation are back at their original levels as well. There is no need for aggregate demand shifts to cause either inflation losses or output-unemployment losses. Both can be avoided by a simple reversal of an aggregate demand shift.

 MACROSOLVE
EXERCISE

Recall the price adjustment equation from Chapter 15 (combine Equations 15.14 and 15.15):

$$\pi = f\hat{Y}_{-1} + \pi_{-1} + Z, \tag{17.1}$$

where π is inflation, π_{-1} is expected inflation (measured by lagged inflation), $\hat{Y}_{-1} = (Y_{-1} - Y^*)/Y^*$ is the lagged GDP gap, and Z represents price shocks, like increases in the price of oil.

We can characterize the policy alternatives in terms of the slope of the macroeconomic policy (MP) curve introduced in Chapter 16, which we now write as

$$\hat{Y} = - g(\pi - \pi^*), \tag{17.2}$$

where π^* is the target inflation rate. Compare Equation 17.2 to 16.11 and note that $g = \delta/(\beta + \sigma)$, so it depends on the policy rule through the response coefficients for output, β, and inflation, δ. In words, the output gap is reduced below zero by g percentage points if inflation rises above target by 1 percentage point. If g is zero, the policy rule keeps output at potential (and unemployment at the natural rate). With g equal to zero, no attempt is made to control inflation. If g is greater than zero, the policy response lowers output and raises unemployment to stabilize inflation. The larger g is, the larger is the reduction in output when an inflation shock occurs, as shown in Figure 17.2. The coefficient g measures how accommodative policy is to inflation. For $g = 0$, policy is fully accommodative to inflation. Larger values of g represent less accommodative policies.

We can use the price adjustment equation to find out how much inflation is reduced by different choices of the response coefficient g. If we substitute the MP curve, Equation 17.2, into the price adjustment equation, we get

$$\pi - \pi^* = (1 - fg)(\pi_{-1} - \pi^*) + Z. \tag{17.3}$$

When g is large, past inflation affects future inflation less and the effects of a single price shock disappear more quickly. Define k as $1 - fg$. The coefficient k measures how long and how much a price shock affects inflation. If g is zero (a fully accommodative policy), so that $k = 1$, then the price shock permanently raises the inflation rate by Z. In this situation, the effects of the price shock are never withdrawn from inflation. If inflation was zero before the price shock, it will be permanently above zero after the price shock. If, at the other extreme, $k = 0$, then the effect of the price shock disappears after only one year. If k is in the intermediate range, between 0 and 1, then the effect of the price shock *gradually* disappears: Excess inflation, $\pi - \pi^*$, is k times the price shock in the year after the shock, k^2 times the price shock in the second year, k^3 in the third year, and so on, eventually back to zero inflation. For example, if k is 0.8, target inflation π^* is 2 percent, and inflation is initially raised from 2 to 12 percent because of the price shock, then the difference between inflation and the tar-

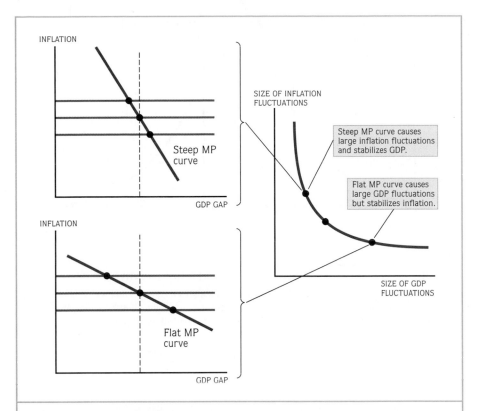

FIGURE 17.2   THE SLOPE OF THE MACROECONOMIC POLICY CURVE REPRESENTS DIFFERENT POLICIES

The slope of the macroeconomic policy (MP) curve (Equation 17.2) depends on the monetary policy rule. If the Fed raises interest rates sharply when inflation rises above target, for example, then the curve is flatter. A flatter curve results in smaller fluctuations in inflation but larger fluctuations in real GDP and employment, as shown in the diagram. A steeper curve due to a more accommodative monetary policy rule results in larger fluctuations in inflation.

get inflation rate is 10 percent in the first year, 8 percent in the next year, 6.4 percent in the third year, 5.1 percent in the fourth year, 4.1 percent in the fifth year, and so on, eventually getting to the target of 2 percent inflation.

A policy that aggressively counters price shocks (with g large and k near zero) results in large fluctuations in output and unemployment. This is clear from Equation 17.2. Suppose that the sensitivity of inflation f to output is 0.2. Then, to achieve a value of k equal to 0.8, we set g equal to 1. With these coefficients, suppose that a positive shock initially raises inflation by 10 percent above target. With $g = 1$, according to the MP curve in Equation 17.2, this reduces output below potential by 10 percent in the period right after the shock. Eventually, output comes back to potential as inflation declines. When g is large, the drop in output is large and, because of Okun's law, the rise in unemployment is large. On the other side, a negative shock that lowers inflation by 10 percent requires output to rise by 10 percentage points above potential if g is 1. According to Okun's law, unemployment falls in this case. A policy that

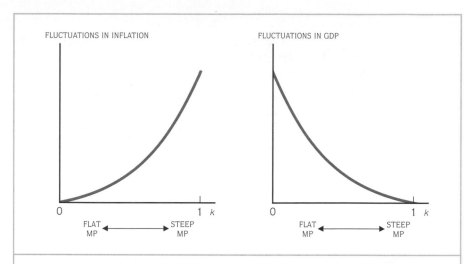

FIGURE 17.3   INFLATION AND OUTPUT LOSSES FOR ALTERNATIVE POLICIES

For $k = 0$, policy changes output enough to make price shocks disappear from inflation after only one year. The average inflation loss is small, but the output loss is substantial. At $k = 1$, policy keeps real GDP equal to potential GDP and lets the price shock influence actual inflation fully.

rolls completely with price shocks (g equal to zero) has a completely stable level of output and employment.

The implications of the choice of the coefficient k for inflation and output losses are shown in Figure 17.3. Because the inflation loss and output loss are related to the squared deviations from normal, the two curves sag as k is raised from zero.

There is another way we can depict the same trade-off. In Figure 17.4, we draw a curve representing the policy frontier in a diagram where average GDP fluctuations are on the horizontal axis and average inflation fluctuations are on the vertical axis. Note how Figure 17.2 demonstrates that the policy rule determines a point on this trade-off.

The Inflation-Output Policy Frontier

1. The optimal policy response to a shift in aggregate demand is to reverse the shift through a change in aggregate demand policy. In that case, the shift causes neither an inflation loss nor an output loss.

2. A general policy for dealing with price shocks is to let the actual amount of inflation be a fraction k of the amount of the shock. The rest of the shock is canceled through aggregate demand policy.

3. An aggressive anti-inflation policy has a value of k close to 0.

4. There is a policy frontier defined by different values of k from 0 to 1. The frontier shows the available combinations of average inflation loss and average output loss. The frontier curves toward the origin.

Finding an Optimal Policy

The policy frontier of Figure 17.4 shows the alternative combinations of inflation and output loss available using different policies. We now show that best policy achieves a compromise between the two types of losses. Remember that the best policy is the one closest to the origin, that is, the one that achieves low values of both output loss and inflation loss. Uncompromising policies are unattractive for two reasons:

1. A policy of strict price stability (a flat MP curve, with $k = 0$, the point at the lower right-hand end of the policy frontier) involves a large amount of output loss. It takes large movements of output to keep inflation exactly at zero in the face of oil price shocks and other shifts in the process.

2. A policy of strict output stability (a vertical MP curve, with $k = 1$, the point at the upper-left-hand end of the policy frontier) involves a large amount of inflation loss. When an inflationary shock occurs, the policy does nothing to offset the shock. Not only does inflation jump upward in the year of the shock, but inflation is higher in future years as well, because the shock raises expected inflation.

Uncompromising policies are unsuitable because, in both cases, the trade-off set by the policy frontier strongly favors making at least a small compromise. From strict inflation stability, a small move toward the middle of the frontier gives a large payoff in reduced output loss with only a small sacrifice of inflation loss. From strict output stability, a small move to the middle gives a large payoff in reduced inflation loss with only a small sacrifice of output loss.

Optimal policy for responding to price shocks is shown in Figure 17.5. To find the optimal compromise, we superimpose the policy frontier of Figure 17.4 on the family of social indifference curves from Figure 17.1. The best point on the frontier is the one tangent to the indifference curve closest to the origin.

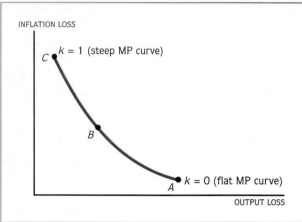

FIGURE 17.4   THE POLICY FRONTIER FOR OUTPUT AND INFLATION LOSSES

Every point on the frontier can be achieved by a policy that lets output respond to inflation. At the upper left is the point of minimal output loss and maximal inflation loss ($k = 1$). At the lower right is the point of low inflation loss and high output loss, corresponding to the other extreme ($k = 0$).

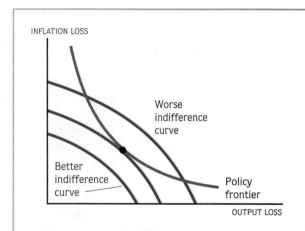

FIGURE 17.5   THE OPTIMAL POLICY FOR RESPONDING TO PRICE SHOCKS

The colored line shows the policy frontier. At the upper left are policies that stabilize output at the cost of higher average inflation loss. At the lower right are policies that stabilize inflation at the cost of higher average output loss. The optimal policy is in the middle, where the frontier is tangent to the indifference curve closest to the origin of all the indifference curves that touch the policy frontier.

In Chapter 16, we looked at the macro performance of the United States from the 1970s to the present in terms of output-inflation loops. In those diagrams, inflation is on the vertical axis and output is on the horizontal axis. Recall that flat loops represent large output fluctuations and small inflation fluctuations, performance corresponding to values of k near zero. The steep (standing-up) loops represent the reverse—large inflation fluctuations and small output fluctuations, performance corresponding to values of k near 1.

The Message for Policy Makers

It is not an easy matter to conduct macro policy in an optimal way. Our analysis has reached two conclusions about the appropriate response to shocks in the economy:

1. If the shock affects only aggregate demand, then a compensating change in aggregate demand policy (monetary or fiscal) eliminates both the inflation loss and the output loss.

2. If the shock affects the price adjustment schedule, then the best policy divides its effects between reducing inflation and unemployment according to the rule that the amount of inflation in excess of the target declines by a fraction k each year.

In general, to develop policy within our model, the policy maker needs to be able to separate shocks into their aggregate demand and price adjustment components and then figure out the magnitude of the response needed to fully offset the aggregate demand shock and partially offset the price adjustment shock. Clearly, some technical analysis is necessary to do this.

The Taylor Rule and Optimal Policy

We showed in Chapter 16 that the Taylor rule is *stabilizing*. When real GDP is greater than potential GDP or when inflation is greater than the target inflation rate, following the Taylor rule smooths out fluctuations. We now show that, when the Taylor rule is stabilizing, it is also consistent with an *optimal* policy for responding to price shocks.

Recall the Taylor rule from Chapter 16,

$$r = (1 + \delta)\pi + B\hat{Y} + R^* - \delta\pi^* \tag{17.4}$$

where π is inflation, π^* is the target inflation rate, $\hat{Y}$ is the GDP gap, and R^* is the equilibrium real interest rate. The Taylor rule is stabilizing, because when inflation rises above the target inflation rate, the Fed raises the nominal interest rate by more than inflation rises, increasing the real interest rate. It is important to understand that, for the Taylor rule to be stabilizing, the coefficient δ must be positive. If $\delta = 0$, the real interest rate does not change when inflation exceeds its target.

The optimal policy for responding to price shocks, as shown in Figure 17.5, is where the policy frontier is tangent to the social indifference curve. This requires a value of k between 0 and 1. Since k is defined as $1 - fg$, this means that g must be between 0 and $1/f$. If the sensitivity of inflation f to output is 0.2, g must be between 0 and 5. Recall that g is defined as $\delta/(B + \sigma)$. As long as the Taylor rule is stabilizing, δ, B, and σ, and therefore g, are all positive. Since g is greater than 0, k is less than 1, and the Taylor rule will not produce a policy of strict output stability. What about the other extreme? While it is possible, according to the equation for the Taylor rule, for the Fed to make δ so large that g is greater than 5 and k is less than 0, this would be an unrealistically aggressive anti-inflationary policy. For the numerical example in Chapter 16, which was used to compare the Taylor rule interest rate with the actual short-term interest rate in Figure 16.8, $\delta = B = 0.5$. Since σ is positive, this produces a value of g less than 1 and therefore nowhere near 5. The Taylor rule with realistic values of δ does not produce a policy of strict price stability.

We have shown that the Taylor rule produces a point on the policy frontier between strict price stability and strict output stability. In terms of Figure 17.4, this would be represented by point B rather than points A or C. This does not mean that, in Figure 17.5, the Taylor rule will necessarily achieve the tangency between the policy frontier and the indifference curve. What it does mean is that, unlike policies of strict price stability or strict output stability, the Taylor rule is consistent with an optimal policy.

Nominal GDP Targeting

There is another, less technical, way to express optimal policy. The alternative begins with the observation that optimal policy tends to stabilize nominal GDP. Suppose that, in some year, a positive aggregate demand shock raises real GDP without much effect on prices. It shows up as above-normal growth of nominal GDP. A rule that calls for steady nominal GDP would automatically offset aggregate demand shocks, just as our optimal policy recommends.

When a positive price-adjustment shock strikes, the optimal policy is to let part of the shock raise prices and part of the shock reduce output and raise unemployment. Keeping nominal GDP on a prescribed growth track does exactly that. Nominal GDP is the product of the price level and real GDP. If the price level jumps, real GDP must fall to keep nominal GDP growth at a prescribed rate. Keeping nominal GDP growth at a prescribed rate is a compromise policy of the type we derived as optimal.

The degree of compromise in a policy that stabilizes nominal GDP seems to favor unemployment stability over price stability. The value of the coefficient of response g for a nominal GDP policy is 1. As we showed, when $g = 1$, the value of k is 0.8 for the numerical example of price adjustment used here.

RESEARCH IN PRACTICE
The Rogoff Principle: Appoint a Central Banker Tougher than Ourselves on Inflation

In 2004, President George W. Bush reappointed Alan Greenspan to a fifth four-year term as chair of the Fed. Greenspan was first appointed by President Ronald Reagan, and was reappointed by Presidents George H. W. Bush and Bill Clinton. He has a reputation and a track record for keeping inflation low. Is there a deeper logic to putting monetary policy into the hands of a proven inflation fighter?

Kenneth Rogoff of Harvard University showed why rational citizens would want a central banker who was a single-minded enemy of inflation, even when the citizens themselves would try to balance inflation against other evils, such as unemployment.

In many arenas of life, we would benefit today if we could commit to taking some future action. For example, parents want their teenage children to believe that the children will lose their driving privileges if they get into an accident. But after an accident occurs, the parents may decide on a less serious punishment, because they find it inconvenient if the kids cannot drive themselves. The children can figure this out in advance, so the announced policy will not make them more careful drivers. In this situation, the parents would rationally choose an arrangement that took the punishment decision out of their hands—they might buy insurance that required teenagers to stop driving after an accident. The parents would turn the punishment decision over to someone tougher than themselves.

Rogoff says that the citizens choosing a central banker are in the same situation. We would like everyone to know that we have a strong anti-inflation policy. The benefits of having that policy exceed the costs of giving up a more flexible policy

in the future. But if we keep monetary policy in our own hands, nobody will believe it will be a strong anti-inflation policy. Our adoption of an anti-inflation policy will not be credible, and the public will not respond to the policy. The answer is to put monetary policy into the hands of a central banker with a strong willingness to fight inflation.

Note what it takes to make this argument valid. First, there must be some benefit to the announcement of a tough policy—teenagers drive more carefully or wage and price increases are moderated. Second, there must be some reason why a simple policy is not credible—parents would not actually follow through or monetary policy will fail to counter inflation because of concerns about high unemployment. Third, the outsider must be credible. The insurance company must enforce its rule and the tough central banker must stick to the anti-inflation policy—and the relevant actors (teenage drivers or wage-price setters) must believe that this will happen.

Appointing a tough individual to be central banker is not the only answer to the problem of credibility. Another would be to put monetary policy on autopilot. Milton Friedman's proposal that the money supply should grow 3 percent per year no matter what happens is one example. Other, more sophisticated autopilot rules that respond directly to inflation might apply the principle more effectively.

The Rogoff principle explains why countries choose central bankers who are tough on inflation. The United States and many other countries have achieved low rates of inflation. President Bush's reappointment of Greenspan is completely consistent with the principle.

Eighty percent of a price adjustment shock is tolerated as a continued increase in inflation the year after it occurs. Twenty percent is extinguished by permitting output to fall. Thereafter, 20 percent of inflation is offset each year, by keeping output below normal. Stabilizing nominal GDP corresponds to a fairly steep MP curve.

Suppose the initial inflation impact from a shock is 10 percent. Under the fixed nominal GDP policy, real GDP falls by 10 percent, and inflation in the following year is reduced to 8 percent. From Okun's law, this means that unemployment rises by 3 percent in the first year.

If the public is so opposed to inflation that the optimal value of k is well below 0.8, then nominal GDP targeting is inappropriate; it gives excessive inflation losses that will not be made up, in the public's view, by the lower unemployment losses it will bring. Or, if the public cares less about inflation, nominal GDP targeting will bring excessive unemployment losses that will not be made up by its favorable influence on inflation losses. In either case, it would be possible to change the policy goal and let nominal GDP respond to the price shock. If $k = 0.8$ is too large, then nominal GDP should be reduced when price shocks occur. If $k = 0.8$ is too small, then nominal GDP could be allowed to grow a bit when a price shock occurs. But the simplicity of a fixed nominal GDP may outweigh the benefits of modifying the path of nominal GDP in this way.[6]

What is the relation between the Taylor rule and nominal GDP targeting? If $\delta = B = 0.5$, g is less than 1 and k is greater than 0.8. This produces a steeper MP curve than nominal GDP targeting. Nothing in the Taylor rule, however, requires δ to equal B. If the parameters in the Taylor rule were set so that $\delta = B + \sigma$, the Fed would raise the nominal interest rate more in response to increases in inflation over its target than increases in the GDP gap. This would produce the same MP curve as nominal GDP targeting. If there were a preference for a flatter MP curve, δ could be raised even further.

17.5 | CHANGING THE POLICY FRONTIER

The policy described in the previous section is optimal in the sense that it tells policy makers how to make the best of a given situation. But the policy does not make the situation better. We should spend at least as much effort thinking about how to move the policy frontier toward the origin as we spend thinking about choosing the best point on the frontier. If the frontier were closer to the origin, both inflation loss and unemployment loss would be lower.

[6]See Robert E. Hall, "Macroeconomic Policy under Structural Change," in *Industrial Change and Public Policy* (Federal Reserve Bank of Kansas City, 1983), pp. 85–111, and James Tobin, "Commentary," in *Industrial Change and Public Policy*, pp. 113–122. A review of the alternative proposals is found in John B. Taylor, "What Would Nominal GNP Targeting Do to the Business Cycle?" *Carnegie-Rochester Conference Series on Public Policy*, Vol. 22 (1985), pp. 61–84.

Implement Monetary Policy Rules

We saw in Chapter 16 how monetary policy rules, if properly implemented, can improve macroeconomic performance. The key insight was that it is not enough to have a policy rule where the Fed raises the nominal interest rate when inflation increases. It is necessary for the nominal interest rate to rise by more than inflation rises, so that the real interest rate increases. This is known as the Taylor principle. The higher real interest rate decreases investment and net exports, stabilizing the economy and bringing inflation down. The specification of the Taylor rule incorporates this stabilizing property.

The historical experience with monetary policy rules for the United States was also discussed in Chapter 16. In the 1970s, the Fed did not raise the nominal interest rate by enough when inflation rose, and monetary policy was not stabilizing. Starting in the mid-1980s, the Fed has raised the nominal interest rate by more than inflation, and monetary policy has been stabilizing.

What are the normative implications of this change in policy? The implementation of a stabilizing monetary policy rule has moved the policy frontier toward the origin. Comparing the 1970s with the 1990s, inflation has been reduced, decreasing inflation loss, and the output gap has narrowed, decreasing output loss. While the specific choice of an optimal policy depends on the location of the indifference curve, a matter of both economic and political debate, that is not the most important point. By implementing a stabilizing monetary policy rule along the lines of the Taylor rule, the Fed has moved the policy frontier closer to the origin, lowering both inflation loss and output loss and enabling the economy to be on a better indifference curve.

Streamline the Labor Market

The policy frontier lies far from the origin because wages do not respond quickly and vigorously to the situation in the labor market. When an inflation shock strikes, policy has to raise unemployment to get inflation back down. When wages are less responsive, a larger rise in unemployment is necessary. If wages could be made to adjust rapidly to surpluses and shortages of labor, then the average unemployment loss needed to keep inflation loss at a given level would be lower. The policy frontier would be closer to the origin.

Because the reasons for sluggish adjustment of wages are not well understood, it is not obvious what types of new policies would speed up the process. Some proposals include the following:

1. *Facilitate Job Matching.* In the highly decentralized labor market of the United States, employers have trouble getting in touch with potential workers. There may be a large number of qualified people ready to work at a particular job at a low wage. If the employer cannot let them know about the job, it may be necessary to hire a nearby worker at a higher wage. Internet job listing makes it possible to draw from a larger number of potential workers. Or, if better information were available about the

number of qualified job seekers, firms would be in a better position to tailor wage offers to the state of the market. Federal and state employment agencies have tried to perform this service for many years, however, and found that employers are reluctant to list most types of jobs. Employers fear having to deal with thousands of unqualified applicants if they list jobs publicly. Instead, they seem to prefer to look at smaller numbers of candidates located privately. There seems to be no basis for hoping that the labor market could be significantly improved by expansion of public job listings.

2. *Eliminate Government Price and Wage Fixing.* Hundreds of government regulations have the effect of either fixing prices and wages directly or limiting the flexibility of businesses in setting prices and wages. The Davis-Bacon Act, for example, prevents contractors from cutting construction costs by taking advantage of slack conditions in markets for construction workers. Local governments regulate bus and taxi fares, so they cannot fall to accommodate the increased supply of drivers in times of higher unemployment. Many government regulations that limited price and wage flexibility have been abolished, however. Airlines are now free to adjust fares whenever market conditions change. Most restrictions on professionals publicizing their prices have been lifted. Still, the scope for further reform in this area is limited.

3. *Reform Unemployment Compensation.* Unemployed workers receive unemployment benefits for up to six months after a job loss. Consequently, their incentives to look for new work and to accept new jobs at lower wages are reduced. Unemployment compensation serves a vital purpose and should not be abolished, but certain types of reforms could improve incentives without making the unemployed suffer. The most important would be to make employers pay more for benefits whenever possible. If an employer had to pay for benefits during a layoff, the employer might prefer to keep an employee at work and cut prices as necessary to sell output. Publicly financed benefits create incentives to lay off a worker, produce less, and maintain a higher price when demand falls.

Improve Indexation

In Chapter 16, we saw that, when wages are linked directly to prices through cost-of-living indexation, the impact of outside price shocks is amplified: A price shock goes immediately into wages, then into costs, and finally into prices again, all within the same year. Although indexation prevents workers from being left behind by general inflation, it is harmful to the economy when wages rise in response to oil or other outside price shocks.

The ideal method of cost-of-living escalation would omit price increases that arise from imports and other materials costs. Although economists have suggested price indexes that would perform better than the CPI for wage indexation, nobody has started to use them for actual wage setting. It is not easy to persuade a skeptical employer or labor union that a new price index is superior to the tried-and-true consumer price index. Proposals to make much smaller changes in the indexes used for wage indexation have encountered stiff resistance. There are no grounds for optimism that wage setters will voluntarily adopt new indexation methods. Nor is it clear that the government can or should try to force changes in this area.

Avoid Government Price Shocks

Sometimes the government itself creates a shock in the price adjustment process. An important example occurred in Britain in 1979. The government cut income taxes and substituted a value-added tax (VAT) to raise the same revenue. Because the value-added tax is imposed on firms, it adds to costs just like an increase in the price of a material input. The VAT is much like a sales tax. In terms of the price adjustment model of Chapter 16, the value-added tax adds an inflationary impetus Z in the year that it goes into effect.

In Britain, the value-added tax shock and the oil price shock occurred simultaneously. The British economy suffered from more inflation and a larger reduction in output than the U.S. economy, which suffered only from the oil price shock. If self-inflicted government price shocks can be kept to a minimum, the policy frontier will be closer to the origin.

Avoiding government price shocks need not prevent tax reform or other useful changes in the government's influence on the economy. For example, a value-added tax can be changed in a simple way that does not change its favorable properties as a tax; it could be instituted so that the cost fell on workers rather than on businesses. Then the switch to the tax would not create a price shock. Changes in all types of economic policies need to be designed with the harmful effects of macro price shocks in mind.

Use Trade Policy

One of the ways the government affects the variability of inflation is through trade policy. Generally, policies that restrict imports raise inflation when they are imposed and lower inflation when they are removed. As noted in Chapter 12, different protectionist policies can have very different effects on U.S. prices. Quotas have a strong and immediate effect on prices. Tariffs have a strong effect if they are not absorbed by foreign sellers. For example, an oil tariff would immediately raise the U.S. price of oil, because it is unlikely that the world oil price would fall by much in response to the tariff. On the other hand, a tariff on Japanese cars might well be absorbed by Japanese automakers, just as they absorbed most of the impact of the appreciating yen in 1995.

Each time a protectionist measure is imposed or tightened, it gives a one-time shock to inflation. If a tariff is on a single important product, such as oil, it can cause a perceptible shock to total inflation. An equal but negative shock occurs if the tariff is taken off. Stabilization policy is significantly more difficult and less successful when protectionist measures are imposed and removed to satisfy other goals, such as protecting ailing domestic industries, fostering energy conservation, or reducing the trade deficit.

Improving the Policy Frontier

1. Policies designed to streamline the labor market could push the inflation-output frontier toward the origin. The same amount of inflation loss would be achieved with less output loss if inflation responded more vigorously to unemployment.

2. Public job placement has not been very successful. Reduced government price and wage fixing might be a small help. Reform in unemployment compensation would also improve the frontier a little.

3. The government should be careful not to create unnecessary price shocks.

REVIEW AND PRACTICE

Major Points

1. The general policy implication of recent research in macroeconomics is that policy should be formulated as a rule or contingency plan.

2. Macroeconomic policy can be logically formulated and evaluated using the target and instrument framework. A social welfare function describes the goals of policy.

3. As in other areas of economics, trade-offs are widespread in macroeconomics.

4. Uncertainty in the models leads to less active use of the policy instruments.

5. High inflation is bad because it causes people to hold too little money. It is also difficult to adjust the tax system to be neutral to inflation. Further, inflation sometimes brings higher uncertainty, which can interfere with efficient resource allocation. Deflation is undesirable for similar reasons.

6. Variations in the rate of unemployment are undesirable because the social costs of periods of high unemployment outweigh the benefits of periods of low unemployment.

7. Indifference curves between inflation loss and unemployment loss curve away from the origin. Higher indifference curves represent poorer macroeconomic performance.

8. Policy rules describe how accommodative monetary policy makers are to inflation. More accommodative policy results in better output performance but worse inflation performance.

9. The Taylor rule is an example of an optimal macroeconomic policy.

10. A rule of keeping nominal GDP constant is another way to characterize an optimal macroeconomic policy.

11. The only type of policy move that could improve both inflation and unemployment performance would be an inward shift of the policy frontier, but unfortunately, the prospects seem limited for this type of policy.

Key Terms and Concepts

new normative macroeconomics	policy frontier
activist policy rules	squared error
discretionary policy	inflation loss
passive policy rule	output loss
social welfare function	

Questions for Discussion and Review

1. If the purpose of the final exam is to motivate students to study, why will the instructor not cancel the final at the last minute, after all studying has occurred, to save everybody's time and effort?

2. What is the basic argument against discretionary policy?

3. If the effect of a policy instrument is uncertain, will policy makers be more or less aggressive in the use of the instrument than they would be under certainty?

4. Give some of the reasons why both inflation and deflation are undesirable.

5. Explain why both high and variable unemployment are undesirable. Why does the policy frontier deal just with the variability and not with the level of unemployment?

6. Explain the consequences for unemployment and inflation if policy makers fully accommodate a price shock. Repeat for zero accommodation and 50 percent accommodation.

7. Describe the axes of the policy frontier diagram and how to find points on the frontier.

8. How should policy makers choose the best point on the frontier?

9. How much accommodation of price shocks occurs if nominal GDP targets are followed?

10. List some of the proposals that have been made to shift the policy frontier inward.

11. Trace out the effects of a restrictive quota on auto imports.

Problems

NUMERICAL

1. Calculate the value of k that corresponds to the policy of keeping nominal GDP at a given level in the year that a price shock occurs. Assume that f equals 1. Assume that the economy starts in equilibrium, with $Y = Y^*$, $\pi^* = 0$, and $\pi = 0$. Then an inflationary shock of 10 percent, $Z = 0.1$, occurs. Compute the change in inflation, using Equation 17.1. Compute the change in output from Equation 17.2. Show that the percentage change in real GDP plus the percentage change in the price level equals zero, the percentage change in nominal GDP.

2. The economy of problem 4, Chapter 16, starts at potential ($\hat{Y} = 0$) with the Fed following a policy rule that implies that $\pi = k\pi_{-1} + Z$. Then it is hit by an inflation shock of $Z = 0.1$. Policy uses a value of k of 0.9. Compute the change in the interest rate necessary to achieve the policy. Also compute the changes in π and $\hat{Y}$. Repeat the calculations for $k = 0.1$. Explain the differences.

3. The purpose of this exercise is to illustrate the trade-off between inflation and unemployment. However, we focus on the output gap rather than on unemployment because the two are so closely related due to Okun's law. Assume $\pi^* = 0$. Suppose that the MP curve

$$\hat{Y} = -g\pi$$

is substituted into the price adjustment equation to get

$$\pi = (1 - 0.2g)\pi_{-1} + Z.$$

a. Starting from $Y = Y^*$ and $\pi = 0$ (zero percent inflation), use the second equation to calculate the effect on inflation for years 1 through 10 of a price shock $Z = 0.1$ (a 10 percent shock to the price level). Set $g = 0.5$.

b. Using the values of inflation you calculated in part a, calculate the value of the GDP gap, $\hat{Y}$, for all 10 years using the policy rule.

c. Plot the values of inflation and the output gap for all 10 years on two time series diagrams (put the variable on the vertical axis and the year on the horizontal axis).

   d. Plot the values of the output gap and inflation on a diagram with inflation on the vertical axis and the output gap on the horizontal axis
(like Figure 17.5).

   e. Calculate the average squared loss for inflation. That is, square each
value of inflation (π^2) for all 10 years, sum up the squares, and divide
by 10. Calculate the average squared loss for the output gap in the
same way. Now repeat the calculations in parts a through d and the inflation loss and output loss for $g = 0.1$ and $g = 0.9$. You should now
have three pairs of inflation loss and output loss, one for each of the
three values of the policy rule g. Plot the three pairs on a diagram with
average inflation loss on the vertical axis and average output loss (output gap) on the horizontal axis. Comment on the position of the three
points. Is a trade-off between inflation loss and output loss evident?
Compare your diagram with that of Figure 17.4. (Note that the output gap loss and the unemployment loss occupy similar relative positions because of Okun's law.)

4. This exercise shows how a stochastic dynamic model with shocks can lead
to business cycle fluctuations. Suppose that the income identity is

$$Y = C + I + G,$$

where $G = 750$. Consumption is equal to

$$C = 80 + 0.63Y_{-1}$$

and investment is a random variable given by

$$I = 650 + (7 - \text{number from a roll of a pair of dice}) \times 10.$$

   a. Roll a pair of dice 20 times, and record the number for each roll. Use
the investment function to calculate investment for each roll. This
gives 20 years of stochastic investment. Investment in year 1 is the
first roll and investment in year 20 is the last roll. Plot the values of investment on a time series chart with investment on the vertical axis
and the year on the horizontal axis. The values should look random,
with investment fluctuating around 650.

   b. Now use the values of investment for the 20 years to calculate income
Y. Substitute the consumption function into the income identity. Start
with Y_{-1} equal to 4,000 and investment equal to the value you calculated for year 1. Then calculate the second year's income by substituting in income for the first year for Y_{-1} and investment in the second
year. Do the same thing for the third year and so on through year 20.

   c. Plot the resulting values of income Y for the 20 years, with the year on
the horizontal axis. The average value should be near 4,000, but you

should see some prolonged fluctuations around this average value that look like business cycles. Compare the prolonged fluctuations of Y with the random but less-prolonged fluctuations of investment I. Calculate the average time between peaks for each series. Unless your dice are loaded, the average time between peaks for income will be longer than that for investment. Try to explain why.

5. Suppose that price adjustment and inflationary expectations are given by Equations 15.14 and 15.15, respectively. Policy is given by Equation 17.2 with $g = 0$. Initially there is an oil price shock of 2.5 percent ($Z = 0.025$).

   a. Calculate inflation and expected inflation over time. Are expectations rational?

   b. Is the monetary authority using a policy rule? Explain your answer.

ANALYTICAL

1. Is the Taylor rule an optimal policy rule?

2. What is the relation between the Taylor rule and nominal GDP targeting?

3. In Chapter 14, we showed how monetary policy affects the economy with a lag. What are the implications of these lags for our suggestions about optimal policy in this chapter? What do lags in the effect of money imply for nominal GDP targeting?

4. Compare a policy of fixing the money stock (as described in Chapter 14) to a policy of fixing the interest rate. Prepare a brief argument in favor of each type of targeting; list advantages and disadvantages.

5. Using the IS-LM method, show what the Fed must do to the money supply to reduce output by a certain percentage when there is a price shock. Could the same actions be undertaken by fiscal policy? Why might a mix of monetary and fiscal policies be used to reduce output after a price shock?

6. Suppose that, in response to a large and unexpected oil price shock, the Fed acts to keep output at potential. Inflationary expectations are given by the expression $\pi^e = 0.9\pi_{-1}$. Prices are sticky and price adjustment is given by an equation like Equation 15.14. The changes in the money stock, prices, and output for the first four years follow:

YEAR	$\%\Delta M$	$\%\Delta P$	$\%\Delta Y$
1	10	10	0
2	9	9	0
3	8.1	8.1	0
4	7.3	7.3	0

  a. How large was the oil price shock?

  b. An economist writing for a popular newsweekly comments: "The Fed is up to its old tricks again, fueling inflation with money-stock growth." The economist goes on to note that, every time the Fed increases the money supply by x percent, it leads to an increase in prices of x percent, just as predicted by the classical model. Is this economist right; that is, has inflation over the last four years been caused by increases in the money stock?

  c. The economist finishes with an admonition to the Fed to stick to a constant money stock rule. This, the economist asserts, will give us noninflationary full employment. If the Fed had held the money stock constant over the last four years, would output have remained constant? Diagram the path the economy would have followed using an output-inflation loop.

7. Suppose that, as a result of the Fed's policy rule, inflation is given by Equation 17.3, where the parameter k lies between 0 and 1. Sketch the output-inflation loop for the case of an oil price shock. Is there overshooting?

MACROECONOMIC POLICY IN THE WORLD ECONOMY

In Chapters 16 and 17, we studied the positive and normative implications of macroeconomic policy making for the United States. In this chapter, we extend the analysis to the world economy. Macroeconomic policy for the United States is conducted under a regime of floating exchange rates, free movement of capital, an implicit inflation target, and a monetary policy where the real interest rate is increased when inflation rises. A number of other countries, including Australia, Canada, and the United Kingdom, and the countries that have combined their national currencies into the euro, conduct macroeconomic policy in a similar manner. Still other countries, including China, fix their exchange rates and restrict capital movement.

We saw in Chapter 12 that changes in U.S. macroeconomic policy can have significant effects on foreign trade and on the exchange rate. This chapter extends our analysis of international macroeconomic issues in a number of ways. First, we look at the international monetary and financial system from a world perspective rather than just considering the role of the United States in the system. In addition to describing the system as it exists in the 2000s, we describe the history of the system. Then we examine monetary policy rules in the world economy and discuss why countries are moving away from fixed exchange rates. We consider the role of the exchange rate in the monetary policy rule and see how the use of policy rules has improved macroeconomic performance in the world economy. Finally, we analyze macroeconomic performance in Japan during the 1990s and early 2000s.

18.1 | THE INTERNATIONAL FINANCIAL AND MONETARY SYSTEM

Within the United States, the financial and monetary system has a seamless quality. It is almost as easy to make a payment or borrow three thousand miles away, over many state borders, as it is in your own state or city. The world economy is not as seamless. With relatively few exceptions, U.S. currency cannot be spent directly in other countries. Borrowing in another country is possible only for larger corporations and then only in a few countries with advanced, open capital markets. In some countries, such as the People's Republic of China, there are detailed controls on the movement of currency and securities across the border in both directions. In many countries, the government tries to push up the price at which foreigners can trade dollars and other currencies for the domestic currency. The result is a black market or a curb market where the traveler gets a better deal but may run into trouble with the law. Currency black markets flourished in the former Soviet Union as law enforcement weakened, but artificially high exchange rates were maintained for the ruble.

There is a strong trend toward making the world economy more integrated. For example, the nations of western Europe have almost completely integrated their financial markets, so that it is as easy for a European business to borrow or lend in another European country as it is for an American business to borrow or lend in another state. In January 1999, 11 European countries—Austria, Belgium, Finland, France, Germany, Ireland, Italy, Luxembourg, the Netherlands, Portugal, and Spain—combined their national currencies to form the euro, and Greece joined in 2001. In January 2002, the individual currencies were eliminated in favor of euro notes and coins. While not a political entity, these countries are called the **Eurozone**. The European Central Bank (ECB) conducts monetary policy for the Eurozone. Following the precedent set by the former German central bank, the Bundesbank, it has a mandate to

ECB: keep inflation low

keep inflation low. Within the Eurozone, movements of labor and capital are almost as free as among the states of the United States. At the same time, there will be a continuing trend toward free movement of currency and financial securities across the borders of countries that have previously controlled those flows.

In the 2000s, the world financial and monetary system can be summarized in the following way: There are economies with sophisticated, integrated financial markets, such as the United States, the Eurozone, Japan, and Britain. These countries have large, active markets in stocks, bonds, options, and other financial instruments. They permit foreigners to trade in their markets on essentially an equal footing with their own citizens, and they do not interfere with their citizens' transactions in foreign markets. There are no inhibitions to completely free markets in their currencies and central bank reserves. Holders of checking accounts in any of the countries can move central bank reserves from one country to another by writing checks, just as account holders in the United States can move them from one bank to another. The major currencies (dollar, yen, euro, and pound) exchange for each other at rates set in extremely fluid, free markets.

Movement btw major currencies = fluid

Although these governments do not control the financial markets directly, the governments influence the behavior of the markets by trading. Central banks such as the Federal Reserve, the Bank of Japan, the ECB, and the Bank of England hold large portfolios of short-term government securities. Each bank usually has large holdings of securities issued by each of the major governments. There are two basic dimensions to central bank policy. One is standard monetary policy, as we discussed in Chapter 14. If the Bank of England buys more British government securities and expands its reserves correspondingly, that is an expansionary move that lowers the British interest rate and stimulates the British economy. The second dimension is the split of the central bank's portfolio between domestic and foreign securities. The Bank of Japan could sell Japanese government securities and use the proceeds to buy U.S. Treasury bills, for example. This move, called a **foreign exchange market intervention,** often is called "selling yen and buying dollars." However, a more detailed description is "selling yen-denominated securities and buying dollar-denominated securities." The effect of the intervention is to raise the exchange rate of the dollar relative to the yen. The magnitude of the exchange-rate effect per billion dollars of intervention may be very small because the securities markets where the intervention occurs are enormous.

selling yen to buy the dollar strengthens $

A number of nations still maintain some degree of insulation from the world financial and monetary system. The most common form of separation is controls on the movement of capital. The governments of these countries require permits for financial transactions across their borders. Often the intention is to trap economic activity within the country's borders. Other times it is to limit foreign entrepreneurs from undertaking profitable activities that might otherwise go to citizens. Controls on the movement of goods are also common. Many countries require permits for some or all types of imports. Finally, some countries try to suppress free-market transactions in their currencies. These currencies are **inconvertible,** meaning that they cannot be bought and sold in open markets.

All around the world there is a powerful trend toward reducing restrictions on financial markets. The specific steps that a country needs to take to free up its financial markets and thereby join the world financial and monetary system are as follows:

1. *Open up currency transactions.* Permit anyone inside or outside the country to exchange the country's currency for any other currency at a market-determined price.

2. *Open up capital movement.* Permit anyone in the country to purchase stocks, bonds, or other financial instruments from other countries or raise funds by selling instruments in other markets. Permit foreigners to buy or sell securities in the country's markets and borrow or lend to businesses or individuals.

3. *Open up movement of goods.* Permit anyone in the country to buy goods and services anywhere else in the world and permit foreigners to buy and sell goods and services in the country.

It is worth noting that the list requires new freedoms, not new government institutions. It is not important that a country have a central bank operating on the same principles as the Federal Reserve. A country need not accumulate foreign reserves (foreign securities owned by the central bank) to function within the world system. But all the major players in the current world system have conventional central banks.

How a Central Bank Carries Out Its Exchange-Rate Policy

Central banks buy and sell government securities to affect exchange rates, interest rates, and ultimately the domestic price level. In Chapter 14, we studied the way the Fed sets the monetary base in the United States. Central banks in other countries operate in almost exactly the same way. The only important difference across countries in central banking is that not all countries have reserve requirements. But all central banks issue reserves as well as currency. Here, we extend the discussion of the central bank to consider foreign reserves as well as domestic assets.

Table 18.1 shows the balance sheet of a central bank. On the asset side of the balance sheet are securities that the central bank has purchased. A similar balance sheet for the Fed was presented in Chapter 14. Here, there are two types of securities: domestic and foreign. Domestic securities are denominated in domestic currency; these may be government bonds or even loans to private firms. The value of domestic securities held by a central bank is frequently called **domestic credit.** Domestic credit is the total credit that the central bank

TABLE 18.1

BALANCE SHEET OF A CENTRAL BANK WITH FOREIGN RESERVES

ASSETS	LIABILITIES
Domestic credit	Currency
Foreign reserves	Bank reserves

has extended to the home economy, whether to the government or the private sector. Foreign securities are denominated in foreign currency. Most frequently these are bonds issued by foreign governments. Foreign securities are **foreign reserves.**

Recall that the monetary base is defined as currency plus bank reserves. Because assets must equal liabilities, we know that domestic credit plus foreign credit equals the monetary base. That is,

$$\text{Monetary base} = \text{Domestic credit} + \text{Foreign reserves.} \qquad (18.1)$$

M_B = domestic credit + foreign reserves

Suppose that the central bank wants to increase the money supply to stimulate the economy. It purchases government bonds in the open market—an open-market purchase; this causes domestic credit to rise. This means that the monetary base and the money supply increase. The increase in the money supply lowers the interest rate. Capital flows out of the country, and the currency starts to depreciate as soon as the interest rate begins to fall below the world interest rate.

What if the central bank wants to prevent depreciation? As foreign-denominated bonds begin to look more attractive relative to domestic bonds, the central bank must provide the increased demand for foreign exchange by selling foreign reserves to prevent the exchange rate from depreciating. It does this by entering the foreign exchange market and selling its foreign reserves for domestic currency. Foreign reserves decrease. The decrease in foreign reserves lowers the monetary base and offsets the previous effect of the open-market operation. In fact, since the interest rate does not fall, we know that the decrease in foreign reserves must be exactly equal to the increase in domestic credit. This keeps the money supply from increasing.

In the case of an open-market sale, the same channels keep the money supply from falling. The upward pressure on interest rates leads the central bank to buy foreign reserves; this increases the money supply. If the bank wants to maintain the exchange rate at parity, it cannot change the money supply. Monetary policy cannot be used both for domestic purposes and to stabilize the exchange rate.

Now suppose that there is an expansionary fiscal policy—an increase in government spending. This increase in government spending does not increase the interest rate if the central bank is fixing the exchange rate, because the money supply automatically increases.

Sterilized Intervention

A central bank can offset a potential depreciation of its currency by selling foreign reserves. Then the money supply contracts, the interest rate rises, and the potential depreciation is offset. However, it is possible for the central bank to sell foreign reserves and buy domestic credit at the same time in the same amount. Such a move is called a **sterilized foreign exchange intervention**. From Table 18.1, it is apparent that a sterilized intervention has no effect on the assets of the central bank. Therefore, it has no effect on the monetary base and no effect on the domestic economy.

Under modern conditions with highly integrated capital markets, a sterilized intervention is unlikely to have much effect. A central bank would have to sell a huge volume of foreign reserves to defend its currency against a threatened depreciation. Its ability to make such a move is limited by its stock of foreign reserves. After exhausting its stock, the bank would have to revert to normal monetary contraction.

Capital or Exchange Controls

Capital controls, such as restrictions on the amount of foreign currency that domestic residents can purchase, would permit the domestic interest rate to be different from the world rate. In fact, capital controls are still used in many small countries for exactly this reason. Although they enable monetary policy to be more effective, capital controls have the disadvantage that they reduce the efficiency of international capital markets. Economic efficiency requires that different types of capital be allocated according to their after-tax rate of return. Many taxes already in the world distort the allocation of capital, so more taxes would distort the allocation even further.

Exchange-Rate Policy

1. With high capital mobility and no expected change in the exchange rate, the domestic interest rate is the same as the world interest rate.

2. Under fixed rates, the central bank must act to keep the domestic interest rate equal to the world rate.

3. Fixed exchange rates can also be achieved with capital controls, but capital controls interfere with the efficient allocation of capital.

18.2 | HISTORY OF THE WORLD FINANCIAL AND MONETARY SYSTEM

Until early in the twentieth century, almost all countries defined their monetary units in terms of gold or silver. Among all the countries on the gold standard, there was no room for variation in exchange rates. The dollar and the pound had a relative value of about $5 per pound because the pound was defined as five times as much gold as the dollar. Under the gold standard, convertibility was not an issue. Further, the prevailing notions of the role of government in the nineteenth century limited government restrictions on flows of capital and goods. In particular, very large flows of capital from Britain to the United States and other rapidly growing countries helped speed the process of economic development.

After World War I and the Great Depression in the 1930s, currencies began to lose their connection with gold. Even though the United States did not formally leave the gold standard until 1971, the Federal Reserve stopped redeeming dollar bills for gold in 1933. Similar changes occurred in other countries. Ever since the 1930s, each country's monetary unit has been defined as its paper currency or reserves, not gold or silver. The type of monetary system described in Chapter 14 has been almost universal. As a result, there has been no automatic determination of exchange rates as there was under the gold standard.

Near the end of World War II, in 1944, representatives of major economies (including John Maynard Keynes for Britain) met in Bretton Woods, New Hampshire, to design a new world financial and monetary system to replace the gold standard. Because large fluctuations in exchange rates in the 1920s and 1930s seemed to be undesirable in contrast to the fixed rates guaranteed under the gold standard, the Bretton Woods system proposed to keep exchange rates almost constant. The dollar was to be the reference point of the system. Other countries adopted dollar values for their currencies (called **par values**), such as $2.80 per British pound. Each central bank agreed to keep its own currency within plus or minus 1 percent of the par value.

Under the Bretton Woods system, central banks held substantial amounts of dollar securities, mostly U.S. Treasury bills. When a country's currency rose a little above par, its central bank would purchase dollar securities and sell securities denominated in its own currency, thus depressing the value of its own currency. When the currency dropped a little below par, the bank would sell dollar securities and buy securities in its own currency. In addition, the central bank might tighten its overall monetary policy by reducing its total holdings of securities (an open-market operation, as described in detail in Chapter 14).

The dollar securities of foreign central banks under the Bretton Woods system constituted their foreign *reserves*. When a central bank prevented an appreciation of its currency by purchasing dollar securities, there was a *reserve inflow*. This was generally considered a favorable sign for that economy. When the central bank was defending its currency by selling dollar securities, there was a *reserve outflow*. A reserve outflow could last only as long as the central bank had a stock of reserves of dollar securities. After the stock ran out, the bank would have to turn to other restrictive measures, or cease its policy of stabilizing the exchange rate. Reserve outflows were a matter of great publicity and concern under the Bretton Woods system.

The Bretton Woods system had a built-in instability that ultimately led to its collapse. Its architects did not completely eliminate the possibility of changes in par values. Once a central bank ran out of dollar securities, it would defend its own currency through monetary contraction or it could **devalue** (reduce the par value of its currency). Monetary contraction is a painful process with adverse political consequences most of the time. But, if traders in the exchange market perceive that a devaluation is likely, they push down the market rate immediately. The result is an exchange-rate crisis. The British pound went through a crisis in 1967. The market perceived that British monetary policy was letting the purchasing power of the pound drop below its earlier relation to the dollar and a reversal of policy was politically unlikely under a Labour government. The Bank of England sold all its dollar securities and borrowed extensively in order to sell even more. But the market saw that the par value of the pound of $2.80 exceeded the value that monetary policy would achieve. Traders started selling pound securities and buying dollar and other securities. The Bank of England lacked the power to keep the exchange rate at par. Finally, in November 1967, the British government validated the traders' judgment by lowering the par value to $2.40.

A second problem with the Bretton Woods system was its vulnerability to mistakes in U.S. monetary policy. To maintain fixed exchange rates, other countries had to keep their inflation rates in line with the U.S. inflation rate. High U.S. inflation in the late 1960s made it difficult for most other countries in the system to keep their currencies from rising above par. They bought huge volumes of U.S. government securities to keep their currencies down, but as in the pound sterling crisis, this type of intervention was not enough. The other countries had to either expand their monetary policies and match U.S. inflation or revalue their currencies.

The Devaluation of the Dollar and the Collapse of Bretton Woods

The Bretton Woods system finally broke down in the early 1970s. On August 15, 1971, the Nixon administration launched a series of moves that effectively ended the system. First, the United States ended its commitment to sell gold to other governments for $35 per ounce. Although few governments had used their right to buy gold at this price, the U.S. move made it clear that the United States was not prepared to make a permanent commitment to a fixed purchasing power for the dollar. Second, the United States used the club of a special tariff to force other countries to revalue their currencies against the dollar. The general revaluation of other currencies was equivalent to a dollar devaluation.

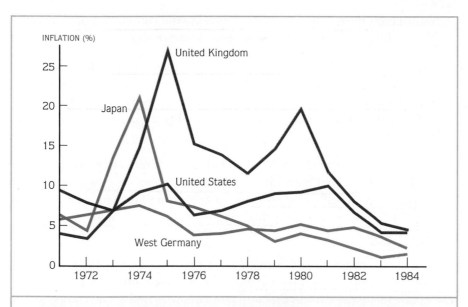

FIGURE 18.1   THE GREAT INFLATION OF THE 1970S

The inflation rate increased in most countries in the 1970s. The increase was larger in Japan and the United Kingdom than in the United States and West Germany. The timing of the increase was also different in different countries.

SOURCE: *International Financial Statistics Yearbook*, International Monetary Fund, 1991, various tables.

The system continued to evolve after 1971. In 1973–74, the price of oil increased fourfold and inflation accelerated. The acceleration was worse for some countries than for others, as shown in Figure 18.1. With widely different inflation rates in different countries, the 1971 parities were soon abandoned as countries found it increasingly difficult to maintain them. The 1974–75 recession, which hit all countries, put additional pressure on existing parities.

The desire of different countries to choose their own macroeconomic policies in response to the 1974–75 recession meant that exchange rates would have to shift further. Eventually most currencies began to float with no set parities, although there were considerable interventions aimed at preventing large movements. The world had emerged from the 1973–74 inflation and the 1974–75 recession with essentially a floating exchange-rate system.

Exchange Rate Policies Today

Countries face a number of policy choices that determine their participation in the international monetary system. Three policy choices that are often considered desirable are

1. *Fixed exchange rates.* Floating exchange rates increase uncertainty, which is often regarded as undesirable. Some economists believe that, by increasing

uncertainty, floating exchange rates decrease the volume of trade, although the evidence supporting this proposition is not strong.

> BUT can't all happen at once...

2. *Free movement of capital.* Controls on capital movements, while allowing a country to keep its interest rate at a different level from the world interest rate, decrease the efficiency of the international financial system and generally (although not universally) are believed to be harmful to the imposing country.

3. *Independent monetary policy.* With an independent monetary policy, such as a Taylor rule, central banks are free to target monetary policy toward the objectives they really care about, such as limiting fluctuations in inflation and GDP, rather than targeting monetary policy toward fixing the exchange rate.

The **macroeconomic policy trilemma** is that only two of these three objectives can be attained simultaneously. The trilemma provides a convenient way to categorize the choices that different countries make. The United States runs an independent monetary policy, allows free capital mobility, and has a flexible exchange rate. As we discussed in Chapter 12, if the Fed wanted to fix the exchange rate, it would have to devote monetary policy to the objective of keeping the U.S. interest rate equal to the world interest rate. This would not be consistent with conducting monetary policy according to the Taylor rule.

The United States has not completely refrained from exchange market intervention. The Federal Reserve Board and the U.S. Treasury can interfere to affect the U.S. exchange rate. The Fed has complete control over the size of its portfolio and therefore the size of the monetary base, and it can exchange dollar-denominated securities for securities of other governments. Although concerns about the value of the dollar in relation to other currencies have been an influence on both dimensions of central bank policy, the United States has permitted the dollar to float in relation to other currencies, with occasional interventions when the dollar reached extreme highs or lows. In 2000, the United States, Germany, Japan, Britain, and France agreed to intervene to bring the dollar down against the euro. Over the years there have been sporadic interventions, like the one in 2000, to counteract large movements in the value of the dollar in both directions, but the United States has had far from fixed exchange rates.

A number of countries have made similar choices. Australia, Canada, and the United Kingdom have flexible exchange rates, allow free movement of capital, and run independent monetary policies that have either implicit or explicit inflation targets. The countries of the Eurozone made a different choice. By combining their national currencies into a single currency, the euro, they committed to irrevocably fix their exchange rates in the same way that the 13 American colonies did in 1792 when they combined their monetary units and formed the U.S. dollar. With free capital mobility among the countries of the

Eurozone, the national central banks gave up the ability to conduct independent monetary policies in the same way that individual U.S. states cannot conduct independent monetary policies.

Asian countries such as China, Hong Kong, and Singapore keep their exchange rates fixed with the U.S. dollar. Other Asian countries, including Japan and Korea, float but intervene much more in foreign exchange markets than the United States and European countries. While the euro has fluctuated by 30 percent up and down against the U.S. dollar between its introduction in 1999 and 2003, the movements in Asian currencies have been much smaller. This has been accomplished by a combination of capital controls and directing monetary policy toward stabilizing the exchange rate.

The International Monetary System

1. From the late 1940s to the early 1970s, the major economies operated under the Bretton Woods system, with fixed exchange rates. Each central bank aimed to keep the value of its currency within a narrow band around its dollar exchange rate.

   1940s – 1970s: Bretton Woods System

2. When inflation rates vary across countries, a system of fixed exchange rates ultimately breaks down. The Bretton Woods system was abandoned in 1971 after inflation worsened in the United States.

3. Under the current system, the dollar floats freely; U.S. policy does little to control its movements.

18.3 | MONETARY POLICY RULES IN THE WORLD ECONOMY

In Chapters 16 and 17, we showed how a monetary policy rule where the Fed increases the real interest rate when inflation rises produces good macroeconomic performance for the United States. One example of this class of policy rules is the Taylor rule, where the interest rate also responds to the output gap. In this section, we extend the analysis of policy rules to the world economy.

 MACROSOLVE EXERCISE

The Demise of Fixed Exchange Rates

An important development of the 1990s and 2000s is that, over time, more countries chose to abandon fixed exchange rates and, instead, adopted a monetary policy based on flexible exchange rates or permanently connected their monetary policy to other countries through monetary union, dollarization, or a currency board. The foremost example of a monetary union is the European Union, where 12 European countries abandoned their national currencies in favor of the euro. Dollarization occurs when a country adopts another country's currency, usually the U.S. dollar, as its national money. Ecuador, El Salvador, and Panama are three countries that have dollarized. A currency board, as in Hong Kong, is a fixed exchange rate where new issues of domestic currency are backed one for one by additional holdings of the key foreign currency.

Forty-seven countries operate a monetary policy with a flexible exchange rate and 50 countries are dollarized, in monetary unions, or use currency boards. These 97 countries endeavor to benefit from the progress made in the practice of monetary policy. They are either tied to a central bank with good price stability goals and instrument setting procedures, or they are trying to pursue an independent monetary policy using these goals and procedures themselves. Seventy-five countries have fixed or heavily managed exchange rates, and seven countries have multiple exchange rates.

One reason for the movement away from fixed exchange rates is the currency crises of the 1990s and 2000s. The crises that occurred in Mexico in 1994, several Asian countries in 1997, Russia in 1998, Brazil in 1999, Turkey in 2000, and Argentina in 2001 had one important feature in common. The crisis countries, for different reasons, found themselves unable to defend a fixed exchange rate when high capital mobility allowed for large and fast capital flows. Since restricting capital flows was not regarded as a desirable option by most of the countries, letting their exchange rates float provided a way to avoid future crises.

Exchange rate policy affects growth and stability. Several large emerging market countries, including Brazil, Korea, and Mexico, have adopted flexible exchange rates combined with clear price stability goals and a system for adjusting the policy instruments. There were no major currency crises in 2002 or 2003, and the movement toward flexible exchange rates and policy rules is one of the reasons for fewer crises and greater stability.

According to the macroeconomic policy trilemma, countries that do not impose controls on currency transactions and capital flows have to choose between a fixed exchange rate and an independent monetary policy. As we saw in Chapter 12, to fix its exchange rate, a country would have to conduct monetary policy so as to keep its interest rate equal to the world interest rate. A monetary policy directed toward keeping the domestic interest rate equal to the world interest rate could not, at the same time, be directed toward raising the real interest rate when inflation increases or responding to changes in the output gap. In other words, a fixed exchange rate is incompatible with a Taylor rule or, more generally, with any monetary policy rule where the central bank responds to anything except the foreign interest rate.

An interesting example of the macroeconomic policy trilemma is the experience of the European Monetary System (EMS). The EMS was the exchange rate system within Europe from 1979 to the establishment of the euro in 1999. While the workings of the EMS were governed by complicated formulas, as a first approximation the member countries agreed to keep their exchange rates within a band of 2.25 percent above or below the German mark. This had the effect of tying countries' monetary policies to those of the German central bank, the Bundesbank, while the Bundesbank assumed responsibility for maintaining low inflation. Like all fixed exchange rate systems, countries could change their exchange rates against the mark.

After a rocky start where, due to incompatible monetary policies between France and Germany, the French frank devalued 11 times against the mark between 1979 and 1984, exchange rates were stabilized within Europe during the second half of the 1980s and early 1990s. During that same period, exchange and capital controls were eliminated so that, by 1990, there was free capital mobility within Europe. According to the macroeconomic policy trilemma, with free capital mobility, member countries of the EMS that wanted to maintain a fixed exchange rate with the German mark had no choice but to keep their interest rates equal to the German interest rate.

The system worked well until German reunification in 1991. Following reunification, there was a large fiscal expansion in an attempt to narrow the gap in living standards between the former East and West Germanys, higher wages in the former East Germany, and higher inflation, which caused the Bundesbank to raise the German interest rate. This left the other members of the EMS in a quandary. They could either raise their own interest rates, a policy incompatible with their domestic objectives, especially during a period of high unemployment and slow growth, or they could devalue their currencies against the German mark. The attempts by France, Italy, and the United Kingdom to keep their exchange rates fixed to the mark once Germany raised its interest rate culminated in a series of currency crises that led to the United Kingdom leaving the EMS in 1992 and France and Italy, while not officially leaving the EMS, adopting very wide bands of plus or minus 15 percent against the mark in 1993.

The experience of the EMS during this period has been studied in the context of the Taylor rule by Richard Clarida of Columbia University, Jordi Gali of Universitat Pompeu Fabra, and Mark Gertler of New York University.[1] Let r denote the actual (nominal) interest rate adopted by France, Italy, or the United Kingdom. Since monetary policy in these countries was directed by the necessity of fixing the exchange rate with the mark, the actual interest rate was also the interest rates that the central banks had to set to keep their exchange rates fixed.

Let r^T denote the (nominal) interest rate for the three countries implied by a Taylor rule for monetary policy, which is interpreted as a proxy for the interest rate that the central banks would have set if monetary policy had been directed toward the domestic objectives of keeping inflation close to target and the GDP gap small. Define **stress** as the difference between the actual interest rate and the Taylor rule interest rate,

$$\text{Stress} = r - r^T. \qquad (18.2)$$

[1]Richard Clarida, Jordi Gali, and Mark Gertler, "Monetary Policy Rules in Practice: Some International Evidence," *European Economic Review*, Vol. 42 (1988), pp. 1033–1068.

The measure of stress is the amount that the central banks of France, Italy, and the United Kingdom had to raise their interest rates above the interest rates implied by the Taylor rule to maintain the fixed exchange rate with Germany. The measure of stress peaks in 1992 for the United Kingdom and in 1993 for France and Italy. This was exactly when the three countries decided that maintaining a fixed exchange rate with the German mark was not worth the cost in terms of their own economies and devalued their exchange rates.

The failure to maintain fixed exchange rates within the EMS produced two very different outcomes. While France and Italy greatly widened their bands, they remained in the EMS and continued negotiations toward a single European currency, the euro. This process culminated in the abandonment of national currencies by France, Germany, and Italy, as well as nine other European countries. The United Kingdom left the EMS, and has chosen to let its currency float against the euro as well as against the U.S. dollar. While the two outcomes are different, both represent movements away from a fixed exchange rate, one to a flexible exchange rate and the other to a single European currency.

The Role of the Exchange Rate in Policy Rules

When we analyzed the positive and normative implications of the Taylor rule for the United States, we did not include the exchange rate in the equation. The Fed raises the interest rate when inflation increases above its target level and when the output gap rises, but not when the exchange rate changes. Recall the Taylor rule from Chapter 16,

$$r = \pi + \delta(\pi - \pi^*) + B\hat{Y} + R^*, \qquad (18.3)$$

where r is the nominal interest rate, π is the inflation rate, π^* is the target inflation rate, Y is the GDP gap, and R^* is the equilibrium real interest rate. The most important thing to remember about the Taylor rule is that $\delta > 0$ and $B > 0$, so that the Fed raises the real interest rate whenever inflation rises above its target level or when the GDP gap increases.

Although the exchange rate does not appear in Equation 18.3, the Taylor rule contains an important *indirect* reaction of the interest rate to the exchange rate.[2] Suppose the exchange rate rises. With sticky prices, a higher nominal exchange rate raises the real exchange rate. According to the net export function, discussed in Chapter 12, the higher real exchange rate decreases net exports, lowering GDP in the short run. This, in turn, decreases the GDP gap, causing the central bank, according to the Taylor rule, to lower the interest rate. For example, if the GDP gap initially was zero, it turns negative, causing the central bank to lower the interest rate. The higher exchange rate also lowers inflation,

---

[2]John B. Taylor, "The Role of the Exchange Rate in Monetary Policy Rules," *American Economic Review*, Vol. 91 (2001), pp. 263–67.

because the price of imported goods does not increase as rapidly with a stronger exchange rate, although, as discussed in Section 12.6, this effect is more important for smaller countries than for the United States. The decrease in inflation also, according to the Taylor rule, causes the central bank to lower the real interest rate.

The same effect works in reverse. Suppose the exchange rate falls, causing, with sticky prices, a lower real exchange rate. This raises GDP and increases the GDP gap, causing the central bank, according to the Taylor rule, to raise the interest rate. For example, if the GDP gap initially was zero, it turns positive, causing the central bank to raise the interest rate. The lower exchange rate also raises inflation because the price of imported goods increases more rapidly with a weaker exchange rate, although, as discussed in the previous paragraph, this effect is more important for smaller countries than for the United States. The increase in inflation also, according to the Taylor rule, causes the central bank to raise the real interest rate.

The Taylor rule can be modified to account for a *direct* effect of the exchange rate on the interest rate set by the central bank. One such modification would be

$$r = \pi + \delta(\pi - \pi^*) + B\hat{Y} + R^* - \alpha(EP/P_w) \tag{18.4}$$

where (EP/P_w) is the real exchange rate and α is a positive coefficient. When the real exchange rate rises, net exports and GDP fall. With coefficient α being positive, the central bank lowers the interest rate, mitigating the contraction. When the real exchange rate falls, net exports and GDP rise, and the central bank raises the interest rate. More-complicated modifications of the Taylor rule have also been proposed. One modification is to include both the current and the lagged real exchange rates, with opposite signs. In that case, an increase in the real exchange rate would cause the central bank to first lower, then subsequently raise, the interest rate.

The possibility of including the exchange rate in the Taylor rule has been studied in both positive, as in Chapter 16, and normative, as in Chapter 17, contexts. In the positive context, empirical research that estimates Taylor rules for the United States finds no additional effect of the real exchange rate on the interest rate beyond the effects of inflation and the GDP gap. In other words, the coefficient α is zero for the United States. For Germany and Japan, Clarida, Gali, and Gertler, using a somewhat more complicated specification, find an effect of the real exchange rate, with the coefficient α approximately equal to 0.10. In the normative context, research that uses social welfare (loss) functions to determine optimal policy rules generally finds at best small improvement, and sometimes even deterioration, of economic performance by including the real exchange rate in the Taylor rule. One reason for this finding is that, as discussed earlier in this section, the Taylor rule already contains an indirect effect of the real exchange rate on the interest rate set by the central bank. Adding a direct effect may not make much difference in practice.

Policy Rules and Macroeconomic Performance in the World Economy

We showed in Chapter 16 that, starting in the mid-1980s, macroeconomic policy in the United States has followed a stabilizing rule where the real interest rate is increased when inflation rises. We also showed that, in comparison with the 1970s, inflation has been lower and GDP fluctuations smaller since the adoption of the stabilizing rule. Macroeconomic performance has improved. In this section, we see that the improvement in macroeconomic performance during this period was not confined to the United States; other countries that adopted similar rules experienced similar improved performance.

Unless a country permanently fixes it exchange rate through a currency board, a common currency, or dollarization, the only monetary policy that can work well in the long run is one based on the *trinity* of (1) a flexible exchange rate, (2) an inflation target, and (3) a monetary policy rule. This section describes the macroeconomic performance of three countries (Australia, Canada, and the United Kingdom) that, like the United States, adopted all three parts of the trinity in the 1990s.

Figure 18.2 depicts inflation in Australia, Canada, and the United Kingdom from 1960 to 2002. There are many similarities between the experience of inflation in these countries and inflation in the United States. For all three countries, inflation was much higher in the 1970s than either before or after. This mimics the Great Inflation in the United States, illustrated in Figure 16.15. Like the United States, inflation in Australia, Canada, and the United Kingdom fell in the early 1980s, picked up in the late 1980s, and fell again in the 1990s.

The inflation rate for all three countries was approximately the same in 1970 as in 1990. Why did inflation rise in the 1970s and fall in the 1990s? The most important reason is that the central banks of all three countries raised the interest rate by much more when inflation started to rise in the late 1980s than when inflation started to rise in the late 1960s and early 1970s. The behavior of the central banks is also shown in Figure 18.2. Look at the bottom panel, for the United Kingdom. In 1971, with inflation at about 8 percent, the overnight interest rate, the equivalent of the federal funds rate for the United States, was 6 percent. In 1990, with the same inflation rate, the overnight interest rate was 15 percent. The same pattern can be seen for Australia and Canada. In the 1990s, the three central banks, like the Fed, followed a policy of raising the interest rate much more when inflation rose than they had followed in the 1970s.

The second aspect of improved macroeconomic performance for the United States, as shown in Figure 16.14, is that the fluctuations in real GDP decreased since the mid-1980s. Figure 18.3 depicts a similar pattern for Australia, Canada, and the United Kingdom. Although there are country-by-country differences as to exactly when the reduction in real GDP fluctuations took place, output volatility fell for each country.

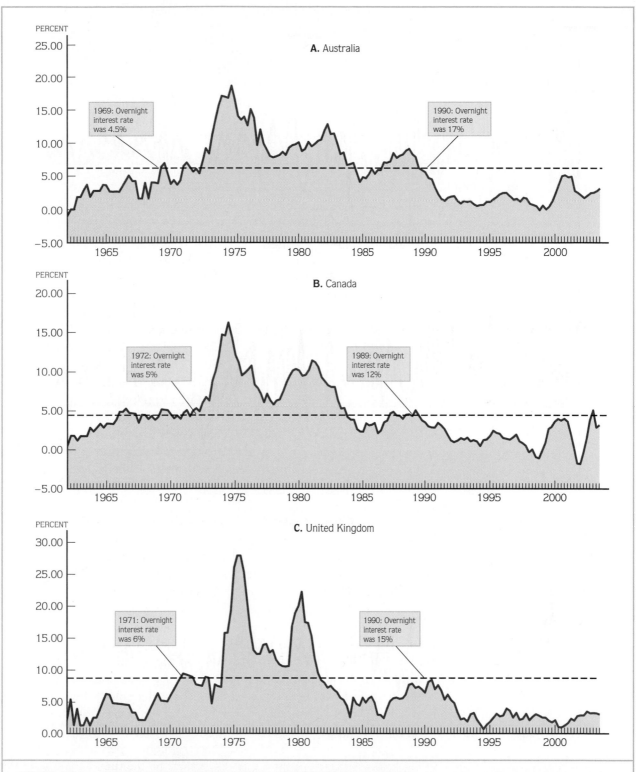

FIGURE 18.2   INFLATION IN AUSTRALIA, CANADA, AND THE UNITED KINGDOM

As in the United States, inflation was much higher for Australia, Canada, and the United Kingdom in the 1970s than in the 1960s, the 1980s, or the 1990s. One explanation is that, like the United States, monetary policy was much more aggressive in fighting inflation in the 1980s and 1990s than in the 1970s.

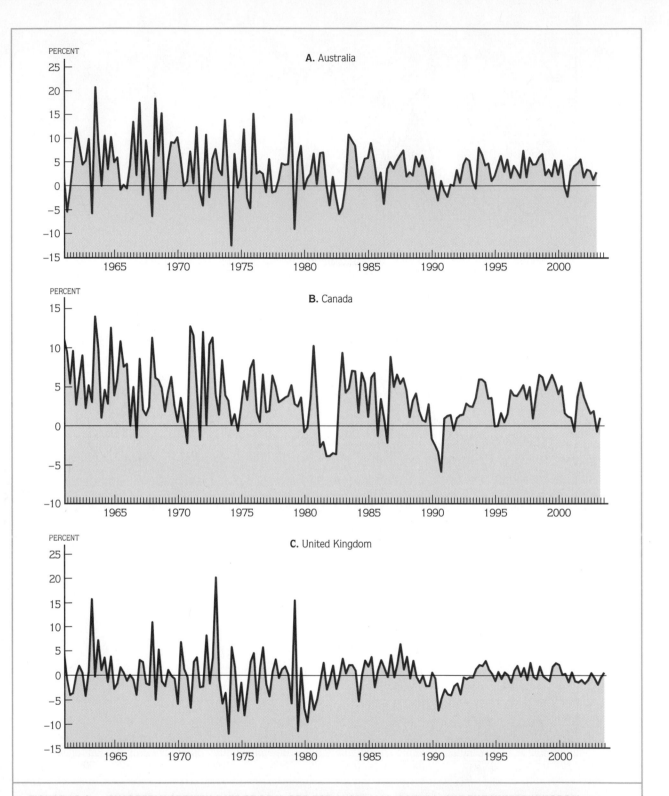

FIGURE 18.3 QUARTERLY GROWTH RATE OF REAL GDP FOR AUSTRALIA, CANADA, AND THE UNITED KINGDOM

As in the United States, the volatility of real GDP fluctuations, measured by the quarterly real GDP growth rate, decreased substantially since the mid-1980s for Australia, Canada, and the United Kingdom. The economies of all three countries have become more stable.

SOURCE: Organization for Economic Cooperation and Development.

Exchange Rates and Policy Rules

1. Unless a country permanently fixes its exchange rate through a currency board, a common currency, or dollarization, the only monetary policy that can work well in the long run is one based on the *trinity* of (1) a flexible exchange rate, (2) an inflation target, and (3) a monetary policy rule.

2. There is an indirect effect of the real exchange rate on the interest rate in the Taylor rule, even if the real exchange rate is not explicitly included as a variable to which the central banks reacts.

3. Countries that adopted monetary policy rules similar to the Taylor rule, Australia, Canada, and the United Kingdom, experienced improved macroeconomic performance similar to that seen in the United States.

18.4 | MACROECONOMIC PERFORMANCE IN JAPAN

Japan's economy is the second largest in the world, about half the size of the United States' and about double the size of Germany's. The improvement in macroeconomic performance since the mid-1980s described in Chapter 16 for the United States and in the previous section for Australia, Canada, and the United Kingdom does not extend to Japan. This stands in contrast with the previous decade, where macroeconomic performance in Japan was much better than in the United States. In this section, we review the historical record and explore some of the reasons for the deterioration in Japan's macroeconomic performance.

The magnitude of the deterioration of Japan's macroeconomic performance is large enough that some have called it the "lost decade." Between 1991 and 2003, real GDP in Japan grew by only 14 percent, compared with 44 percent in the United States. There was virtually no economic growth during the first half of the decade. Real GDP was 20 percent below potential GDP by 1995, a shortfall nearly as large as in the Great Depression of the 1930s in the United States. Following an enormous increase in asset prices that was not sustainable, an **asset price bubble,** in the 1980s Japan's major stock market index, the Nikkei, fell 79 percent from its peak in 1989 to 2003 and the land price index fell by 70 percent. Eight fiscal stimulus packages produced the highest debt to GDP ratio among industrialized countries, 140 percent, compared with 60 percent for the United States. Unemployment rose from 2 percent in 1990 to 5 percent in 2003, the highest level in almost 50 years.[3]

We start by depicting, in Figure 18.4, inflation rates in Japan and the United States from 1978 to 2003. Two patterns are immediately evident. First,

"Lost Decade"

---

[3]See Jahyeong Koo, "Japan's Economic Policy Conundrums," *Southwest Economy* (July/August 2003), Federal Reserve Bank of Dallas.

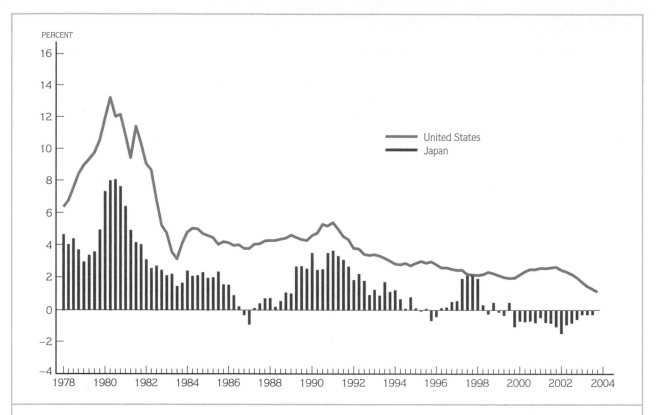

FIGURE 18.4   INFLATION RATES IN JAPAN AND IN THE UNITED STATES

Inflation rates have been consistently lower in Japan than in the United States from the late 1970s to the early 2000s. While the United States went from high inflation to low inflation, Japan went from low inflation to deflation or near-negative inflation.

SOURCE: Organization for Economic Cooperation and Development.

inflation in both countries was brought down in the early 1980s, and has stayed low (relative to the 1970s) ever since. Second, inflation in Japan has been consistently lower than inflation in the United States. The inflation experience in the two countries can be categorized as follows: *High inflation*, the United States in the late 1970s and the early 1980s; *low inflation*, Japan in the late 1970s and the 1980s and the United States in the late 1980s and 1990s; **deflation** (negative inflation) or **near-negative inflation** (inflation close to zero), Japan in the 1990s.

bad [

We proceed to depict, in Figure 18.5, real GDP in Japan and the United States during two periods. The top panel of Figure 18.5 covers the period 1978–1986. Real GDP in Japan was much smoother than real GDP in the United States. There were no recessions in Japan comparable in magnitude to the recessions of 1980 and 1981–1982 in the United States. In fact, *real* GDP in Japan was almost as smooth as a trend line that would depict *potential* GDP in the United States. Japanese policy makers were very successful in keeping

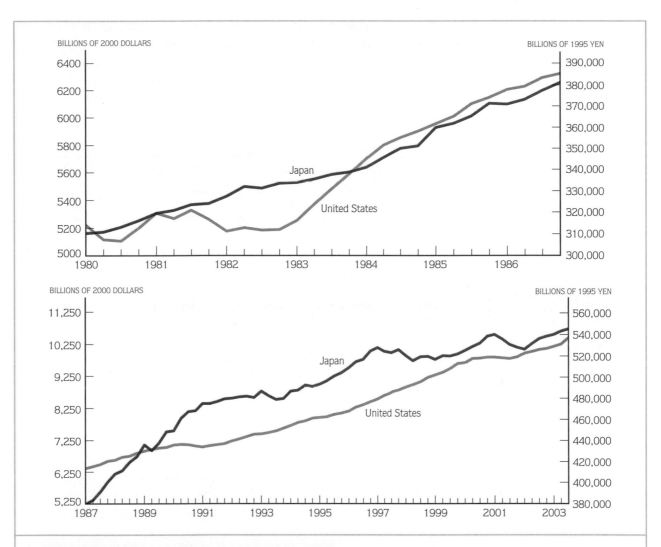

FIGURE 18.5   REAL GDP IN JAPAN AND THE UNITED STATES

From 1973 to 1986, real GDP in Japan was much smoother than real GDP in the United States. The opposite is true for 1987 to 2003. Real GDP in the United States was much smoother than real GDP in Japan during the latter period.

SOURCE: Organization for Economic Cooperation and Development.

the economy moving along a steady growth path—in the face of oil and other shocks—during a period in which other countries had huge cyclical swings.

Now look at the bottom panel of Figure 18.5, which covers the period 1987–2002. The differences in the two periods are striking. Real GDP in the United States was much smoother than real GDP in Japan during the latter period. Real GDP in the United States, not real GDP in Japan, looks like a smooth trend line during the 1990s. The recession in the United States in 1990–1991 looks very small compared to the fluctuations in Japan, the long slowdown starting in the early 1990s and the downturn in the late 1990s.

Combining the information contained in Figures 18.4 and 18.5, an interesting pattern emerges. The two periods of low inflation, the late 1970s and the 1980s in Japan and the late 1980s and 1990s in the United States, were associated with good macroeconomic performance; steady growth without large recessions. The periods of high inflation, the United States in the late 1970s and the early 1980s, and deflation or near-negative inflation, Japan in the 1990s, were associated with poor economic performance.

If low inflation is good for macroeconomic performance, why is near-negative inflation and deflation bad for macroeconomic performance? The answer lies in the zero bound on the nominal interest rate. As discussed in Chapter 14, the nominal interest rate cannot fall below zero because, if it did, everyone would rather hold money, which pays no interest, than an interest bearing asset that pays negative interest. Once the nominal interest rate hits zero, the Fed and other central banks cannot stimulate the economy by pushing the interest rate any lower through open market operations. While there are proposals for the Fed and other central banks to conduct monetary policy by purchasing assets that are not perfect substitutes for money, we do not know how such policies would work in practice.

The relation between near-negative inflation, or deflation, and the zero bound on the nominal interest rate can be seen by examining the Taylor rule in Equation 18.3. Consider a numerical example where the coefficient $\delta = 0.5$, the coefficient $B = 0.5$, the inflation target $\pi^* = 0.02$, and the equilibrium real interest rate $R^* = 0.02$. This is the same numerical example used in Chapter 16. Suppose that the inflation rate π is zero. If the economy is on its long-run growth path, so that GDP equals potential GDP, then $\hat{Y} = 0$ and the policy rule would be to set the nominal interest rate equal to 1 percent. From Equation 18.3 with inflation equal to zero, $r = 0 + 0.5(0 - 0.02) + 0.5(0) + 0.02 = 0.01$. With the nominal interest rate so low in normal times, the central bank would have very little scope to lower it further to stimulate the economy in the event of a slowdown or a recession.

The situation becomes worse in the case of deflation. Using the same numerical example, consider what happens if inflation is minus 1 percent. From Equation 18.3, $r = -0.01 + 0.5(-0.01 - 0.02) + 0.5(0) + 0.02 = -0.005$. But this is impossible because the central bank cannot lower the nominal interest rate below zero. The scenario becomes even worse if the deflation intensifies. Suppose, using the numerical example, inflation is minus 2 percent (deflation is 2 percent). From Equation 18.3, $r = -0.02 + 0.5(-0.02 - 0.02) + 0.5(0) + 0.02 = -0.04$. The zero bound on the nominal interest rate makes it impossible for the central bank to stimulate the economy along the lines suggested by the Taylor rule.

How did Japan get into the conundrum of near-negative inflation or deflation? Following the bursting of the asset price bubble in 1989, a sharp decline in money growth was associated with a sharp decline in nominal GDP growth. This can be seen in Figure 18.6. Another perspective can be found by comparing the overnight call rate, Japan's equivalent of the federal funds rate, with the

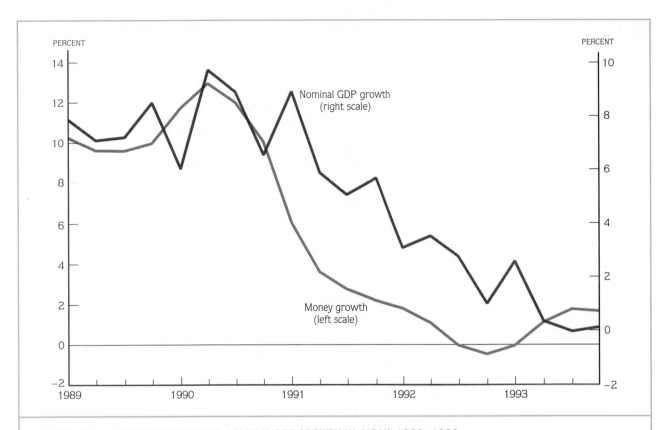

FIGURE 18.6   MONEY GROWTH AND NOMINAL GDP GROWTH IN JAPAN, 1989–1993

Monetary policy in Japan was very restrictive in the early 1990s. A sharp decline in money growth was associated with a sharp decline in nominal GDP growth.

interest rate implied by the Taylor rule. Using the parameters from Equation 18.3, Figure 18.7 shows that both a more rapid rise in the interest rate in the late 1980s and a more rapid fall in the interest rate from 1991 to 1994 would have been more appropriate than the policies actually followed by the Bank of Japan.

Why was Japanese monetary policy so restrictive in the early 1990s? There are several possible reasons. First, the initial motivation for restrictive monetary policy was to lower inflation and counteract the asset price bubble. The Bank of Japan was unwilling to let money growth rise again for fear of causing another bubble. Second, during this period, interest rates were very low and some monetary policy officials felt that lowering them further would not do any good. But, as we have seen, interest rates were not so low in real terms. Because there was deflation, the real interest rate was greater than the market interest rate. Third, some argued that the depression was caused by nonmonetary factors, such as the need to restructure businesses, and increasing money growth would not increase real economic growth.

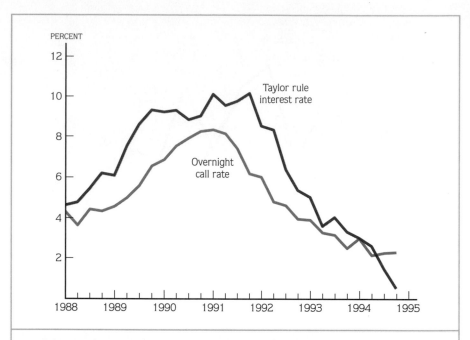

FIGURE 18.7   OVERNIGHT CALL RATE AND THE TAYLOR RULE INTEREST RATE IN JAPAN, 1988–1994

Comparing the overnight call rate with the interest rate implied by the Taylor rule, both a more rapid rise in the interest rate in the late 1980s and a more rapid fall in the interest rate in the early 1990s would have been more appropriate than the policies that were actually followed by the Bank of Japan.

Once Japan found itself in the situation of near-negative inflation or deflation, monetary policy making became very difficult. Starting in September 1995, the Bank of Japan lowered the overnight call rate to 0.5 percent, and in February 1999, it brought the rate to virtually zero. With the exception of a short period at the end of 2000, it stayed at zero through 2003. The difficulty, as discussed here and in Chapter 14, is that even a zero nominal interest rate can produce a too high real interest rate with near-negative inflation or deflation and the zero bound on the nominal interest rate makes lowering the real interest rate problematic. Even with a zero nominal interest rate, there has been deflation. Economic growth, while positive, is still very low by historical standards.

In Chapter 14, we discussed several ways where, in theory, a central bank can conduct expansionary monetary policy even at the zero nominal interest rate bound. While manipulating the exchange rate has been the most discussed option, it does not seem promising. Contrary to popular opinion, Japan is not much of a trading country. With an export/GDP ratio below 10 percent, depreciating the currency would not provide much stimulus. In addition, South Korea and China might respond by devaluations of their currencies, countering the expansionary effect.

Restoring economic growth in Japan will require changes in both monetary and banking policy. First, deflation must be stopped. Deflation raises real interest rates, discourages investment, and encourages people to postpone consumption. Deflation is also damaging to the operation of the banking system because, with near-zero interest rates, banks can avoid dealing with problem loans.

In March 2001, the Bank of Japan announced that it would provide ample liquidity until deflation was ended. While the monetary base increased by 34 percent in the following 18 months, the money supply hardly increased at all and deflation continued. In Chapter 14, we learned how increases in the monetary base are translated into larger increases in the money supply through increases in bank lending, a process called the *money multiplier*. Japanese banks, however, actually decreased their lending, and so the money multiplier process was not operative. We saw in Chapter 9 that sustained increases in money supply growth produce higher inflation. While this is usually considered in light of the negative consequences of going from low to high inflation, it is equally applicable to the positive consequences of gong from deflation to low inflation. Escaping from deflation requires sustained increases in the growth rate of the money supply.

This brings us to banking policy. An important reason why the increase in the monetary base did not quickly end deflation is the large number of nonperforming, or bad, loans in the banking sector. Banks that are burdened by **nonperforming loans** do not seek out new loan opportunities, which are necessary to translate monetary base growth into money supply growth, even when they have excess reserves. The magnitude of the bad loan problem is immense; it dwarfs the savings and loan crisis in the United States in the 1980s. The Japanese government's estimate of bad loans is $266 billion (6 percent of GDP), and other estimates are higher. While the costs of addressing the bad loan problem will be high, the longer Japan takes to resolve the problem the higher the costs will be.

Another issue that needs to be addressed to promote economic growth is productivity. Japan combines industries where productivity is the highest in the world with industries that lag behind their counterparts in other countries. For example, food processing employs 11 percent of Japan's manufacturing workforce. If the productivity in Japan's food processing could be raised to the level in France, productivity in the Japanese economy as a whole would rise by 1.64 percent.

Some improvement in Japan's macroeconomic performance occurred in 2003 and 2004. Economic growth increased during 2003 and the first half of 2004, and the increased growth appeared to be sustainable. The shift by the Bank of Japan in March 2001 to a policy of sharply raising monetary base growth until deflation was eliminated continued through 2003—the monetary base increased by 68 percent between March 2001 and December 2003—and consumer prices excluding fresh food rose for the first time in five years in October 2003. There was a reduction in nonperforming loans which, combined with the increased growth of the money supply, provided hope that deflation had finally ended.

Japan

1. In contrast with the 1980s, macroeconomic performance in Japan has been much worse than macroeconomic performance in the United States in the 1990s and early 2000s.

2. Japan has experienced sustained *near-negative inflation* (inflation close to zero) and even periods of *deflation* (negative inflation).

3. Overly restrictive monetary policy in the early 1990s was a major cause of Japan's deflation.

4. Escaping from deflation and restoring economic growth requires changes in both monetary and banking policy.

REVIEW AND PRACTICE

Major Points

1. Free trade in goods and assets is a characteristic of an integrated global economy.

2. In an open economy, central bank policy takes two forms: monetary policy and foreign exchange market intervention. Monetary policy refers to measures that change the total liabilities of the central bank. Exchange-rate policy refers to measures that alter the mix of foreign and domestic assets in the central bank's portfolio.

3. Under a fixed exchange-rate system the central bank must use monetary policy to keep the domestic interest rate equal to the world rate. A fixed exchange rate is incompatible with a Taylor rule.

4. Fixed exchange-rate systems require the nations involved to have similar rates of domestic inflation. The Bretton Woods system failed in the early 1970s when U.S. inflation increased above the rate other members of the system considered acceptable.

5. The macroeconomic policy trilemma is that, among the policy objectives of fixed exchange rates, free movement of capital, and independent monetary policy, only two of the three objectives can be attained simultaneously. The trilemma provides a way to categorize the choices different countries make.

6. In the last few years, a number of countries have chosen to abandon fixed exchange rates and, instead, adopt a monetary policy based on flexible exchange rates or permanently connect monetary policy to other countries through monetary union, dollarization, or a currency board.

7. Moderate inflation leads to better macroeconomic performance than either high inflation, as in the United States in the late 1970s and early 1980s, or deflation or near-negative inflation, as in Japan in the 1990s and early 2000s.

Key Terms and Concepts

Eurozone

foreign exchange market
    intervention

inconvertible

domestic credit

foreign reserves

sterilized foreign exchange
    intervention

par values

devalue

macroeconomic policy trilemma

stress

asset price bubble

deflation

near-negative inflation

non-performing loans

Questions for Discussion and Review

1. Compare the Bretton Woods system with the Eurozone.

2. What are the similarities and differences between a foreign exchange market intervention and an open market operation?

3. What is the macroeconomic policy trilemma?

4. What is the concept of stress in a fixed exchange-rate system?

5. How can the Taylor rule be modified to account for a direct effect of the exchange rate on the interest rate set by the central bank?

6. Why did macroeconomic performance improve for Australia, Canada, and the United Kingdom since the mid-1980s?

7. Compare and contrast Japan's and the United States' experience with inflation from the late 1970s to the early 2000s.

8. Compare and contrast the fluctuations of real GDP in Japan and the United States from the late 1970s to the early 2000s.

Problems

NUMERICAL

1. Suppose the balance sheet of the central bank is (billions of dollars):

| Domestic credit | 450 | Currency | 425 |
| Foreign reserves | 50 | Bank reserves | 75 |

What would be the effect on domestic credit, foreign reserves, currency, and bank reserves of

    a. An open market purchase of $10 billion?

    b. A foreign exchange market intervention to prevent a depreciation of $10 billion?

    c. A sterilized foreign exchange intervention of $10 billion?

2. Suppose Canada and the United States kept their exchange rate fixed, with each country conducting monetary policy according to the Taylor rule,

$$r = \pi + B\hat{Y} + \delta(\pi - \pi^*) + R^*,$$

where $B = 0.5$, $\delta = 0.5$, $\pi = 0.02$, and $R^* = 0.02$.

    a. If Canada conducts an expansionary fiscal policy, so that its equilibrium real interest rate increases from 0.02 to 0.03, show why this is incompatible with maintaining a fixed exchange rate with the United States.

    b. Following the change in Canada's fiscal policy, what would the United States need to do to keep the exchange rate fixed?

3. Suppose the economy has an IS curve with a direct effect of the real exchange rate,

$$R - R^* = -\sigma\hat{Y} - \gamma(EP/P_w)$$

and a Taylor rule with a direct effect of the real exchange rate

$$r = \pi + B\hat{Y} + \delta(\pi - \pi^*) + R^* - \alpha(EP/P_w),$$

where (EP/P_w) is the real exchange rate and α and γ are positive coefficients.

    a. Derive the equation for the macroeconomic policy curve.

    b. What is the effect of a rise in the real exchange rate on the output gap $\hat{Y}$ if there is no direct effect of the real exchange rate in the Taylor rule $(\alpha = 0)$.

    c. What would the coefficient α in the Taylor rule need to be to eliminate any effect of a rise in the real exchange rate on the output gap $\hat{Y}$?

4. Suppose that the Taylor rule is given by

$$r = \pi + B\hat{Y} + \delta(\pi - \pi^*) + R^*,$$

where $B = 0.5$, $\delta = 0.5$, $\pi^* = 0.01$, and $R^* = 0.01$

a. Suppose that the inflation rate $\pi = 0$. According to the Taylor rule, what would the nominal interest rate be if the output gap $\hat{Y} = 0$.

b. Now suppose that the inflation rate π = minus 1 percent. Can monetary policy be conducted according to the Taylor rule?

ANALYTICAL

1. Explain why high U.S. inflation in the 1960s caused the collapse of the Bretton Woods system of fixed exchange rates.

2. Using the concept of stress, explain why German reunification caused crises in the European Monetary System.

3. Explain why the Taylor rule in Equation 18.3 contains an important indirect reaction of the interest rate to the exchange rate even though the exchange rate does not appear in the equation.

4. Using the modified Taylor rule in Equation 18.4, show how there can be a direct, as well as an indirect, effect of the exchange rate on the interest rate.

5. Show why, in the case of deflation, the zero bound on the nominal interest rate can make it impossible for the central bank to stimulate the economy along the lines suggested by the Taylor rule in Equation 18.3.

GLOSSARY

accelerationist property Attempts to keep output above normal in the long run result in accelerating prices. (15)

accelerator The principle that investment is higher when GDP is growing, because businesses must enlarge their capital stocks to meet higher demand. (11)

accommodative policies Policies that increase the money supply in response to positive price shocks. (9)

activist policy rules Fiscal or monetary policies that respond to current developments in the economy. (17)

actual capital stock The same as capital stock. Actual capital stock is used to distinguish between the desired and the actual capital stock. (11)

aggregate demand Total demand for goods and services. (7)

aggregate demand curve Downward-sloping relation between GDP and the price level such that spending balance occurs and the money market is in equilibrium. (8)

aggregate demand shock An event other than a change in policy that shifts the aggregate demand curve. (9)

appreciation The exchange rate rises. (12)

asset price bubble An increase in asset prices that is too large to be sustainable. (18)

augmented Solow model An economic model based on the Solow growth model, which focuses on human capital. (6)

automatic stabilizers Changes in taxes and transfers during recessions and booms, which have a stabilizing effect on disposable income. (10)

balanced growth path A path of economic growth along which the growth rates of capital and labor are equal. (4)

boom-bust cycle The combination of a boom, disinflation, recession, and recovery. (16)

borrowed reserves The part of bank reserves borrowed from the Fed. (12)

budget The federal government budget summarizes all three of the types of effects on aggregate demand: purchases, transfers, and taxes. (13)

budget deficit A budget deficit exists when the sum of government spending, government transfers to the private sector, and interest on the government debt is greater than taxes. (2)

budget surplus A budget surplus exists when the sum of government spending, government transfers to the private sector, and interest on the government debt is less than taxes. (2)

buffer stock A portion of inventory maintained to accommodate unexpected changes in demand. (11)

business cycles The recurrent cycles of expansions, recessions, and recoveries in the economy. (1)

capital deepening Growth of capital per hour of labor. (5)

capital stock The amount of factories and machines in the economy. (11)

catch up An initially poorer country grows faster than an initially richer country and eventually achieves the same level of per-capita income. (6)

classical dichotomy Describes an economy where monetary policy affects only prices and where employment and output are determined purely by nonmonetary factors. (9)

conditional convergence The hypothesis that income per capita in a given country converges to that country's steady-state value. (6)

constant steady-state growth hypothesis The prediction of the Solow model that growth rates eventually return to a constant long-run value. (6)

consumer price index (CPI) A price index that measures the cost of living for a typical urban family. (2)

consumption Spending by households, including purchases of durable goods, nondurable goods, and services. (2)

consumption expenditures Spending on goods and services measured at the time they are acquired. (10)

consumption function Relation between total consumption and income. (7)

convergence hypothesis The prediction of the Solow model that, over time, gaps in per capita income among countries will narrow. (6)

countercyclical stabilization policy The use of monetary and fiscal policy to reverse, or counter, the effects of aggregate demand shocks. (9)

cross-country growth regressions An equation that explains the variation of growth rates across countries by variations in savings rates, population growth rates, and other variables. (6)

cross-country level regressions An equation that explains the variation of levels of income per capita across countries by variations in savings rates, population growth rates, and other variables. (6)

crowding out Reduction in investment and net exports as a result of higher interest rates caused by higher government purchases of goods and services. (8)

currency The government's paper money and coins. (14)

currency ratio The amount of currency that people want to hold as a ratio of their deposits. (12)

current account The balance of payments account that keeps track of net exports of goods and services, net interest payments, and net international transfers such as government grants and remittances. (2)

cyclical deficit The difference between the actual deficit and the structural deficit. (12)

deflation A negative rate of inflation, so that prices fall. (18)

deflator A price index calculated by dividing a component of nominal GDP by the same component of real GDP. (2)

depreciation The exchange rate falls. (12)

desired capital stock The amount of capital input chosen by firms given the demand for their products and the rental price of capital. (11)

desired stock of housing The public's demand function for housing, which can be found where the rental price of housing intersects the demand curve. (11)

devalue A move by a central bank to reduce the par value of its currency. (18)

discount rate The interest rate on loans made by the Fed to banks. (14)

discretionary changes Changes in tax law made by Congress to mitigate the drop in aggregate demand during recessions. (13)

discretionary policy One-time changes in monetary and fiscal policy in response to a specific shock or combination of shocks. (9)

disposable personal income Income available to families for spending, net of taxes and including transfers. (2)

divergence Countries that are initially poorer grow slower than countries that are initially richer, so that gaps in per capita income widen. (6)

domestic credit The value of domestic securities held by a central bank. (18)

economic shocks Events other than changes in policy that move real GDP away from potential GDP. (9)

elasticity The percentage change in one variable induced by a one-percent change in another variable. (13)

endogenous growth theory A theory in which increases in technology are explained by forces within the model. (5)

equilibrium real interest rate The real interest rate when the economy is at full employment. (16)

euro The single currency used by 12 European countries. (2)

Eurozone The twelve European countries that have combined their national currencies to form the euro. (18)

excess reserves The amount of reserves, beyond required reserves, that banks keep at the Fed. (12)

exchange rate The price at which exchanges of dollars for foreign currencies take place. (2)

expansion Period following a recovery when output and employment are rising above their trends. (1)

exports Goods and services produced in the United States and purchased by foreign consumers, businesses, or governments. (2)

federal government budget A statement of the receipts and outlays of the federal government. (12)

final goods New goods that undergo no further processing before they are sold to consumers. (2)

financial account The balance of payments account that keeps track of international borrowing and lending. (2)

financial variables Interest rates and the supply of money. (8)

fiscal policy The use of tax rates and government spending to influence the economy. (8)

fixed investment The purchase of new factories, machines, and houses. (2)

flexible exchange-rate system The international monetary system when countries do not try to fix their exchange rates within narrow bands. (12)

foreign exchange market The global market where dollars and other currencies are traded. (12)

foreign exchange market intervention Policy move by a central bank to buy or sell government securities to raise or lower an exchange rate. (18)

foreign reserves The value of foreign securities held by a central bank. (18)

forward-looking theory of consumption Theory where consumers consider their likely future incomes in making current consumption decisions. (10)

full employment Situation where labor demand equals labor supply and unemployment is at its natural level. (4)

full-employment deficit The deficit that would occur if the economy were at full employment. (13)

full-employment level of output The amount of output that would be produced if everyone who wanted to work could find a job. (4)

GDP gap The percentage departure of actual GDP from potential GDP. (3)

geography hypothesis Most of the differences on income per capita across countries can be explained by geographic, climatic, and ecological differences. (6)

government purchases Purchases of goods and services by federal, state, or local governments. (2)

Great Inflation The high inflation in the United States from the late 1960s to the early 1980s. (16)

growth accounting formula A formula which says that the rate of growth of output equals technology growth plus the weighted rates of growth of labor and capital. (5)

human capital Schooling and on-the-job training. (6)

imports Goods and services produced abroad and purchased by United States consumers, businesses, or governments. (2)

income inequality The gap between rich and poor. (6)

inconvertible Refers to currencies that cannot be bought and sold in open markets. (18)

inflation The percentage increase in the price level over time. (1)

inflation loss The economic loss caused by inflation, which is summarized as the average of the squared deviation of the inflation rate from its target. (17)

institutions hypothesis Differences in economic performance across countries are caused by the organization of society. (6)

interest rate The amount charged for a loan by a bank or other lender per dollar per year, expressed as a percent. (1)

intermediate goods Goods produced by businesses and used as inputs by other businesses, such as steel. (2)

intermediation role The role of banks to take deposits from some individuals and make loans to others. (14)

intertemporal budget constraint The total amount of consumption must equal total resources, now and in the future, in terms of present discounted value. (10)

inventory investment The change in stocks of unsold goods at business firms from one year to another. (2)

investment Purchases of newly produced plant, equipment, inventories, and houses. (2)

investment demand Level of purchases of new capital chosen by firms given the demand for their products and the rental price of capital. (11)

investment demand function Tells how much capital equipment a firm will purchase given its planned level of output and the rental price of capital. (11)

investment function Relation between investment and the interest rate. (8)

investment supply Decisions made by producers of investment goods about how much to supply. (11)

IS curve Downward-sloping relation between GDP and the interest rate such that spending balance is preserved—at a higher interest rate, investment and net exports are lower, so spending balance occurs at a lower level of GDP. (8)

job-losing rate The percentage of the labor force who become unemployed each month. (3)

job-finding rate The percentage of the unemployed who leave unemployment each month. (3)

labor force The number of people 16 years of age or over who are either working or unemployed. (3)

labor force participation rate The percentage of the working-age population in the labor force. (4)

labor productivity Output per hour of labor. (5)

labor quality Improvements in the measurable skills of the workforce. (5)

lag The time that elapses between a firm's realization that new capital is needed and the completion of the capital installation. (11)

leakage A portion of the increase in spending that occurs as GDP rises, that goes overseas and does not enter domestic aggregate demand. (12)

life-cycle theory A theory that consumption depends on a family's present and future resources, not just on current income. (10)

liquidity constraints Consumers cannot always borrow as much as they would need to maintain their level of consumption during temporary falls in income. (10)

LM curve Upward-sloping relation between GDP and the interest rate such that the money market is an equilibrium—at a higher interest rate, money demand is lower, so the level of income where the money market is in equilibrium is higher. (8)

Long Boom The back-to-back expansions in the United States during the 1980s and the 1990s. (16)

longitudinal surveys Surveys that collect information on individuals over a number of years. (10)

long-run economic growth The study of the general upward path of output over time. (4)

long-run growth model A model designed to explain differences in growth rates across countries and over time. (4)

long-run marginal propensity to consume A measure of how much consumption increases over the long run when personal disposable income rises. (10)

Lucas supply curve Upward-sloping relation between GDP and the price level arising from imperfect information about monetary policy. (15)

macroeconomic policy curve The negative relation between the GDP gap and the amount that inflation is above the target inflation rate where the economy is on its IS curve and monetary policy is determined by the Taylor rule. (16)

macroeconomic policy trilemma The principle that only two of three desirable monetary policy objectives can be achieved simultaneously. (18)

macroeconomics The branch of economics that tries to explain how and why the economy grows and fluctuates over time. (1)

Malthusian model An economic model that explains the absence of economic growth during most of recorded history. (4)

Malthusian stagnation The prediction of the Malthusian model that there is no economic growth. Output per worker is just sufficient to sustain life. (4)

marginal benefit of capital Profit contributed by another unit of capital—the avoided cost of labor and other factors saved by the use of more capital. (11)

marginal cost of capital The rental cost of capital charged by the renting firm. (11)

marginal product of labor The additional output produced by one additional unit of work. (4)

marginal propensity to consume (MPC) A measure of how much an additional dollar of disposable income is spent on consumption. (7)

marginal propensity to import Increase in imports per unit of additional GDP, the negative of the slope of the net exports function. (7)

means of payment The methods that people use to pay for goods—money is one means of payment, credit cards are another. (14)

menu costs Costs a firm incurs to change the price of a product. (15)

microeconomics The branch of economics that studies the behavior of individual consumers, firms, and markets. (1)

monetary base Total amount of currency and reserves. (14)

monetary policy Movements of the interest rate and money supply determined by the Federal Reserve Board. (1)

monetary policy rule Systematic use of monetary policy. (1)

money Total amount of currency and checking deposits. Money is used synonymously with the money supply. (8)

money demand The sum of the demand for currency and the demand for checking deposits. (14)

money demand function Relation between the demand for money, income, the interest rate, and the price level. (8)

money multiplier Relation between the monetary base and the money stock—there can be several dollars in money for each dollar of the monetary base because reserve requirements are around 10 percent. (14)

money supply Amount of money available to the public, as determined by the Fed. The money supply consists of the total amount of currency and checking deposits. (1)

multiplier The amount by which GDP is higher in an economy with a higher level of government purchases in comparison to an otherwise identical economy with lower government purchases. (7)

national income Total income of all residents of the United States. (2)

natural rate of unemployment The amount of unemployment when the labor market is in equilibrium. (3)

natural rate property A property of the price adjustment equation which says that if real GDP is permanently above potential GDP, inflation rises without bound. (9)

near-negative inflation An inflation rate that, while positive, is very close to zero. (18)

neoclassical growth revival The argument that long-term growth in the United States is consistent with the predictions of the Solow growth model. (5)

net export function A function that summarizes the relation between income and net exports. (7)

net exports Exports less imports. (7)

net investment Gross investment minus depreciation. (2)

neutrality of money The property by which money supply has no influence on output or the interest rate in the long run. (9)

new normative macroeconomics Policy research that focuses on "what should be" rather than endeavors to explain the actual behavior of the Fed and other central banks. (17)

nominal GDP A dollar measure of production or final goods and services during one year. (2)

nominal money The same as money. Nominal money is used if you want to make sure that the distinction between money and real money is clear. (8)

nonaccommodative policies Policies that hold the money supply constant in response to price shocks. (9)

nonperforming loans Loans owed to banks that are not expected to ever be repaid. (18)

nonresidential fixed investment Spending on structures and equipment for use in business. (2)

nonrivalry One person's use of technology does not limit another person's use of the same technology. (5)

Okun's law A formula which says that for each percentage point by which the unemployment rate is above the natural rate, real GDP is 3 percent below potential GDP. (3)

open-economy multiplier The multiplier when net exports depend on income (7)

open-market operations The purchases or sales of government bonds by the Fed. (14)

outlays Government purchases of goods and services plus government transfers for social security and other purposes. (13)

output loss The economic loss from unstable output, measured by the average squared GDP gap. (17)

panel surveys Surveys that collect information on individuals over a number of years. (10)

partial excludability The inventor or owner of a technology cannot completely prevent other people from using it. (5)

par values The dollar values adopted for their currencies by countries during the Bretton Woods system. (18)

passive policy rule A policy rule without feedback. (17)

permanent-income theory Theory that consumption depends on a family's perception of its permanent income, or present and future resources, not just on current income. (10)

personal income Total income received by the public before income taxes. (2)

Phillips curve The relation between a change in the price level and its determinants describes the process of price adjustment. (9)

physical capital Equipment, structures, and other productive facilities. (6)

pipeline function Firms hold stocks of products as inventories as a normal part of the production process—for example, partly built cars moving through an auto plant are in the pipeline and counted as inventories. (11)

policy frontier Curve that shows the set of different combinations of output loss and inflation loss than can be achieved in the economy. (17)

policy ineffectiveness theorem With a Lucas supply function, a policy rule based on the same information available to the public cannot affect output and employment. (15)

policy rule Procedure for using a policy instrument such as taxes to respond to developments in the economy. (13)

potential GDP The amount of GDP the economy produces in normal times absent temporary influences such as booms and recessions. (1)

precautionary motive One of three motives in people's demand for money, under which individuals save some wealth in the form of money in case of an emergency need for funds. (14)

precautionary savings In choosing a consumption path, people put more weight on what is happening today than on their expectations of what will happen in the future. (10)

price index A measure of the cost of living or general price level obtained by averaging over the prices of many goods and services. (2)

price rigidity Firms wait to change prices after new conditions develop; prices are rigid during this period. (15)

price shock An event that shifts the price adjustment relationship. (9)

producer price index (PPI) A price index that measures the prices charged by producers at various stages in the production process. (2)

production function A representation of how much output can be produced from given amounts of labor, capital, and technology. (4)

production function for technology Relation between improved technology and the inputs devoted to research and development. (5)

purchasing power parity Situation where a dollar spent in the United States buys the same amount of goods as converting the dollar into a foreign currency and spending the proceeds in that country. (12)

rate of depreciation Reduction in the stock of capital as a result of aging. (11)

rate of time preference Tendency to choose current against future consumption—with a rate of time preference of 5 percent, the marginal utility of consumption is 5 percent higher this year than next year, when the levels of consumption are the same in both years. (10)

rational expectations A hypothesis that holds that firms and consumers make the most of the information available to them. (1)

reaction function Equation describing a procedure for using a policy instrument such as taxes to respond to developments in the economy. (13)

real exchange rate A measure of the exchange rate adjusted for differences in price levels between the United States and the ROW. (12)

real gross domestic product (GDP) A measure of the total output of goods in the economy, in constant dollars. (1)

real interest rate The interest rate minus the expected rate of inflation. (1)

real money The money supply divided by the price level. (8)

real wage The dollar wage divided by the price level. (4)

recession A period when real GDP declines. (1)

recovery A period of positive growth with the economy still below its trend. (1)

reserve ratio The fraction of their checking deposits that banks are required to hold on reserve at the Fed. (12)

residential fixed investment Spending on construction of new houses and apartment buildings. (2)

reversal of fortune The possibility that, over time, countries that are relatively rich can become relatively poor, and vice versa. (6)

Ricardian equivalence A proposition holding that it makes little difference if the government earns tax revenue this year or in future years; all that matters is the total amount of spending. (13)

saving supply Decisions made by consumers about the amount to save. (11)

scale effects The implication of endogenous growth models that an increase in the number of workers doing research increases the long-run growth rate. (5)

search theory Job seekers balance the benefit of starting an available job right away against the benefit of taking a better job that might come along later, net of the cost of waiting. (3)

short-run marginal propensity to consume A measure of how much consumption rises over the short run (during one year or one business cycle) when disposable income rises. (10)

social infrastructure The institutions and government policies that determine the economic environment in a country. (6)

social welfare function Expression of the public's preferences about inflation and output loss. (17)

Solow growth model A model of growth that focuses on the production function. (4)

speculative motive One of three motives in people's demand for money, according to which individuals hold money because they believe that other forms of holding wealth, such as the stock market, will decline in value. (14)

spending balance Situation where the public's planned level of spending is sufficient to generate the level of income they assumed when they made their spending plans. (7)

squared error The difference between the actual level of a variable that policymakers care about, such as inflation, and its target level, squared. (17)

square-root rule A theorem for inventories which says that stores should hold inventories proportional to the square root of sales, and which also applies to the demand for money. (14)

sterilized foreign exchange intervention Central bank buys or sells foreign government securities and sells or buys an equal amount of domestic government securities, in an effort to influence the exchange rate without changing the monetary base. (18)

stress The difference between the interest rate necessary to keep the exchange rate fixed and the Taylor rule interest rate. (18)

structural deficit Another name for the full-employment deficit. (12)

subsistence line The minimum level of output per worker necessary to avoid starvation. (4)

target inflation rate The level of inflation that a central bank, such as the Fed, would like to see on average over the long term. (16)

Taylor principle The principle that, in order to conduct good monetary policy, the Fed (or other central bank) needs to increase the real interest rate when inflation rises. (1, 16)

Taylor rule The Fed raises the overnight interest rate when inflation exceeds an inflation target and when GDP exceeds potential GDP. (1, 16)

terms of trade The ratio of the price of exports to the price of imports. (12)

total factor productivity Output per generalized unit of input—including labor, capital, energy, and materials. (5)

trade deficit Amount by which imports exceed exports. (7)

trade surplus Amount by which exports exceed imports. (7)

trade-weighted exchange rate An average of several different exchange rates, each one weighted according to the amount of trade with the United States. (12)

transactions motive One of three motives in people's demand for money, under which individuals hold money because they expect to need it soon to purchase goods or make other transactions. (14)

transition period A period of time in the Solow growth model where the economy is off its balanced growth path. (4)

unemployment rate The percentage of those in the labor force who are not working but looking for work. (1)

unit of account The nationally agreed upon unit for measuring value, keeping accounts, and quoting prices; in the United States, the dollar. (14)

value added The difference between the revenue a firm earns by selling its products and the amount it pays for the products of other firms it uses as intermediate goods. (2)

wage-price spiral With substantial indexation, a price shock will drive up wages, which will then drive up prices, and so on, for many rounds. (15)

INDEX